THIRD EDITION

Cognition

THIRD EDITION

Cognition

EXPLORING THE SCIENCE OF THE MIND

Daniel Reisberg

Reed College

W. W. Norton & Company
New York · London

W. W. Norton & Company has been independent since its founding in 1923, when William Warder Norton and Mary D. Herter Norton first published lectures delivered at the People's Institute, the adult education division of New York City's Cooper Union. The Nortons soon expanded their program beyond the Institute, publishing books by celebrated academics from America and abroad. By mid-century, the two major pillars of Norton's publishing program—trade books and college texts—were firmly established. In the 1950s, the Norton family transferred control of the company to its employees, and today—with a staff of four hundred and a comparable number of trade, college, and professional titles published each year—W. W. Norton & Company stands as the largest and oldest publishing house owned wholly by its employees.

Composition: GGS Book Services, Atlantic Highlands
Manufacturing by: Courier, Westford
Director of Manufacturing / College: Roy Tedoff
Editors: Jon Durbin and Aaron Javsicas
Copy Editor: Stephanie Hiebert
Production Editor: Chris Granville
Editorial Assistant: Kelly Rolf

Library of Congress Cataloging-in-Publication Data
Reisberg, Daniel.
     Cognition: exploring the science of the mind / Daniel Reisberg—3rd ed.
         p. cm.
     Includes bibliographical references and index.

ISBN 0-393-92542-0

   1. Cognitive psychology.   I. Title.
BF201.R45 2005
153—dc22

                                                                    2005040451

W. W. Norton & Company, Inc., 500 Fifth Avenue, New York, NY 10110
www.wwnorton.com

W. W. Norton & Company Ltd., Castle House, 75/76 Wells Street, London W1T 3QT
1 2 3 4 5 6 7 8 9 0

FOR FRIDERIKE

CONTENTS

PART FOUR
Knowledge 249

PART FIVE

Thinking 401

I was a college sophomore when I took my first course in cognitive psychology, and I've been excited about this field ever since. Why? First, cognitive psychologists are asking terrific questions. Some of the questions concern broad issues that have intrigued humanity for thousands of years. Why do we think the things we think? Why do we believe the things we believe? What are the limits of human ability? How can we make ourselves better, as individuals, and as a species?

Other questions asked by cognitive psychologists are of a more immediate, personal, concern: How can I help myself to remember more of the material that I'm studying in school? Is there some better way to solve the problems I encounter? Why is it that my roommate can study with the radio on, but I can't?

And sometimes the questions have important consequences for our social institutions: If an eyewitness reports what he saw at a crime, should we trust him? If a newspaper raises questions about a candidate's integrity, how will the voters react?

Of course, we want more than interesting questions. We would like some answers as well, and this is the second reason I find cognitive psychology so exciting: In the last half century, the field has made extraordinary progress on many fronts, providing us, now, with a rich understanding of the nature of memory, the processes of thought, and the content of knowledge. There are, to be sure, many things still to be discovered—that's part of the fun. Even so, we already have something to say about all of the questions just posed, and many more as well. We can speak to the specific questions and to the general, to the theoretical issues and to the practical. Our research has provided data of interest to scholars engaged in a range of intellectual pursuits; we have uncovered principles useful for improving the educational process; and we have made discoveries of considerable importance for the courts. What I've learned, as a cognitive psychologist, has changed how I think about my own memory; it's changed how I make decisions; it's changed how I draw conclusions when I'm thinking about events in my life.

On top of all this, I'm excited about the intellectual connections that cognitive psychology makes possible. In the modern academic world, intellectual disciplines are becoming more and more sophisticated, with their own methods and their own conceptual framework. As a consequence, these disciplines often become isolated from each other, sometimes working on closely related problems without even realizing it. In contrast, cognitive psychology has, in the last decades, actively sought out contact with neighboring disciplines, and, in this book, we will touch on topics in philosophy, economics, biology, linguistics, politics, computer science, and medicine. These connections bring obvious benefits, since insights and information can be traded back and forth between the domains. In addition, these connections highlight the importance of the material we will be examining, and provide a strong signal that we are working on a project of considerable power and scope.

I have tried, in this text, to convey all this excitement. I've done my best to put in view the questions being asked within my field, the substantial answers we can provide for these questions, and finally, some indications of how cognitive psychology is (and has to be) interwoven with several other intellectual endeavors.

I have also had other goals in writing this text. In my own teaching, I work hard at maintaining a balance among several different elements—the nuts and bolts of how our science proceeds, the data provided by the science, the practical implications of our findings, and the theoretical framework that holds all of these pieces together. I've tried to find the same balance in this text. In particular, I've tried to make certain that the presentation of our science—the procedures we use, the exact nature of our data, and so on—is fully integrated with a presentation of the ideas and theories that derive from cognitive psychology research. These ideas provide the narrative that binds the pieces of the science together, and, indeed, it is these ideas that make the research interesting; it is these ideas that drive our endeavor forward. Therefore, I have tried, within each chapter, and from one chapter to the next, to convey how the various pieces fit together into a coherent package. In short, I have tried to emphasize what the result mean, and what the science is telling us.

I have also aimed at a text that is broad in its coverage and up-to-date in its presentation. Our field changes quickly, and students are entitled to a text that stays close to the current state of the art. Moreover, our theories are often rich and subtle in their treatments of a topic, and students deserve a text that conveys this sophistication. I've therefore tried, overall, to write a book that is deep enough, serious enough, but also clear enough so that by the book's close, students will have a full, rich, and contemporary understanding of cognition.

Perhaps most important, I have tried to write this book with language that is compatible with all these goals. To help students see how the pieces of our field fit together, the prose needs to emphasize the flow of ideas in research. To help students grasp the technical material, the prose needs to be approachable, but to provide real understanding of these issues, the prose needs to be precise. I hope my writing style will achieve these aims—but you, the reader, will need to be the judge of this.

Indeed, in general, others will have to decide whether I've accomplished what I set out to. In fact, I look forward to hearing from my readers—both the students I'm hoping to reach and the colleagues I'm hoping to serve. I would be happy to hear from both constituencies what I have done well in the book, and what I could have done better; what I've covered (but should have omitted) and what I've left out. It is unlikely that I'll be able to respond to every comment, but I do welcome the comments, either via regular mail (through W. W. Norton) or via e-mail (cogtext@ reed.edu).

The book's fifteen chapters are designed to cover the major topics within cognitive psychology. The first section of this book lays the foundation. Chapter 1 provides the conceptual and historical background for the subsequent chapters. In addition, this chapter seeks to convey the extraordinary scope of this field and why, therefore, research on cognition is so important. This chapter also highlights the relationship between theory and evidence in this domain, and discusses the logic on which the field of cognitive psychology is built.

Chapter 2 then offers a brief introduction to the study of the brain. Most of cognitive psychology is concerned with the functions that our brains make possible, and not the brain itself. Nonetheless, our understanding of cognition has certainly been enhanced by the study of the brain, and, throughout this book, we will use biological evidence as one means of evaluating our theories. Chapter 2 is designed to make this evidence fully accessible to the reader—by providing a quick survey of the research tools used in studying the brain, and overview of the brain's anatomy, and also an example of how we can use brain evidence as a source of insight into cognitive phenomena.

In the second section of the book, we consider the problems of object recognition, and then the problem of attention. Chapter 3 discusses how we recognize the objects that surround us. This seems a straightforward matter—what could be easier than recognizing a telephone, or a coffee cup, or the letter "Q"? As we will see, however, recognition is surprisingly complex. Chapter 4 considers what it means to "pay attention." The first half of the chapter is concerned largely with selective attention, in which one seeks to focus on a target while ignoring distractors. The second half of the chapter is concerned with divided attention, in which one seeks to focus on more than one target, or more than one task, at the same time. Here, too, we will see that seemingly simple processes often turn out to be more complicated than one might suppose.

The third section turns to the broad problem of memory. Chapters 5, 6, and 7 starts with a discussion of how information is "entered" into long-term storage, but then turn to the complex interdependence between how information is first learned and how that same information is subsequently retrieved. A recurrent theme in this section is that learning that is effective for one sort of task, one sort of use, may be quite *in*effective for other uses. This theme is examined in several contexts, and leads to a discussion of current research on "memory without awareness." These chapters also offer a broad assessment of human memory: How accurate are our memories? How complete? How long-lasting? These issues are pursued both with regard to theoretical treatments of memory, and also the practical consequences of memory research, including the application of this research to the assessment, in the courtroom, of eyewitness testimony.

The book's fourth section is about knowledge. Earlier chapters showed over and over that humans are, in many ways, guided in their thinking and experiences by the broad pattern of things they already know. This invites the questions posed by Chapters 8, 9, 10, and 11: What is knowledge? How is it represented in the mind? Chapter 8 examines the idea that knowledge can be represented via a complex network, and includes a discussion of associative networks in general and connectionist modeling in particular. Chapter 9 turns to the question of how "concepts," the building blocks of our knowledge, are represented in the mind. Chapters 10 and 11 focus on two special types of knowledge. Chapter 10 examines our knowledge about language, with discussion both of "linguistic competence" and "linguistic performance." Chapter 11 considers "visual knowledge" and examines what is known about mental imagery.

The chapters in the fifth section are concerned with the topic of thinking. Chapter 12 examines how each of us draws conclusions from evidence—including cases in which we are trying to be careful and deliberate in our judgments, and also cases of informal judgments of the sort we often make in our everyday lives. Chapter 13 turns to the question of how we reason from our beliefs—how we check on whether our beliefs are correct, and how we draw conclusions, based on things we already believe. Both of these chapters examine the strategies that guide our thinking, and some of the ways that these strategies can, on occasion, lead to error. The chapters then turn to the pragmatic issue of how these errors can be diminished through education. Chapter 13 also discusses how we make decisions and choices, with a special focus first on "economic" theories of decision-making, and then on some of the seeming, "irrationality" in human decision-making. Next, Chapter 14 considers how we solve problems. The first half of the chapter discusses problem-solving strategies of a general sort, useful for all problems; the chapter then turns to more specialized strategies, and with this, the topic of expertise. The chapter concludes with a discussion of the role of creativity and insight within problem solving.

The final chapter in the book does double service. First, it pulls together many of the strands of contemporary research relevant to the topic of consciousness—what consciousness is, and what consciousness is for. In addition, most students will reach this chapter at the end of a full semester's work, a point at which students are well served by a review of the topics already covered, and also a point at which students are ill served by the introduction of much new material. Therefore, this chapter draws most of its themes and evidence from previous chapters, and in that fashion serves as a review for many points that appear earlier in the book. By the same token, Chapter 15 highlights the fact that we are using these materials to approach some of the greatest questions ever asked about the mind, and, in that way, this chapter should help to convey some of the power of the material we have been discussing throughout the book.

This basic structure of the book is the same as it was in the previous (second) edition. In addition, though, much has changed in this, the third, edition. I have, of course, updated all chapters, to include important new research published since the previous edition. In some cases, this new research served largely to confirm previous claims (and, of course, it's always gratifying to see that the field had been on the right track, and that old hypotheses are confirmed by new data). In other cases, the new evidence has filled gaps in our previous knowledge, and so the presentation in this edition is, with these new findings, more filled-in than it had been before. For many topics, this involves presentation of the relevant neuroscience, in light of our remarkable progress in exploring the biological bases for cognitive processes.

In other cases, though, the field's claims have had to evolve in response to new data, and so several sections of the book contain theoretical conceptions new to this edition. And, finally, new evidence has brought clarity to some issues that had been unclear in the past, and this has allowed a presentation that is more straight-forward and more compact.

I have also taken steps to make this edition more accessible and more attractive to students. As part of this effort, the third edition is notably shorter than the previous two. I hope that this has not in any way reduced the sophistication or the richness of the book; the shortening was instead made possible by trimming of detail that wasn't crucial for the presentation, and removing some issues that were separate from the book's main themes. As a result, the book is not just shorter; it is more cohesive and more focused.

Also new for this edition are several ancillaries, including *supplemental essays,* available on the book's website, for each chapter. (The web site can be found at www.wwnorton.com/web/cognition) These essays were designed directly to address two requests I've often heard: First, many students want to explore various applied issues connected to cognitive psychology, both to deepen their understanding of the field, and also to put their understanding to good use. To help students with this, I've written a brief essay for each chapter exploring how the chapter's materials can be applied to a specific domain that is of enormous importance, and also of considerable interest to me—namely, the interface between psychology and the legal system. Some of these essays explore issues of eyewitness memory; others explore how juries make decisions; still others explore how legal concepts can be defined. In each case, I have tried to illustrate how legal issues can be influenced and illuminated by psychological research.

Another frequent request, both from students and from colleagues who use the book, was for fuller treatment of research methods. Within the book, I've always tried to integrate the discussion of what psychologists know with some explanation of how they know it. In the *supplemental essays* on the web for this edition, however, I've also covered some more fundamental points about how research gets done (and so have written on counterbalancing, and the importance of control groups, and the need to control for experimental demand, and so on). These essays are designed to accompany individual chapters, and so in each case are connected to the content of that chapter. In addition, these essays are designed so that, overall, the sequence of essays will provide a reasonable background in how studies get designed and interpreted.

Finally, let me turn to the happiest of chores—thanking all of those who have contributed to this book. I begin with those who helped with the previous editions: Bob Crowder (Yale University) and Bob Logie (University of Aberdeen) both read the entire text of the first edition, and the book was unmistakably improved by their insights. Other colleagues read, and helped me enormously with, specific chapters: Enriqueta Canseco-Gonzalez (Reed College); Rich Carlson (Pennsylvania State University); Lila Gleitman (University of Pennsylvania); Henry Gleitman (University of Pennsylvania); Peter Graf (University of British Columbia); John Henderson (Michigan State University); Jim Hoffman (University of Delaware); Frank Keil (Cornell University); Mike McCloskey (John Hopkins University); Hal Pashler (UCSD); Steve Pinker (MIT); and Paul Rozin (University of Pennsylvania).

The second edition was markedly strengthened by the input and commentary provided by these colleagues: Martin Conway (University of Bristol); Kathleen Eberhard (Notre Dame); Howard Egeth (Johns Hopkins University); Bill Gehring (University of Michigan); Steve Palmer (University of California, Berkeley); Henry Roediger (Washington University); and Eldar Shafir (Princeton University).

And in the present edition, once again, I've been fortunate to have the advice, criticism, and insights provided by a number of colleagues who, together, have made the book better than it otherwise could have been, and I'd like to thank: Bill Gehring and Ellen Hamilton (University of Michigan); Steve Luck (University of Iowa); Evan Palmer, Melinda Kunar, & Jeremy Wolfe (Harvard University); Randall Engle (Georgia Tech); Nancy Kim (Rochester Institute of Technology); Daniel Simons (University of Illinois); Chris Shunn (University of Pittsburgh); Michael Miller, (UC Santa Barbara); Richard Catrambone (Georgia Tech); and Rich Carlson (Penn State).

I also want to thank the people at Norton. Jon Durbin and I have now been working together for a dozen years, and have built a bond of trust, respect and good will that is an enormous resource for me. Aaron Javsicas, as Assistant Editor, is better at managing book projects than anyone I have ever encountered. I'm grateful to Stephanie Hiebert for her skilled and careful editing, even if she is fonder of the APA style manual than I am. Kelly Rolf and Chris Granville have also been tremendously helpful in getting this edition to the finish line.

Finally, it is Jacob, Solomon and Friderike who make this all worthwhile. They forgive me the endless hours at the computer, but also (thank heavens) tug me away from the computer at the right moments. They remind me of what is important, and also keep my life on track. I couldn't do any of this without them.

Daniel Reisberg
Portland, Oregon

PART ONE

THE FOUNDATIONS OF COGNITIVE PSYCHOLOGY

WHAT IS COGNITIVE PSYCHOLOGY? In Chapter 1, we will define this discipline and, with that, we'll offer an early sketch of what this field can teach us—both in terms of theory and in terms of practical applications. We will also provide a brief history, in order to explain why cognitive psychology takes the form that it does.

Chapter 2 has a different focus: In the last decade or two, cognitive psychology has formed a productive partnership with the field of cognitive neuroscience. Investigators in these two fields work together to describe how the mind works, what is involved in various mental processes, and how the brain makes these achievements and processes possible. In this book, our main emphasis will be on psychology, not neuroscience, but we'll make use of neuroscience evidence at many points in our discussion. To do this, though, we first need to provide some background, and this is the main purpose of Chapter 2. We'll include a rough map of what's where in the brain, but we must be clear from the start about what this means: Each area of the brain performs a specific function, but that doesn't mean that there are large-scale "centers" in the brain—a "reading center," for example, or a "memory center." Instead, any mental achievement you can name depends on the coordinated functioning of many different brain regions, with each region contributing its own small bit to the overall achievement. We'll show evidence for this pattern of "cerebral teamwork" at the very beginning of Chapter 2, when we consider a bizarre form of brain damage. This pattern will then remain in view throughout the chapter, and will certainly be evident late in the chapter when we'll zoom in on the visual system as a case study of how the brain functions.

The Science of the Mind

This is a book about intellectual functioning. It will take us several pages to spell out just what this means, but some of the questions to be asked are obvious from the start:

There you are, studying for next Wednesday's exam, but for some reason, the material just won't "stick" in your memory. You find yourself wishing, therefore, for a better strategy to use in studying and memorizing. What would that strategy be? Is it possible to have a "better memory"?

While you're studying, your friend is moving around in the room, and you find this terribly distracting. Why can't you just shut out your friend's motion? Why don't you have better control over your attention and your ability to concentrate?

A police officer is interviewing a witness to a crime and is dismayed by how little the witness remembers. You've been introduced to a woman at a party, but minutes later, you realize (to your embarrassment) that you have forgotten her name. Why do we forget? What sorts of things are we likely to forget, and what sorts of things are we likely to remember?

You pick up the morning newspaper and are horrified to learn how many people have decided to vote for candidate X. How do people decide whom to vote for? For that matter, how do people decide what college to attend, or which car to buy, or even what to have for dinner? What forces drive our decisions?

■ This chapter begins with a sketch of the scope of cognitive psychology. The domain of this field includes activities that are obviously "intellectual" (like remembering, or attending, or making judgments), and also a much broader range of activities that turn out to *depend on* these intellectual achievements.

■ A brief review of the history of cognitive psychology highlights two essential themes. One is the idea that we cannot study the mental world by means of direct observation. The second theme is that we *must* study the mental world, if we are to understand behavior; this is because our behavior depends in crucial ways on how we *perceive* and *understand* the world around us.

■ Combining these themes, we are led to the view that we must study the mental world *indirectly*, but, as we will see, the (inferential) method for doing this is the same method used by other sciences, including physics.

■ Finally, we consider an example of research in cognitive psychology, to illustrate the types of data that psychologists consider and the logic they use in testing their theories.

Cognitive psychologists know an enormous amount about all these topics, and before we are through, we will have considered evidence pertinent to each of the scenarios just mentioned. In addition, note that in the cases just described, things aren't going as you might have wished: You fail to remember; you are unable to ignore a distraction; the voters make a choice you don't like. But what about the other side of things? What about the remarkable intellectual feats that humans achieve—brilliant deductions or creative solutions to complex problems? Before we are done, we will also have a lot to say about how these are possible, and thus how it is that we accomplish the great things we do.

The Scope of Cognitive Psychology

The examples we've mentioned so far—remembering, paying attention, making judgments about evidence, and making decisions—all fall squarely within the realm of cognitive psychology, and, when this field was first launched, it was generally understood as the *scientific study of knowledge*. How is knowledge acquired? How is knowledge retained so that it's available when needed? How is knowledge used, as a basis for action or as a basis for generating further knowledge?

These topics do a decent job of conveying the breadth of cognitive psychology, but perhaps a better way is to look within these various topics, examining what each includes. Consider, for example, the study of memory: When we investigate how memory functions, what exactly is it that we are investigating? Or, to turn this around, what tasks rely on memory?

When you are taking an exam, you obviously rely on memory—memory for what you have learned during the term. Likewise, you rely on memory when you are at the supermarket and trying to remember the cheesecake recipe, so you can buy the ingredients. You rely on memory when you are reminiscing about childhood. But what else draws on memory?

Consider this simple story (adapted from Charniak, 1972):

"Betsy wanted to bring Jacob a present. She shook her piggy bank. It made no sound. She went to look for her mother."

This four-sentence tale is trivially easy to understand, but this is true only because you provided some important bits of background. For example, you weren't at all puzzled, as you read the story, about why Betsy was interested in her piggy bank; you weren't puzzled, specifically, about why the story's first sentence led naturally to the second. This is because you already knew (a) that the things one gives as presents are often things bought for the occasion (rather than things already owned), (b) that buying things requires money, and (c) that money is stored in piggy banks. Without these facts, you would have been bewildered about why a desire to give a gift would lead someone to their piggy bank. (Surely you did not think she intended to give the piggy bank itself as the present!) Likewise, you immediately understood why Betsy *shook* her piggy bank. You didn't suppose that she was shaking it in frustration, or trying to find out if it would make a good percussion instrument. Instead, you understood that she was trying to determine the bank's contents. But you knew this only because you already knew (d) that children don't keep track of how much money is in their bank, and (e) that one cannot simply look into the bank to learn its contents. Without these facts, Betsy's shaking of the bank would make no sense. Similarly, you understood what it meant that the bank made no sound. That's because you know (f) that it's usually coins (not bills) that are kept in piggy banks, and (g) that coins make noise when they are shaken. If you didn't know these facts, you might have interpreted the bank's silence, when it was shaken, as good news, indicating perhaps that the bank was jammed full of $20 bills—an inference, of course, that would have led you to a very different expectation for how the story would unfold from there.

Of course, there's nothing special about the Betsy and Jacob story, and so it seems likely that we'll encounter a similar reliance on background knowledge in many other settings. This clearly suggests that, in general, our understanding of stories, or ordinary conversations, depends on memory—depends on our drawing key bits of information from our storehouse of knowledge. Indeed, if we didn't supply this information, then anyone telling the Betsy and Jacob story would need to spell out all the connections and all the assumptions. That is, the story would have to include all the background facts that, *with* memory, are supplied by you. As a result, the story would have to be 50 times longer than it currently is, and the telling of it 50 times slower. The same would be true for every story we hear, every conversation we participate in. Memory is thus crucial for each of these activities.

The importance of memory is also evident in another setting: Whenever you learn something, you are gaining new information, or perhaps a new skill, and then somehow carrying that new information with you so that it's ready for use at some future point. Of course, that new information has to be stored somewhere, and that *somewhere* is memory. Therefore, without memory, you wouldn't be able to retain anything you've learned—and so, no memory, no learning; no memory, no ability to benefit in any way from experience.

Here is a different sort of example: In Chapter 6, we will consider various cases of clinical amnesia—cases in which someone, because of brain damage, has lost the ability to remember certain materials. These cases are fascinating at many levels, including the fact that they provide us with key insights into what memory is for: Without memory, what is disrupted?

One well-studied amnesia patient was a man identified as H.M. We'll have more to say about H.M. in Chapter 6, but a few observations are pertinent here: H.M.'s memory loss was the unanticipated by-product of brain surgery intended to control his epilepsy, and the loss is quite profound. H.M. has no trouble remembering events prior to the surgery, but he seems completely unable to recall any event that occurred after his operation. If asked who the president is, or about recent events, he reports events that were current at the time of the surgery. If asked questions about last week, or even an hour ago, he recalls nothing.

The memory loss has, of course, had massive consequences for H.M.'s life, and some of the consequences are perhaps surprising. For example, he had an uncle of whom he was very fond, and H.M. often asks about his uncle: How is he? What's he doing these days? Unfortunately, the uncle died some time after H.M.'s surgery, and H.M. was told this sad news. The information came as a horrible shock, triggering enormous grief, but because of his amnesia, H.M. soon forgot about it.

Some time later, H.M. again asked about his uncle and was once more told of the uncle's death. With no memory of having heard this news before, H.M. was again hearing it "for the first time," with the shock and grief every bit as strong as it was initially. Indeed, each time he hears this news, he is hearing it "for the first time." With no memory, he has no opportunity to live with the news, to adjust to it. Hence, his grief cannot subside. Without memory, H.M. cannot come to terms with his uncle's death.

A different glimpse of memory function comes from H.M.'s poignant comments about his state and about "who he is." Each of us has a conception of who we are, of what sort of person we are. That conception is supported by numerous memories: We know whether we're deserving of praise for our good deeds or blame for our transgressions because we remember our good deeds and our transgressions. We know whether we've kept our promises or achieved our goals because, again, we have the relevant memories. None of this is true for people who suffer from amnesia, and H.M. sometimes comments on the fact that, in important ways, he doesn't know who he is. He doesn't know if he should be proud of his accomplishments or ashamed of his crimes; he doesn't know if he's been clever or stupid, honorable or dishonest, industrious or lazy. In a sense, then, it would seem that, without a memory, there is no self. (For broader discussion see Hilts, 1995; and M. Conway & Pleydell-Pearce, 2000.)

What, then, is the scope of cognitive psychology? As we mentioned earlier, this field is sometimes defined as the scientific study of the acquisition, retention, and use of knowledge. This makes it sound like the field is concerned with purely intellectual matters; it makes it sound like the field has a fairly narrow scope. We have just considered some examples, though, that show the opposite to be true: Our self-concept, it seems, depends on our knowledge (and, in particular, on our episodic knowledge). Our emotional adjustments to the world, as we have seen, rely on our memories. Or, to take much more ordinary cases, our ability to understand a story we've read, or a conversation, or, presumably, any of our experiences, depends on our supplementing that experience with some knowledge.

In short, cognitive psychology, and a reliance on our knowledge, and on our ability to learn, remember, and make judgments, is relevant to virtually every waking moment of our lives. Activities that don't, on the surface, appear intellectual would nonetheless collapse without the support of our cognitive functioning. This is true whether we're considering our actions, our social lives, our emotions, or almost any other domain. This is the scope of cognitive psychology and, in a real sense, is the scope of this book.

A Brief History

In its modern form, cognitive psychology is a relatively young endeavor—about 40 or 50 years old. Despite this youth, cognitive psychology has had an enormous impact—so much so that many speak of the "cognitive revolution" within psychology. This "revolution," taking place across the 1950s and 1960s, represented a striking change in the style of research and theorizing employed by most psychologists. The new styles were intended initially for studying problems we have already met: problems of learning, memory, and so on. But these new styles were soon exported to other domains and have provided important insights in these domains. In important ways, then, the cognitive revolution changed the intellectual map of our field.

The Years of Introspection

To understand all of this, we need some historical context. In the late 19th century, scholars—notably Wilhelm Wundt (1832–1920) and his student Edward Bradford Titchener (1867–1927)—launched the new enterprise of research psychology, defining their field for the first time as an endeavor separate from philosophy or biology.

In those years, psychologists were concerned largely with the study of conscious mental events—our feelings, thoughts, perceptions, and recollections. Moreover, there was just one way, they argued, to study these events. They started with the obvious fact that there is no way for you to experience my thoughts, or I yours. The only person who can experience or observe your thoughts is you. They concluded, therefore, that the only way to study thoughts is for each of us to **introspect**, or "look within," to observe and record the content of our own mental lives, and the sequence of our own experiences.

Wundt and Titchener insisted, though, that the introspection could not be casual. Instead, introspectors had to be meticulously trained: They were given a vocabulary to describe what they observed; they were trained to be as careful and as complete as possible; and above all, they were trained simply to report on their experiences, with a minimum of interpretation.

This style of research was quite influential for several years, but psychologists soon became disenchanted with it, and it is easy to see why. As one concern, these early investigators were forced to acknowledge that some thoughts are *un*conscious, and this meant that introspection was inevitably limited as a research tool. This follows from the fact that introspection, by its nature, is the study of conscious experiences, and so can tell us nothing about unconscious events.

Indeed, we now know that unconscious thought plays a huge part in our mental lives. For example, what is your phone number? Odds are good that, the moment this question was asked, the number "popped" into your thoughts without any effort, noticeable steps, or strategies on your part. But, in fact, there's good reason to think that this simple bit of remembering requires a complex series of steps (see, for example, Chapter 8). These steps take place outside your awareness, and so, if we rely on introspection as our means of studying mental events, then we have no way of examining these processes.

But there are also other problems with introspection: In order for any science to proceed, there must be some way of testing its claims; otherwise we have no way of separating correct assertions from false ones, accurate descriptions of the world from fictions. Hand in hand with this requirement, science needs some way of resolving disagreements: If you claim that there are ten planets in our solar system, and I insist that there are nine, we need some way of determining who is right. Otherwise, we have no way of locating the fact of the matter, and so our "science" will become a matter of opinion, not fact.

With introspection, though, this testability of claims is often unattainable. To see why this is, let's imagine that you insist your headaches are worse than mine. How could we ever test your claim? It might be true that you describe your headaches in extreme terms: You talk about your "unbelievable, agonizing, excruciating" headaches. But that might simply mean that you are inclined toward extravagant descriptions; it might reflect your verbal style, not your headaches. Similarly, it might be true that you need bed rest whenever one of your headaches strikes. Does that mean your headaches are truly intolerable? It might mean instead that you are self-indulgent and rest even in the face of mild pain. Perhaps our headaches are identical, but I'm stoic about mine and you're not.

How, therefore, should we test your claim about your headaches? What we need is some means of directly comparing your headaches to mine, and that would require transplanting one of your headaches into my experience, or vice versa. Then one of us could make the appropriate comparison. But there is no way to do this, leaving us, in the end, truly unable to determine if your headache reports are exaggerated or not, distorted or accurate. We're left, in other words, with no access to the objective facts. Our only information about your headaches is what comes to us through the filter of your description, and we have no way to know how (or whether) that filter is coloring the evidence.

For purposes of science, this is not acceptable. For science, we need objective observations, observations that we can count on. We need observations that aren't dependent on a particular point of view, or a particular descriptive style. It is not enough to consider "the world as one person sees it." Instead, we want to consider the world as it objectively is. In scientific discourse, we usually achieve this objectivity by making sure all the facts are out in plain view, so that you can inspect my evidence, and I yours. In that way, we can be certain that neither of us is distorting or misreporting or exaggerating the facts. And that is precisely what we cannot do with introspection.

The Years of Behaviorism

The concerns just raised led many psychologists, particularly those in the United States, to abandon introspection as a research method. Psychology could not be a science, they argued, if it relied on introspective data. Instead, psychology needed objective data. That means we needed to focus on data that were out in the open, for all to observe.

An organism's *behaviors* are observable in the right way: You can watch my actions, and so can anyone else who is appropriately positioned. Therefore, data concerned with behavior are objective data, and so grist for the scientific mill. Likewise, *stimuli* in the world are in this same "objective" category: These are measurable, recordable, physical events.

In addition, you can arrange to record the stimuli I experience day after day after day and also the behaviors I produce each day. This means that you can record how the pattern of behaviors changes with the passage of time and with the accumulation of experience. Thus, my *learning history* can also be objectively recorded and scientifically studied.

Of course, my beliefs, wishes, goals, and expectations are all things that cannot be directly observed, cannot be objectively recorded. Thus we need to rule out any discussion of these "mentalistic" notions. These can be studied only via introspection (or so the argument goes), and introspection, we have suggested, is worthless as a scientific tool. Hence, a scientific psychology needs to avoid these invisible internal processes or events.

It was this perspective that led researchers to the **behaviorist** movement, a movement that dominated psychology in America for roughly the first half of the 20th century. This movement was in many ways a success and uncovered a range of broad principles concerned with how our behavior changes in response to different configurations of stimuli (including those stimuli we call "rewards" and "punishments"). Many of these principles remain in place within contemporary psychology and provide the base for an important enterprise called "learning theory," as well as a wide range of practical applications. (For a description of these principles, see B. Schwartz, Wasserman, & Robbins, 2001.)

By the late 1950s, however, psychologists were convinced that a great deal of our behavior could not be explained in this way. The reason, to put it plainly, is that we can easily show that the way people act, and the things that they say, and the way that they feel, are guided, not by the objective situation itself, but instead by how they *understand* or *interpret* the situation. Therefore, if we follow the behaviorists' instruction and focus only on the objective situation, we will regularly misunderstand why people are acting as they are and make the wrong predictions about how they will behave in the future. Or, to put this point another way, the behaviorists' perspective demands that we not talk about mental entities like beliefs, memories, and so on, because there is no way to study these entities directly, and so no way to study them scientifically. Yet it seems that these subjective entities play a pivotal role in guiding behavior, and so we *must* consider these entities if we want to understand behavior!

Evidence pertinent to these assertions is threaded throughout the chapters of this book. Over and over, we will find it necessary to mention people's perceptions and strategies and understanding, as we strive to explain why (and how) they perform various tasks and accomplish various goals. Indeed, we've already seen an example of this pattern: Imagine that we present the "Betsy and Jacob" story to people and then ask them various questions about the story: Why did Betsy shake her piggy bank? Why did she go to look for her mother? Their responses will surely reflect their understanding of the story, which in turn depends on far more than the physical stimulus—that is, the 29 syllables of the story itself. If we wanted to predict their responses, therefore, we would need to refer to the stimulus (the story itself) *and also* to the persons' knowledge and understanding of, and contribution to, this stimulus.

Here's a different example that makes the same general point: There you sit in the dining hall. A friend produces this physical stimulus: "Pass the salt, please." You immediately produce a bit of salt-passing behavior. So far, this seems fine from the behaviorists' perspective: There was a physical stimulus (the words that your friend uttered) and an easily defined response (your passing of the salt). But notice that things would have proceeded in the same way if your friend had offered a different stimulus. "Could I have the salt?" would have done the trick. Ditto for "Salt, please!" or "Hmm, this sure needs salt!" If your friend is both loquacious and obnoxious, the utterance might have been, "Excuse me, but after briefly contemplating the gustatory qualities of these comestibles, I have discerned that their sensory qualities would be improved by the addition of a number of sodium and chloride ions, delivered in roughly equal proportions and in crystalline form; could you aid me in this endeavor?" You might giggle (or snarl) at your friend, but you would still pass the salt.

Now let's work on the science of salt-passing behavior. When is this behavior produced? Since we've just observed that the behavior is evoked by all of these different stimuli, we would surely want to ask: What do these stimuli have in common? If we can answer that question, we're well on our way to understanding why all of these stimuli have the same effect.

If we focus entirely on the observable, objective aspects of these stimuli, they actually have little in common. After all, the actual sounds being produced are rather different in that long utterance about sodium and chloride ions and the utterance, "Salt, please!" And, in many circumstances, *similar* sounds would not lead to salt-passing behavior. Imagine that your friend says, "Salt the pass," or "Sass the palt." These are acoustically similar to "pass the salt" but wouldn't have the same impact. Or imagine that your friend said, "She has only a small part in the play. All she gets to say is, 'Pass the salt, please.'" In this case, exactly the right syllables were uttered, but you wouldn't pass the salt in response.

It seems, then, that our science of salt-passing won't get very far if we insist on talking only about the physical stimulus. Stimuli that are physically different from each other ("Salt, please" and the bit about the ions) have similar effects. Stimuli that are physically similar to each other ("Pass the salt" and "Sass the palt") have different effects. Physical similarity, therefore, is plainly not what unites the various stimuli that evoke salt-passing.

It should be obvious, though, that the various stimuli that evoke salt-passing do have something in common with each other: They all *mean the same thing*. In some cases, this meaning derives easily from the words themselves ("Please pass the salt"). In other cases, the meaning depends on certain pragmatic rules. (For example, we pragmatically understand that the question, "Could you pass the salt?" is not a question about arm strength, although, interpreted literally, it might be understood that way.) In all cases, though, it seems plain that, to predict your behavior in the dining hall, we need to ask what these stimuli mean to you. This seems an extraordinarily simple point, but it is a point, echoed over and over by countless other examples, that indicates the impossibility of a complete behaviorist psychology.[1]

The Roots of the Cognitive Revolution

We seem to be nearing an impasse: If we wish to explain or predict behavior, we need to make reference to the mental world—the world of perceptions, understandings, and intentions. This is because how people act is shaped by how they perceive the situation they're in, how they understand the stimuli, and so on. But how should we study the mental world? We can't employ introspection, because

---

[1]We should mention briefly that the behaviorists themselves quickly realized this point. Hence, modern behaviorism has abandoned the radical rejection of mentalistic terms, and, indeed, it's hard to draw a line between modern behaviorism and a field called "animal cognition," a field that often employs mentalistic language! The behaviorism being criticized here is a historically defined behaviorism, and it's this perspective that, in large measure, gave birth to modern cognitive psychology.

we've argued that introspective data are (at best) problematic. It would seem, then, that we're caught in a trap: We need to talk about the mental world, if we hope to explain behavior. But the only direct means for studying the mental world turns out to be unworkable.

The solution to this impasse was actually suggested many years ago, perhaps most clearly by the philosopher Immanuel Kant (1724–1804), and it is his method that, in many ways, underlies the principal research strategy of cognitive psychology. To use this **transcendental method,** one must begin with the observable facts and then work backward from these observations. In essence, one asks: How could these observations have come about? What must the *causes* be that produced these *effects?*

This method, sometimes called "inference to best explanation," is at the heart of most modern science. Physicists, for example, routinely use this method to study objects or events that cannot be observed directly. To take just one case, no physicist has ever observed an electron, but this has not stopped physicists from learning a great deal about electrons. How do they proceed? Even though electrons themselves are not observable, their presence often leads to observable results—in essence *visible effects* from an *invisible cause.* Thus, among other things, electrons cause observable tracks in cloud chambers, and they produce momentary fluctuations in a magnetic field. Physicists can then use these observations the same way a police detective uses clues—asking, in essence, what the "crime" must have been like if it left this and that clue. (A size 11 footprint? That tells us what size feet the criminal has, even though no one observed his feet. A smell of tobacco smoke? That suggests the criminal was a smoker. And so on.) In the same fashion, physicists observe the clues that electrons leave behind, and from this information they form hypotheses about what exactly electrons must be like, in order to have produced these specific effects.

Of course, physicists (and other scientists) have a huge advantage over a police detective, and, indeed, this is crucial for the distinction between science and "ordinary" police work: If a police detective has insufficient evidence, she can't arrange for the crime to happen again, so that more evidence will be produced. But scientists do have this option; they can arrange for new experiments, with new measures. Better still, they can set the stage in advance, to maximize the likelihood that the "culprit" (in our example, the electron) will leave useful clues behind. In this way, the scientist can gather more and more data, including data that are crucial for testing the specific predictions of a particular theory. This prospect—of reproducing experiments, and varying experiments to test hypotheses—is, of course, what gives science its power. It's what allows scientists to assert that their hypotheses have been rigorously tested, and it's what gives scientists assurance that their theories are correct.

Psychologists work in the same fashion. We know that we need to study mental processes; that's what we learned from the limitations of behaviorism. But we also know that mental processes cannot be observed directly; we learned that from the downfall of introspection. Our path forward, therefore, has to rely on the fact that mental processes, themselves invisible, have visible consequences: measurable delays in producing a response, performances that can be assessed for accuracy, errors that can be scrutinized and categorized. By examining these and other effects produced by mental processes, we can develop—and then *test*—hypotheses about what the mental processes must have been. In this fashion, we use Kant's method, just as physicists do, to develop a science that does not rest on direct observation.

The Computer as Metaphor

In Kant's method, one starts with observed data and seeks to reconstruct the unseen processes that led to these data. But what form should this reconstruction take? What sort of mechanisms might one propose for our ability to remember, or our ability to solve problems? Should we seek to explain the data in terms of magnetic fields, or biochemistry, or divine intervention? If we seek the best explanation for the observed data, then in what terms should that explanation be cast?

In the 1950s, a new approach to psychological explanation became available, and it turned out to be immensely fruitful. This new approach was suggested by the rapid developments in electronic information processing, including developments in computer technology. From the start, it was clear that computers were capable of tremendously efficient information storage and retrieval ("memory"), as well as performance that seemed to involve decision-making and problem-solving. Psychologists therefore began to explore the possibility that the human mind employed processes and procedures similar to those used in computers, and so psychological data were soon being explained in terms of "buffers" and "central processors," terms borrowed from computer technology. (See, for example, Broadbent, 1958; and G. A. Miller, Galanter, & Pribram, 1960.)

The computer metaphor provided a new language for describing psychological processes and explaining psychological data. Given a particular performance, say, on a memory task, one could hypothesize a series of information-processing events that made the performance possible. In this way, the computer metaphor allowed us to run the Kantian logic: Given a set of data, one could propose a particular sequence of information-processing events as the hypothesized source of those data. One could then ask whether some other, perhaps simpler, information-processing sequence could also explain the data, or whether some other sequence could explain both these data and some other findings. In this fashion, we could do more than ask how the data came about; we could, in addition, ask what the *best* way is to think about the data. More important, one could then test these proposed sequences: If such-and-such mechanism lies behind these data, then things should work differently in this circumstance or that one. (We'll offer an example of how this works in just a moment.) If these predictions are confirmed, that is strong argument that the proposed hypothesis was correct; if these predictions are not confirmed, then a new hypothesis is needed.

Let's be clear, though, that the use of the computer metaphor does not commit us to claiming that "the mind is just like a computer" or "the mind is nothing more than a complex computer." Instead, we are suggesting only that the mind is *enough* like a computer that we can profitably explain much about the mind by using the language of computer processing. Likewise, the mind seems to be enough like a computer that the use of such language leads to the discovery of new facts about intellectual performance.

Research in Cognitive Psychology: An Example

How does this method work in practice? Let's explore this point with a concrete example. We will return to this example in Chapters 4 and 5, and there put it into a richer theoretical context. For now, though, our focus is on the method, rather than on the theory itself.

Working Memory: Some Initial Observations

Many of the sentences in this book—including the present one, which consists of 19 words—are rather long. In many of these sentences, words that must be understood together (such as "sentences . . . are . . . long") are widely separated (note the 12 words interposed between "sentences" and "are"). Yet you have no trouble understanding these sentences.

We begin, therefore, with a simple fact—that you are able to read, even though ordinary reading requires you to integrate words that are widely separated on the page. How should we explain this fact? What is the (unseen) cause that leads to this (easily observed) fact? The obvious suggestion is that you're relying on some form of *memory*, which allows you to remember the early words in the sentence as you forge ahead. Then, once you have read enough, you can integrate what you have decoded so far. In this section's very first sentence, you needed to remember the first seven words ("Many of the sentences in this book") while you read the interposed phrase ("including . . . 19 words"). Then you had to bring those first seven words back into play, to integrate them with the sentence's end ("are rather long").

The form of memory proposed here is generally called **working memory**, to emphasize that this is the memory you use for information that you are actively working on. Working memory is relatively small, but it holds information in an easily accessible form, so that the information is, so to speak, at your fingertips, instantly available when you need it. Thus, having decoded the first part of a sentence, you store its semantic content in working memory, so that it is ready at hand a moment later, when you are all set to integrate this content with the sentence's end.

In Chapter 5 we'll have much more to say about the relationship between working memory and other forms of memory. For now, though, let's consider just a few facts and use those as basis for refining our claims about working memory.

First, we suggested that working memory is relatively small, and, in fact, its size may be important for its functioning: With relatively few items in working memory, there will never be a problem in locating just the item you want. (If you have only two keys on your key ring, it's easy to find the one that unlocks your door. If you had a hundred keys on the ring, the situation would be rather different.) That's useful, because you want items in working memory to be accessible, ready to use.

Can we test this proposal? One way to measure working memory's capacity is via a **span test**. In this test, we read to someone a list of, say, four items, perhaps four letters ("A D G W"). The person has to report these back, immediately, in sequence. If she succeeds, we try it again with five letters ("Q D W U F"). If she can repeat these back correctly, we try six letters, and so on, until we find a list that the person cannot report back accurately. Generally, people start making errors with sequences of seven or eight letters. Most people's letter span, therefore, is about seven or eight. This confirms our hypothesis that working memory is limited in size and, just as important, provides a simple example of how we can learn about this memory's properties by seeing how this (unseen) memory influences observable performance.

Working Memory: A Proposal

There are other facts that also need to be explained, and so we'll need to elaborate our account of working memory in order to explain all the evidence, to account for all the "clues." For example, people often make errors in the span test, and when they do, the errors are often systematic. Generally, people inadvertently substitute one letter for another with a similar sound. Having heard "S," they'll report back "F"; or having heard "V," they'll report back "B." The problem is not in hearing the letters in the first place: We get similar sound-alike confusions if the letters are presented visually. Thus, having *seen* "F," people are likely to report back "S"; they are not likely, in this situation, to report back the similar-looking "E."

Alan Baddeley and Graham Hitch (1974) proposed a model to explain both this finding and many other results as well. Their model starts by stipulating that working memory is not a single entity. Instead, working memory has several different parts, and so they prefer to speak of a **working-memory system**. At the heart of the system is the **central executive**. This is the part that runs the show and that does the real work.

The executive is helped out by a number of low-level "assistants." These assistants are not at all sophisticated; they are useful for mere storage of information and not much more. If any work needs to be done on the information—interpretation or analysis—the assistants can't do it; the executive is needed. Nonetheless, these assistants are highly useful: Information that will soon be needed, but isn't needed right now, can be sent off to the assistants for temporary storage. Therefore, the executive isn't burdened by the mere storage of this information and is freed up to do other tasks.

In effect, the assistants serve the same function as a piece of scratch paper on your desk. When you're going to need some bit of information soon (a phone number, perhaps), you write it down on the scratch paper. Of course, the scratch paper has no mind of its own, and so it can't do anything with the "stored" information; all it does is hold on to the information. But that's helpful enough: With the information stored in this manner, you can cease thinking about it, and so you are free to think about something else instead. That is the gain. Then, once you are ready for the stored information, you glance at your notes, and there the information is.

Working memory's assistants provide the same benefit. One of the most important assistants is the **articulatory rehearsal loop.** To use the loop, the central executive launches the activity of pronouncing the items to be remembered (e.g., pronouncing the phone number you want to remember). The pronunciation isn't out loud; instead, you talk to yourself—you go through the motions of speaking but without making a sound. This silent **subvocalization** causes a record of this "speech" to be loaded into a sort of internal echo box, part of the mental apparatus normally used for hearing. More technically, subvocalization creates a record in a **phonological buffer**. Once in that buffer, though, the record begins to fade away. At this point, the executive must intercede: The executive "reads" the contents of the buffer and starts another cycle—again launching the subvocalization, which causes a new record to be loaded into the buffer, and so on. (See Figure 1.1.)

Using this loop, therefore, places only an occasional demand on the executive. The executive has to launch each cycle, but then, once launched, the subvocalization—often referred to as the "inner voice"—can run pretty much on its own, thanks to the fact that speech is enormously well practiced and so largely automatic. That gets the information into the buffer, sometimes called the "inner ear." The buffer is a passive storage device—information simply arrives there, with no action needed. Before long, though, the information in the buffer starts to decay, and then the executive *is* needed, to read the buffer's contents (before the information is lost), and start the next cycle. But in the interim—during the subvocalization and prior to the decay—the executive is free to work on other matters, and this is the advantage of using this loop. Just as you're free to think about other matters once you've written a number on your scratch pad, the executive is free for other tasks while the loop is running.

Evidence for the Working-Memory System

Baddeley and Hitch proposed this model as an explanation for the available evidence; it was, in their view, the best way to explain the facts collected so far. This is the first step of the Kantian logic we have described. It is crucial, though, that their model also leads to many new predictions, and these allow us to test the model's accuracy. This is the step that turns a "mere" hypothesis into solid scientific knowledge.

For example, imagine that we ask people to take the span test while simultane-ously saying "tah-tah-tah" over and over, out loud. This **concurrent articulation** task obviously requires the mechanisms for speech production. Therefore, these mechanisms are not available for other use, including subvocalization. (See Figure 1.2.) This is because, simply, you can't use muscles in two different ways at the same time, and so you cannot subvocalize one sequence while overtly vocalizing some-thing else.

According to the model, how will this constraint matter? First, note that our initial span test measures the combined capacities of the central executive and the

---

FIGURE 1.1   The Working-Memory System

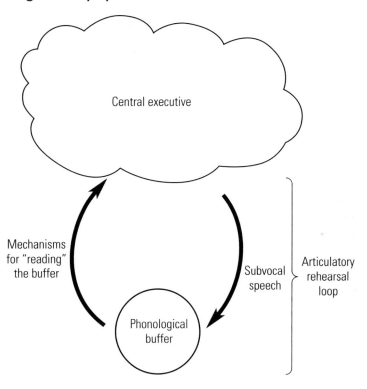

The central executive controls all functions within working memory, but the executive is supported by a number of low-level assistants. One assistant, the articulatory rehearsal loop, involves two components—subvocal speech (the "inner voice") and a phonological buffer (the "inner ear"). Items are rehearsed by using subvocalization to "load" the buffer. While this is going on, the executive is free to work on other matters. However, the executive is needed to "read" the contents of the buffer before they decay; the executive can then pronounce the items again, launching another cycle through the loop.

FIGURE 1.2   The Effects of Concurrent Articulation

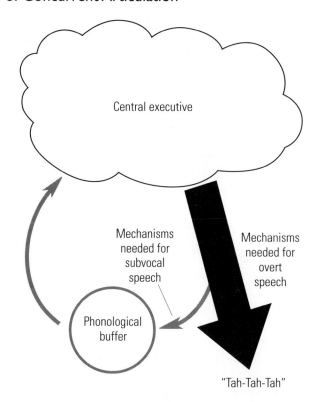

The mechanisms needed for subvocal speech (the "inner voice") overlap heavily with those needed for actual, overt speech. Therefore, if these mechanisms are in use for actual speech, they are not available for subvocal rehearsal. Hence, many experiments block rehearsal by requiring participants to say "tah-tah-tah" out loud.

loop. That is, when people take a span test, they store some of the to-be-remembered items in the loop, and other items via the central executive. With concurrent articulation, though, the loop isn't available for use, and so we are now measuring the capacity of working memory without the rehearsal loop. We should predict, therefore, that concurrent articulation, even though it's extremely easy, should cut memory span drastically. This prediction turns out to be correct. Span is ordinarily about seven items; with concurrent articulation, it drops to three or four.

Second, with visually presented items, concurrent articulation should eliminate the sound-alike errors. To see why, consider the sequence of events in rehearsal: With visual presentation, items are initially seen and registered by the central executive. The executive then launches the subvocalization of the to-be-remembered items, using the "inner voice," and this loads a record of these items into the phonological buffer, the "inner ear." It is here, in the inner ear, that the sound-alike errors arise. (This is because the phonological buffer involves mechanisms that are literally part of the auditory system, and so things that sound alike when heard also sound alike in the buffer.) This sequence of events is blocked, however, by concurrent articulation: With the inner voice unavailable, there's no way for the executive to "load" the items into the inner ear. Therefore, the to-be-remembered items never reach the place in which the sound-alike errors arise. Hence, there should be no sound-alike errors. This prediction is, once again, correct: With concurrent articulation, sound-alike errors are largely eliminated.

Third, we can also test people's memory spans by using complex visual shapes. People are shown these shapes and then must echo the sequence back by drawing what they have just seen. If we choose shapes that are not easily named, then the shapes cannot be rehearsed via the inner-voice/inner-ear combination. (What would one subvocalize to rehearse these?) With such stimuli, there should be no effect of concurrent articulation: If people aren't using the rehearsal loop, there is no cost attached to denying them use of the loop. This prediction is also correct.

Finally, here is a different sort of prediction: We have claimed that the rehearsal loop is required only for storage; this loop (like all of working memory's assistants) is incapable of any more sophisticated operations. Therefore, these other operations should not be compromised if the loop is unavailable. This turns out to be correct: Concurrent articulation blocks use of the loop but has no effect on someone's ability to read brief sentences, to do logic problems, and so on. Likewise, we can present people with a string of three or four letters and ask them to remember these while solving a simple problem. After they've solved the problem, they report back the original letters. It turns out that half filling working memory in this fashion has virtually no impact on problem-solving; performance is just as fast and just as accurate under these circumstances as it is without the memory load. The reason is that this memory load is accommodated within the rehearsal loop, placing no burden on the executive. And it is the executive, not the loop, that is needed for problem-solving, again in accord with the overall model.

The Nature of the Working-Memory Evidence

No one has ever seen the "inner voice" or "inner ear" directly. Nonetheless, we're confident that these entities exist, because they are essential parts of our explanation for the data and there seems to be no other way to explain the data. Moreover, our claims about the inner voice and inner ear have consistently led us to new predictions that have then been confirmed by further testing. It's in this way that we can use the observable evidence to reconstruct what the unobserved structures and processes must be.

Let's note also that, in supporting our account, we have many forms of data available to us. We can manipulate research participants' activities, as we did with concurrent articulation, and look at how this manipulation changes their performance (i.e., the size of the measured memory span). We can also manipulate the stimuli themselves, as we did in testing memory for visual shapes, and see how this changes things. We can also look in detail at the nature of the performance, asking not just about the overall level of performance, but also about the specific errors (sound-alike vs. look-alike). We can also measure the speed of participants' performance and ask how this is influenced by various manipulations. We did this, for example, in asking whether problem-solving is compromised by a concurrent memory load. The obvious assumption here is that mental processes are very quick but nonetheless do take a measurable amount of time. By timing how quickly participants answer various questions or perform various tasks, we can ask what factors speed up mental processes and what factors slow them down.

Other sorts of data can also be brought into play. For example, what exactly is the nature of subvocalization? Does it literally involve covert speech and thus movements (perhaps tiny movements) of the tongue, the vocal cords, and so on? One way to find out would be to paralyze these various muscles. Would this disrupt use of the rehearsal loop? As it turns out, we don't have to perform this experiment; nature has performed it for us. Because of specific forms of neurological damage, some individuals have no ability to move these various muscles and thus are unable to speak. These individuals are **anarthric**—that is, without speech. Data indicate, however, that these individuals show sound-alike confusions in their data, just as ordinary participants do. This observation suggests that actual muscle movements are not needed for subvocalization. Instead, "inner speech" probably relies on the brain areas responsible for *planning* the muscle movements of speech. This is by itself an interesting fact, but for present purposes, note the use of yet another type of data: observations from **neuropsychology**, concerned with how various forms of brain dysfunction influence observed performance.

We can pursue similar questions by examining the brain activity of people without any brain damage. Recent developments in brain-imaging technology tell us that when a participant is engaged in working-memory rehearsal, considerable brain activity is observed in areas that we know (from other evidence) are crucially involved in the production of spoken language, as well as in areas that play an important role in the perception and understanding of spoken language. These data are drawn from **cognitive neuroscience**—the study of the biological basis for cognitive functioning—and lend further support to the idea that claims about the inner voice and inner ear are more than casual metaphors.

Finally, it is crucial that we have built our argument with *multiple lines* of evidence. That's because, in most cases, no single line of evidence is by itself decisive. There are, after all, probably other ways to explain our initial observations about span, if those results were all we had to go on. There are also other ways to explain the other individual findings we have mentioned, if these likewise were considered in isolation. It's only when we take the results as a package that we can make headway, and if we have done our work well, there will be just one theoretical account that fits with the entire data pattern. At that point, with no other way to explain the data, we will conclude that we have understood the evidence and that we have correctly reconstructed what is going on in the mind, invisibly, never directly observed.

Working Memory in a Broader Context

Having made all of these methodological points, let us round out this section with one final comment: Why should we care about the structure of working memory? Why is working memory interesting? The memory-span task itself seems quite unnatural: How often do we need to memorize a set of unrelated numbers or letters? For that matter, how often do we need to work on a problem while simultaneously saying "tah-tah-tah" over and over? In short, what does this task, and this procedure, have to do with things we care about?

The answer to these questions allows us to replay an issue we have already discussed: We rely on working memory in a vast number of circumstances, and so, if we understand working memory, we move toward an understanding of this far broader set of problems and issues. For example, bear in mind our initial comments about the role of working memory in reading, or in any other task in which you must store early "products," keeping them ready for integration with later products. One might imagine that many tasks have this character; reading, reasoning, and problem-solving are a few. If you make effective use of working memory, therefore, you will have an advantage in all of these domains. Indeed, some scholars have suggested that "intelligence" in many domains amounts to nothing more than excess capacity in working memory. (See, for example, Kyllonen & Cristal, 1990.)

In a similar vein, the use of articulatory rehearsal seems a simple trick—a trick you use quite spontaneously, a trick in which you take no special pride. But it is a trick you had to learn, and young children, for example, often seem not to know the trick. There is some indication that this can be a problem for these children in learning to read: Without the option of relying on articulatory rehearsal, reading becomes much more difficult. It also appears that the rehearsal loop plays an important role when someone is learning new vocabulary, including vocabulary in a new language (Baddeley, Gathercole, & Papagno, 1998; Gathercole, Service, Hitch, Adams, & Martin, 1999). So here, too, is an important function of the working-memory system.

These examples can easily be multiplied but, by now, the point should be clear: Working memory and articulatory rehearsal are relevant to a wide range of mental activities, in adults and in children. Understanding working memory, therefore, may give us insight into a broad range of tasks. Similar claims can be made about many other cognitive resources: By understanding what it means to pay attention, we move toward an understanding of all the contexts in which attention plays a role. By understanding how we comprehend text, or how we use our knowledge to supplement our perceptions, we move toward an understanding of all the contexts in which these play a part. And in each case the number of such contexts is vast.

We end this section, therefore, by echoing a comment we have already made: The machinery of cognition is essential to virtually all of our waking activities (and perhaps some of our sleeping activities as well). The scope of cognitive psychology is broad indeed, and the relevance of our research is wide.

Chapter Summary

1. Cognitive psychology is concerned with how people remember, pay attention, and think. The importance of all these issues arises in part from the fact that most of what we do, think, and feel is guided by things we already know. One example is the comprehension of a simple story, which turns out to be heavily influenced by the knowledge we supply.

2. Cognitive psychology emerged as a separate discipline in the late 1950s, and its powerful impact on the wider field of psychology has led many to speak of this emergence as the cognitive revolution. One predecessor of cognitive psychology was the 19th-century movement that emphasized introspection as the main research tool for psychology. Psychologists soon became disenchanted with this movement, however, for several reasons: Introspection cannot inform us about unconscious mental events. Even with conscious events, claims rooted in introspection are often untestable, because there is no way for an independent observer to check on the accuracy or completeness of an introspective report.

3. The behaviorist movement rejected introspection as a method, insisting instead that psychology speak only of mechanisms and processes that were objective and out in the open for all to observe. However, evidence suggests that our thinking, behavior, and feelings are often shaped by our perception or understanding of the events we experience. This is problematic for the behaviorists: Perception and understanding are exactly the sorts of mental processes that the behaviorists regarded as subjective and not open to scientific study.

4. In order to study mental events, psychologists have turned to a method in which one focuses on observable events but then asks what (invisible) events must have taken place in order to make these (visible) effects possible. In many cases, this method involves hypotheses about information-processing events, so that, in general, human mental processes can be described in terms similar to those used to describe computer processes.

5. Research in working memory provides an example of how cognitive psychologists use evidence. One theory of working memory proposes that this memory consists of a central executive and a small number of low-level assistants, including the articulatory rehearsal loop, which stores material by means of covert speech. Many forms of evidence are used in supporting this account: measures of working memory's holding capacity in various circumstances, the nature of errors people make when using working memory, the speed of performance in working-memory tasks, evidence drawn from the study of people with brain damage, and evidence drawn from brain-imaging technology.

The Neural Basis for Cognition

C ognitive psychologists rely on many sorts of evidence: response times, error rates, questionnaire responses, and so on. No one source of data is more important than the others; all contribute to the broad fabric of evidence that allows us to test our theories.

One form of evidence, however, does need its own presentation: evidence concerning the brain functioning that makes cognition possible. We will encounter this biologically rooted evidence throughout this book, woven together with other sorts of data, as we develop and test our theories. But first we need to lay the appropriate foundation—some background information about the brain and the methods used to study the brain.

- We explore the example of *Capgras syndrome* to illustrate how seemingly simple achievements actually depend on many parts of the brain; we also highlight the ways that the study of the brain, and brain damage, can illuminate questions about the mind.

- We then survey the brain's anatomy, emphasizing on the function carried out by each brain region. The identification of these functions is supported by neuroimaging data,

which can assess the activity levels in different brain areas, and also by studies of the effects of brain damage.

- We consider the *visual system* as an illustration of what we can learn from closer scrutiny of brain function. Here we see that the analysis of the visual input begins the moment visual information enters the nervous system, and depends on many highly specialized brain areas, all working in parallel with the others.

Capgras Syndrome: An Initial Example

The human brain is an extraordinarily complex organ in which the functioning of the whole is dependent on many interconnected systems. Because of this complexity, the brain's functioning can break down in many different ways, and damage virtually anywhere in the brain will produce specific—and sometimes highly disruptive—symptoms. These symptoms are often tragic for the afflicted persons and their families, but they can also be a rich source of insight into how the brain functions.

Consider, for example, a remarkable disorder known as **Capgras syndrome** (Capgras & Reboul-Lachaux, 1923). This disorder is rare on its own, but seems to be one of the accompaniments to Alzheimer's syndrome, and so is sometimes observed among the elderly (Harwood, Barker, Ownby, & Duara, 1999). More directly, though, the disorder can result from various injuries to the brain (Ellis & De Pauw, 1994).

Someone with Capgras syndrome is fully able to recognize the people in her world—her husband, her parents, her friends—but she is utterly convinced that these people are not who they appear to be. The real husband or the real son, the afflicted person insists, has been kidnapped (or worse). The person now on the scene, therefore, isn't the genuine article; instead, he or she must be a well-trained, well-disguised impostor.

Imagine what it is like to have this disorder. You turn to someone you know extremely well—perhaps your father—and say, "You look like my father, sound like him, and act like him. But I can tell that you're not my father. Who are you?"

Often a person with Capgras syndrome insists that there are slight differences between the impostor and the person he or she has replaced—subtle changes in personality, or tiny changes in appearance. Of course, no one else detects these (nonexistent) differences, compounding the bewilderment experienced by the Capgras sufferer. These feelings spiral upward, with the patient developing all sorts of paranoid suspicions about why a loved one has been replaced, and why no one seems to acknowledge this replacement. In the extreme, the Capgras sufferer may be led to desperate steps, in some instances murdering the supposed impostor in an attempt to end the charade and relocate the "genuine" character. In one case, a Capgras patient was convinced his father had been replaced by a robot and so decapitated him in order to look for the batteries and microfilm in his head (Blount, 1986).

What is going on here? The answer, according to some researchers, lies in the fact that facial recognition involves two separate systems in the brain, one of which leads to a cognitive appraisal ("I know what my father looks like, and I can perceive that you closely resemble him") and the other to a more global, somewhat emotional appraisal ("You look familiar to me and also trigger a warm response in me"). The concordance of these two appraisals then leads to the certainty of recognition ("You obviously are my father"). In Capgras syndrome, though, the latter (emotional) processing is disrupted, leading to the intellectual identification without the familiarity response (Ellis & Lewis, 2001; Ellis & Young, 1990; Ramachandran & Blakeslee, 1998): "You resemble my father but trigger no sense of familiarity, so you must be someone else."

The Neural Basis For Capgras Syndrome

A crucial step in examining this hypothesis about Capgras syndrome is to examine the brains of people with this disorder. This examination is made possible by **neuroimaging techniques,** developed in the last few decades, that allow researchers to take high-quality, three-dimensional "pictures" of living brains, without in any way disturbing the brains' owners. We will have more to say about neuroimaging later, but first, what do these techniques tell us about Capgras syndrome?

One form of neuroimaging data comes from PET scans, and these tell a great deal about the structure of the brain—including abnormalities in the brain tissue (PET will be described in more detail later in this chapter). These scans suggest a link between Capgras syndrome and abnormalities in several brain areas (Edelstyn & Oyebode, 1999; also O'Connor, Walbridge, Sandson, & Alexander, 1996; see Figure 2.1). One site of damage is in the temporal lobe, particularly on the right side of the head. This damage probably disrupts circuits involving the **amygdala,** an almond-shaped structure that—in the intact brain—seems to serve as an "emotional evaluator," helping an organism to detect stimuli associated with threat or danger. The amygdala is also important for detecting *positive* stimuli—indicators of safety, or indicators of available rewards. It seems likely, then, that the amygdala, the "evaluator," is essential for making the judgment of "you look familiar to me and trigger a warm emotional feeling"—one half of our two-systems hypothesis.

Patients with Capgras syndrome also have brain abnormalities in the frontal lobe, specifically in the **right prefrontal cortex.** What is this area's normal function? To find out, we turn to a different neuroimaging technique, fMRI, which allows us to track moment-by-moment activity levels in different sites in a living brain. (We'll say more about fMRI in a later section.) This allows us to answer such questions as, When a person is reading, which brain regions are particularly active?

FIGURE 2.1 The Lobes of the Human Brain

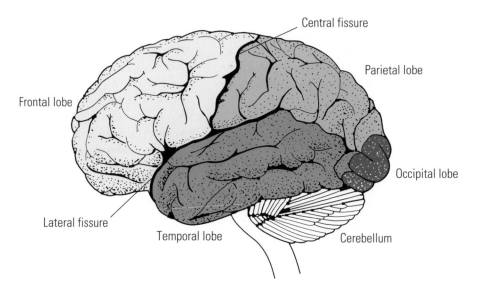

The four lobes of the forebrain surround (and hide from view) the midbrain and most of the hindbrain. (The cerebellum is the only part of the hindbrain that is visible.) This side view shows the brain's left cerebral hemisphere (and so, here, the left-hand side of the drawing is the front of the head); the structures on the right side of the brain are similar. However, the two halves of the brain do have somewhat different functions, and so the results of brain injury depend on which half is damaged. The symptoms of Capgras syndrome, for example, result from damage to specific sites on the right side of the frontal and temporal lobes.

How about when a person is listening to music? With data like these, we can ask which tasks make heavy use of a brain area, and from that base we can draw conclusions about what the brain area's function is.

An important hint about Capgras syndrome comes from fMRI scans of patients suffering from an entirely different problem: schizophrenia (Silbersweig et al., 1995). Neuroimaging reveals diminished activity in the patients' frontal lobes whenever the patients are experiencing hallucinations. One plausible interpretation of this is that the diminished activity reflects a decreased ability to distinguish internal events (thoughts) from external ones (voices), or to distinguish imagined events from real ones. (For supporting data, see Glisky, Polster, & Routhieaux, 1995.)

How is this relevant to Capgras syndrome? With damage to the frontal lobe, Capgras patients may be less able to keep track of what is real and what is not, what is plausible and what is not. As a result, weird beliefs can emerge unchecked, including delusions (about robots and the like) that you or I would find utterly bizarre.

What Do We Learn from Capgras Syndrome?

As it turns out, multiple lines of evidence support this account of Capgras syndrome (e.g., Ellis & Lewis, 2001; Ramachandran & Blakeslee, 1998). Some of the evidence comes from the psychology laboratory and confirms that memory for factual knowledge is indeed separable from the warm sense of familiarity (see Chapter 6). Thus (for example) we know that familiarity and memory for factual knowledge are responsive to different sorts of influences, just as we would expect if they depend on different mechanisms with each mechanism responsive to its own set of factors.

In addition, some of the relevant evidence is obviously biological, telling us the location of the brain damage in Capgras patients, and also telling us the likely functions of these brain sites when they're *not* damaged. Specifically, and as we've just seen, the biological evidence confirms that some of the damage involves the amygdala, and this is probably the reason why Capgras patients experience no sense of familiarity when they look at faces they know quite well. And some of the damage involves the prefrontal cortex, which allows Capgras patients, when they experience this lack of familiarity, to offer crazy hypotheses about their skewed perception.

Note, then, that our understanding of Capgras syndrome depends on a combination of evidence drawn from cognitive psychology and from cognitive neuroscience; we use both perspectives to test (and, ultimately, to confirm) the hypothesis we've offered. In addition, just as both perspectives can illuminate Capgras syndrome, both can be *illuminated by* the syndrome. That is, we can use Capgras syndrome (and other biological evidence) to illuminate broader issues about the nature of the brain and of the mind.

For example, Capgras syndrome suggests that the amygdala plays a crucial role in supporting the feeling of familiarity. Other biological evidence suggests that the amygdala also plays a central part in helping people remember the emotional events of their lives (e.g., Buchanan & Adolphs, 2004). Still other evidence indicates that the amygdala plays a role in decision-making (e.g., Bechara, Damasio, & Damasio, 2003), and this may be especially important for decisions that rest on emotional evaluations, and perhaps also decisions that rest on *hunches*. Facts like these tell us an enormous amount about the various functions that make cognition possible, and in this case, the facts tell us that our theorizing needs to include a broadly useful "emotional evaluator," involved in many cognitive processes. Moreover, Capgras syndrome tells us that this emotional evaluator works in a fashion separate from our evaluation of factual information, providing us a way to think about the occasions in which our evaluation of the facts points toward one conclusion, while an emotional evaluation points toward a different conclusion. These are clues of enormous value as we put together our theories about the ordinary functioning of cognitive processes like memory or decision-making.

Cases like Capgras syndrome are just as valuable in helping us understand how the brain functions in normal people—that is, when all the neural systems are intact. As an illustration, consider what this syndrome teaches us about how the various parts of the brain work together for even the simplest achievement. In order to recognize your father, for example, one part of the brain needs to store the factual memory of what your father looks like. Another part of the brain is responsible for analyzing the visual input you receive when looking at a face. Yet another brain area has the job of comparing this now-analyzed input to the factual information provided from memory, to determine if there's a match or not. Another site provides the emotional evaluation of the input. A different site presumably assembles the data from all these other sites, and so registers the fact that the face being inspected does match the factual recollection of your father's face and also produces a warm sense of familiarity. Ordinarily, all of these brain areas work together, allowing the recognition of your father's face to go smoothly forward. If they don't work together—that is, if the coordination among these areas is disrupted—yet another area works to make sure you offer plausible hypotheses about this, and not zany ones. (And so, if your father looks less familiar to you on some occasion, you're more likely to explain this by saying, "I guess he must have gotten new glasses," rather than "I bet he's been replaced by a space alien.")

Unmistakably, then, this apparently easy task—seeing one's own father and recognizing who he is—requires multiple brain areas. The same is true of most tasks, and, in this way, Capgras syndrome illustrates this crucial aspect of brain function.

The Principal Structures of the Brain

In order to discuss Capgras syndrome, we had to refer to different brain areas; we also had to rely on several different research techniques. Thus, the syndrome also illustrates another point—namely, that this is a domain in which we need some technical foundations before we can develop our theories. Let's start building those foundations.

The human brain weighs between 3 and 4 pounds; it's roughly the size of a small melon. Yet this structure has been estimated to contain a trillion nerve cells (that's 10^{12}), each of which is connected to 10,000 or so others—for a total of roughly 10 million billion connections. How should we begin our study of this densely packed, incredibly complex organ?

One place to start is with a simple fact that we've already met—namely, that different parts of the brain perform different jobs. We've known this fact about the brain for many years, thanks to clinical evidence showing that the symptoms produced by brain damage depend heavily on the location of the damage. In 1848, for example, a horrible construction accident caused Phineas Gage to suffer damage in the frontmost part of his brain; this damage led to severe personality and emotional problems. In 1861, physician Paul Broca noted that damage in a different location, on the left side of the brain, led to a disruption of language skills. In 1911, Édouard Claparède (1911–1951) reported his observations with patients who suffered from profound memory loss, a loss produced by damage in still another part of the brain.

Clearly, therefore, we need to understand brain functioning with reference to brain anatomy. Where was the damage that Gage suffered? Where exactly was the damage in Broca's patients, or Claparède's? In this section, we fill in some basics of brain anatomy.

Hindbrain, Midbrain, Forebrain

The human brain is divided into three main structures: the hindbrain, the midbrain, and the forebrain. The **hindbrain** sits directly atop the spinal cord and includes several structures crucial for controlling key life functions. It's here, for example, that the rhythm of heartbeats is controlled, and the rhythm of breathing. The hindbrain also plays an essential role in maintaining the body's overall tone, and so, specifically, the hindbrain helps maintain the body's posture and balance, and also helps regulate the brain's level of alertness.

The largest area of the hindbrain is the **cerebellum**. For many years, investigators believed the cerebellum's main role was in the coordination of our bodily movements and balance. Recent studies, however, suggest that the cerebellum also plays a diverse set of other roles, and damage to this organ can cause problems in spatial reasoning, in discriminating sounds, and in integrating the input received from various sensory systems (J. M. Bower & Parsons, 2003).

The **midbrain** also has several roles. It plays an important part in coordinating our movements, including the skilled, precise movements of our eyes as we explore the visual world. Also in the midbrain are circuits that relay auditory information from the ears to the areas in the forebrain where this information is processed and interpreted. Still other structures in the midbrain help to regulate our experience of pain.

For our purposes, though, the most interesting brain region (and, in humans, the largest region) is the **forebrain**. Pictures of the brain (like the one in Figure 2.1) show little other than the forebrain, because this structure surrounds (and hides from view) the entire midbrain and most of the hindbrain. Of course, it is only the outer surface of the forebrain that is visible in such pictures; this is the **cortex** (from the Latin word for "tree bark").

The cortex is just a thin covering on the outer surface of the brain; on average, it is a mere 3 mm thick. Nonetheless, there is a great deal of cortical tissue; by some estimates, the cortex comprises 80% of the human brain. This considerable volume is made possible by the fact that the cortex, thin as it is, consists of a very large sheet of tissue; if stretched out flat, it would cover roughly 2 square feet. But the cortex isn't stretched flat; instead, it is all crumpled up and jammed into the limited space inside the skull. It's this crumpling that produces the brain's most obvious visual feature—the wrinkles, or **convolutions**, that cover the brain's outer surface.

Some of the "valleys" in between the wrinkles are actually deep grooves that anatomically divide the brain into different sections. The deepest groove is the **longitudinal fissure**, running from the front of the brain to the back, and separating the left **cerebral hemisphere** from the right. Other fissures divide the cortex in each hemisphere into four lobes (Figure 2.1), and these are named after the bones that cover them—bones that, as a group, make up the skull. The **frontal lobes** form the front of the brain—right behind the forehead. The **central fissure** divides the frontal lobes on each side of the brain from the **parietal lobes**, the brain's topmost part. The bottom edge of the frontal lobes is marked by the **lateral fissure**, and below this are the **temporal lobes.** Finally, at the very back of the brain, connected to the parietal and temporal lobes, are the **occipital lobes**.

Subcortical Structures

Hidden from view, underneath the cortex—and so **subcortical**—are many other parts of the forebrain. One of these is the **thalamus**, a brain region that acts as a relay station for nearly all the sensory information going to the cortex. Directly underneath the thalamus is the **hypothalamus**, a structure that plays a crucial role in the control of motivated behaviors such as eating, drinking, and sexual activity.

Surrounding the thalamus and hypothalamus is another set of interconnected structures that together form the **limbic system** (see Figure 2.2). Included here are the **hippocampus** and the amygdala, both located underneath the cortex in the temporal lobe. These structures play a crucial role in learning and memory, and in

---

FIGURE 2.2 The Limbic System

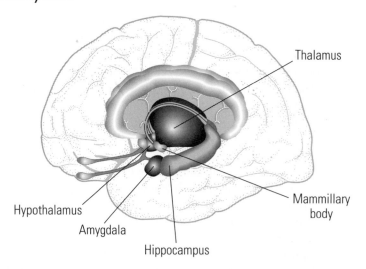

In this drawing, we have pretended that the left cerebral hemisphere is transparent, so that we can see through it to the limbic system underneath. This system includes a number of subcortical structures that play a crucial role in learning and memory and in emotional processing.

emotional processing. The patient H.M., whom we discussed in Chapter 1, developed his profound amnesia after surgeons removed these structures—a strong confirmation of their role in the formation of new memories.

Like most parts of the brain, these various structures come in pairs, and so there is a hippocampus on the left side of the brain and another on the right, a left-side amygdala and a right one. Of course, the same is true for the cortex itself: There is a temporal cortex in the left hemisphere and another in the right, a left occipital cortex and a right one, and so on. In all cases, cortical and subcortical, the left and right structures in each pair have roughly the same shape, the same position in their respective sides of the brain, and the same pattern of connections to other brain areas. Even so, there are differences between the left-side and right-side structures, and in many cases, we can document differences in function, with the left-hemisphere structure involved in somewhat different tasks, and playing a different role, from the corresponding right-hemisphere structure.

Let's bear in mind, though, that the two halves of the brain work together; the functioning of one side is closely integrated with that of the other side. This integration is made possible by the **commissures**, thick bundles of fibers that carry information back and forth between the two hemispheres. The largest commissure is the **corpus callosum**, but several other structures also ensure that the two brain halves work together as partners in virtually all mental tasks.

Neuroimaging Techniques

As we have noted, the specific symptoms that result from brain damage depend heavily on the site of the damage. A **lesion** (a specific area of damage) on the hippocampus produces memory problems but not language disorders; a lesion on the occipital cortex produces problems in vision but spares the other sensory modalities. The consequences of brain lesions also depend on which hemisphere is damaged: damage to the left side of the frontal lobe, for example, is likely to produce a disruption of language use; damage to the right side of the frontal lobe doesn't have this effect. All of these facts obviously confirm that different brain areas perform different functions.

A similar conclusion follows from neuroimaging data. As we mentioned in our discussion of Capgras syndrome, neuroimaging techniques allow us to take precise three-dimensional pictures of the brain. Several such techniques are available, including **computerized axial tomography**, or CT scans, and **positron emission tomography**, or PET scans. CT scans use X-rays to study the brain's anatomy. PET scans provide a precise assessment of how blood is flowing through each region of the brain, to study the brain's functioning. (This method rests on the fact that, when a particular brain area is more active, it needs—and receives—a greater blood flow, see Figure 2.3.)

In general, these techniques rely on a bank of detectors surrounding the head—a bank of X-ray detectors for CT scans, a bank of photon detectors for PET scans. A

FIGURE 2.3 PET Scan and Visual Stimulation

PET scans measure how much glucose (the brain's fuel) is being used at specific locations within the brain; this provides a measurement of that location's activity level at a certain moment in time. In the figure, the brain is viewed from above, with the front of the head at the top of the drawing, and the back at the bottom. As the figure shows, visual processing involves increased activity in the occipital cortex. (Photograph by Dr. John Mazziotta et al./Photo Researchers)

computer then compares the signals received by each of the detectors and uses this information to pinpoint the source of each signal. In this way, the computer can reconstruct a three-dimensional map (or image) of the brain—a map, in CT scans, that tells us what *structures* are where or, in PET scans, that tells us about *activity levels* and, specifically, what regions are particularly active or inactive at any point in time.

In recent years, investigators have relied more on two newer techniques: **magnetic resonance imaging** (MRI; see Figure 2.4) and **functional magnetic resonance imaging** (fMRI). MRI scans start by passing a magnetic field through the brain to align the spinning of the nuclei of all the atoms that make up the brain tissue; then a brief pulse of electromagnetic energy is used to disrupt these spins. After this disruption, the spins of the nuclei shift back into alignment with the magnetic field, and as this shift happens, the atoms give off electromagnetic energy. This energy is recorded by a bank of detectors arrayed around the person's head, analyzed by a computer, and assembled into a detailed three-dimensional representation of the brain. An fMRI scan uses similar principles but measures the oxygen content in the blood flowing through each region of the brain; this turns out to be an accurate index of the level of neural activity in that region. In this way, fMRI scans provide an incredibly precise picture of the brain's moment-by-moment activities.

FIGURE 2.4   Magnetic Resonance Imaging

Magnetic resonance imaging produces magnificently detailed pictures of the brain. The left panel shows a "slice" of the brain viewed from the top of the head (the front of the head is at the top of the image); clearly visible is the longitudinal fissure, which divides the left cerebral hemisphere from the right. The middle panel shows a slice of the brain viewed from the front; again, the separation of the two hemispheres is clearly visible, and so are some of the commissures linking the two brain halves. The right panel shows a slice of the brain viewed from the side; many of the structures in the limbic system (Figure 2.2) are easily seen.

PET and fMRI scans show us that the pattern of activation across the brain depends heavily on what task the person is performing. Again, this tells us that different brain areas perform different functions and so make different contributions to whatever task is under way. Thus, if a brain area performs a function that is particularly relevant to a task, that brain area will be highly activated during that task; if a brain area's function is not relevant to a task, then its activity level will be lower.

Neuroimaging: An Example

As an example of the power of neuroimaging techniques, consider a study by Tong, Nakayama, Vaughan, and Kanwisher (1998). In one condition of their study, participants were looking at pictures of *faces* while their brains were scanned; the data showed high levels of activation in an area called the **fusiform face area** (FFA), an area that seems highly responsive to faces and much less responsive to other visual stimuli (Figure 2.5A). In a second condition, participants were looking at pictures of houses while their brains were scanned; now the data showed high levels of activity in a different region: the **parahippocampal place area** (PPA), a brain site that seems to respond actively whenever pictures of *places* are in view (Figure 2.5B).

FIGURE 2.5 Brain Activity and Awareness

Panel A shows an fMRI scan of a subject looking at *faces*. Activation levels are high in a brain area called the fusiform face area (FFA); apparently, this area is more responsive to faces than to other visual stimuli. Panel B shows a scan of the same subject looking at pictures of *places*; now activity levels are high in the parahippocampal place area (PPA). Panel C compares the activity in these two brain areas when a picture of a face is in front of one eye, and a picture of a house is in front of the other eye. When the subject becomes aware of the face, activation is higher in the FFA. When the subject becomes aware of the house, activation in the PPA increases. Clearly, then, the activation level reflects what the subject is aware of, and not just the pattern of incoming stimulation.

Data like these make it clear that different areas of the brain are specialized not just for vision but for specific types of visual targets.

The most interesting condition of the Tong et al. study, however, was one in which a picture of a face was put in front of one of the participant's eyes while a picture of a house was put in front of the other eye. This is a situation known to produce **binocular rivalry:** The visual system is unable to handle both stimuli at once, or to fuse the stimuli into a single complex perception. Instead, the visual system seems to flip-flop between the stimuli, so that, for a while, the person is aware only of the face; then, for a while, aware of only the house; and so on.

In the Tong et al. study, participants pressed buttons to indicate, at each moment in time, whether they were aware of seeing the house or aware of seeing the face. At the same time, the researchers used an fMRI scan to keep track of the activity levels in the FFA (again, normally responsive to faces) and the PPA (normally responsive to places).

What should we expect here? If these brain areas respond simply to the stimuli that are available, then the activity levels would not have varied as the experiment progressed. The stimuli, after all, were never changed. But if these brain areas reflect the participants' conscious perception, then activity should fluctuate, with a change in brain activity each time the binocular rivalry produces a new perception.

To analyze the data, the researchers relied on the **BOLD** signal (for *blood oxygenation level dependent*). This signal measures how much oxygen the blood's hemoglobin is carrying in each part of the brain, and this provides a quantitative basis for comparing activity levels in different brain areas.

Figure 2.5C shows the key result. At moments in which the participant reported a conscious switch from seeing the face to seeing the house, activity in the PPA went up, and activity in the FFA went down. At moments in which the participant reported the reverse switch, the activity levels in these two brain areas showed the opposite pattern.

Note, then, the power of these techniques. We can use brain scanning, first, to figure out the special function of different brain regions, and thus to learn (for example) which brain regions are crucial for the perception of faces, and which for the perception of other stimuli. Second, we can use measurements like the BOLD signal to track activity levels across time, and ask how the brain activity changes in response to new stimuli or new thoughts. Third, we can ask what exactly a brain state corresponds to: Does activity of the FFA, to put it crudely, tell us only what stimuli are present, sending their images to the nervous system? Or does activity of the FFA tell us what the person is consciously perceiving? The Tong et al. data favor the second option, with the striking suggestion that we can use brain scans as a means of studying some of the bases for conscious awareness. (For more on consciousness, see Chapter 15.)

Correlation Versus Causation

Neuroimaging data strongly suggest that different jobs are carried out by different bits of the brain, inviting us to ask questions like, What job does the occipital cortex do? What work does the temporal lobe do? Answering these questions is referred to as the **localization of function**.

There is, however, a limitation to the neuroimaging data: We have already seen, for example, that activity levels increase in the FFA when a face is being perceived, but does this mean the FFA is needed for face perception? Perhaps the FFA activation is just a by-product of face perception, and not playing a crucial role. As an analogy, think about the fact that a car's speedometer becomes "more activated" (i.e., shows a higher value) whenever the car goes faster. That doesn't mean that the speedometer *causes* the speed or is *necessary* for the speed. Indeed, the car would go just as fast and would, for many purposes, perform just as well if the speedometer were removed. The speedometer's state, in other words, is *correlated* with the car's speed, but in no sense causes (or promotes, or is needed for) the car's speed.

In the same way, neuroimaging data tell us which areas are correlated with a particular function, but we need other data to ask whether those brain sites play a role in causing (or supporting, or allowing) that function. In many cases, those other data come from the study of brain lesions: If damage to a brain site disrupts a function, that's obviously an indication that the site does play some role in supporting that function.

Also helpful here is a technique called **transcranial magnetic stimulation** (TMS). This techniques creates a series of strong magnetic pulses at a specific location on the scalp, causing a (temporary!) disruption in the small brain region directly underneath this scalp area (Helmuth, 2001). In this way, we can ask, in an otherwise normal brain, what functions are compromised when a particular bit of brain tissue is temporarily "turned off." As a result, we can ask, in a normal brain, whether that brain tissue plays a causal role in supporting the appropriate brain function.

Primary Motor Projection Areas

We've now said a lot about the general issue of localization of function. Let's turn to some specific brain areas and ask exactly what functions they serve.

Certain areas of the brain seem to be the arrival points for information coming from the eyes, ears, and other sense organs. Other areas are the departure points for signals leaving the forebrain and controlling muscle movement. The arrival points are contained within regions known as the **primary sensory projection areas**, one projection area for each of the sensory modalities. The departure points are contained in regions known as the **primary motor projection area**.

Evidence for the motor projection area comes from studies in which investigators apply mild electrical current to this area in anesthetized animals. This stimulation often produces specific movements, so that current applied to one site causes a movement of the left front leg, while current applied to a different site causes the ears to perk up. These movements show a pattern of **contralateral control**, with stimulation to the left hemisphere leading to movements on the right side of the body, and vice versa.

The sites stimulated in these studies are in a strip of tissue toward the rear of the frontal lobe (Figure 2.6A), and this is the primary motor projection area. The term "projection" is borrowed from geography because this area seems to form a

FIGURE 2.6 The Primary Motor Projection Area

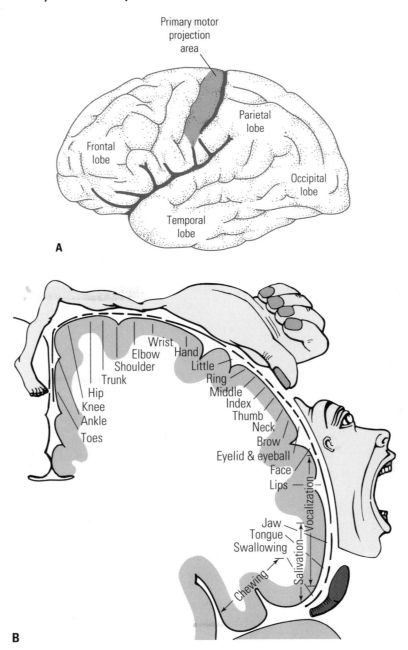

The primary motor projection area, located toward the rear of the frontal lobe (Panel A), sends out the signals that ultimately result in muscle movement. Panel B shows which parts of the body are controlled by different parts of the projection area; clearly, more cortical space is devoted to the body parts that we can move with greatest precision.

"map" of the body, with particular positions on the cortex corresponding to particular parts of the body.

Investigators have been able to draw these maps in some detail, and Figure 2.6B shows one representation of the result. In the figure, a drawing of a person has been overlaid on a depiction of the brain, with each part of the little person positioned on top of the area of the brain that controls its movement. As the figure shows, areas of the body that we can move with great precision (fingers and lips, for instance) have a lot of cortical area devoted to them; areas of the body over which we have less control (the shoulder or the back, for instance) receive less cortical coverage. (For a possible complication in this picture, though, see Graziano, Taylor, & Moore, 2002.)

Primary Sensory Projection Areas

Information arriving from the skin senses (your sense of touch or your sense of temperature) is projected to a region in the parietal lobe, just behind the motor projection area; this is labeled the "somatosensory" area in Figure 2.7. If a patient's

---

FIGURE 2.7 The Primary Sensory Projection Areas

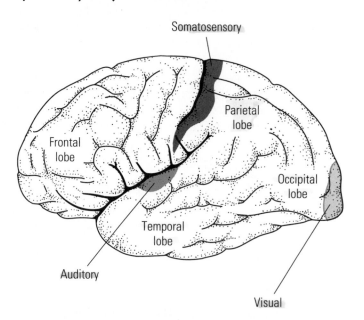

Information arriving from the skin senses is projected to a region in the parietal lobe (the somatosensory projection area). Information arriving from the eyes is projected to the occipital lobe; information from the ears, to the temporal lobe.

brain is stimulated in this region (with electrical current or touch), the patient will typically report a tingling sensation in a specific part of the body. Figure 2.7 also shows the region in the temporal lobes that functions as the primary projection area for hearing (the "auditory" area). If directly stimulated here, patients hear clicks, buzzes, and hums. An area in the occipital lobes serves as the primary projection area for vision; stimulation here produces the experience of seeing flashes of light or visual patterns.

These sensory projection areas differ from each other in important ways, but they also have features in common, and they're features that parallel the attributes of the motor projection area. First, each of these areas provides a map of the sensory environment. In the somatosensory area, each part of the body's surface is represented by its own region on the cortex; areas of the body that are near to each other are typically represented by similarly nearby areas in the brain. In the visual area, each different region of visual space has its own cortical representation, and again, adjacent areas of space are usually represented by adjacent brain sites. In the auditory projection area, different frequencies of sound each have their own cortical sites, and adjacent brain sites are responsive to adjacent frequencies.

Second, in each of these maps the assignment of cortical space is governed by function, not by anatomical proportions. In the parietal lobes, parts of the body that are not very discriminating with regard to touch, even if they're physically large, get relatively little cortical area (Figure 2.8). Other, more sensitive, areas of the body (the lips, tongue, and fingers) get far more space. In the occipital lobes, more cortical surface is devoted to the fovea, the part of the eyeball that is most sensitive to detail.

Finally, these projection areas all respect the principle of contralateral control: The left parietal lobe receives its main input from the right side of the body, for example; the right temporal lobe receives its main input from the left ear. The same principle applies to the visual projection areas, but here the projection is not contralateral with regard to body parts; instead, it's contralateral with regard to physical space. Specifically, the visual projection area in the right cerebral hemisphere receives information from both the left eye and the right, but the information it receives corresponds to the left half of visual space (i.e., all of the things you see toward the left when you are looking straight ahead). The reverse is true for the left cerebral hemisphere: It receives information from both eyes, but from only the right half of visual space.

Association Areas

The projection areas described so far—both motor and sensory—make up only a small part of the human cortex—roughly 25%. The remaining cortical areas are traditionally referred to as the **association cortex**, on the idea that this section of the brain performs the task of associating simple ideas and sensations in order to form more complex thoughts and behaviors.

| FIGURE 2.8 | The Sensory Homunculus |

In the somatosensory projection area, a lot of cortical space is devoted to parts of the body that are extremely sensitive to touch (e.g., the lips, tongue, and fingers). Relatively little space is devoted to parts of the body that are less sensitive (e.g., the shoulders or the legs). Here is an artist's rendition of what a person would look like if his actual appearance were proportional to the cortical area allotted to each body part! (Courtesy of the Natural History Museum, London)

This terminology, however, may be misleading. Among other reasons, the terminology does nothing to reflect the fact that this large volume of brain tissue can be subdivided further on both functional and anatomical grounds. These subdivisions are perhaps best revealed by the diversity of symptoms that can result if the cortex is damaged in one or another specific location. For example, some lesions in the frontal lobe produce **apraxias,** disturbances in the initiation or organization of voluntary action. Other lesions (generally in the occipital cortex, or in the rearmost part of the parietal lobe) lead to **agnosias,** or disruptions in a person's ability to identify familiar objects. Agnosias usually affect one modality only, so a patient with visual agnosia, for example, can recognize a fork by touching it, but not by looking at it. A patient with auditory agnosia, by contrast, might be unable to identify familiar voices but might still recognize the face of the person speaking.

Still other lesions (usually in the parietal lobe) produce **neglect syndrome,** in which the individual seems to ignore half of the visual world. A patient afflicted with this syndrome will shave only half of his face and eat food from only half of his plate. If asked to read the word "pigpen," he will read "pen," and so on.

Damage in other areas causes still other symptoms. We mentioned earlier that lesions in the left frontal lobe, usually at sites just above the lateral fissure, can result in disruption to language capacities, a problem referred to as **aphasia.**

Finally, damage to the frontmost part of the frontal lobe, the **prefrontal area**, causes a variety of different problems. In many cases, these are problems of planning and implementing strategies. In other cases, patients with damage here show problems in inhibiting their own behaviors, relying on habit even in situations for which habit is inappropriate. Frontal lobe damage can also (as we mentioned in our discussion of Capgras) lead to a variety of confusions, such as whether a remembered episode actually happened or was simply imagined.

We will have more to say about many of these diagnostic categories—aphasia, agnosia, neglect, and more—in upcoming chapters. There we'll be able to consider these disorders in the context of other things we know about object recognition, attention, and so on; this will allow us to draw important lessons from these clinical data. Our point for the moment, though, is a simple one: These various clinical patterns make it clear that the so-called association cortex contains many subregions, each specialized for a particular function, but with all of the subregions working together in virtually all aspects of our daily lives.

The Visual System

So far, we have taken a fairly coarse view of the brain, discussing large-scale structures. But it is also useful to take a closer look at the brain, to see how the brain's functions are actually carried out. In this section, we'll illustrate this sort of closer look by considering the brain systems that allow us to see, and to recognize the objects that we see. We take the visual system as our example for two reasons. First, it is a modality through which humans acquire a huge amount of information, whether by reading or simply by viewing the objects and events that surround us. If we understand vision, therefore, we understand the processes that bring us much of our knowledge. Second, investigators in this area have made enormous progress, providing us with a rich portrait of how the visual system operates, and so the study of vision provides an excellent illustration of how the close study of the brain can proceed, and what it can teach us.

The Photoreceptors

You look around the world, and, instantly, effortlessly, you recognize the objects that surround you—the words on this page, objects in the room in which you're sitting, things you can view out the window. You know the identities of these objects, and you also perceive that each has a particular size, position, color, and texture. What makes all of this possible? The sequence of events begins, of course, with the eye.

Light is produced by many objects in our surroundings—the sun, candles, lamps, and so on—and this light then reflects off of most other objects. It is usually this reflected light—reflected from this book page, or from a friend's face—that launches the processes of vision. Some of this light hits the front surface of the eyeball, passes through the **cornea** and the **lens**, and then hits the **retina**, the light-sensitive tissue that lines the back of the eyeball (Figure 2.9). The cornea and lens focus the incoming light, just as a camera lens might, so that a sharp image is cast onto the retina. The cornea is fixed in its shape, but the shape of the lens can be adjusted by a band of muscle that surrounds it. When the muscle tightens, the lens bulges somewhat, creating the proper shape for focusing images cast by nearby objects; when the muscle relaxes, the lens returns to a flatter shape, allowing the proper focus for objects farther away.

On the retina, there are two types of **photoreceptors**, cells that respond directly to the incoming light. The **rods** are sensitive to much lower levels of light and so play an essential role whenever we're moving around in semidarkness, or whenever we're trying to view a fairly dim stimulus. But the rods are also color-blind: They distinguish among different intensities of light (and so contribute to our percep-

---

FIGURE 2.9   ## The Human Eye

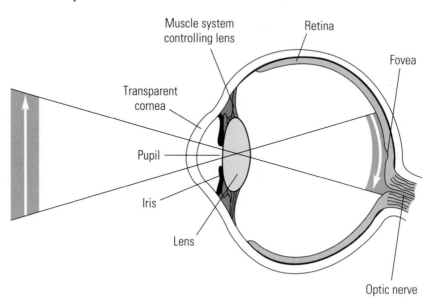

Light enters the eye through the pupil and is focused by the cornea and the lens so that a sharp image is projected onto the light-sensitive retina. The fovea is the region of the retina with the greatest sensitivity to detail.

tion of brightness), but they provide no means of discriminating one hue from another.

Cones, in contrast, are much less sensitive than rods and so need more incoming light to operate at all. But cones are sensitive to color differences. More precisely, there are three different types of cones, each having its own pattern of sensitivities to different wavelengths. We perceive color, therefore, by comparing the outputs from these three cone types. Strong firing from only the cones that prefer short wavelengths, for example, accompanied by weak (or no) firing from the other cone types, signals purple. Blue is signaled by equally strong firing from the cones that prefer short wavelengths and those that prefer medium wavelengths, with only modest firing by cones that prefer long wavelengths. And so on.

Cones also have another crucial function: They allow us to discern fine detail. The ability to see detail is referred to as **acuity**, and acuity is much higher for the cones than it is for the rods. This explains why we point our eyes toward a target whenever we wish to perceive it in detail. What we are actually doing is positioning our eyes so that the image of the target falls onto the **fovea**, the very center of the retina. Here cones far outnumber rods, and as a result, this is the region of the retina with the greatest acuity.

As one moves away from the fovea and into the visual periphery, the rods predominate; well out into the periphery, there are no cones at all. This is why we're better able to see very dim lights out of the corner of our eyes. Sailors and astronomers have known this for years; when looking at a barely visible star, they know that it's best not to look directly at the star's location. By looking slightly away from the star, they ensure that the star's image will fall outside of the fovea, and onto a region of the retina dense with the more light-sensitive rods.

Lateral Inhibition

Rods and cones do not report directly to the brain. Instead, the photoreceptors stimulate **bipolar cells**, which in turn excite **ganglion cells**. The ganglion cells collect information from all over the retina and then gather together to form the bundle of nerve fibers that we call the **optic nerve**. The optic nerve leaves the eyeball and carries information to various sites in the brain. Most of the fibers go first to an important way station in the thalamus called the **lateral geniculate nucleus**, or LGN; from there, information is transmitted to the primary projection area for vision, in the occipital cortex (Figure 2.10).

Let's be clear, though, that the optic nerve is far more than a mere cable that conducts signals from one site to another. Instead, the cells that link retina to brain are already engaged in the task of analyzing the visual input. One example of this lies in the phenomenon of **lateral inhibition**, a pattern in which cells, when stimulated, inhibit the activity of neighboring cells. To see why this is important, consider two cells, each receiving stimulation from a brightly lit area (Figure 2.11). One cell (Cell B in the figure) is receiving its stimulation from the middle of the lit area.

FIGURE 2.10 **The Path from Eyeball to Brain**

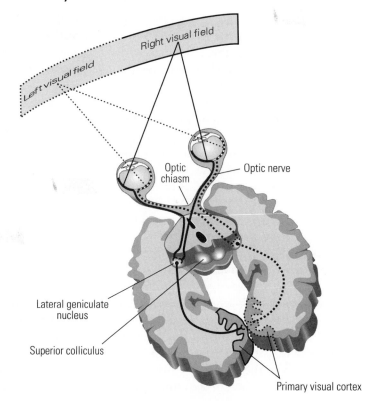

Ganglion cells collect information from all over the retina and then gather together to form the bundle of nerve fibers we call the optic nerve. Most of the fibers pass through the lateral geniculate nucleus and project from there to the primary visual cortex in the occipital lobe. Notice that half of the fibers in the optic nerve cross (at the optic chiasm) from one side to the other; as a result, the left cerebral hemisphere receives visual information from the right side of space, and the right hemisphere receives visual information from the left side of space.

It is strongly stimulated, but so are its neighbors, and so all of the cells in this area are inhibiting each other. As a result, the activity level of Cell B is *increased* by the stimulation but *decreased* by the lateral inhibition it is receiving. This combination leads to only a moderate level of activity overall.

In contrast, another cell (Cell C in the figure) is receiving its stimulation from the edge of the lit area. It is strongly stimulated, and so are its neighbors *on one side*. Therefore, this cell will receive inhibition from one side but not from the other, and so it will be less inhibited than Cell B (which is receiving inhibition from all sides). So, in short, cells B and C initially receive the same input, but C is less inhibited than B and will therefore end up firing more strongly than B.

| FIGURE 2.11 | Lateral Inhibition and Edge Enhancement |

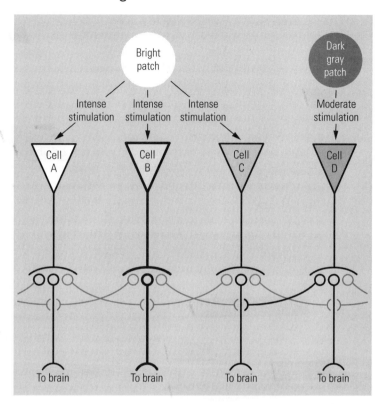

Cell B is strongly stimulated by the bright patch but receives lateral inhibition from both of its (strongly activated) neighbors, A and C. As a result, Cell B sends a diminished signal to the brain. Cell C initially receives the same input as B but ends up sending a stronger signal to the brain. This is because C receives lateral inhibition from only one of its neighbors. (Its other neighbor, Cell D, is only slightly activated and so is sending out only a small amount of inhibition.) In this fashion, lateral inhibition creates a pattern in which cells receiving input from the edge of a surface send out stronger signals.

The pattern of lateral inhibition, then, actually leads to stronger responses from cells detecting the edge of a surface (such as Cell C) than from cells detecting the middle of a surface (such as Cell B). This will, in effect, lead to an exaggerated response along the surface's edges, making those edges easier to detect. This process, called **edge enhancement**, makes it easier for the visual system to discern the shapes contained within the incoming visual information. And, importantly, this edge enhancement is done at a very early stage of the visual processing. In other words, the information sent to the brain isn't a mere copy of the incoming stimulation; instead, the steps of interpretation and analysis begin immediately, in the eyeball.

Single Neurons and Single-Cell Recording

Part of what we know about the optic nerve, and indeed, part of what we know about the entire brain, comes from a technique called **single-cell recording**. As the name implies, this is a procedure through which investigators can record, microsecond by microsecond, the pattern of electrical changes within a single neuron.

To understand this technique, it will be useful to know a bit more about **neurons**, the cells that do the main work of carrying information back and forth in the nervous system. Neurons come in many shapes and sizes, but they generally have three identifiable regions (see Figure 2.12): The **dendrites** are the part of the neuron that usually detects incoming signals. The **cell body** contains the neuron's nucleus and the metabolic machinery that sustains the cell. Finally, the **axon** is the part of the neuron that transmits a signal to another location. Axons vary considerably in length. The axons of the retinal ganglion cells, for example, stretch from the retina to the LGN, a distance of a couple of inches. In contrast, the axons that send command signals from the spinal cord to the legs can be a full meter in length.

The axon often has several branches that terminate on other neurons. They do not touch these other neurons directly; instead, there is a small gap between the adjacent neurons. Communication across this gap is generally done via chemical signals: **Neurotransmitters** are released through the membrane at the end of the axon; these chemicals drift across the gap and stimulate the next neuron. This site—the end of the axon, plus the gap, plus the receiving membrane of the next neuron—is called a **synapse**. The axon's end is therefore called the **presynaptic membrane**; the receiving membrane (typically on the next neuron's dendrites) is the **postsynaptic membrane**.

When the neurotransmitters arrive at the postsynaptic membrane, they cause changes in the membrane that allow certain ions to flow into and out of the postsynaptic cell. If these ionic flows are relatively small, then the postsynaptic cell quickly recovers and nothing more happens. But if the ionic flows are large enough, this triggers a response from the postsynaptic cell. In formal terms, if the incoming signal reaches the postsynaptic cell's **threshold**, then the cell **fires;** that is, it sends a signal down its axon, which in turn releases neurotransmitters at the next synapse, potentially causing the next cell to fire.

Notice, therefore, that the postsynaptic neuron's initial response can vary in size; the incoming signal can cause a small ionic flow or a large one. The magnitude of this response depends on several factors: How much neurotransmitter did the presynaptic cell release? How sensitive is the postsynaptic cell at this site? Both of these measures can vary from one neuron to the next and also can be altered with experience; this alteration is likely to be the neural basis for much of what we call "learning." In addition, the presynaptic cell may fire many times in succession; these inputs can accumulate, and so small ionic flows may eventually lead to a response in the postsynaptic cell. Likewise, the postsynaptic cell is likely to be receiving inputs from many other cells; these inputs, too, can accumulate, leading to a response.

FIGURE 2.12 A Typical Neuron

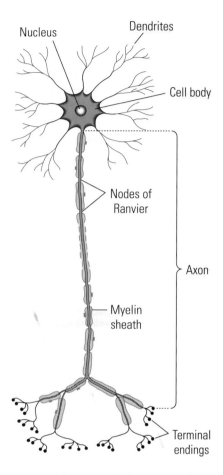

Neurons come in many shapes and sizes, but most have three identifiable regions: The dendrites are the part of the neuron that usually detects incoming signals. The cell body contains the metabolic machinery that sustains the cell. The axon is the part of the neuron that transmits a signal to another location. When the cell fires, neurotransmitters are released from the terminal endings at the tip of the axon. (After B. Katz, 1952)

Crucially, though, once these inputs reach the postsynaptic neuron's firing threshold, the signal that is produced does not vary in size. Either a signal is sent down the axon or it is not; if the signal is sent, it is always of the same magnitude, a fact referred to as the **all-or-none law**. If the cell is stimulated strongly, it may fire more frequently, or it may keep firing for a longer time, but the size of the signal that is sent along the axon never changes.

When investigators record the activity of a single neuron, therefore, what they are recording is the cell's firing—in particular, its firing rate. This rate can then be examined in conjunction with a scrutiny of the circumstances in order to figure out what event—either in the external world or elsewhere in the nervous system—triggered the firing. In this way, we can figure out roughly what job the neuron does within the broad context of the entire nervous system.

The technique of single-cell recording has been used with enormous success in the study of vision. In a typical study, the animal being studied is first immobilized. Then, electrodes are placed just outside a neuron in the animal's optic nerve or brain. Next a computer screen is placed in front of the animal's eyes, and various patterns are flashed on the screen: circles, lines at various angles, or squares of various sizes at various positions. Researchers can then ask, Which patterns cause that neuron to fire? To what visual inputs does that cell respond?

By analogy, we know that a smoke detector is a smoke detector because it "fires" (makes noise) when smoke is on the scene. We know that a motion detector is a motion detector because it "fires" when something moves nearby. But what kind of detector is a given neuron? Is it responsive to any light in any position within the field of view? In that case, we might call it a "light detector." Or is it perhaps responsive only to certain shapes at certain positions (and therefore is a shape detector)? With this logic, we can map out precisely what it is that the cell responds to; this is referred to as the cell's **receptive field**—that is, the size and shape of the area in the visual world to which that cell responds. With that, we learn what kind of detector the cell is.

Multiple Types of Receptive Fields

Classic data from single-cell recording come from studies by David Hubel and Torsten Wiesel (1959, 1968), who were awarded the Nobel Prize for their work; many subsequent studies have elaborated and extended their findings. Hubel and Wiesel documented the existence of several types of neurons within the visual system, each of which has a different kind of visual trigger, a different type of receptive field. Some neurons in the visual system seem to function as "dot detectors." These cells fire at their maximum rate when light is presented in a small, roughly circular area, in a specific position within the field of view. Presentations of light just outside of this area cause the cell to fire at *less* than its usual "resting" rate, so the input must be precisely positioned to make this cell fire. Figure 2.13 depicts such a receptive field.

Such cells are often called **center–surround cells,** to mark the fact that light presented to the central region of the receptive field has one influence, whereas light presented to the surrounding ring has the opposite influence. If both the center and the surround are strongly stimulated, the cell will fire neither more nor less than usual; for this cell, a strong uniform stimulus is equivalent to no stimulus at all.

FIGURE 2.13   Center–Surround Cells

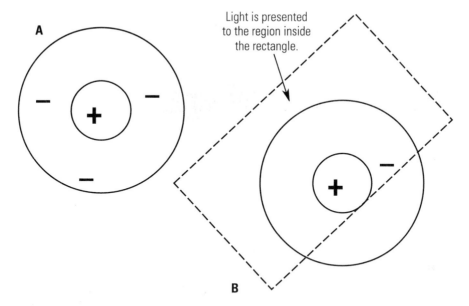

Light is presented to the region inside the rectangle.

A

B

Some neurons function as dot detectors, and have receptive fields with a center–surround organization. If light shines onto the central region, the cell increases its firing rate; this is why the center is marked "+". If light shines onto the peripheral region, the cell decreases its firing. If both regions are illuminated, the cell will not change its firing rate in either direction. Stimuli presented outside the periphery have no effect on the cell. If we present a stimulus as shown in B, the entire center is stimulated, but only a portion of the surround. Therefore, the positive signal outweighs the negative, and so the cell's firing rate will increase somewhat.

Other cells fire at their maximum only when a stimulus containing an edge of just the right orientation appears within their receptive fields. These cells, therefore, can be thought of as "edge detectors." Some cells prefer vertical edges, some prefer horizontal, some prefer orientations in between. If a cell's preference is, say, for horizontal edges, then nearly horizontal edges will evoke some response from the cell, but the response will be less than that for the cell's favored orientation. Edges sharply different from the cell's preferred orientation (say, a vertical edge for a cell that prefers horizontal) will elicit no response (see Figure 2.14).

Other cells, elsewhere in the visual cortex, fire maximally only if an angle of a particular size appears in their receptive fields; others fire maximally in response to corners and notches. Still other cells appear to be movement detectors and will fire strongly if a stimulus moves, say, from right to left across the cell's receptive field. Other cells favor left-to-right movement, and so on through the various possible directions of movement.

| FIGURE 2.14 | Orientation-Specific Visual Fields |

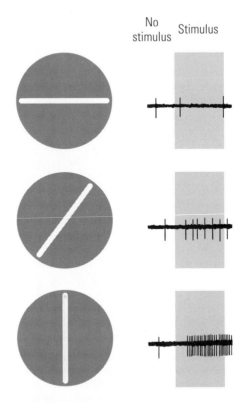

Some cells in the visual system fire only when the input contains a line segment at the proper orientation. For example, one cell might fire very little in response to a horizontal line, fire only occasionally in response to a diagonal, and fire at its maximum rate only when a vertical line is present. (After Hubel, 1963)

Parallel Processing in the Visual System

This proliferation of cell types suggests that the visual system relies on a "divide and conquer" strategy, with different types of cells, and different areas of the brain each specializing in a particular kind of analysis. This pattern is certainly visible in **V1**, the site on the occipital lobe where axons from the LGN first reach the cortex (see Figure 2.15). The pattern becomes all the more evident as we consider other brain areas. Figure 2.16, for example, reflects one recent summary of the brain areas known (on the basis of single-cell recording) to be involved in vision. Some of these areas (V1, V2, V3, V4, PO, and MT) are in the occipital cortex; other areas are in the parietal cortex; others are in the inferotemporal cortex (we'll have more to

FIGURE 2.15 Area V1 in the Brain

A

B

V1, primary
visual cortex

Area V1 is the site on the occipital lobe where axons from the LGN first reach the cortex.
Panel A shows the brain as if sliced down the middle; Panel B shows the brain viewed from
the side. As the two panels show, most of Area V1 is located on the cortical surface between
the two cerebral hemispheres.

say in a moment about these areas outside of the occipital cortex). Each area seems
to have its own function. Neurons in Area MT, for example, are acutely sensitive to
direction and speed of movement. Cells in Area V4 fire most strongly when the
input is of a certain color and a certain shape.

This pattern of specialization makes it clear that the visual system relies on **parallel processing**—a system in which many different steps (in this case, many different kinds of analysis) are going on at the same time. (Parallel processing is usually

FIGURE 2.16	The Visual Processing Pathways

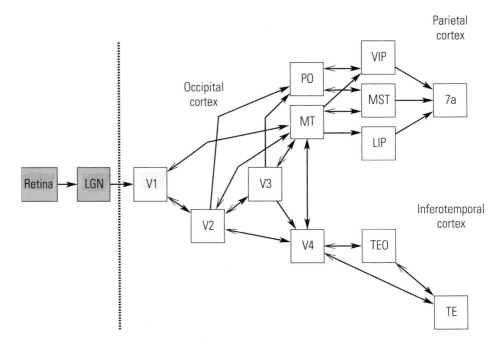

The visual system relies heavily on parallel processing, with different brain areas engaged in their own specific analyses. Information from the LGN is sent primarily to Area V1, but from there, information is sent along several different pathways. (Adapted from art by Steven Luck)

contrasted with **serial processing**, in which steps are carried out one at a time—that is, in a series.) One advantage of this simultaneous processing is speed: Brain areas trying to discern the shape of the incoming stimulus don't need to wait until the motion analysis or the color analysis is complete. Instead, all of the analyses go forward in parallel, with no waiting time.

Another advantage of parallel processing is the possibility of mutual influence among multiple systems. To see why this is important, consider the fact that sometimes our interpretation of an object's motion depends on our understanding of the object's three-dimensional shape. This suggests that it might be best if the perception of shape happened first. That way, we could use the results of this processing step as a guide to later analyses. In other cases, though, it turns out that the relationship between shape and motion is reversed: In these cases, our interpretation of an object's three-dimensional shape depends on our understanding of its motion. To allow for this possibility, it might be best if the perception of motion happened first, so that it could guide the subsequent analysis of shape.

How do we deal with these conflicting demands? The visual system has evolved a pattern in which both sorts of analysis go on simultaneously, so that each type of analysis can be enriched and informed by the other. Put differently, neither the shape-analyzing system nor the motion-analyzing system gets priority. Instead, the two systems work concurrently and "negotiate" a solution that satisfies both systems (Van Essen & DeYoe, 1995).

Parallel processing is evident in virtually every aspect of the visual system. Within the optic nerve itself, there are (at least) two different types of cells, **P cells** and **M cells**, and these provide the main inputs for the corresponding types of cells in the LGN: P cells provide input for the LGN's **parvocellular cells;** M cells, for the LGN's **magnocellular cells.** (The terms refer to the relative sizes of these cells; *parvo* derives from the Latin word for "small" and *magno* from the word for "large.") P cells and M cells are different in several ways: P cells have smaller receptive fields than do M cells, and they also have a different pattern of firing: P cells continue to fire if a stimulus remains unchanged; M cells fire when the stimulus appears and then again when it disappears, but not in between.

What purpose is served by this specialization? The P cells in the optic nerve and the parvocellular cells in the LGN appear to be specialized for spatial analysis and the detailed analysis of form. The M cells in the optic nerve and the magnocellular cells in the LGN are probably specialized for the detection of motion and the perception of depth.[1]

Evidence for parallel processing continues as we move beyond the occipital cortex. As Figure 2.17 indicates, some of the information is transmitted from the occipital lobe to the cortex of the temporal lobe. This pathway, often called the ***what system***, plays a major role in the identification of visual objects, telling us whether the object is a cat, an apple, or whatever. A second pathway, which carries information to the parietal cortex, is often called the ***where* system** and seems to perform the function of guiding our action, based on our perception of where an object is located—above or below us, to our right or to our left (Goodale & Milner, 2004; Ungerleider & Haxby, 1994; Ungerleider & Mishkin, 1982).

The contrasting roles of these two systems can be revealed in many ways, including studies of brain damage. Patients with lesions in the occipital-temporal pathway show visual agnosia—an inability to recognize visually presented objects, including such common things as a cup or a pencil. On the other hand, these patients show little disorder in recognizing visual orientation or in reaching. The reverse pattern is observed with patients who have suffered lesions in the occipital-parietal pathway: difficulty in reaching, but no problem in object identification (Damasio, Tranel, & Damasio, 1989; Farah, 1990; Goodale, 1995; F. Newcombe, Ratcliff, & Damasio, 1987).

---

[1]Many students find it useful to think of the P cells as specialized roughly for the perception of *pattern*, and M cells as specialized for the perception of *motion*. These descriptions are somewhat crude, but they're easy to remember.

| FIGURE 2.17 | The *What* and *Where* Pathways |

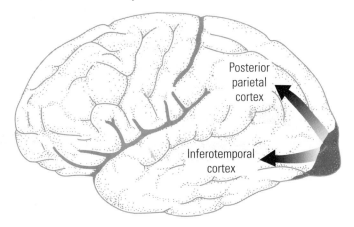

Information from the primary visual cortex (located at the back of the head) is transmitted both to the inferotemporal cortex (the so-called *what* system) and to the posterior parietal cortex (the *where* system).

Other clinical data echo this broad theme of parallel processing among separate systems. For example, we noted earlier that different brain areas are critical for the perception of color, motion, and form. If this is right, then someone who has suffered damage in just one of these areas should show problems in the perception of color but not the perception of motion or form, or problems in the perception of motion but not the perception of form or color.

These predictions are correct: Some patients do suffer a specific loss of color vision through damage to the central nervous system, even though their perception of form and motion remains normal (Gazzaniga, Ivry, & Mangun, 1998; Meadows, 1974). To them, the entire world is clothed only in "dirty shades of gray."[2] Other patients suffer damage to the motion system and so develop a disorder dubbed "akinetopsia" (Zihl, Von Cramon, & Mai, 1983). For such patients, the world is described as a succession of static photographs. They're unable to report the speed or direction of a moving object; as one patient put it, "When I'm looking at the car first, it seems far away. But then when I want to cross the road, suddenly the car is very near." Cases like these provide dramatic confirmation of the separateness of our visual system's various elements, and the ways in which the visual system is vulnerable to very specific forms of damage. (For further evidence, with neurologically intact participants, see Bundesen, Kyllingsbaek, & Larsen, 2003.)

---

[2]This is different from ordinary color blindness, which is usually present from birth and results from abnormalities that are outside the brain itself—for example, abnormalities in the photoreceptors.

Putting the Pieces Back Together

It should be clear, then, that our intellectual achievements depend on an array of different brain areas working together. This was evident in our consideration of Capgras syndrome, and the same pattern emerged in our description of the visual system. Here, too, many brain areas must work together: the *what* system and the *where* system, areas specialized for the detection of movement and areas specialized for the identification of simple forms.

We have identified certain advantages that derive from this cerebral division of labor and the parallel processing it allows. But the division of labor also creates a problem: If multiple brain areas contribute to an overall task, how is their functioning coordinated? When we see a ballet dancer in a graceful leap, the leap itself is registered by motion-sensitive neurons, but the recognition of the ballet dancer depends on shape-sensitive neurons. How are the pieces put back together? When we reach for a coffee cup but stop midway because we see that the cup is empty, the reach itself is guided by the *where* system; the fact that the cup is empty is registered by the *what* system. How are these two streams of processing coordinated?

Investigators refer to this broad issue as the **binding problem**—the task of reuniting the various elements of a scene, elements that are initially dealt with by different systems in different parts of the brain. And obviously this problem is solved: What we perceive is not an unordered catalogue of sensory elements. Instead, we perceive a coherent, integrated perceptual world. Apparently, then, this is a case in which the various pieces of Humpty Dumpty are reassembled to form an organized whole.

Visual Maps and Firing Synchrony

Look around you. Your visual system registers whiteness and blueness and brown-ness; it also registers a small cylindrical shape (your coffee cup), a medium-sized rectangle (this book page), and a much larger rectangle (your desk). How do you put these pieces together so that you see that it's the coffee cup, and not the book page, that's blue; the desktop, and not the cup, that's brown?

There is still debate about how the visual system solves this problem, but we can identify three elements that certainly contribute to the solution. One element is spatial position. The part of the brain registering the cup's shape is separate from the parts registering its color or its motion; nonetheless, these various brain areas all have something in common: They each keep track of where the target is—where the cylindrical shape was located, and where the blueness was; where the motion was detected, and where things were still. Thus, the reassembling of these pieces can be done with reference to spatial position. In essence, you can overlay the map of *which forms are where* on top of the map of *which colors are where* to get the right colors with the right forms, and likewise for the map showing *which motion patterns are where.*

Information about spatial position is of course important for its own sake: You have an obvious reason to care whether the tiger is close to you or far away, or whether the bus is on your side of the street or the other. But, in addition, location information apparently provides a frame of reference used to solve the binding problem. Given this double function, we shouldn't be surprised that spatial position is a major organizing theme within all the various brain areas concerned with vision, with each area seeming to provide its own map of the visual world.

We mentioned earlier that these maps are readily detectable in the sensory projection areas. Single-cell recording confirms that adjacent cells within a bit of brain tissue are usually responsive to adjacent positions within the visual field—so that, in fact, the receptive fields really do form a map of visual space. But if there are multiple brain areas responsible for different aspects of vision, then there must be multiple maps; indeed, more than 30 such maps have been documented (Gazzaniga et al., 1998).

However, spatial position, as important as it is, is not the whole story. Evidence is accumulating that the brain also uses a special *rhythm* to identify which sensory elements belong with which. Imagine two groups of neurons in the visual cortex. One group of neurons fires maximally whenever a vertical line is in view; another group fires maximally whenever a stimulus is in view moving from left to right. Let's also imagine that, right now, a vertical line is presented, and it is moving in the right way, and so, as a result, both groups of neurons are firing strongly. How does the brain encode the fact that these attributes are bound together, different aspects of a single object? The visual system seems to mark this fact by means of **neural synchrony.** If the neurons detecting a vertical line are firing in synchrony with those signaling movement, then these attributes are registered as belonging to the same object. If they are not in synchrony, the features are not bound together. Moreover, the synchrony is made possible by the fact that the neurons are firing at roughly the same rate: about 40 times per second, a rate called the **gamma-band oscillation** (Buzsáki & Draguhn, 2004; Csibra, Davis, Spratling, & Johnson, 2000; Elliot & Müller, 2000; Fries, Reynolds, Rorie, & Desimone, 2001).

What causes this synchrony? How do the neurons become synchronized in the first place? Here another factor appears to be crucial: *attention.* We will have more to say about attention in Chapter 4, but for now let's just note that attention plays a key role in binding together the separate features of a stimulus. (For a classic statement of this argument, see Treisman, Sykes, & Gelade, 1977, and Treisman & Gelade, 1980. For a more recent, and more complex view, see Quinlan, 2003, and also Chapter 4.)

Evidence for attention's role comes from many sources, including the fact that, when we overload someone's attention, she is likely to make **conjunction errors**—correctly detecting the features present in a visual display, but making mistakes about how the features are bound together (or *conjoined*). Thus, someone shown a blue *H* and a red *T* might report seeing a blue *T* and a red *H*—an error in binding. Similarly, individuals who suffer from severe attention deficits (because of brain damage in the parietal cortex) are particularly impaired in tasks that require them to judge how features are conjoined to form complex objects (e.g., Robertson, Treisman, Friedman-Hill, & Grabowecky, 1997). Finally, studies suggest that the pattern of gamma-band oscillation is typically observed in an animal's brain when the animal is attending to a specific stimulus, but is not observed in neurons activated by an unattended stimulus. Results like these argue both that attention is crucial for the binding problem and that attention is linked to the pattern of neural synchrony that seems to unite a stimulus's features.

Once again, therefore, we see that seemingly simple mental achievements depend on multiple brain areas and, crucially, the coordination of action across these areas. In addition, these factors, helping to "bind" together different elements of the stimulus, remind us that information is represented in the brain in several different ways: in terms of *which* cells are firing, *how often* they are firing, and also, it seems, the *rhythm* in which they are firing. Finally, note that our account of vision requires discussion of "lower level" activities (such as what happens just one or two synapses into the brain) and also "higher level" activities (including the influence of attention on neural activity). In a sense, then, our account of brain functioning will need to depend on an understanding of cognition at the same time that our account of cognition will rely heavily on what is known about the brain.

Chapter Summary

1. The brain is divided into several different structures, but of particular importance for cognitive psychology is the forebrain. In the forebrain, each cerebral hemisphere is divided into the frontal lobe, parietal lobe, temporal lobe, and occipital lobe. In understanding these brain areas, one important source of evidence comes from studies of brain damage, allowing us to examine what sorts of symptoms result from lesions in specific brain locations. This has allowed a localization of function, an effort that is also supported by neuroimaging research, which shows that the pattern of activation in the brain depends heavily on the particular task being performed.

2. Different parts of the brain perform different jobs, but for virtually any mental process, different brain areas must work together in a closely integrated fashion. When this integration is lost (as it is, for example, in Capgras syndrome), bizarre symptoms result.

3. The primary motor projection areas are the departure point for nerve cells that initiate muscle movement. The primary sensory projection areas are the main points of arrival for information from the eyes, ears, and other sense organs. All of these projection areas show the pattern of contralateral control, with tissue in the left hemisphere sending or receiving its main signals from the right side of the body, and vice versa. The projection areas each provide a map of the environment or the relevant body part, but the assignment of space in this map is governed by function, not by anatomical proportions.

4. Most of the forebrain's cortex has traditionally been referred to as the association cortex, but this area is itself subdivided into specialized regions. This subdivision is reflected in the varying consequences of brain damage, with lesions in the occipital lobe leading to visual agnosia, damage in the temporal lobes leading to aphasia, and so on. Damage to the prefrontal area causes many different problems, but these are generally problems in the forming and implementing of strategies.

5. One brain area that has been mapped in considerable detail is the visual system. This system takes its main input from the rods and cones on the retina. Then, information is sent via the optic nerve to the brain. Importantly, cells in the optic nerve do much more than transmit information; they also begin the analysis of the visual input. This is reflected in the phenomenon of lateral inhibition, which leads to edge enhancement.

6. Part of what we know about the brain comes from single-cell recording, which can record the electrical activity of an individual neuron. In the visual system, this recording has allowed researchers to map the receptive fields for many cells, and this mapping has provided evidence for a high degree of specialization among the various parts of the visual system, with some parts specialized for the perception of motion, other parts specialized for the perception of color, and so on. These various areas function in parallel, and this parallel processing allows great speed; it also allows mutual influence among multiple systems.

7. Parallel processing begins in the optic nerve and continues throughout the visual system. For example, the *what* system (in the temporal lobe) appears to be specialized for the identification of visual objects; the *where* system (in the parietal lobe) seems to tell us where an object is located.

8. The reliance on parallel processing creates a problem of reuniting the various elements of a scene so that these elements are perceived in an integrated fashion. This is called the binding problem. One key in solving this problem, though, lies in the fact that different brain systems are organized in terms of maps, so that spatial position can be used as a framework for reuniting the separately analyzed aspects of the visual scene.

PART TWO

LEARNING ABOUT THE WORLD AROUND US

I N THE PREVIOUS SECTION, we described some of the early steps involved in vision, but we emphasize that these are only the *early* steps. We begin Chapter 3, therefore, with a discussion of the various ways in which the perceiver analyzes, organizes, and interprets the visual input. We then turn to the broad issue of how we recognize the various objects that surround us in the world, and here we'll discover the ways in which object recognition is influenced by expectations and prior knowledge. We'll describe how a mechanism made up of very simple components can be sensitive to this knowledge, and that will lead us into a discussion of how complex knowledge can be "distributed" across an entire system. (This notion of "distributed processing" is important in Chapter 3 and in other settings, and we'll return to this idea later in the book.)

Chapter 4 then turns to the study of attention. As we'll see, paying attention is a complex achievement involving many different elements. Some of the steps needed for attention will be the same no matter what it is a person is paying attention to; other steps will depend on the particular task. In either case, paying attention requires that one commit some mental resources, and in the absence of those resources, performance drops off markedly. In addition, these resources are available only in limited quantities, and this constraint may set boundaries on human performance. Part of what's at stake in Chapter 4, therefore, is a discussion of what people can or cannot accomplish, and whether there may be ways to escape the apparent limits on attention.

Recognizing Objects in the World

As we saw in Chapter 2, information about the visual world is picked up by a large array of neural detectors, with each detector tuned to a particular aspect of the stimulus information. Some detectors specialize in horizontal line segments, others detect vertical lines or diagonals. Still others pick out specific patterns of movement or fire only when certain angles or notches are in view. For that matter, there are even neurons (in the monkey's brain) that fire only when a monkey's hand is in view (whether the fingers are stretched out or clenched in a fist) or only when another monkey's face is in view!

However, visual perception involves far more than a simple detection of the stimulus input's properties. As one consideration, we have already mentioned that the input's various attributes are detected by separate brain systems, and so a further step is required to reunite these various attributes so that we recognize that it is the squirrel that is brown and moving and the leaves that are green and still, rather than some other combination of these features. But the complexities of perception do not stop there. In this chapter, we consider some of the other steps involved in perceiving the visual world, and with that, we discuss just how large a role the perceiver plays—not just as a detector of incoming information, but as an active interpreter of that information.

We should emphasize at the start, however, that we'll survey only some of the complexities involved in perception.

- In important ways, perception goes "beyond the information given" in interpreting a stimulus. Various points of organization are imposed by the perceiver, and determine what a stimulus looks like and what the stimulus is seen to resemble.

- Recognition of visual inputs begins with features, but how easily we recognize a pattern depends on several factors: We have an easier time recognizing frequently or recently viewed patterns, and also patterns that are well formed (such as letter sequences with "normal" spelling patterns). We explain these findings in terms of a feature net, a network of detectors each "primed" according to how often or how recently it has fired. The network relies on distributed knowledge to make inferences, and this process gives up some accuracy in order to gain a reasonable level of efficiency.

- The feature net can be extended to other domains, including the recognition of three-dimensional objects or the identification of sounds. However, the recognition of faces requires a different sort of model, sensitive to configurations rather than to parts.

- Finally, we consider top-down influences on recognition. The existence of these influences tells us that object recognition is not a self-contained process; instead, knowledge external to object recognition is imported into and clearly shapes the process.

We'll hold to the side, for example, the question of how you perceive movement, or how you figure out how far away from you a stimulus is. We'll also leave untouched the problem of constancy—that is, how you manage to perceive the objects in the world as having a constant shape, size, and color, despite the fact that the visual stimulation you receive from these objects changes as your viewing circumstances change. (Thus, the image that an object casts on your retina grows in size as you approach the object, yet you perceive the actual size of the object as unchanged.)

The topics of movement, depth, and constancy are all deeply important, and they are covered in detail in courses on visual perception. In this text, however, we will focus instead on the aspects of visual perception that allow us to recognize the objects we encounter every day in the world around us.

Visual Perception

We receive information about the world through various sensory modalities: We hear the sound of the approaching train, we smell the chocolate cake almost ready to come out of the oven, we feel the tap on our shoulder. There is no question, though, that for humans vision is the dominant sense. This is reflected in how much brain area is devoted to vision compared to how much is devoted to any of the other senses. It is also reflected in many aspects of our behavior. For example, if visual information conflicts with information received from other senses, we usually place our trust in vision. This is the basis for ventriloquism, in which we see the dummy's mouth moving, while the sounds themselves are coming from the dummy's master. Vision wins out in this contest, and so we experience the illusion that the voice is coming from the dummy.

But how does vision operate? You open your eyes, and you see around you a world filled with familiar objects—chairs and desks, windows and walls, telephones and pencils. As you read this page, you can see the individual letters printed here, and they are letters that you know and can identify. The letters form words, which you also can recognize; you could say them out loud if requested, and you know the meaning of the words, so that you easily understand these sentences.

How is any of this possible? How do you manage to perceive, and then recognize, the objects you see every day? This is the problem, first, of **form perception**, the process through which you manage to see what the basic shape and size of an object are. Next is the problem of **object recognition**, the process through which you identify what the object is.

Why Is Object Recognition Crucial?

Virtually all knowledge and all use of knowledge depend on form perception and object recognition. To see this, think about a physician who might know how to treat diabetes, but who doesn't know how to recognize a case of diabetes. In this case, the physician's knowledge about treatment becomes useless, because the physician doesn't know when (or with which patients) to use the treatment. Likewise, you know a great deal about telephones, and you use that knowledge in many ways. But you could not do this if you couldn't recognize a telephone when you saw one. Without recognition, one cannot bring one's knowledge to bear on the world.

In a similar fashion, object recognition is also crucial for learning. In virtually all learning, one must combine new information with information learned previously. But for this to happen, one must categorize things properly. Today you learn something about Solomon. Yesterday you learned something about Solomon. If you are to integrate the new knowledge with the old, you need to realize that the person before you today is the same person as the one you met yesterday. Without proper categorization, there is no way to combine and integrate information.

Thus, object recognition may not be a glamorous skill, but it is crucial for virtually all of our commerce with the world. Moreover, it is the essential base for learning and memory. For our purposes, therefore, we will start our inquiry where much of knowledge starts: with the recognition and identification of objects in the world.

Beyond the Information Given

In Chapter 2, we saw how the process of object recognition begins: with the detection of simple visual features. But we've known for many years that there is more to the process than this. Early in the 20th century, a group of psychologists called the "Gestalt psychologists" noted that our perception of the visual world is organized in ways that the stimulus input is not.[1] They argued, therefore, that the organization must be contributed by the perceiver; this is why, they claimed, the perceptual whole is often different from the sum of its parts. Some years later, Jerome Bruner voiced similar claims and coined the phrase "beyond the information given" to describe some of the ways that our perception of a stimulus differs from (and goes beyond) the stimulus itself (Bruner, 1973).

Consider the form shown in the top of Figure 3.1: the Necker cube. This drawing is called an ambiguous figure because there is more than one way to perceive it. As one option, it can be perceived as a cube viewed from above (in which case it is similar to the cube marked "A" in the figure); alternatively, it can be perceived as a cube viewed from below (in which case it is similar to the cube marked "B"). Both perceptions fit perfectly well with the information received by your eyes, and so the drawing itself is fully compatible with either of these perceptions. Put differently, the lines on the page are neutral with regard to the shape's configuration in depth; the lines on the page don't specify which is the "proper" interpretation.

Your perception of the cube, however, is not neutral. Instead, you perceive the cube as having one configuration or the other—similar either to Cube A or to Cube

FIGURE 3.1 The Necker Cube

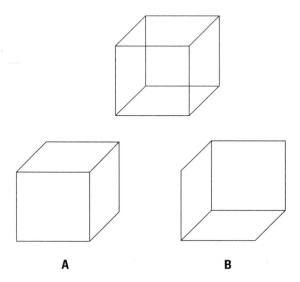

A　　　　　　　**B**

The top cube can be perceived as if viewed from above (in which case it is a transparent version of Cube A) or as if viewed from below (i.e., a transparent version of Cube B).

[1] *Gestalt* is the German word for "shape" or "form." The Gestalt psychology movement was, overall, committed to the view that our theories need to pay attention to the organization of the entire shape, and not just focus on how we register the shape's parts.

FIGURE 3.2 The Vase/Profiles Figure

This figure can be perceived either as a white vase against a black background or as two black profiles against a white background.

B. Your perception, in other words, goes beyond the information given in the drawing, by specifying an arrangement in depth.

The same point can be made for many other stimuli. Consider Figure 3.2, for example. This figure can be perceived as a vase centered in the picture, or it can be perceived equally well as two profiles facing each other. The drawing by itself, it seems, is fully compatible with either of these perceptions, and so, once again, the drawing is neutral with regard to perceptual organization. In particular, it is neutral with regard to **figure/ground organization,** the determination of what is the figure (the central object, displayed against a background) and what is the ground. Your perception of this figure, however, is not neutral about this point. Instead, your perception somehow specifies that you are looking at the vase and not at the profiles, or that you are looking at the profiles and not at the vase.

In both of these examples, your perception contains information—about how the form is arranged in depth, or about which part of the form is figure and which ground—that is not contained within the stimulus itself. Apparently, then, this is information contributed by you, the perceiver.

Parsing

Does the pattern shown in Figure 3.3A contain the numeral 4? Is the pattern in 3.3C contained in Figure 3.3B? In each case, the answer is yes, although this usually is not obvious without some close scrutiny of the figures. More specifically, whether the embedded figure is detected depends on how the perceiver **parses** the

FIGURE 3.3 Embedded Figures

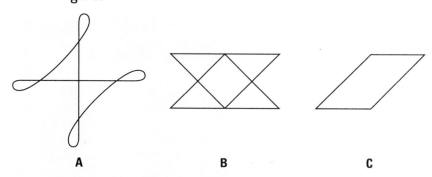

A   B   C

Pattern A contains the numeral 4, but most participants fail initially to detect the numeral. Likewise, Pattern B contains Pattern C, but this isn't obvious until you search for the "hidden" form. Thus, perception of forms depends on how one "dissects" the overall pattern.

stimulus—which parts are perceived as going together, and which are perceived as separate. And once again, this organization, this grouping of the parts, is not in the stimulus itself; it is, instead, another contribution by the perceiver.

These examples obviously involve simple drawings on an otherwise blank ground. The real importance of parsing, though, and of perceptual organization in general, comes into view when we consider more complex scenes, like the one shown in Figure 3.4. In this scene, you easily recognize the banana, the pitcher, and so on, but to do this, you first have to parse the scene appropriately. For example, you have to unite Portion B (one half of the apple) with Portion E (the other half of the apple), even though they are separated by Portion D (the banana). Portion B must not be united with Portion A (a bunch of grapes), even though they are adjacent and approximately the same color. The bit of the apple hidden from view by the banana must also be somehow filled in, so that you can perceive an intact apple rather than two apple slices. In all of these ways, the perceiver must organize the sensory input, making distinctions between some bits, uniting other bits, filling in gaps, and more. These steps are all needed if the perceiver is to recognize the intact forms, and if the perceiver is to recover an orderly scene from incomplete and, in some ways, disordered sensory information.

The Logic of Perception

In short, the stimulus by itself does not tell you which elements of the input are figure and which are ground, or how those elements should be parsed, or how the form is arranged in three dimensions. Instead, these crucial organizing themes must be imposed on the stimulus by the perceiver, so that, in effect, the organization is "in the eye of the beholder," and not in the stimulus itself. And, of course, it

FIGURE 3.4   The Importance of Parsing

To determine what these various objects are, the perceptual system must first decide what goes with what—for example, that Portion B and Portion E are different bits of the same object (even though they are separated by Portion D), that Portion B and Portion A are different objects (even though they are adjacent and the same color).

is possible for the perceiver to organize the same stimulus in different ways on different occasions. When this happens, very different perceptions are produced—so that a stimulus is perceived once as a vase and then later as profiles, or is perceived first as a cube viewed from below and then later as one viewed from above, and so on.

This perceptual organization then turns out to matter in important ways. For one, the organization determines our most immediate impressions of the stimulus. The stimulus we "see," in other words, and the way that stimulus looks to us, and what it appears to resemble, are all determined not just by the pattern in front of our eyes, but by the pattern as we have interpreted it—the pattern with the organizing themes we've added.

The perceptual organization also plays a powerful role in deciding whether a form will be recognized as familiar or not: Imagine that we show a series of forms to participants, and Figure 3.2 is presented as part of the series. Via instructions, we manage to suggest to the participants that this figure shows a vase. Later in the series, we again show Figure 3.2, but this time we suggest that it shows two profiles. In this setting, it's quite likely that participants will not realize they've seen this figure before, will not realize the form is familiar. Apparently, what matters for familiarity is not the objective stimulus, not the pattern of pixels that literally hits your eye. Instead, what matters for familiarity is the figure as *perceived*—the figure *plus* the specifications added by the perceiver—and if these specifications change, the familiarity is lost.

Similarly, our ability to identify a form also depends on organization. For instance, will the perceiver detect the vase in Figure 3.2 or the parallelogram in Figure 3.3B? It turns out that, with one organization, the form is instantly visible; with another, the form is, for all practical purposes, simply absent. (For another example, see Figure 3.5).

FIGURE 3.5   A Hidden Figure

Whether an object is recognized or not depends on the physical stimulus and also on how the stimulus is interpreted and organized by the perceiver. In this figure, most people do not recognize the familiar form. Changing their understanding of what is figure and what is ground, however, helps. (Try thinking of the form as a white shape on a black background.) Likewise, changing their understanding of the form's orientation helps too. (Try thinking of the left side as being the form's top.) (After Kanizsa, 1979)

But how does this perceptual interpretation happen? What are the processes through which the interpretation is generated? We do not yet have a full account, although investigators are making impressive progress in understanding how these processes unfold. Some of the progress involves detailing the relevant brain mechanisms, and this work connects well with the materials described in Chapter 2. (Hoffman, 2000, and Palmer, 1999, provide recent reviews.) Other lines of research focus more on the "logic" of the processes, rather than the biological steps implementing this logic (e.g., Rock, 1983).

In what sense is perception "logical"? Let's note, first, that the interpretation achieved by the perceptual system—the organization of figure and ground, the parsing, and so on—must fit with all the incoming stimulus information. Just like a good scientist, your perceptual apparatus requires a hypothesis that fits with all the data. Second, the perceptual system seems to prefer the simplest explanation of the stimulus. Here, too, the perceptual system acts just like a scientist—avoiding overly elaborate explanations of the "data," if a simpler explanation will do. Third, the perceptual system also seems to avoid interpretations that involve coincidences. As an example, consider Figure 3.6. Most people immediately perceive this form as two lines crossing, but notice that other perceptions are possible: The form could, for example, be parsed as two *V* shapes, one on the top and one on the bottom. However, this interpretation would depend on the two *V* shapes being in exactly the right positions—just touching, with no overlap. In any other position, the combined *V*s would look quite different. Therefore, interpreting Figure 3.6 as

---

FIGURE 3.6   Avoiding Coincidences

This form could be perceived as two *V* shapes, one on the top and one on the bottom. Or it could be parsed as two *V* shapes with one on the left and one on the right. The visual system seems to avoid these interpretations, however, because they involve an element of coincidence: This is what two *V*s would look like if they just happened to be positioned perfectly, touching and aligned, but with no overlap.

two *V*s would rely on a coincidence—that the forms just happen to be in exactly the right positions—and this is why other interpretations of the form seem to be preferred.

Let's be clear, though, that we are not proposing that there really is a little scientist inside your brain, generating hypotheses about the input, calculating the likelihood of this or that coincidence. The perceptual system does work as if it were generating hypotheses and the like, but the key phrase here is "as if." Neural mechanisms somehow function in a way that leaves us, overall, with a process that seems quite logical and seems to analyze and interpret the evidence just as a scientist might. We do not know yet what all those neural mechanisms are, but in the meantime, these logical principles can help us make sense of a great deal of evidence concerning how people interpret the visual forms they encounter.

Object Recognition

In Chapter 2, we saw how the nervous system begins its analysis of the visual input, with a large set of detectors operating in parallel, each detecting a specific attribute of an image. Next, these various attributes are somehow bound together, so that the perceiver knows that the green-ness he detected was a property of the horizontal line and not the vertical one. The processes of perception then have to organize this information: Were the horizontal and vertical lines part of the same object, or parts of different objects? This is the step of parsing, in which the perceiver figures out which elements go with which. Also necessary is the step of figure/ground organization and an interpretation of both the figure's orientation and its configuration in depth.

With the form organized in this fashion, we are ready (at last) to take the next steps toward identifying what the form actually is—a truck, a tree, or a character in a video game. Let's turn, therefore, to these next steps. Our goal in this chapter is to describe how we recognize the huge variety of objects we encounter in our day-to-day world. We'll start, though, with a narrower focus: examining how we recognize the letters and words that make up printed language. Later in the chapter, we'll return to a discussion of visual targets other than print.

Recognition: Some Early Considerations

You are obviously able to recognize a huge number of different patterns—different objects (cows, trees, hats), various actions (running, jumping, falling), and different sorts of situations (crises, comedies).

Not only do you recognize all these things, but you can also recognize many variations of each. You recognize cats standing up and cats sitting down, cats running and cats asleep. And of course the same is true for your recognition of pigs, chairs, and any other object in your recognition repertoire.

You also recognize objects even when your information is partial. For example, you can still recognize a cat if only its head and one paw are visible behind a tree. You recognize a chair even when someone is sitting on it, despite the fact that the person blocks much of the chair from view.

All of this is true for print as well: You can recognize tens of thousands of different words, and you can recognize them whether the word is printed in large type or small, italics or straight letters, upper case or lower. You can even recognize handwritten words, for which the variation from one to the next is huge.

In addition, your recognition of various objects, whether print or otherwise, is influenced in important ways by the *context* in which the objects are encountered. For example, consider Figure 3.7. The middle character is the same in both words, but the character doesn't look the same. Instead, the character looks more like an *H* in the left word and more like an *A* in the right. Likewise, one unhesitatingly reads the left word as "THE" and not "TAE," and the right word as "CAT" and not "CHT."

How should we think about all this? What mechanism underlies all of these effects? In the next sections, we will develop a proposal for such a mechanism.

Features

One plausible suggestion is that many objects are recognized by virtue of their parts. You recognize an elephant because you see the trunk, the thick legs, the large body. You know a lollipop is a lollipop because you can see the circle shape on top of the straight stick. But how do you recognize the parts themselves? How, for example, do you recognize the circle in the lollipop? Perhaps you do so by virtue of its parts—the constituent arcs, for example.

To put this more generally, recognition might begin with the identification of **features** in the input pattern—features such as vertical lines, curves, or diagonals. With these features appropriately catalogued, you can start assembling the larger units: If you detect a horizontal together with a vertical, you know you're looking at a right angle. If you've detected four right angles, you know you're looking at a square. And so on. (For a complication, though, see Figure 3.8.)

FIGURE 3.7 | Context Influences Perception

TAE CAT

Pattern recognition is influenced by the fact that "THE" is a commonly observed sequence of letters; "TAE" is not. Likewise, "CAT" is often encountered; "CHT" is not. Given this knowledge, one is likely to read this sequence as "THE CAT," reading the middle symbol as an *H* in one case and as an *A* in the other. (After Selfridge, 1955 ©1955 IRE [now IEEE]).

FIGURE 3.8 ## What Is a Triangle?

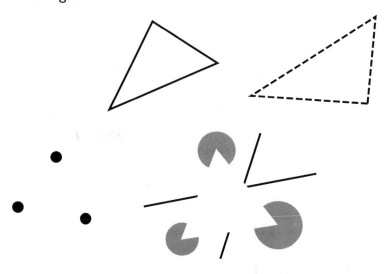

The features that we use in object recognition are not the features of the raw input. Instead, the features that we use are the ones in our organized perception of the input. This is evident in the fact that we recognize all of these forms as triangles—even though the essential features (three lines, three angles) are present in only one of them. The features are present, however, in our *organized perception* of the forms.

How are the features themselves recognized? A simple possibility is that we have a memory for each feature, telling us, in effect, just what that feature looks like. These memory patterns can then be compared to the pattern before your eyes. If some part of this input matches one of the patterns in your repertoire, then you know that the relevant feature is present. "That bit matches my 'corner' pattern, so I know a corner is present. That bit matches my 'curve' pattern, so I know a curve is present."

Some advantages of this system are obvious immediately. First, features such as line segments and curves could serve as general-purpose building blocks. Not only would these features serve as the basis for recognizing letters; they could also serve as the basis for recognizing other, more complex visual patterns (chairs, jackets, smiling faces), opening the possibility of a single pattern recognition system able to deal with patterns of many sorts.

Second, we have noted that we recognize many variations on the objects we encounter—cats in different positions, *A*s in different fonts or different handwritings. But although the various *A*s are different from each other in overall shape, they do have a great deal in common: two inwardly sloping lines and a horizontal crossbar. Focusing on features might allow us to concentrate on what is common to the various *A*s, and so might allow us to recognize *A*s despite their apparent diversity.

The Separateness of Feature Detection

The considerations just sketched indicate that features might be useful as a base for recognition. But can we find more direct evidence for the existence of features? One line of evidence comes from studies of individuals who have suffered brain damage in the parietal cortex. These patients appear relatively normal in tasks that require them simply to detect whether particular features are present or absent from a display. They are markedly impaired, however, in tasks that require them to judge how the features are bound together to form complex objects (A. Cohen & Rafal, 1991; Friedman-Hill, Robertson, & Treisman, 1995; Robertson, Treisman, Friedman-Hill, & Grabowecky, 1997).

Converging evidence comes from a study in which *transcranial magnetic stimulation* (TMS) was used to disrupt portions of the brain in healthy individuals. (For more on TMS, see Chapter 2.) Ashbridge, Walsh, and Cowey (1997) found that disruption of the parietal lobe had no impact on performance when participants were searching a display for targets defined by a single feature (e.g., "Find the red shape"). However, the TMS slowed performance when participants were searching for a target defined by a conjunction of features ("Find the shape that is red and round").

These results—from a case of brain damage on the one hand, and from TMS procedures on the other hand—make it clear that the *detection* of features is separate from the processes needed to put features together, to form more complex wholes. These findings confirm the claim we are after—namely, that the detection of features does have special status in the perception and recognition of objects.

Word Recognition

The evidence does suggest, therefore, that pattern recognition begins with the detection of simple features. But how are the features assembled to allow the recognition of larger units—whole words, for example, or Chihuahuas or fire hydrants? Before we tackle this question, let's fill in some more facts that we can use as a guide to our theory-building.

The Logic of Word-Recognition Studies

It requires no great effort to see that a telephone is a telephone, nor do you have any difficulty in identifying the letters on this page. It would seem, then, that ordinary circumstances do little to challenge your well-practiced recognition skills, and as a result, ordinary object recognition may not tell us much about your abilities.

By analogy, think of a spelling test in which you are asked to spell words like "CAT" or "DOG." Surely you would do well on this test, but this wouldn't tell us how good a speller you are, since most people, good spellers or bad, would do well on such an easy test. Formally, we would say that performance in this test will be at ceiling levels, and so the test will be insensitive, unable to discriminate good spellers from poor ones. To make the test more informative, therefore, we need to make it more sensitive, and this requires that we increase the difficulty of the test so that it will challenge your abilities.

By the same logic, if we want to uncover how recognition works, we need a test that challenges the participants, to get performance away from ceiling levels. To create such a challenge, one option is simply to present the stimuli to participants very quickly, for fractions of a second. Older research did this by means of a **tachistoscope**, a device that allows presentation of stimuli for precisely controlled amounts of time, including very brief presentations. More modern research uses computers for this purpose, rather than tachistoscopes, but the brief presentations are still called "tachistoscopic presentations."

In an ordinary procedure, the participant is shown a series of stimulus words on a computer screen, each for some brief duration—perhaps 20 or 30 ms (milliseconds). Each word is followed by a post-stimulus **mask**—often just a random jumble of letters, such as "XJDKEL." The mask serves to interrupt any continued processing that participants might try to do for the stimulus just presented, and this allows researchers to be certain that a stimulus presented for (say) 20 ms is visible for exactly 20 ms and no longer.

Factors Influencing Recognition

Whether someone can recognize a word shown tachistoscopically depends on many factors, including the word's frequency in the language. We can assess this frequency by literally counting how often each word appears in newspapers, magazines, and books (Kucera & Francis, 1967; Thorndike & Lorge, 1963); these counts turn out to be excellent predictors of tachistoscopic recognition. The classic demonstration comes from a study by Howes and Solomon (1951); their results showed, in essence, that the more frequently a word appears in print, the easier that word will be to recognize in a tachistoscopic presentation. In a more recent experiment, Jacoby and Dallas (1981) showed their participants words that were either very frequent (appearing more than 50 times in every million printed words) or infrequent (occurring only 1 to 5 times per million words of print). In one of their studies, participants viewed these words for 35 ms, followed by a mask. On average, participants recognized 65% of the frequent words under these conditions, but only 33% of the infrequent words—a striking two-to-one advantage for frequent words.

Another factor influencing recognition is recency of view. If participants view a word and then, a little later, view it again, they will recognize the word much more readily the second time around. The first exposure primes the participant for the second exposure; more specifically, this is a case of **repetition priming**.

As an example, participants in one study read a list of words aloud. The participants were then shown a series of words in a tachistoscope. Some of the tachistoscopic words were from the earlier list and so had been primed; others were not from the earlier list and so were unprimed. For words that were high in frequency, 68% of the unprimed words were recognized, compared to 84% of the primed words. For words low in frequency, 37% of the unprimed words were recognized, compared to 73% of the primed words (Jacoby & Dallas, 1981, Exp. 3).

The Word-Superiority Effect

Words frequently viewed are easier to perceive, as are words viewed recently. It also turns out that words themselves are easier to perceive, as compared to isolated letters. This finding is referred to as the **word-superiority effect**.

This effect is usually demonstrated with a "two-alternative, forced-choice" procedure. Thus, in some trials, we might tachistoscopically present a single letter—let's say *K*—followed by a post-stimulus mask, and follow that with a question: "Was there an *E* or a *K* in the display?" In other trials, we present a word—let's say "DARK"—followed by a mask, followed by a question: "Was there an *E* or a *K* in the display?"

Notice that a participant has a 50-50 chance of guessing correctly in either of these situations, and so any contribution from guessing is the same for the letters as it is for the words. Note in addition that, for the word stimuli, both of the letters we've asked about are plausible endings for the stimulus; either ending would create a common word ("DARE" or "DARK"). Therefore, a participant who saw only part of the display (perhaps "DAR") couldn't use his knowledge of the language to figure out what the display's final letter was. In order to choose between *E* and *K*, the participant really needs to have seen the relevant letter—and that, of course, is exactly what we want.

The results from this procedure are clear: Accuracy rates are higher in the word condition, and so, apparently, recognizing words is easier than recognizing isolated letters. To put this more precisely, participants are more accurate in identifying letters if those letters appear within a word, as opposed to appearing all by themselves (Reicher, 1969; Rumelhart & Siple, 1974; Wheeler, 1970).

In some ways, this is a peculiar result: In order to know what word you're looking at, you need to identify the word's letters. That's because the identity of a word is determined by the letters. (If the letters were different, then obviously the word would be different.) Cast in these terms, the step of identifying letters seems to be part of the overall task of identifying a word, and thus common sense says that identifying letters should be easier than identifying words. Surely it's easier to do part of a job than it is to do the whole job! Yet the evidence says otherwise.

Degrees of Well-Formedness

The evidence tells us, therefore, that it's easier to recognize an *E*, say, if the letter appears in the context "CASE" than if the letter appears on its own. But will any context produce this effect? It turns out that it is also easier to recognize an *E* if it appears within the string "FIKE" than it is if the *E* appears in isolation. Apparently, having a context is helpful even if the context is neither familiar nor meaningful. However, not all contexts provide an advantage. Recognition of the letter *H* (for example) is helped very little if it appears in a context such as "HGFD" or "HXXX."

As a related point, consider these two strings of letters: "JPSRW" and "GLAKE." Strings like "JPSRW" are very difficult to recognize when presented tachistoscopically. With exposures of 20 or 30 ms, participants will identify one or two letters from a string like this, but no more. The nonword "GLAKE," however, is far easier to recognize, even though it's no more familiar than "JPSRW." A string like "GLAKE" will often be read correctly with a 20- or 30-ms exposure.

To put this more generally, it turns out that the word-superiority effect is obtained, and recognition is aided, if a letter appears within a context that is well formed according to the rules of the language. Moreover, the more regular the context, the stronger the facilitation. Thus, for English speakers, the more a string resembles English, the easier it is to recognize. This is a well-documented pattern and has been known for a long time (Cattell, 1885).

How do we assess "resemblance to English"? One way is via pronounceability (e.g., "GLAKE" is easy to say; "JPSRW" is not); in general, pronounceable strings are more easily recognized with tachistoscopic presentations than are unpronounceable strings. Alternatively, one can assess resemblance to English in statistical terms. One can count up, in English, how often the letter *P* follows the letter *J*, how often the letter *S* follows the letter *P*, and so forth. In this way, one can ask which letter combinations are likely and which are rare. With this done, one can then evaluate any new string in terms of how likely its letter combinations are. Well-formedness measured in this way is also a good predictor of tachistoscopic performance (Gibson, Bishop, Schiff, & Smith, 1964; G. A. Miller, Bruner, & Postman, 1954).

Making Errors

It seems, then, that our perception of words is influenced by spelling patterns, and so we have an easier time recognizing sequences that use common letter combinations, a harder time with sequences that involve unusual combinations. The influence of spelling patterns also emerges in another way: in the mistakes we make. With tachistoscopic exposures, word recognition is good, but not perfect, and the errors that occur are quite systematic: There is a strong tendency to misread less-common letter sequences as if they were more-common patterns; irregular patterns are misread as if they were regular patterns. Thus, for example, "TPUM" is likely to be misread as "TRUM" or even "DRUM." But the reverse errors are rare: "DRUM" is unlikely to be misread as "TRUM" or "TPUM."

These errors often involve the misreading of a feature or two (e.g., misperceiving the *P* as an *R*, or an *O* as a *Q*). But larger errors also occur; for example, someone shown the four letters "TRUM" might instead perceive "TRUMPET". Both the large and the small errors show the pattern described: Misspelled words, partial words, or nonwords are read in a way that brings them into line with normal spelling. In effect, people perceive the input as being more regular than it actually is, and so these errors are referred to as **over-regularization errors**. This phenomenon suggests once again that our recognition is guided by (or, in this case, misguided by) some knowledge of spelling patterns.

One other point about these errors should also be emphasized. Participants in these procedures usually do not realize when they have made an error (e.g., Pillsbury, 1897). From their point of view, they are reporting what they see, and so, apparently, the misspelled or mangled letter sequences actually look correct to them. It seems, therefore, that people don't merely misidentify the stimuli; they misperceive them.

Feature Nets and Word Recognition

How can we explain this broad pattern of evidence? Key elements of the explanation derive from a theory of pattern recognition first published more than 40 years ago (Selfridge, 1959).

The Design of a Feature Net

Imagine that we want to design a system that will recognize the word "CLOCK" whenever it is presented. How might this "CLOCK" detector work? Perhaps the detector is "wired" to a *C*-detector, an *L*-detector, an *O*-detector, and so on. Whenever these letter detectors are all activated, this activates the word detector. But what activates the letter detectors? Perhaps the *L*-detector is "wired" to a horizontal-line detector, and also a vertical-line detector, and maybe also a corner detector, as shown in Figure 3.9. When all of these feature detectors are activated as a group, this activates the letter detector.

The idea here is that there is a network of detectors, organized in layers, with each subsequent layer concerned with more complex, larger-scale objects. The "bottom" layer is concerned with features, and that is why networks of this sort are often referred to as **feature nets.**

At any point in time, each detector in the network would have a particular **activation level**, which reflects how activated the detector is at just that moment. When a detector receives some input, its activation level increases. A strong input will increase the activation level by a lot, and so will a series of weaker inputs. In either case, the activation level will eventually reach the detector's **response threshold**, and at that point the detector will **fire**—that is, send its signal to the other detectors to which it is connected.

These points obviously parallel our description of neurons in Chapter 2, and that is no accident. If the feature net is to be a serious candidate for how humans recognize patterns, then the net has to employ the same sorts of building blocks

FIGURE 3.9 Networks of Detectors

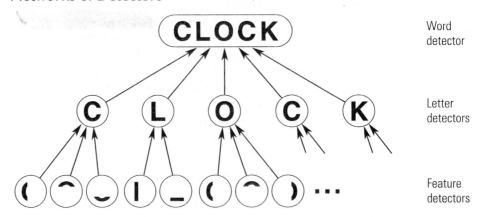

Word detector

Letter detectors

Feature detectors

Word detectors might be triggered by letter detectors, so that the word detector would fire whenever the appropriate letters were presented. The letter detectors in turn might be triggered by feature detectors, so the letter detectors would fire whenever the features were on the scene.

that the brain does. However, let's be careful not to overstate this point: No one is suggesting that detectors are neurons, or even large groups of neurons. Instead, detectors would presumably involve much more complex assemblies of neural tissue. Nonetheless, it's plainly attractive that the hypothesized detectors, within the feature net, function in a way that's biologically sensible.

Within the net, some detectors will be easier to activate than others—that is, some detectors require a very strong input to make them fire, while other detectors have a "hair trigger" and so will fire even with a weak input. This readiness to fire is determined in part by how activated the detector was to begin with. If the detector was moderately activated at the start, then only a little input is needed to raise the activation level to threshold, and so it will be easy to make this detector fire. If the detector was not at all activated at the start, then a strong input is needed to bring the detector to threshold, and so it will be more difficult to make this detector fire.

We therefore need to ask, What determines a detector's starting activation level? A number of factors contribute, but among them, detectors that have fired recently will have a higher activation level (think of it as a "warm-up" effect). Detectors that have fired frequently in the past will also have a higher activation level (think of it as an "exercise" effect). Thus the activation level is dependent on principles of recency and frequency.

We now can put this mechanism to work. Why are frequent words in the language easier to recognize than rare words? Frequent words have, by definition, appeared often in the things you read. Therefore, the detectors needed for recognizing these words have been frequently used, and so they have relatively high levels of activation. Thus, even a weak signal (e.g., a very brief presentation of the word) will bring these detectors to their response threshold and so will be enough to make these detectors fire. Thus, the word will be recognized even with a weak or degraded input.

Repetition priming is explained in similar terms. Presenting a word once will cause the relevant detectors to fire. Once they have fired, activation levels will be temporarily lifted, because of recency of use. Therefore, only a weak signal will be needed to make the detectors fire again. As a result, the word will be more easily recognized the second time around.

The Feature Net and Well-Formedness

The net we've described so far cannot explain all of the data. Consider the effects of well-formedness—for instance, the fact that people are able to read strings like "PIRT" or "HICE," when they're presented tachistoscopically, but not strings like "ITPR" or "HCEI." This difference can't be explained in terms of letter detectors, since, as it turns out, the same letters are used in "PIRT" and "ITPR," yet one is easy to recognize and one is not. Likewise for "HICE" and "HCEI." The difference also can't be explained in terms of word detectors: None of these letter sequences is a word, and so word detectors would play no role in the recognition of these strings.

How, therefore, should we accommodate these results? One option is to add another layer to the net, a layer filled with detectors for letter combinations. In Figure 3.10, we have added a layer of **bigram detectors**—detectors of letter pairs. These detectors, like all the rest, will be triggered by lower-level detectors and send their output to higher-level detectors. And just like any other detector, each bigram detector will start out with a certain activation level, influenced by the frequency with which the detector has fired in the past, and also the recency with which it has fired.

This turns out to be all the theory we need. Why are English-like nonwords more easily recognized than strings not resembling English ("RSFK" or "IUBE")? Well-formed words involve familiar letter combinations. You have never seen the sequence "HICE" before, but you have seen the letter pair *HI* (in "HIT," "HIGH," or "HILL") and the pair *CE* ("FACE," "MACE," "PACE"). The detectors for these letter groups, therefore, have high activation levels at the start, and so they don't need much additional input to reach their threshold. As a result, these detectors will fire with only weak input. That will make the corresponding letter combinations easy to recognize, facilitating the recognition of strings like "HICE." None of this is true for "RSFK." None of these letter combinations is familiar, and so this string will receive no benefits from priming. A strong input will therefore be needed to bring the relevant detectors to threshold, and so the string will be recognized only with difficulty. (For more on bigram detectors, and how they work, see Grainger & Whitney, 2004; and Whitney, 2001.)

FIGURE 3.10	Bigram Detectors

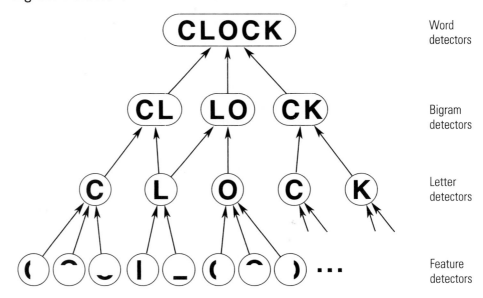

It seems plausible that a layer of bigram detectors is interposed between letter detectors and word detectors.

Recovery From Confusion

The bigram detectors also provide some further advantages. Imagine that we present the word "CORN" for 20 ms. With this brief presentation, the quantity of incoming information is small, and so some of the word's features may not be detected. Figure 3.11 shows how this might play out: The fast presentation of the *O* wasn't enough to trigger all of the feature detectors appropriate for the *O*. In fact, only the bottom-curve detector is firing. Therefore, the *O*-detector will receive input from just one of its features, and so will be only weakly activated. But, of course, the same is true for the *U*-detector, the *Q*-detector, and the *S*-detector: These, too, are responsive to the bottom-curve feature detector, and so, with this detector firing, they also will be weakly activated.

But now look what happens at the next level. The *C*-detector is strongly activated, because the *C* was clearly visible. The detectors for *O*, *U*, *Q*, and *S* are all weakly activated, because only one of their feature detectors is firing. As a result, the bigram detectors for *CO*, *CU*, *CQ*, and *CS* are all receiving the same input: a strong signal from one of their letters, and a weak signal from the second letter. Despite this equivalence in the input, though, these bigram detectors won't all respond in the same way: The *CO*-detector is well primed (because this is a frequent

| FIGURE 3.11 | Error Trapping |

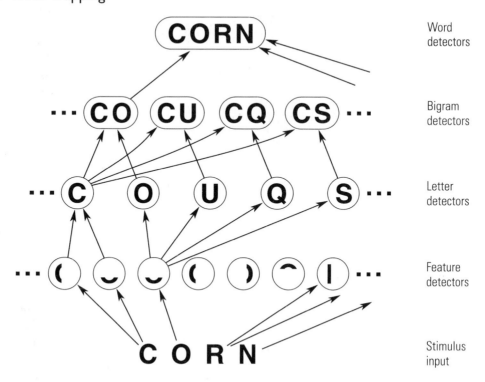

If "CORN" is presented briefly, not all of its features will be detected. Imagine, for example, that only the bottom curve of the O is detected, and not the O's top or sides. This will (weakly) activate the O-detector, but will also activate the detectors of various other letters having a bottom curve, including U, Q, and S. This will, in turn, send weak activation to the appropriate bigram detectors. The CO-detector, however, is well primed and so is likely to respond even though it is receiving only a weak input. The other bigram detectors (for CQ or CS) are less well primed and so will not respond to this weak input. Therefore, "CORN" will be correctly perceived, despite the confusion at the letter level caused by the weak signal.

pattern), and so the input probably will be enough to fire this detector. The *CU*-detector is less primed (because this is a less frequent pattern); the *CQ*- or *CS*-detectors, if these even exist, are not primed at all. The input will therefore not be enough to activate these detectors.

Thus, at the letter level, there was confusion about the input letter's identity: Several detectors were firing, and all were firing equally. At the bigram level, only one detector responds, and so the confusion has been sorted out and an error has been avoided.

Ambiguous Inputs

The mechanism just described also helps in explaining some other evidence. Look again at Figure 3.7 (p. 73). The second character shown is exactly the same as the fifth, but the left-hand string is perceived as "THE" (and the character is identified as an *H*), and the right-hand string is perceived as "CAT" (and the character as an *A*).

This observation is now easily explained. When the ambiguous character is in view, it will trigger some of the features normally associated with an *A* and some normally associated with an *H*. This will cause the *A*-detector to fire, but only weakly (because only some of the *A*'s features are present), and likewise for the H-detector. At the letter level, therefore, there is uncertainty about what the incoming character is.

The uncertainty is resolved at subsequent levels. With the *T*-detector firing well, and the *A*- and *H*-detectors firing weakly, there will be a moderate signal sent to both the *TH*- and the *TA*-detectors, and likewise to the *THE*- and *TAE*-detectors. But the *TH*-detector is enormously well primed; so is the *THE*-detector. If there were a *TAE*-detector, it would be barely primed, since this is a string rarely encountered. Thus the *THE*- and *TAE*-detectors might be receiving similar input, but this input is sufficient only for the well-primed *THE*-detector, and so only it will respond. In this way, the net will recognize the ambiguous pattern as "THE," not "TAE." The same is true for the ambiguous pattern on the right, perceived as "CAT," not "CHT."

A similar explanation will handle the word-superiority effect (see, for example, Rumelhart & Siple, 1974). To take a simple case, imagine that we present the letter *A* in the context "AT." If the presentation is brief enough, participants may see very little of the *A*, perhaps just the horizontal crossbar. This would not be enough to distinguish among *A*, *F* or *H*, and so all these letter detectors would fire weakly. If this were all the information the participants had, they'd be stuck. But let us imagine that the participants did perceive the second letter in the display, the *T*. It seems likely that the *AT* bigram is far better primed than the *FT* or *HT* bigrams. (That is because you often encounter words like "CAT" or "BOAT"; words like "SOFT" or "HEFT" are less frequent in the English language.) Thus, the weak firing of the *A*-detector would be enough to fire the *AT* bigram detector, while the weak firing for the *F* and *H* might not trigger their bigram detectors. In this way, a "choice" would be made at the bigram level that the input was "AT" and not something else. Once this bigram has been detected, answering the question, "Was there an *A* or an *F* in the display?" is easy. In this manner, the letter will be better detected in context than in isolation. This is not because context allows you to see more; instead, context allows you to make better use of what you see.

Recognition Errors

There is, however, a downside to all this: Imagine that we present the string "CQRN" to participants. If the presentation is brief enough, participants will register only a subset of the string's features. Let's imagine, in line with an earlier example, that they register only the bottom bit of the string's second letter. This detection of the bottom curve will weakly activate the *Q*-detector, and also the *U*-detector and the *O*-detector. The resulting pattern of network activation is shown in Figure 3.12, which, as you can see, is nearly identical to Figure 3.11.

We have already argued that the pattern of priming within the network will lead to a "CORN" response in the situation shown in Figure 3.11. But the "grist" for the network is exactly the same in Figure 3.12: The same feature detectors are firing. Therefore, this input, too, will lead to "CORN." Hence, in the first case (when the stimulus actually is "CORN"), the dynamic built into the net aids performance, allowing the network to recover from its initial confusion. In the second case (with "CQRN" as the stimulus), the same dynamic causes the network to misread the stimulus.

FIGURE 3.12 Recognition Errors

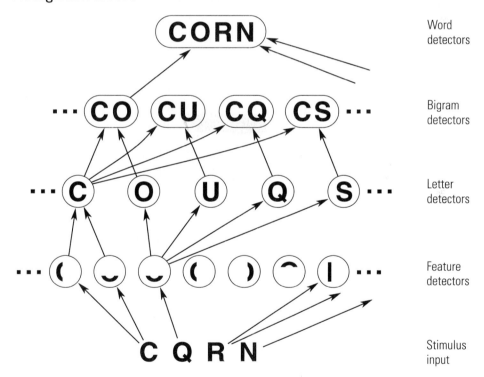

If "CQRN" is presented briefly, not all of its features will be detected. Perhaps only the bottom curve of the *Q* is detected, and this will (weakly) activate various other letters having a bottom curve, including *O*, *U*, and *S*. However, this is the same situation that would result from a brief presentation of "CORN" (as shown in Figure 3.11), and therefore, by the logic we have already discussed, this stimulus is likely to be misperceived as "CORN."

This example illustrates how over-regularization errors come about. In essence, the network is biased, always favoring frequent letter combinations over infrequent ones. This bias facilitates perception if the input is, in fact, a frequent word. But the bias will pull the network toward errors if the input has an unusual spelling pattern, and the errors will always be of the same sort, turning irregular spelling into more frequent combinations.

Let's note, though, that these errors are usually unproblematic. Low-frequency words are, as we've just discussed, likely to be misperceived. But, by definition, low-frequency words aren't encountered that often. The network's bias promotes the perception of frequent words, and these (by definition) are the words you encounter most of the time. Hence, the network's bias aids recognition in the more frequent cases and hurts recognition only in the rare cases. Necessarily, then, the network's bias helps perception more often than it hurts.

Why Aren't the Mistakes Noticed?

We mentioned earlier that research participants don't merely misidentify the input; they seem instead to misperceive it. In other words, when people in tachistoscopic procedures make errors, they often insist that they are reporting what they clearly saw. What produces this illusion?

Consider the similarity between Figures 3.11 and 3.12. In Figure 3.11, the firing of the *CO*-detector is a legitimate detection. In Figure 3.12, the firing of this same detector constitutes a **false alarm**, a "detection" even though there's no "CO" present. In other words, these two situations differ with regard to the *input* to the *CO*-detector. However, the situations are identical if we consider the *output* from this detector. In both cases, the detector fires, and this triggers subsequent detectors. And, of course, those subsequent detectors have no way to tell *why* the *CO*-detector is firing; all they know is that it *is* firing, and that's what they respond to. As a result, those subsequent detectors will react in exactly the same way to a sequence that began with a real detection and to one that began with a false alarm.

Said differently, there really is no difference, as far as the network is concerned, between stimuli that actually occurred and stimuli that were merely inferred. Either of these can lead to a detector response, and in either case, the impact on subsequent events will unfold in the same way. It's no wonder, then, that the network can't distinguish actual recognitions from errors, and no wonder that the network's mistakes go entirely unnoticed.

Distributed Knowledge

We are almost ready to leave our discussion of the feature net. In closing, though, we need to work through two last points: first, the nature of the "knowledge" built into the network; and second, the broader question of why the network should function as it does.

We've seen many indications that, somehow, knowledge of spelling patterns is "built into" the network. For example, the network "knows" that *CO* is a common bigram in English, while *CF* is not. As a result, it's literally true that the system is better prepared for one of these patterns than for the other. One might say that the system "expects" one of these patterns (*CO*) to appear often, and is ready for it when it does appear, but has no such expectation for the other (*CF*). Likewise, when in doubt (if, for example, the input is barely seen), the system is more likely to "infer" a *CO* is present than a *CF*. And so on.

However, the sense in which the net "knows" these facts about spelling is worth emphasizing, since we will return to this idea in later chapters. This knowledge is not explicitly stored anywhere. Nowhere within the net is there a sentence like "*CO* is a common bigram in English; *CF* is not." Instead, this memory, if we even want to call it that, is manifest only in the fact that the *CO*-detector happens to be more primed than the *CF*-detector. The *CO*-detector doesn't "know" anything about this advantage, nor does the *CF*-detector know anything about its *dis*advantage. Each simply does its job, and in the course of doing their jobs, occasions will arise that involve a "competition" between these detectors. (This sort of competition was illustrated in Figures 3.11 and 3.12.) When these competitions occur, they'll be "decided," in a straightforward way, by activation levels: The better-primed detector will be more likely to respond, and so that detector will be more likely to influence subsequent events. That's the entire mechanism through which these "knowledge effects" arise. That's how "expectations" or "inferences" emerge—as a direct consequence of the activation levels.

To put this into technical terms, the network's "knowledge" is not **locally represented** anywhere; it is not stored in a particular location or built into a specific process. Thus, we cannot look just at the level of priming in the *CO*-detector and conclude that this detector represents a frequent bigram, nor can we look at the *CF*-detector to conclude that it represents a rare bigram. Instead, we need to look at the *relationship* between their levels of priming, and we also need to look at how this relationship will lead to one detector being more influential than the other. The knowledge about bigram frequencies, in other words, is **distributed knowledge**—that is, represented in a fashion that's distributed across the network, and detectable only if we consider how the entire network functions.

What is perhaps most remarkable about the feature net, then, lies in how much can be accomplished with a distributed representation, and thus with simple, mechanical elements, correctly connected to one another. The net appears to make inferences and to know the rules of English spelling. But the actual mechanics of the net involve neither inferences nor knowledge (at least not in any conventional sense). You and I can see how the inferences unfold by taking a bird's-eye view and considering how all the detectors work together as a system. But nothing in the net's functioning depends on the bird's-eye view. Instead, the activity of each detector is locally determined—influenced by just those detectors feeding into it. When all of these detectors work together, though, the result is a process that acts as if it knows the rules. But the rules themselves play no role in guiding the network's moment-by-moment activities.

Efficiency Versus Accuracy

One other crucial fact about the network is that it does make mistakes: misreading some inputs and misinterpreting some patterns. But, as we've seen, these mistakes are produced by exactly the same mechanisms that are responsible for the network's main advantages—its ability to deal with ambiguous inputs, for example, or to recover from its own errors.

Perhaps, therefore, we should view the errors as simply the price one pays in order to gain the benefits associated with the net: If one wants a mechanism that's able to deal with unclear, or partial, inputs, one simply has to live with the fact that sometimes the mechanism will make mistakes. But this invites a question: Do we really need to pay this price? After all, outside of the lab we're unlikely to encounter tachistoscopic inputs. Instead, we see stimuli that are out in view for long periods of time, stimuli that we can inspect at our leisure. Why, therefore, don't we take the moment to scrutinize these inputs, so that we can rely on fewer inferences and assumptions, and in that fashion gain a higher level of accuracy in recognizing the objects we encounter?

Think back to the "Betsy and Jacob" story discussed in Chapter 1. This story leaves a great deal unsaid, relying on the fact that listeners (or readers) can fill in the missing information. Of course, this carries a risk: There's always a chance that the reader might make bad inferences or mistaken assumptions. To avoid this risk, we could spell out everything in the story, but if we did, the story would need to be intolerably long, and the telling of it impossibly slow.

Moreover, the gains of spelling out everything in this story would be tiny, because we'd be forced to include tons of information that, in truth, should be blindingly obvious (e.g., the fact that people need money to buy things, or that piggy banks contain money, not olives). Thus, spelling out everything would have an enormous cost and would gain us very, very little. If we insist on greater efficiency, then—that is, if we insist on leaving out many elements of the story and letting the reader fill these in with inference—we are not being impatient; we are simply being reasonable.

The same is true for word recognition. To maximize accuracy, we could, of course, scrutinize every character on the page. That way, if a character were missing or misprinted, we would be sure to detect it. But the cost associated with this strategy would be insufferable: Reading would be unspeakably slow (in part because the speed with which we move our eyes is relatively slow—no more than four or five eye movements per second). In contrast, one can make inferences about a page with remarkable speed, and this leads readers to adopt the obvious strategy: They read some of the letters and make inferences about the rest. And for the most part, those inferences are safe—thanks to the simple fact that our language (like most aspects of our world) contains some redundncies, so that one doesn't need every lettr to identify what a wrd is; oftn the missng letter is perfctly predctable from the contxt, virtually guaranteeing that inferences will be correct.

Thus, the efficient reader is not being careless, or hasty, or lazy. Given the redundancy of text, and given the slowness of letter-by-letter reading, the inferential strategy is the only strategy that makes sense.

Descendants of the Feature Net

As we mentioned early on, we have been focusing on one of the simpler versions of the feature net. This has allowed us to bring a number of important themes into view—such as the trade-off between efficiency and accuracy, and the notion of distributed knowledge built into a network's functioning. However, it should be said that many variations on the feature-net idea are possible, each differing somewhat from the specific proposal we have discussed, and each with its own advantages and disadvantages. In this section, we consider some important variations on the network idea.

The McClelland and Rumelhart Model

An influential model of word recognition was proposed by McClelland and Rumelhart (1981); a portion of their model is illustrated in Figure 3.13. Once again, there is a feature base and a network of connections, as various detectors serve to influence one another. This net, like the one we have been discussing, is better able to identify well-formed strings than irregular strings; this net is also more efficient in identifying characters in context, as opposed to characters in isolation. However, several new features of this net make it possible to accomplish all this without bigram detectors.

In the network proposal we have considered so far, activation of one detector serves to activate other detectors. These **excitatory connections** are shown in Figure 3.13 with arrows; for example, detection of a *T* serves to "excite" the "TRIP" detector. In the McClelland and Rumelhart model, however, detectors can also inhibit each other, so that detection of a *G*, for example, inhibits the "TRIP" detector. These **inhibitory connections** are shown in the figure with dots. In addition, this model allows for more complicated signaling than we have employed so far. In our discussion, we have assumed that lower-level detectors trigger upper-level detectors, but not the reverse. The flow of information, it seemed, was a one-way street. In the McClelland and Rumelhart model, though, higher-level detectors (word detectors) can influence the lower-level detectors, and detectors at any level can also influence the other detectors at the same level (e.g., letter detectors inhibit other letter detectors; word detectors inhibit other word detectors).

FIGURE 3.13 **Alternative Conceptions of the Feature Network**

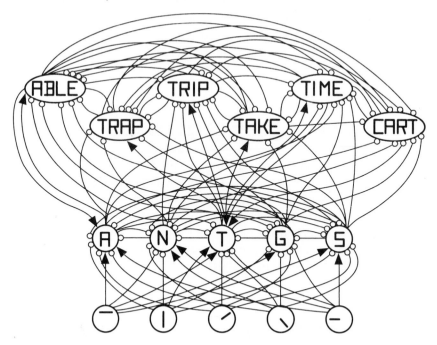

McClelland and Rumelhart (1981) offered a pattern-recognition model with no detectors for letter combinations. Instead, letter detectors directly activate word detectors. This model includes both excitatory connections (indicated by arrows) and inhibitory connections (indicated by connections with round heads). Connections within a specific level are also possible—so that, for example, activation of the "TRIP" detector will inhibit the detectors for "TRAP", "TAKE", or "TIME".

To see how this would work, let's say that the word "TRIP" is briefly shown, allowing a viewer to see enough features to identify, say, only the *R*, *I*, and *P*. Detectors for these letters will therefore fire, in turn activating the detector for "TRIP." Activation of this word detector will inhibit the firing of all the other word detectors (e.g., detectors for "TRAP" or "TAKE"), so that, in a sense, these other words are less likely to arise as distractions or competitors with the target word. At the same time, activation of the "TRIP" detector will excite the detectors for its component letters—i.e., detectors for *T*, *R*, *I*, and *P*. The *R*-, *I*-, and *P*-detectors, we've assumed, were already firing, so this extra activation "from above" has little impact. But the *T*-detector, we've supposed, was not firing before. The relevant features were on the scene but in a degraded form (thanks to the brief presentation); this weak input was insufficient to trigger an unprimed detector. However, once the excitation from the "TRIP" detector primes the *T*-detector, it is more likely to fire, even with a weak input.

In effect, then, activation of the word detector for "TRIP" implies that this is a context in which a *T* is quite likely. The network therefore responds to this suggestion by "preparing itself" for a *T*. Once the network is suitably prepared (by the appropriate priming), detection of this letter is facilitated. In this way, the detection of a letter sequence (the word "TRIP") makes the network more sensitive to elements that are likely to occur within that sequence. That is exactly what we need for the network to be responsive to the regularities of spelling patterns. And, of course, we've seen that there is ample evidence that humans are sensitive to (and exploit) these regularities.

There are actually several reasons one might prefer this kind of net over the kind considered earlier. As one consideration, there is ample evidence that higher-level detectors can activate lower-level detectors, just as the McClelland and Rumelhart model proposes. We will return to these "top-down" effects in a few pages, and similar effects will be discussed in Chapter 4. Second, we can also find biological evidence for this sort of two-way communication in the nervous system: Neurons in the eyeballs send activation to the brain but also receive activation from the brain; neurons in the LGN send activation to the visual cortex but also receive activation from the cortex. These facts make it clear that visual processing is not a one-way process, with information flowing simply from the eyes toward the brain. Instead, signaling occurs in both an ascending (toward the brain) and a descending (away from the brain) direction, just as the McClelland and Rumelhart model claims.

Recognition by Components

What about the recognition of things other than print? For example, what about three-dimensional objects? Can these also be recognized by a network?

There are, to be sure, many differences between recognition of print and recognition of solid objects. Nonetheless, it does seem that the recognition of objects can be achieved through a feature net similar to the one we have described here. For illustration, let's look at two different conceptions of how object recognition might proceed.

Hummel and Biederman (1992; also Hummel & Stankiewicz, 1998) have offered a network theory dubbed the **recognition by components** (or RBC) model. The crucial innovation in this model is an intermediate level of detectors, sensitive to **geons** (short for "geometric ions"). Hummel and Biederman's proposal is that geons serve as the basic building blocks of all the objects we recognize; geons are, in essence, the alphabet from which all objects are constructed. Geons are simple shapes, such as cylinders, cones, and blocks (Figure 3.14A). And only a small set of these shapes is needed: According to Biederman (1987, 1990), we need (at most) three dozen different geons to describe every object in the world, just as 26 letters are all that are needed to produce all the words of English. These geons can then be combined in various ways—in a top-of relation, or a side-connected relation, and so on, to create all the objects we perceive (see Figure 3.14B).

FIGURE 3.14   Geons

Biederman (1987, 1990) has proposed that geons serve as the basic building blocks of all the objects we recognize. In other words, we recognize objects by first recognizing their component geons. Panel A shows five different geons; Panel B shows how these geons can be assembled into objects. The numbers in Panel B identify the specific geons; for example, a bucket contains Geon 5 top-connected to Geon 3.

The RBC model, like the network we have been discussing, uses a hierarchy of detectors. The lowest-level detectors are feature detectors, which respond to edges, curves, vertices, and so on. These detectors in turn activate the geon detectors. Higher levels of detectors are then sensitive to combinations of geons. More precisely, geons are assembled into more complex arrangements called "geon assemblies," which explicitly represent the *relations* between geons (such as top-of or side-connected). These assemblies, in turn, activate the object model, a representation of the complete, recognized object.

The presence of the geon and geon-assembly levels, within this hierarchy, buys us several advantages. For one, geons can be identified from virtually any angle of view, and so recognition based on geons is **viewpoint-independent**. Thus, no matter what your position relative to a cat, you'll be able to identify its geons and thus identify the cat. Moreover, it seems that most objects can be recognized from just a few geons (in the appropriate configuration). As a consequence, geon-based models like RBC can recognize an object even if many of the object's geons are hidden from view.

In addition, several lines of evidence seem to confirm that geons do play a role in recognition. For example, recognition of simple objects is relatively easy if the geons are easy to discern; recognition is much more difficult if the geons are hard to identify (Biederman, 1985). As an illustration, consider the objects shown in Figure 3.15. In Columns B and C, about two thirds of the contour has been deleted from each drawing. In Column B, this deletion has been carefully done so that the geons can still be identified; as you can see, these objects can be recognized without much difficulty. In Column C, however, the deletion has been done in a fashion that obscures geon identity; now object recognition is much more difficult. Thus, it really does seem that the geons capture something crucial for identification of these objects.

Recognition via Multiple Views

A number of researchers, prominently including Michael Tarr (1995; also Hayward & Williams, 2000; Tarr & Bülthoff, 1998; Vuong & Tarr, 2004; Wallis & Bülthoff, 1999), have offered a different approach to object recognition. They propose that people have stored in memory a number of different views of each object they can recognize: an image of what the cat looks like when viewed head-on, a view of what it looks like from the left, and so on. To recognize the object, therefore, one must match the current view of the object with one of these views in memory. However, the number of views in memory is limited—perhaps a half dozen or so—and so, in many cases, the current view won't line up with any of the available images. In that case, one needs a time-consuming process of "rotating" the remembered view into alignment with the current view. (See Chapter 11 for more on mental rotation.) As a result, ease of recognition will be faster from some viewpoints than from others, and so, in this fashion, recognition will be **viewpoint-dependent**.

A growing body of data suggests that recognition actually is viewpoint-dependent in this way. To be sure, we can recognize objects from many different angles, but our recognition is faster from some angles than others, in a fashion consistent with this multiple-views proposal.

For our purposes, though, what is crucial is how you manage to do the comparison between an object now before your eyes and an image currently in memory. One prominent proposal involves processes very much like those in the networks we've been discussing (Riesenhuber & Poggio, 1999, 2002; for an explicit comparison between this model and feature nets, see Tarr, 1999). In this model, there is a hierarchy of detectors, with each successive layer within the network concerned with more complex aspects of the whole. Thus, low-level detectors respond to lines at certain orientations; higher detectors respond to corners and notches. At the top of the hierarchy are detectors that respond to the sight of whole objects. It is important, though, that these detectors each represent what the object looks like from

FIGURE 3.15 Recognizing Degraded Pictures

In Column B, one can still identify the objects' geons, and so the forms are easily recognized. In Column C, it is difficult to identify the geons, and correspondingly difficult to identify the objects. This evidence adds strength to the claim that geon identification plays an important role in object recognition.

a particular vantage point, and so the detectors fire when there is a match to one of these view-tuned representations.

A number of proposals have been offered for how this model might be implemented in the nervous system (and, in particular, in the tissue we identified as the *what* system, in Chapter 2). For example, the view-tuned representations are probably supported by tissue in the inferotemporal cortex, near the terminus of the *what* pathway. Recording from cells in this brain area has shown that many neurons here seem object-specific—that is, fire preferentially when a certain type of object is on the scene. Crucially, most of these neurons are view-tuned: They fire most strongly to a particular view of the target object. This is, of course, just what one might expect with the multiple-views proposal.

We should emphasize, though, that there continues to be debate between advocates of the RBC approach (with its claim that recognition is largely viewpoint-independent) and the multiple-views approach (with its argument that recognition is viewpoint-dependent). Obviously, further data are needed to resolve this disagreement. In the meantime, let's be clear that both proposals involve the sort of hierarchical network we've been discussing. In other words, no matter how this debate about object recognition turns out, it looks like we're going to need a network model along the lines we've considered.

Different Objects, Different Recognition Systems?

We have now shifted our focus away from print: A network can also be designed, it seems, to recognize three-dimensional objects. But how far can we travel on this path? Can other sorts of recognition—recognition of sounds, recognition of faces, recognition of smells—be approached in the same way?

The evidence suggests a mixed answer. As we will see, many domains, rather distant from print, do show effects similar to the ones we have reviewed, suggesting that similar mechanisms are in play. Other domains, however, reveal a different dynamic, implying that, for these domains, we need a different sort of theory.

Recognition Errors in Hearing

Many of the principles surveyed so far do generalize to other domains. For example, it is usually true that more frequently viewed (or more frequently heard) patterns are easier to recognize. Likewise, repetition priming can be demonstrated with many different kinds of stimuli. It is also true in general that regular or well-formed patterns are easier to recognize than ill-formed patterns. And when recognition errors occur, they are, in general, in the direction of regularizing the input, just as in the case of print. All of this invites the conclusion that a uniform theoretical treatment will be possible across diverse domains.

As an illustration of the relevant research, consider studies of the so-called **restoration effect.** In these procedures, sounds are tape-recorded and then carefully modified. For example, the "s" sound in the word "legislature" might be removed and replaced by a brief burst of noise. When people hear this degraded input, however, they do not detect the omission; instead, they report hearing the complete word, "legislature," accompanied by a burst of noise. In effect, they supply the missing sound on their own. If they are asked exactly when the accompanying noise occurred (simultaneous with the first syllable? the second?), they often cannot tell (Repp, 1992; Samuel, 1987, 1991; for further discussion of the recognition of speech, see Chapter 10).

These restoration errors are plainly related to the errors we have described in print recognition. In both cases, the perceiver goes beyond the information actually provided, filling in the information that "should" be there. In the case of print, we attributed this to well-primed detectors. Thanks to priming, these detectors will fire even in response to a weak input; that makes the network robust. Unfortunately, though, we can find circumstances in which the detectors fire in the absence of an input—producing what we called a false alarm response. Apparently, the same is true with auditory stimuli such as speech and also, it turns out, with nonlinguistic stimuli, such as musical phrases (DeWitt & Samuel, 1990).

Faces

However, one category of input does seem to require a different sort of recognition system: faces. Several pieces of evidence support the claim that face memory is served by specialized structures and mechanisms. One indication comes from individuals who have suffered brain damage leading to agnosia. It turns out that there are many subtypes of agnosia, one of which is called **prosopagnosia.** People with this disorder lose their ability to recognize faces, even though their other visual abilities seem to be intact. This seems to imply the existence of a special neural structure involved almost exclusively in the recognition and discrimination of faces (Burton, Young, Bruce, Johnston, & Ellis, 1991; Damasio, Tranel, & Damasio, 1990; De Renzi, Faglioni, Grossi, & Nichelli, 1991; Sergent & Poncet, 1990).

A second distinguishing principle of face recognition is its strong dependence on orientation. As we have seen, there is debate about whether the recognition of houses, or teacups, or automobiles, is viewpoint-dependent. But there can be no question for faces: Recognition of faces is heavily dependent on orientation. In one study, for example, four categories of stimuli were considered: right-side-up faces, upside-down faces, right-side-up pictures of common objects other than faces, and upside-down pictures of common objects. As can be seen in Figure 3.16, performance suffered for all of the upside-down stimuli. However, this effect was much larger for faces than it is for other kinds of stimuli (Yin, 1969).

FIGURE 3.16 Memory for Faces Presented Upright or Upside-Down

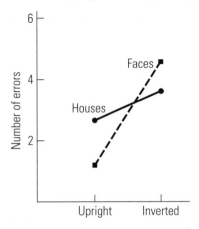

People's memory for faces is quite good, compared with memory for other pictures (in this case, pictures of houses). However, performance is very much disrupted when the pictures of faces are inverted. Performance with houses is also worse with inverted pictures, but the effect of inversion is far smaller. (After Yin, 1969)

The same point can be made informally. Figure 3.17 shows two upside-down photographs of former British prime minister Margaret Thatcher (from P. Thompson, 1980). You can probably detect that something is odd about them, but now try turning the book upside down, so that the faces are right side up. As you can see, the difference between these faces is immense, and yet this rather fiendish contrast is largely lost when the faces are upside down. Once again, it seems that the perception of faces is strikingly different when we view the faces upside down. (Also see Rhodes, Brake, & Atkinson, 1993; and Valentine, 1988.)

All of this seems to imply that face recognition is different from recognition of other sorts—served by its own neural apparatus and particularly dependent on orientation. However, we need to fine-tune this claim a bit because other stimuli, and not just faces, also rely on this special recognition system.

Consider first the evidence of prosopagnosia. Our understanding of this syndrome has grown as a greater number of cases have been examined. For example, there is a case of a prosopagnosic farmer who not only lost the ability to recognize faces, but also lost the ability to recognize his individual cows. Likewise, there is a case of a prosopagnosic bird-watcher who has, it seems, lost both the ability to discriminate faces and also the ability to discriminate warblers (Bornstein, 1963; Bornstein, Sroka, & Munitz, 1969). Still another patient has lost the ability to tell cars apart; she is able to locate her car in a parking lot only by reading all the license

FIGURE 3.17 Perception of Upside-Down Faces

The left-hand picture looks somewhat odd, but the two pictures still look relatively similar to each other. Now try turning the book upside down (so that the faces are upright). In this position, the left-hand face (now on the right) looks ghoulish, and the two pictures look very different from each other. Perception of upside-down faces is apparently quite different from our perception of upright faces. (From Thompson, 1980)

plates until she finds her own (Damasio, Damasio, & Van Hoesen, 1982). Thus, prosopagnosia is not strictly a disorder of face recognition.

Likewise, in Chapter 2, we considered neuroimaging data showing that a particular brain site—the so-called fusiform face area (FFA)—is specifically responsive to faces. It turns out, though, that tasks requiring subtle distinctions among birds, or among cars, also produce high levels of activation in this area (Gauthier, Skudlarski, Gore, & Anderson, 2000). Apparently, the neural tissue "specialized" for faces isn't used only for faces.

In the same way, other categories of stimuli, not just faces, show the upside-down effect we have already described. For example, one study examined people who were highly experienced judges in dog shows, people who knew particular breeds extremely well. Diamond and Carey (1986) compared how well these judges recognized right-side-up and upside-down stimuli in each of two categories: faces and dogs in the familiar breed. Not surprisingly, performance was much worse with upside-down faces than with right-side-up faces, replicating the pattern of Figure 3.16. The critical result, though, is that performance suffered just as much with upside-down pictures of dogs.

None of these results challenge the claim that we have a specialized recognition system, using its own brain tissue, and especially sensitive to orientation. The key, though, is that this system doesn't operate only on faces. Instead, the system seems crucial whenever a task has two characteristics: The task has to involve recognizing specific individuals within a category, and the category has to be an extremely familiar one (Diamond & Carey, 1986; Gauthier, 2000). The recognition of faces certainly meets these requirements, but other tasks do as well. Thus, this special system is used when expert bird-watchers are recognizing individual birds, when a farmer (enormously familiar with his herd) is recognizing individual cows, and so on.

How does this second system work? Several authors have suggested that humans have one object-recognition system specialized for the recognition of a pattern's *parts* (features, geons) and the assembly of those parts into larger wholes. That's the system we've been discussing for most of this chapter. In addition, a second system is specialized for the recognition of *configurations*. This system is less able to analyze patterns into their parts and less able to recognize these parts, but it is more sensitive to larger-scale patterns. Presumably it is this system that is crucial for the recognition of faces and the other cases discussed in this section (for a broad review, see Farah, Wilson, Drain, & Tanaka, 1998).

Damage to either of these systems would cause difficulties—but difficulties of different sorts. Damage to the second (configuration) system is presumably what underlies prosopagnosia. Damage to the first (part) system disrupts the ability to recognize words, objects, or any other target that is identified by its inventory of parts. Consistent with this proposal, prosopagnosia and object agnosia do appear to be separate disorders, with patients typically showing one of these but not the other, just as we would expect if the patient has suffered brain damage in just one of these systems (Farah et al., 1998).

Further work is needed to specify how the configurational system functions. In the meantime, it appears that the feature-net approach we have discussed in this chapter is powerful and applicable to a wide variety of patterns, but simply is not the whole story. Some patterns, including faces, seem to involve a different sort of pattern recognition. (For examples of other research on memory for faces, see Hancock, Bruce, & Burton, 2000; Hay, Young, & Ellis, 1991; and Murray, Yong, & Rhodes, 2000.)

Top-Down Influences on Object Recognition

The previous section had a two-part message: On the one side, we saw that the feature-net idea is applicable to a great many domains: Not only is it useful for the recognition of print, but it is also applicable to the recognition of common objects, speech sounds, and more. At the same time, there are also domains for which the feature net is not well suited. The suggestion, then, is that we need multiple recognition systems: the part-based system we've been focusing on, designed specifically to recognize objects by identifying their elements; and then a configurational system, crucial for faces and some other patterns.

In this last section, we explore a different limit on the feature net. Our concern here is with targets for which the feature net is useful—print, common objects, and so on. Even in this domain, it turns out that the feature net must be supplemented with additional mechanisms. This requirement doesn't undermine the importance of the feature-net idea; the net is plainly needed as part of our theoretical account. The key word, however, is *part* because, as we'll see, we need to place the feature net within a larger theoretical frame.

The Benefits of Larger Contexts

Let us begin with some evidence. We have already seen that letter recognition is improved by context, so that the letter *V*, for example, is easier to recognize in the context "VASE," or even the nonsense context "VIMP," than it is if presented alone. It turns out that the same is true for words: These, too, are better recognized in context—in particular, in the context of a sentence.

There are many formal demonstrations of this effect (e.g., Rueckl & Oden, 1986; Spellman, Holyoak, & Morrison, 2001; Tulving & Gold, 1963; Tulving, Mandler, & Baumal, 1964), but for our purposes, an informal example will be sufficient: Imagine that we tell research participants, "I am about to show you a word very briefly on a computer screen; the word is the name of something that you can eat." If we forced the participants to guess the word at this point, they would be unlikely to name the target word. (There are, after all, many things you can eat, and so your chances are slim of guessing just the right one.) But if we now tachistoscopically show the word "ARTICHOKE," we are likely to observe a large priming effect; that is, participants are more likely to recognize "ARTICHOKE" with this cue than they would have been without the cue.

Consider what this priming involves. First, the person needs to understand all of the words in the instruction. If she did not understand the word "eat" (if, for example, she mistakenly thought we had said, "something that you can beat"), we would not get the priming. Second, the person must understand the syntax of the instruction and, specifically, the relations among the words in the instruction. Again, if she mistakenly thought we said "something that can eat you," we would expect a very different sort of priming. Third, the person has to know some facts about the world—namely, the kinds of things that can be eaten; without this knowledge, we would expect no priming.

To explain how a word context benefits letter recognition, all we needed was a couple hundred bigram detectors and a suitable pattern of priming. The example we have just considered, though, is different, simply because it relies on a huge range of background knowledge. We could, after all, have given the instruction that the word about to be shown is the name of a historical figure, and so *that* knowledge would need to be included in our account. We could have said that the word is related to the *Lord of the Rings*, so *that* knowledge would have to be included as well. And so on. Plainly, if we're going to explain all of these priming effects, we'll need to hook up our pattern-recognition system to a much broader library of information!

Interactive Models

Psychologists find it useful to distinguish two sorts of priming and, with that, two sorts of processing. Our focus so far has largely been on **data-driven**, or **bottom-up**, processing. That is, we have discussed how the incoming information (the "data") triggers a response by feature detectors, which in turn triggers a response by letter detectors (or geon detectors), and so on. The data take the initiative; the data get things going. Moreover, most of the priming we have considered has also been data-driven: If the *TH*-detector (for example) is well primed, it is simply because of the data this detector has received in the past—that is, the inputs it has encountered recently or frequently.

But object recognition also involves **concept-driven**, or **top-down**, processing—processing that is driven by a broad pattern of knowledge and expectations, including knowledge that cannot easily be understood as an echo of frequent or recent experiences. The examples of priming given in the previous section are illustrations of top-down priming.

Most contemporary models of object recognition involve both top-down and bottom-up components and so are said to be **interactive models**. In fact, we have already mentioned one interactive model: the McClelland and Rumelhart word-recognition model. (Recall that this model has activation flowing upward from lower-level units, like letter detectors, and downward from higher-level units, like word detectors.) But this model clearly needs to be expanded to incorporate the sort of broad knowledge effects we've now considered—priming effects that cannot be explained simply in terms of someone's stimulus history (i.e., what stimuli the person has seen recently).

To put this more broadly, concept-driven priming relies on knowledge that is separate from one's knowledge about letters, words, and letter combinations. This is why, for example, the McClelland and Rumelhart model, while interactive, is not interactive enough; that is, it does not draw on a wide enough knowledge base to handle the effects we are now considering.

Notice, though, where this brings us: The evidence is telling us that we cannot view object recognition as a self-contained process. Instead, knowledge that is external to object recognition (e.g., knowledge about what is edible) is imported into and clearly influences the process. Put differently, the "ARTICHOKE" example (and many others as well) does not depend on stimulus history, at least not in any straightforward way. Instead, what is crucial for priming is what a person knows coming into the experiment, and also how this knowledge is used.

We have, therefore, reached an important juncture. We have tried in this chapter to examine object recognition in isolation from other cognitive processes, considering how a separate object-recognition module might function, with the module then handing its product (the object it had recognized) on to subsequent processes. We have made good progress in this attempt and have described how a significant piece of object recognition might proceed. But in the end we have also run up against a problem—namely, concept-driven priming. This sort of priming depends on what is in memory, and on how that knowledge is accessed and used, and so we really cannot tackle concept-driven priming until we have said a great deal more about memory, knowledge, and thought. We therefore must leave object recognition for now in order to fill in some other pieces of the puzzle. We will have more to say about object recognition in later chapters, once we have some more theoretical machinery in place.

Chapter Summary

1. Visual perception is a highly active process in which the perceiver goes beyond the information given in organizing and interpreting the visual input. The process includes specifying a figure/ground organization for the input, parsing the figure into its components, and specifying how the figure is organized in depth. To describe these processes, some investigators speak of the "logic of perception," referring to the fact that perception, like a good scientist, arrives at an interpretation that fits with all the evidence, and without appeals to coincidence.

2. We easily recognize a wide range of objects in a wide range of circumstances. Our recognition is heavily influenced by context, which can determine how or whether we recognize an object. To study these achievements, investigators have often focused on the recognition of printed language, using this case as a microcosm within which to study how object recognition in general might proceed.

3. Many investigators have proposed that recognition begins with the identification of features in the (parsed, organized) input pattern. Crucial evidence for this claim comes from neuroscience studies that show that the detection of features is separate from the processes needed to assemble these features into more complex wholes.

4. To study word recognition, investigators often use tachistoscopic presentations. In these studies, words that appear frequently in the language are easier to identify, and so are words that have been recently viewed—an effect known as repetition priming. The data also show a pattern known as the word-superiority effect; this refers to the fact that words are more readily perceived than isolated letters. In addition, well-formed nonwords are more readily perceived than letter strings that do not conform to the rules of normal spelling. Another reliable pattern is that recognition errors, when they occur, are quite systematic, with the input typically perceived as being more regular than it actually is. These findings together indicate that recognition is shaped by learning, often relying on inference, and certainly influenced by the regularities that exist in our environment (e.g., the regularities of spelling patterns).

5. These results can be understood in terms of a network of detectors. Each detector collects input and fires when the input reaches a threshold level. A network of these detectors can accomplish a great deal; for example, it can interpret ambiguous inputs, recover from its own errors, and make inferences about barely viewed stimuli. This provides a powerful demonstration of how complex intellectual achievements can sometimes be built up out of very simple components.

6. The feature net seems to "know" the rules of spelling and "expects" the input to conform to these rules. However, this knowledge is distributed across the entire network and emerges only through the network's parallel processing. This setup leads to enormous efficiency in our commerce with the world because it allows us to recognize patterns and objects with relatively little input and under highly diverse circumstances. But these gains come at the cost of occasional error. This trade-off may be necessary, though, if we are to cope with the informational complexity of our world.

7. A feature net can be implemented in different ways—with or without inhibitory connections, for example. With some adjustments (e.g., the addition of geon detectors), the net can also recognize three-dimensional objects, and with other adjustments, it may be able to recognize sounds. However, some stimuli—for example, faces—probably are not recognized through a feature net, but instead require a different sort of recognition system.

8. The feature net also needs to be supplemented to accommodate top-down influences on object recognition. These influences can be detected in the benefits of larger contexts in facilitating recognition, and also in forms of priming that are plainly concept-driven rather than data-driven. These other forms of priming demand an interactive model, which merges bottom-up and top-down processes.

Paying Attention

Consider your circumstances right now. You are paying attention to this page, reading these words. However, there are literally thousands of other inputs available to you, things you could pay attention to if you chose. For example, you're paying attention to the meanings of these words, but you could choose instead to look at the shapes of the letters, rather than the words themselves. You could, if you chose, contemplate the color of the paper, or its texture. If you wanted to, you could look up from the page and look at any of the people or objects in the room with you. And these are just the *visual* inputs. There are also many sounds in the room. Perhaps the radio is on, or perhaps you can hear someone at the next desk turning pages. Perhaps the room is silent, but even so, you could focus on the silence, much as a sentry listens carefully to detect intruders.

In the same spirit, you could, if you wished, pay attention to the weight of the book in your hands, or to the pressure of your chair against your body. Or, if you liked, you could pay attention to none of these things and choose instead to think about what you did last weekend, or what you'll write in your term paper.

This list could easily be extended, but by now the point should be clear: The stimulus you're attending to is only one of many that are available to you, and that simple fact invites two crucial observations. First, it seems clear that you could choose to pay attention to any of the things just mentioned, and if you did, you would be virtually oblivious to the other things on the list. Indeed, until you read the previous

- In this chapter, we argue that multiple mechanisms are involved in the seemingly simple act of paying attention. In particular, people must take many different steps to facilitate the processing of desired inputs; in the absence of these steps, our ability to pick up information from the world is dramatically reduced.

- Many of the steps we take in order to perceive have a "cost" attached to them: They require the commitment of mental resources. These resources are limited in availability, and this is part of the reason why we cannot pay attention to two inputs at once: This would require more resources than we have.

- Divided attention (the attempt to do two things at once) can also be understood in terms of resources: We can perform two activities at the same time provided that the activities do not require more resources than we have available.

- Some of the mental resources we use are specialized, and so are required only for tasks of a certain sort. Other resources are more general, needed for a wide range of tasks. The resource demand of a task can be diminished through practice, although this often means having less control over the task.

- We emphasize that attention is best understood not as a process or mechanism, but as an *achievement*. Like most achievements, paying attention involves many different elements, all of which help us to be aware of the stimuli we're interested in, and not pulled off track by irrelevant distractors.

paragraph or two, you probably were oblivious to the other stimuli we mentioned! How do you do this? How do you manage to avoid the distractors and focus your attention in just the manner you wish, selecting only one input of many? Second, there seems to be one thing you cannot easily do: pay attention to all of these things at once. If you start musing about your weekend, you are likely to lose track of what's on the page; if you start planning your paper, you won't finish the reading assignment. Of course, it is possible in some circumstances to divide your attention, to deal with two different inputs at once. You can, if you choose, hum a melody while reading these words; most people can walk and chew gum at the same time; and so on. But where are the limits? When can you do two (or more) things at the same time, and when can't you?

These questions set the agenda for the present chapter. We will start with **selective attention**—the processes through which you somehow select one input and "tune out" the rest. We will then turn to questions about **divided attention**, examining when (and if) you can do multiple tasks at once. Selective and divided attention are clearly linked to each other (since one has to select when one cannot divide!), but it will be useful to start by treating them separately.

Selective Listening

Many early studies of attention employed a task called **shadowing**. In this task, participants hear a tape recording of someone speaking and must echo this speech back, word for word, while they are listening to it. Shadowing is initially quite difficult, but it becomes relatively easy after a few minutes' practice. (You might try it, shadowing a voice on the radio or TV.)

In most experiments, the message to be shadowed, the **attended channel**, is presented through stereo headphones, so that participants hear the attended channel through, say, the right earphone. A different message—the **unattended channel**—is presented in the left earphone, and participants are instructed simply to ignore this message. This overall setup is referred to as **dichotic listening**.

Under these circumstances, participants easily follow one message, and their shadowing performance is generally near perfect. At the same time, however, they hear remarkably little from the unattended channel. If we ask them, after a minute or so of shadowing, to report what the unattended message was about, they cannot (Cherry, 1953). They cannot even tell if the unattended channel contained a coherent message or just random words. In fact, in one study, participants shadowed coherent prose in the attended channel, while, in the unattended channel, they heard a text in Czech, read with English pronunciation. Thus, the individual sounds (the vowels, the consonants) resembled English, but the message itself was (for an English speaker) gibberish. After a minute of shadowing, only 4 of 30 participants detected the peculiar character of the unattended message (Treisman, 1964).

More recent studies have documented a similar pattern with *visual* inputs. Participants in one study watched a TV screen that showed a team of players in white shirts passing a ball back and forth; the participants had to signal each time the ball changed hands. Interwoven with these players (and visible on the same TV screen) was another team, wearing black shirts, also passing a ball back and forth; participants were instructed to ignore these. Participants easily did this selective task, and they were so intent on the white team that they failed to notice other rather peculiar events that appeared on the screen, right in front of their eyes. For example, they entirely failed to notice when another player, wearing a gorilla costume, walked through the middle of the game, pausing briefly to thump his chest before exiting! (Figure 4.1; Neisser & Becklen, 1975; Simons & Chabris, 1999).

However, people are not altogether oblivious to the unattended channel: In selective listening experiments, they easily and accurately report whether the unattended channel contained human speech, musical instruments, or silence. If the unattended channel contains human speech, they can report whether the speaker was male or female, had a high or low voice, was speaking loudly or softly. (For reviews of this early work, see Broadbent, 1958; and Kahneman, 1973.) It seems, then, that physical attributes of the unattended channel are heard, even though participants seem oblivious to the unattended channel's semantic content.

Some Unattended Inputs Are Detected

However, some results do not fit this pattern. Some bits of the unattended input seem to "leak" through, and are noticed. In one study, people were asked to shadow one passage while ignoring a second passage. Embedded within the unattended

| FIGURE 4.1 | Visual Attention |

In this experiment, subjects were instructed to keep track of the ballplayers in the white shirts. Intent on their task, they were oblivious to what the black-shirted players were doing. They also failed to see the person in the (black) gorilla suit, strolling through the scene.

channel, though, was a series of names, including the participant's own name. Overall, participants heard very little of the unattended message, in keeping with the other studies mentioned. Nonetheless, about a third of them did hear their own name (Moray, 1959). As we commonly say, the name seemed to "catch" their attention. Other contents will also catch your attention, if you are suitably primed for them: Mention of a movie you just saw, or mention of your favorite restaurant, will often be noticed in the unattended channel. More generally, words with some personal importance will also be noticed (A. R. A. Conway, Cowan, & Bunting, 2001; Wood & Cowan, 1995).

These results are often referred to under the banner of the **cocktail party effect**: There you are at a cocktail party, engaged in conversation. Many other conversations are taking place in the room, but somehow you're able to "tune them out." You are aware that other people in the room are talking, but you don't have a clue what they're saying. All you hear is the single conversation you're attending, plus a buzz of background noise. But now imagine that someone a few steps away from you mentions the name of a close friend of yours. Your attention is immediately caught by this, and you find yourself listening to that other conversation and (momentarily) oblivious to the conversation you had been engaged in. This experience, easily observed outside the laboratory, is of course precisely parallel to the pattern of experimental data.

How can we put all of these results together? How can we explain both our general insensitivity to the unattended channel and also the cases in which the unattended channel "leaks through"?

Perceiving and the Limits on Cognitive Capacity

At the very start, we have two broad options for how we might think about attention. One option focuses on what we do with the *unattended* input. Specifically, the proposal is that we somehow block processing of the inputs we're not interested in, much as a sentry blocks the path of unwanted guests but simply stands back and allows legitimate guests to pass. This sort of proposal was central for early theories of attention, which suggested that we erect a filter that shields us from potential distractors. Desired information (the attended channel) is not filtered out and so goes on to receive further processing (Broadbent, 1958).

Evidence suggests that we do sometimes shut out distractors in this way, but it turns out that this shutting out does not involve a skill of blocking distractors *in general*. We can't, in other words, decide to block out all sounds so that we can focus on something we're reading; likewise, we can't decide to block out all noises in the room except the lecturer's voice, which we're trying to hear. Instead, it seems that our skills of blocking distraction are much more specific: We learn to inhibit our responses to a particular distractor, or to a particular unwanted input. This skill obviously helps whenever that distractor is on the scene, but it won't help with other distractors. For these, we need to develop a new skill, aimed specifically at blocking the new distraction (M. C. Anderson & Spellman, 1995; Fox, 1994, 1995; Jacoby, Lindsay, & Hessels, 2003; Hirst, DeFockert, & Viding, Lavie, 2004; Milliken, Joordens, Merikle, & Seiffert, 1998; Milliken & Tipper, 1998; Reisberg, Baron, & Kemler, 1980).

Other evidence, though, suggests that this is only a part of the story. That's because not only do we block the processing of distractors, but we are also able to *promote* the processing of *desired* stimuli.

Inattentional Blindness

Perceiving seems extraordinarily easy: You open your eyes and you see. You don't feel like you're expending any effort, and even when your resources are sharply limited (when you're extremely tired, for example), you're still able to perceive! As we saw in Chapter 3, however, perception involves a considerable amount of activity—as you parse and organize and interpret the incoming stimulus information. One might think that this activity should require some initiative and some resources from you. The evidence suggests that it does.

In one experiment, participants were told that they would see large "+" shapes on a computer screen, presented for 200 milliseconds, followed by a pattern mask. If the horizontal bar of the "+" was longer than the vertical, the participants were supposed to press one button; if the vertical was longer, then they had to press a different button. As a complication, participants weren't allowed to look directly at the "+." Instead, they fixated (pointed their eyes at) a mark in the center of the computer screen—a **fixation target**—and the "+" shapes were shown just off to one side.

For the first three trials of the procedure, events proceeded just as the participants expected, and the task was relatively easy. On Trial 3, for example, participants made the correct response 78% of the time. On Trial 4, though, things were slightly different: While the target "+" was on the screen, the fixation target disappeared and was replaced by one of three shapes—a triangle, a rectangle, or a cross. Then the entire configuration (the "+" target and this new shape) was replaced by a pattern mask.

Immediately after the trial, participants were asked, Was there anything different on this trial? Was anything present, or anything changed, that wasn't there on previous trials? Remarkably, 89% of the participants reported that there was no change; they had apparently failed to see anything other than the (attended) "+." To probe the participants further, the researchers then told them (correctly) that, during the previous trial, the fixation target had momentarily disappeared and had been replaced by a shape. The participants were then asked what that shape had been and were explicitly given the choices of a triangle, a rectangle, or a cross. The responses to this question were essentially random. Even when probed in this fashion, participants seemed not to have seen the shape that had been directly in front of their eyes (Mack & Rock, 1998; see also Mack, 2003).

Perhaps the 200-millisecond exposure was simply too brief. As a check on this, the investigators ran another procedure: Participants were given the same task of judging the "+," but they were also told, before the experiment began, that they should report any other stimuli that appeared on the screen. In essence, this instruction warned participants that other stimuli might appear, and so participants were alert for these other stimuli. With this warning, the vast majority of the participants did detect the targets. Plainly, then, the targets were visible, if one was looking for them.

What's going on in this study? Some researchers have proposed that the participants in the main experiment did see the target shapes but, a moment later, couldn't *remember* what they had just seen (Wolfe, 1999). Mack and Rock, however, offer a stronger claim: They note that the participants were not expecting any shapes to appear and were not in any way prepared for these shapes. As a consequence, Mack and Rock claim, the participants literally failed to see the shapes, even though they were staring straight at them. This failure to see, caused by inattention, has been dubbed **inattentional blindness** (Mack & Rock, 1998; see also Mack, 2003).

Which of these accounts is correct? Did participants fail to see the input? Or did they see it but, just a few milliseconds later, forget what they'd seen? For purposes of theory, this distinction is crucial, but for the moment, let's emphasize what the two proposals have in common: By either account, our normal ability to see what's around us, and to make use of what we see, is dramatically diminished in the absence of attention.

Conscious Perception, Unconscious Perception

Mack and Rock, the investigators who documented the inattentional blindness phenomenon, draw a strong claim from these data: There is no perception, they claim, without attention. But what exactly is meant by "perception"? To be more precise, Mack and Rock argue that there is no *conscious* perception without attention (Mack & Rock, 1998, p. 14).

To see why this refinement is needed, consider the following experiment (Moore & Egeth, 1997; for other data pertinent to this claim, see Mack, 2003; and Mack & Rock, 1998). Participants were shown a series of images on a computer screen; each image contained two horizontal lines surrounded by a pattern of black and white dots (Figure 4.2A), and the participants' task was to decide which of the two lines was longer, the top one or the bottom.

For the first three trials of this procedure, the background dots on the computer screen were arranged randomly. On Trial 4, however, and with no warning to participants, the pattern of dots shown was like the one in Figure 4.2B, creating a stimulus configuration that reproduces a standard geometric illusion, the Müller-Lyer illusion. Focusing their attention on the two horizontal lines, however, the participants didn't perceive this pattern. When they were asked immediately after the trial whether they had noticed any pattern in the dots, none reported seeing the pattern. They were then told directly that there had been a pattern and were asked to choose it (out of four choices available); 90% selected one of the incorrect patterns. Plainly, then, this experiment reproduces the finding of inattentional blindness.

Nonetheless, the participants were influenced by the dot pattern. In the standard Müller-Lyer display, the "fins" make the top horizontal line in Figure 4.2C appear longer than the bottom horizontal line, even though both lines are exactly the same length. The dot pattern in the Moore and Egeth displays did the same, and 95% of the participants reported that the top line in Figure 4.2B was longer than the bottom one, even though, in the display, both were the same length.

Notice, then, that even though the participants were completely unaware of the fins, they were still heavily influenced by them. No participant reported seeing the

FIGURE 4.2 Unconscious Perception

A

B

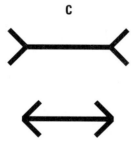

C

Participants were shown a series of images, each containing a pair of horizontal lines; their task was to decide which of the two lines was longer. For the first three trials, the background dots were arranged randomly (Panel A). For the fourth trial, the dots were arranged as shown in Panel B, roughly reproducing the configuration of the Müller-Lyer illusion; Panel C shows the standard form of this illusion. The participants in this study did not perceive the "fins" consciously, but they were nonetheless influenced by the fins—judging the top horizontal line in Panel B to be longer, fully in accord with the usual misperception of this illusion.

fins, but virtually all responded in the length judgment in a fashion consistent with the fins. The obvious conclusion, then, is that participants did perceive the fins in some way, but did not consciously perceive them. We will return to issues of consciousness and unconscious perception in Chapter 15, but for now, it seems attention may not be needed for unconscious perception.

Change Blindness

Similar conclusions emerge from studies of **change blindness**. This term refers to observers' remarkable inability to detect changes in scenes they are looking at. In some experiments, participants are shown pairs of pictures separated by a brief blank interval (e.g., Rensink, O'Regan, & Clark, 1997). The pictures in the pair are identical except for some single aspect: an "extra" engine shown on the airplane in one picture and not in the other; a man not wearing a hat in one picture, but wearing one in the other; and so on. Participants know from the start that their task is to detect these changes, but even with this clear understanding of the task, the task is quite difficult. If the change involves something central to the scene, observers may need as many as a dozen alternations between the pictures before they detect the change. If the change involves some peripheral aspect of the scene, then as many as 25 alternations may be required.

A related pattern emerges when participants watch movies. In one study, observers watched a movie of two women having a conversation. During the film, the camera first focused on one woman, then on the other, just as it would in an ordinary TV show or movie. The crucial element of this experiment, though, was that aspects of the scene changed every time the camera angle changed. For example, when the camera was pointing at Woman A, you could plainly see the red plates on the table between the women. When the camera was shifted to point at Woman B, just a fraction of a second later, the plates had miraculously turned white. Most observers, however, noticed none of these changes. In one experiment, a film containing a total of nine changes was shown to ten participants. Only one participant claimed to notice the changes, and when pressed, this participant merely said there was a difference in "the way people were sitting." When allowed to watch the film again and told explicitly to look out for changes, observers noticed (on average) only two of the nine changes (D. T. Levin & Simons, 1997; Shore & Klein, 2000; Simons, 2000).

Incredibly, the same result pattern can be documented with live (not filmed) events. In a remarkable study, an investigator (let's call him "A") approached pedestrians on a college campus, and asked for directions to a certain building. During the conversation, two men carrying a door approached, and deliberately walked *between* A and the research participant. Therefore, A was momentarily hidden (by the door) from the participant's view, and in that moment, A traded places with one of the men carrying the door. A second later, therefore, A was able to walk away, unseen, while the new fellow (who had been carrying the door) stayed behind and continued the conversation with the participant.

Roughly one third of the participants failed to notice this switch. They continued the conversation as though nothing had happened—despite the fact that A and his replacement were wearing different clothes, had easily distinguishable voices, and so on. When asked directly whether anything odd had happened in this event, many participants commented only that it was rude that the guys carrying the door had walked right through their conversation (Simons & Levin, 1998; for other studies of change blindness, see Most et al., 2001, and Rensink, 2002; for similar effects with auditory stimuli, see Vitevitch, 2003).

Once again, we can debate whether these results show limits of perception or limits of memory. Perhaps participants didn't notice the color of the plates, or the presence of the plane engine. Or perhaps they did notice these things and briefly stored this information in memory. A moment later, though, they perceived the next scene, or the next view, and placed this into memory, overwriting or displacing the memory of the first perception. As a consequence, participants' memory would contain only the scene most recently viewed, and this would, of course, make it impossible to compare the successive views to detect any changes.

In either case—that is, with an emphasis on perception or on memory—we draw the same conclusion: The perception of the visual world is far from automatic; putting a stimulus directly in front of your eyes provides no guarantee that you'll detect and respond to that stimulus. Perhaps you need to take some steps to *perceive* the stimulus. Perhaps you need to spend some effort to make sure you'll *remember* the stimulus for more than a millisecond or two. On either account, the pickup of information from a sensory input requires some work.

Selective Priming

We've just argued that the pickup of information from the world requires "work," but what is the nature of this work? If looking directly at something isn't by itself enough to allow conscious perception, then what else is needed? We'll offer a several-part answer to these questions before we're through, but one important element involves the mechanisms we discussed in Chapter 3.

In Chapter 3, we proposed that recognition requires a network of detectors, and we argued that these detectors fire most readily, and most quickly, if they are suitably primed. But what does that priming involve? In some cases, priming is produced by one's visual experience—specifically, whether each detector has been used recently or frequently in the past. But, as we suggested at the end of Chapter 3, priming can also come from another source: your hypotheses and expectations about what the stimulus will be.

Notice, then, that people can literally prepare themselves for perceiving, by priming the suitable detectors. Let's hypothesize in addition that this priming isn't free. Instead, you must spend some effort or allocate some resources in order to do the priming, and let's suppose that these resources are in limited supply.

This simple idea, on its own, helps explain several findings we've already met. Why don't participants notice the shapes in the inattentional blindness studies? It may be that they don't expect any stimulus, and so they have no reason to prepare for any stimulus. As a result, the stimulus, when it's presented, falls on unprepared—and so unresponsive—detectors.

What about selective listening? In this case, one does not want to hear the distractor, and so devoting resources to the distractor would be, at best, a waste of these resources. Therefore the detectors needed for the distractor are unprimed, literally making it more difficult to hear the distractor. But why, on this account, does attention sometimes "leak," so that we do hear some aspects of the unattended input? Think about what will happen if your name is uttered on the unattended channel. The detectors for this stimulus are already primed, simply because this is a stimulus you have frequently encountered in the past. Thanks to this prior exposure, the activation level of these detectors is already high; you don't need to prime them further. So these detectors will fire even if your attention is elsewhere.

This seems, therefore, to be a promising way to think about attention: with resources needed to prime detectors, but with those resources in limited supply. We've already flagged the fact that this cannot be our entire account of attention, and we'll need to add more elements to our theory before we are through. But can we find evidence to confirm more directly that detector priming is part of the story?

Two Types of Priming

In a classic series of studies, Posner and Snyder (1975) gave people a straightforward task: A pair of letters was shown on a computer screen, and participants had to decide, as swiftly as they could, whether the letters were the same or different. So someone might see "A A" and answer "same," or might see "A B" and answer "different."

Before each pair, participants saw a warning signal. In the neutral condition, the warning signal was a plus sign ("+"). This signal notified participants that the stimuli were about to arrive but provided no other information. In a different condition, the warning signal was itself a letter and actually matched the stimuli to come. So someone might see the warning signal "C" followed by the pair "C C." In this case, the warning signal actually served to prime the participants for the stimuli. In a third condition, though, the warning signal was misleading. The warning signal was again a letter, but it was a letter different from the stimuli to come. Participants might see "C" followed by the pair "F F." Let's call these three conditions *neutral*, *primed*, and *misled*.

In each condition, Posner and Snyder recorded how swiftly people responded; that is, they measured **response times**, or RTs. By comparing RTs in the *primed* and *neutral* conditions, we can ask what benefit there is from the prime. Likewise, by comparing RTs in the *misled* and *neutral* conditions, we can ask what cost there is, if any, from being misled.

Before we turn to the results, though, we need one further complication: Posner and Snyder ran this procedure in two different versions. (The design is depicted in Table 4.1.) In one version, the warning signal was an excellent predictor of the upcoming stimuli: For example, if the warning signal was an *A*, there was an 80% chance that the upcoming stimulus pair would contain *A*s. In Posner and Snyder's

TABLE 4.1	Design of Posner and Snyder's Experiment

		Typical Sequence		Provides Repetition Priming?	Provides Basis for Expectation?
	Type of Trial	Warning Signal	Test Stimuli		
Low-validity condition	Neutral	+	AA	No	No
	Primed	G	GG	Yes	No
	Misled	H	GG	No	No
High-validity condition	Neutral	+	AA	No	No
	Primed	G	GG	Yes	Prime leads to correct expectation
	Misled	H	GG	No	Prime leads to incorrect expectation

The sequence of events was the same in the high-validity and low-validity conditions. What distinguished the conditions was how often the various events occurred. In the low-validity condition, *misled* trials occurred four times as often as *primed* trials (80% vs. 20%). Therefore, participants had reason not to trust the primes, and correspondingly had no reason to generate an expectation based on the primes. In the high-validity condition, things were reversed: Now *primed* trials occurred four times as often as *misled* trials. Therefore, participants had good reason to trust the primes, and good reason to generate an expectation. For most of the trials, this expectation will be correct. Note, though, that if participants base their expectations on the prime, then they will generate the wrong expectation in the *misled* trials.

terms, the warning signal provided a "high validity" prime. In a different version of the procedure, the warning signal was a poor predictor of the upcoming stimuli: If the warning signal was an *A*, there was only a 20% chance that the upcoming pair would contain *A*s. This is the "low validity" condition.

Let's consider the low-validity condition first, and let's focus on those rare occasions in which the prime did match the subsequent stimuli. That is, we are focusing on 20% of the trials and ignoring the other 80%. In this condition, the participant can't use the prime as a basis for predicting the stimuli because, after all, the prime is a poor indicator of things to come. Therefore, the prime should not lead to any specific expectations. Nonetheless, we do expect faster RTs in the *primed* condition than in the *neutral* condition: Thanks to the prime, the relevant detectors have just fired, and so the detectors should still be warmed up. When the target stimuli arrive, therefore, the detectors should fire more readily, allowing a faster response. This is, in effect, a case of repetition priming, as described in Chapter 3.

The results bear this out. RTs were reliably faster in the *primed* condition than in the *neutral* condition; Figure 4.3 shows this as a 30-millisecond difference between

FIGURE 4.3   The Effects of Priming on Stimulus Processing

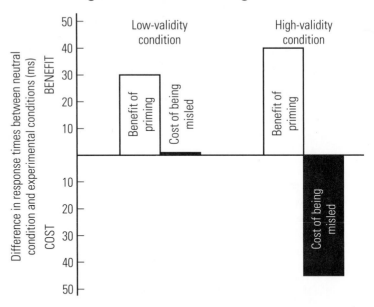

As one way of assessing the Posner and Snyder (1975) results, we can subtract the response times for the *neutral* condition from those for the *primed* condition; in this way, we measure the benefits of priming. Likewise, we can subtract the response times for the *neutral* condition from those for the *misled* condition; in this way, we measure the costs of being misled. In these terms, the low-validity condition shows a small benefit (from repetition priming) but zero cost from being misled. The high-validity condition, in contrast, shows a larger benefit, but also a substantial cost. The results shown here reflect trials with a 300-ms interval between the warning signal and the test stimuli; the results were somewhat different at other intervals.

the *primed* and *neutral* conditions. Apparently, the detectors can be primed by mere exposure to a stimulus. Or, to put it differently, priming is observed even in the absence of expectations. This priming seems truly stimulus-based.

What about the *misled* condition? With a low-validity prime, misleading participants had no effect: Performance in the *misled* condition was the same as performance in the *neutral* condition. Priming the "wrong" detector, it seems, takes nothing away from the other detectors—including the detectors actually needed for that trial. This fits with our discussion in Chapter 3: Each of the various detectors works independently of the others. Thus, priming one decector obviously influences the functioning of that specific detector, but neither helps nor hinders the other detectors.

What about the high-validity primes? In this case, people might see, for example, a "J" as the warning signal, and then the stimulus pair "J J." Presentation of the prime itself will fire the *J*-detectors, and so it should, once again, "warm up" these detectors, just as the low-validity primes did. Thus, we expect a stimulus-driven benefit from the prime. However, the high-validity primes may also have another influence: High-validity primes are excellent predictors of the stimulus to come. Participants are told this at the outset, and they have lots of opportunity to see that it is true. High-validity primes will therefore produce a warm-up effect and also an expectation effect, whereas low-validity primes produce only the warm-up. Consequently, we can explore the influence of expectations by comparing the impact of high- and low-validity primes.

As Figure 4.3 shows, high-validity primes produced a larger benefit than low-validity primes. The combination of warm-up and expectations produces a larger benefit than warm-up alone. From the participants' point of view, it pays to know what the upcoming stimulus might be.

Just as important, though, is what happened in the *misled* condition: With high-validity primes, responses in the *misled* condition were *slower* than responses in the *neutral* condition. That is, misleading participants actually hurt performance. As a concrete example, *F*-detection was slower if *G* was primed, compared to *F*-detection when the prime was simply the neutral warning signal ("+").

Explaining the Costs and Benefits

The message of these data is clear: There are two types of primes. One type is produced merely by presentation of the priming stimulus, with no role for expectations. This sort of priming seems truly stimulus-based. The other type of priming is expectation-based, and is created only when the participant believes the prime allows a predicton of what's to come. The expectation-based priming is larger in magnitude than the stimulus-based priming, and, the data suggest, it's also slower: Stimulus-based priming can be observed immediately after the prime; priming based on expectations takes roughly a half second to develop (Neely, 1977).

The two types of priming can also be distinguished in another way: in terms of whether each has a cost attached to it. Stimulus-based priming appears to be "free," and so we can prime one detector without taking anything away from the other detectors. We see this in the low-validity condition, in the fact that the *misled* trials lead to responses just as fast as those in the *neutral* trials. Expectation-based priming, on the other side, does have a cost, as we see in the high-validity condition. Here, priming the "wrong" detector does take something away from the other detectors, and so participants are worse off when they're misled than when they received no prime at all.

What produces this cost? As an analogy, think about being on a limited budget. Imagine, for example, that you have just $50 to spend on groceries. You can spend more on ice cream if you wish, but if you do, you'll have that much less to spend on other foods. Any increase in the ice cream allotment must be covered by a decrease somewhere else. This trade-off arises, though, only because of the limited budget. If you had unlimited funds, you could spend more on ice cream and still have enough money for everything else.

Expectation-based priming shows the same pattern. If the *Q*-detector is primed, this takes something away from the other detectors. Getting prepared for one target seems to make people less prepared for other targets. But we just said that this sort of pattern implies a limited "budget." If an unlimited supply of activation were available, one could prime the *Q*-detector and leave the other detectors just as they were. And that is the point: Expectation-based priming, by virtue of revealing costs when misled, reveals the presence of a **limited-capacity system**.

We can now put the pieces together: Ultimately, we need to explain the facts of selective attention, including the fact that, while listening to one message, you hear little content from other messages. To explain this, we have proposed that perceiving involves some work, and this work requires some limited mental resources. That is why you can't listen to two messages at the same time: Doing so would demand more resources than you have. And now, finally, we are seeing evidence for those limited resources: The Posner and Snyder research (and many other results) reveals the workings of a limited-capacity system, just as our hypothesis demands.

Chronometric Studies and Spatial Attention

The Posner and Snyder study shows us how a person's expectations about an upcoming stimulus can influence the processing of that stimulus. But what exactly is the nature of these expectations? How precise, or how vague, are they? To see the point, imagine that participants are told, "The next stimulus will be a *T*." In this case, they know exactly what to get ready for. But now imagine that participants are told, "The next stimulus will be a letter," or "The next stimulus will be on the left side of the screen." Will these cues allow people to prepare themselves?

In these latter cases, participants obviously can't prepare for the content of the upcoming stimulus, but they can prepare in a more general sense: They can, for example, prepare for a stimulus coming at a particular time, at a specific position in space. Are these more general expectations helpful?

This issue has been examined in many studies of **spatial attention**—that is, our ability to focus on a particular position in space, and thus to be better prepared for any stimulus that appears in that position. In one early study, Posner, Snyder, and Davidson (1980) required their participants simply to detect letter presentations; their task was just to press a button as soon as a letter appeared. Participants kept their eyes pointed at a central fixation mark, and letters could appear either to the left or to the right of this mark.

For some trials, a neutral warning signal was presented, so that participants knew a trial was about to start but had no information about stimulus location. For other trials, an arrow was used as the warning signal. Sometimes the arrow pointed left, sometimes right; and the arrow was generally an accurate predictor of the stimulus-to-come's location: If the arrow pointed right, the stimulus would be on the right side of the computer screen. (In the terms we used earlier, this is a high-validity cue.) On 20% of the trials, however, the arrow misled participants about location.

The results show a familiar pattern (Posner et al., 1980, Exp. 2): With high-validity priming, the data show a benefit from cues that correctly signal where the upcoming target will appear. Concretely, with a neutral warning signal, people took 266 ms to detect the signal. With a correct prime, they were faster: 249 ms. This isn't a huge difference, but keep the task in mind: All participants had to do was detect the input. Even with the simplest of tasks, therefore, it pays to be prepared.

What about the trials in which participants were misled? RTs in this condition averaged 297 ms, 31 ms (about 12%) slower than the neutral condition. Once again, therefore, we're seeing evidence of a limited-capacity system: In order to devote more attention to (say) the left position, one has to devote *less* attention to the right. If the stimulus then shows up on the right, one is less prepared for it—hence the cost of being misled.

The Binding Problem

Studies of spatial attention have suggested to some psychologists that visual attention can profitably be compared to a searchlight beam that can "shine" anywhere in the visual field. The "beam" marks the region of space for which one is prepared, so inputs within the beam are processed more efficiently and more swiftly. The beam can be wide or narrowly focused, and it can be moved about at will as one explores (attends to) one aspect of the visual field or another. We hasten to add that there are some complexities here, and we will have more to say about this searchlight idea before we are done. Even so, the metaphor of attention as a searchlight does convey many of attention's properties, and so, many investigators find it instructive to think of attention in these terms.

Let's emphasize, though, that the searchlight idea is referring to movements of *attention*, and not movements of the eyes. Of course, eye movements do play an important role in our selection of information from the world: Obviously, if we want to learn more about something, we look at it! But even so, movements of the eyes can be separated from movements of attention, and it's attention that's moving around in the Posner et al. study. We know this because of the timing of the effects: Eye movements are surprisingly slow, requiring 180 to 200 ms. But the benefits of primes can be detected within the first 150 ms after the priming stimulus is presented. Thus the benefits of attention occur prior to any eye movement, and so they cannot be a consequence of eye movements.[1]

But what exactly does the "searchlight" accomplish? What is different, in our processing of an input, when the light is "shining" on that input? Part of the answer, we've said, involves priming: When we say that the searchlight of attention is shining on a stimulus, this is just another way of saying that a person is priming the

---

[1]In fact, it's actually quite important that the "searchlight" of attention can be moved more rapidly than the eyes can. That capability allows us to use attention to explore a visual target in a preliminary way, in order to decide whether to move our eyes toward the target or not. In other words, fast movements of attention allow us to do some advance scouting, in order to guide the (slower) movements of the eyes.

relevant detectors for that stimulus. This priming allows the detectors to work more swiftly and more efficiently, promoting our perception of the input. Without this priming, the detectors would be much less responsive, and this helps explain why we typically do not perceive unattended inputs.

Priming also has another role: By promoting the response to a stimulus, we make it more likely that we'll *remember* the stimulus. That way, our impression of the input won't be displaced the moment a new impression, or a new input, comes into view. (See Chapter 5 for more on the steps that will promote memory.)

But the searchlight of attention also has another role, and it's connected to a topic we discussed in Chapter 2: As we discussed there, separate detectors within the nervous system respond to different aspects of the input. Some detectors respond to the input's shape; others, to its color; others, to whether the input is moving or not. This parallel processing has certain advantages, but it also creates a problem for us: We need to reunite these various elements in the scene, in order to perceive a coherent, integrated object. In Chapter 2, we called this the "binding problem."

In Chapter 2 we also argued that attention plays a crucial part in solving the binding problem, and we mentioned several findings in support of this claim. For example, if we overload someone's attention when they are looking at a display, we disrupt the binding, and this often leads to conjunction errors—mistakes about how the features in the display are bound together (or conjoined). Thus, someone looking at a yellow square and a green circle might mistakenly perceive a yellow circle and a green square (Treisman & Gelade, 1980; for other evidence, see Chapter 2).

But how does attention help? The answer is easy: If you shine the searchlight on just one object and so attend to only one item at a time, you eliminate any chance for confusion about how the stimulus features within the display are assembled. By focusing your mental searchlight on just a single stimulus, you know that the color you are now perceiving came from that stimulus, and also that the shape you are now perceiving came from that stimulus. In this way, you avoid the risk of confusion about which elements belong with which (Treisman & Gormican, 1988; also see Wolfe, 2003).

The "Searchlight" of Attention

As we mentioned earlier, the searchlight analogy reflects many facts about attention, but the analogy is also misleading in some ways. (For a broad assessment of the searchlight metaphor, see Cave & Bichot, 1999.) Let's therefore take a more detailed look at the analogy.

Think about how an actual searchlight works. If, for example, a searchlight shines on a donut, then part of the beam will fall on the donut's hole and so illuminate the plate underneath the donut. Similarly, if the searchlight isn't aimed quite accurately, it may also illuminate the plate just left of the donut. The region illuminated by the beam, in other words, is defined purely in spatial terms: a circle of light at a particular position. That position may or may not line up with the boundaries of the object you're shining the beam on.

Is this how attention works—so that we pay attention to whatever it is that falls in a certain region of space? In this case, we might on some occasions end up paying attention to part of this object, part of that. An alternative is that we pay attention to *objects*, rather than to *positions in space*. To continue the example, the target of our attention might be the donut itself, rather than the donut's location. In that case, the plate just to the left, and the bit of plate visible through the donut's hole, might be close to our focus, but they aren't part of the attended object and so aren't attended.

Which is the correct view of attention? Do we pay attention to regions in space, whatever the objects (or parts of objects) are that fall in that region? Or do we pay attention to objects? It turns out that each view captures part of the truth.

One important line of evidence comes from the study of people who have suffered forms of brain damage (typically in the parietal cortex) that produce extraordinary problems in paying attention. For example, patients with **unilateral neglect syndrome** seem simply to ignore all inputs coming from one side of the body. A patient with neglect syndrome will eat food from only one side of the plate, will wash only half of his or her face, and will fail to locate sought-for objects if they are on the neglected side (Heilman, Watson, & Valenstein, 1985; Sieroff, Pollatsek, & Posner, 1988). This syndrome usually results from damage to the *right* parietal lobe, and so the neglect is for the *left* side of space. (Remember the brain's contralateral organization; see Chapter 2.) Thus, in the laboratory, neglect patients will read only the right half of words shown to them; that is, they will read "pigpen" as pen, "parties" as ties, and so on. If asked to cross out all the *E*s on a page, the patient will cross out the *E*s on only the right side of the page.

One influential account of these patients hinges on a hypothesis about how the searchlight beam of attention is controlled. According to this proposal, several brain areas are involved in the control of the beam. One area seems to disengage the beam from its current focus; another area controls the movement of the beam to its new target; a third area serves to lock the beam into its new focus (Corbetta, Kincade, Ollinger, McAvoy, & Shulman, 2000; Posner, Walker, Friedrich, & Rafal, 1987). Damage to each of these brain areas has its own effects, but the patients with neglect syndrome seem to have suffered damage in the brain area (in the parietal cortex) crucial for disengaging attention from its current focus. Thus, if their attention has just been drawn to one position, they respond very slowly (or not at all) to a stimulus presented at some other position. It is as if their attention, once locked in to a position, cannot be unlocked to move elsewhere.

With this base, let's return to our question about how best to describe attention: Do we pay attention to *locations in space*, independent of what objects are in those locations? Or do we pay attention to *objects*, only loosely guided by location in space? Taken at face value, the symptoms of neglect syndrome seem to support the space-based acount: The afflicted patient seems insensitive to all objects within a spatially defined region—namely, everything to the left of their current focus. If an object falls half within the region and half outside of it, then it's the spatially defined region that matters, not the object's boundaries. This is evident, for example, in how these patients read words—responding only to the word's right half, apparently oblivious to the word's overall boundaries.

Other evidence, however, demands further theory. In one study, patients with neglect syndrome had to respond to targets that appeared within a barbell-shaped frame (Figure 4.4). Not surprisingly, they were much more sensitive to the targets

---

FIGURE 4.4   ## Space-Based or Object-Based Attention?

Patient initially sees:

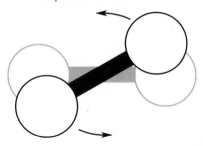

As the patient watches:

Patient now sees:

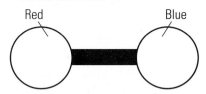

Patients with unilateral neglect syndrome were much more sensitive to targets appearing within the red circle (on the right) and missed many of the targets appearing within the blue circle (on the left); this observation simply confirms their clinical diagnosis. Then, as the patients watched, the "barbell" frame rotated, so that now the red circle was on the left and the blue circle was on the right. After this rotation, participants were still more sensitive to targets in the red circle (now on the left), apparently focusing on this attended object even though it had moved into their "neglected" side.

appearing within the red circle (on the right) and missed many of the targets appearing in the blue circle (on the left); this result simply confirms the patients' diagnosis. What is crucial, though, is what happened next: While the patient watched, the barbell frame was slowly spun around, so that the red circle, previously on the right, was now on the left, and the blue circle, previously on the left, was now on the right.

What should we expect in this situation? If the patients consistently neglect a region of space, they should now be more sensitive to the right-side blue circle. A different possibility is more complicated: Perhaps these patients have a powerful bias to attend to the right side, and so initially attend to the red circle. Once they have "locked in" to this circle, however, it is the object, and not the position in space, that defines their focus of attention. According to this view, if the barbell form rotates, they will continue attending to the red circle (this is, after all, the focus of their attention), even though it now appears on their "neglected" side. This prediction turns out to be correct: When the barbell rotates, the patients' focus of attention seems to rotate with it (Behrmann & Tipper, 1999).

To describe these patients, therefore, we need a two-part account. First, the symptoms of neglect syndrome plainly reveal a spatially defined bias: These patients neglect half of space. But, second, once attention is directed toward a target, it is the target itself that defines the focus of attention; if the target moves, the focus moves with it. In this way, the focus of attention is object-based, not space-based. (For more on these issues, and on neglect syndrome in general, see Awh, Dhaliwal, Christensen, & Matsukura, 2001; Bisiach, 1996; Duncan et al., 1999; Halligan & Marshall, 1994; Logie, 1995; O'Craven, Downing, & Kanwisher, 1999; and Scholl, 2001.)

Could it be that this complex pattern appears only in neglect patients, so that the pattern is somehow a by-product of their brain damage? The answer to this is clearly no. Normal participants, too, show a mix of space-based and object-based attention. We have already seen evidence for the spatial base: The Posner et al. (1980) study and many results like it show that participants can focus on a particular region of space *in preparation* for a stimulus. In this situation, the stimulus has not yet appeared; there is no object to focus on. Therefore, the attention must be spatially defined.

In other cases, though, attention is heavily influenced by object boundaries. For example, several studies have shown participants displays with visually superimposed stimuli, as if a single television set were showing two channels at the same time (Neisser & Becklen, 1975; Simons & Chabris, 1999). Participants can easily pay attention to one of these stimuli and ignore the other. This selection cannot be space-based (because both stimuli are in the same place) and so must be object-based.

Similarly, Egly, Driver, and Rafal (1994) had their participants look at a computer screen that showed two rectangles, one on the left side of the screen and one on the right. The participants' task was to respond as soon as they saw a target at one end (top or bottom) of one of the rectangles. In the majority of trials, a cue signaled in advance where the target would appear—in which rectangle, and at which end of the rectangle. In other trials, though, the cue was misleading: It signaled a location, but the target appeared elsewhere. Sometimes the target appeared in the same rectangle as the cue, but at the rectangle's opposite end; sometimes the target appeared in the other rectangle.

Not surprisingly, participants were fastest when the cue accurately signaled where the target would be; this observation echoes other results we have already discussed. What's crucial, though, is the comparison between misleading cues that at least signaled the proper rectangle, and misleading cues that signaled the *wrong* rectangle. According to a space-based account, there should be no difference between these two cases, because the display had been arranged so that both of the targets were the same distance from the misleading cue. According to an object-based account, though, these two cases will be different: Let's say that the cue draws attention to the top of the left-hand rectangle, and the target then appears in the bottom of that rectangle. In that case, the cue at least led participants to focus on the proper rectangle, and so attention will (on an object-based account) include that rectangle. Hence, responses will be quicker in this condition than they would be if the cue signaled the wrong rectangle altogether.

The latter prediction turns out to be correct. The cues in this study didn't just draw attention to a *location*. They also drew attention to the *object* that was in that location. Hence, in this way, our description of attention needs to be object-based, as well as space-based.

Neuroscience Evidence and Early Selection

The previous section was concerned with the attention "searchlight," but it also illustrated another point: the way in which the study of attention can draw on many types of evidence, including behavioral evidence (e.g., the data on spatial cueing) and also neuroscience evidence (e.g., data concerned with the effects of brain damage). What else can we learn from this partnership between psychology and neuroscience?

We know that people seem largely oblivious to unattended inputs, but why is this? One suggestion is simply that these inputs are not processed in any serious way. According to this view, the input to be attended is identified at a very early stage of processing, and steps are taken to ensure that this input receives full analysis. Unattended inputs, in contrast, receive only the most basic sensory analysis and nothing more.

There is, however, a different possibility: Perhaps the unattended inputs do pass through the normal steps needed for peception, but the results of these steps never reach consciousness. In other words, we do extract information from the unattended inputs, but we are generally not aware of this information. Or, as a closely related idea, perhaps we are briefly aware of this information but rapidly forget it.

These various proposals all share the idea that attention is selective, so that the attended input is handled differently from the unattended input. What is at issue, though, is *when* the selection takes place: The **early selection** hypothesis says that the attended input is identified and privileged from the start, so that the unattended input receives little analysis. The **late selection** hypothesis, on the other hand, says that all inputs are processed fully; it is only the attended input, however, that reaches consciousness, or (as a related idea) it is only the attended input that is remembered.

We first met this issue in our discussion of change blindness, when we asked whether an absence of attention disrupts *perception* or disrupts *memory*. We can now return to this issue, though, building on what we've learned about mental resources, and also what we've learned about the biological mechanisms underlying attention.

As is often the case, it turns out that both the early selection and the late selection proposals capture elements of the truth, because the amount of processing of the unattended input may depend on the circumstances. If, for example, the attended input is particularly complex, then the processing of this input will demand a lot of resources. In this case, little capacity will be left over for other stimuli, with the consequence that the other stimuli receive less processing. In contrast, imagine that the attended input is relatively simple. Processing this input will demand few resources, leaving more available for the unattended inputs. Here the unattended inputs will probably receive more analysis (after Lavie, 1995, 1997, 2001; for some challenges to this claim, though, see Mack, 2003).

On this basis, it is not surprising that we can identify two very different sorts of cases. Earlier in the chapter, we considered a case in which people seem fully unaware of the distractors, but are nevertheless strongly influenced by them (pp. 108–109). Apparently, in this case, the distractors were perceived, but that perception—even if influential—was not conscious. But, on the other side, we can also find the opposite pattern, with the distractor stimuli receiving remarkably little analysis, and indeed falling out of the stream of processing at a very early stage. Relevant evidence comes, for example, from studies that record the electrical activity of the brain in the milliseconds after a stimulus has arrived. These studies confirm that the brain activity for attended inputs is distinguishable from that for unattended inputs just 60 or 70 ms after the stimulus presentation—a time interval in which the earliest sensory processing is still under way (Hillyard, Vogel, & Luck, 1998). Apparently, in these cases, the attended input is priviliged from the very start.

Other data show directly that attention can modulate events early in the sequence of visual processing; this confirms that attended inputs are treated differently from unattended inputs from the very start. For example, recording from neurons in area V4 of the visual cortex shows that the neurons are more responsive to attended inputs than to unattended ones, almost as if attention made the light areas seem brighter and dim areas seem darker (Carrasco, Ling, & Read, 2004;

Carrasco, Penpeci-Talgar, & Eckstein, 2000; Reynolds, Pasternak, & Desimone, 2000). This makes it seem undeniable that attention doesn't just change what we remember or what we're aware of. Attention also literally changes what we perceive.

Perceiving and the Limits on Cognitive Capacity: An Interim Summary

Our account is growing complex, so let's pause to take stock of where we are. At the broadest level, we have suggested that two different mechanisms are involved in selective attention. One mechanism serves to *inhibit,* or block out, the processing of *unwanted* inputs; this is, in effect, a mechanism for "ignoring" inputs in which we have no interest. A second mechanism *facilitates* the processing of *desired* inputs. This is a mechanism for "paying attention."

We've also seen, though, that the mechanism for paying attention has many parts. In other words, we take many different steps to promote the processing of inputs we're interested in: If we know the target's identity in advance, we can prime the relevant detectors. If we know only *where* the target will appear, we can prime detectors for the appropriate region of space, and then, once we locate the object in that region, we prime detectors for that object. This priming, in turn, also involves multiple steps: We have to unlock attention from its current focus, move the focus, and then lock it in at the new focus. We also move our eyes, so that stimulation from the attended object falls onto our foveas. All of this also allows us to narrow our attention so that we can figure out which elements of the sensory input belong together, as part of a single object, and which do not. And, finally, we've suggested that we also take some steps so that we'll remember the attended input, so that it leaves more than a fleeting impression.

To put all of this succinctly, then, the term "attention" seems not to label a particular process or a particular mechanism. Instead, we probably need to think of paying attention as an *achievement*, something that you are able to do. Like many other achievements (doing well in school, staying healthy, earning a good salary), paying attention requires many elements. The exact set of elements varies from occasion to occasion. Sometimes a strong distractor is on the scene, making it essential that you inhibit your response to that distractor. Sometimes, though, no distractors are in view, so inhibition plays a smaller role. Sometimes you know in advance what the stimulus will be, and so you can prime just the right detectors. Sometimes stimuli are less predictable, and so your priming must be more diffuse. In all cases, though, multiple steps are needed, to ensure that you end up aware of (and able to remember) the stimuli you're interested in, and not pulled off track by irrelevant inputs.

In addition, we've also seen that many of these steps have a cost attached to them; that is, they require the commitment of mental resources, and these resources are in limited supply. This constraint sets limits on our performance: We can pay attention to multiple inputs only if the combined demand from these inputs is within our "budget." Often, though, the expense of tracking multiple inputs will be beyond our budget, and this is why we're typically aware of so little in the unattended channel.

Divided Attention

So far in this chapter, we have been concerned with selective attention. That is, we have emphasized situations in which you wanted to focus on a single input. If other tasks and other stimuli were on the scene, they were mere distractors. Our concern, therefore, has been on how you manage to select just the desired information, while avoiding irrelevant distraction.

There are also circumstances, however, in which you want to do multiple things at once, in which you try to divide your attention among various tasks or various inputs. In some cases you can do this, but your ability to perform concurrent tasks is clearly limited. Almost anyone can walk and talk simultaneously, but it is far harder to solve calculus problems while reading a history text. Why are some task combinations difficult, while others are easy?

Our initial answer to these questions is already in view. We have proposed that perceiving requires resources that are in short supply; the same is presumably true for other mental tasks—remembering, reasoning, problem-solving. They, too, require resources, and without these resources, these processes cannot go forward. All of this provides a straightforward account of divided attention: One can perform concurrent tasks only if the sum of the tasks' demands is within the "cognitive budget." Thus, for example, solving calculus problems requires some mental resources, and so does reading a text. You have enough resources to do either one of these tasks by itself, but not enough for both; if you try to do both at the same time, you will fail.

But what are these hypothesized mental resources? Do all tasks, no matter what they involve, draw on the same mental resources? Or are mental resources somehow specialized, so that the resources required by a task depend on the exact nature of the task? Once again, we'll see that both proposals capture part of the truth, and so, once again, we'll be driven toward a theory of attention with multiple elements.

The Specificity of Resources

Some mental resources do seem relatively specialized and thus are drawn on only by certain sorts of tasks. This is why it is more difficult to combine two verbal tasks than it is to combine a verbal task with a spatial task. To make this idea concrete, imagine that you are trying to read a list of words while simultaneously listening to someone give a speech. Both of these tasks draw on resources that are specialized for verbal tasks, and so if (for example) listening to the speech exhausts the verbal resources, then reading while listening will be impossible: The reading requires resources that aren't available. But now imagine that you are trying to look at pictures while listening to the speech. This will be much easier because picture-viewing presumably doesn't require verbal resources, and so it won't matter if those resources have been exhausted by some other task.

This pattern—greater interference among more similar tasks—is easily demonstrated. In an early study by D. Allport, Antonis, and Reynolds (1972), participants heard a list of words presented through headphones into one ear, and their task was to shadow these words. At the same time they were also presented with a second list. No immediate response was required to this second list, but later on, memory was tested for these items. In one condition, these memory items consisted of words presented into the other ear, so the participants were hearing (and shadowing) a list of words in one ear while simultaneously hearing the memory list in the other. In a second condition, the memory items were presented visually. That is, while the participants were shadowing one list of words, they were also seeing, on a screen before them, a different list of words. Finally, in a third condition the memory items consisted of pictures, also presented on a screen.

These three conditions have similar requirements, namely shadowing one list while memorizing another. But the first condition (hear words + hear words) involves very similar tasks; the second condition (hear words + see words) involves less similar tasks; the third condition (hear words + see pictures), even less similar tasks. If performance is limited by task-specific resources, then it seems most likely that the first pair of tasks will compete with each other for resources, and least likely that the last pair will. Thus, in terms of task-specific resources, we would expect the most interference in the first condition, the least in the third. And that is what the data show. (For further evidence, see Brooks, 1968; Hirst, 1986; and Hirst & Kalmar, 1987.)

However, it is also possible to document interference among tasks that are very different from each other. This suggests that some mental resources are rather general in their use and so are drawn on by virtually all tasks, no matter what the nature of the task. Evidence comes from many sources, including one often-discussed case: talking on a cell phone while driving. The conversation requires an auditory input and speech as output; the material being attended to is verbal. Driving, on the other hand, involves a visual input and hand and foot motion as output; the material being attended to is spatial. One might therefore think that there is little or no overlap in the resources required for these two tasks, and so little chance that the tasks will compete for resources.

It turns out, however, that driving and cell-phone use do interfere with each other; this is reflected, for example, in the fact that phone use has been implicated in many automobile accidents (Lamble, Kauranen, Laakso, & Summala, 1999). The interference can be observed even if the phones are of the hands-free type so that the driver can keep his/her hands on the wheel. Even with a hands-free phone, drivers engaged in cell-phone conversations are more likely to be involved in accidents, and slower to hit the brakes when they need to. As another measure of performance, drivers engaged in phone conversations are less likely to note and re-member billboards they pass along the way, even if they look straight at the bill-boards (Strayer, Drews, & Johnston, 2003; Strayer & Johnston, 2001; also Spence & Read, 2003).

Identifying General Resources

Clearly, then, some mental resources are general-purpose, not specialized, and so drawn on by tasks as different as talking and driving. But what exactly are these general resources? Different authors have offered different proposals, but their sug-gestions are not mutually exclusive, and it is likely that there are several task-general resources, with each one contributing to the limits on how (or whether) we can divide attention between tasks.

Some authors, for example, liken mental resources to an energy supply or a bank account, drawn on by all tasks, and we have used this analogy in much of our discussion. For example, Kahneman (1973) hypothesized that mental tasks require the expenditure of mental effort (also see Eysenck, 1982). The term "effort" was meant rather literally here, so that mental tasks require effort in about the same fashion that physical tasks do.

Other authors, however, have offered a different view, conceiving of these re-sources more as "mental tools," rather than as some sort of mental "energy supply." Thus, there is a task-general resource needed for planning, another needed for re-sponse initiation, and so on (A. Allport, 1989; Baddeley, 1986; Duncan, Emslie, Williams, Johnson, & Freer, 1996; Johnson-Laird, 1988; Just, Carpenter, & Hemphill, 1996; Norman & Shallice, 1986).

As one illustration of a task-general resource, Pashler and Johnston (e.g., McCann & Johnston, 1992; Pashler, 1991, 1992, 1996; Pashler & Johnston, 1989) have proposed a mental mechanism that is required for *selecting* and *initiating* re-sponses, including both physical responses and mental ones (such as the beginning of a memory search, or the making of a decision). This **response selector** presum-ably plays a key role in coordinating the timing of our various activities, and so serves (in part) as a mental traffic cop, controlling which processes go forward at any moment in time. A crucial point, though, is that, this mechanism can initiate only one response at a time, and so it is not possible to divide this resource in any literal sense. If two concurrent tasks each require the response selector, then one of them must wait its turn while the selector deals with the other task.

Let's be clear, though, that this does not imply that we can, at a broad level, do only one task at a time. If, for example, you are trying to divide your attention be-tween Task A and Task B, you could first select and launch some action that is part of Task A. Doing so will require the response selector, and so the selector will, at that moment, not be available for Task B. However, the response selector is needed to *launch* your actions, but it isn't needed to *oversee* those actions while they are under way. As a result, after you've launched the first step for Task A, the response selector is momentarily free—and so can be used to select and launch a step for Task B. Then, while that step is being carried out, you can use the response selector to launch the next step of A. This kind of back-and-forth, turn-taking arrangement is referred to as **time-sharing.**

Working Memory as a Limited Resource

Time-sharing allows us to make efficient use of the response selector, but the fact remains that the selector can initiate only one action at a time, and this constraint places limits on our performance in many settings. As we have noted, though, the response selector is only one of the task-general resources, and other resources also limit our performance, including the resource that we call "working memory."

We will have more to say about working memory in Chapter 5, but, in brief, modern conceptions of working memory treat it as a several-part system. Some of the parts are relatively passive storage vessels—allowing you to hold on to information that you'll need soon, but don't need right now. A more sophisticated part of working memory, though, is a control mechanism that serves as a "central executive" for the mind, and that directs the function of many cognitive processes (Baddeley, 1986, 1996; Conway, Kane, & Engle, 2003; for some possible complications, see Logan, 2003).

Several variations of this proposal have been developed; let's look at one in particular (Engle & Kane, in press): Engle and his associates have suggested that much of our day-to-day functioning is guided by habit and prior associations. After all, most of the situations we find ourselves in resemble those we've encountered in the past, and so we don't need to start from scratch in figuring out how to behave. Instead, we can rely on the responses or strategies we've used previously.

In some cases, though, we want to behave in a fashion that's different from how we've behaved in the past—perhaps because our goals have changed, or perhaps because the situation has changed in some way that makes prior habits no longer useful. In such cases, we need to overrule the action or strategy supplied by memory. To do this, Engle proposes, we need to spend special effort to keep our current goal in mind, so that it, and not habit, will guide our actions. As a related problem, some settings contain triggers that powerfully evoke certain responses. If we wish to make some *other* response, we need to spend effort to avoid the obvious trap.

With this context, Engle's proposal is that **executive control** is a task-general mental resource needed whenever someone wants to avoid interference from previous habit. This control provides two essential functions: On the one side, it works to maintain the desired goal in mind; simultaneously, it serves to *inhibit* automatic or habitual responses.

Evidence for this view comes from studies that compare people with a larger working-memory capacity (WMC), and so, by hypothesis, a greater degree of executive control, with people who have a smaller WMC. (We'll describe in Chapter 5 how this capacity is measured.) It turns out that people with a larger WMC have an advantage in many tasks, both simple and complex. As an example of a very simple task, in one study participants were initially required to fix their eyes on a target (Kane, Bleckley, Conway, & Engle, 2001). When a cue arrived, participants were asked, in one condition, to move their eyes *toward* the cue. This was easy, because this requirement is in line with ordinary habit: Whenever a stimulus appears suddenly in our view, we tend to move our eyes toward the stimulus to inspect it, just as this condition requires. In another condition, however, participants were asked to do something more difficult: They were asked to override habit, and, as soon as the cue arrived, they were required to make an eye movement in the opposite direction, *away from* the cue.

The first condition in this experiment should not require executive control; there is no need to override the habitual response. Consistent with this prediction, individuals with smaller WMC were just as fast and just as accurate in making the desired response, as individuals with a larger capacity. The second condition, though, is different and should require executive control, overriding habit. And, consistent with the theory, individuals with larger WMC were uniformly more successful in the task—faster, and less likely to fall into the trap of moving their eyes (contrary to instructions) toward the cue.

This eye-movement task fits well with the hypotheses we are discussing, but of course the task is not deeply interesting for its own sake. It is important, therefore, that measures of WMC are also correlated with a wide range of other tasks. Thus, individuals with a greater working-memory capacity are also likely to score higher on the verbal SAT, to be better in reading comprehension and the following of directions, better at reasoning tasks and computer-language learning, and so on (Engle & Kane, in press). All of this is sensible if we assume that each of these complex tasks requires, as one of its components, an ability to maintain goals in mind and to resist various forms of interference.

Moreover, this list makes it clear that the mental resources being assessed when we measure WMC are indeed mental resources of broad application—just as we would expect from a limited-availability, task-general mental resource. This is not to say that this resource is needed for all tasks; it is not. Many tasks, as we said, can be performed with routines automatically supplied by memory, or can rely on habits triggered by the situation. For tasks like these, executive control will be unnecessary, and so there will be no relationship between how well someone performs the task, and how large or small that person's working-memory capacity is. But for many other tasks, this sort of control will be necessary, and these will include simple tasks and complex, verbal tasks and spatial ones. It is in this sense that this resource is task-general. (For more on the task-general status of working memory, see Kane et al., 2004; for a different conception, but one that also identifies executive control as a general resource, see Logan, 2004.)

Finally, we should note that researchers have also made headway in identifying the neural underpinnings of WMC, and two separate areas of the brain appear to be involved. First, the prefrontal cortex (roughly, the brain area right behind the eyes) seems to play a crucial role in "goal maintenance"—the process of keeping one's current goal in mind. This is reflected, for example, in the finding that people who have suffered damage to the prefrontal cortex often show a pattern of "goal neglect"—falling into habit and failing to work toward their assigned goals in a particular task, even though they remember and understand the current goals perfectly well (Duncan, Burgess, & Emslie, 1995; Duncan et al, 1996). Other evidence comes from a study in which participants had to perform a Stroop task (described in the next section), which requires a response *different from* the one provided by habit. Data from fMRI scans showed that activation in the prefrontal cortex increased in the seconds leading up to each trial, and, the greater the activation, the lower the chance of error—i.e., the *greater* the chance that participants would be able to resist the force of habit (Braver & Cohen, 2001; MacDonald, Cohen, Stenger, & Carter, 2000).

On the other side, different evidence suggests that another brain structure—the anterior cingulate—may play a role in detecting situations that seem to call for two conflicting responses. In such situations, this structure seems to trigger increased activation in other areas, including the prefrontal cortex, which then work to overcome the conflict (Botvinick, Braver, Barch, Carter, & Cohen, 2001).

These two brain functions—goal maintenance (supported by the prefrontal cortex) and conflict detection (supported by the anterior cingulate)—fit well with the claims that Engle and others have made about working memory. More generally, these neuroscience findings add support to the claim that there are certain processes, certain mechanisms, that will be needed for a wide range of tasks, and that therefore are the task-general mental resources described by our theories.

Divided Attention: An Interim Summary

Again, let's pause to take stock of where we are. Our consideration of *selective* attention drove us toward a several-part account, with one mechanism apparently serving to block out unwanted distractors, and then a list of other mechanisms, all serving to promote the processing of interesting stimuli. Now, in our discussion of *divided* attention, we again seem to require several elements in our theory. Interference between tasks is plainly increased if the tasks are similar to each other, presumably because similar tasks overlap in their processing requirements and so make competing demands on mental resources that are specialized for that sort of task. It is on this basis, then, that our overall account of divided attention needs to take these task-specific resources into account.

At the same time, interference can also be demonstrated with tasks that are entirely different from each other—driving and talking on a cell phone, for example. Thus, our account also needs to include resources general enough in their use that they're drawn on by almost any task. We've argued that there are likely to be several of these general resources: an energy supply needed for mental tasks; a response selector needed whenever a task involves the launching of successive steps; executive control, needed whenever a task requires "rising above" prior habits and tendencies; and probably others as well. Different tasks will draw on these resources to different degrees, but, crucially, a wide variety of tasks will draw on each of these resources; that is why we're categorizing them as *general* resources. And in all cases the principle will be the same: Tasks will interfere with each other if their combined demand for a resource is greater than the amount available—that is, if the demand exceeds the supply.

Practice

We still need to add a complication to our account—namely, the effect of *practice*. To introduce the issue, let's return to the example of talking on a cell phone while driving. For a skilled driver, this task combination is easy *if* the driving is straightforward and the conversation relatively simple. Indeed, many drivers manage this pair of simultaneous tasks every day, without causing traffic accident after traffic accident. Things fall apart, though, the moment the conversation becomes complex, or the driving becomes challenging (e.g., because you have to merge into traffic or negotiate a complex turn). That's when the two tasks visibly interfere with each other: Engaged in deep conversation, the driver misses a turn; while maneuvering through the intersection, the driver suddenly stops talking.

These facts can easily be fit into our framework: It seems likely that there's a close relationship between how complicated a task is and how resource-demanding it is. Concretely, driving in ordinary circumstances makes only a light demand on working memory and only occasional demands on the response selector, whereas driving in a challenging situation makes a much heavier demand on these resources. The same is true for conversation: A casual chat with a friend requires few resources; a profound interview requires more. It's no wonder, then, that you *can* combine these tasks (driving and talking) when they're easy, but not when they're hard: Difficult driving requires a lot of resources, and so does difficult conversation. Together, they'll demand more resources than you have available.[2]

The Effects of Practice

What we've just said is true only for a skilled driver. For a *novice* driver, the task of driving is difficult all by itself, even on a straight road with no traffic. If, therefore, we ask the novice to do anything else at the same time—whether it's talking on a cell phone or even listening to the radio—we put the driver (and other cars) at substantial risk.

---

[2]As a practical note, let's emphasize that challenges like a sudden increase in the demands of driving, or a sudden shift in the conversation's complexity, can arise without warning. As a result, you never know when the conversation and driving will demand more resources than you've got (and thus cause interference), and this is why most psychologists would recommend that you never talk on the cell phone while driving. If you follow that advice, then there's obviously no risk that interference might unexpectedly arise. Whether drivers (including the psychologists themselves) heed this advice, however, is a separate matter.

Why are things so different after practice than before? The main proposal should be obvious: We have already said, first of all, that mental tasks require resources, with the particular resources required, and the *amount* of those resources required, dependent on the nature of the task. Let's now add the claim that, as a task becomes more practiced, it requires *fewer* resources.

Why should this be? Why does practice diminish a task's resource demand? Actually, the answer to these questions flows naturally from the way we've defined some of the resources. For example, the executive control that's measured by working-memory capacity (WMC) is needed whenever one has to rise above habit and has to do things in a new way. Early in practice, though, there are no habits to fall back on—because the task is brand-new. As a result, executive control is needed all the time. With practice, the person acquires a repertoire of habits, associations, and procedures, and so can rely more and more on these routine thoughts and actions. Thus, the demand for executive control decreases.

The same is true for the response selector: Early in practice, you have to decide what the first step of your performance should be, then launch that step. Then you have to choose the second step and launch it. And so on. Thus the response selector is needed a lot—for the selection and launching of each individual step. After practice, though, you can handle things differently. Because you know in advance what the steps of the task will be, you can approach the task with the entire sequence in mind and so use the response selector just once: to launch the whole sequence. Thus, there's no need for a series of choices ("What do I do next?") and, with that, no need for a series of launches, one for each of the task's steps. Instead, you simply do a single memory lookup ("What was the sequence of steps I used last time?"), and then the response selector is needed to launch the overall routine. Once that's done, you can just run off the routine, with no further need for the selector.

Cast in these terms, it is not surprising that, with practice, tasks make smaller demands on mental resources. These resources, it seems, are intimately tied up with the *control* of our mental performance—making plans for what to do, launching each step, and so on. Once a routine is established, there is less need for this control, and with that, less need for the resources.

Why Does Practice Improve Performance?

We have so far discussed why practice makes a task less resource-demanding. But what about the other obvious effect of practice—namely, the fact that it makes performance *better*? After all, there is no question that a pianist plays more beautifully after rehearsing a piece for a while, or that athletes play more skillfully after practice. Similar observations can be made for mental skills, such as solving problems, or reading, or doing calculations. These, too, are more successful after practice than before. What produces this improvement?

One reason for improvement with practice is that often there's more than one way to approach a task, and with practice, one can try them all and stick with the ones that work. Another reason is that tasks often involve procedures or information that must be memorized, and memorization is made possible by the repeated exposures that practice allows. This memorization, too, contributes to the visible improvements made possible by practice.

But another factor hinges on resource availability. The key idea here is that most tasks that you do have multiple components, and you will succeed in the task only if you can handle all the components. To continue our example of driving, a skilled driver needs to keep track of her steering *and* how fast she is going *and* how far she is from the car in front of her, and so on. If the driver neglects any of these elements, the result could be disastrous.

Cast in these terms, it appears that complex tasks, all by themselves, can create problems in divided attention: To do the task, you need to be able to divide your attention among the task's parts, and that's where practice comes in: Early in practice, the various parts of a task will each require resources, and that makes it impossible to think about all the tasks' parts at once. Thus the novice tennis player, getting ready to serve the ball, will focus all his resources on how he tosses the ball upward. As a result, the player won't have any resources left over for other aspects of the serve—like choosing where to aim.

With practice, however, the *elements* of a task each become easier, thereby freeing up resources for dealing with other elements of the same task. This is what allows the driver (or the tennis player) to deal with multiple elements simultaneously, and this is precisely what skilled performance requires.

In addition, this shift in resource demand also makes it possible to think about *new* elements of a task—elements that are beyond the reach of any novice. As an example, a skilled chess player is, of course, sensitive to the locations of the various pieces on the board, and is alert to how these pieces might move in the next few steps of the game. But for the expert, these elements are so obvious, and thinking about them is so automatic, that resources are left over for other, more abstract aspects of the game: What long-term strategy does the player want to develop? Are there hints in the opponent's moves so far that might signal her long-term strategy? The novice has no resources for these "higher-order" elements, and this lack of resources places powerful limits on the quality of the novice's play.

Automaticity

In all of these ways, then, practice can make tasks easier (so that it's possible to combine the now-practiced task with other, simultaneous, tasks) and also better (and thus the quality of the performance goes up). This is made possible, in large part, by the fact that practice decreases resource demands, and this decrease, as we have seen, comes from the fact that practice diminishes the need for *control* of a task.

All of this has an important implication: If, after practice, a task is no longer drawing on mechanisms that provide control, then the task is, in a sense, *uncon-trolled*. Consistent with this suggestion, many psychologists distinguish **controlled tasks** and **automatic tasks**. Controlled tasks are typically novel tasks or tasks that require considerable flexibility in one's approach. These tasks require many mental resources and so are difficult to combine with other tasks. But controlled tasks—as their name implies—are under the person's control. They happen when the person wishes, and can be stopped and restarted as the person wishes.

Automatic tasks have the opposite properties. These tasks are highly familiar and do not require great flexibility. The person approaches these tasks with a well-learned routine—a sequence of responses (often triggered by specific stimuli) that have gotten the task done in the past. Usually the routine has been learned through practice, but it can also be learned from some good advice or a skilled teacher. In any case, once the routine is acquired, the automatic task doesn't need to be supervised or controlled, and so it requires few resources. As a result, an automatic task is unlikely to compete for resources with other tasks, and so it can easily be combined with other tasks. But since automatic tasks are *not* well controlled, they can, in some circumstances, act as if they were "mental reflexes."

A striking example of this **automaticity** involves an effect known as **Stroop interference.** In the classic demonstration of this effect, participants were shown a series of words and asked to name aloud the color of the ink used for each word. The trick, though, was that the words themselves were color names. So people might see the word "BLUE" printed in green ink and would have to say "green" out loud, and so on (Stroop, 1935).

This task turns out to be enormously difficult. There is a strong tendency to read the printed words themselves, rather than naming the ink color, and people make many mistakes in this task. Presumably, this reflects the fact that word recognition, especially for college-age adults, is enormously well practiced and, as a consequence, can proceed automatically. This is a condition, therefore, in which mental control should be minimal, and that is certainly consistent with the errors that we observe. (For a variant of Stroop interference, see Figure 4.5. We note, though, that there is still debate over the exact mechanisms that produce this interference; for some of that debate, see Besner & Stolz, 1999; Besner, Stolz, & Boutilier, 1997; Durgin, 2000; Engle & Kane, in press; Jacoby et al., 2003; and Kane & Engle, 2003. For some discussion of how automatic actions may be shaped by circumstances, see Bargh, 1989; and Bargh & Chartrand, 1999.)

Where Are the Limits?

We are nearing the end of our discussion of attention, and so it again may be useful to summarize where we are, especially since our discussion of mental resources has grown somewhat complicated. At the heart of our account, though, are two very simple ideas: First, tasks require resources, and, second, you cannot "spend" more resources than you have. These claims are central for almost everything we have said about selective and divided attention.

The complications in this account arise from the fact that there seem to be different types of resources, and the exact resource demand of a task depends on sev-

| FIGURE 4.5 | Stroop Interference |

How many items are in each row?	How about these rows?
# #	4 4
? ? ? ?	2 2 2 2
&	3
& &	3 3
/ / / /	1 1 1 1
#	4
? ?	2 2
/ / /	1 1 1
# # #	4 4 4
& & & &	3 3 3 3
?	2
/ /	1 1

Stroop's original demonstration involved color-naming, but many variations on this effect can be demonstrated. For example, scan down the left column, saying out loud how many items are in each row. Now do the same with the right column. Here the task is more difficult, because of the strong tendency to read the numerals rather than counting them.

eral factors. The nature of the task matters, of course, so that the resources required by a verbal task (like reading) are different from those required by a spatial task (like remembering a shape). The novelty of the task and how much flexibility the task requires also matter. Connected to this, *practice* matters, with well-practiced tasks requiring fewer resources.

What, then, sets the limits on divided attention? When can you do two tasks at the same time, and when not? The answer varies, case by case. If two tasks make competing demands on task-specific resources, the result will be interference. If two tasks make competing demands on task-general resources (such as the response selector, or working-memory capacity), again the result will be interference. In addition (and here we return to a point we made much earlier in the chapter), it will be especially difficult to combine tasks if the tasks involve similar stimuli—if both involve printed text, for example, or both involve hearing speech. This is because these cases will make the binding problem (again, the problem of figuring out which features belong with which input) especially difficult. As a result, there is a greater danger of "crosstalk" with similar inputs (i.e., leakage of bits of one input into the other input).

In short, then, it looks like we do need a multipart theory of attention, with performance limited by different factors on different occasions. This draws us once more to a claim we made earlier in the chapter: Attention cannot be thought of as a skill, or a mechanism, or a capacity. Instead, attention is an *achievement*—an achievement of performing multiple activities simultaneously, or an achievement of successfully avoiding distraction when you wish to focus on a single task. And, as we have seen, this achievement rests on an intricate base, so that many skills, mechanisms, and capacities contribute to our ability to attend.

Finally, one last point: We have discussed various limits on human performance—that is, limits on how much you can do at any one time. How rigid are these limits? We have discussed the improvements in divided attention that are made possible by practice, but are there boundaries on what practice can accomplish? Can one perhaps gain new mental resources or, more plausibly, find new ways to accomplish a task in order to avoid the bottleneck created by some limited resource? At least some evidence indicates that the answer to these questions may be yes, and if so, many of the claims made in this chapter must be understood as being claims about what is *usual*, and not claims about what is *possible* (Spelke, Hirst, & Neisser, 1976; Hirst, Spelke, Reaves, Caharack, & Neisser, 1980). With this, many traditions in the world—Buddhist meditation traditions, for example— claim it is possible to *train* attention, so that one has better control over one's mental life; how do these claims fit into the framework we have developed in this chapter? These are issues in need of further exploration, and in truth, what is at stake here is a question about the boundaries on human potential, making these issues of deep interest for future researchers to pursue.

Chapter Summary

1. People are often quite oblivious to unattended inputs; they are unable to tell if an unattended auditory input is coherent prose or random words, and often fail altogether to detect unattended visual inputs, even though they are right in front of the viewer's eyes. However, some aspects of the unattended inputs are detected. For example, people can report on the pitch of the unattended sound and whether it contained human speech or some other sort of noise. Sometimes they can also detect stimuli that are especially meaningful; some people, for example, hear their own name if it is spoken on the unattended channel.

2. These results suggest that perception may require the commitment of mental resources, with some of these resources helping to prime the detectors needed for perception. This proposal is supported by studies showing that we do perceive more efficiently when we can anticipate the upcoming stimulus (and so can prime the relevant detectors). In many cases, this anticipation is spatial—if, for example, we know that a stimulus is about to arrive at a particular location. This priming, however, seems to draw on a limited-capacity system, and so priming one stimulus or one position takes away resources that might be spent on priming some other stimulus.

3. Neuroimaging techniques and clinical data indicate that many brain areas and many mechanisms are needed to make these perceptual anticipations possible. For example, different brain mechanisms are needed to disengage the searchlight beam of attention from its current position, to move it to a new position, and then to lock the beam into the new position. Disruption to any of these mechanisms causes problems in attending, but the most striking problems are those evident in unilateral neglect syndrome, in which an individual attends to only one half of space.

4. Perceiving, it seems, requires the commitment of resources, and so do most other mental activities. This provides a ready account of divided attention: It is possible to perform two tasks simultaneously only if the two tasks do not in combination demand more resources than are available. Some of the relevant mental resources are task-general, and so called on by a wide variety of mental activities. These include the response selector, mental effort, and working-memory capacity. Other mental resources are task-specific, required only for tasks of a certain type.

5. Divided attention is clearly influenced by practice, and so it is often easier to divide attention between familiar tasks than between unfamiliar tasks. In the extreme, practice may produce automaticity, in which a task seems to require virtually no mental resources but is also difficult to control. One proposal is that automaticity results from the fact that decisions are no longer needed for a well-practiced routine; instead, one can simply run off the entire routine, doing on this occasion just what one did on prior occasions.

PART THREE

MEMORY

I N THIS SECTION, we'll discuss how people learn new things and how they remember this information later. We'll also consider some of the apparent failures of memory, including cases in which people "draw a blank" and can't remember anything at all, and also cases in which people seem to remember but are actually recalling things that never happened! Throughout the section, we'll be concerned with both theoretical and practical questions—for example, questions about how students should study their class materials, and also questions about how much trust a jury can place in an eyewitness's recollection of a crime.

One theme in this section concerns the active nature of memory. For example, our discussion of learning will lead us to recognize the importance of how the learner engages (thinks about) the material to be remembered. As we'll see, passive exposure to information, with no intellectual engagement, leads to poor memory later on. In addition, we'll learn why some forms of engagement lead to good memory and other forms do not.

The active nature of memory will also be visible in our discussion of what it means to remember. Here we'll see that in many cases what seems to be remembering is really after-the-fact reconstruction, and we'll need to consider how this reconstruction proceeds and what it implies for memory accuracy.

A second theme—the role of memory connections—will be equally prominent. In Chapter 5, we'll see that, at its essence, learning involves the creation of connections, and the more connections formed, the better the learning. In Chapter 6, we'll explore the idea that these connections are helpful because they serve as retrieval paths later on—paths, one hopes, that will lead you from your memory search's starting point to the information you're trying to remember. This idea of connections as retrieval paths has powerful implications for when you will succeed in remembering and when you will fail, and we'll explore in particular why excellent preparation for one type of test may be poor preparation for another type of test. We'll use this idea as a means of exploring the contrasts between conscious and unconscious remembering.

Chapter 7 explores a different ramification of the connections idea: Memory connections can actually be a source of memory errors. In learning, you create connections that knit together the new material with things you already know. These connections are helpful (because they serve as retrieval paths), but the more connections you create, the harder it will be to keep track of which of the remembered elements were contained within the episode itself and which are connected to that episode only because you connected them during the learning process. We'll learn what this means for memory accuracy overall, and we'll also learn what one can do to minimize error and to improve the completeness and accuracy of human memory.

The Acquisition of Memories and the Working-Memory System

How does new information—whether it's a friend's phone number or a fact we hope to memorize for the Bio exam—become established in memory? Are there more or less effective ways to learn? Why do we sometimes forget? And, finally, how much trust should we place in our memories? How accurate and how complete is our recollection of previous events? These questions will be our focus for the next three chapters.

In tackling these questions, there is an obvious way to organize our inquiry. Before there can be a memory, some learning must occur; that is, new information must be acquired. Therefore, **acquisition** should be our first topic for discussion. Then, once information has been acquired, it must be held in memory until it is needed. We refer to this as the **storage** phase. Finally, we use the information that is in memory; we remember. Information is somehow found in the vast warehouse that is memory and brought into active use; this is called **retrieval.**

This organization probably strikes you as intuitively sensible; it fits, for example, with the way most "electronic memories" (e.g., computers) work. Information ("input") is

- We begin the chapter with a discussion of the broad architecture of memory. We then turn to a closer examination of one component of the model—namely, working memory.

- We emphasize the active nature of working memory—activity that is especially evident when we discuss working memory's "central executive," a mental resource that serves to order, organize, and control our mental lives.

- The active nature of memory is also evident in the process of *rehearsal*: Rehearsal is effective only if the person engages the materials in some way; this is reflected, for example, in the contrast between deep processing (which leads to excellent memory) and mere maintenance rehearsal (which produces virtually no memory benefit).

- The activity during learning appears to establish *memory connections*, and these can then serve as retrieval routes when it comes time to remember the target material. For complex material, the best way to establish these connections is to seek to understand the material; the better the understanding, the better the memory will be.

provided to a computer (the acquisition phase). The information then resides in some dormant form, perhaps in the computer's memory or perhaps on the hard drive (the storage phase). Finally, the information can be brought back from this dormant form, often via a search process that hunts through the memory or disk (the retrieval phase). Of course, there's nothing special about a computer here; "low-tech" information storage works the same way. Think about a file drawer: Information is acquired (i.e., filed), then rests in this or that folder, and then is retrieved.

Guided by this framework, we'll begin our inquiry by focusing on the acquisition of new memories, leaving discussion of storage and retrieval for later. As it turns out, though, we will soon find reasons for challenging this overall approach to memory. In discussing acquisition, for example, we might wish to ask: What is good learning? What guarantees that material is firmly recorded in memory? As we will see, the evidence indicates that what is good learning depends on how the memory is to be used later on, so that good preparation for one kind of use may be poor preparation for a different kind of use. Claims about acquisition, therefore, must be interwoven with claims about retrieval. These interconnections between acquisition and retrieval will be the central theme of Chapter 6.

In the same way, we cannot separate claims about memory acquisition from claims about memory storage. To put it simply, how you learn and how well you learn depend heavily on what you already know. That relationship needs to be explored and explained, and it will provide a recurrent theme for both this chapter and Chapter 7.

With these caveats in view, we will nonetheless begin by describing the acquisition process. Our approach will be roughly historical: We will start with a simple model, emphasizing data collected largely in the 1970s. We will then use this as the framework for examining more recent research, adding refinements to the model as we proceed.

The Route into Memory

Starting in the late 1950s, much theorizing in cognitive psychology was guided by a new way of thinking about mental events—a perspective known as **information processing**. Details aside, the notion was that complex mental events such as learning, remembering, or deciding actually involved a large number of discrete steps. These steps occurred one by one, each with its own characteristics and its own job to do, and with each providing as its "output" the input to the next step in the sequence. Within this framework, theories could often be illustrated with charts such as the one in Figure 5.1. In this diagram, each enclosed shape represents a separate event or process, and the arrows represent the flow of information from one event to the next. The research goal was to make the charts more and more complete by analyzing each box into still smaller boxes, continuing until the entire process could be described in terms of elementary **information-processing components**.

A great deal of information-processing theory focused on the processes through which information was detected, recognized, and entered into memory storage—that is, on the process of information acquisition. Although there was disagreement about the details, there was reasonable consensus on the bold outline of events. An early version of this model was described by Waugh and Norman (1965); later refinements were added by R. C. Atkinson and Shiffrin (1968). The consensus model came to be known as the **modal model**, and it is on this model that we will focus.

FIGURE 5.1   An Information-Processing View of Memory

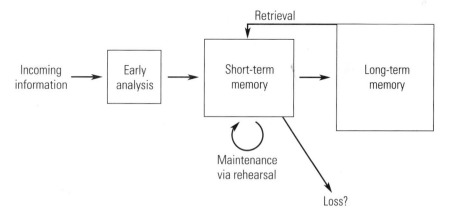

In this view, the boxes represent separate events, processes, or storage spaces; arrows represent the flow of information from one process to another.

The Modal Model

According to the modal model, our information processing involves different kinds of memory, two of which are short-term memory and long-term memory. **Short-term memory** holds on to information currently in use, much as your desk contains the papers or books with which you are currently working. Just like your desk, short-term memory is limited in how much it can hold but, most important, information in short-term memory is instantly and easily available to you.

We first mentioned short-term memory in Chapter 1, although there we used the more modern terminology, **working memory**—a term that emphasizes the function of this memory. (We also talked about working memory in Chapter 4, when we talked about executive control. We'll return to the issue of the executive later in this chapter.) We noted in Chapter 1 that virtually all mental tasks rely on working memory because virtually all mental tasks involve inputs or sequences of steps that are stretched out in time. That creates a short-lived memory demand: You need to hang on to the early parts of the input, or the early steps, while you're working on what comes next. Only then, with the later steps finished, can you put all of the pieces together.

To make this point concrete, let's return to an example we described in Chapter 1: As you read this sentence, your interpretation of the early words will depend on what comes later; therefore, you will need to store the early words for a few moments, until you have read the entire sentence. Those early words, presumably, would be stored in working memory. That way, the words (or, at least, the *meanings* of the words) are available to you when you need them, at the sentence's end, when you're ready to think about what the entire sentence means.

It is in this fashion, then, that working memory provides a mental "desk space"—a resource that lets you hang on to ideas, images, and memories while you're working on them. But you also need another type of memory—one that's much larger, and that includes all the information that you're not thinking about right now, but that is nonetheless part of your knowledge base. This is **long-term memory** (LTM), and it contains all of the information you remember: your memories of what you did yesterday, how you spent your childhood, a vast number of facts about your favorite topic, the names and faces of a hundred acquaintances, and so on.

Although there is a close association between working memory and the contents of your current thinking, there is no such association for long-term memory. At any point in time, much of the material in LTM lies dormant, neither influencing nor influenced by your current thoughts. Correspondingly, the process of retrieving information from LTM, and thus making the information available for use, often requires some hunting, and this can sometimes be effortful and slow.

Working Memory and Long-Term Memory: One Memory or Two?

Many pieces of evidence demand this distinction between working memory and LTM, but much of the evidence comes from a single task: Participants are read a series of words, like "bicycle, artichoke, radio, chair, palace." The length of the list can vary, and so can the rate at which the words are presented. Typical experiments, though, use lists of about 30 words, presented at a rate of about one word per second. Immediately after the last word is read, participants are asked to repeat back as many words as they can. They are free to report the words in any order they choose, which is why this is referred to as a **free recall** procedure.

People usually remember 12 to 15 words in such a test, in a consistent pattern: They are extremely likely to remember the first few words on the list, something known as the **primacy effect**; and they are also likely to remember the last five or six words on the list, a **recency effect**. This pattern is illustrated in Figure 5.2, with a *U*-shaped curve describing the relation between position within the series (or **serial position**) and likelihood of recall (Baddeley & Hitch, 1977; Deese & Kaufman, 1957; Glanzer & Cunitz, 1966; Murdock, 1962; Postman & Phillips, 1965).

This serial-position curve is easily explained by the modal model. At any point in time, according to our model, working memory contains the material someone

---

FIGURE 5.2 | The *U*-Shaped Serial Position Curve

Participants are read a list of words, and then, immediately after this presentation, they must recall as many of the words as they can. They are most likely to remember the first few words presented to them and the last few words. (After Glanzer & Cunitz, 1966)

is working on at just that moment. So what are participants working on during the list presentation? Presumably, they are thinking about the words they are hearing, and so it is these words that are in working memory. This memory, though, is limited in its size, capable of holding only five or six words. Therefore, as participants try to keep up with the list presentation, they will be placing the words *just heard* into working memory, and this will bump the previous words out of this memory. Consequently, as participants proceed through the list, their working memories will, at each moment, contain only the half dozen words that arrived most recently. Any words earlier than these will have been pushed out by later arrivals.

Of course, the last few words on the list don't get bumped out of working memory, because obviously no further input arrives to displace these words. Therefore, when the list presentation ends, those last few words stay in place. Moreover, our hypothesis is that materials in working memory are readily available—easily and quickly retrieved. When the time comes for recall, therefore, working memory's contents (the list's last few words) are accurately and completely recalled.

In a nutshell, then, the proposal is that the list's ending is still in working memory when the list ends, and working memory's contents are easy to retrieve. This is the source of the recency effect. The primacy effect, on the other hand, comes from a different source. According to the modal model, the transfer of material from working memory to LTM depends on processes that require time and attention, so let's examine how participants allocate their attention to the list items. As participants hear the list, they do their best to be good memorizers, and so, when they hear the first word, they repeat it over and over to themselves ("bicycle, bicycle, bicycle")—a process referred to as **memory rehearsal**. When the second word arrives, they rehearse it, too ("bicycle, artichoke, bicycle, artichoke"). Likewise for the third ("bicycle, artichoke, radio, bicycle, artichoke, radio, . . ."), and so on through the list. Note, though, that the first few items on the list are privileged: For a brief moment, "bicycle" was the only word participants had to worry about, and so it had 100% of their attention lavished on it; no other word received this privilege. For a brief moment, "artichoke" had 50% of the participants' attention, more attention than any word except the first. When "radio" arrived, it had to compete with "bicycle" and "artichoke" for the participants' time, and so it received only 33% of their attention.

Words later in the list receive even less attention. Once six or seven words have been presented, the participants need to divide their attention among all of these, which means that each word receives only a small fraction of the participants' efforts. As a result, words later in the list literally are rehearsed fewer times than words early in the list—a fact we can confirm simply by asking participants to rehearse out loud (Rundus, 1971).

This easily provides an explanation of the primacy effect—that is, the observed memory advantage for the early list items. These early words didn't have to share attention with other words, and so more time and more rehearsal were devoted to these early words than to any others. This means that the early words have a greater chance of being transferred into LTM—since, as we've already said, this transfer depends on processes requiring time and attention. And, of course, with a greater chance of being transferred into LTM, the list's early words also have a greater chance of being recalled after a delay, and that's what shows up in our data as the primacy effect.

This account of the serial-position curve leads to many further predictions. First, note that the model claims that the recency portion of the curve is coming from working memory, while the other items on the list are being recalled from LTM. Therefore, any manipulation of working memory should affect recall of the recency items, but not recall of the other items on the list. To see how this works, consider a modification of our procedure: In the standard procedure, we allow participants to recite what they remember immediately after the list's end. In place of this, we can delay recall by asking participants to perform some other task prior to their report of the list items. For example, we can ask them, immediately after hearing the list, to count backward by threes, starting from 201. They do this for just 30 seconds, and then they try to recall the list.

We have hypothesized that, at the end of the list, working memory still contains the last few items heard from the list. But the chore of counting backward will itself require working memory (e.g., to keep track of where one is in the counting sequence). Therefore, this chore will *displace* working memory's current contents; that is, it will bump the last few list items out of working memory. As a result, these items obviously won't benefit from the swift and easy retrieval that working memory allows, and, of course, that retrieval was the presumed source of the recency effect. On this basis, the simple chore of counting backward, even if only for a few seconds, will eliminate the recency effect. In contrast, the counting backward should have no impact on recall of the items earlier in the list: These items are (by hypothesis) being recalled from long-term memory, not working memory; and there's no reason to think the counting task will interfere with LTM. (That's because LTM, unlike working memory, is not dependent on current activity.)

Figure 5.3 shows that these predictions are correct: An activity interpolated between the list and recall essentially eliminates the recency effect, but it has no influence elsewhere in the list (Baddeley & Hitch, 1977; Glanzer & Cunitz, 1966; Postman & Phillips, 1965). Note that merely delaying the recall for a few seconds after the list's end, with no interpolated activity, has no impact. In this case, participants can continue rehearsing the last few items during the delay and so can maintain them in working memory. With no new materials coming in, nothing displaces the recency items from working memory, and so a normal recency effect is observed.

The model makes a very different set of predictions for experiments that manipulate long-term memory rather than working memory. In this case, the manipulation should affect all performance *except* for recency. For example, what happens if we slow down the presentation of the list? Now participants will have

| FIGURE 5.3 | The Impact of Interpolated Activity on the Recency Effect |

With immediate recall, or if recall is delayed by 30 seconds with no activity during this delay, a strong recency effect is detected. In contrast, if participants spend 30 seconds on some other activity between hearing the list and the subsequent memory test, the recency effect is eliminated. This interpolated activity has no impact on the pre-recency portion of the curve.

more time to spend on all of the list items, increasing the likelihood of transfer into more permanent storage. This should improve recall for all items coming from LTM. Working memory, in contrast, is limited by its size, not by ease of entry or ease of access. Therefore, the slower list presentation should have no influence on working-memory performance. As predicted, Figure 5.4 shows that slowing the list presentation improves retention of all the pre-recency items but does not improve the recency effect. Other variables that influence entry into long-term memory have comparable effects. Using more familiar or more common words, for example, would be expected to ease entry into long-term memory and does improve pre-recency retention, but it has no effect on recency (Sumby, 1963).

Over and over, therefore, the recency and pre-recency portions of the curve are open to separate sets of influences and obey different principles. This strongly indicates that these portions of the curve are the products of different mechanisms, just as the modal model proposes.

| FIGURE 5.4 | Rate of List Presentation and the Serial-Position Effect |

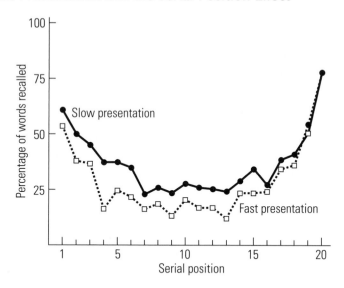

Presenting the to-be-remembered materials at a slower rate improves pre-recency performance but has no effect on recency. The slow rate in this case was 9 seconds per item; the fast rate was 3 seconds per item.

A Closer Look at Working Memory

There is more to be said about memory acquisition and, in particular, about how materials are entered into long-term memory. Before turning to these matters, though, we should pause to consider working memory more fully. This will allow us to fill in some details about this store and to say more about this memory's function.

The Function of Working Memory

As we have discussed, virtually all mental activities require the coordination of several pieces of information or several inputs. We often need to start by working on these ideas or inputs one at a time, and only afterward integrate them into a full package. We mentioned the example of reading a sentence, in which you have to decipher the sentence's early words, then place these on "hold" while working on the sentence's later words. Then, once these have been identified, you can integrate all the words to understand the full phrase. Likewise, consider a simple plan: You must first choose your goal, but then you put this choice on hold in order to concentrate on the early steps needed to reach this goal. Then, once these early steps are taken, you have to think about the goal again, in order to select your next steps.

Of course, the memory making this possible is working memory. When information is currently in use or likely to be needed soon, it is held in working memory. This plainly implies that working memory will be involved in a wide range of tasks, and this suggestion has been confirmed in many studies. As we mentioned in Chapter 4, some of these studies exploit the fact that working memory's capacity varies somewhat from one individual to the next. One can therefore ask about this memory's function by asking what tasks are facilitated by a slightly larger working memory, and what tasks are compromised by a smaller memory.

This research tells us, as one example, that someone with a larger-capacity working memory is likely also to be a more efficient reader, confirming the role for working memory in reading (Baddeley, Logie, Nimmo-Smith, & Brereton, 1985; Daneman & Carpenter, 1980; Just & Carpenter, 1992). Likewise, people with a larger capacity are better off in many types of reasoning skills, making it clear that working memory matters here, too. Other studies show similar positive correlations between working-memory capacity and performance on the SATs, computer-language learning, the following of directions, and more (e.g., Carpenter, Just, & Shell, 1990; Engle & Kane, in press; Kyllonen & Cristal, 1990).

The Holding Capacity of Working Memory

What does it mean to say that someone has a larger-capacity working memory, or a smaller working memory? Where do these measurements come from? For many years, working memory's capacity was measured with a **digit-span task**. In this task, people are read a series of digits (e.g., "8, 3, 4") and must immediately repeat them back. If they do this successfully, they are given a slightly longer list (e.g., "9, 2, 4, 0"). If they can repeat this one without error, they're given a still longer list, and so on. This continues until the person starts to make errors—something that usually happens when the list contains more than seven or eight items.

Procedures such as this imply that working memory's capacity is around seven items or, more cautiously, at least five items and probably not more than nine items. These estimates are often summarized by the statement that this memory holds **"7 plus-or-minus 2"** items (Chi, 1976; Dempster, 1981; G. A. Miller, 1956; Watkins, 1977).

However, these "measurements" of working memory may be misleading. If working memory can hold 7 plus-or-minus 2 items, what exactly is an "item"? Can we remember seven sentences as easily as seven words? Seven letters as easily as seven equations? In a classic paper, George Miller proposed that working memory holds 7 plus-or-minus 2 **chunks** (G. A. Miller, 1956). The term "chunk" is a deliberately unscientific-sounding term, in order to remind us that a chunk does not hold a fixed quantity of information. Instead, Miller proposed, working memory holds 7 plus-or-minus 2 packages, and what those packages contain is largely up to the individual person.

The flexibility in how people "chunk" the input can easily be seen in the span test because performance in this task turns out to depend enormously on how the person thinks about or organizes the items. For example, someone might hear a list like "H, O, P, T, R, A, E, G," etc. If the person thinks of these as individual letters, then he or she will remember 7 of them, more or less. If the same person instead thinks of the list as composed of syllables ("ho, pit, rah, egg"), then he or she will remember approximately 7 syllables, or 14 letters. If the person happens to form three-letter syllables ("hop, tra, . . ."), he or she may remember close to 21 letters, and so on (Postman, 1975; Simon, 1974).

This chunking process, however, does have a cost attached. In remembering the chunks, the person can sometimes lose track of what the original items actually were. If, for example, a person memorizes the sequence "H, O, P, T, . . .") by chunking it as "ho, pit," and so on, this could easily produce a memory error: The person might remember "I" as the fourth letter in the sequence, when, in truth, this letter was inserted merely to make the second chunk pronounceable.

In addition, the chunking process takes some effort. We can see this in the fact that working memory seems able to hold 7 plus-or-minus 2 digits or letters, but slightly fewer syllables, and slightly fewer words, and even fewer sentences. The reason is that attention is required to "repackage" the materials (assembling the letters into syllables, or the syllables into words). With some amount of attention spent in this way, less attention is available for maintaining these items in working memory. Hence, the greater the amount of repackaging, the fewer the items that can be retained. (For more on this trade-off, with increased processing leading to fewer resources available for storage, see Daneman & Carpenter, 1980; and Hitch, Towse, & Hutton, 2001.)

Even with these costs of repackaging, though, we should not understate the power of the chunking strategy and, consequently, the flexibility of what working memory can hold. Consider a remarkable individual studied by Chase and Ericsson (Chase & Ericsson, 1978, 1979, 1982; Ericsson, Chase, & Faloon, 1980; for a broader review, see Ericsson, 2003). This fellow happens to be a fan of track events, and when he hears numbers, he thinks of them as finishing times for races. The sequence "3, 4, 9, 2," for example, becomes "3 minutes and 49 point 2 seconds, near world-record mile time." In this fashion, four digits become one chunk of information. This person can then retain seven finishing times (seven chunks) in memory, and this can involve 20 or 30 digits! Better still, these chunks can then be grouped into larger chunks, and these into even larger chunks. For example, finishing times for individual racers can be chunked together into heats within a track meet, so that, now, four or five finishing times (more than a dozen digits) become one chunk. With strategies like this and with a considerable amount of practice, this person has increased his apparent memory span from the "normal" 7 digits to 79 digits!

However, let's be clear that what has changed through practice is merely this person's chunking strategy, not the size of working memory itself. This is evident in the fact that, when tested with sequences of letters, rather than numbers, so that he can't use his chunking strategy, this individual's memory span is a (perfectly normal) six consonants. Thus, the seven-chunk limit is still in place for this fellow, even though (with numbers) he is able to make extraordinary use of these seven slots.

The Active Nature of Working Memory

Chunking, therefore, provides one complication in our measurement of working memory's capacity. Another, and more important, complication grows out of the very nature of working memory. Specifically, the language of the modal model seems to imply that working memory is something like a box in which information is stored or, continuing our earlier desk analogy, something like a location in which information can be displayed. In this view, learning would be a matter of transferring information from one position (working memory) to another (long-term memory), as though working memory were the loading dock just outside the large memory warehouse.

In truth, though, this conception of working memory is far too static. We've already seen that some amount of repackaging takes place on the memory loading dock. And later in the chapter, we'll see that the "work" in working memory often involves sophisticated analysis of the materials to be remembered, as well as the finding of connections between these materials and other information already in storage. Given these points, the notion of a loading platform may be misleading, as is the notion of mechanical transfer between one position and another. If working memory is a place at all, it's not a mere box. It is instead more like the office of a busy librarian who is energetically categorizing, cataloguing, and cross-referencing new material.

But if working memory is an active place, then perhaps we need to rethink how we *measure* this memory's capacity. As we've discussed, this capacity has traditionally been measured with a span test. However, this test is essentially designed to count the number of "slots" in working memory, with each item on the test being placed in its own slot. This method does little to measure working memory's capacity *to do things* with these slots, and this concern has led researchers to develop more dynamic measures of working memory—so-called measures of **operation span,** designed specifically to measure the efficiency of working memory when it is "working."

For example, research participants might be asked to read aloud a series of sentences, like

Due to his gross inadequacies, his position as director was terminated abruptly.

It is possible, of course, that life did not arise on the Earth at all.

Immediately after reading the sentences, the participant is asked to recall the final words in the sentences—in this case, "abruptly" and "all." If the participant can do this successfully with these two sentences, she is asked to do the same task with a group of three sentences, and then with four, and so on, until the limit on her performance is located.

This task might seem peculiar, but look at what it involves: storing some materials (the ending words) for later use in the recall test, while simultaneously working with other materials (the full sentences). This juggling of processes, as you move from one part of the task to the next, is exactly what working memory must do in its functioning in day-to-day life. Therefore, performance in the operation-span test is likely to reflect the efficiency with which working memory will operate in more natural settings.

The data confirm this prediction. We have mentioned that people with a larger working-memory capacity (WMC) have an advantage on many other measures: the verbal SAT, tests of reasoning, reading comprehension, and so on (Ackerman, Beier, & Boyle, 2002; Cantor & Engle, 1993; Daneman & Hannon, 2001; Engle & Kane, in press; Gathercole & Pickering, 2000; Gray, Chabris, & Braver, 2003; Howe, Rabinowitz, & Powell, 1998; Just & Carpenter, 1992). In other words, there are strong *positive correlations* between WMC and these other measures. Similar results have been found with children, and so the size of working-memory capacity is, for example, positively correlated with problem-solving performance in schoolchildren (Passolunghi, Cornoldi, & De Liberto, 1999). These correlations are all obtained when the more active measure of working memory—namely, operation span—is used. These correlations are not observed with the more traditional (and more static) span measure, confirming the advantage of the more dynamic measures. These findings, in turn, strengthen the overall claim that working memory is not a passive storage box but is instead a highly active information processor.

The Working-Memory System

When we measure people's operation spans, we're asking them to do two things with working memory at the same time: They need to process the sentences we're presenting, and they also need to hold on to the sentences' final words, for later recall. This is, we've proposed, exactly what working memory has to do all the time: temporarily holding on to one bit of information while simultaneously working on something else. And, in fact, the *structure* of working memory is set up for precisely this function.

In Chapter 1, we introduced the idea that working memory is actually not a single entity, but is instead a *system* built out of several components (Baddeley, 1986, 1992; Baddeley & Hitch, 1974; Salame & Baddeley, 1982). At the center of the system is the **central executive**, a multipurpose processor capable of running many different operations on many different types of material. Our discussion of working-memory capacity (WMC) in Chapter 4 provided some description of the executive, and we will have more to say on this topic before we are through. It is the central executive that does the real "work" in working memory, and so if one has to plan a response or make a decision, these steps require the executive. But, in addition, many tasks place a different, less complicated demand on working memory—namely, that it serve literally as a *memory*, a temporary resting spot for information that isn't needed yet but soon will be. This function is crucial for many purposes, but all it requires is mere maintenance, and there's no reason to burden the executive with this simple task. Instead, this chore can be turned over to one of working memory's less sophisticated "helpers," leaving the executive free to work on more difficult matters.

The proposal, then, is that working memory often relies on low-level helpers, which serve, roughly, as internal scratch pads, storing information you will need soon but don't need right now. And there are different types of scratch pads: the **visuospatial buffer**, used for storing visual materials (such as mental images; see Chapter 11); and also the **rehearsal loop**, used for storing verbal materials. To see how this works, try reading the next few sentences while holding on to this list of numbers: "1, 4, 6, 4, 9." Got them? Now read on. You are probably repeating the numbers over and over to yourself, rehearsing them with your inner voice. But this turns out to require very little effort, so you can continue reading while doing this rehearsal. Nonetheless, the moment you need to recall the numbers (what were they?), they are available to you. The claim, of course, is that the numbers were maintained by one of working memory's helpers—namely, the rehearsal loop. While the helper provided this maintenance, the central executive was free to continue reading. And that is the advantage of this system: With mere storage handled by the helpers, the executive is available for other, more demanding tasks.

The Rehearsal Loop

How does the rehearsal loop function? We worked through this issue in Chapter 1, but let's quickly review the main points, using the example mentioned in the previous section: storing numbers while reading. (Also see Baddeley, 1986, 2000.)

To manage this task, working memory's central executive must first identify the numbers (i.e., read them off the page), but then the executive needs to shuffle these numbers off to storage so that it's not burdened with them. That way, the executive will be free to work on other things (such as reading the rest of the page). To do this, the executive relies on the rehearsal loop. Specifically, the executive uses the process of **subvocalization** to pronounce the numbers. In essence, you silently say the numbers to yourself. Of course, the activity of speaking is immensely well practiced, and so there's no need for the executive to monitor or supervise this activity. Thus, once the executive has initiated the speech, and once the speaking is under way, the executive can turn to other matters, and that is exactly what we want: The burden of holding on to the numbers is now carried by the "inner voice," not the executive.

Subvocalization, in turn, produces a representation of these numbers in the **phonological buffer**. In other words, an auditory image is created in the "inner ear." This image will fade away after a second or two, and before it does, the executive is needed once again: The executive "reads" the contents of the buffer, as if listening to the "echo" in order to remind itself what the numbers were. Then the executive initiates the next pronunciation by the inner voice, to begin another cycle, and at that point it can go back to its other business.

In this way, the executive is needed only once per cycle: to read the contents of the buffer and launch the next round of subvocalization. For the remainder of the cycle, the numbers to be remembered are maintained by the rehearsal loop, not the executive, leaving the executive free to focus on other, more demanding, activities. (For more on the rehearsal loop and the evidence supporting this account, see Chapter 1.)

The Central Executive

What can we say about the main player within working memory—the central executive itself? We offered one proposal in Chapter 4, building on the idea that mental activities rely on a number of task-general mental resources. Some of these resources certainly involve executive functions, such as the selection and launching of responses (Pashler, 1991, 1992, 1994), or planning and the setting of goals (A. R. A. Conway, Kane, & Engle, 2003; Duncan, 1995; Duncan, Emslie, Williams, Johnson, & Freer, 1996; Engle & Kane, in press), or the steps needed to resist falling into mere habit or routine (Engle & Kane, in press). With this said, the proposal, quite simply, is that these mental resources *are* the central executive, or more plausibly, that they are key elements within the executive. Put differently, the central executive is just the name we give for the use of these cognitive resources.

This view of the central executive is supported by several lines of evidence. We know, for example, that many sites in the prefrontal cortex are particularly active when people are engaged in tasks that make heavy use of working memory (Courtney, Petit, Maisog, Ungerleider, & Haxby, 1998; Goldman-Rakic, 1995). This leads us to ask what symptoms result if someone has suffered brain damage in these areas, and the answer is intriguing: Often people who have suffered frontal lobe damage can still lead relatively normal lives. In much of their day-to-day behavior, they show no obvious symptoms; they perform normally on conventional tests of intelligence.

Nonetheless, with appropriate tests we can reveal the disruption that results from frontal lobe damage, and it turns out that the disruption takes several different forms. We mentioned one of the problems in Chapter 4: Patients with frontal lesions show a pattern of "goal neglect"—relying on habitual responses even if those responses won't move them toward their assigned goal in a particular task. Closely related is a problem known as **perseveration**. This pattern emerges in many aspects of the patients' behavior and involves a strong tendency to produce the same response over and over, even when it's plain that the task requires a change in the response. For example, in one commonly used task, the patients are asked to sort a deck of cards into two piles. At the start of the task, the patients have to sort the cards according to color; later they need to switch strategies and sort according to the shapes shown on the cards. The patients have enormous difficulty making this shift, and they continue to sort by color (i.e., they *persevere* in their original pattern) even though the experimenter tells them again and again that they are placing the cards onto the wrong piles (Goldman-Rakic, 1998).

A somewhat different pattern is revealed when patients with frontal lobe damage are asked to make a copy of a drawing. For example, one patient was asked to copy Figure 5.5A; the patient produced the drawing shown in Figure 5.5B. The copy preserves many features of the original, but close inspection makes it clear that the patient drew the copy with no particular plan in mind. The large rectangle that defines much of the shape was never drawn; the diagonal lines that organize the figure were drawn in a piecemeal fashion. Many details are correctly reproduced but were not drawn in any sort of order; instead, these details were added whenever they happened to catch the patient's attention (Kimberg, D'Esposito, & Farah, 1998). Another patient, asked to copy the same figure, produced the drawing shown in Figure 5.5C. This patient started to draw the figure in a normal way, but then got swept up in her own artistic impulses, adding stars and a smiley face (Kimberg et al., 1998).

All of these data make it clear that the prefrontal cortex does not have just one function. This area of the brain seems pivotal in allowing people to plan and organize their activities (that seems to be the difficulty with the patient who drew Figure 5.5B); it also seems crucial for the inhibition of impulses (lack of inhibition led to the drawing in Figure 5.5C). The prefrontal cortex also seems crucial for "turning off" responses once they have been launched (the problem in perseveration). All of these functions are likely to contribute to what we are here calling the central executive—the mental resource (or, more likely, the *set* of resources) that serves to order, organize, and control our mental lives. (For further treatment of this complex topic, see Duncan, 1995; S. J. Gilbert & Shallice, 2002; Kane & Engle, 2003; Kimberg et al., 1998; and Stuss & Levine, 2002.)

The Nature of Working Memory

Let's pause to take stock and to ask, in particular, how our discussion over the last few pages fits into the larger picture with which we began this chapter. With that, where are we with regard to the modal model, introduced several sections ago?

Our understanding of working memory has certainly evolved in recent years, and as we've seen, the evidence now makes it clear that working memory is not a mere box or storage container. Instead, working memory is much more dynamic than that, and, indeed, "working memory" may actually be just the name we give to an organized set of *activities*, especially the complex activities of the central executive.

FIGURE 5.5 Drawings by Patients with Prefrontal Brain Damage

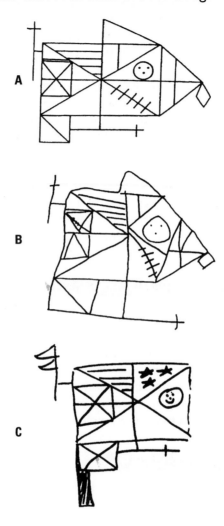

Two patients with damage to the prefrontal cortex were asked to copy the figure shown in Panel A. The drawing shown in Panel B, by one of the patients, is reasonably accurate, but it was plainly drawn in a feature-by-feature fashion, with no overall plan in mind. The patient who drew the image in Panel C started out in a normal way but then ended up following her own artistic impulses, rather than carrying out the task as she'd first intended.

Even so, some claims in the modal model remain unchanged: In current conceptions, working memory is still understood to be crucial for storing the information that you're currently thinking about, limited in its storage capacity, but easily loaded and easily accessed. In addition—and still in accord with the modal model—current conceptions view working memory as being quite fragile, since each shift in attention brings new information into working memory, and the newly arriving materials displace earlier items. Storage in working memory, therefore, is plainly temporary. All of this is in clear contrast to long-term memory, which is far larger in capacity, less easily loaded or accessed, and far more enduring.

With all of this said, we're now ready to move on. We've discussed the broad "architecture" of memory—with a working-memory system and a long-term store, connected more or less as shown in Figure 5.1. We've also said a great deal about working memory—its structure and its function. But if we are to understand memory acquisition, we still need to tackle the most important part of the puzzle: how information becomes established in long-term memory, so that it can be remembered an hour, or a day, or even a decade after the original event of learning.

Entering Long-Term Storage: The Role of the Intent to Learn

We've already seen one important clue about how information becomes established in long-term storage: In discussing the primacy effect, we suggested that the more an item is rehearsed, the more likely it is that you will remember that item later on. In order to pursue this clue, however, we need to ask what exactly rehearsal is, and how it might work to promote memory.

Two Types of Rehearsal

The term "rehearsal" really means little beyond "thinking about." When a research participant rehearses an item on a memory list, she's simply thinking about that item—perhaps once, perhaps over and over; perhaps mechanically, or perhaps with close attention to what the item means. Clearly, therefore, there is considerable variety in the sorts of activity that count as rehearsal, and, in fact, psychologists find it useful to sort this variety into two broad types.

As one option, people can engage in **maintenance rehearsal**, in which they simply focus on the to-be-remembered items themselves, with little thought about what the items mean or how they are related to each other. This is a rote, mechanical process, recycling items in working memory simply by repeating them over and over. In contrast, **relational**, or **elaborative**, **rehearsal** involves thinking about what the to-be-remembered items mean, and how they are related to each other, and to other things in the surroundings, and to other things you already know.

In general, relational rehearsal is vastly superior to maintenance rehearsal for establishing information in memory. Indeed, in many settings, maintenance rehearsal provides no long-term benefits whatsoever. As an informal demonstration of this point, consider the following common experience: You want to telephone a friend, and so you call directory assistance to get his number, or perhaps you look up the number in the telephone book. Once you've learned the number in this way, you recite it over and over to yourself while pressing the appropriate sequence of buttons on your phone. But it turns out that the line is busy, so you wait a minute or two and then try again. The moment you start to dial, though, you realize that you don't have a clue what the number is, even though you knew it perfectly well just a few seconds earlier. What went wrong? While dialing the number the first time, you held onto it via maintenance rehearsal. This kept the number in your thoughts while you were dialing but did nothing to establish the number in long-term storage. And when you try to dial the number the second time, it's long-term storage that you need.

Here is a more formal demonstration of the same point: Participants in one study were asked to listen to a series of word lists, and at the end of each list, their task was to report the most recent word they'd heard that began with the letter *B* (Craik & Watkins, 1973). Thus, the participants might hear "basket, spoon, telephone, cub, lamp, fish, hair, plant, lake, book, chair, foot, baby, hill, tree"; for this list, they would report "baby"—the last *B*-word in the series. Then they would hear a new list, and again they had to report its most recent *B*-word. And so on. Things proceeded in this fashion until the end of the session when, to the participants' surprise, they were asked to write down all of the *B*-words they had heard during the entire session. Up until that moment, they had no idea their memories were being tested, and no idea that they had reason to remember any *B*-word other than the most recent one.

While listening to these lists, therefore, participants believe they need to keep track of only one word—namely, the most recent *B*-word. Thus, continuing with the example from before, when they hear "basket," they try to remember it, on the chance that the list will contain no other *B*-words; in that case, "basket" would be the word to be reported. The moment they hear "book," they can stop thinking about "basket," because they now know that "basket" won't be the last *B*-word on the list.

In addition, participants have no reason to think about these words in any complicated way; all they need to do is maintain the most recent *B*-word in memory so that it's available for report. This "mere maintenance" does require the participant to keep thinking about the word, over and over, but that's not a problem here: In this simple task, participants have little else to do, and so nothing will interrupt their continued maintenance of this single item.

Let's now add one complication. The stimuli in this experiment were actually devised with a scheme in mind. Sometimes the *B*-words were positioned very closely together on the list (like "book" and "baby" in our example, with just two words in between). Other words (like "basket" in our example) were followed by several words not beginning with B. How should this matter for memory? Words like "book" were presumably kept in working memory for only a short time, because this word was quickly followed by (and so displaced by) another B-word. Consequently, "book" was rehearsed only a few times. Words like "basket" were kept in working memory for a longer period and so were rehearsed many times.

If participants are doing only maintenance rehearsal, then memory performance in this procedure should be very poor. In addition, it should not matter how much of this rehearsal participants did: If maintenance rehearsal is an ineffective preparation for the memory test, then it is irrelevant whether they did a lot or a little of this futile activity. Therefore, we should expect similar results if a B-word was quickly followed by another (and so rehearsed only briefly) or if a B-word was followed by another only after a long interval. All of this is exactly what the data show.

It would appear, therefore, that rehearsal promotes memory only if it's rehearsal of the right sort. We know from the primacy effect that, sometimes, more rehearsal leads to more memory. However, if you spend many seconds thinking about something, but think about it only in a mindless mechanical fashion (i.e., through maintenance rehearsal), the item will not be established in your memory.

In exactly the same way, long-lasting memories are not created simply by repeated exposures to the items to be remembered. If you encounter an item over and over but, on each encounter, barely think about it (or think about it in a mechanical fashion), then this, too, will not produce a long-term memory. As a demonstration, consider the ordinary penny. Adults in the United States have probably seen pennies tens of thousands of times. Adults in other countries have seen their own coins just as often. If sheer exposure is what counts for memory, then people should remember what these coins look like perfectly.

But, of course, most people have little reason to pay attention to the penny. Pennies are a different color from the other coins, so they can be identified at a fast glance, with no need for further scrutiny. If it's scrutiny that matters for memory, or, more broadly, *if we remember what we pay attention to and think about*, then memory for the coin should be quite poor.

The evidence on this point is clear: People's memory for the penny is remarkably bad. For example, most people know that Lincoln's head is on the "heads" side, but which way is he facing? Is it his right cheek that's visible, or his left? What other words or markings are shown on the coin? Most people do very badly with these questions; their answers to the "which way is he facing" question are close to random (Nickerson & Adams, 1979); performance is similar for people in other countries remembering their own coins. (Also see Bekerian & Baddeley, 1980; and Rinck, 1999.)

Overall, then, it seems that merely having an item in front of your eyes is not enough to get it into your memory—even if the item is in front of your eyes over and over and over. Likewise, having an item in your thoughts doesn't, by itself, establish a memory. That's shown by the fact that maintenance rehearsal seems entirely ineffective at promoting memory.[1] But all of this simply demands the next question: What *is* enough to establish a bit of information in long-term storage? Some pages back, we introduced a contrast between maintenance rehearsal and elaborative, or relational, rehearsal. If—as it seems to be—maintenance rehearsal is a poor way to memorize, is elaborative rehearsal more effective?

Incidental Learning, Intentional Learning, and Depth of Processing

Consider a student taking a course in college. The student knows that his memory for the course materials will be tested later (e.g., in the course's final exam). And presumably the student also takes various steps to help himself remember: He may read through his notes again and again, he may discuss the material with friends, he may try outlining the material, and so on.

Will these various techniques work—so that the student will have a complete and accurate memory when the exam arrives? And notice that the student is taking these steps in the context of wanting to memorize, hoping to memorize. How do these elements influence performance? Or, put another way, how does the *intention to memorize* influence how or how well we learn?

These questions have been addressed in many experiments, and in order to summarize the broad pattern of data, it will be helpful to present a composite experiment, summarizing the results of many different studies. This composite is a bit complicated, so we have illustrated its design in Table 5.1. (An early procedure by Hyde & Jenkins, 1969, is quite close to the composite we're about to describe, but related data have been reported by Bobrow & Bower, 1969; Craik & Lockhart, 1972; Hyde & Jenkins, 1973; Jacoby, 1978; Lockhart, Craik, & Jacoby, 1976; Parkin, 1984; Slamecka & Graf, 1978; and many others.)

Some of the participants in this experiment are told that we are studying how quickly they can make judgments about letters. No indication is given that we are actually interested in memory. The participants are then shown a series of word pairs on a computer screen. For each pair, they decide as quickly as possible whether the two words are typed in the same case (both capitalized or both not) or typed in different cases. Let's refer to this as **shallow processing**, since participants are engaging the information in a relatively superficial fashion. (Other examples of shallow processing would be decisions about whether the words are printed in red or in green, high or low on the screen, and so on.) At the end of this sequence, the participants are surprised to learn that their memories are being tested, and they are asked to write down as many of the words as they can remember. This is the top

---

[1] We should acknowledge that maintenance rehearsal does have a lasting impact if memory is tested in just the right way, and we will return to this point in Chapter 6. (Some of the relevant evidence is in Wixted, 1991; or Kelly, Burton, Kato, & Akamatsu, 2001.) However, this leaves in place the point we are making here: Maintenance rehearsal is nearly worthless for establishing the sorts of memories one needs when simply trying to remember, "Is this what I saw yesterday?" or "Is this what I heard ten minutes ago?" and so on.

| TABLE 5.1 | Studying the Effects of Intention and the Effects of Levels of Processing on Memory |

Type of processing	Incidental learning	Intentional learning
Shallow	Are these words in the same typeface? "HOUSE—trick"	Are these words in the same typeface? "HOUSE—trick" *and*, in addition, you'll have to remember these words later on!
Medium	Do these words rhyme? "BALL—TALL"	Do these words rhyme? "BALL—TALL" *and*, in addition, you'll have to remember these words later on!
Deep	Are these words synonyms? "CAR—AUTOMOBILE"	Are these words synonyms? "CAR—AUTOMOBILE" *and*, in addition, you'll have to remember these words later on!

Illustrated here is a composite of many procedures examining how memory performance is shaped by the intention to memorize, and also by how, at the time of learning, one approaches the material to be remembered.

left cell in the design shown in Table 5.1. This sort of procedure assesses **incidental learning**—that is, learning in the absence of any intention to learn.

A second group of participants is given the same instructions, but with one change. Like the first group, these participants are told that we want them to make judgments about whether the words in each pair are in the same case or in different cases. This group, therefore, is also doing shallow processing. However, this group is also told that their memories will be tested, so that when the memory test arrives, it comes as no surprise. These participants, therefore, are doing shallow processing in the context of the intention to learn. This is the top right cell in Table 5.1, and examines **intentional learning**.

A third group of participants is brought into the lab and told that we are studying how quickly people can make judgments about rhyme. If the two words shown on the computer screen rhyme, they press one button; if not, they press a different button. Again, a surprise memory test follows this presentation. These participants are doing what we might call "medium processing," and because the memory test was unexpected, this is another instance of incidental learning.

A fourth group is given the same rhyme task but is told in advance about the upcoming memory test. Members of this group are doing medium processing with the intention to memorize the words they are viewing.

The fifth and sixth groups (the bottom row in Table 5.1) are led to do **deep processing**—that is, to think about the meaning of the items. Participants in the fifth group are shown pairs of words on a computer screen, with the instruction that they should press one button if the words on the screen are synonymous, another button if they are not. No warning is given about a memory test, and therefore these participants presumably have no intention to memorize the words. Participants in the sixth group are given the same task but are warned about the memory test, so this group is doing deep processing with the intention to learn.

What are the results of all this? Let's frame the answer in terms of Table 5.1. When the time comes for recall, participants from the bottom left cell (deep processing with no intention to learn) perform quite well, whereas participants from the top left cell (shallow processing with no intention to learn) do rather poorly. In other words, attention to meaning really pays off for recall, while attention to surface characteristics produces little memory benefit. Moderate levels of processing (attention to rhyme) produce a moderate level of recall performance.

What about the right column of the table? Here the result is quite straightforward: There is no difference between the left and right columns of the table. That is, the intention to learn seems to add nothing. For purposes of memorizing, there is no difference between shallow processing with the intention to learn and shallow processing without this intention. Likewise, there is no difference between deep processing with the intention to learn and deep processing without this intention.

The Intention to Learn

In the experiment just sketched, depth of processing had a powerful effect, such that the deeper the processing, the better the memory. However, incidental learning and intentional learning yielded identical patterns, indicating little role for the intention to learn. But let's take a closer look at the importance of intentions, by considering one last group of participants: This group is told that they are about to be shown words on a computer screen, and they are asked to memorize these words. No further instructions are given, so they are free to approach this memorization in any way they choose. These participants are then shown a sequence just like the ones described in the previous section.

When people are instructed to memorize, each uses the strategy that he or she thinks best. And, in fact, different people have different beliefs about the best way to memorize. Some of us, for example, have discovered that thinking about meaning is an effective strategy and so, if asked to memorize, spontaneously draw on deep processing. Others seem to believe that the best way to memorize is by listening to the sound of the word over and over. These people will end up indistinguishable from the participants in the middle right of Table 5.1, while people who spontaneously employ deep processing will end up equivalent to participants in the lower right. Of course, the participants we were discussing before had been instructed to use a particular form of processing, and the people we are now considering have "self-instructed." But, as it turns out, this difference between instruction and self-instruction is irrelevant to performance.

All of this leads to the expectation that results from this "just memorize" condition will be rather variable, depending on how participants self-instruct—that is, on what strategy they choose. This prediction is correct. If participants have figured out, on their own, that attention to meaning aids memory, then they perform quite well. More precisely, they perform as well as—but no better than—participants specifically told to do deep processing. If they select a less-than-optimal strategy, then they perform at a lower level. And, in fact, many people do have peculiar beliefs about what works in placing material into memory. These people then choose their memorizing strategy on the basis of these (faulty) beliefs, and their performance on memory tests is correspondingly poor. (For studies of people's spontaneous strategies, see J. R. Anderson & Bower, 1972; A. L. Brown, 1979; Hyde & Jenkins, 1969; T. O. Nelson, 1976; and Postman, 1964.)

What, therefore, should we conclude about the role of intention in guiding the learning process? Clearly, intention does matter: Someone who has no intention to learn may end up doing maintenance processing rather than elaborative processing, and this obviously will affect what is remembered. Likewise, someone who intends to learn will select the strategy he or she thinks best, and, as we have seen, this choice of strategy will also affect the quality of memory. But these effects of intention are all *indirect.* The intention to learn leads people to approach the materials in a certain fashion, and it is the approach, not the intention, that matters for memory. If we can lead people to approach the materials in the same way without the intention, we get the same memory results.

The Role of Meaning and Memory Connections

Where are we so far? Every day we experience many things—new sights, new sounds, new ideas. Some of these we'll remember; some of these we will not. We're extremely unlikely to remember those sights and sounds for which we did only maintenance rehearsal—even if we did a lot of it. Our chances of remembering are better if we did elaborative rehearsal—that is, if we thought about how these experiences are related to each other, or to other things we know. But much depends on *what sort* of elaborative rehearsal we did: If we thought about the things we saw, or the things we heard, only in superficial terms (shallow processing), we're much less likely to remember them than we would be if we thought about them in terms of their meaning. And we should emphasize that this difference between shallow and deep processing is quite large: In many experiments, people are three, or four, or five times more likely to remember items that were processed deeply than they are to remember items processed in a shallow manner.

Clearly, then, a great deal depends on how we engage the materials we encounter at the time of learning—whether we do deep processing, shallow processing, or mere maintenance. But what exactly does this "engagement" with the materials accomplish? Why is it, for example, that attention to meaning leads to such good recall? Let's start with a broad proposal; we'll then need to circle back and fill in the evidence for this proposal.

Perhaps surprisingly, the benefits of deep processing may not lie in the learning process itself. Instead, deep processing may influence *subsequent* events. More precisely, attention to meaning may promote recall by virtue of facilitating *retrieval* of the memory, later on. To understand the issue, consider what happens whenever a library acquires a new book: On its way into the collection, the new book must be catalogued and shelved appropriately. These steps happen when the book arrives, but the cataloguing doesn't literally influence the arrival of the book into the building. The moment the book is delivered, it's physically in the library, catalogued or not, and the book doesn't become "more firmly" or "more strongly" in the library, thanks to the cataloguing.

But, of course, the cataloguing is crucial. If the book were merely tossed on a random shelf somewhere, with no entry in the catalogue, users might never be able to find it. Indeed, without a catalogue entry, users of the library might not even realize that the book was in the building. Notice, then, that cataloguing happens at the time of arrival, but the benefit of cataloguing isn't for the arrival itself. (If the librarians all went on strike, so that no books were being catalogued, books would continue to arrive, magazines would still be delivered, and so on. Again: The *arrival* doesn't depend on cataloguing.) Instead, the benefit of cataloguing is for events subsequent to the book's arrival: Cataloguing makes it possible (and maybe makes it *easy*) to find the book later on.

The same is true for the vast library that is our memory: The task of learning is not merely a matter of placing information into long-term memory. Learning also needs to establish some appropriate indexing; it must, in effect, pave a path to the newly acquired information, so that this information can be retrieved at some future point. In essence, then, one of the main chores of memory acquisition is to lay the groundwork for memory retrieval.

But what is it that facilitates memory retrieval? There are, in fact, several ways to search through memory, but a great deal depends on memory *connections*. Connections allow one memory to trigger another, and then that memory to trigger another, so that, like a series of dominoes falling, one is "led" to the sought-after information. If remembering the experimenter's shirt reminds you of materials you learned during the experiment, this will help you to locate these materials in memory. In this case, there must have been some connection in your thoughts between the shirt and the target materials, and this connection is what triggered the reminding. Likewise, if remembering the third word on a list reminds you of the fourth and fifth, these connections among the items will improve memory performance.

This line of reasoning easily accounts for why attention to meaning promotes memory. Attention to meaning involves thinking about relationships: "What words are related in meaning to the word I'm now considering?" "What is the relationship between the start of this story and the way the story turned out?" Thinking about points like these will help you to find (or, in some cases, to *create*) connections among your various ideas, and it's these connections, we're proposing, that really matter for memory.

Elaborate Encoding

These are, as we've noted, broad claims, and, in fact, it will take us several chapters to work through all the evidence for these claims. One bit of evidence, though, is immediately accessible: On the hypotheses just sketched, attention to meaning should not be the only way to improve memory. Other strategies should have similar effects, provided that these strategies help the memorizer to establish memory connections.

As an example, consider a study by Craik and Tulving (1975). Participants were shown a word, and then were shown a sentence with one word left out. Their task was to decide whether the word fit into the sentence. For example, they might see the word "chicken," then the sentence "She cooked the _____." The appropriate response would be yes, since the word does fit in this sentence. After a series of these trials, there was a surprise memory test, with participants asked to remember all the words they had seen.

This experiment was arranged so that some of the sentences shown to participants were simple, while others were more elaborate. For example, "She cooked the _____" would be a simple sentence, while a more complex sentence might be, "The great bird swooped down and carried off the struggling _____." The data showed that words were more likely to be remembered if they appeared with these rich, elaborate sentences.

To make their decisions about these sentences, the research participants obviously have to think about the meanings of the words in the sentences. It would seem, then, that participants must think about the meaning of every word presented to them, and if this were all that mattered for memory, then all of the words should be remembered equally. But that's not what the data show. Instead, deep and elaborate processing led to much better recall than deep processing alone.

Why does elaborate processing help memory? The answer hinges on memory connections. Perhaps the "great bird swooped" sentence calls to mind a barnyard scene, with the hawk carrying a chicken away. Or perhaps it calls to mind thoughts about predator–prey relationships. One way or another, the richness of this sentence offers the potential for many connections, as it calls other thoughts to mind, each of which can be connected, in your thinking, to the target sentence. These connections, in turn, provide potential **retrieval paths**—paths that can, in effect, guide your thoughts toward the content to be remembered. All of this seems less likely for the impoverished sentences. These will evoke fewer connections and will establish a narrower set of retrieval paths. Consequently, they'll be less likely to be recalled later on.

Organizing and Memorizing

Sometimes memory connections link the to-be-remembered material to other information already in memory. In other cases, the connections link one aspect of the to-be-remembered material to another aspect of the same material. Such a connection ensures that, if any part of the material is recalled, then all will be recalled.

In all cases, though, the connections are obviously important, and that leads us to ask, How does one go about discovering (or creating) these connections? More than 60 years ago, a German psychologist, George Katona, argued that the key lies in *organization* (Katona, 1940). Katona's argument, in fact, was that the processes of organization and memorization are inseparable: We memorize well when we discover the order within the material. Conversely, if we find (or impose) an organization on the material, we will easily remember it. These suggestions are, of course, fully compatible with the conception we are developing, since what organization provides is, once again, memory connections.

Mnemonics

For thousands of years, people have wished for "better" memories; they have wished to learn more quickly, and to remember more accurately. Motivated by these wishes, a number of techniques have been designed to "improve" memory—techniques known as **mnemonic strategies**. Some of these mnemonics are modern inventions, but most are very old, dating back to ancient Greece.

Most mnemonics involve a straightforward and familiar principle—namely, that organization helps. If an organization can be found within the materials, then this will lead to good memory. If an organization cannot be found, then often an "external" organization can be imposed on the material, with the same memory benefit.

Let us take a concrete case. You want to remember a list of largely unrelated items, perhaps the entries on your shopping list, or a list of questions you want to ask when you next see your adviser. You might try to remember this list using one of the so-called **peg-word systems**. These systems begin with a well-organized structure, such as this one:

One is a bun.

Two is a shoe.

Three is a tree.

Four is a door.

Five is a hive.

Six are sticks.

Seven is heaven.

Eight is a gate.

Nine is a line.

Ten is a hen.

This rhyme provides ten "peg words" ("bun," "shoe," "tree," and so on), and in memorizing something, you can "hang" the materials to be remembered on these "pegs." Let's imagine, therefore, that you are trying to memorize the list of topics you want to discuss with your adviser. If you want to discuss your unhappiness with your chemistry class, you might form an association between chemistry and the first peg, "bun." You might, for example, form a mental image of a hamburger bun floating in an Erlenmeyer flask. If you also want to discuss your after-graduation plans, you might form an association between some aspect of those plans and the next peg, "shoe." (Perhaps you might think about how you plan to pay your way after college by selling shoes.) If you continue in this fashion, then when the time comes to meet with your adviser, all you have to do is think through that silly rhyme again. When you think of "one is a bun," it is highly likely that the image of the flask (and therefore of chemistry lab) will come to mind. When you think of "two is a shoe," you'll be reminded of your job plans. And so on.

Hundreds of variations on this strategy are possible, some taught in self-help courses (you've probably seen the ads—"How to Improve Your Memory!"), some presented by corporations as part of management training, and on and on. Some mnemonic strategies rely heavily on visualization (e.g., we mentioned that you might form an image of the bun floating in the flask), others do not. (See Chapter 11.) All the variations, though, employ the same basic scheme. To remember a list with no apparent organization, you impose an organization on it, by employing a skeleton or scaffold that is itself tightly organized. The number rhyme provides one such scaffold, but other scaffolds are easily located.

In later chapters, we will have more to say about why these systems work. Our point for now is simply that they do work, not only helping you to remember individual items, but also helping you to remember those items in a specific sequence (G. H. Bower, 1970, 1972; G. H. Bower & Reitman, 1972; Christen & Bjork, 1976; Higbee, 1977; Roediger, 1980; J. Ross & Lawrence, 1968; Yates, 1966). All of this confirms our central claim: Organizing improves recall. Mnemonics work because they impose an organization on the materials to be remembered, thus establishing connections between the material and some other easily remembered structure.

Mnemonics obviously contribute to our theoretical understanding of memory, but in addition, they have important practical uses. Many students, for example, use a first-letter mnemonic to remember the standard colors of the rainbow, turning the list of seven colors (red, orange, yellow, . . .) into a single integrated unit: the name "Roy G. Biv." Likewise, many students use the sentence "King Phillip crossed the ocean to find gold and silver" to remember the taxonomic categories: kingdom, phylum, class, order, family, genus, and species. Students of anatomy also make heavy use of mnemonics. For example, there are 12 pairs of nerves that exit the brain directly. (All other commands to and from the brain flow through the nerves that make up the spinal cord.) To learn these 12 cranial nerves, many students memorize the sentence shown in Figure 5.6 and use the first letter in each word to remember the nerves: olfactory, optic, and so on.

FIGURE 5.6 ⸱A Mnemonic for Neuroanatomy

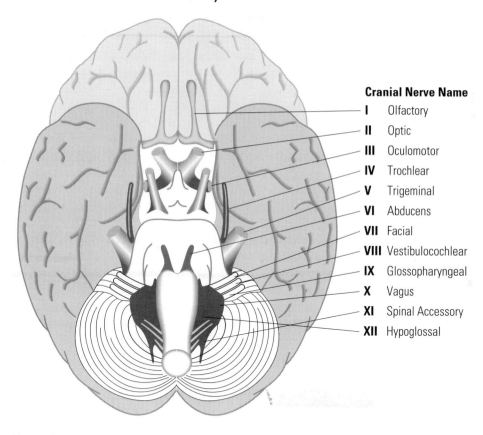

Cranial Nerve Name

I	Olfactory
II	Optic
III	Oculomotor
IV	Trochlear
V	Trigeminal
VI	Abducens
VII	Facial
VIII	Vestibulocochlear
IX	Glossopharyngeal
X	Vagus
XI	Spinal Accessory
XII	Hypoglossal

Almost all signals coming into or out of the brain pass through the spinal cord. Twelve nerves, however, exit the brain directly. These are the cranial nerves, and they are visible in this diagram of the bottom surface of the brain. Students are often asked to memorize the names of these nerves, and they can make their task easier by memorizing this sentence: "On old Olympus towering top, a famous vocal German viewed some hops," with the words' first letters corresponding to the first letters of the nerves' names.

These techniques serve students well, underscoring the fact that mnemonics are indeed effective. A first-letter mnemonic, just like any other mnemonic, imposes organization and unity on a list, and here, as always, organization aids memory.

But let's also note that there's a downside to using mnemonics in a classroom setting: In using a mnemonic, you typically focus on just one aspect of the material to be remembered—just the first letter of the word to be remembered, for example, or (returning to an earlier case) just some specific relationship between "bun" and chemistry. This focus guarantees that the selected link receives much attention and so is well established in memory. But focusing in this way also means that you *won't* pay much attention to *other* aspects of the material to be remembered. In many settings, this means that you'll cut short your effort toward understanding this material, and likewise your effort toward finding multiple connections between the material and other things you know.

Notice, then, that mnemonic use involves a trade-off: More attention focused on one or two memory connections means less attention spent on thinking about other connections, including the other connections that might help you to understand the material. This trade-off will be fine if you don't care very much about the meaning of the material. (Do you care why biologists count "order" as a subset of "class," rather than the other way around?) But this trade-off is troubling if you're trying to memorize material that is meaningful. In this case, you would be better served by a memory strategy that leads you to seek out multiple connections between the material you're trying to learn and things you already know. Indeed, this effort toward multiple links will help you in two ways. First, it will obviously foster your understanding of the material to be remembered, and so will lead to better, richer, deeper learning. Second, the multiple links will also help you to retrieve this information later on: We've already suggested that memory connections serve as retrieval paths; and the more paths there are, the easier it will be to find the target material later.

For all of these reasons, mnemonic use may be ill-advised in many situations. Nonetheless, the fact remains that mnemonics are immensely useful in some settings (what were those rainbow colors?), and this in turn confirms our initial point: Organization promotes memory.

Understanding and Memorizing

So far, we've said a lot about how people memorize rather impoverished stimulus materials—lists of randomly selected words, or colors that have to be learned in exactly the right sequence. In our day-to-day lives, however, we typically want to remember more meaningful, and more complicated, material. We wish to remember the episodes we experience, the details of rich scenes we have observed, the plots of movies we have seen, or the many-step arguments we have read in a book. Do the same memory principles apply to these cases?

The answer to this question is clearly yes. Our memory for events, or pictures, or complex bodies of knowledge is enormously dependent on our being able to organize the material to be remembered. We remember best what we have organized best; we remember poorly when we can neither find nor create an organizing scheme.

With these more complicated materials, though, and as we've already suggested, our best bet for organization is not some arbitrary skeleton, like those used in peg-word systems. Instead, the optimal organization of these complex materials is generally dependent on understanding. That is, we remember best what we understand best. There are many ways to show that this is true. For example, one can give people a sentence or paragraph to read and test their comprehension by asking questions about the material or by asking them to paraphrase the material. Some time later, we can test their memory for this material. Moreover, we can use memory materials difficult enough so that understanding is not guaranteed, and in this way, we can look at different degrees of success in understanding and ask how this success influences memory.

The results are straightforward: The better the participants' understanding of a sentence or a paragraph, the greater the likelihood that they will remember it later. The more accurately they could answer questions immediately after reading the material, the greater the chance that they will remember the material after a delay. (For reviews of the relevant research, see Baddeley, 1976; and Bransford, 1979. For some complications, see Kintsch, 1994; we'll return to these complications in Chapters 6 and 7.)

This pattern can be demonstrated in the laboratory; it can also be demonstrated in people's day-to-day lives. For example, consider the material you are learning right now, in the courses you are taking. Will you remember this material 5 years from now, or 10, or 20? The answer depends on how well you understand the material. One measure of understanding is the grade you earn in a course: With full and rich understanding, you are likely to earn an A; with poor understanding, your grade is likely to be lower! One would expect, therefore, that the higher someone's grade in a course, the more likely that person is to remember the course contents, even many years later. This is exactly what the data show. Plainly, the better your understanding, the better (and longer-lasting) your memory will be (M. Conway, Cohen, & Stanhope, 1992).

The relationship between understanding and memory can also be demonstrated in another way, by *manipulating* whether people understand the material or not. For example, in an experiment by Bransford and Johnson (1972), participants read this passage:

The procedure is actually quite simple. First you arrange items into different groups. Of course one pile may be sufficient depending on how much there is to do. If you have to go somewhere else due to lack of facilities that is the next step; otherwise you are pretty well set. It is important not to overdo things. That is, it is better to do too few things at once than too many. In the short run, this may not seem important but complications can easily arise. A mistake can be expensive as well. At first, the whole procedure will seem complicated. Soon, however, it will become just another facet of life. It is difficult to foresee any end to the necessity for this task in the immediate future, but then, one never can tell. After the procedure is completed one arranges the materials into different groups again. Then they can be put into their appropriate places. Eventually they will be used once more and the whole cycle will then have to be repeated. However, that is part of life. (p. 722)

You are probably puzzled by this passage; so are most research participants. The story is easy to understand, though, if we give it a title: "Doing the Laundry." In the experiment, some participants were given the title before reading the passage; others were not. Participants in the first group easily understood the passage, and were able to remember it after a delay. The second group, reading the same words, were not confronting a meaningful passage and did poorly on the memory test. (For related data, see Bransford & Franks, 1971; and Sulin & Dooling, 1974.)

Similar effects can be documented with nonverbal materials. Consider, for example, the picture shown in Figure 5.7. This picture at first looks like a bunch of meaningless blotches; with some study, though, you may discover that a familiar

---

FIGURE 5.7 | Comprehension Also Aids Memory for Pictures

People who perceive this picture as a pattern of meaningless blotches are unlikely to remember the picture. People who perceive the "hidden" form do remember the picture. (After Wiseman & Neisser, 1974)

object is depicted. Wiseman and Neisser (1974) tested people's memory for this picture. Consistent with what we have seen so far, their memory was good if they understood the picture, and bad otherwise. (Also see G. H. Bower, Karlin, & Dueck, 1975; Mandler & Ritchey, 1977; Rubin & Kontis, 1983.)

Chunking and Entry Into Long-Term Memory

One might object to these examples, however, on the grounds that they involve a trick: In the "laundry" study, we are not really testing people's memory for the passage. All the participants need to remember is the passage's title. Given their prior knowledge about how one washes clothes, that would be enough to allow them to reconstruct the passage at the time of test. Likewise for pictorial materials: To do well on a memory test, participants don't need to remember the complex pattern of blotches in Figure 5.7. Instead, remembering a one-word summary (e.g., "dalmatian") might be enough. In either case, it is no surprise that understanding aids memory, because understanding might literally reduce the amount of information to be remembered—a title instead of a passage, a summary instead of a complicated pattern.

This suggestion—that understanding reduces the load on memory—turns out to be well founded. The only bit of confusion in the preceding paragraph lies in the idea that this is some sort of memory "trick." Instead, what is at stake here is an important principle of memory, a principle with wide application. As we have already noted, understanding a story depends in part on the discovery of various connections—among the various elements of the story, and between the story and other things you know. We have argued that one function of these connections is to render the story findable in memory later on. But an equally important function of the connections is to unify the elements of the story, so that we think of them not as individual elements but as constituents in an interconnected whole. It is then this whole that enters memory, rather than the separate items—one unit rather than many.

There are a great many illustrations of this point, but a classic example was devised by Katona, whose work we have already mentioned. Katona asked his research participants to learn the following string of digits:

$$1\,4\,9\,1\,6\,2\,5\,3\,6\,4\,9\,6\,4\,8\,1\,1\,0\,0\,1\,2\,1$$

The data follow a familiar pattern. People remember well the first two or three digits (a primacy effect) and the last few (recency), but they cannot easily remember the full list. We then point out to the participants that the list follows a simple pattern. To help them see the pattern, we add some punctuation:

$$1, 4, 9, 16, 25, 36, \ldots$$

In this form, you probably recognize the series as being $1^2, 2^2, 3^2, 4^2, 5^2, 6^2, \ldots, 11^2$. Once participants see this, the results are rather different. They can now remember the entire list perfectly and, in fact, can remember the list even if we extend it ($\ldots 1\,4\,4\,1\,6\,9$).

When participants find the connections that unify this list, they turn the 21 separate digits into a single whole. In effect, they are translating the number series into a rule or a sentence ("The list consists of the squares of the integers from 1 to 11"), and the sentence is appreciably easier to remember than the original series was. Ironically, this translation from a number series to a sentence actually increases the sophistication and complexity of what is being remembered: Memorizing the original number series required that one merely recognize the various digits. In contrast, the summary sentence requires comprehension of English syntax, and of the mathematical terms "squares" and "integers." But this is not what is crucial for memory. The number of memory packages is more important than the internal complexity of these packages, and so there is considerable gain from translating 21 packages into one.

Notice that all of this precisely parallels claims that we made earlier in the chapter about working memory. We discussed then that more information could be packed into this memory if the information was "chunked." Thus, for example, a list of seven letters might fill working memory if the person thinks of the list as containing individual letters. If the same list is chunked into two- or three-letter syllables, then the load on working memory is much reduced. By integrating and unifying the materials, you decrease the number of chunks, and this helps memory. Earlier we made this point with regard to short-term remembering, but the idea is exactly the same when we are talking about longer-term remembering: Understanding serves to unify material, and this makes remembering easier.

There is also another parallel between our earlier comments about chunking and the issues now before us: We have already noted that chunking can be a source of error: If the letters C and R are chunked into the syllable "car," then there is a chance that someone might mistakenly remember that an A was present in the original material. In other words, errors can arise in the "unpacking" of chunks. The same is true of long-term storage: It's much easier to remember the single phrase "a story about laundry" than it is to remember the 180 words in the original stimulus. But, later on, on the basis of this phrase in memory, one might recall a mention of "detergent," or a reference to "water temperature," even though there was none. Chunking clearly improves memory, but with a potential cost, and we will have much more to say about this cost in Chapter 7.

The Study of Memory Acquisition

This chapter has ostensibly been about memory acquisition. How do we acquire new memories? How is new information, new knowledge, established in long-term memory? Or, in more pragmatic terms, what is the best, most effective, most efficient way to learn? We now can answer these questions, but in important ways our discussion has also indicated that we need to place these questions into a broader context—looking not just at acquisition, but also at the substantial contribution from the memorizer, as well as the powerful interconnections among acquisition, retrieval, and storage.

The Contribution of the Memorizer

Over and over, we have seen that memory is facilitated by organizing and understanding the materials to be remembered. Hand in hand with this, it appears that memories are not established by sheer contact with the items you're hoping to remember. If people are merely exposed to the items, without giving those items any thought, then subsequent recall of those items will be poor.

These points immediately draw our attention to the role played by the memorizer. If we wish to predict whether this or that event will be recalled, it is not enough to know that someone was exposed to the event. Likewise, if we wish to predict memory performance, it is not enough to describe the memory "equipment" possessed by each of us—e.g., a working memory with various components, a long-term memory with a specific structure. Instead, if we wish to predict someone's recall performance, we need to pay attention to what the person was doing at the time of learning. Did she elect to do mere maintenance rehearsal, or did she engage the material in some other way? If the latter, how did she think about the material? Did she pay attention to the appearance of the words or to their meaning? If she thought about meaning, was she able to understand the material? Did she think about the material as involving separate bits, or did she find some unifying theme? It is these considerations that are crucial for predicting the success of memory.

The contribution of the memorizer is also visible in another way: We have argued that learning depends on the person's making connections, but connections to what? If someone wants to connect the to-be-remembered material to other knowledge, to other memories, then the person needs to have that other knowledge; she needs to have other (potentially relevant) memories. Thus, what people contribute to learning also includes their own prior knowledge. If someone happens to enter the learning situation with a great deal of relevant knowledge, then he or she arrives with a considerable advantage—a rich framework onto which the new materials can be "hooked." If someone enters the learning situation with little relevant background, then there is no framework, nothing to connect to, and learning will be correspondingly more difficult. Thus, if we wish to predict the success of memorizing, we also need to consider what other knowledge the individual brings into the situation.

The Links Among Acquisition, Retrieval, and Storage

These points lead us to another theme of immense importance. Our emphasis in this chapter was on memory acquisition, but we have now seen several indications that claims about acquisition cannot be separated from claims about memory storage and memory retrieval. For example, why is recall improved by organization and understanding? We have suggested that organization provides retrieval paths, making the memories "findable" later on, when the time comes to remember the target information. Therefore, our claims about acquisition rest on assumptions about memory retrieval and the usefulness of memory connections within retrieval.

Likewise, we have just noted that a person's ability to learn new material depends, in part, on having a framework of prior knowledge to which the new materials can be tied. In this way, claims about memory acquisition must be coordinated with claims about the nature of what is already in storage.

The same can be said about chunking, both in working memory and in long-term storage. In most cases, chunking depends on understanding, and understanding rests on things you already know. The number series, "1 4 9 1 6 . . ." can be chunked as the squares of the digits only if you already know what the squares of the digits are. The passage about laundry is understood only by virtue of your prior knowledge about how clothing is washed. In both of these cases, therefore, chunking at the time of memory acquisition is completely tied up with knowledge you already have, and so again we see the interdependence of memory acquisition and knowledge already in storage.

We close this chapter, then, with a two-sided message. We have offered many claims about memory acquisition and about how memories are established. In particular, we have offered claims about the importance of memory connections, organization, and understanding. At the same time, though, these claims cannot stand by themselves. At the level of theory, our account of acquisition has already made references to the role of prior knowledge and to the nature of memory retrieval. At the level of data, we will soon see that these interactions among acquisition, knowledge, and retrieval have important implications—for learning, for forgetting, and for memory accuracy. We turn next to some of those implications.

Chapter Summary

1. It is convenient to think of memorizing as having separate stages: First, one acquires new information (acquisition). Next, the information remains in storage until it is needed. Finally, the information is retrieved. However, this separation among the stages may be misleading: For example, in order to memorize new information, one forms connections between this information and things one already knows. In this fashion, the acquisition stage is intertwined with the retrieval of information already in storage.

2. Information that is currently being considered is stored in working memory; information that is not currently active but is nonetheless in storage is in long-term memory. Working memory is sometimes likened to the mental "desk space," long-term memory to the mental "library." The distinction between these two forms of memory is often described in terms of the modal model and has been examined in many studies of the serial-position curve. The primacy portion of this curve reflects those items that have had extra opportunity to reach long-term memory; the recency portion of this curve reflects the accurate retrieval of items currently in working memory.

3. Working memory is more than a passive storage container. Instead, this is where the mind's filing, cross-referencing, and active contemplation take place. This activity is carried out by working memory's central executive. For mere storage, the executive often relies on a small number of low-level assistants, including the articulatory rehearsal loop and the visuospatial buffer, which work as mental scratch pads. The activity inherent in this overall system is reflected in the flexible way material can be chunked in working memory; the activity is also reflected in current measures of the active memory span.

4. Working memory's "central executive" may simply be the name we give to a small number of mental resources that serve to order, organize, and control our mental lives. These resources rely heavily on brain tissue in the prefrontal cortex; this is reflected in the fact that damage to the prefrontal cortex causes difficulties in tasks that require someone to plan and organize their activities.

5. Maintenance rehearsal serves to keep information in working memory and requires little effort, but it has little impact on subsequent recall. To maximize one's chances of recall, elaborative rehearsal is needed, in which one seeks connections within the material to be remembered, or connections between the material to be remembered and things one already knows.

6. In many cases, elaborative processing takes the form of attention to meaning. This attention to meaning is called deep processing, in contrast to attention to sounds or visual form, which is considered shallow processing. Many studies have shown that deep processing leads to good memory performance later on, even if the deep processing was done with no intention of memorizing the target material. In fact, the intention to learn has no direct effect on performance; what matters instead is how someone engages or thinks about the material to be remembered.

7. Deep processing has its beneficial effects by creating effective retrieval paths that can be used later on. Retrieval paths depend on connections linking one memory to another; each connection provides a path potentially leading to a target memory. Mnemonic strategies build on this same idea and focus on the creation of specific memory connections, often tying the to-be-remembered material to a frame (a familiar location or a strongly structured poem, for example).

8. Perhaps the best way to form memory connections is to understand the material to be remembered. In understanding, one forms many connections within the material to be remembered, and also between this material and other knowledge. With all of these retrieval paths, it becomes easy to locate this material in memory. Consistent with these suggestions, studies have shown a close correspondence between the ability to understand some material and the ability to recall that material later on; this pattern has been demonstrated with stories, visual patterns, number series, and many other sorts of stimuli.

Interconnections Between Acquisition and Retrieval

Putting information into long-term memory helps us only if we can retrieve it later on. Otherwise, it would be like putting money into a savings account from which no withdrawals are possible, or like writing books that could never be read. And it is equally clear that there are different ways to retrieve information from memory. We can try to recall the information ("What was the name of your tenth-grade homeroom teacher?") or to recognize it ("Was the name perhaps Miller?"). If we try to recall the information, a variety of cues may or may not be available (we might be told, as a hint, that the name began with an *M* or rhymed with "tiller").

In Chapter 5, we largely ignored these variations in retrieval. We talked as if material was well established in memory or was not, with no regard for how the material would be retrieved from memory. We spoke about certain principles as promoting memory, as though these claims held true independently of how the memory would be used. There is every reason to believe, however, that we cannot ignore these variations in retrieval, and in this chapter we will examine the interactions between how exactly a bit of information was learned, and how it is retrieved later on.

- Learning does not simply place information in memory; instead, learning prepares you to retrieve the information in a particular way. As a result, learning that is good preparation for one sort of memory retrieval may be inadequate for other sorts of retrieval.

- In this chapter, we examine several lines of evidence showing a clear linkage between how material is learned and how it can be retrieved. In general, the idea is that retrieval will be best if your mental perspective is the same during learning and during retrieval.

- Some experiences also seem to produce unconscious memories, and an examination of these "implicit memory" effects will help us understand the broad set of ways in which memory influences us, and also help us see where the feeling of familiarity comes from.

- Finally, an examination of amnesia confirms a central theme of the chapter—namely, that we cannot speak of "good" or "bad" memory in general, but need to evaluate memory by considering how, and for what purposes, the memory will be used.

Retrieval Hints and Cues

Why should there be a relationship between the particular way you learn and the particular form of memory retrieval? Let's start with an informal example. Then, as we move forward in the chapter, we can look at the evidence that confirms the pattern implied by the example, and we can also develop the theory that goes with this pattern.

Imagine that you hear a history lecture in which Professor Jones speaks about the early days of the Vietnam War, and let's say that, during the lecture, you find yourself thinking about how this lecture is similar to other lectures you have heard by Professor Jones. These thoughts will establish a number of memory connections between this lecture and the others you have heard, and these connections can serve as retrieval paths—that is, paths that will guide your thoughts if you later want to work your way back to the target memory (i.e., your memory of the Vietnam lecture).

It is easy to see how these retrieval paths might help you: Imagine that, a month later, someone asks you, "What are Professor Jones's views about the Vietnam War?" This question may call the relevant lecture to mind, and if so, then you can answer immediately. But after a month's time, the question may not be enough to trigger thoughts about that lecture. Even so, the question will get you thinking about Professor Jones and his various lectures. And because you've established memory connections between Jones's other lectures and the lecture you seek, these connections are likely to guide your thoughts from the lectures that first come to mind to the target material: the class on Vietnam (Figure 6.1).

But now imagine that you try to locate this same memory via a different retrieval path: "Does the current political situation remind you of anything you have learned recently?" Under these circumstances, what you need is some memory connection between "the current political situation" and the target memory. That

FIGURE 6.1   Memory Retrieval Paths

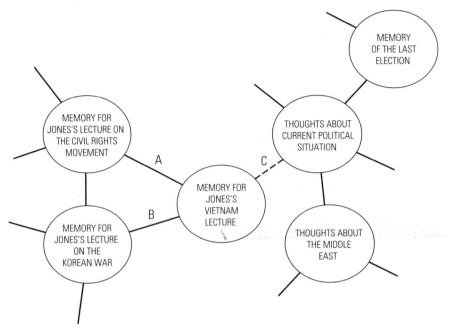

Imagine that, when hearing Professor Jones's lecture about Vietnam, you thought about the relationship between this lecture and other lectures you had heard from Professor Jones. Thinking about these relationships would establish in your memory the connections labeled here "A" and "B." As a result, the next time you thought about, say, Jones's lecture on the civil rights movement, you would be guided (via connection A) back to your memory for the Vietnam lecture. These connections might not help you, though, if someone later asks you, "Have you learned anything recently that's related to the current political situation?" In order for this question to trigger the Vietnam memory, you would need connection C, but that's not a connection you created when you thought about the Vietnam lecture. As a result, a question about the "current political situation" might not call the Vietnam lecture to mind.

connection would lead you from your starting point (the question you've just been asked) to your goal. It is of little use in this setting that you've established connections between Jones's other lectures and the target memory, since those are not the connections you need. Therefore, for this memory search, your earlier learning may not be helpful. When you heard the lecture, you did form connections, but they turn out not to be the connections you need right now: They won't bring you from your starting point in this search to the target material.

To put this into broader terms, the idea here is that any bit of learning might prepare you for some forms of memory retrieval but not others. If your learning produces, say, a connection between memory X and memory Y, your thoughts will be guided toward Y whenever you're thinking about X. But this memory connection will have no impact if you happen not to be thinking about X. It's on this basis that learning prepares you to access (and thus to retrieve) a memory *from a particular starting point*, and the learning will help you if you're currently at that starting point. Otherwise, the path may be of little use.

State-Dependent Learning

All of this fits well with the suggestions we made in Chapter 5. There we argued that memory depends on connections, either connections within the material to be remembered, or connections between this material and other things you already know. We also suggested that these connections function by making memories "findable." In other words, these connections serve as retrieval paths along which you can "travel" in order to reach information in long-term storage.

These ideas, as simple as they are, have many implications, and our "Professor Jones" example highlights one of the implications: We may not be able to speak of any bit of learning as "good" or "bad," as "effective" or "ineffective." Instead, learning involves the formation of connections, and these connections will be effective for some purposes (e.g., for retrieving the information from a certain set of starting points), but less effective for other purposes. By analogy: Is it a good thing or bad to build a new highway going into Chicago from the south? The answer depends on the situation: This highway will be very useful if later you want to reach Chicago from the south. But the highway won't be helpful if you hope later to enter Chicago from the west. Memory connections work the same way.

Evidence for these claims comes from many sources. Consider first a broad class of studies on **state-dependent learning** (J. E. Eich, 1980; Overton, 1985). In these studies, there are typically two different learning situations and two different tests. One of the test formats is matched to one of the learning situations, and one to the other learning situation. Hence, we end up with what psychologists call a "2 × 2" design.

In one such study, Godden and Baddeley (1975) asked deep-sea divers to learn various materials. Some of the divers learned the material while sitting by the edge of the water, not wearing their diving masks. Others learned the material while 20 feet underwater, hearing the material via a special communication set. Within each group, half of the divers were then tested while above water, and half were tested below (Figure 6.2).

Underwater, the world has a different look, feel, and sound, and this could easily influence what thoughts come to mind for the divers when they're in this situation. This will set the mental context for learning and so will shape the sorts of memory connections the divers form during the learning, and thus what retrieval paths are available later on. To put this concretely, imagine that a diver is thinking about the sound of his breathing while underwater. This might lead the diver to form some memory connection between these thoughts about breathing and the

FIGURE 6.2 The Design of a State-Dependent Learning Experiment

Test while

	On land	Underwater
On land	Learning and test circumstances match	
Underwater		Learning and test circumstances match

Learn while

Half of the participants (deep-sea divers) learned the test material while underwater; half learned while sitting on land. Likewise, half were tested while underwater; half were tested on land. We expect a retrieval advantage if the learning and test circumstances match. Hence, we expect better performance in the top left and bottom right cells.

materials to be remembered. If this diver is then back underwater at the time of the memory test, the sound of underwater breathing is again on the scene and may lead the diver back into the same thoughts. Once thinking these thoughts, the diver is likely to benefit from the memory connection linking these thoughts to the target materials. In contrast, if the diver is on land during the memory test, then the sound of breathing is absent, and so those thoughts won't be triggered and the connections will have no influence.

With this logic in mind, we would expect the divers who learned material while underwater to remember the material best if tested underwater; this will increase the chance that they're able to use the memory connections they established earlier. Likewise, the divers who learned on land should do best if tested on land. This is exactly what the data show (Figure 6.3).

Related results have been obtained with odors present or absent during learning (Cann & Ross, 1989; Schab, 1990): Memory is best if the olfactory environment is the same during memory retrieval as it was during the initial learning. Similar data have been obtained in studies designed to mimic the real-life situation of a college student: The research participants read a two-page article on psychoimmunology, similar to the sorts of readings they might encounter in their college courses. Half the participants read the article in a quiet setting; half read it in noisy

| FIGURE 6.3 | State Dependency From a Change in Physical Circumstances |

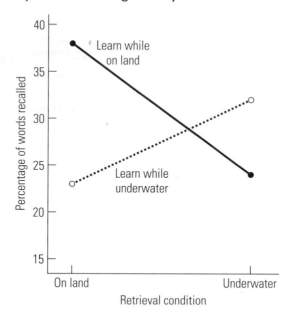

Materials learned while on land are best recalled while on land. Materials learned while underwater are best recalled while underwater. The change in circumstances doesn't obliterate the benefits of learning (in all conditions, performance is considerably better than 0%); nonetheless, the differences between conditions are substantial.

circumstances. When given a short-answer test later on, those who read the article in quiet did best if tested in quiet—67% correct answers, compared to 54% correct if tested in a noisy environment. Those who read the article in a noisy environment did better if tested in a noisy environment—62% correct, compared to 46% (Grant et al., 1998; also see Balch, Bowman, & Mohler, 1992; S. Smith, 1985; S. M. Smith & Vela, 2001).

S. M. Smith, Glenberg, and Bjork (1978) report the same pattern if learning and testing simply take place in different rooms: Recall is best if done in the room in which the initial learning took place. Here, though, there is an interesting twist: In one procedure, the participants learned materials in one room and were tested in a different room. Just before testing, however, the participants were urged to think about the room in which they had learned—what it looked like, and how it made them feel. When tested, these participants performed as well as those participants for whom there was no room change (S. Smith, 1979). What seems to matter, therefore, is not so much the physical context, but the psychological context—a result that's entirely consistent with our account of this effect.

Changes in One's Approach to the Memory Materials

In a number of settings, therefore, recall performance is best if someone's state (internal or external) at the time of testing matches their state at the time of learning. This pattern shows the benefit of **context reinstatement**—that is, improved memory performance if we re-create the context that was in place during learning.

Let's emphasize, though, that the context has its effect only because it influences how the person thinks about the materials to be remembered; it's these thoughts, and the perspective the person has during learning, that really matter for memory, and not the physical environment. On this basis, we should be able to get the same result with no change in physical context, but instead by manipulating someone's perspective directly.

Fisher and Craik (1977) presented their participants with a series of word pairs. The participants were instructed to learn the second word in each pair, and to use the first word in each pair only "as an aid to remembering the target words." For half of the pairs, the "context word" was semantically associated with the target word; for example, if participants were shown "cat," they were also shown the context word "dog." This association should have encouraged them to think about the words' meanings. For the other pairs, the context word was one that rhymed with the target (e.g., if shown "cat," they were also shown the context word "hat"). This association should have encouraged participants to think about the target word's sound.

When the time came for a test, participants were given either a hint concerning meaning ("Was there a word on the list associated with 'dog'"?) or a hint concerning sound ("Was there a word on the list associated with 'hat'"?). Table 6.1 shows the results. Note, first, the column all the way to the right (averaging together trials with meaning hints and trials with sound hints). Consistent with the data in Chapter 5, thinking about meaning generally leads to better memory, in this case with an impressive 30.5-to-21.5 advantage. That is, people who thought about meaning at the time of learning remembered about 50% more than people who thought about

TABLE 6.1 Percentage of Words Recalled on Testing After Prior Association With Either Meaning or Sound

	Type of Hint		
	Meaning	Sound	Both Combined
Type of processing at time of learning			
Meaning	44%	17%	30.5%
Sound	17%	26%	21.5%

After Fisher & Craik, 1977.

sound. But now look at the table's other two columns. If participants thought about meaning at the time of learning, they did considerably better in the test if the cues provided by the experimenter concerned meaning. The same was true for sound: If they thought about sound at the time of learning, then they did better with a cue concerning the word's sound.

In fact, the table shows two separate influences on memory working at the same time: an advantage for thinking about meaning (overall, performance is better in the top row) and an advantage for matched learning and test conditions (overall, performance is best in the main diagonal of the table). In the table's top left cell, these effects combine, and here performance is better than in any other condition. These effects clash in the column showing the results of the sound hint. The advantage from thinking about meaning favors the top cell in this column; the advantage from matched learning and test conditions favors the bottom cell. As it turns out, the match effect wins over the levels-of-processing effect: "Deep but unmatched" (17%) is inferior to "not so deep, but matched" (26%). Thus, the advantage for deep processing is simply overturned in this situation.

Encoding Specificity

It is possible to view the data presented so far in a slightly different way: When you hear Jones's lecture about Vietnam, what goes into your memory is not just a record of that lecture; what's in your memory is that lecture *plus* some record of what you were thinking about, in response to the lecture. In the terms we used earlier, what is preserved in your memory is some record of the lecture plus the set of connections you established, in thinking about the lecture.

This extra material in your memory can obviously influence your search for the target information. That's what we have been emphasizing so far, in showcasing the role of these connections as retrieval paths. But this extra material can, in a sense, also change the *meaning* of what is remembered: In some situations, "memory plus *this* set of connections" has a different meaning from "memory plus *that* set of connections." That change in meaning, in turn, can have profound consequences for how you remember the past. To see this, let's consider experiments on **encoding specificity.**

In these experiments, people are typically asked to memorize a list of words. Midway down the list might be the word "jam," and by manipulating the context, we can arrange things so that participants understand this word as indicating the stuff one makes from berries or grapes. (We can arrange this, for example, by preceding the word "jam" with a word like "jelly" or "fruit." For more on this sort of priming effect, see Chapter 8.) A short time later, we test memory by presenting various items and asking whether or not these appeared on the previous list. "Jam" is presented, but now we arrange the context so that "jam" is understood as in "traffic jam." Under these circumstances, people usually will say that the word was not on the previous list, even though their memory for the list seems to be quite good. That is, people are quite likely to remember most of the other words on the list, even though they don't remember seeing our test word.

This kind of demonstration has been reported in numerous forms by Endel Tulving (Tulving, 1983; also see Hunt & Ellis, 1974; Light & Carter-Sobell, 1970). Why is this called "encoding specificity"? This label reminds us that what one encodes (i.e., places into memory) is indeed specific—not just the physical stimulus as it was encountered, but the stimulus together with its context. In the experiment just described, the context would include what one thinks and understands about the word. As a result, when participants are later presented with the word in some other context, they ask themselves, "Does this match anything I learned previously?" and they *correctly* answer no. And their answer is indeed correct. It is as if the participants learned the word "other" and were later asked whether they had been shown the word "the." In fact, "the" does appear as part of "other" or, more precisely, the letters *T H E* do appear within the word "other." But it is the whole that people learn, not the parts. Therefore, if you've seen "other," it's entirely sensible to deny that you have seen "the" or, for that matter, "he" or "her," even though all these letter combinations are contained within "other."

Learning a list of words works in much the same way. The letters *J A M* were contained in what the research participants learned, just as *T H E* is contained in "other." In both cases, however, what was learned was the broader, integrated experience: the word as the perceiver organized it, the word as the perceiver understood it. Therefore "jam" as in "traffic jam" *isn't* what participants learned earlier, and so they're correct in asserting that this item wasn't on the earlier list.

Many other results also fit with these assertions. For example, we can show people the pattern in Figure 6.4, and arrange things so that they perceive the pattern as a vase on a black background. (As before, we can use a priming procedure, perhaps previously showing the participants pictures of other white figures on black backgrounds.) A few minutes later, we show the picture again, but this time we prime participants so that they see two profiles against a white background. We now ask them whether they have ever seen this figure before. This should be an extremely easy task because, after all, they have just seen this pattern. Nonetheless, people often assert that they have not seen the figure before (Kanizsa, 1979; Rock, 1983). Apparently, what matters for picture memory is, just as with words, the *stimulus as understood*, not the geometrically defined picture itself. (We considered a number of related results in the early pages of Chapter 3, when we discussed the interpretive nature of perception.)

Once again, therefore, we are led to some familiar themes. What happens during learning is the establishment of a memory that can be retrieved in a certain way, from a certain perspective. If the perspective changes—if, in particular, your understanding of the test item changes—then the original memory may not be retrieved. In light of this, we're led once more to the suggestion that we should not speak of "good learning" (or "less good learning") in general. Instead, what counts

FIGURE 6.4   The Ambiguous Vase/Profiles Figure

This figure, which we first met in Chapter 3, can be perceived either as a white vase against a black background or as two black profiles against a white background.

as good learning depends on later events: Whether it is better to learn underwater or on land depends on where one will be tested. Whether it is better to learn while listening to jazz or while sitting in a quiet room depends on the music background of the memory test. Even whether it is best to attend to meaning depends to some extent on whether meaning will be prominent when the time comes for memory retrieval.

Different Forms of Memory Testing

Our discussion so far has focused on the learner's circumstances and perspective, and whether these are the same during memory retrieval as they were during the original learning. Similar conclusions emerge when we consider another way memory retrieval can vary: in the nature of the memory test itself.

Both in the laboratory and in day-to-day life, we often want to **recall** information we encountered earlier. This means that we're presented with some cue that broadly identifies the information that we seek, but then we need to come up with the information on our own: "What was the name of that great restaurant that your parents took us to?" "Can you remember the words to that song?" "Where were you last Saturday?"

This stands in contrast to memory tests that hinge on **recognition**. In this case, information is presented to us, and we must decide whether it's the sought-after information or not. "Is this the man who robbed you?" "I'm sure I'll recognize the street when we get there." "If you let me taste that wine, I'll tell you if it's the same one we had last time."

These two modes of retrieval—recall and recognition—turn out to be fundamentally different from each other. Recall, by its very nature, requires memory *search,* because you have to come up with the sought-after item on your own; you need to locate that item within memory. As a result, recall depends heavily on memory connections because it is the connections (serving as retrieval paths) that support the search. It's no surprise, then, that forms of learning that promote connections are particularly useful for recall testing. Specifically, recall is much more likely if you thought about relationships during the original learning—relationships between the materials to be remembered and other things you know, or between the materials to be remembered and other aspects of the learning environment. Thinking about these relationships creates connections, and these can (potentially) lead you to the information you seek.

In some cases, recognition also depends on memory search, but unlike recall, it's not a search for the item to be remembered. Instead, it's a search for the earlier episode in which you encountered this item, and, if you can remember the episode, that will lead to a successful recognition. For example, imagine that you are taking a recognition test, and the fourth word on the test is "loon." You might say to yourself, "Yes, I remember seeing this word on the previous list, because I remember the image that came to mind when I saw this word." In this example, the test word ("loon") has triggered a memory for an episode (namely, the episode in which you saw the word in the study list), and this allows you to make the decision that, yes, you did see this word earlier. Your performance on the memory test, therefore, will be promoted by memory connections that lead your thoughts from the word "loon" to the memory of the earlier encounter, and so success, as with recall, will be more likely if you formed the relevant connections during learning.

But recognition can also proceed in a different fashion: Let's say that you're taking a recognition test, and the fifth word on the test is "butler." In response to this word, you might say to yourself, "I don't specifically remember seeing this word on the list, but this word feels extraordinarily familiar. If the word wasn't on the list, then it wouldn't seem so familiar. Therefore, it must have been on the list." In this case you do not have what's called **source memory**; that is, you do not have any recollection of the source of your current knowledge. But you do have a strong sense of **familiarity,** and you're willing to make an inference about where that familiarity came from. In other words, you attribute the familiarity to the earlier encounter, and thanks to this **attribution,** you will probably respond yes on the recognition test.

Familiarity and Source Memory

Familiarity and source memory are clearly distinct from each other. We know this from many observations, including the fact that it is possible to have either one of these without the other. For example, the "butler" case just described is one in which you have familiarity but no source memory. The same pattern can easily be observed outside of the lab: Consider the relatively common experience in which you are walking down the street, or perhaps turn on the television, and see a familiar face. Immediately you know the face is familiar, but you are unable to say just why the face is familiar. Is it someone you saw in a movie last month? Is it the driver of the bus you often take? You are at a loss to answer these questions; all you know is that the face is familiar.

In (maddening!) cases like these, you cannot "place" the memory, you cannot identify the episode in which the face was last encountered. But you are certain the face is familiar, even though you don't know why. This is familiarity without source memory.

The inverse case (source memory without familiarity) is less common but can also be demonstrated. For example, we considered an illustration of this pattern in Chapter 2 when we considered Capgras syndrome: In this syndrome, the patient has detailed, complete, accurate memories of the past, but no sense at all of familiarity, and faces (of family members, of friends) seem hauntingly *un*familiar.

Source memory and familiarity can also be distinguished on the basis of various neuroscience findings. For example, the pattern of brain waves is different when participants are making judgments based largely on familiarity, in comparison to cases in which they are making judgments influenced by both familiarity and source memory.[1] This difference indicates that these two forms of memory depend on distinguishable brain areas and distinguishable types of brain activity. (Rugg & Yonelinas, 2003, review these and other neuroscience findings pertinent to the distinction between source memory and familiarity; also see Yonelinas, 2001. For a broad hypothesis about how familiarity and source memory are supported by the nervous system, see Hodges & Graham, 2001.)

Finally, source memory and familiarity are also distinct in terms of the sorts of learning that promote each of these, and that brings us back to our main theme: the interaction between type of learning and type of memory retrieval. Source memory, we've said, is promoted by learning that creates memory connections: In a recall test, these connections can lead you from thoughts about the setting ("What was the name of that restaurant?") to the target information ("Oh yeah, it was Reuben's Place"). In a recognition test, these connections can lead you from thoughts about the test item ("loon") to thoughts about where it was that you last met that item. In either case, what you need is a link between the test item and a setting, and that's why attention to connections during learning—attention to relationships—promotes source memory.

---

[1]Brain waves are observed by means of precise voltage measurements at various positions on the scalp. Remember that the activity of individual neurons is essentially electrical in nature (see Chapter 2), and when large populations of neurons are active at the same time, their combined electrical activity produces changes that are big enough to be measured on the scalp. This is the basis for electroencephalography, or EEG recording, and provides one of our tools for observing the activity of the intact brain.

What about familiarity? Here it turns out that merely focusing on the material to be learned, with no thought about connections, can be quite helpful. In this case, no retrieval paths will be established, and so this will be poor preparation for any task that requires you to tie the material to its setting, or any task that requires you to search through memory later to find this material. But this sustained *exposure* to the material will establish familiarity, and so it will be good preparation for tasks that depend on familiarity (e.g., Bartz, 1976; Glenberg & Adams, 1978; Glenberg, Smith, & Green, 1977; Woodward, Bjork, & Jongeward, 1973).

Implicit Memory

We certainly know that some stimuli—a face that you see, a song that you hear, a scent that reaches your nose—instantly seem familiar to you. You're sure you've encountered the stimulus before; you know that it is somehow connected to your past. But what are the memory processes that produce these feelings? As we'll see, our best path toward this issue begins with cases in which stimuli *are* familiar (are part of your past) but don't *feel* familiar.

Memory Without Awareness

In a study by Jacoby (1983; also Jacoby & Dallas, 1981; Winnick & Daniel, 1970), participants were initially shown a series of words. In the *no context* condition, the words were simply shown on a computer screen. For example, participants might see "XXXX, Dark" on the screen, and their task was to read "dark" aloud. In the *context* condition, participants saw each word along with its antonym. For example, they were shown "Hot, Cold" and had to read "cold" aloud. Finally, in the *generate* condition, participants saw the antonym only ("Low, ????") and had to say out loud what the target word was (in this case "high").

In this procedure, the *generate* condition involves the most conceptual activity because the participant must attend to the cue word's meaning and come up with the antonym. In contrast, the *no context* condition provides neither reason nor encouragement to think about the word's meaning; it seems likely that people in this condition will read the word without thinking much about it. The *context* condition will probably involve an intermediate level of activity because this condition does draw attention to meaning (via the antonym) but does not require the participants to do anything with the antonym.

In Chapter 5, we argued that attention to meaning is usually an effective way to memorize; mere exposure, in contrast, seems to provide little memory benefit. On this basis, we would expect the participants to remember words encountered in the *generate* condition, but probably not those encountered in the *no context* condition. That is what the data show: After viewing all of the words, half of the participants were tested via a conventional recognition procedure, and in this test, performance was best for words presented in the *generate* condition, worse if the words had appeared in the *context* condition, and worst of all in the *no context* condition (Figure 6.5).

So far, then, this looks just like studies we have already seen. The twist, though, comes from the other half of the participants, tested in a different fashion. They were seated in front of a tachistoscope and shown a series of briefly presented words. Their task was simply to say what the words were—that is, to read them out loud. Some of the words presented had also been presented during the learning phase, and some of the words were novel—i.e., had not been recently viewed.

As we saw in Chapter 3, word recognition can be difficult, especially if the presentations are brief. Crucially, though, repetition helps: If we show a word to participants and then, a short time later, show them the word again, they're much more likely to recognize the word on the second presentation than they were on the first. In Chapter 3, we referred to this as "repetition priming," and, of course, this priming involves some sort of memory: If there was no record of the first presentation, then how could it influence the second presentation? But what kind of memory is this? And what creates this memory? This brings us back to the Jacoby study.

FIGURE 6.5

Preparation for Direct and Indirect Memory Tasks

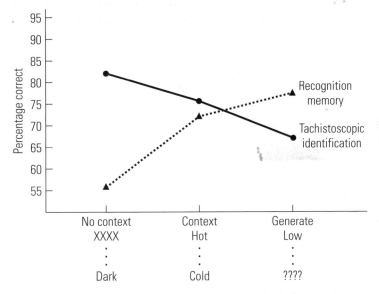

Participants in the *no context* condition saw words and read them aloud; those in the *generate* condition had to generate the words (antonyms) on their own (and did not see them). Participants in the *context* condition saw the words but had a meaningful context (antonyms) and so only had to glance at the words in order to identify them. The *generate* condition was the best preparation for a direct test ("Are these the words you saw before?") but worst for an indirect test (tachistoscopic identification). (After Jacoby, 1983)

Figure 6.5 shows the data. With tachistoscopic testing, performance was best if participants had encountered the words in the *no context* condition, worst if they had encountered the words in the *generate* condition. These results are exactly the opposite of the results from the standard recognition test. In that condition, performance was, it seems, dependent on *thinking about* the words. The more of this conceptual work the participants had done, the better their recognition memory was. In contrast, tachistoscopic performance seems dependent on perceptual "work"—that is, on literally seeing the items. Participants obviously see the words in the *no context* condition, and this produces strong priming. They don't see the words at all in the *generate* condition, and this condition produces negligible priming. The *context* condition again takes an intermediate position: Given the context, participants do not need to look at the word with any great care. Having seen "hot," the participant can confirm, with a quick glance, what the next word ("cold") must be. Hence, there will be some "perceptual contact" with the stimulus, but it will be slight. It makes sense, therefore, that this condition produces an intermediate level of priming.

All of this suggests that we are seeing two different types of memory here. One type, relevant to the standard recognition test, is promoted by conceptual engagement with the materials. This is consistent with what we saw in Chapter 5. The other type of memory, though, is different: It's somehow relevant to the tachistoscopic test and is promoted by *perceptual* work with the materials. Moreover, these two types of memory seem independent of each other, and one can have either without the other. In particular, after the *no context* condition, participants are likely to have the sort of memory relevant for the tachistoscopic task, but not the sort of memory needed for ordinary recognition. As a result, they'll be influenced by a specific past experience, even though they seem (on a direct test of memory) not to remember that experience at all—a pattern that some researchers refer to as "memory without awareness."

Similar results have been obtained with other tasks. For example, in a **lexical-decision task**, participants are shown strings of letters ("STAR," "LAMB," "NIRE"); their task is to indicate (by pressing one button or another) whether the string of letters is a word in English or not. Lexical decisions are appreciably quicker if the person has recently seen the test word; that is, lexical decision shows its own version of repetition priming. This priming is observed even when participants have no explicit memory for having encountered the stimulus words before (Oliphant, 1983).

How is this demonstrated? We can show participants a list of words and then later test them in two different ways. The direct test uses a standard recognition procedure: "Which of these words were on the list I showed you earlier?" The indirect test is a lexical decision: "Which of these letter strings form real words?" In this setup, the two tests will often yield different results: At a sufficient delay, the direct memory test is likely to show that the participants have completely forgotten the words presented earlier; according to the lexical-decision results, however, they still remember the words (i.e., show a robust priming effect). Once again, people demonstrate an influence by a past event, even though they seem to have no conscious memory of that event.

The same pattern has been observed with a task called **word-stem completion**. In this task, people are given the first few letters of a word and must produce a word with this beginning. For example they might be asked to name a word that begins "CLA." In some versions of this task, an obscure word is required to complete the word stem. In this situation, people are more likely to come up with the word if they have encountered it recently—even if, when asked directly, they report no memory at all of that earlier encounter. In other versions of this task, more than one word provides a plausible ending to the stem (e.g., "CLAM," "CLASS," "CLATTER"), and the question of interest is which of these words the person produces. If one of these words has been seen recently, people are likely to produce it, rather than a legitimate alternative, as the completion to the word stem. Once again, though, this priming effect is observed even if participants, when tested directly, show no memory of having seen the word recently (Graf, Mandler, & Haden, 1982).

Thus, in a range of settings, it seems that people are influenced by a previous encounter even if they have no conscious recollection of the encounter. (For reviews, see Richardson-Klavehn & Bjork, 1988; and Schacter, 1987.) Results like these have led psychologists to distinguish two types of memories. **Explicit memories** are those usually revealed by **direct memory testing**—testing that specifically urges you to remember the past. Recall is a direct memory test; so is the standard recognition test. **Implicit memories**, on the other hand, are those typically revealed by **indirect memory testing** and are often manifested as priming effects. In this form of testing, one's current behavior or judgments are demonstrably influenced by a prior event, but one may be quite unaware of this. Tachistoscopic recognition, lexical decision, word-stem completion, and many other tasks provide indirect means of assessing memory.

The Breadth of Implicit Memory

The effects of implicit memory can be demonstrated in a wide range of circumstances. To describe the evidence, though, we first need to say more about how implicit memory feels from the rememberer's point of view. This will then lead us back into our discussion of familiarity and source memory.

Let's say that we show people a stimulus and then, sometime later, show them the same stimulus again. Let's imagine further that we allow enough time to pass between the first encounter and the second so that, when the second encounter comes along, our participants no longer have an explicit memory for the first time they met this stimulus. As a result, they're not aware that the second encounter *is* a second encounter; they believe they're meeting the stimulus for the first time.

In this situation, people may still have an implicit memory for the stimulus, but how will they be influenced by this memory? The answer depends on the context.

Thanks to the implicit memory, the stimulus is likely to feel in some way "special." We have several expressions in English that seem to capture this specialness: We sometimes say that something "rings a bell" or "strikes a chord." But exactly what this means, and exactly how this feels, seems to depend on the circumstances.

Several experiments will help to illustrate this point. Jacoby, Kelley, Brown, and Jasechko (1989) presented participants with a list of names to read out loud. The participants were told nothing about a memory test; they thought the experiment was concerned with how they pronounced the names. Sometime later, though, the participants were given the second step of the procedure. They were shown a new list of names and asked to rate each person named on this list according to how famous each was. The list included some real, very famous people; some real but not-so-famous people; and also some fictional names. Crucially, the fictional names were of two types: Some were names that had occurred on the prior list, and some were simply new names. A comparison between those two types will tell us how the prior familiarization (during the "pronunciation task") influenced the judgments of fame.

For some participants, the "famous" list was presented right after the "pronounce" list; for other participants, there was a 24-hour delay between these two steps. To see how this delay matters, imagine yourself in the place of a participant in the immediate-testing condition: When you see one of the fictional-but-familiar names, you might decide, "This name rings a bell, but that's because I just saw it on the previous list." In this case, you have a feeling of familiarity, and you also remember the source of this familiarity. Therefore, there's nothing here to persuade you that the name belongs to someone famous, and you respond accordingly. But now imagine yourself in the place of a participant in the other condition, with the 24-hour delay. Thanks to this time span, you may not recall the earlier episode of seeing the name in the pronunciation task. Nonetheless, the familiarity remains, and so, in this setting, you might say, "This name rings a bell, and I have no idea why. I guess this must be a famous person." And this is indeed the pattern of the data: When the two lists are presented one day apart, the participants are likely to rate the made-up names as being famous.

Apparently, the participants noted (correctly) that some of the names did "ring a bell" and so did have a certain feeling of familiarity. The false judgments of fame, however, come from the way the participants *interpreted* this feeling, and what conclusions they drew from it. To put it simply, participants in the 24-hour delay condition forgot the real source of the familiarity (appearance on a recently viewed list) and instead filled in a bogus source ("Maybe I saw this person in a movie?"). And it's not hard to see why they made this particular misattribution. After all, the experiment was described to them as being about fame, and other names on the list were indeed those of famous people. From the participants' point of view, therefore, it is a reasonable inference under these circumstances that any name that "rings a bell" belongs to a famous person. Of course, this misattribution is possible only because the feeling of familiarity produced by these names was ill-defined enough that it was open to misinterpretation, and that's the point: Implicit memories seem to leave people only with a vague sense that a stimulus is somehow distinctive; what happens after this depends on how they interpret that feeling.

Implicit Memory and the "Illusion of Truth"

A different example is somewhat frightening. Participants in one study heard a series of statements and had to judge how interesting each statement was (Begg, Anas, & Farinacci, 1992). As an example, one sentence was, "The average person in Switzerland eats about 25 pounds of cheese each year." (This is false; the average is closer to 18 pounds.) Another was, "Henry Ford forgot to put a reverse gear in his first automobile." (This is true.) After hearing these sentences, the participants were presented with some more sentences, but now they had to judge the credibility of these sentences, rating them on a scale from *certainly true* to *certainly false*. Needless to say, some of the sentences in this "truth test" were repeats from the earlier presentation; the question of interest is how sentence credibility is influenced by sentence familiarity.

The result was a propagandist's dream: Sentences heard before were more likely to be accepted as true; that is, familiarity increased credibility (Begg, Armour, & Kerr, 1985; A. S. Brown & Halliday, 1990; Hasher, Goldstein, & Toppino, 1977). To make things worse, this effect emerged even when the participants were explicitly warned in advance not to believe the sentences in the first list. In one procedure, the participants were told that half of the statements had been made by men, and half by women. The women's statements, they were told, were always true; the men's always false. (Half the participants were told the reverse.) Then participants rated how interesting the sentences were, with each sentence attributed either to a man or a woman. "Frank Foster says that house mice can run an average of four miles per hour," or "Gail Logan says that crocodiles sleep with their eyes open." Later, participants were presented with more sentences and had to judge their truth, with these new sentences including the earlier assertions about mice, crocodiles, and so forth.

Let's focus on the sentences initially identified as being false—in our example, Frank's claim about mice. If someone explicitly remembers this sentence ("Oh yes—Frank said such and such"), then he should judge the assertion to be false ("After all, the experimenter said that all the men's statements were lies"). But what about someone without this explicit memory? Since the person doesn't remember whether the assertion came from a male or a female, he or she can't use the source as a basis for judging the sentence's veracity. Nonetheless, the person might still have an implicit memory for the sentence, left over from the earlier exposure ("Gee, that statement rings a bell"), and this might increase the credibility of the statement ("I'm sure I've heard that somewhere before; I guess it must be true").

This is exactly the pattern of the data: Statements plainly identified as false when they were first heard still created the so-called **illusion of truth**; that is, these statements were subsequently judged to be more credible than sentences never heard before.

The relevance of this result to the political arena, or to advertising, should be clear. A newspaper headline inquires, "Is Mayor Wilson a crook?" Or perhaps the headline declares, "Known criminal claims Wilson is a crook!" In either case, the assertion that Wilson is a crook has now become familiar. The Begg et al. data indicate that this familiarity will, by itself, increase the likelihood that you'll later believe in Wilson's dishonesty. This will be true even if the paper merely raised the question; it will be true even if the allegation came from a disreputable source. Malicious innuendo does in fact work nasty effects (Wegner, Wenzlaff, Kerker, & Beattie, 1981).

Attributing Implicit Memory to the Wrong Stimulus

In both the illusion-of-truth and the false-fame experiments, participants are misinterpreting a sense of familiarity: They know that a name or a sentence is familiar, but they don't realize that this is because it was on the previous list. Instead, they falsely conclude that the name is familiar because it belongs to someone famous, or that the sentence is familiar because they read it in some authoritative source.

In other cases, this misinterpretation can go even further: In one experiment, participants were presented with bursts of noise and asked to judge how loud each noise was (Jacoby, Allan, Collins, & Larwill, 1988). Embedded within each burst of noise, though, was a sentence. Some of the sentences were new to participants, but crucially, some of the sentences had been presented earlier.

In this study, memory appeared in an odd way: If a sentence was one of the previously presented ones, participants had an easier time hearing it against the backdrop of noise. This is just another case of repetition priming and so is consistent with results already described. But then the participants seemed to reason in this fashion: "Well, that sentence was easy to hear. I guess, therefore, the noise couldn't have been so loud." Likewise, for the unfamiliar sentences, they seemed to reason like this: "Gee, that noise must have been loud, since it really drowned out the sentence." As a result of these (completely unconscious) inferences, if the noise contained sentences that had been heard before, the noise was (mis)perceived as being softer than it actually was. Noise containing novel sentences was (mis)perceived as being loud.

In this experiment, therefore, the participants seem not to realize at all that the previously presented sentences are, in fact, familiar. All they realize is that it's easier to perceive the sentences in one condition than it is in the other, and they mistakenly attribute this difference to differing noise levels. In other words, it is the sentences that are (objectively) familiar, but there's no subjective sense of familiarity. Indeed, the implicit memory doesn't at all change how participants feel about the sentences. Instead, the memory shows its influence by changing how the participants feel about an entirely different stimulus—namely, the noise in which the sentences are embedded.

Attributing Implicit Memory to the Wrong Source

One last example will illustrate the range of cases in which we are influenced by misplaced familiarity, and it is an example of some consequence: In a study by E. Brown, Deffenbacher, and Sturgill (1977), research participants witnessed a staged crime. Two or 3 days later, they were shown "mug shots" of individuals who supposedly had participated in the crime, but as it turns out, the people in these photos were different from the people who were actually involved in the crime; no mug shots were shown for the truly "guilty" individuals. Finally, after 4 or 5 more days, the participants were shown a lineup of 4 persons and asked to select from this lineup the individuals seen in Step 1—namely, the original crime.

The data in this study show a pattern known as **source confusion**: The participants correctly realized that one of the people in the lineup looked familiar, but they were confused about the source of the familiarity. They falsely believed they had seen the person's face in the original "crime," when, in truth, they'd seen it only in a subsequent photograph. In fact, the likelihood of this error was quite high, with 29% of the participants (falsely) selecting from the lineup an individual they had seen only in the mug shots.

Does this sort of confusion happen outside of the laboratory? It certainly does. One example comes from a court case in England in which a crime victim confidently identified a sailor as the person who had robbed him. The sailor, however, was able to prove that, at the time of the crime, he was many miles away. How did this mistaken identification arise? It turns out that the crime victim was a ticket agent in a train station, and the sailor had, on several prior occasions, purchased tickets at this station. Apparently, the ticket-seller correctly realized that the sailor's face was familiar but (unwittingly) drew the wrong conclusion about why the face was familiar (D. F. Ross, Ceci, Dunning, & Toglia, 1994). Similar examples are easy to find. (Findings like these clearly have implications for how the police should run eyewitness identification procedures; for the U.S. Supreme Court's views on this point, see, for example, *Simmons v. United States*, 1968; also Gorenstein & Ellsworth, 1980.)

Theoretical Treatments of Implicit Memory

One unmistakable message coming from all of these studies is that we are often better at remembering *that* something is familiar than we are at remembering *why* it is familiar. This is why it's possible to have a sense of familiarity with no source memory ("I've seen her somewhere before, but I can't figure out where!"), and also why it's possible to be correct in judging familiarity but mistaken in judging source.

This latter pattern was evident in many of the examples we have just considered, and in other cases as well (e.g., Anand & Sternthal, 1991; Peretz, Gaudreau, & Bonnel, 1998; Seamon et al., 1995; Zajonc, 1980).

In addition, it is important that, in many of these studies, participants are being influenced by memories they are not aware of. In some cases, participants do realize that a stimulus is somehow familiar, but they have no memory of the encounter that produced the familiarity. In other cases, people don't even have a sense of familiarity for the target stimulus; nonetheless, they're influenced by their previous encounter with the stimulus. We saw this pattern in the experiment involving noise judgments. Other experiments show that participants often *prefer* a previously presented stimulus over a novel stimulus, even though they have no sense of familiarity with either stimulus. In such cases, people don't realize at all that their preference is being guided by memory (S. T. Murphy, 2001).

It does seem, then, that the term "memory without awareness" really is appropriate, and it does seem sensible to describe these memories as *implicit* memories. But what exactly are implicit memories? What is the content of these memories? It is to these questions that we now turn.

Implicit Memory: A Hypothesis

We have already noted (e.g., in Chapter 4) that perceptual processes are improved by practice. The practice raises the activation level of the relevant detectors (and so it makes it easier to fire these detectors in the future); it also strengthens the connections linking one detector to the next, so that communication between detectors is improved. All of this makes it easier to perceive that same stimulus the next time you meet it.

Presumably, though, the same can be said for other bits of intellectual performance: Just as perceiving a word leads to fluency in perceiving, perhaps contemplating a word's meaning leads to fluency of a parallel sort. The next time you contemplate the same word's meaning, you might be a little quicker or more efficient.

We would expect these practice effects to be rather specific. Exercising your legs makes your legs stronger, not your arms. In the same way, practice at perceiving Gladys will help you when next you see Gladys; the practice will not improve your ability to perceive Sally or Lola. More generally, practice in perceiving a stimulus will improve your ability to perceive that stimulus; similarly, practice in thinking through a specific chain of associations will make it easier to retrace those mental steps, and not some others.

With these points as backdrop, here is a hypothesis: Implicit memory is simply the name we give to these practice effects and the resulting increase in **processing fluency**. For some tasks, this increase in fluency is by itself enough to influence performance. Consider, for example, implicit memory's effect on tachistoscopic identification or on lexical decisions. These tasks require little more than the identification of the presented stimuli, and so these tasks would benefit directly from anything that speeds up processing. Thus, when we say these tasks are influenced by implicit memory, we're simply acknowledging the fact that, once a stimulus has been perceived, it will be easier to perceive the next time around.

To explain other implicit-memory effects, though, we need a further assumption—namely, that people are sensitive to the *degree* of processing fluency. That is, people know when they have perceived easily and when they have perceived only by expending more effort. They likewise know when a sequence of thoughts was particularly fluent and when the sequence was labored. Note that we are not claiming that people experience the fluency as fluency. When a stimulus is easy to perceive, people do not experience something like, "That stimulus sure was easy to recognize!" Instead, they merely register a vague sense of specialness. They feel that the stimulus "rings a bell." No matter how it is described, though, our hypothesis is that the sense of specialness has a simple cause—namely, ease in processing, brought on by fluency, which in turn was created by practice.[2]

We still need one more step in our hypothesis, but it is a step we have already introduced: When a stimulus feels special, people typically want to know why. Thus, the vague, hard-to-pinpoint feeling of specialness (again, produced by fluency) triggers an attribution process, as people seek to ask, "Why did that stimulus stand out?" In many circumstances, that question will be answered correctly, and so the specialness will be (correctly) interpreted as familiarity, and the familiarity will in turn be attributed to the correct source. In other situations, though, things may not go so smoothly. People can sometimes interpret the specialness correctly as familiarity, but then make a mistake about the familiarity's source. Or they can go even further off track and interpret the specialness in some other fashion altogether. For example, they might register that a stimulus seems special, but mistakenly conclude that this specialness isn't because the stimulus is familiar in some way; instead, they might interpret the specialness as a preference, or a reaction to the stimulus's beauty, and so on. Thus a wide range of interpretations is possible for the feeling of specialness, and it's this range that tells us just how large a role the attribution process plays.

It also seems likely that we can detect *decreases* in perceptual fluency, as well as increases. Imagine that someone you know well changes her hairstyle or gets new eyeglasses. In such cases, you often have the uncomfortable feeling that something in your friend's appearance has changed, but you can't figure out what it is. In our terms, your friend's face was a stimulus that you had seen often, and therefore a

---

[2]Actually, what people detect, and what makes a stimulus feel "special," may not be fluency per se. Instead, what they detect may be a *discrepancy* between how easy (or hard) it was to carry out some mental step, and how easy (or hard) they expected it to be, in light of the context and their experience. (See, for example, Whittlesea, 2002.) A stimulus is registered as distinctive, or "rings a bell," when this discrepancy reaches too high a level. Having acknowledged this, however, we will, for simplicity's sake, ignore this complication in our discussion.

stimulus you were fluent in perceiving. Once the stimulus is changed, however, your well-practiced steps of perceiving don't run as smoothly as they have in the past, and so the perception is less fluent than it had been. This lack of fluency is detected and produces the "something is new" feeling. But then the attribution step fails: You cannot identify what produced this feeling. This case provides the mirror image of the cases we have been considering, in which familiarity leads to an increase in fluency, so that something "rings a bell" but you cannot say why.

The Nature of Familiarity

All of these arguments provide us—at last—with a proposal for what "familiarity" is: In general, a stimulus will seem familiar whenever the following list of requirements is met: First, you have encountered the stimulus before. Second, because of that prior encounter (and the "practice" it afforded), you are now faster and more efficient in your processing of that stimulus; that's what we're calling "processing fluency." Third, you detect that fluency (or, more precisely, you detect the fact that the fluency is greater than you'd expected), and this leads you to register the stimulus as somehow distinctive or special. Fourth, you reach a particular decision about that specialness—namely, that the stimulus has this distinctive quality *because* it is a stimulus you have met before, in some prior episode. And then, finally, you draw a conclusion about when and where it was that you encountered the stimulus—in the experimenter's list of words, or yesterday in the newspaper, and so on. (For some possible problems with this proposal, though, see Rugg & Yonelinas, 2003.)

In essence, then, familiarity isn't a *feeling* that is directly triggered by a stimulus. Instead, it is a *conclusion* that you draw, *based on a feeling* (of specialness) that is triggered by the stimulus. Let's be clear, though, that none of these steps happen consciously; you're certainly not aware of seeking an interpretation or trying to explain why a stimulus feels distinctive. All you experience consciously is the end product of all these steps: the sense that a stimulus feels familiar.

Moreover, this conclusion about a stimulus isn't one you draw capriciously; instead, you draw this conclusion, and decide a stimulus is familiar, only when you have supporting information. Thus, imagine that you encounter a stimulus that "rings a bell." You're certainly more likely to decide the stimulus is familiar if you also have an (explicit) source memory, so that you can recollect where and when you last encountered that stimulus. ("I know this stimulus is familiar *because I can remembering seeing it yesterday*.") You're also more likely to decide a stimulus is familiar if the surrounding circumstances support it: If you are asked, for example, "Which of these words were on the list you saw earlier?" then the question itself gives you a cue that some of the words were recently encountered, and so you're more likely to attribute fluency to that encounter.

However, this interpretive process can go wrong, leading, as we've seen, to the false-fame effect, the illusion of truth, and other demonstrations of misplaced fluency. Thus, a stimulus that is objectively familiar (i.e., has been presented in the past) may not seem subjectively familiar (i.e., may not "feel familiar"). And even if a stimulus does seem subjectively familiar, it is possible to be entirely mistaken about why!

The Specificity of Implicit Memories

This account of implicit memory also leads to another prediction. The proposal we are considering is that implicit memory is, in essence, a skill—one that is created by your practice with a stimulus, when last you met it. It's then this skill that leads to processing fluency and all that follows from it.

If this is right, then implicit memories should be quite specific: As we said earlier, practice in perceiving Gladys will help you to recognize Gladys later on; it won't help you to recognize Lola. For that matter, practice in perceiving Gladys from the side will increase your skill in recognizing her from that angle; this may not help if, later on, you need to recognize her from another perspective.

Consistent with these ideas, implicit memories are indeed specific, but the nature of the specificity varies from one case to the next in a sensible fashion. That is because some implicit memories depend on *perceptual skill*—skill in recognizing a particular stimulus. For those memories, the skill will emerge the next time you encounter that stimulus; other stimuli won't trigger the skill. In contrast, some implicit memories depend on *conceptual skill*— skill in thinking about a particular combination of ideas. For these memories, the exact stimulus isn't crucial, and so altering the stimulus in some way will have no effect on the memory.

Let's look at how this distinction shows up in the data. Considerable priming is observed if (for example) participants are asked to complete word fragments (e.g., What is this word: "_L_P_A_T"?) and are subsequently retested with the same fragments. However, virtually no priming is observed if participants initially see one fragment (e.g., "_L_P_A_T") and are then tested with a different fragment of the same word (e.g., "E_E_H_N_"). Why is this? The initial exposure provided skill in working with a particular fragment. To reveal that skill, therefore, we need to present again the same fragment. If you've acquired skill in moving from Point A to Point B, that skill won't help you if we ask you to move from Point C to Point B!

In the same fashion, consider the priming effect observed in lexical-decision tasks. In the standard version of this procedure, participants first see a list of words, and then they see the lexical-decision test items. In an alternate version of this procedure, participants first *hear* a tape-recorded list of words, and then they *see* the test items. This shift in modality tremendously reduces the priming effect. Apparently, practice with an auditory presentation of a word doesn't help you if you later need skill in recognizing a visual presentation of the same word (Jacoby & Witherspoon, 1982; Kirsner, Milech, & Standen, 1983; Roediger & Blaxton, 1987).

In contrast, though, let's consider the priming effect that we earlier called the "illusion of truth," in which prior exposure to a sentence increases subsequent ratings of how credible that sentence is. In the illusion-of-truth procedures, the stimuli are clearly presented and in view for a long time; the task involves no time pressure. In this setting, perceiving the stimuli should be extremely easy, and so there's little need here for great perceptual skill. As a consequence, there should be little benefit in this task from any *increase* in perceptual skill. If, therefore, we interpret the illusion of truth in terms of fluency, it's probably not *perceptual* fluency that's critical. Instead, the key must be *conceptual* fluency—fluency in thinking about an idea's meaning or an idea's implications.

To put this concretely, imagine that we show participants the sentence, "Henry Ford forgot to put a reverse gear in his first automobile." Showing them this sentence will give them some practice in perceiving the words, but because perceiving is so easy in this situation, the practice won't have much of an impact. However, showing them the sentence will also give them some practice in thinking about the relevant ideas: Ford, absent minded inventors, and so on. This will produce fluency with these ideas, and it's this conceptual fluency that produces the illusion of truth.

In light of all this, what should we expect if participants first hear the sentence about Henry Ford and then see it in our subsequent test? In this case, they won't be able to use their earlier-practiced perceptual skill, but we just suggested that perceptual skill isn't crucial here. What is crucial is fluency in thinking about the ideas, and the ideas will be the same whether the stimulus is heard or seen. Therefore, we shouldn't expect stimulus specificity in this situation. This prediction turns out to be correct: The illusion-of-truth effect is still observed, even if the sentences are heard the first time around and then seen in the actual test. This shift in modality, in other words, removes any benefits of perceptual skill, but that skill doesn't matter here, and so the shift in modality has no effect (Begg, Anas, & Farinacci, 1992; for related data, see A. Brown, Neblett, Jones, & Mitchell, 1991; Craik, Moscovitch, & McDown, 1994; Srinivas, 1993; and Weldon, 1993).

All of this fits well into the theoretical picture we are presenting: Implicit memory involves processing fluency, and fluency effects are quite specific. But the nature of the specificity depends on the type of fluency we're considering: Fluency in perceiving is fluency in dealing with a particular stimulus, and therefore the fluency is specific to that stimulus. For this reason, if a procedure depends on perceptual fluency, then the implicit-memory effects will be lost if the stimulus format is changed. In contrast, fluency in thinking about meaning is not dependent on the format of the stimulus, and so, if this is the sort of fluency needed for a particular task, the results will be unchanged if the stimulus format is altered. (For further discussion of these points, see Jacoby, Levy, & Steinbach, 1992; and Weldon, 1993.)

Process Purity

Throughout this section, we've said many things about how, and in what circumstances, people are influenced by implicit memory. We've made it sound, though, as if there were one set of tasks influenced by implicit memory, and a different set influenced by explicit memory. Indirect tests of memory (like lexical decision, or word-stem completion) would be in the first category; direct tests (like recall or recognition) would be in the second.

As it turns out, though, this isn't quite right. Instead, many tasks are influenced by *both* implicit and explicit memory. Acknowledging this fact helps us to understand how these memories work and also, as we'll see, raises a challenge for us.

Imagine a participant trying to solve the word stem "S T U ___". We've been assuming that this is an implicit-memory task, and, without question, recent priming with the word "stupor" would influence the participant's response. But perhaps the participant also has an explicit memory of recently seeing the word "stupor." This, too, might guide the response so that this word, and not "stupid" or "stuck" or "stuff", would be used to complete the fragment.

In this way, word-stem completion is not a **process-pure task**. That is, it's not a task influenced by just one process. And, of course, the same is probably true for lexical decision or any other indirect task. Each of these tasks, designed to tap implicit memory, might also be affected by explicit memory. And the converse is also true: Tasks like recognition or recall, designed to assess explicit memory, may well be influenced by implicit memory, so these tasks, too, are not process-pure. Thus, a participant might be taking a standard recognition test and encounter the word "warehouse." If this word really "rings a bell," even if the participant has no idea why, this perceived familiarity could influence the participant's response.

The *absence* of process purity substantially broadens the range of tasks that may be influenced by implicit memory. Even tasks that seem, on the face of things, to involve the explicit recollection of previous events may be subtly shaped by these unconscious memories. But, in addition, the absence of process purity creates a problem for us: Let's imagine, for example, that we want to ask whether deep processing helps establish implicit memories. We already know that deep processing promotes explicit memory (Chapter 5), but does it have the same effect on implicit memory? To find out, we might have half of our participants do deep processing of some words, and half do shallow processing. Then we could ask, Do the groups differ in how much priming they show in, say, a word-stem completion task? (For examples of studies actually asking this sort of question, see A. Brown & Mitchell, 1994; Challis & Brodbeck, 1992; D. Nelson, Schreiber, & Holley, 1993; Srinivas & Roediger, 1990; and Thapar & Greene, 1994.)

Let's say that the data do show greater priming after deep processing than after shallow. This difference *might* indicate that deep processing promotes implicit memory, and thus creates stronger priming effects. But there's also another interpretation: Perhaps the deep processing in this study made it more likely that participants would have an *explicit* memory for the priming words; and since (as we've now seen) explicit memory can contribute to this task, perhaps it's the explicit memory that leads to the effect we observed. In that case, deep processing would promote priming, even if deep processing had no effect on implicit memory!

What should we do about cases like this? This has been a topic of some debate. Jacoby and his colleagues have proposed a clever way to analyze the data from priming experiments in order to derive process-pure measurements from process-impure tasks (e.g., Jacoby, 1991; Jacoby & Kelley, 1992; also see Blum & Yonelinas, 2001; Kinoshita, 2001). In other words, they have proposed a method for obtaining separate estimates of the contributions of implicit memory and explicit memory to task performance, and with this method, they can draw conclusions about whether a particular factor (such as deep processing) influenced one of these memories, or the other, or both. This seems, in a straightforward way, to solve the problem just sketched. However, others have expressed reservations about this form of data analysis, in some cases arguing that the analysis works only under certain circumstances, and in other cases arguing for a different mode of analysis (see, for example, Brainerd, Reyna, & Mojardin, 1999; Curran & Hintzman, 1995; Hirshman, 1998; Humphreys et al., 2003; Jacoby, 1998; Richardson-Klavehn & Gardiner, 1998).

It is too soon to tell how this debate will be resolved. The concern about process purity must be taken seriously, and our standard measures of task performance are almost certainly not process-pure. How (or whether) we can obtain process-pure measures is less clear, and until this point is resolved, it may be difficult to gain a precise picture of exactly which factors influence implicit memory.

Amnesia

Before moving on, let's pause to put the last few sections into proper context. There can be no question that we are often influenced by the past without being aware of that influence. We often respond differently to familiar stimuli, even if we have no subjective feeling of familiarity. Thus, our conscious recollection seriously underestimates what is in our memories. Moreover, it is clear that an attribution step plays a crucial role in determining how we are influenced by these unconscious memories, with that attribution step often going astray. And above all, it seems certain that we have only begun to document the many unconscious influences of memory on what we do, what we say, and what we think.

In addition, the evidence makes it plain that there are at least two different kinds of memory: one typically conscious and deliberate, one typically unconscious and automatic. It turns out that there has been some disagreement about how we should define these two types of memory, but there is no disagreement about the need for some distinction, some categorization scheme.

In fact, two further lines of evidence also speak to the need to distinguish these categories of memory. One, which we'll simply mention, involves the attempt to chart memory performance across the life span. Many studies are pertinent to this point, but in general, the pattern is that implicit memory can be documented at all ages, from very early childhood to very old age. Indeed, what is remarkable is the similarity in implicit-memory performance by people at very different ages. Performance on explicit-memory tasks, on the other hand, is strongly age-dependent, with children and the aged both outperformed by those in their middle years (Graf & Masson, 1993; N. S. Newcombe, Drummey, Fox, Lie, & Ottinger-Alberts, 2000). These observations obviously add to the evidence that a distinction is needed here, with the memory systems distinguishable developmentally as well as functionally.

The distinction is also demanded by clinical evidence—in particular, evidence from cases of brain damage.

Anterograde Amnesia

A variety of injuries or illnesses can lead to a loss of memory, or amnesia. Some forms of amnesia are retrograde, meaning that they disrupt memory for things learned prior to the event that initiated the amnesia. Retrograde amnesia is often caused, for example, by blows to the head; often one is unable to recall events occurring just prior to the blow. Other forms of amnesia have the reverse effect, causing disruption of memory for experiences after the onset of amnesia; these are cases of anterograde amnesia. (We should note that many cases of amnesia have both retrograde and anterograde memory loss.) Here we will focus on anterograde amnesia; as we will see, this form of memory loss can tell us a great deal about the issues we have been discussing. (For more on retrograde amnesia, see A. S. Brown, 2002; M. Conway & Fthenaki, 1999; Kapur, 1999; Kopelman & Kapur, 2001; Nadel & Miscovitch, 2001; and Riccio, Millin, & Gisquet-Verrier, 2003.)

We discussed a famous case of anterograde amnesia in Chapter 1: the patient H.M. (For a review of H.M.'s case, see Milner, 1966, 1970.) H.M. suffered from profound epilepsy, and a variety of attempts at curing him had all failed. As a last resort, doctors sought to contain H.M.'s disease by brain surgery, specifically by removing portions of the brain that seemed to be the source of the seizures. In a very narrow sense, the surgery was a success, because it did improve the epilepsy. But even so, the surgery was a disaster, because the cure for epilepsy came at an incredible cost: H.M. seems now unable to learn anything new.

H.M. can function normally in some regards and can, for example, hold a coherent, meaningful conversation. Within the conversation, he may even talk about prior events in his life, since he is fully able to recall events that took place *prior to* the surgery. However, he can't recall anything that has taken place since the surgery. Episodes he's experienced, people he's met, books he's read—all seem to leave no enduring record, as though nothing new can get into his long-term storage. The severity of H.M.'s amnesia is visible in many ways, but the problem becomes instantly clear if a conversation with him is interrupted for some reason: If you speak with him for a while, then (for example) leave the room and come back 3 or 4 minutes later, H.M. seems to have totally forgotten that the earlier conversation ever took place; if the earlier conversation was your first meeting with H.M., he will, after the interruption, be quite certain he is now meeting you for the very first time.

H.M.'s specific case is unique, but a similar amnesia can be found in patients who have been longtime alcoholics. The problem is not the alcohol itself; the problem instead is that alcoholics tend to have inadequate diets, getting most of their nutrition from whatever they are drinking. It turns out, though, that most alcoholic beverages are missing several key nutrients, including vitamin B_1 (thiamine). As a result, longtime alcoholics are vulnerable to a number of problems caused by thiamine deficiency, including **Korsakoff's syndrome** (Rao, Larkin, & Derr, 1986; Ritchie, 1985).

A Korsakoff's patient seems in many ways similar to H.M. There is typically little problem in remembering events that took place before the onset of alcoholism. Current topics can also be maintained in the mind as long as there is no interruption. New information, though, if displaced from the mind, is seemingly lost forever. Korsakoff's patients who have been in the hospital for decades will casually mention that they arrived only a week ago; if asked the name of the current president or events in the news, they unhesitatingly give answers appropriate for two or three decades back, whenever the disease began (Marslen-Wilson & Teuber, 1975; Seltzer & Benson, 1974).

Learning From Amnesia

These cases of amnesia can teach us a great deal about memory. For example, what is the biological basis for memory? A partial answer comes from the fact that amnesia is typically associated with damage that involves the hippocampus and neighboring brain areas; this obviously implies that these brain sites play a crucial role in memory. Let us be clear, though, that the evidence does not imply that the hippocampus is the "seat" of memory in the brain. We know this because damage to the hippocampus does not disrupt already-established memories. (Hippocampus damage is associated with *anterograde* amnesia, not retrograde.) Instead, the hippocampus plays its main role in memory acquisition, so that, with hippocampal damage, H.M. and the Korsakoff's patients seem unable to create *new* memories. (For more on the role of the hippocampus, and also the role played by other brain sites, see Aggleton & Shaw, 1996; Baddeley, 1999; Nadel & Jacobs, 1998; and J. M. Reed & Squire, 1997.)

The study of amnesia can also provide important lessons about the function of memory in our daily lives. As one illustration, consider again the patient H.M. We mentioned that H.M. can function normally in some arenas: He can, for example, hold a reasonable conversation. But he is also limited in profound ways. If, for example, in the midst of a conversation H.M. notices that the other person is smiling, he often does not know why. Was there a funny joke in the conversation a moment ago? Or did someone say something embarrassing? Or is it a smile of sympathy because someone said something sad? Because of this sort of ambiguity, H.M. lives with a constant sense of awkwardness: "Right now, I'm wondering, have I done or said anything amiss? You see, at this moment everything looks clear to me, but what happened just before? That's what worries me" (a quote from H.M. in Hilts, 1995, p. 138). Examples like this make it clear what a crucial role memory plays in many settings—including our ordinary everyday social interactions. (For further discussion of memory's role in our lives, see Chapters 1 and 7.)

The study of amnesia can also help us with a number of theoretical questions—including the question that was before us a few pages back: the contrast between implicit and explicit memory.

Another Look at Amnesia: What Kind of Memory Is Disrupted?

Patients suffering from anterograde amnesia can remember events from before the amnesia's start, suggesting that there is nothing wrong with their long-term memories. The patients also seem to have intact working memories; that is how they remember events as they think about them. In H.M.'s case, for example, these intact parts of his memory are what allow him to participate in a normal conversation: As long as the conversation is coherent and uninterrupted, he can maintain the stream of ideas in his intact working memory. It's only when an interruption occurs, pushing the conversation momentarily out of working memory, that he needs to draw on long-term storage, and then his amnesia becomes fully visible.

What, then, is the problem with amnesic patients? For many years, their amnesia was described as a "disconnection syndrome." The idea was that their problem was lodged in the *connection* between working memory and long-term memory, so that they were unable to move information from working memory into long-term storage. That is why no new memories could be established.

Other evidence, though, demands significant revision in this account of amnesia, and some of the evidence has been available for a long time: In 1911, Édouard Claparède (1911/1951) reported the following incident: He was introduced to a young woman suffering from Korsakoff's amnesia, and he reached out to shake the patient's hand. However, Claparède had secretly positioned a pin in his own hand so that, when they clasped hands, the patient received a painful pinprick. (Respect for patient's rights would prevent any modern physician from conducting this cruel experiment, but ethical standards for physicians were obviously different in 1911.) The next day, Claparède returned and reached out to shake hands with the patient. Not surprisingly for someone with Korsakoff's amnesia, the patient initially gave no indication that she recognized Claparède or remembered anything about the prior encounter. Nevertheless, when the time came to clasp hands, the patient at the last moment abruptly withdrew her hand and would not shake hands with Claparède. Claparède asked her why, and after some confusion, the patient simply said vaguely that "sometimes pins are hidden in people's hands."

This patient seemed to have no explicit memory of the prior encounter with Claparède. She did not mention the encounter in explaining her refusal to shake hands; if questioned closely about the prior encounter, she indicated no knowledge of it. Nonetheless, some sort of memory was retained. The patient knew something about the previous day's mishap but could not report on the knowledge.

This peculiar kind of remembering can be demonstrated with Korsakoff's patients in many other ways. In one experiment, Korsakoff's patients were asked a series of trivia questions (Schacter, Tulving, & Wang, 1981). For each question, possible answers were offered in a multiple-choice format, and the patient had to choose which was the right answer. If the patient did not know the answer, he or she was told it, and then (unbeknownst to the patient) the question was replaced in the stack. Sometime later, therefore, as the game continued, the question came up again, and this time the patient was quite likely to get it right. Apparently, the patient had "learned" the answer in the previous encounter and "remembered" the relevant information. Consistent with their diagnosis, though, the patients had no recollection of the learning: They were consistently unable to explain why their answers were correct. They did not say, "I know this bit of trivia because the same question came up just five minutes ago." Instead, they were likely to say things like, "I read about it somewhere," or "My sister once told me about it."

A different experiment makes a similar point: In a procedure by M. K. Johnson, Kim, and Risse (1985), patients with Korsakoff's amnesia heard a series of brief melodies. A short time later, they were presented with a new series and told that some of the tunes in the second batch were repeats from the earlier presentation. The amnesic patients' assignment was to tell which tunes were the repeats and which tunes they were hearing for the first time. As expected, these patients did poorly on this task; indeed, their memory responses were close to random. This result is, of course, consistent with their clinical diagnosis. Remarkably, though, when asked which melodies they preferred, the amnesic patients uniformly preferred the familiar ones. The patients had no (explicit) memory for these tunes, but a memory did emerge with indirect testing—emerged, in this case, as a preference.

A great many results show this pattern, with amnesic patients showing profound memory loss on some measures but looking perfectly normal on other measures (N. J. Cohen & Squire, 1980; Graf & Schacter, 1985; Moscovitch, 1982; Schacter, 1996; Schacter & Tulving, 1982; Squire & McKee, 1993). Thus, on the one side, these patients seem completely incapable of recalling episodes or events. In the terms we have been using, these patients seem to have no "explicit memory." At the same time, these patients do learn and do remember; they seem to have intact "implicit memories." Indeed, in most tests of implicit memory, amnesic patients seem indistinguishable from ordinary individuals.

These results obviously add to the package of evidence we have been considering in the last several sections. As we've seen, many experiments indicate that explicit and implicit memory can be distinguished on functional grounds, with these two types of memory apparently created by different sorts of learning and evoked by different sorts of tests. The amnesia data indicate that these two types of memory can also be distinguished on neurological grounds—with specific forms of brain damage disrupting some sorts of memory but sparing others.

Explicit Memory Without Implicit?

If explicit memory is truly independent of implicit memory, then it should be possible to identify two types of brain damage: one that disrupts explicit memory but leaves implicit memory intact, and one that disrupts implicit memory but leaves explicit memory intact. This pair of complementary cases provides what neuroscientists call a **double dissociation**, and it is a powerful argument for the independence of two mental capacities.

We have already seen half of the evidence we need: In Korsakoff's syndrome, implicit memory seems to function normally, even though explicit memory is massively disrupted. Can we find the opposite case? In one study, three patients were studied: One had damage to the hippocampus but not the amygdala; another had damage to the amygdala but not the hippocampus; the third had damage to both structures (Bechara et al., 1995). The patients were exposed to a series of trials in which a particular stimulus (a blue light) was reliably followed by a loud boat horn, while other stimuli (green, yellow, or red) were not followed by the horn. Later on, the patients were exposed to the blue light on its own and their bodily arousal was measured; would they show a fright reaction in response to this stimulus? In addition, the patients were asked directly, "Which color was followed by the horn?"

The two patients with damage to the hippocampus did show a fear reaction to the blue light, but when asked directly, they could not explicitly recall which of the lights had been associated with the boat horn. In contrast, the two patients with damage to the amygdala showed exactly the opposite pattern. They were able to report calmly that just one of the lights had been associated with the horn, and that the light's color had been blue—demonstrating fully intact explicit memory. When presented with the blue light, however, they showed no fear response.

Related evidence comes from a patient who had damage to his occipital lobe, in areas crucial for vision (Gabrieli, Fleischman, Keane, Reminger, & Morell, 1995). The patient was first shown a list of words and then tested in two different ways: In one test, the words were mixed together with new words, and the patient had to judge which words were old and which were new. In the other test, the words were presented tachistoscopically, and the question was whether words shown earlier would be more easily identified. The results were clear-cut: In the test of explicit recognition memory, the patient performed normally. In the tachistoscopic task, however, the patient showed no evidence of repetition priming.

In both of these studies, therefore, we see evidence of diminished implicit memory (no fear response in the first study, no priming in the second), even though the patients have normal explicit memories. This is, of course, the mirror image of the pattern shown by H.M. and Korsakoff's patients, and it makes it clear that explicit and implicit memory are indeed separate and independent from each other.

Optimal Learning

The amnesia data also draw us back to the issues with which this chapter began. Throughout the chapter, we've argued that we cannot make claims about learning or memory acquisition without some reference to how the learning is going to be used later on, or how the memories are going to be retrieved. That is because we've seen, over and over, that learning that works perfectly well as preparation for one sort of memory retrieval may be worthless as preparation for a different sort of retrieval. Learning that will allow you, later on, to remember well in one set of circumstances may not allow you to remember at all in a different set of circumstances.

This theme is obviously echoed in our discussion of implicit memory, and in the amnesia data. Experiences that create explicit memories are distinct from those that create implicit memories. Whether an experience is "good" or "bad" for creating memories therefore depends on how, and in what situation, the memory is going to be used. Likewise, it would be too coarse to say that amnesia (or brain damage more generally) disrupts the capacity to acquire new memories. Instead, some forms of brain damage make it difficult to acquire explicit memories; and some, implicit memories. Therefore, the nature of the disruption again depends on how the memories will be used later on, how they will be retrieved.

All of this seems to have a powerful practical implication: If you are trying to learn some new material, then the ideal form of learning will be one that is "aligned with" the approach to the material that you'll need later. If later on you'll be tested explicitly, you want to learn the material in a fashion that prepares you for that form of retrieval. If later on you'll be tested underwater, or while listening to music, then, again, you want to learn the material in a way that prepares you for that context and the mental perspective it produces.

The problem, though, is that during learning, you often don't know how you'll be approaching the material later—whether your focus during retrieval will be on meaning or on sound, whether you'll need the information implicitly or explicitly, and so on. As a result, maybe the best strategy in learning would be to employ *multiple perspectives*. To pick up an analogy we used early in the chapter, if you think that, at some point in the future, you'll want to reach Chicago, but you don't know yet whether you'll be approaching the city from the north, the south, or the west, your best bet might be to build multiple highways, so that you can reach your goal from any direction. Memory works the same way. If you initially think about a topic in different ways, and in conjunction with many other ideas, then you will establish many paths leading to the target material. This multiperspective approach, therefore, might provide something close to an optimal learning strategy.

The fact is, though, that we usually don't adopt this multiperspective approach. Hence, our memories are typically bound to the particular perspective we had in mind at the time of learning. The limitations that this approach creates in our memories have been in plain view throughout the chapter, and they lead to an important set of principles about when our remembering will succeed and when it will fail.

Chapter Summary

1. In general, the chances that someone will remember an earlier event are greatest if the physical, mental, and emotional circumstances in place during memory retrieval match those in place during learning. This is reflected in the phenomenon of state-dependent learning, in which one is most likely to remember material learned while underwater if tested underwater, most likely to remember material learned while listening to music if again listening to music during the test, and so on.

2. In the same vein, if one focused on the meaning of some material while learning it, then hints concerned with meaning will be especially helpful when the time comes to recall the material. If one focused on the sound of the material during learning, then hints concerned with sound will be most helpful at the time of recall.

3. A similar pattern is reflected in the phenomenon of "encoding specificity." This term refers to the idea that one usually learns more than the specific material to be remembered itself; one also learns that material within its associated context. As a result, remembering is most likely if that context is re-created at the time of recall.

4. All these results arise from the fact that learning establishes connections among memories, and these connections serve as retrieval paths. Like any path, these lead from some starting point to some target. To use the path, therefore, one must return to the appropriate starting point. In the same way, if there is a connection between two memories, then activating the first memory is likely to call the second to mind. If the first memory is not activated, however, this connection, no matter how well established, will not help in locating the second memory, just as a large highway approaching Chicago from the south will not be helpful if you are trying to reach Chicago from the north.

5. In the same way, some learning strategies are effective as preparation for some sorts of memory tests but ineffective for other sorts of tests. Some strategies, for example, are effective at establishing source memory rather than familiarity; other strategies do the reverse. Source memory is essential for recall; recognition can often be achieved either through source memory or through familiarity.

6. Different forms of learning also play a role in producing implicit and explicit memories. Implicit memories are those that influence us even when we have no awareness that we are being influenced by a specific previous event. In many cases, implicit-memory effects take the form of priming—for example, in tachistoscopic recognition or word-stem completion. But implicit memories can also influence us in other ways, producing a number of memory-based illusions.

7. Implicit memory may be the consequence of processing fluency, produced by experience in a particular task with a particular stimulus. The fluency is sometimes detected and registered as a sense of "specialness" attached to a stimulus. Often, this specialness is then attributed to some cause, but this attribution can be inaccurate. Because the fluency is created by a particular task and stimulus, the fluency will have its effects only when the same task and stimulus are encountered again.

8. Investigators disagree about the specifics of how implicit memory should be described, and this disagreement is in part a reflection of a mixed data pattern, with implicit memory showing slightly different characteristics in different experiments. However, this data pattern may reflect only the fact that our measures of implicit memory are not process-pure.

9. Implicit memory is also important in understanding the pattern of symptoms in anterograde amnesia. Amnesic patients perform badly on tests requiring explicit memory and may not even recall events that happened just minutes earlier. However, they often perform at near-normal levels on tests involving implicit memory. This disparity underscores the fact that we cannot speak in general about good and bad memories, good and poor learning. Instead, learning and memory must be matched to a particular task and a particular form of test; learning and memory that are excellent for some tasks may be poor for others.

Remembering Complex Events

In the last two chapters, we have said a great deal about how memory functions—how information is lodged in storage in the first place, and then how the information is retrieved later. Notice, though, that almost all of the data we have considered come from studies that have used relatively simple materials: Research participants have been asked to memorize word lists or short sentences. We've probed memory for single pictures or brief bits of melody.

In our daily lives, however, we obviously encounter much more complex materials. We encounter (and then try to remember) complicated episodes involving many actions and, often, many players. And, crucially, these episodes are integrated into the fabric of our lives. Thus, we enter the episode knowing certain things about the situation. Then, afterward, we're likely to encounter other episodes and other information pertinent to the event we experienced initially.

How does all this complexity influence memory? In this chapter, we will tackle this issue in two separate ways. First, we'll consider some of the *errors* that can arise when people try to remember episodes that are related to other things they know and other things they have experienced. Second, we'll consider some of the factors that are directly pertinent to memory as it functions in day-to-day life. For example, we'll consider the impact of the *emotion* that is often part of an event, asking how it influences memory. We'll also consider the effect of *time*, asking how people remember events that happened years, or even decades, earlier.

213

- Outside the lab, we often try to remember materials that are related in some fashion to other things we know or have experienced. Over and over, we will see that this other knowledge, the knowledge we bring to a situation, helps us to remember by promoting retrieval, but also hurts memory by promoting error.

- The memory errors produced by our prior knowledge tend to be quite systematic, and so we often end up recalling the past as more "normal," more in line with our expectations, than it actually was.

- Even if we acknowledge the memory errors, our overall assessment of memory can be quite positive. This is because our memories are accurate most of the time, and the errors that do occur can be understood as the by-products of mechanisms that generally serve us well.

- Finally, we will consider three factors that play an important role in shaping memory outside of the laboratory: our *involvement* with an event, *emotion*, and also the *passage of time*. These factors each require some additional principles as part of our overall theory, but they also confirm the power of more general principles— principles hinging (for example) on the role of memory connections.

Memory Errors, Memory Gaps

Where did you spend last summer? Have you ever been in a canoe? Where were you 5 minutes ago? These are, of course, extremely easy questions. The sought-after information is in your memory, and you effortlessly retrieve the information the moment you need it. And the same is true for countless other bits of information; these, too, are at your fingertips, swiftly and easily recalled whenever you wish.

Simple observations like these testify to the breadth, efficiency, and general success of human memory. Each of us carries a huge quantity of information in memory, and we can usually retrieve this information with ease. But of course there are also circumstances in which remembering is less successful. Sometimes you try to remember an episode and you simply draw a blank. Or you recall something, but with no conviction that you're correct: "I think her nickname was Dink, but I'm not sure."

Memory can also fail in another way: Sometimes you recall a past episode, but then it turns out that your memory is mistaken. Perhaps details of the event were different from the way you recall them. Or perhaps your memory is altogether wrong, misrepresenting large elements of the original episode. In some cases, you even remember entire events that never happened at all!

How, and how often, do these errors arise? In tackling these broad questions, let's start with some examples.

Memory Errors: Some Initial Examples

In 1992, an El Al cargo plane lost power in two of its engines just after taking off from Amsterdam's Schiphol Airport. The pilot attempted to return the plane to the airport but could not make it; a few minutes later, the plane crashed into an 11-story apartment building. The building collapsed and burst into flames; 43 people were killed, including the plane's entire crew.

Ten months later, researchers questioned 193 people about the crash, asking them in particular, "Did you see the television film of the moment the plane hit the apartment building?" More than half of the participants (107 of them) reported seeing the film, even though there was no such film. No camera had recorded the crash; no film (or any reenactment) was shown on television. The participants were remembering something that never took place (Crombag, Wagenaar, & van Koppen, 1996; for similar data, with people remembering a nonexistent film of the car crash that killed Princess Diana and Dodi Fayed, see Ost, Vrij, Costall, & Bull, 2002).

In a follow-up study, the investigators surveyed another 93 people about the crash. These people were also asked whether they had seen the (nonexistent) TV film, and then they were asked some more detailed questions about exactly what they had seen in the film: Was the plane burning when it crashed, or did it catch fire a moment later? In the film, did you see the plane come down vertically with no forward speed, or did it hit the building while still moving horizontally at a considerable speed?

Two thirds of these participants remembered seeing the film, and most of them confidently provided details about what they had seen. When asked about the plane's direction and speed of movement, for example, only 23% prudently said that they couldn't remember. The others gave various responses, presumably based on their "memory" of the film; as it turns out, only 11% gave the correct answer.

This is not a case of one or two people making a mistake; instead, a large majority of the people questioned seemed to have a detailed recollection of the nonexistent film. In addition, let's emphasize that the El Al crash was an emotional, important, and much-discussed event for these Dutch participants; the researchers were not asking them to recall a minor occurrence.

Perhaps these errors emerged simply because the research participants were trying to remember something that had taken place almost a year earlier. Is memory more accurate when the questions come after a shorter delay? In a study by Brewer and Treyens (1981), the participants were asked to wait briefly in the experimenter's office, prior to the procedure's start. After 35 seconds, participants were taken out of this office and told that there actually was no experimental procedure. Instead, the study was concerned with their memory for the room in which they had just been sitting.

The participants' recollections of the office were plainly influenced by their prior knowledge—in this case, their knowledge about what an academic office typically contains. For example, participants surely knew, in advance of the study, that academic offices usually contain a desk and a chair, and as it turns out, these pieces of furniture were present in this particular office. This agreement between prior knowledge and the specific experience led to accurate memory, and 29 of 30 participants correctly remembered that the office contained a desk and chair. In other regards, however, this office was different from what the participants might have expected. Specifically, participants would surely expect an academic office to contain shelves filled with books, yet in this particular office no books were in view (Figure 7.1). As it turns out, though, the participants' recall was often in line with their expectations, and not with reality: Almost one third of them (9 of 30) remembered seeing books in the office when, in fact, there were none.

How could this be? How could so many Dutch participants be wrong in their recall of a significant emotional episode? How could intelligent, alert college students fail to remember what they had seen in an office just moments earlier? The

---

| FIGURE 7.1 | The Office Used in the Brewer and Treyens Study |

No books were in view in this office, but participants, biased by their expectations for what should be in a scholar's office, often remembered seeing books! (After Brewer & Treyens, 1981)

answer lies in a point we mentioned at the very start of this discussion: the interconnections between the episode being remembered and the other knowledge in our memories.

Memory Errors: A Hypothesis

Memory errors can actually happen in many different ways, starting with errors that arise during your initial exposure to the episode to be remembered, and continuing through the moment of recall. In all cases, though, the errors involve the same simple mechanism: In Chapters 5 and 6, we emphasized the importance of memory connections, linking each bit of knowledge in your memory to other bits. Sometimes these connections tie together similar episodes, so that this trip to the beach ends up connected in memory to your recollections of other trips. Sometimes the connections tie an episode to certain ideas—ideas, perhaps, that were part of your understanding of the episode, or ideas that were triggered by some element within the episode.

With all of these connections in place, information ends up being stored in memory in a system that looks like a vast spiderweb, with each bit of information connected by many threads to other bits of information elsewhere in the web. And within this spiderweb, there are no clear boundaries, keeping the contents of one memory separate from the contents of other memories. The memories, in other words, are not stored in separate "files," each distinct from the others. What is it, therefore, that holds together the various elements within a remembered episode? It is simply the density of connections: There are many connections linking the various aspects of your "trip to the beach" to each other. There are fewer connections linking this event to other events. This is the only marker, within the system, that identifies which elements are truly *part of* the remembered episode, and which are merely *related to* the episode.

As we have discussed, the connections linking one memory to the next play a crucial rule in memory retrieval: Whenever you are looking for some bit of information, you follow the connections from one information bit to the next until you find the information you want. For this reason, the connections are plainly a good thing, and the more connections there are, the easier it will be for you to find the information you seek.

However, these same connections can also create problems for you: As you add links between the bits of this episode and the bits of that episode, you are gradually knitting these two episodes together. As a result, it becomes very easy to lose track of which bits of information were contained within which episode, and with that, you become vulnerable to what we might think of as "transplant" errors, in which a bit of information encountered in one context is transplanted into another context. In the same fashion, as your memory for an episode becomes more and more interwoven with other thoughts you had about the episode, it becomes difficult to keep track of which elements are linked to the episode because they were, in truth, part of the episode, and which are linked because they were merely *associated with* the episode in your thought. This, too, can produce transplant errors—as elements that were part of your thinking get (mis)remembered as if they were actually part of the original experience.

Understanding Both Helps and Hurts Memory

This hypothesis clearly suggests that having memory connections both helps and hurts recollection. It helps because the connections promote retrieval. It hurts because the connections make it difficult to see where the remembered episode stops and other, related, knowledge begins. As a result, the connections encourage intrusion errors, errors in which other knowledge intrudes into the remembered event.

Consistent with this view, many experiments show that factors that encourage the creation of connections do both help and hurt memory. As one example, consider the role of *understanding* itself. In one study, half of the participants in the experiment read the following passage (Owens, Bower, & Black, 1979):

> Nancy arrived at the cocktail party. She looked around the room to see who was there. She went to talk with her professor. She felt she had to talk to him but was a little nervous about just what to say. A group of people started to play charades. Nancy went over and had some refreshments. The hors d'oeuvres were good but she wasn't interested in talking to the rest of the people at the party. After a while she decided she'd had enough and left the party.

Other participants read the same passage, but with a prologue that set the stage:

> Nancy woke up feeling sick again and she wondered if she really were pregnant. How would she tell the professor she had been seeing? And the money was another problem.

All participants were then given a recall test in which they were asked to remember the sentences as exactly as they could. As can be seen in Table 7.1, partici-

| TABLE 7.1 | Number of Propositions Remembered by Participants |

	Theme condition[a]	Neutral condition
Studied propositions (those in story)	29.2	20.2
Inferred propositions (those not in story)	15.2	3.7

After Owens et al., 1979.

[a]In the *theme* condition, a brief prologue set the theme for the passage that was to be remembered.

pants who had read the prologue recalled considerably more of the original story. This is consistent with claims made in Chapter 5: The prologue provided a meaningful context for the remainder of the story, and this helped understanding. Understanding, in turn, promoted recall.

At the same time, the story's prologue also led participants to include many things in their recall that were not mentioned in the original episode. In fact, participants who had seen the prologue made *four times* as many intrusion errors as did participants who had not seen the prologue. For example, they might recall, "The professor had gotten Nancy pregnant." This is not part of the story but is certainly implied, and so will probably be part of the participants' understanding of the story. It is then this understanding (including the imported element) that is remembered.

The DRM Paradigm

Similar effects can even be demonstrated with word lists, provided that the lists are carefully arranged, so that they make appropriate contact with prior knowledge. For example, in many experiments, participants have been presented with lists like this one: "bed, rest, awake, tired, dream, wake, snooze, blanket, doze, slumber, snore, nap, peace, yawn, drowsy." Then, immediately after hearing this list, participants are asked to recall as many of the words as they can.

As you may have noticed, all of the words in this list are associated with the word "sleep," and the presence of this theme helps memory: The words that are on the list are relatively easy to remember. It turns out, though, that "sleep," the root of the list, is not itself included in the list. Nonetheless, the participants spontaneously make the connection between the list words and this associated word, and this almost invariably leads to a memory error: When the time comes for recall, participants are extremely likely to recall that they heard "sleep." In fact, they are just as likely to recall "sleep" as they are to recall the actual words on the list!

This same pattern emerges in recognition testing: If participants are shown test words and asked which of these appeared in the original list, they are just as likely to recognize "sleep" as being one of the list words as they are to recognize actually presented list words. When asked how confident they are in their memories, participants are just as confident in their (false) recognition of "sleep" as they are in their (correct) recognition of genuine list words (Roediger & McDermott, 1995, 2000; also see Brainerd & Reyna, 1998; Bruce & Winograd, 1998; Deese, 1957; McEvoy, Nelson, & Komatsu, 1999; and Stadler, Roediger, & McDermott, 1999).

This paradigm is referred to as the **Deese–Roediger–McDermott** (or DRM) procedure, in honor of the investigators who developed it. The procedure yields striking results—with a very simple task leading to large numbers of memory errors. The errors are observed even if participants are put on their guard before the procedure begins. In one experiment, participants were warned that their task was "trickier than it seems at first." Next, everything about the procedure was put out in plain view. In particular, the participants were told explicitly that each memory list would revolve around a single theme, and they were warned, "Many people have a tendency on the memory test to recall words that fit with the theme even if those words actually weren't on the original list. Try not to do that; try to be careful, and recall only words you actually heard on the list." Even with this clear warning, participants still made the DRM errors—although they did make slightly fewer errors than participants who received no warning (Reisberg, 1999; also Gallo, Roberts, & Seamon, 1997; McDermott & Roediger, 1998). Apparently, the mechanisms leading to these memory errors are quite automatic, and not mechanisms that people can somehow inhibit.

Schematic Knowledge

In the DRM procedure, intrusion errors come from words (or ideas) merely associated with the materials being learned. In other settings, though, intrusion errors come from the background knowledge that we bring to most situations. This knowledge is usually helpful: It guides us as we explore, think about, and interpret the situations we find ourselves in. But this knowledge can also be a powerful source of memory error.

To make this concrete, imagine that you go to a restaurant with a friend. This is a familiar experience for you, and you have knowledge about what normally happens in each visit: You'll be seated; someone will bring you menus; you'll order, then eat. Eventually, you'll pay the check and leave. Knowledge like this is called generic knowledge; it's knowledge about how things unfold in general, and knowledge about what's typical in a particular sort of setting. This knowledge is often referred to by the Greek word schema (plural: schemata). Schemata summarize the broad pattern of what's "normal" in a situation, and so your kitchen schema tells you that a kitchen is likely to have a stove in it, but no piano; your dentist's office schema tells you that there are likely to be magazines in the waiting room; and so on.

Schemata help us in many ways. For one, they tell us what's important in a situation and what's not, and this influences what we pay attention to. In addition, schemata help us to understand a situation. In the restaurant, for example, you're not puzzled by the fact that someone keeps filling your water glass, or that someone drops by the table to ask, "How is everything?" You know that these are normal occurrences in a restaurant, and so you instantly understand how they fit into the broader script.

Schemata also help you when the time comes to recall an event later. Often there are gaps in our recollection—either because there were things we didn't notice in the first place, or because we have gradually forgotten some aspects of an experience. (We will say more about forgetting in a moment.) In either case, we can rely on our schemata to fill these gaps. In recalling your restaurant visit, for example, you might not remember anything about the menus. Nonetheless, you can be reasonably sure that there were menus, and that they were given to you early on and taken away right after you placed your order. You might not remember this information, but you can reconstruct it on the basis of your schematic knowledge.

Evidence for Schematic Knowledge

Once again, therefore, we are led to a familiar theme: Schematic knowledge helps us, we've just argued, because it guides our attention and our understanding and can help us to reconstruct things we cannot remember. But schematic knowledge can also hurt us, promoting error in both our perception and our memory.

Moreover, the *types* of errors promoted by schema use will be quite predictable. In general, a reliance on schemata will make the world seem more "normal" than it really is, and will make the past seem more "regular" than it actually was. Imagine, for example, that you read a story about a visit to the dentist's office, and in the story there's no mention of any magazines in the waiting room. Nonetheless, you might remember the magazines anyhow because they are "supplied" by your dentist's office schema. (If you're using your schema to reconstruct what the story contained, the schema will suggest magazines, whether they were in the story or not.) Likewise, if you hear about some people going to a restaurant, you're likely to recall that they ate food, whether you heard that information or not. Here, too, your schema invites you to assume that which is normal, and to reconstruct that which is ordinary—with the consequence that you'll end up "regularizing" your recollection of the past.

The classic demonstration of these effects comes from research published many years ago in Frederick Bartlett's book *Remembering*. Bartlett presented his participants with stories taken from the folklore of Native Americans (Bartlett, 1932). When tested later, the participants did reasonably well in recalling the gist of the stories, but they made many errors in recalling the particulars. Often, details of the original story were simply omitted from their recall; other details were either added to the original or changed. The pattern of errors, though, was quite systematic: The details omitted tended to be details that made little sense to Bartlett's British participants. Likewise, aspects of the story that were unfamiliar were changed into aspects that were more familiar; steps of the story that seemed inexplicable were supplemented to make the story seem more logical.

In this study, participants' memories seem to have "cleaned up" the story—making it more coherent (from their perspective), more sensible, than it first seemed. This is exactly what we would expect if the memory errors derived from the participants' attempts to understand the story, and with that, their efforts toward fitting the story into a familiar schematic frame. Elements that fit with the frame remained in their memories, or could perhaps be reconstructed later. Elements that did not fit dropped out of memory or were changed.

In the same spirit, consider the Brewer and Treyens study we mentioned at the very start of this chapter—the study in which participants remembered seeing bookshelves full of books, even though there were none. This error was produced by schematic knowledge: During the event itself (i.e., while the participants were sitting in the office), this knowledge told the participants that academic offices usually contain many books and this biased what the participants paid attention to. (If you're already certain that the shelves contain books, why should you spend time looking at the shelves? This would only confirm something that you already know.) Then, when the time came to recall the office, participants used their schema to reconstruct what the office *must* contain—a desk, a chair, and of course lots of books. In this fashion, the memory for the actual office was eclipsed by generic knowledge about what a "normal" office contains.

Likewise, think back to our other early example—the misremembered plane crash. Here, too, the memory error distorts reality by making the past seem more regular, more typical, than it really was. After all, the Dutch survey respondents probably hear about most major news events via a television broadcast, and this broadcast typically includes vivid video footage. So here, too, the past as remembered seems to have been assimilated into the pattern of the ordinary. The event as it unfolded was unusual, but the event *as remembered* is quite typical of its kind. This is just as we would expect if understanding and remembering were guided by schemata, with those schemata representing the way things generally unfold. (For other evidence, see, among others, G. H. Bower, Black, & Turner, 1979; Bransford & Johnson, 1972, 1973; Lampinen, Copeland, & Neuschatz, 2001; and Spiro, 1977.)

The Causes of Forgetting

Schematic knowledge sometimes plays a large role in shaping memory, and sometimes a smaller role. The influence of schematic knowledge is smaller, for example, if, at the time of an event, you think carefully about how exactly the event unfolded, rather than what the event meant; what was distinctive about the episode, rather than what the event had in common with other, similar, events. Paying attention to these particulars will decrease the need later on for schema-based reconstruction, and will also decrease the chance that, in recalling the episode, you'll confuse it with other, related episodes.

Another important factor, not surprisingly, is the passage of time. As the retention interval (i.e., the amount of time that elapses between the initial learning and the subsequent retrieval) grows, you will gradually forget more and more of the earlier event, and this can promote errors in two different ways. First, you're likely to rely on after-the-fact reconstruction to "plug" these gaps in the memory record, filling in with inference the bits that you cannot recall. This by itself will increase the influence of schematic knowledge (which is, after all, the basis for the reconstruction). Second, as you forget the details of an episode, it will become more difficult to distinguish which elements were actually part of the event, and which were merely associated with the event in your thoughts. This will increase the likelihood of intrusion errors. (For some of the many, many demonstrations that retention interval is a crucial variable, see Jobe, Tourangeau, & Smith, 1993.)

But why does the passage of time matter? Why, in brief, does forgetting happen? Actually, there are several hypotheses. One possibility is **decay**. With the passage of time, memories may fade or erode. Perhaps this is because the relevant brain cells die off. Or perhaps the connections among memories need to be constantly refreshed; if not, the connections may gradually weaken. In any event, it is largely the passage of time that triggers these events.

A different possibility is that new learning somehow works against or interferes with older learning. According to this **interference** account, less is remembered about older events because, as time passes, there is more and more opportunity for interference. That's because the passage of time allows new learning, and it is this new learning that interferes with older memories.

A third hypothesis blames **retrieval failure**. After all, the retrieval of information from memory is far from guaranteed, and we argued in Chapter 6 that retrieval is most likely if your perspective (mental, emotional, and physical) at the time of retrieval matches that in place at the time of learning. If we now assume that your perspective is likely to change more and more as time goes by, we can make a prediction about forgetting: The greater the retention interval, the greater the likelihood that your perspective has changed, and therefore the greater the likelihood of retrieval failure.

There is no doubt that retrieval failure does occur. In many circumstances, we are unable to remember some bit of information, but then, a while later, we do recall that information. Because the information eventually was retrieved, we know that it was not "erased" from memory through decay or interference. Our initial failure to recall the information, therefore, must be counted as an example of retrieval failure. But what about the other mechanisms—decay and interference? Do they contribute to forgetting?

The evidence on this point is mixed. On the one side, there is evidence that memories do decay with the passage of time (e.g., Altmann & Gray, 2002). On the other side, we will later look at evidence showing that some memories last an extremely long time; this tells us that decay is far from inevitable. In addition, a number of studies have directly compared the effects of decay and interference, and show that interference, not decay, seems the more prominent source of ordinary forgetting.

Here's one example of how the evidence unfolds: Baddeley and Hitch (1977) asked rugby players to recall the names of the other teams they had played against over the course of a season. Not all players made it to all games, because of illness, injuries, or schedule conflicts. These differences allow us to compare players for whom "two games back" means 2 weeks ago, to players for whom "two games back" means 4 weeks ago. Thus, we can look at the effects of retention interval (2 weeks vs. 4) with the number of intervening games held constant. Likewise, we can compare players for whom the game a month ago was "three games back" to players for whom a month means "one game back." Now we have the retention interval held constant, and we can look at the effects of intervening events. In this setting, Baddeley and Hitch report that the mere passage of time accounts for very little; what

FIGURE 7.2 **Forgetting From Interfering Events**

Members of a rugby team were asked to recall the names of teams they had played against. Their performance was influenced by the number of games that intervened between the game to be recalled and the attempt to remember. This pattern fits with an interference view of forgetting. (After Baddeley & Hitch, 1977)

really matters is the number of intervening events (Figure 7.2). This is just what we would expect if interference, and not decay, is the major contributor to forgetting.

Interference: Blurring of Similar Episodes

Why does memory interference occur? Why can't the newly acquired information peacefully coexist with older memories? Part of the answer is "source confusion." This term (which we first met in Chapter 6) refers to the fact that we are often able to remember things we have learned or conversations we have heard, but may be mistaken about the source of this knowledge—where it was, or when it was, that we learned the facts or heard the conversations. (For discussion of source confusion, see, for example, Bornstein & LeCompte, 1995; Dodson, Holland, & Shimamura, 1998; Jurica & Shimamura, 1999; and Marsh & Landau, 1995.)

Source confusion can actually take many forms. One form involves the intrusion of schematic knowledge into a memory for some specific event: Let's say, for example, that you visit a farm and, 6 months later, remember seeing the farmer's tractor, even though, in truth, no tractor was in sight during your visit. In this case, the "memory" of the tractor was probably supplied by your generic knowledge because, of course, you know in general that farms do have tractors. Thus, you would be correct in thinking that the idea of a tractor is *associated with* your memory of the farm visit. Your mistake, though, lies in your belief about the source of this idea: You think the barn was part of the episode you're recalling, even though, in fact, the real source for this idea is your generic knowledge.

Source confusion can also result when memory for one episode "blurs together" with memories for other, similar, episodes. This is why memory errors are less likely when people are remembering some unique event, as opposed to one episode within a series of similar episodes (Brewer, 1988). If you've seen only one ballet in your life, there's no risk of confusion when you try to remember in which ballet you saw the dancing fireflies. But, in contrast, let's say that you're trying to remember a train ride with a truly comical conductor. Will you remember which train ride it was? You may not, simply because the many train rides in your experience have blurred together in memory. As a result, interference is observed, with new learning (many train rides) impeding memory for the specific event you're trying to recall. The new learning doesn't *erase* the old learning, but it does erode memory accuracy, as details are exchanged from one episode to another. (For examples of this pattern, see Jobe et al., 1993; Neisser, 1981; Reinitz, Lammers, & Cochran, 1992; and Roberts & Blades, 1998.)

Interference: The Effect of Leading Questions

Yet another type of source confusion involves cases in which an event that actually occurred blurs together with a different event that merely refers to, or is related to, the target event. For example, imagine that you witness a crime, and then, later, are asked questions about the crime. The two events in this case are, first, experiencing the crime itself, and then, second, the experience of being questioned. If these two events blur together in memory, then it's possible that information you pick up during the questioning may be merged with information from the original episode, and this may change how you remember the original!

Many experiments have examined this issue and have asked, more specifically, what happens if a witness to a crime is asked leading questions (by a friend, or another witness, or a police investigator). In one of the early studies, Loftus and Palmer (1974) showed participants a series of projected slides depicting an automobile collision. Sometime later, half the participants were asked, "How fast were the cars going when they hit each other?" Others were asked, "How fast were the cars going when they smashed into each other?" The difference between these questions ("hit" vs. "smashed") is slight, but it turned out to be enough to bias the participants' estimates of speed. Participants in the first group estimated the speed to have been 34 miles per hour; participants in the second group estimated 41 miles per hour. But what is critical comes next: One week later, the participants were asked in a perfectly neutral way whether they had seen any broken glass in the slides. Participants who had initially been asked the "hit" question tended to remember (correctly) that no glass was visible; only 14% said they had seen glass. Participants asked the "smashed" question, though, were reasonably likely to remember glass; 32% asserted that glass was visible. It seems, therefore, that the change of just one word within the initial question can have a large effect—in this case, more than doubling the likelihood of memory error.

Across the last quarter century, researchers have tried many variations on this procedure, and to put it broadly, all have the same effect. In some studies, the misinformation is merely implied (as it was in the "hit" vs. "smashed" experiment). In other studies, the misinformation is subtly mentioned as part of the questioning. Participants might, for example, be asked, "How fast was the car going when it raced by the barn?" when, in truth, no barn was in view. In still other studies, participants have been exposed to descriptions of the target event that allegedly were written by "other witnesses," and again, these descriptions contain some misinformation. Finally, in other cases, participants have been asked questions about an event that required the participants themselves to *make up* the misinformation. For example, participants can be asked, "In the video, was the man bleeding from his knee or from his elbow after the fall?" Even though it was clear in the video that the man was not bleeding at all, participants are still forced to choose one of these options (Zaragoza, Payment, Ackil, Drivadahl, & Beck, 2001).

All of these procedures have roughly the same impact, because all are variations on the same theme: In all cases, the participant experiences an event and then is exposed to misinformation about the event. Then some time is allowed to pass. At the end of this interval, the participant's memory is tested. And in all cases the outcome is the same: A substantial number of participants—sometimes as many as one third of the participants in the study—end up incorporating the misinformation into their memory for the original event. (For recent summaries of all of this research, see Ayers & Reder, 1998; and Loftus, 2003.)

In this fashion, researchers have reliably been able to create **false memories**, memories that misrepresent how an event actually unfolded. As a result, broken glass is remembered when really there was none; barns are remembered when there were no buildings at all; screwdrivers originally seen are remembered as hammers, and blue sedans are remembered as brown pickup trucks. Similar procedures have altered how people are remembered—so that clean-shaven men are remembered as bearded, and so on.

This overall pattern of results is often referred to as the **misinformation effect** because the participants' memory is plainly being influenced by misinformation they received after an episode was over. Note, though, that this effect is really just another example of source confusion: In the misinformation studies, the participants *correctly* recall that, at some point in their past, they encountered (for example) the idea of broken glass or the idea of a barn. They're also correct in believing that these ideas are somehow connected to the episode they're trying to recall. Their error, however, lies in their belief about the *source* of this memory: They believe these items were contained in the original episode they witnessed, when really they were contained in the misinformation they acquired subsequently.

Are There Limits on the Misinformation Effect?

Obviously, suggestions and leading questions can change the details of how an event is remembered, and they can even add whole objects (barns, for example) to a memory for an event. Further research, however, suggests that misinformation can do much more than this, and can create memories for entire episodes that never happened at all.

In one study, college students were told that the investigators were trying to learn how different people remember the same experience. The students were then given a list of events that they were told had been reported by their parents; the students were asked to recall these events as well as they could, so that the investigators could compare their recall with their parents' (Hyman, Husband, & Billings, 1995).

Some of the events on the list had, in fact, been reported by the participants' parents. Other events were bogus—made up by the experimenters. (In fact, the experimenters checked with the parents to make certain that these bogus events really had not happened.) One of the bogus events was an overnight hospitalization for a high fever; in a different experiment, the bogus event was attending a wedding reception and accidentally spilling a punch bowl on the parents of the bride.

The college students were easily able to remember the genuine events (i.e., the events actually reported by their parents). In an initial interview, more than 80% of these events were recalled; by a second interview, this number had climbed to almost 90%. In the first interview, none of the students recalled the bogus events, but repeated attempts at recall changed this pattern: By the third interview, 25% of the participants were able to remember the embarrassment of spilling the punch bowl, and many were able to supply the details of this (fictitious) episode. Other studies have yielded similar results, with participants led to recall details of particular birthday parties that, in truth, they never had (Hyman et al., 1995) or an incident of being lost in a shopping mall, even though this event never took place (Loftus, 1997; Loftus & Pickrell, 1995; also see Porter, Yuille, & Lehman, 1999). In other studies, participants have been led in a similar fashion to recall a hot-air balloon ride that, in reality, never happened, and also to recall a (fictitious) event in which they were the victim of a vicious animal attack (Loftus, 2003).

The same sort of result has been documented with children, and, in fact, the evidence suggests that children are more vulnerable than adults to this sort of memory "planting." In one study, children participated in an event with "Mr. Science," a man who showed them a number of fun demonstrations. Afterward, the parents (who were not at the event) were asked to discuss the event with their children—and were, in particular, urged to discuss several elements that (unbeknownst to the parents) actually had never occurred. Later on, the children were interviewed about their visit with Mr. Science, and many of them confidently remembered the (fictitious) elements they had discussed with their parents—including a time (that never happened) in which Mr. Science put something "yucky" in their mouths, or a time in which Mr. Science hurt the child's tummy (by pressing too hard when applying a sticker; Poole & Lindsay, 2001). Such results obviously echo the misinformation results with adults, but they are also extremely important for their own sake, because (among other concerns) these results are relevant to children's testimony in the courtroom (Bruck & Ceci, 1999; Ceci & Bruck, 1995).

Clearly, then, entire events can be planted in someone's memory, so that the person ends up recalling—confidently and in detail—an episode that never took place. Moreover, it seems relatively easy to plant these memories: Two or three brief interviews, with no particular pressure, no effort toward coercion, are all that is needed.

Of course, it is easier to plant *plausible* memories than implausible ones (although memories for implausible events can also be planted; Hyman, 2000; Mazzoni, Loftus, & Kirsch, 2001; Pezdek, Finger, & Hodge, 1997; Pezdek & Hodge, 1999; A. K. Thomas & Loftus, 2002). It is easier to plant a memory if the false suggestion is repeated, rather than delivered just once (Bruck & Ceci, 1999; Zaragoza & Mitchell, 1996). False memories are also more easily planted if the research participants are urged to imagine how the suggested event unfolded—an effect referred to as "imagination inflation" (Garry & Polaschek, 2000; Goff & Roediger, 1998; Mazzoni & Memon, 2003; A. K. Thomas, Bulevich, & Loftus, 2003). Finally, it appears that some individuals are more susceptible than others to false memories (Bremner, Shobe, & Kihlstrom, 2000; Clancy, Schacter, McNally, & Pitmann, 2000; Heaps & Nash, 1999; Hyman & Billings, 1998; Scullin, Kanaya, & Ceci, 2002; Winograd, Peluso, & Glover, 1998).

Across all of these variations, though, the basic points remain: False memories can easily be planted, through a variety of procedures, and the memory errors thus created can be large (e.g., entire events). Once the false memories are planted, the target "events" seem to be "remembered" fully and in detail. All of this raises many troubling questions—including questions about how much each of us can trust our own recollection, and also questions, as we've noted, about the degree to which the *courts* can trust the memory of eyewitnesses to crimes. Returning to our main agenda, though, the various forms of the misinformation effect provide compelling support for the claim that *memory interference* and (more specifically) *source confusion* are powerful sources of forgetting and memory error.

Evaluating Human Memory

Where, then, does all of this leave us? Obviously the accuracy of our memories is far from guaranteed, and the past as we remember it may, in some cases, be markedly different from the past as it really was. This clearly has implications for how we should think about the past, and for how much faith we should put in our own memories. As we have mentioned, it also has important pragmatic implications—for example, for the legal system: Eyewitness testimony is taken very seriously by the courts, but of course this testimony relies on what the witness remembers. The research we have discussed raises important concerns about such testimony.

Overall, though, how worried should we be about memory accuracy? To put the point bluntly, how often is our recollection of the past actually wrong?

Accurate Memories

It would probably be a mistake to give a single broad assessment of human memory. This is because, in some settings, memory errors are quite likely, while in other settings they are unlikely. Nonetheless, the overall pattern of evidence suggests that, in our daily lives, we usually *can* trust our memories. More often than not, our recollection is complete, detailed, long-lasting, and *correct*.

Many lines of evidence are pertinent to this claim. For example, Yuille and Cutshall (1986) interviewed 13 witnesses to an actual crime, 4 to 5 months after the event. The witnesses' memory for the crime was impressively accurate, despite this delay, and despite the fact that the investigators used stringent criteria in evaluating the witnesses' recall: Reported ages of the perpetrators, for example, had to be within 2 years to be counted as correct; reported weights, within 5 pounds. No leeway was given for the estimation of the number of shots fired in the incident. Even with these strict rules, the witnesses were correct in 83% of the details reported about the action itself within the episode, 90% correct in their descriptions of objects on the scene. (Also see Fisher, Geiselman, & Amador, 1989; and Yuille & Kim, 1987.)

Similar levels of accuracy have been observed in other studies. For example, H. Howes, Siegel, and Brown (1993) asked their adult participants to recall events from very early in childhood. When checked, most of these memories turned out to be reasonably accurate. Likewise, Brewin, Andrews, and Gotlib (1993) summarize a number of studies showing that our autobiographical recollection is correct most of the time.

Therefore, we can document cases of wonderfully accurate memory, and also examples of huge memory errors. What shapes this pattern? When is memory accurate, and when not? We have already mentioned some of the key factors: Gaps in memory, thanks either to inattention during an event, or the passage of time afterward, make memory errors more likely. Having a source of intrusion (e.g., misinformation encountered after the event, or some related episode that can be confused with the event being remembered) also promotes memory errors. With these factors in play, memory errors are astonishingly likely. But this doesn't change the fact that, in most circumstances, our memories serve us very well.

Memory Confidence

Is there a way to protect ourselves against the memory errors that do occur? Can we somehow scrutinize our own recall (or, just as important, scrutinize the memory reports we hear from other people), and separate the memories that can be trusted from those that are potentially false? The evidence on this point is disappointing, and, unfortunately, memory errors seem to be largely undetectable.

It's certainly true that we put more trust in some memories than others. Thus we sometimes announce that we're confident in our recall ("I distinctly remember her yellow jacket; I'm sure of it") and sometimes we say the opposite ("Gee, I think he was wearing blue, but I'm not certain"). And the evidence suggests that we take these assessments quite seriously. In our own recall, we're more willing to take action based on confident memories than hesitant ones. And the same is true when we're listening to others: In the courtroom, for example, juries place much more weight on a witness's evidence if the witness expresses confidence during the testimony; conversely, juries are usually skeptical about testimony that is hesitant or hedged. Apparently, then, juries believe that *confident* recall is likely to be *accurate* recall (Brigham & Wolfskiel, 1983; Cutler, Penrod, & Dexter, 1990; Loftus, 1979; Wells, Lindsay, & Ferguson, 1979). And it is not just juries who hold this view: Judges believe the same, and so judges typically instruct juries to put more faith in confident witnesses, less faith in hesitant ones (*Neil v. Biggers*, 1972, is a key ruling on this point in federal court; for a parallel ruling from a state court, see *State of Oregon v. Classen*, 1979).

This is a case, however, in which common sense, juries, and the courts are all mistaken. Many studies have systematically compared research participants' confidence when they are reporting a correct memory with their confidence when they are reporting a false memory. This research has employed many of the procedures we have discussed in this chapter—memory for sentences, the DRM technique, the misinformation paradigm—and also a number of studies designed to mimic the situation of an actual eyewitness to a crime. Across all of these procedures, the pattern is quite clear: There is little or no relationship between memory confidence and memory accuracy. Any attempt to categorize memories as correct or incorrect, therefore, based on the rememberer's confidence, will be riddled with errors. (For some of the evidence, see Busey, Tunnicliff, Loftus, & Loftus, 2000; Chandler, 1994; Roediger & McDermott, 1995; Sporer, Penrod, Read, & Cutler, 1995; W. B. Thompson & Mason, 1996; and Wells, Luus, & Windschitl, 1994.)

How could this be? How could we be so poor in evaluating our own memories? The main reason is that our confidence in a memory is influenced by several variables that have no influence on accuracy. When these variables are on the scene, confidence will change (sometimes upward, sometimes downward) with no change in the accuracy level, and this will undermine any correspondence between confidence and accuracy.

As one example, participants in one study were witnesses to a (simulated) crime, and then, sometime later, they were asked if they could identify the "culprit" from a group of pictures. Some of the participants were then given feedback ("Good, you identified the suspect"), and some were not. This feedback could not possibly influence the *accuracy* of the identification, because the feedback arrived only after the identification was done. But the feedback did influence *confidence*, and witnesses who had received the feedback expressed a much higher level of confidence in their choice than did witnesses who received no feedback (Wells & Bradfield, 1999; Wells, Olson, & Charman, 2002, 2003). Thus, with confidence inflated but accuracy unchanged, the linkage between confidence and accuracy was necessarily diminished.

In short, then, memory confidence is a poor indicator of memory accuracy, and with this, we can easily find examples of memories that are recalled with enormous confidence but are nonetheless filled with errors (e.g., Neisser & Harsch, 1992). As a result, memory confidence is (at best) an unreliable means of detecting memory mistakes.

Remembering Versus Knowing

Perhaps we can distinguish correct memories from false memories in some other way. Investigators have asked whether false memories are perhaps less detailed than genuine memories, or perhaps more detailed. There is typically little difference. Investigators have also tried urging their participants to be extremely careful in these experiments—to respond, "Yes, this is familiar" only if they are quite certain about their judgments. These warnings do reduce the number of errors somewhat, suggesting that at least some errors are detectable and avoidable. Even with these warnings, however, many memory errors remain (e.g., K. L. Chambers & Zaragoza, 2001; Greene, Flynn, & Loftus, 1982; Tousignant, Hall, & Loftus, 1986).

Still other investigators have tried timing their participants' responses, on the idea that responses based on false memories should be somewhat slower than responses based on clear, detailed, accurate memories. Typically, though, there is no difference in speed of responding between correct and incorrect answers (e.g., Begg & Wickelgren, 1974; Bransford, Barclay, & Franks, 1972; Bransford & Franks, 1971; Paris & Lindauer, 1976).

Other researchers have considered the emotion attached to a memory. We know that people often become quite emotional when recalling the events of their lives—and so they feel proud when thinking about some past triumph, upset when thinking about some past tragedy, and so on. Are they perhaps less emotional when remembering some memory fiction—an event that never occurred? If so, then we could use the degree of emotion as a way of distinguishing accurate memories from false ones. But this, too, turns out to be a dead end. False memories, memories of events that never actually happened, can be just as upsetting, just as emotional, as memories for real events (McNally et al., 2004).

Nonetheless, investigators continue to hunt for measures that might allow us to distinguish accurate memories from inaccurate ones. For example, consider the way a memory "feels" from the point of view of the person doing the remembering (Rajaram, 1993; Tulving, 1985). Sometimes, the person feels like he actually remembers the past; perhaps he remembers where he was when an event occurred, or what he was doing at the time: "I remember that this word was on the list because I remember that, when I saw the word, it reminded me of my math professor." Sometimes, though, our recollection does not contain these episodic details; in this case, we might speak of "knowing" something rather than "remembering" it: "This word seems very familiar, and so I know it was on the list, but I don't remember the experience of seeing it."

A great deal of research has explored this subjective difference and has asked why a memory sometimes arrives in your thoughts with the feeling of remembering, and why it sometimes arrives with the feeling of knowing (e.g., Gardiner, 1988; Hicks & Marsh, 1999; Jacoby, Jones, & Dolan, 1998). But will this distinction help us in detecting false memories? The evidence suggests that the feeling of remembering is, in fact, somewhat more likely with correct memories than it is with false memories (e.g., M. Conway, Collins, Gathercole, & Anderson, 1996; Lane & Zaragoza, 1995). Put differently, false memories often arrive with only a general sense of familiarity and no recollection of a particular episode. ("I'm sure there were books there, although, to tell you the truth, I don't remember anything about what they looked like.") But there are numerous exceptions to this pattern, and so in many cases fully correct memories arrive in your thoughts with only a feeling of knowing, and fully false memories arrive with a detailed sense of remembering. As a result, this subjective distinction between knowing and remembering, like the other efforts we have described, cannot serve as a reliable means of distinguishing correct memories from false ones (Frost, 2000; Holmes, Waters, & Rajaram, 1998; Roediger & McDermott, 1995; for other research, pursuing still other leads in distinguishing true memories from false ones, see Geiselman, Schroppel, Tubridy, Konishi, & Rodriguez, 2000; Heaps & Nash, 2001; Lamb, 1998; Leippe, Manion, & Romanczyk, 1992; and Pickel, 1999).

Exotic Strategies for Improving Memory

We are moving toward a mixed evaluation of human memory. On the positive side, people seem to remember accurately most of the time; correct memories are certainly more common than incorrect ones. On the negative side, though, when memory errors do occur, the errors can be large, and the errors seem to be virtually undetectable: Memories that contain errors, or memories that are wholly false, can be just as vivid, just as detailed, just as emotional, and recalled with just as much speed and confidence as memories that are completely accurate. These errors can occur when we are remembering actual events in our own lives (e.g., Neisser & Harsch, 1992); they can occur when we are trying to remember events important to us professionally (Vicente & Brewer, 1993); they can even occur in contexts in which the false memory leads us to confess to a crime we never committed (Kassin, 1997; Kassin & Kiechel, 1996; Ofshe, 1992).

Is there anything we can do to improve this situation? Can we somehow become better rememberers? As one option, a great deal has been asserted about the value of hypnosis in helping people to remember. Indeed, the suggestion is sometimes made that, under hypnosis, witnesses to an earlier event can remember everything about the event, including aspects they did not even notice (much less think about and interpret) at the time.

Many studies have examined these claims, and the evidence is clear: Hypnotized participants who are instructed to remember do their very best to comply, and this means that they will give a full and detailed reporting of the target event. However, it is not the case that the hypnotized participants remember more. Instead, they simply *say* more, in order to be cooperative. By saying more things, they will (just by chance) say some things that happen to be true. But most of the memory report by hypnotized people turns out not to be true, and, worse, the hypnotized individuals cannot tell you which of the reported details are correct and which are made up or are guesses. In other words, hypnosis does not improve memory; it just changes the willingness to talk (Dinges, Whitehouse, Orne, Powell, Orne, & Erdelyi, 1992; Hilgard, 1968; M. Smith, 1982; Spiegel, 1995).

Worse, there is reason to believe that hypnosis may actually compromise memory accuracy rather than improve it. Under hypnosis, people tend to be quite compliant, quite cooperative. Therefore, suggestions made to someone who is hypnotized will be taken very seriously—including suggestions about how a previous event unfolded. As a result, people who are hypnotized are more susceptible to the misinformation effect than people not under hypnosis.

Similar observations apply to various drugs alleged to improve memory—sodium amytal, for example. Many of these drugs work (in part) as sedatives, and this puts an individual in a less guarded, less cautious state of mind. This state of mind allows people to report more about the past—not because they remember more, but simply because, in this relaxed state, they are willing to say more. Likewise, this less guarded state leaves an individual more vulnerable to the effects of leading or misleading questions, which of course can undermine memory accuracy. Plainly, then, these techniques are not the way to improve recollection.

A more exotic way to improve recall is suggested by reports of people whose brains have been directly stimulated, usually as part of brain surgery. Patients are typically awake during this surgery, and the surgeon uses their responses to brain stimulation as a way of locating certain structures and regions within the brain. Sometimes, though, when the brain is prodded or poked, the patient suddenly remembers scenes from long ago, often in clear and remarkable detail. Could this be the way to defeat forgetting and to recover one's "lost past"?

In fact, only a small number of patients report recollections in response to this stimulation of the brain. But the memories evoked in this fashion are extraordinary—clear and detailed, as though the patients were reliving the earlier experience. Unfortunately, though, we have no way of knowing whether these are really memories. These experiences might, for example, be hallucinations of some sort. Or these experiences might be very vivid reconstructions. Because this evidence comes from an extreme circumstance, it has been difficult to track down the historical facts to confirm (or disconfirm) these patients' recollections. Until this is done, we have no evidence that they are remembering, much less remembering accurately. Hence, we have no basis for claiming that this technique promotes memory retrieval.

Memory: An Overall Assessment

Over and over in this chapter, we have seen that memory errors do occur. People sometimes confidently, sincerely, and vividly recall events that never took place. In other settings, they recall actual events, but in a fashion that is systematically different from the way the events really unfolded.

Most of these errors have been documented in the laboratory, but it is easy to identify the same sorts of errors in various real-world settings—including settings in which the stakes are extremely high. Errors by eyewitnesses to crimes, for example, have been well documented by investigators (e.g., Ceci & Bruck, 1995; Loftus & Ketcham, 1991; Schacter, 1999; Wright & Davies, 1999; Wright & McDaid, 1996) and acknowledged as a problem by the U.S. Department of Justice (Connors, Lundregan, Miller, & McEwan, 1996).

One might argue, though, that these errors are simply the price we pay in order to gain other advantages: Bear in mind that the errors arise (in part) because our memories are densely interconnected with each other. This is what allows elements to be transplanted from one remembered episode to another. But the connections are, of course, there for a purpose: They are the retrieval paths that make memory search possible. Thus, to avoid the errors, we would need to restrict the connections, but if we did that, we would lose the ability to locate our own memories within long-term storage!

In addition, the memory connections that lead to error often help us in other ways. Our environment, after all, is in many ways predictable, and it is enormously useful for us to exploit that predictability. There's little point in scrutinizing a kitchen to make sure there is a stove in the room, because, in the vast majority of cases, there is. Why take the time, therefore, to confirm the obvious? Likewise, there's little point in taking special note that, yes, this restaurant does have menus and that, yes, people in the restaurant are eating and not having their cars repaired. These, too, are obvious points, and it would be a waste of effort to give them special notice.

On these grounds, reliance on schematic knowledge is a good thing: Schemata guide our attention to what's informative in a situation, rather than what's self-evident; and they also guide our inferences at the time of recall. If this use of schemata sometimes leads us astray, this may be a tiny price to pay for the gain in efficiency that schemata allow. (For a parallel argument, see Chapter 3.)

Finally, what about forgetting? Remarkably, this, too, may be a blessing in disguise, for sometimes it is to our advantage to remember less, and to forget more. For example, think about all the times in your life when you've been with a particular friend. These episodes are related to each other in an obvious way, and so they are likely to become interconnected in your memory. This will cause interference, because you will have difficulty remembering which episode is which, and whether you had a particular conversation in this episode or in that one. However, rather than lamenting this as an example of forgetting (caused by interference), perhaps we should *celebrate* what's going on here: Because of the "interference," all of the episodes will merge together in your memory, so that what resides in memory is one integrated package, containing, in united form, all of your knowledge about your friend. In this way, *general knowledge* is created. In other words, the same blurring together that makes it difficult to remember episodes also makes it possible to think in a general way, to think about what's in common among diverse experiences, rather than what it is that makes each experience unique. Without this blurring together, our capacity for thinking in general terms might be dramatically impaired.

It seems, then, that our overall assessment of memory can be reasonably upbeat. We have, to be sure, discussed a wide range of memory errors, but we have also emphasized that errors are the exception rather than the rule. In addition, we have now pointed out that the errors are, in most cases, a side product of mechanisms that otherwise help us—to locate our memories within storage, to be efficient in our contact with the world, and to form general knowledge. Thus, even with the errors, even with forgetting, it seems that human memory functions in a fashion that serves us well.

Autobiographical Memory

We began this chapter by acknowledging that much of the evidence in Chapters 5 and 6 was concerned with memory for very simple stimuli—word lists, for example, or short sentences. In this chapter, we've considered memories for more complex materials, and this discussion has drawn our attention to the way in which someone's knowledge (whether knowledge of a general sort, or knowledge about related episodes) can both improve memory and also interfere with it.

In making these points, we've now considered memories in which the person was actually involved in the remembered episode, and not just an external witness (e.g., the children remembering the Mr. Science visit). We've also looked at studies that involved memories for emotional events (e.g., the plane crash we discussed at the chapter's start), and memory over the very long term (e.g., memories for childhood events "planted" in adult participants).

These three factors—involvement, emotion, and long delay—are, of course, often relevant to the sorts of remembering people do outside of the laboratory, and, indeed, all three are crucial factors for **autobiographical memory**. This is the memory that each of us has containing the full recollection of our lives, and this memory plays a central role in shaping how each of us thinks about ourselves, and thus how we behave. (For more on the distinction between autobiographical memory and the broader category of *episodic* memory, see Baddeley, Aggleton, & Conway, 2002. For more on the distinction between episodic memory and semantic, or generic, memory, see Hodges & Graham, 2001; Kopelman & Kapur, 2001; Schachter, 1996; and Tulving, 1993, 2002.)

All of this leads us to ask, How do the three factors we've mentioned, each crucial for autobiographical memory, influence what we remember?

Memory and the Self

Having some involvement in an event, rather than passively witnessing the event, turns out to have a powerful effect on memory. This is probably because involvement in the event leads naturally to the idea that the event is relevant to you and who you are, and relevance to the self is a powerful force in shaping memory. As one consideration, information perceived to be relevant to the self is, in general, better remembered—a result referred to as the **self-reference effect** (Symons & Johnson, 1997). This effect emerges in many forms, including an advantage in remembering things you have said as opposed to things others have said, better memory for adjectives that apply to you relative to adjectives that do not, better memory for names of places you have visited relative to names of places you have never been, and so on.

One reason for all this is, quite simply, attention: Each of us tends to take special interest in events that are related to our own lives, and so we are likely to attend to these events with special care. This may account for much of the self-reference effect. Schemata are another factor: Each of us knows an enormous amount about ourselves, and so we are likely to have a rich and detailed self-schema. This schema will serve as a powerful mnemonic device, organizing and interconnecting any self-relevant information.

A separate role for the self arises from our earlier argument that some "remembering" is, in fact, reconstruction based on current knowledge and current understanding. When, for example, you try to recall what you did last Tuesday, you're likely to rely on your understanding of how, in general, your Tuesdays unfold; that understanding will guide your memory search and also help you to fill any gaps in your recollection. Similarly, when you're trying to recall how you acted, say, at last year's New Year's party, you will probably draw on your understanding of what things you're likely to have done at this party and what things you're likely not to have done. This will depend, in turn, on how you view yourself: If you think of yourself, say, as a quiet and polite person, you're unlikely to reconstruct a drunken dance on the table. If you think of yourself as a funny person, you're unlikely to reconstruct your sitting quietly in the corner.

Does our self-perception influence memory in this way? Consider the fact that many people believe they have been reasonably consistent, reasonably stable, over their lifetimes. They believe, in other words, that they've always been pretty much the same as they are now. If memory for the past is to some extent a reconstruction, based on current ideas, then people with this belief about themselves should end up recalling their past in a biased fashion—one that maximizes the (apparent) stability of their lives. This turns out to be right: They recall their attitudes in the past, and the past status of their romantic relationships, and their health, in a fashion that emphasizes consistency, and thus makes the past look more like the present than it really was. In contrast, people who happen to have the opposite view of themselves—namely, the belief that they have changed a lot over the years—show a different memory pattern. They also remember the past in a biased way, but it's a bias that overstates how much they've changed (M. Conway & Ross, 1984; Holmberg & Homes, 1994; for other results, also showing how current views of self change memory, see L. J. Levine, 1997; G. B. Marcus, 1986; Ochsner & Schacter, 2000; and M. Ross & Wilson, 2003).

It's also true that most of us would prefer to have a positive view of ourselves, including a positive view of how we have acted in the past. This, too, can shape memory. As one illustration, Bahrick, Hall, and Berger (1996) asked college students to recall their high school grades as accurately as they could. The data showed some amount of forgetting, and, perhaps surprising, the forgetting was independent of what the grade was: Students were just as likely to forget good grades as bad. Nonetheless, self-service did play a role: When students forgot a good grade, their (self-serving) reconstruction led them to the (correct) belief that the grade must have been a good one; consistent with this, 89% of the A's were correctly remembered. But when students forgot a poor grade, reconstruction led them to the (false) belief that the grade must have been okay, and as a result, only 29% of the D's were correctly recalled. Overall, then, students consistently recalled their grades as being better than they actually were. (For other mechanisms through which current motivations can color autobiographical recall, see M. Conway & Holmes, 1999; M. Conway & Pleydell-Pearce, 2000; Kunda, 1990; and Mather, Shafir, & Johnson, 2000.)

Memory and Emotion

Another factor that is extremely important for autobiographical memory is *emotion.* We don't get emotional when memorizing a researcher's list of words, or a story that we read in the lab. But plainly many of our experiences in life *do* cause emotion; how does this influence memory?

In general, emotion helps us to remember. At a biological level, emotional events trigger a series of events in our bodies that (among other effects) leads to an increase in the level of glucose in the blood, which then promotes the process of memory **consolidation**—the process through which memories are biologically "cemented in place." (For reviews, see Buchanan & Adolphs, 2004; Dudai, 2004; Hamann, 2001; and Öhman, 2002.) In addition, emotional events are likely to be important to us, virtually guaranteeing that we will pay close attention as the event unfolds, and this obviously helps memory. Furthermore, we tend to mull over emotional events in the minutes (or hours) following the event, and this is tantamount to memory rehearsal. For all of these reasons, then, it is unsurprising that emotional events are well remembered (Reisberg & Heuer, 2004).

Many authors have argued in addition that emotion changes what we pay attention to, within an event, and this changes the pattern of what is and what is not remembered from an emotional episode. One proposal is that emotion leads to a "narrowing" of attention so that, in an emotional event, all of one's attention will be focused on just a few aspects of the scene (Easterbrook, 1959). This helps to guarantee that these attended aspects are firmly placed into memory, but it also implies that the rest of the event, excluded from this narrowed focus, won't be remembered later. As a result, people will have good memory for the emotional event's "center" but poor memory for the event's "periphery."

Many studies have documented this sort of memory narrowing, both in the laboratory and in the recollection of emotional events occuring in people's lives (e.g., Burke, Heuer, & Reisberg, 1992; Christianson, 1992; Steblay, 1992). But this narrowing is not always observed, for reasons that are as yet unclear. One suggestion is that much depends on *why* someone is emotional—whether it is because the person has seen a particular stimulus that caused the arousal (a weapon, the sight of a bloody wound) or because the person experienced some frightening thought, or perhaps because of empathy. At least some evidence suggests that memory narrowing is produced by only the first (stimulus-based) type of arousal (Laney, Campbell, Heuer, & Reisberg, in press; Reisberg & Heuer, 2004), but other evidence on this point is needed.

Flashbulb Memories

One group of emotional memories, however, seems to be in a category all its own. These are the so-called flashbulb memories—memories of extraordinary clarity, typically for highly emotional events, retained despite the passage of many years. When R. Brown and Kulik (1977) introduced the term "flashbulbs," they pointed as a paradigm case to the memories people have of first hearing the news of President Kennedy's assassination. Their participants, interviewed more than a decade after that event, remembered it "as though it were yesterday," recalling details of where they were at the time, what they were doing, and whom they were with. Many participants were able to recall the clothing worn by people around them, the exact words uttered, and the like. Memories of comparable clarity have also been reported for other, more recent, events, including the 1995 reading of the verdict in the O. J. Simpson trial, the news of Princess Diana's death in 1997, and the attack on the World Trade Center in 2001 (see, for example, Pillemer, 1984; and Rubin & Kozin, 1984; see also Weaver, 1993; and Winograd & Neisser, 1993).

Flashbulb memories seem extraordinarily vivid and are rich in detail, but are these memories *correct*—that is, an accurate reflection of how the event really did unfold? Research indicates that at least some flashbulb memories do contain large-scale errors. For example, Neisser and Harsch (1992) interviewed college students one day after the 1986 explosion of the space shuttle *Challenger*, asking the students how they first heard about the explosion, what they were doing at the time, and so on. They then reinterviewed these students 3 years later, asking the same questions about the shuttle explosion. The results show remarkably little agreement between the immediate and delayed reports, even with regard to major facts such as who delivered the news or where the person was when the news arrived. It appears, then, that the 3-year reports are mostly false, although it should be said that the students were highly confident about the accuracy of these reports. (For similar data, see Christianson, 1989; Talarico & Rubin, 2003; and Wagenaar & Groeneweg, 1990.)

Other data, though, tell a different story, suggesting that flashbulb memories *are* remembered accurately. Why should this be? Why are some flashbulb events remembered well, while others are not? One key factor seems to be the **consequentiality** of the flashbulb event. If the event matters directly for the participant's life, then the event tends to be remembered accurately. If the event is largely inconsequential for that person, then memory accuracy will be poor. This point is well illustrated in a study that examined how accurately people remembered the 1989 San Francisco earthquake. For individuals who lived in Georgia, thousands of miles from the earthquake's epicenter, memory accuracy was quite low. For people who lived in Santa Clara (at the epicenter), the earthquake was remembered accurately and in detail (Neisser, Winograd, & Weldon, 1991; Palmer, Schreiber, & Fox, 1991). Similarly, another study examined people's memories for the abrupt and unexpected resignation of British Prime Minister Margaret Thatcher. People differed widely in the accuracy of their recall for this event, but this accuracy was closely linked to their assessments of how important the event was for them: If it was important for them, they were much more likely to remember it, so that, again, consequentiality predicted accurate recollection (M. Conway et al., 1994).

In summary, some flashbulb memories do turn out to be marvelously accurate, while others turn out to be filled with error. From the point of view of the person doing the remembering, however, there is no difference between the accurate memories and the inaccurate ones: Both are recalled with great detail; both are recalled with enormous confidence. In both cases, the memory can be intensely emotional. This obviously adds strength to our earlier claim that memory errors can occur even in the midst of our strongest, most confident recollection.

Traumatic Memories

Flashbulb memories tend to be highly emotional: Some people still cry when they think about Princess Diana's death, even though her death was several years ago; other people still grow angry (or, in some cases, relieved) when they think of O. J. Simpson's acquittal. But, sadly, we can easily find cases of much stronger emotion, evoked by much more consequential events. How are these events remembered? If someone has witnessed wartime atrocities, can we count on the accuracy of their testimony in a war crimes trial? If someone reports a sexual assault, can we count on the accuracy of her recall? And for that matter, if someone suffers through the horrors of a sexual assault, will the painful memory eventually fade? Or will the memory remain as a horrific remnant of the experience?

The evidence suggests that most traumatic events are well remembered for many years, and indeed, victims of some atrocities seem plagued by a cruel enhancement of memory, leaving them with extra-vivid and long-lived recollections of the terrible event (Brewin, 1998; Golier, Yehuda, & Southwick, 1997; G. S. Goodman et al., 2003; Harber & Pennebaker, 1992; Horowitz & Reidbord, 1992; Pope, Hudson, Bodkin, & Oliva, 1998). But there are exceptions to this pattern, and some people who suffered through truly extreme events seem to have little or no recall of the horrors (e.g., Arrigo & Pezdek, 1997).

What produces this pattern? Several factors contribute to the fact that some traumatic events seem to be completely forgotten. In some cases, the trauma occurred when the person was very young. (This includes cases, for example, of children who have suffered some form of abuse.) Forgetting these early traumas probably reflects the fact that, in general, people have considerable difficulty in recalling events (traumatic or otherwise) from the first years of life. As a result, the failure to recall the trauma is just part of the broader pattern of what's called *childhood amnesia.*

In other cases, the traumatic events are accompanied by sleep deprivation, head injuries, or alcohol and drug abuse, and each of these can disrupt memory (McNally, 2003). In still other cases, the extreme stress associated with the event can disrupt the biological processes needed for establishing the memory in the first place; as a result, no memory is ever established (Hasselmo, 1999; McGaugh, 2000; Payne, Nadel, Britton, & Jacobs, 2004).

It is far more common, though, for traumatic events to be remembered extremely well—so much so that people who have experienced trauma sometimes complain of "too much" memory, and wish they remembered *less*. This enhanced memory is probably best understood in terms of the biological processes through which memories are established. As we have mentioned, some of these processes (especially those involving the amygdala and related areas) are promoted by the conditions that accompany bodily arousal (Buchanan & Adolphs, 2004; Hamann, 2001).

Finally, one last hypothesis is highly controversial: Several authors have argued that highly painful memories will be repressed. Repressed memories, it is claimed, will not be consciously available later on, but will still exist in a person's long-term storage. As a result, these memories may continue to influence a person in one form or another and, in suitable circumstances, may be "recovered"—that is, made conscious once again. (For modern versions of this hypothesis, see, for example, Freyd, 1996, 1998; and Terr, 1991, 1994; for some deep reservations about this hypothesis, see, among others, Shobe & Kihlstrom, 1997.)

Most memory researchers are skeptical about the repression idea, arguing that the evidence for repression is at best ambiguous. Consider, for example, the evidence of memory "recovery." If an event is completely forgotten for years, and then is finally remembered, isn't this proof that memories can be repressed and then recovered? Unfortunately, it is no proof at all. Some "recovered memories" were probably remembered all along; the person simply refused to discuss them (presumably because the remembered events were quite painful). In this case, the "recovery" reflects the fact that the person is at last willing to discuss these memories out loud. Such a recovery may be extremely consequential—emotionally and perhaps legally—but it does not tell us anything about how memory works.

In other cases, memories lost and then found may reveal the effects of ordinary retrieval failure. This certainly is a mechanism that can hide memories from view for long periods of time, only to have the memories reemerge once a suitable retrieval cue is available. In this case, too, the recovery is of enormous importance for the person finally remembering the long-lost episodes, but again, this merely confirms the role of an already documented memory mechanism; there is no need here for any exotic theorizing about repression.

Finally, and most troubling, we need to entertain the possibility that at least some of these "recovered memories" are, in fact, false memories. After all, we know that false memories occur, and that they are more likely when one is recovering the distant past than when one is trying to remember recent events. It is also worth mentioning that many recovered memories emerge only with the assistance of a therapist who is genuinely convinced that the client's psychological problems stem from childhood abuse. Even if the therapist scrupulously avoids leading questions, bias might still lead him or her to shape the client's memory in other ways—by giving signs of interest or concern if the client hits on the "right" line of exploration, by spending more time on topics related to the alleged memories, and so forth. In these ways, the climate within a therapeutic session could guide the client toward finding exactly the "memories" the therapist expects to find.

These are, of course, difficult issues, especially when we bear in mind that recovered memories often involve horrible episodes, such as episodes of sexual abuse; if these memories are true, therefore, they are evidence for repugnant crimes. But here, as in all cases, the veracity of recollection cannot be taken for granted. This caveat is obviously important in evaluating any memory, and it is far more so for anyone wrestling with this sort of traumatic recollection. (For discussion of this difficult issue, see, among others, Kihlstrom & Schacter, 2000; Loftus & Guyer, 2002; Read, 1999; and Schooler, in press.)

Long, Long-Term Remembering

Our discussion has several times touched on the fact that people sometimes seek to recall events that happened long, long ago—perhaps several decades earlier. Of course, distant events are often difficult to remember, and some of our memories from long ago will certainly turn out to be mistaken. But, impressively, our memories from long ago can also turn out to be wonderfully accurate.

Bahrick, Bahrick, and Wittlinger (1975) tracked down the graduates of a particular high school—people who had graduated in the previous year, and the year before, and the year before that, and, ultimately, people who had graduated 50 years before. All of these alumni were shown photographs from their own year's high school yearbook. For each photo, they were given a group of names and had to choose the name of the person shown in the picture. The data show remarkably little forgetting; performance was approximately 90% correct if tested 3 months after graduation, the same after 7 years, and the same after 14 years. In some versions of the test, performance was still excellent after 34 years (Figure 7.3).

FIGURE 7.3 Memory Over the Very Long Term

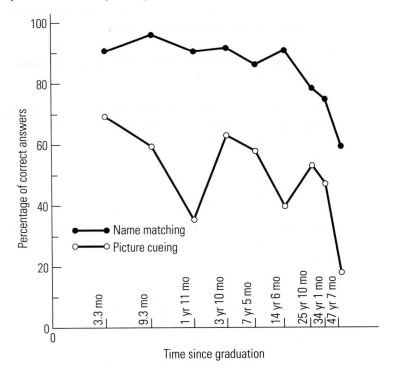

People were tested for how well they remembered names and faces of their high school classmates. In one version, the research participants were given a group of names and had to select which name belonged to the face shown. In this task ("name matching"), participants were 90% correct even 14 years after graduation. In a different version, participants were shown the pictures and had to come up with the names on their own ("picture cueing"). In this test, participants were still 60% accurate after 7 years. The data do show a drop-off after 47 years, but it is unclear whether this reflects an erosion of memory or a more general drop-off in performance caused by the normal process of aging. (After Bahrick et al., 1975)

Recall performance in this study was slightly worse than recognition but was still impressive. When asked to come up with the names on their own, rather than choosing the correct name from a list, the participants were able to name 70% of the faces when tested 3 months after graduation, and 60% after 9 months. Remarkably, they were still able to name 60% of their classmates after 7 years.

As a different example, what about the material you are learning right now? You are presumably reading this textbook as part of a course on cognitive psychology. Five years from now, will you still remember things you have learned in this course? How about a decade from now? M. Conway, Cohen, and Stanhope (1991) explored precisely these questions, testing students' retention of a cognitive psychology course taken years earlier. The results broadly echo the pattern we have already seen: Some forgetting of names and specific concepts was observed during the first 3 years after the course. After the third year, however, performance stabilized, so that students tested after 10 years still remembered a fair amount and, indeed, remembered just as much as did students tested after 3 years. Memory for more general facts and memory for research methods showed even less forgetting.

Some loss of memories is observed in these studies, but what is remarkable is how much people do remember, and for how long. In study after study, there is an initial period of forgetting, generally for the first 3 or 4 years. After that, performance remains impressively consistent, despite the passage of several decades. In other words, if you learn the material well enough to retain it for 3 years, odds are that you will remember it for the rest of your life. Indeed, Bahrick (1984) has claimed that memories can achieve a state of **permastore** (short for "permanent storage"), although he argues that only some memories achieve this status. Permastore is more likely, for example, if the material is extremely well learned in the first place (Bahrick, 1984; Bahrick & Hall, 1991; M. Conway, Cohen, & Stanhope, 1991, 1992). Permastore is also more likely if the person continues to learn new materials in that domain. Thus, students who take calculus courses in college are likely to remember their high school algebra even 50 years after high school (Bahrick & Hall, 1991). Some learning strategies also seem more likely to produce permastore (Bahrick, Bahrick, Bahrick, & Bahrick, 1993).

Very long-term retention is also helped by one additional factor: rehearsal. For many years, M. Linton (1975, 1978, 1982, 1986; also Wagenaar, 1986) has kept careful notes on the events that fill each of her days, sort of like keeping a detailed diary. After certain intervals, she selects events from the diary and tests her own memory for what transpired; this memory can then be checked against the written record. Linton reports impressive memory accuracy for these mundane events—over 65% remembered after 3 years, roughly the same after 4 years. In addition, Linton often retests her memory for a given event. This way, we can ask about the effects of rehearsing these memories, since, after all, the experience of testing memory constitutes a reencounter with the original episode. (Thus, the first test provides a rehearsal that may then benefit the second test.) This rehearsal turns out to have enormous impact. For those events previously tested (rehearsed), forgetting after 3

FIGURE 7.4   Remembering Events in One's Life

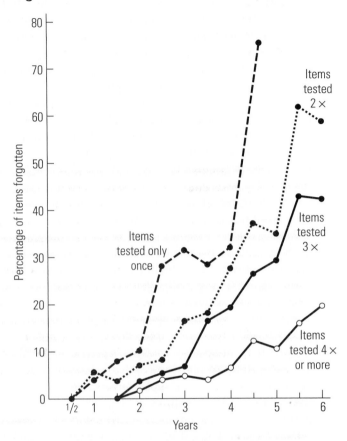

Each day, the author of this study recorded what had happened during that day. At various later times she tested her memory for different events. Some events were tested only once; two thirds of these were still remembered after 3 or 4 years. Other items were tested multiple times; each test served to remind the subject of the event, and so "refreshed" the memory. Even a single "refresher" can markedly decrease forgetting. (After M. Linton, 1978)

years was cut in half, from 32% forgotten with no rehearsals, to 16% with one rehearsal (Figure 7.4).

How General Are the Principles of Memory?

Where does this brief survey of autobiographical memory leave us? In some ways this form of memory seems different from other sorts of remembering, and in some ways it is the same. Autobiographical memories can last for years and years, but so can memories that do not refer directly to one's own life. Autobiographical remembering is far more likely if the person occasionally revisits the target memories; these rehearsals dramatically reduce forgetting. But the same is true in non-autobiographical remembering.

Autobiographical memory is also open to error, just as other forms of remembering are. We saw this in cases of flashbulb memories that turn out to be false. We have also seen that misinformation and leading questions can plant false autobiographical memories—about birthday parties that never happened, and trips to the hospital that never took place.

These facts strengthen a claim that has been implicit in much of our discussion over the last three chapters: Certain principles seem to apply to memory in general, quite independent of what it is that is being remembered. All memories depend on connections. The connections promote retrieval. The connections also facilitate interference because they allow one memory to blur into another. The connections can fade with the passage of time, producing memory gaps, and the gaps are likely to be filled via reconstruction based on generic knowledge. All of these things seem to be true whether we are talking about relatively recent memories or memories from long ago, emotional memories or memories of calm events, memories for complex episodes or memories for simple word lists.

But of course this does not mean that all principles of memory apply to all types of remembering. As we saw in Chapter 6, for example, the rules that govern implicit memory may be different from those that govern explicit memory. And, as we have seen here, some of the factors that play a very large role in shaping autobiographical remembering (e.g., the role of self-flattery) may be irrelevant to other sorts of memory.

In the end, therefore, our overall theory of memory is clearly going to need more than one level of description. We will need some principles that apply only to certain types of memory (e.g., principles specifically aimed at autobiographical remembering). But we will also need broader principles, reflecting the fact that some themes seem to apply to memory of all sorts (e.g., the importance of memory connections). As we have seen over the last three chapters, these more general principles have moved us forward considerably in our understanding of memory in many different domains and have allowed us to illuminate many aspects of learning, of memory retrieval, and of the sources of memory error.

Chapter Summary

1. Our memories are usually accurate, but errors do occur and can be quite large. In general, these errors are produced by the connections that link our memories to each other and link memories for specific episodes to other, more general, knowledge. These connections help us, because they serve as retrieval paths. But the connections can also "knit" separate memories together, making it difficult to keep track of which elements belong in which memory.

2. Some memory errors are produced by our understanding of an episode. The understanding promotes memory for the episode's gist but also encourages memory errors. A similar pattern emerges in the DRM procedure, in which a word related to other words on a list is (incorrectly) recalled as being part of the list.

3. Similar effects arise from schematic knowledge. This knowledge helps us to understand an episode and also guides our attention during the episode. But a reliance on the schematic knowledge can lead us to remember an episode as being more "regular," more "normal," than it actually was.

4. Memory errors are more likely in recalling distant events rather than recent ones. One reason for this is decay of the relevant memories; another reason is retrieval failure. Perhaps the most important source of forgetting, though, is interference.

5. Memory interference can take many forms. In some cases, generic knowledge interferes with the recall of a specific episode. In other cases, related episodes are blurred together in memory, and this can produce source confusion with regard to which elements occurred in which episode. Interference can also be produced by misinformation received after an event—delivered either in leading questions or in suggested descriptions for how the event took place. In either case, misinformation can change how we remember the people or the actions within an event, and in some cases it can plant memories for entire events that never happened at all.

6. While memory errors are easily documented, cases of accurate remembering can also be observed and are probably more numerous than cases involving memory error. However, people seem unable to tell apart their accurate and inaccurate memories. This is because false memories can be recalled with just as much detail, emotion, and confidence as a historically accurate memory. Memory errors also cannot be defeated with exotic techniques such as hypnosis or "memory-improving" drugs.

7. Although memory errors are troubling, they may simply be the price we pay in order to obtain other advantages. For example, many errors result from the dense network of connections that link our various memories. These connections sometimes make it difficult to recall which elements occurred in which setting, but these same connections serve as retrieval paths, and without the connections, we might have great difficulty in locating our memories in long-term storage. Even forgetting may have a positive side, by virtue of trimming details from memory in a fashion that may foster abstract thinking.

8. Autobiographical memory is influenced by the same principles as any other form of memory, but it is also shaped by its own set of factors. For example, episodes connected to the self are, in general, better remembered—a pattern known as the self-reference effect. Autobiographical memories are also often emotional, and this has multiple effects on memory. Emotion seems to promote memory consolidation, but it may also produce a pattern of memory narrowing.

9. Some events give rise to very clear, long-lasting memories called flashbulb memories. Despite their subjective clarity, these memories, like memories of any other sort, can contain errors and, in some cases, can be entirely inaccurate. Flashbulb memories are most likely to be accurate if the remembered events were perceived to be consequential at the time they occurred.

10. At the extreme of emotion, trauma has mixed effects on memory. Some traumatic events are not remembered, probably because of interrupted consolidation. Other traumatic events are remembered for a long time and in great detail. There is also great controversy over recovered memories, but at least some of these memories are likely to be false memories of events that did not occur.

11. Some events can be recalled even after many years have passed. In some cases, this is because the knowledge was learned so well that it reached a state of permastore. In other cases, occasional rehearsals preserve a memory for a very long time.

PART FOUR

KNOWLEDGE

I N Parts II and III, we saw case after case in which our interactions with the world are guided by knowledge. In perceiving, we make inferences guided by knowledge about the world's regular patterns. In attending, we anticipate inputs guided by knowledge about what's likely to occur. In learning, we connect information to things that we already know. And so on. But what is knowledge? How is knowledge represented in the mind? How do we locate knowledge in memory when we need it?

These questions will be at the heart of this section. In Chapter 8, we'll develop a proposal for how knowledge is represented in memory and use this proposal to put some flesh on the suggestion—so crucial for Chapters 5, 6, and 7—that learning consists of the creation of memory connections, and that these connections then serve as retrieval paths. In Chapter 8 we'll also return to an idea that complex processes can be built up from a network of simple elements relying on distributed representations and parallel processing. In Chapter 3, we applied this idea to the recognition of objects; here we'll apply it to the learning and use of knowledge.

In Chapter 9, we'll look at the building blocks of our knowledge—our individual concepts. What is it we know when we know what a "dog" is, or when we know what "reading" is? We'll consider several hypotheses about what this knowledge might be, and we'll see that each hypotheses captures a part of the truth, and so we'll be driven toward a several-part theory, combining these various views. In the process, we'll also be driven toward an overall framework in which our knowledge about "dog," "reading," and the like turns out to depend in interesting ways on our knowledge about many other concepts. As we'll see, therefore, one cannot know what a "dog" is without also understanding what an "animal" is, what a "living thing" is, and so on. As a result, connections among ideas again enter our view—this time, connections that play a central role in representing our conceptual knowledge.

Chapters 10 and 11 look at two special types of knowledge: our knowledge about language, and our knowledge about visual images. In Chapter 10, we will see that our knowledge of language is highly creative, in the sense that we can produce new words and new sentences that no one has ever used before. But, at the same time, the creativity is somehow constrained, and there are some words and sentences that are considered unacceptable by virtually any speaker. In order to understand this pattern of "constrained creativity," we'll consider the possibility that language knowledge involves abstract rules that are, in some fashion, known and honored by every user of the language.

In Chapter 11, we'll discuss the fact that mental images seem to involve representations that are qualitatively distinct from those involved in other forms of knowledge, but we will also consider some of the ways in which memory for visual appearances is governed by the same principles as other forms of knowledge.

Associative Theories of Long-Term Memory

L ong-term memory is huge. It has to be, in order to contain all of the information we remember— memories for episodes and for mundane facts, phone numbers, lyrics for songs, the faces of a thousand different acquaintances, the layout of our hometown, the definitions of 50,000 to 60,000 different words, and on and on and on.

How do we ever find anything in this huge storehouse? How do we manage to locate a particular bit of information among the millions and millions of other bits contained within this vast library? We saw in Chapter 7 how seamlessly we integrate remembered information with current environmental input, so that we are often not aware that we have supplemented the actual input with information supplied from memory. Apparently, then, we don't merely *succeed* in retrieving information from memory; we succeed swiftly, effortlessly, and unwittingly.

We have also suggested that memory search is aided by *connections* between the materials to be learned and things one already knows, and we have claimed that these connections provide retrieval paths, routes that one can take when searching for a particular memory. But what are these connections? Who or what does the "traveling" on these retrieval paths? We turn now to these questions, and more broadly to the questions of how all of our knowledge is stored in long-term memory, and how that information is located when needed.

■ In this chapter, we pursue the idea that *connections* among memories don't merely link the memories together. Instead, those connections are actually the building blocks out of which memories are created.

■ This approach, with individual memories built up out of "nodes" within a "network," can explain many of the results we have discussed in the previous three chapters. The approach also leads to new predictions, and the success of these predictions makes it undeniable that memory does involve a system in which activation flows from one node to the next.

■ Less clear, though, is whether the spread of activation through a network is *part* of how memory search proceeds, or whether this simple mechanism might provide our *entire account* of memory search.

■ In addition to our general evaluation of network models, we'll consider two specific ways a network might represent knowledge: via a system of locally represented propositions, or via a system of distributed representations. As we'll see, there are powerful arguments in favor of each approach, and it is simply too soon to tell which is the preferred way to think about how knowledge is represented in the mind.

The Network Notion

Much of this chapter will be devoted to exploring a single idea: that memory connections provide much more than retrieval paths; instead the connections *are* our memories. For example, you know your mother's name; this fact is recorded in your memory. The proposal to be considered is that this memory is literally represented by a memory connection, in this case a connection between some memory content representing your mother and some memory content representing the sound pattern of her name. That connection isn't some appendage to the memory. Instead, the connection *is* the memory. Likewise for all the other facts you know (the opposite of "hot," how you spent last Thanksgiving, the color of rubies), so that all of knowledge is represented via a sprawling network of these connections, a vast set of associations.

The notion that memory contains a network of associations is hardly new. The idea has been discussed, both in philosophy and in psychology, for several centuries. Modern conceptions of the network, however, differ from their predecessors in important ways; we will discuss some of these differences as we proceed. Our initial focus, though, will not be on the modern conceptions per se. Instead, we will be concerned with broader themes: What motivates this approach to memory? Why should we think that memory has an associative base? Then, once we have discussed these issues, we will turn to some of the specific ways an associative theory might be implemented. We will first consider a form of theorizing patterned after the work of Collins and Loftus (1975) and J. R. Anderson (1976, 1980; J. R. Anderson & Bower, 1973). Later in the chapter, we will turn to the most recent version of associative theorizing, a sophisticated treatment known as "connectionism."

How Might the Network Work?

The essence of a memory network is straightforward. First, we need some means of representing individual ideas; these representations will be the **nodes** within the net, just like the knots within a fisherman's net. (In fact, the word "node" is derived from the Latin word for knot, *nodus*.) These nodes are then tied to each other via connections that we will call **associations** or **associative links**. If you like, you can think of the nodes as being akin to cities on a map, and associations as being the highways that link the cities. Learning, within this metaphor, would be similar to building a highway between two cities, or perhaps improving an existing highway so that it is more easily and quickly traveled.

In this view, what it means to search through memory is to begin at one node (one "city") and to travel via the connections until the target information is reached. Critically, not all associations are of equal strength. Some "cities" are linked by superhighways, others only by country roads. Other cities are not linked to each other at all, but you can get from one to the next by traveling via some intermediate cities. This will immediately provide part of our account for why some memories are easily called up, while others are not: For example, if asked, "When is your birthday?" you answer quickly and easily. Presumably, this is because there is a strong connection between the MY BIRTHDAY node and the node representing a specific date. This connection has been established by the fact that this date and the idea of birthdays have frequently been thought about in conjunction with each other, creating an easily traveled path from one to the other. (Throughout this chapter, we will use small capital letters when we are referring to a NODE in memory; we will use normal type when referring to the word or stimulus represented by that node.)

Even at this early stage of presentation, though, we reach a point in which modern versions of the network differ from older versions. According to philosophers like John Locke and George Berkeley, associations among ideas are largely stamped in by the environment: If you heard the word "birthday" and then heard a date, this would be enough to create a mental association. As we have seen in earlier chapters, however, this claim is not correct; memory connections are not established in this passive manner. (See, for example, our discussion of maintenance rehearsal and elaborative rehearsal in Chapter 5.)

Modern network theories therefore require a more active role for the learner. Memory connections will be established only if, during the learning episode, the learner pays attention to the items to be remembered. Likewise, a great deal depends on how the learner engages the items. For example, thinking about the material in several different ways will create multiple connections, each of which can later be used as a retrieval path. The learner will also be helped if he or she thinks about the material in distinctive ways. For example, if you establish an association between THE LIST I STUDIED EARLIER and SOME CAPITALIZED WORDS, this connection isn't very informative and probably won't help you later on to recall the words to be remembered. In contrast, an association between THE LIST I STUDIED EARLIER and, say, THE OPPOSITE OF LOVE is distinctive and will help you to remember.

Spreading Activation

Theorists speak of a node becoming activated when it has received a strong enough input signal, sort of like a lightbulb being turned on by incoming electricity. This implies that what travels through the associative links is akin to energy or fuel, and the associative links themselves can be thought of as "activation carriers"—hoses carrying the fuel or wires carrying electricity. Then, once a node has been activated, it can in turn activate other nodes: Energy will spread out from the just-activated node, via its associations, and this will activate nodes connected to the just-activated node.

To put all of this more precisely, nodes receive activation from their neighbors, and as more and more activation arrives at a particular node, the **activation level** for that node increases. Eventually, the activation level will reach the node's **response threshold**. Once this happens, we say that the node **fires**. This firing has several effects, including the fact that this node will now itself be a source of activation, sending energy to its neighbors and so activating them. In addition, firing of the node will summon attention to that node; this is what it means to "find" a node within the network.

Activation levels below the response threshold, so-called **subthreshold activation**, also have an important role to play: Activation is assumed to accumulate, so that two subthreshold inputs may add together, or **summate**, and bring the node to threshold. Likewise, if a node has been partially activated recently, it is, in effect, already "warmed up," so that even a weak input will be sufficient to bring the node to threshold.

These claims mesh well with points we raised in Chapter 2, when we considered how neurons communicate with each other. Neurons receive activation from other neurons; once a neuron reaches its threshold, it fires, sending activation to other neurons. All of this is precisely parallel to the suggestions we are offering here, and this invites the hope that our theorizing about the network will be easily translated into biological terms. Let's be clear that this is not a suggestion that nodes *are* neurons; instead, the biological realization of nodes is likely to be far more complicated than this. Even so, nodes (like any other construct in our theorizing!) can exist only through the functioning of neural tissue, and in this case, the close parallels between the way nodes work and the way neurons work suggest that it will be a straightforward matter to translate the psychological claims into biological ones. If so, we can look forward to a point at which we will understand both how the memory network functions and how it is realized in the nervous system.

In addition, the claims we are developing here parallel those we offered in Chapter 3, when we described how a network of detectors might function in object recognition. Detectors receive their activation from other detectors; they can accumulate activation from different inputs; once activated to threshold levels, they fire. We will return to these parallels later in this chapter, when we will argue that the network of nodes in long-term memory includes the network of detectors we considered in Chapter 3.

Returning to long-term storage, however, the key idea is that activation travels from node to node via the associative links. As each node becomes activated and fires, it serves as a source for further activation, spreading onward through the network. This process, known as **spreading activation**, allows us to deal with a key issue. How does one navigate through the maze of associations? If you start a search at one node, how do you decide where to go from there? Our initial proposal is that you do not "choose" at all. Instead, activation spreads out from its starting point in all directions simultaneously, flowing through whatever connections are in place. Think of fuel flowing through hoses: If two hoses radiate out from a starting point, the fuel does not "choose" the left hose or the right. If there are two hoses in place, the fuel will flow through both.

This is not to say, however, that all pathways are equally effective in carrying the activation, and in fact, we have already suggested that they're not. Some associative links, thanks to recent or frequent use, are particularly effective; others are less so. (To push the metaphor a bit further, some of the hoses are tiny and so can carry only a small amount of fuel; other hoses are much larger.) For that matter, perhaps some associations are "built in"—that is, are innately strong. In any event, the stronger or better-established links will carry activation more efficiently and so will be more successful at activating subsequent nodes.

Evidence Favoring the Network Approach

This sketch of the network leaves a great deal unspecified, but that is deliberate: Associative nets can be implemented in various ways, and we are not ready yet to talk about the details of any particular implementation. We first need to ask whether we are even on the right track. Is this a sensible approach at all? What can be explained in these terms?

Hints

Why do hints help us to remember? Why is it, for example, that you just draw a blank if asked, "What's the capital of South Dakota?" but then remember if given the hint, "Is it perhaps a man's name?"

Here's one likely explanation: Mention of South Dakota will activate the nodes in memory that represent your knowledge about this state. Activation will then spread outward from these nodes, eventually reaching nodes that represent the capital city's name. It is possible, though, that there is only a weak connection between the SOUTH DAKOTA nodes and the nodes representing "Pierre." Perhaps you are not very familiar with South Dakota, or perhaps you haven't thought about this state, or its capital, for some time. In these cases, insufficient activation will flow into the PIERRE nodes, and so these nodes won't reach threshold and won't be "found."

Things will go differently if a hint is available. If you are told, "South Dakota's capital is also a man's name," this will activate the MAN'S NAME node, and so activation will spread out from this source at the same time that activation is spreading out from the SOUTH DAKOTA nodes. Therefore, the nodes for "Pierre" will now receive activation from two sources simultaneously, and this will probably be enough to lift the nodes' activation to threshold levels. In this way, question plus hint accomplishes more than the question by itself (see Figure 8.1).

Context Reinstatement

As we saw in Chapter 6, memory is best if the state you're in during memory retrieval is the same as the state you were in during learning. If you were underwater during learning, you'll have an easier time remembering what you learned

---

FIGURE 8.1 — Activation of a Node From Two Sources

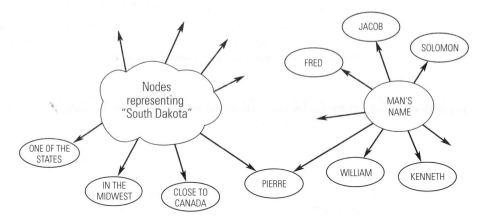

A participant is asked, "What is the capital of South Dakota?" This activates the SOUTH DAKOTA nodes, and activation spreads outward from there to all of the associated nodes. However, it is possible that the memory connection between SOUTH DAKOTA and PIERRE is weak; in that case, PIERRE may not receive enough activation to reach threshold, and so the desired information will not be located. Things will go differently, though, if the participant is also given the hint, "The capital is a man's name." Now, the PIERRE node will receive activation from two sources: the SOUTH DAKOTA nodes and the MAN'S NAME nodes. With this double input, it is more likely that the PIERRE node will reach threshold. This is why the hint ("man's name") makes the memory search easier.

if you're again underwater during the memory test. If you were thinking about sounds during learning, you'll do better if you think about sounds during the test.

Why should this be? Being underwater will bring certain thoughts to mind during the learning, and it seems likely that some of these thoughts will become associated with the materials being learned. In the terms we're using in this chapter, being underwater will activate certain thoughts, and the nodes representing these thoughts will become connected to the nodes representing the materials to be remembered.

With this base, the logic here is the same as it was in our discussion of hints: Imagine that you learn a list of words, including the word "pointer," while underwater. If asked later on, "What words were on the list?" activation will flow outward from the nodes representing your general thoughts about the list. Perhaps enough of this activation will reach the POINTER nodes to activate them, but perhaps not. If, however, you are again underwater at the time of the test, then this will trigger certain thoughts, and we just suggested that the nodes representing these thoughts may be linked to the nodes representing the learned material—including the POINTER nodes. As a result, the POINTER nodes will be receiving a double input: They'll receive activation from the nodes representing thoughts about the list, and also from the nodes representing the underwater thoughts. This double input makes it more likely that the POINTER nodes will be activated, leading to the memory advantage that we associate with context reinstatement.

More Direct Tests of the Network Claims

It seems, then, that the network proposal provides a natural way to bring together the evidence presented in the last few chapters. And, in some ways, this should be no surprise. After all, we have been talking all along about the importance of *connections*, and the proposal now before us simply develops this idea—by being a notch more precise about what the connections are and how they work. It's no wonder, then, that the network notion provides a coherent and useful way to think about memory—a single framework into which we can bring many different findings. But in addition, the network approach makes its own predictions about memory, allowing a more direct test of the claim that memory does indeed have an associative base.

Spread of Activation and Priming

A key idea of the associative network is that subthreshold activation can accumulate, so that insufficient activation received from one source can add to the insufficient activation received from another source. This was, for example, the heart of our proposal for why hints work, and why context reinstatement helps memory. More direct evidence for this claim, though, comes from several paradigms, one of which is the **lexical-decision task**.

In a lexical-decision experiment, participants are shown a series of letter sequences on a computer screen. Some of the sequences spell words; other sequences are **pseudowords**—that is, letter strings that look like words but aren't (e.g., "blar" or "plome" or "tuke"). The participants' task is to hit a "yes" button if the sequence spells a word and a "no" button otherwise. Presumably, they perform this task by "looking up" these letter strings in their "mental dictionary," and they base their response on whether they find the string in the dictionary or not. We can therefore use the participants' speed of response in this task as an index of how quickly they can locate the word in their memories. (We have already encountered this task in Chapter 6.)

Meyer and Schvaneveldt (1971; Meyer, Schvaneveldt, & Ruddy, 1974) presented their participants with *pairs* of letter strings, and participants had to respond "yes" if both strings were words, and "no" otherwise. Thus, participants would say "yes" in response to "chair, bread," but "no" in response to "house, fime." In addition, if both of the strings were words, sometimes the words were semantically related (e.g., "nurse, doctor"), and sometimes they were not ("lake, shoe"). What was of central interest was how this relationship between the words would influence performance.

Consider a trial in which participants see a related pair, like "bread, butter." To choose a response, they first need to "look up" the word "bread" in memory. This means they'll search for, and presumably activate, the relevant nodes, and in this fashion decide that, yes, this first string is a legitimate word. Then they're ready for the second word in the pair. But notice that, in the process of looking up the first word, the BREAD node in memory has now been activated. This will, we've hypothesized, trigger a spread of activation outward from this node, bringing activation to other, nearby nodes. These nearby nodes will surely include BUTTER, since the association between "bread" and "butter" is a strong one. Therefore, once BREAD is activated, some activation should also spread to the BUTTER node.

To see how this matters, let's think through what happens next, when the participant turns his or her attention to the second word in the pair. To select a response, the participant must locate "butter" in memory. If the participant finds this word (or, more precisely, finds the relevant nodes), then he or she knows that this string, too, is a word, and can hit the "yes" button. But of course the process of activating the BUTTER node has already begun, thanks to the activation this node just received from BREAD. This should accelerate the process of bringing this node to threshold (since it's already partway there!), and so it will require less time to activate. Hence, we expect quicker responses to "butter" in this context, compared to a context in which "butter" was preceded by some unrelated word, and therefore not primed.

This prediction is correct. In the Meyer and Schvaneveldt experiment, participants' lexical-decision responses were faster by almost 100 ms if the stimulus words were related, so that the first word could prime the second in the fashion we just described. This is exactly as we would expect on the model we are developing. (For reviews of other relevant studies, including some alternative conceptions of priming, see Lucas, 2000; and Hutchison, 2003.)

Sentence Verification

When one searches through the network, activation spreads from node to node to node. Search through the network, therefore, is like travel, and so the farther one must travel, the longer it should take to reach one's destination. In a classic experiment, Collins and Quillian (1969) tested this claim using a **sentence verification task.** The participants were shown sentences on a computer screen, such as, "A robin is a bird," or "A robin is an animal"; or "Cats have claws," or "Cats have hearts." Mixed together with these obviously true sentences were a variety of false sentences ("A cat is a bird"). Participants had to hit a "true" or "false" button as quickly as they could.

Collins and Quillian reasoned that participants perform this task by "traveling" through the network, seeking a connection between nodes. Thus, when the participant finds the connection from the ROBIN node to the BIRD node, this confirms that there is, in fact, an associative path linking these two nodes, and this tells the participant that the sentence about these two concepts is true. This travel will require little time, of course, if the two nodes are directly linked by an association, as ROBIN and BIRD probably are. In this case, participants should answer "true" rather quickly. The travel will require more time, however, if the two nodes are connected only indirectly (like ROBIN and ANIMAL), and so we should expect slower responses to sentences that require a "two-step" connection than to sentences that exploit a single connection.

In addition, Collins and Quillian noted that there is no point in storing in memory the fact that cats have hearts and the fact that dogs have hearts and the fact that squirrels have hearts. Instead, they proposed, it would be more efficient just to store the fact that these various creatures are animals, and then the separate fact that animals have hearts. Hence the property "has a heart" would be associated with the ANIMAL node rather than the nodes for each individual animal, and the same is true for all the other properties of animals, as shown in Figure 8.2. According to this logic, we should expect relatively slow responses to sentences like "Cats have hearts," since, to choose a response, a participant must locate the linkage from CAT to ANIMAL and then a second linkage from ANIMAL to HEART. We would expect a quicker response to "Cats have claws," because here there would be a direct connection between CAT and the node representing this property: Although all cats have claws, other animals do not, and so this information could not be entered at the higher level.

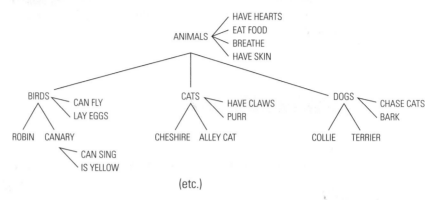

FIGURE 8.2 Hypothetical Memory Structure for Knowledge About Animals

(etc.)

Collins and Quillian proposed that memory has a hierarchical structure. This system avoids redundant storage of connections between CATS and HAVE HEARTS, and between DOGS and HAVE HEARTS, and so on for all the other animals. Instead, HAVE HEARTS is stored as a property of all animals. To confirm that cats have hearts, therefore, one must traverse two links: from CATS to ANIMALS, and from ANIMALS to HAVE HEARTS. This should take more time than it would to confirm that cats have claws and that cats purr, which require traversing only one link. (After Collins & Quillian, 1969)

As Figure 8.3 shows, these predictions are all borne out. Responses to sentences like "A canary is a canary" take approximately 1,000 ms (1 second). This is presumably the time it takes just to read the sentence and to move one's finger on the response button. Sentences like "A canary can sing" require an additional step of traversing one link in memory and yield slower responses. Sentences like "A canary can fly" require the traversing of two links, from CANARY to BIRD and then from BIRD to CAN FLY, and are correspondingly slower.

We should note, though, that subsequent data have clouded this picture somewhat. For example, Collins and Quillian were correct in arguing that response times depend heavily on the number of associative steps that must be traversed to support a response, but it turns out that this is not the whole story: In addition, some connections can be traversed more quickly than others. This is why participants are quicker to assent to "A robin is a bird" than to "A peacock is a bird" (Rosch, 1973, 1975; E. E. Smith, Rips, & Shoben, 1974). If we were simply to count nodes, these are both one-step connections and so should yield similar response times. In general, though, the more "typical" the exemplar (robins are typical birds, peacocks are not), the faster the response times. (We will say more about typicality in Chapter 9.)

In addition, the principle of nonredundancy envisioned by Collins and Quillian turns out to be often, but not always, true. Thus, for example, from the standpoint of economy, the property of "having feathers" should be associated with the

| FIGURE 8.3 | Time Needed to Confirm Various Semantic Facts |

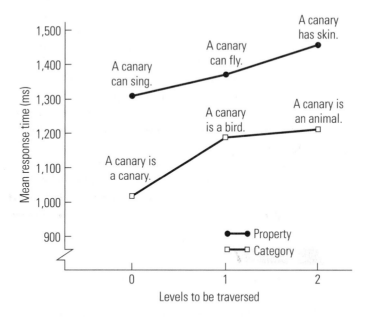

Participants must answer "true" or "false" to sentences such as "A canary is a bird." The graph shows the relation between the type of sentence and how long it took participants to respond to each sentence (response time). Participants were fastest when no links in the network had to be traversed, slower when the necessary ideas were separated by one link, and slower still if the ideas were separated by two links. (After Collins & Quillian, 1969)

BIRD node rather than (redundantly) with the ROBIN node, the PIGEON node, the EAGLE node and so forth. This fits with the fact that responses are relatively slow to sentences like, "Sparrows have feathers." Verifying this sentence requires a two-step connection—from SPARROW to BIRD and then from BIRD to HAS FEATHERS—and that's the reason for the slowness. However, it turns out that participants respond very quickly to a sentence like "Peacocks have feathers." This is because, in observing peacocks or speaking of peacocks, one often thinks about their prominent tail feathers (Conrad, 1972). Even though it is informationally redundant, a strong association between PEACOCK and FEATHERS is likely to be established.

Finally, there is reason to be skeptical about the proposal that our knowledge, in general, can be represented via neat hierarchies like the one shown in Figure 8.2. This is because, to put it simply, most things can be classified in more than one way, yielding a complex pattern of multiple, overlapping hierarchies. For example, the concept PERSONAL COMPUTERS might be represented within the hierarchy of ELEC-TRONIC DEVICES, and so would be represented along with RADAR, CELL PHONES, and

STEREO AMPLIFIERS. However, PERSONAL COMPUTERS can also be represented within the hierarchy of OFFICE EQUIPMENT, and so would now be joined by STAPLERS, PENCILS, and FILE CABINETS. For that matter, PERSONAL COMPUTERS can also be represented within the hierarchy of MODERN INVENTIONS, with yet a different set of conceptual cousins. This complexity obviously speaks against a strict hierarchical organization such as the one depicted in Figure 8.2.

For these reasons, psychologists have moved away from the exact model proposed by Collins and Quillian. However, let's not lose sight of the contribution here: It does seem that, all other things being equal, we can predict memory access by counting the number of nodes participants must traverse in answering a question. This observation by itself strengthens the claim that associative links play an important role in memory representation. But we cannot neglect the phrase "all other things being equal." Speed of memory access also depends on several other factors, including the efficiency of individual associations, the existence of special connections, and also something referred to as the "degree of fan."

Degree of Fan

Imagine a sentence verification task in which a participant confronts (on separate trials) the following two sentences: "A robin has wings," and "An aardvark has legs." The associations between ROBIN and its properties are likely to be stronger than those between AARDVARK and its properties, simply because participants in these experiments have probably thought about robins far more often than they've thought about aardvarks. In addition, the participants *know more* about robins than they do about aardvarks, and so there are more associations radiating out from ROBIN than there are from AARDVARK. As illustrated in Figure 8.4, this implies that the ROBIN node will look like the hub of a many-spoked wheel, whereas the AARDVARK node will not. In the standard terminology, ROBIN has a high **degree of fan** (many things fanning out from it), AARDVARK has a low degree of fan.

Why should degree of fan matter? Recall that, once a node is activated, the links radiating out from this node will all receive activation energy simultaneously; that is, the links will be activated in parallel with each other, rather than in some serial order. In addition, it seems sensible to assume that the quantity of activation is limited. Therefore, the more the activation is divided, the less will go to each recipient. Activation spreading outward from AARDVARK will be divided only five ways, and so each link will receive 20% of the total. The activation spreading outward from ROBIN will be much more thinly divided, and so each link will receive a smaller share of the whole.

Does degree of fan matter for memory retrieval? This question is difficult to ask with "robin" and "aardvark," because these concepts differ both in degree of fan and in strength of association. Imagine that we asked participants to verify the sentences "Aardvarks have legs" and "Robins have wings." The prediction is that the ROBIN node has a greater degree of fan, and this will slow down verification of the "robin" sentence. At the same time, the links radiating from ROBIN are likely to be

| FIGURE 8.4 | Degree of Fan for Two Nodes |

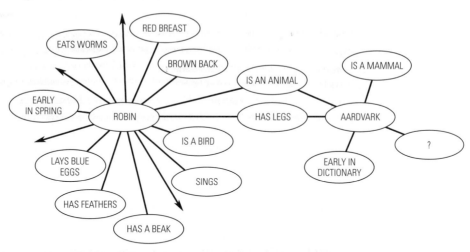

Most people know many facts about robins, and so there are many linkages radiating out from the ROBIN node—a high degree of fan. In contrast, people typically know relatively few facts about aardvarks, and so few linkages radiate out from the AARDVARK node—a low degree of fan.

more efficient, thanks to frequency of use, and this will speed up verification of the "robin" sentence. Hence, we have two effects on the scene, working in opposite directions, and potentially canceling each other out.

To ask whether degree of fan matters, we need to find a case in which two nodes differ *only* in degree of fan. One way to do this is to start, so to speak, from scratch. For example, J. R. Anderson (1974) taught his research participants a set of sentences about people in locations: "The doctor is in the bank." "The fireman is in the park." "The lawyer is in the church." "The lawyer is in the park." And so on. In the full set of sentences, some of the actors (e.g., the doctor) appeared in only one location (the bank); others (the lawyer) appeared in two locations. Likewise, some locations (the church) contained only one person; other locations (the park) contained two. In this way, Anderson controlled the degree of fan from the nodes representing each of these terms; there was greater fan for PARK than for CHURCH, and greater fan for LAWYER than for DOCTOR.

All of these were new facts for the participants, since Anderson had just made them up. Therefore, the strength of the association for these sentences started out at zero. Then, by controlling the learning process, Anderson controlled the growth of association strength and, in particular, made certain that association strength was the same for all of the sentences. In this way, Anderson ended up with a set of nodes that differed in degree of fan, but not in the strength of their connections to other nodes.

Once the participants had memorized these sentences, they were given a recognition test in which they had to decide as quickly as possible whether each of the test sentences had been presented as part of the learning set. The data showed a clear effect of fan: Response times were fastest when only one sentence mentioned a specific person or a specific place; response times were slowest when multiple sentences named a specific person or place. This is exactly what we would expect if activation were a fixed quantity and so, the more ways divided, the less to each recipient. The less to each recipient, the longer it takes for the target node to be fully activated and so, finally, the longer for the response to be chosen. (For other research on the fan effect, and also some complications, see Anderson & Reder, 1999a, 1999b; McGuire & Maki, 2001; Radvansky, 1999; and Radvansky & Zacks, 1991.)

Is There a Cost to Knowing Too Much?

Note an odd consequence of the experiment just described, and of the notion of fan: In some circumstances, there may be a cost attached to knowing "too much." If you know just one fact about aardvarks, then this fact will be easily remembered whenever you think about aardvarks. That is because, with such a low degree of fan, all the activation spreading out from the AARDVARK node will flow down this single association; there's nowhere else for it to go. However, if you learn more and more about aardvarks, the AARDVARK node's degree of fan will increase, and so now, when this node is activated, its activation will be divided among many associations, with each getting just a small share of the total. As a result, thinking about aardvarks may no longer remind you of that very first fact you knew. That fact is still in memory and still associated with the AARDVARK node, and so it will still receive some activation whenever you are thinking aardvark thoughts. But because of the greater fan, it will receive only a small slice of the activation, and this may not be enough for it to become activated itself.

In this way, new knowledge about a topic is interfering with older learning. More precisely, the new knowledge (and the corresponding increase in fan) makes it more difficult to access the older memory, so that in this case, the interference is actually leading to a form of retrieval failure.

These points require some revisions in the claims about interference that we offered in Chapter 7. There we suggested that interference can arise because the new and old memories get blurred together, or because the rememberer gets confused about which memory is which. But here we see another contributor to interference—new learning literally competing with the old learning for activation energy. In addition, Chapter 7 presented retrieval failure and interference as separate mechanisms, each making its own contribution to forgetting. We now see, however, that these two mechanisms are sometimes overlapping. There are, to be sure, cases of interference that do not involve retrieval failure, and cases of retrieval failure that do not involve interference. But now before us is a case in which retrieval failure is actually caused by interference. (For more on forgetting within a network, see M. C. Anderson, Bjork, & Bjork, 1994, 2000.)

Let's be very careful, though, not to overstate all these points. Sometimes, learning new facts can cause interference, for the reasons just described. But in many cases, things turn out quite differently, so that new learning actually *promotes* retrieval of previously learned facts. To see why, consider the three situations shown in Figure 8.5. Situations 1 and 2 here are exactly like the case we just discussed with aardvarks. Situation 1 shows a very early stage of learning, with the person knowing just a single fact (represented by node B) about a topic (node A). In this situation, there is just a single association radiating out from node A, and so whenever A is activated, all of its activation will be channeled to node B. Activation of node A, therefore, is almost certain to activate B.

Degree of Fan Versus Number of Retrieval Paths

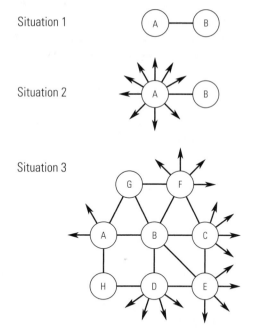

Early in learning (Situation 1), a person knows only a single fact about A—namely, that it is associated with B. Later in learning (Situation 2), the person may have learned more about A. Thanks to the increased fan, less of A's activation spreads to B. This makes it more difficult to activate node B in Situation 2 than in Situation 1. As an alternative, the person may learn a rich network of interconnected facts (Situation 3). In this case, A's degree of fan is increasing, so that less of A's activation spreads to B. At the same time, however, B is receiving activation from many new sources. As a result, B will be easier to activate in this case than in Situation 1.

Situation 2 shows a later stage of learning, in which more has been learned about A, and so the degree of fan from node A has increased. Now node B receives only a fraction of A's activation; as a consequence, thinking about A is less likely to remind you of B in Situation 2 than it was in Situation 1. This is the case in which new learning leads to retrieval failure.

Let's be clear, though, that Situation 2 involves a case in which someone has learned a group of separate, individual facts, all about the same topic, but with the facts not connected to one another. In contrast, consider the learning you are doing right now, as you read this chapter. You are not (we hope) simply learning a list of individual facts, each associated with the concept "associative networks." Instead, you are learning a set of *interrelated* facts, so that you are acquiring a whole network of new connections, more closely modeled by Situation 3 than by Situation 2. In Situation 3, A's degree of fan has once again increased, relative to Situation 1, and so here too, B receives less input from A than it did initially. At the same time, however, B can now receive input from many other sources, and as a result, node B will be *easier* to activate in Situation 3 than in the other situations—receiving less input from A, but receiving more input overall. Hence, the fan effect gave an advantage to Situation 1, but Situation 3 has a greater advantage: the advantage created by the existence of multiple retrieval paths. It is in this fashion that, even with the fan effect, learning new facts can aid retrieval. (For more on these issues, see M. C. Anderson, Bjork, & Bjork, 1994, 2000; M. C. Anderson & McCulloch, 1999; and Van Overschelde & Healy, 2001.)

Retrieving Information From a Network

So far, things look good for the network model. We have easily encompassed the findings described in Chapters 5, 6, and 7, and many new results confirm our claims about spreading activation and fan. In addition, the network idea offers us one further benefit: It holds the promise of explaining how we search through memory so quickly and easily.

Searching Through the Network via Associative Links

Think about how an encyclopedia is organized. There is obviously a vast amount of information contained within the encyclopedia, neatly compartmentalized into individual entries. Therefore, if you want to learn about dogs, you turn to the entry on that topic; if you want to learn about glaciers, you turn to that topic, and so on.

But what if you don't know which entry in the encyclopedia contains the information you seek? Imagine that your dog is ill, and you are trying to figure out what the problem is. You might start by reading the entry about dogs, but let's say you find nothing useful there. You probably wouldn't conclude at that point that the information you want wasn't in the encyclopedia. You'd realize instead that the information might be contained in some other entry. But which one? Perhaps there are separate entries for individual dog illnesses, and so the information you want is in an entry on, say, "doffinitis." The problem, though, is that, if you don't know this name, you have no reason to turn to the relevant page, and so you might not find the information you're hunting.

Editors of encyclopedias, however, have anticipated these situations, and they have done something to help you out: At the end of most entries, you will find a series of pointers, saying something like, "For related information, see the entry on X or the entry on Y." If the right pointers are in place, you will be led to the entry containing the information you want. In some cases, you may need to repeat this process (perhaps the entry on "dogs" leads you to the entry on "veterinary medicine," and from there, a new series of pointers leads you to the entry talking about "doffinitis"). Indeed, with enough of these pointers in place, one could imagine leading a reader to "doffinitis" from several different starting points. We've just described how a search might start with "dog" and get from there to your target. Likewise, the "disease" entry might have a pointer that leads you to the "medicine" entry, which has a pointer that leads to the "veterinary medicine" entry, which would lead you to the desired information. And so on.

This idea of pointers is, of course, also crucial for another information-storage system: the World Wide Web. To search the Web, you often begin with a search engine (Google, Yahoo, etc.), but in many cases, this does not bring you directly to the information you want. Nevertheless, you can often find the desired information by using the labeled hyperlinks that lead from one site to the next. These links are the equivalent of pointers saying, "For more information, see . . . ." One great advantage of the Web, though, is that (unlike an encyclopedia) you don't have to flip pages to find the related entries; instead, the entries are promptly displayed on your monitor the moment you request them. Even so, the idea is the same, and so one can imagine finding information on "doffinitis" by first locating a Web page on pets that contains links to pages on veterinary medicine, and so forth.

Of course, all this depends on having the right pointers and, indeed, on having a lot of pointers; otherwise, bridges between related topics may be omitted. However, the system won't work if you have too many pointers. Imagine that, at the bottom of a Web page, you found the message, "For more information, check out these sites!" and this was followed by a list of 343,912 links to other pages. This wouldn't be helpful, because it provides too many links (and so you might need weeks to sift through the options to find the one that was useful). Thus, *too few* links can be a problem, and so can *too many*. But presumably, an appropriate middle number of links can be found, so that we could end up with a Web page providing useful guidance to your further searching.

All of this is easily translated into network terms. Associative links can guide search through memory, just as the pointers guide search through an encyclopedia. To continue our example, let's imagine that, at some prior point, you have thought about the relationship between disease and medicine, and the relationship between medicine and veterinary medicine. Therefore, the corresponding nodes will be linked, and so activating the DISEASE node will cause activation to spread to the MEDICINE node. Activation of that node will in turn activate the VETERINARY MEDICINE node, and so on, leading eventually to the material you seek.

It is also important that activation can spread from more than one source simultaneously; we relied on this claim in our discussion of hints and context reinstatement. This is actually better than what you do with an encyclopedia or the World Wide Web. It is the equivalent of looking up one encyclopedia entry and finding its list of pointers, and then looking up a different entry, with its own list of pointers, and then, finally, asking which pointers appear on both lists. Obviously, this could narrow your search considerably, but with the encyclopedia or the Internet it would be a cumbersome process. In the associative net that supports your memory, however, this process is achieved automatically: Activation will simply spread out from both of the entry points and, with no intervention and no guidance, will converge on the sought-after node.

Finding Entry Nodes

We've now described how activation of one node can lead you to the next, and that can lead you to the next, thus allowing a search through memory. To get this process started, though, we need to get the very first node activated, to launch the entire process. How does this happen?

Imagine that someone asks you a question like, "How excited were you when you got your driver's license?" This question will (among other things) make you think about your driver's license, and this involves activating the relevant nodes. As a result, activation will spread out from those nodes—setting off the memory search process we just described. But how did the *question* (something you heard) trigger *memory* nodes in the first place?

Likewise, imagine that you smell an aroma and are reminded of your childhood. Or you hear a song and find yourself thinking about the last time you heard that song. In these cases, a perceptual cue obviously brings certain ideas to mind, and these set off the search via spreading activation. But how does the sensory cue manage to trigger an idea in the first place?

One option is simply to link the memory network directly to the mechanisms of perception, so that some nodes within the net are **input nodes**. In their functioning, these nodes will be like any others: They will receive activation via associative links; once triggered, they will send activation to other nodes. What is special about these input nodes is that they receive most of their input activation from appropriate *detectors*, with these in turn connected to the eyes, ears, and so on.

In fact, this is perfectly compatible with claims we made in Chapter 3, when we discussed how you recognize words. We suggested there that detectors for *words* might be triggered by detectors for the appropriate *letter combinations*. These in turn would be triggered by *letter detectors*, which would themselves be triggered by *feature detectors*. All we need to do now is notice that these various detectors are actually nodes within a network, functioning just like any other nodes: accumulating activation, eventually reaching threshold, and then sending activation to other nodes. And because they are nodes, there is no problem with these perceptually driven "input nodes" (the detectors) sending their activation to the long-term memory nodes we are describing in this chapter.

To put this in different words, there's really no difference between the feature net we described in Chapter 3 and the memory network we're describing here. They are seamlessly joined, with detectors (nodes that receive their input from the outside world) sending activation to memory nodes, and in that fashion allowing cues from the outside to trigger events in the memory network.

In this setting, we should acknowledge that we still need more theory, to explain how inputs (especially complex, structured inputs) are recognized, and so our simple network-based proposal will be an important part of the story, but not the whole story. (For more on this point, see Chapter 3 and also Chapter 10.) Even so, we have taken a large step toward answering the question of what it is that launches memory search in the first place. The key idea is that perceiving and identifying an input will involve, among other steps, the locating and activating of that input's node in the network. Perceiving, itself, will launch memory search.

Unpacking the Nodes

We have so far spoken of nodes as representing ideas or memories. But what does this mean? Could a node contain, for example, "my full memory of last semester's courses"? A node such as this would create two problems. First, this node would encompass a great deal of information. We would then need to figure out how one searches through the information *inside* of a node, in addition to the problem of how one finds nodes in the first place. Second, if we build a lot of information into a single node, we invite a worry about how one interprets, or reads, the information in a node. If each node contained a book-length description of an event or episode, we would need to incorporate into our theorizing some device capable of reading and interpreting this corpus of material. Conversely, the simpler we keep each node's informational content, the less we need to rely on some interpretive device.

These claims apply to any network model, to any model seeking to describe memory in terms of a pattern of associations. To say more than this, however, we need to start distinguishing among the various types of associative models, and in particular, we need to distinguish the most recent versions of associative theory from earlier versions. Let's start with the older perspective; we will consider the more recent innovations later on.

Different Types of Associative Links

One proposal is that nodes represent single concepts, and nothing more complicated than that. This is consistent with the examples we have used so far, in which nodes have stood for concepts such as "chair" or "doctor." This still leaves many questions: How does a node represent a concept? Does the DOG node contain a brief definition of the concept "dog"? A small picture of a dog? It turns out that neither of these proposals is satisfactory, and we will need most of Chapter 9 to work through the problem of how concepts are represented in the mind.

In the meantime, though, we can use the network notion to help us with a related problem—namely, how we might represent more complex ideas, such as "George Washington was the first president" or "My favorite movie is *Casablanca*." For that matter, how do we represent an idea as complicated as "my understanding of Darwin's theory of evolution," or a memory as complicated as "how I spent last summer"?

These complex ideas are represented, oddly enough, with more network. As a first approximation, an associative link may exist between "George Washington" and "first president," and a set of links may tie together "movie" and "favorite" and "*Casablanca*." But this is too simple. How, for example, would one represent the contrast between "Sam has a dog" and "Sam is a dog"? If all we have is an association between SAM and DOG, we won't be able to tell these two ideas apart. Early theorizing sought to deal with this problem by introducing different types of associative links, with some links representing equivalence (or partial equivalence) relations and other links representing possessive relations. These links were termed "isa" links, as in "Sam isa dog," and "hasa" links, as in "A bird hasa head" or "Sam hasa dog" (Norman, Rumelhart, & Group, 1975).

Propositional Networks and ACT

There are clear limits, however, on what we can accomplish with these labeled associations. The problem is that we are able to remember, and to think about, a wide range of relationships, not just equivalence and possession. We can, for example, consider the relationship "is the opposite of" or the relationship "is analogous to," and a thousand others as well. If each type of relationship is represented by a specific type of associative link, then we risk losing the simplicity that made the network idea so attractive in the first place. Worse, if we have too many types of links, we'll end up needing a "link reader" of some sort, and a reader is one of the things we were hoping to avoid.

Researchers have therefore sought other mechanisms through which network models might represent complex ideas. Their proposals differ in many ways, so once again we cannot talk about network models in general; we are forced instead to consider a specific model. Let's look at a model developed by John Anderson

(1976, 1980, 1993; J. R. Anderson & Bower, 1973), bearing in mind that this is just one way a network might be implemented; other implementations are possible.

Central to Anderson's conception is the idea of **propositions**; these are defined as the smallest units of knowledge that can be either true or false. For example, "Children love candy" is a proposition, but "Children" is not; "Susan likes blue cars" is a proposition, but "blue cars" is not. Propositions are easily represented as sentences, but this is merely a convenience. In fact, the same proposition can be represented in a variety of different sentences: For example, "Children love candy," "Candy is loved by children," and "Kinder lieben Bonbons" all express the same proposition. For that matter, this same proposition can also be represented in various nonlinguistic forms, including a structure of nodes and linkages, and that is exactly what Anderson's model does.

Anderson's theory is embodied in a computer program known as ACT (and, in later versions, as ACT-R; see J. R. Anderson, 1993, 1996). Within ACT, propositions are represented as shown in Figure 8.6. The ellipse identifies the proposition itself; associations connect the ellipse to the ideas that are the proposition's constituents. The associations are labeled, but only in general terms. That is, the associations are identified in terms of their syntactic role within the proposition. This allows us to distinguish the proposition "Dogs chase cats" from the proposition "Cats chase dogs."

FIGURE 8.6 Network Representation of the Proposition "Dogs Chase Cats"

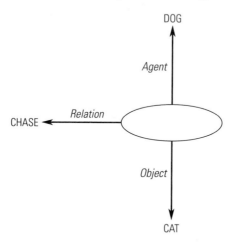

The ellipse denotes a proposition; the ellipse is, in essence, the "meeting point" for the various elements of the proposition. Three nodes are involved in this proposition: DOG, CAT, and the action CHASE. Arrows indicate associations among the nodes; labels on the arrows specify the nature of the association. (After J. R. Anderson, 1980)

FIGURE 8.7   Network Representation of Some of the Concepts Associated With "Dog"

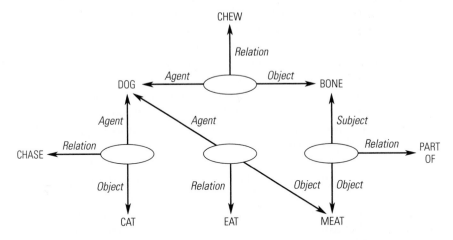

One's understanding of dogs—what dogs are, what they are likely to do—is represented by an interconnected network of propositions, with each proposition indicated by an ellipse. Thus, one's understanding involves the propositions "Dogs chase cats," "Dogs eat meat," "Dogs chew bones," and so on. A complete representation of knowledge about dogs would, of course, include a far greater number of propositions. (After J. R. Anderson, 1980)

This simple network can be expanded to represent more complex bits of knowledge. Figure 8.7 shows the proposition "Dogs chew bones" in the context of other propositions about dogs; the overall structure represents (part of) our knowledge about what a dog is and how it behaves.

To represent specific episodes, or a specific object (rather than a category), ACT makes a distinction between **type nodes** and **token nodes**. "Type" refers to a general category, and type nodes are embedded in propositions true for the entire category. A "token" is a specific instance of a category, and token nodes are therefore found in propositions concerned with specific events and individuals. Note that type and token nodes are typically connected to each other as shown in Figure 8.8.

In addition, the ACT model distinguishes between timeless truths like "Jacob feeds the pigeons," and more specific statements, like "Last spring, Jacob fed the pigeons in Trafalgar Square." ACT does this by incorporating time and location nodes as part of propositions, and in this fashion it can mark when and where the proposition was true. This additional information allows ACT to represent facts about specific episodes (Figure 8.9).

The ACT model shares many claims with other network models: Nodes are connected by associative links. Some of these links are stronger than others, with the strength of the link depending on how frequently and recently it has been used.

FIGURE 8.8 Networks Contain Information About Categories and About Individuals

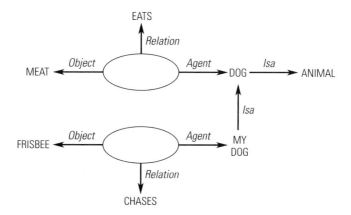

This fragment of a network contains a type node, representing dogs in general, and a token node, representing a specific dog (MY DOG). The type node is linked to propositions true for all dogs; the token node is linked to propositions true only for MY DOG. That is, all dogs eat meat. Not all dogs chase Frisbees, although my dog does. The type node and token node are linked to each other, indicating that "my dog" is a member of the category "dogs."

FIGURE 8.9 Representing Episodes Within a Propositional Network

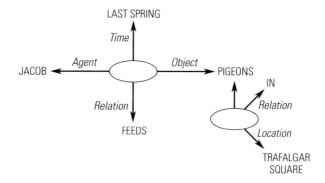

In order to represent episodes, the propositional network includes time and location nodes. This fragment of a network represents two propositions—the proposition that Jacob fed pigeons last spring, and the proposition that the pigeons are in Trafalgar Square. Note that no time node is associated with the proposition about pigeons being in Trafalgar Square. Therefore, what is represented is that the feeding of the pigeons took place last spring, but the pigeons are generally in the square.

Once a node is activated, the process of spreading activation causes the nearby nodes to become activated as well. ACT is distinctive, however, in its attempt to represent knowledge in terms of propositions, and the promise of this approach has attracted the support of many researchers in this area.

Evaluating Network Models

Associative theories of memory have generated much research, and they strike many as our best hypothesis about how knowledge is represented in the mind. At the same time, these models have been controversial. Let's look at some of this debate.

How Can We Test Network Models?

The evidence is clear that mechanisms such as spreading activation and subthreshold priming do play a role in memory search. However, the data presented so far do not speak to a larger and more interesting issue: Are these mechanisms merely *involved* in memory search? Or could it be that these mechanisms, by themselves, *provide our entire account* of memory retrieval, so that we need no further theory? Up until now in this chapter, we've considered no mechanisms other than associations, spreading activation, and the like. Therefore, we've been on a path toward suggesting that these are the only mechanisms we'll need to explain memory retrieval. Is this suggestion right?

Perhaps the best way to address these questions might be simply to give networks a serious try. Specifically, if one has a theory of how memory operates, one powerful test of the theory would be to build a working model based on the theoretical claims, and to examine how well the model performed as an information storage and retrieval device. On this basis, many psychologists are seeking to construct such models of memory, usually implemented as a computer program that functions according to the rules and procedures specified by the theory. (We mentioned earlier, for example, that Anderson's ACT model is embodied in such a system.) This allows us to see how well the computer does in "learning"—that is, in storing new information—and then in retrieving facts, based on some cue or hint. If the computer fails in these tasks, or doesn't do as well as humans do, we know that something is missing (or wrong) in the theory. What if the computer succeeds? Success would indicate that the processes and strategies programmed into the computer are sufficient to accomplish the tasks of learning and remembering. This would not, by itself, show that humans use the same processes and strategies. It would, however, be a strong argument that the theory must be taken seriously as an account of human performance.

It would take us rather far afield to evaluate these modeling efforts in any detail. To make a long story short, though, it is not possible to point to an associative network that successfully simulates all of human memory. The available models work reasonably well, but all are limited in their scope, representing just a narrow slice of knowledge—knowledge about a particular topic or a particular domain. How should we think about this? One possibility is that these limitations are necessary and reflect some inadequacies in the network approach. But it is also possible that the limitations merely reflect the early state of the models' evolution. With further work and refinements, perhaps these limits will be overcome.

It's too soon to know which of these interpretations is correct. What we can do in the meantime, though, is to look at some of the specific reasons why the models have (so far) been limited; this will help us understand some of the potential problems for the network approach. We'll then consider ways that a network might handle these challenges.

Retrieval Blocks and Partial Retrievals

One attractive feature of the associative net is that activation spreads out indiscriminately through all of the available connections. We need no means of directing the activation or supervising the search. Instead, one simply allows the activation to travel wherever the connections lead.

This approach keeps our theorizing simple, but do things always work in a fashion consistent with this "automatic" view? Try to think of the word that means a type of carving done on whalebone, often depicting whaling ships or whales. Try to think of the name of the navigational device used by sailors to determine the positions of stars. Try to think of the name of the Russian sled drawn by three horses. Chances are that, in at least one of these cases, you found yourself in a frustrated state—certain you knew the word but unable to come up with it. The word was, as they say, right on the "tip of your tongue"; following this lead, psychologists refer to this as the **TOT phenomenon**. People in the TOT state often know correctly that the word is somewhere in their vocabulary, they often correctly remember what letter the word begins with, how many syllables it has, and approximately what it sounds like. Thus a person might remember "It's something like Sanskrit" in trying to remember "scrimshaw," or "something like secant" in trying to remember "sextant" (A. Brown, 1991; R. Brown & McNeill, 1966; Harley & Brown, 1998; W. James, 1890; Read & Bruce, 1982; Reason & Lucas, 1984; B. L. Schwartz, 1999). Similar results have been obtained when people try to recall specific names: Who played the nervous man with the knife in the shower scene in Hitchcock's *Psycho*? What was the name of the Greek orator who taught himself to speak clearly by practicing speeches with pebbles in his mouth? With clues like these, research participants are often able to recall the number of syllables in the name and the name's initial letter, but not the name itself (Brennen, Baguley, Bright, & Bruce, 1990; Yarmey, 1973). (The orator was Demosthenes, and Anthony Perkins was the nervous man with the knife. The Russian sled is a troika.)

On first inspection, these findings seem not to fit with the network view. It seems clear that a person in the TOT state has reached the memory vicinity of the sought-after word. After all, the person is able to come up with the correct starting letter and the correct number of syllables. In addition, the nodes in this area of memory are presumably receiving a great deal of activation, given the time and effort one spends in trying to find the word. But this activation seems not to spread to the sought-after node, or if it does, the activation of this node is not being recognized or acknowledged. In short, you are in the right neighborhood; there is lots of activation on the scene, but the activation does not reach the target. All of this is peculiar if we conceive of spreading activation as a purely mechanical process whose success is guaranteed once one is in the correct memory vicinity.

Finding More Distant Connections

A different concern is, in a sense, the mirror image of the points just raised. In the TOT state, we fail to locate a target memory, despite our being in the right memory vicinity with plenty of activation. Here is the inverse case: How do we succeed in locating memories when there are no close connections between our starting point and our target?

The crux of the issue here is part psychology, part arithmetic. Consider first the range of jobs we want associative links to do for us: They tie together episodic memories, they tie together generic memories, they tie together aspects of our concepts (e.g., the "possession of feathers" is presumably part of, or closely tied to, our concept of "bird," and the linkage between these is, once again, a memory association). Given all this, it becomes clear that the number of associative links radiating out from any individual concept—that is, the realistic degree of fan—will be very high indeed.

We have already said that only some of the links radiating out from a node will be efficient carriers of activation—namely, those links that are used frequently or recently. But realistically, what is the number of these likely to be? How many strong associations does one have, for example, to "water"? Is 100 a halfway plausible number? This is probably a gross underestimate, but it will serve for the moment. Using this estimate, think about what happens when activation spreads outward from the WATER node. One hundred new nodes each receive some activation (Figure 8.10). If the sought-for information is directly associated with the WATER node, things will now go well: One only has to choose which among these hundred is the node one seeks.

But what if the sought-for node is not directly tied to WATER? What if it is tied by means of one intermediate step? We have already said that 100 nodes receive activation directly from WATER; now, activation spreads out from these. If each of these 100 is connected to 100 more nodes, we end up with activation reaching 10,000 nodes. And, of course, if the sought-for node is still one more step removed, we need to let activation spread once again, so that now activation reaches a million nodes ($100 \times 100 \times 100$).

It would seem, then, that we will create problems if we let the spreading activation spread too far. Even if the spread is only three or four steps, we will end up with too many nodes activated, and so we will lose the selective guidance we hoped

FIGURE 8.10 How Many Associations Are There to "Water"?

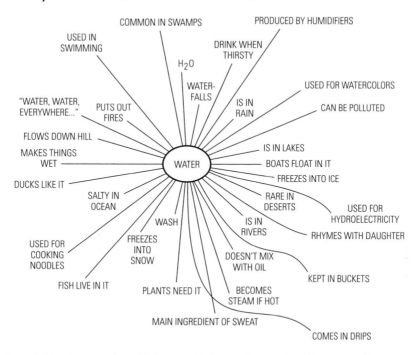

There is probably a huge number of linkages radiating out from each node; we have shown here only some of the ideas associated with the node for WATER. Each of these associations leads to some other node(s), and there are many linkages radiating out from those other nodes. If activation spreads out just one step, a large number of nodes will be activated. If activation spreads out two steps, how many nodes receive activation?

for in the first place. You were hunting for one memory, but you've activated a million memories instead!

Of course, we can avoid this danger if we place limits on how far the activation can spread, or equivalently, if we arrange things so that the spreading activation gets weaker and weaker as it moves outward from its source. In either of these cases, we will avoid the risk of activating too many nodes, but we also risk not finding the node we seek: If the activation peters out, for example, after a single link, then your memory search will never find information that is two links away from your starting point.

Winner Takes All

How should we address these various challenges? Let's start with the fact that whenever you hunt through memory, activation spreads outward from the nodes representing your search's starting point. In many cases, this will activate the nodes representing the information you seek, but it will also activate many nodes irrele-vant to your current concerns. What you need, therefore, is some means of narrow-ing things down, of picking out just a subset of the now-activated nodes. In this way, you could focus on the nodes representing the desired information and ignore the nodes representing irrelevancies.

One way to achieve this is by launching a process of *competition* among the nodes. More specifically, let's imagine a process in which each node can sometimes send out inhibition, rather than activation, to the nodes associated with it, *deacti-vating* its neighbors, rather than activating them. Let's also imagine that the more active a node is, the more strongly it will inhibit its neighbors. As a result, we might start with, say, 100 nodes activated, some more strongly than others. The most strongly activated node, however, will "shut down" the other (more weakly acti-vated) nodes, so that many are activated initially, but only one—the strongest—survives the competition. This is called a **winner-takes-all system.**[1]

A winner-takes-all system could help us with both of the network problems we described earlier. Concretely, let's say that you're in a chemistry exam and trying to remember some facts about water. Your thinking about water will activate the node for this concept, and this will send activation to many nodes that are entirely irrele-vant for your current purposes—the nodes representing your memory of the vaca-tion at the lake, or the nodes representing your annoyance at the rainy weather. These nodes will be shut down, however, thanks to the competition we have de-scribed: In this setting, it's likely that the node H_2O will receive activation both from the WATER node and from the CHEMISTRY node; this will make the H_2O node strong enough to win the winner-takes-all contest, shutting down the other distracting thoughts. If activation now spreads outward from the H_2O node, you are likely to find the information you seek. And, crucially, with the RAINY WEATHER nodes now shut down, and also the VACATION AT THE LAKE nodes, you won't activate *their* associ-ated nodes, and so the distracting thoughts won't trigger other distracting thoughts. This will, of course, keep your thinking on track. In this way, the winner-takes-all system provides a selective mechanism that reduces distraction and helps you swiftly cull through the nodes activated in your search.

Sometimes, though, this mechanism will work against you. Imagine that you are trying to remember the name of the main character in the movie *The Matrix*. You'll start by activating nodes representing your recall of the movie, and activation will then spread from there to the associated nodes. One of those nodes might be MORPHEUS, and this is close (Morpheus was in the movie) but not quite right (Mor-pheus wasn't the main character). But perhaps the MORPHEUS node becomes strongly activated. This launches the winner-takes-all process, which weakens the

---

[1] The terminology here is borrowed from politics. In most parliamentary systems—the United Kingdom's, for example, or Germany's—each party gets a share of power corresponding to its share of votes. If the X party, therefore, gets 28% of the votes, then it gets 28% of the seats in parliament. In contrast, the United States has a winner-takes-all system: If a presidential candidate gets 58% of the vote, she doesn't get just 58% of the presidency; she gets 100%.

other associated nodes—which include the node you want! At this point, your early activation of MORPHEUS will actually work against your finding the information you seek. (Who was the main character, by the way?) In this fashion, the winner-takes-all system can produce a **retrieval block** and can, in particular, produce the pattern we have labeled the TOT state.

Your best bet in this situation, therefore, may be simply to give up on your search for now. This will allow the MORPHEUS activation to decay, which will then weaken the inhibition now attached to this node's neighbors, which will then make it easier to activate these neighbors. (For more on competition among nodes, and how, in particular, this might apply to the TOT phenomenon, see Anderson & Bell, 2001; M. C. Anderson & Spellman, 1995; L. E. James & Burke, 2000; S. K. Johnson & Anderson, 2004; Macleod & Macrae, 2001; and B. L. Schwartz, 1999.)

Do We Need a Guide?

We mentioned earlier that a memory network needs the right number of connections. With too few, activation will not reach the desired target. With too many, activation will spread too far. In exactly the same fashion, the network needs the proper balance between activation and inhibition. If the inhibition is too weak or starts too late, then too many memories will be activated and we lose the advantages we hoped to gain from inhibition. But if the inhibition is too strong or starts too early, then it may deactivate nodes that represent the target information, and this will obviously defeat the memory search.

How does one find the appropriate balance? This is an issue for which computer modeling is particularly helpful: By trying out different configurations, one can ask how best to set up the network. Of course, it may turn out that no configuration gets the job done. In that case, we'll need some other mechanism to guide search within the network, so this, too, is something we can hope to learn from modeling.

What if the model doesn't work out? The network as we have described it has the advantage of working in an extremely straightforward manner: There's no complex guidance system for the spread of activation; instead, activation simply flows wherever the connections lead. Inhibition likewise requires no guidance system but works in a fashion that seems automatic and mechanical. If these processes get the job done, then we end up with a model that is impressively simple (and, one might even say, elegant). But if these processes do not get the job done, perhaps we need some less mechanical, more intelligent means of searching through the network. And then, of course, we'll need some more theory to explain exactly how this "intelligent process" functions.

We leave this section, therefore, with a number of dangling questions. It is clear that we can productively think of memory as being a network of associations, with activation flowing from one node to another. This simple conception has allowed us to explain a wide range of data in this chapter; the conception also makes good biological sense (see Chapter 2). What is unclear, though, is whether this is all the theory we need. Will spreading activation plus some sort of node competition be enough to explain memory search and memory retrieval? Or will we need to supplement these mechanisms with some sort of "memory executive," guiding memory search? For these difficult questions, we do not yet have answers.

The Newest Chapter: Connectionism

In the last 25 years or so, an important descendant of the network idea has appeared on the scene and has generated enormous excitement in psychology, as well as in computer science and philosophy. This development seeks to address (among other things) exactly the worries we have just been considering. However, rather than adding a more intelligent component to the network, guiding memory search, this new approach goes in the opposite direction and tries to show just how much we can accomplish with network and more network.

Distributed Processing, Distributed Representations

A small number of important innovations have spurred this new wave of theorizing, a wave referred to as **connectionism**, or **parallel distributed processing** (PDP). (For excellent introductions to this domain, see Churchland, 1989; Flanagan, 1991; Haugeland, 1997; and Rumelhart, 1997.)

In the networks we have considered so far, what it means to "think about" or "remember" a particular idea is to activate the node for that idea. This assumes a system of **local representations**, with one idea per node, or one content per location. In a connectionist system, in contrast, there are only **distributed representations**, so that any particular idea is represented not by a single node, but by a pattern of activation across the network. To take a simple case, the concept "birthday" might be represented by a pattern in which nodes B, F, H, and R are firing, whereas the concept "computer" might be represented by a pattern in which nodes C, G, H, and S are firing. Note that node H is part of both of these patterns and probably part of the pattern for many other concepts as well. Thus, we can't attach any meaning or interpretation to this node by itself; we can only learn what is being represented by looking at many other nodes simultaneously to find out what pattern of activation exists across the entire network. (For more on local and distributed representations, see Chapter 3.)

This reliance on distributed representation has important consequences for how a connectionist network functions. Imagine being asked what sort of computer you use. In order for you to respond, the idea "computer" needs to trigger the idea "iBook" (or "Dell" or "Compaq" or whatever it is you have). In a distributed network, this means that the many nodes representing "computer" have to manage collectively to activate the many nodes representing "iBook." To continue our simple illustration, node C has to trigger node L at the same time that node G triggers node A, and so on, leading ultimately to the activation of the L-A-J-T combination that, let's say, represents "iBook." In short, then, a network using distributed representations must employ processes that are similarly distributed, so that one wide-spread activation pattern can have broad enough effects to evoke a different (but equally widespread) pattern. In addition, the steps bringing this about must all occur simultaneously—in parallel—with each other, so that one entire representation can smoothly trigger the next. This is why connectionist models are said to involve parallel distributed processing (PDP).

Notice, though, that there is a conspicuous disadvantage attached to this sort of model: With no local representations, there can be no centralized pooling of information and no centralized control. In a connectionist model, different parts of a process are carried out by different (and largely independent) operators, and there is no mechanism in place to coordinate the overall process. This by itself might make connectionist models look implausible as a conception of how our mental processes work.

At the same time, though, distributed processing carries some important advantages. After all, mental processes often do have many parts; memory searches often must satisfy multiple demands (Figure 8.11). Rather than trying to coordinate all of

FIGURE 8.11 Satisfying Multiple Constraints

Imagine that you live in an apartment on the tenth floor of a building, and you want to hang a picture on the wall. All you need to do is bang a nail into the wall, but you have no hammer. What should you use? You need to search memory for something that is hard enough to bang a nail, lightweight enough so that you can swing it, strong enough so that it can take the impact, likely to be within your apartment, portable enough so that you can move it to the "job site," preferably belonging to you and not your roommate, and so on. If the cast-iron frying pan comes to mind, it's because the pan satisfied all these requirements. How do you manage to search through memory in order to honor all of these constraints?

these demands, perhaps it would be easier to let one part of the network worry about one demand; another part, another demand; and so on. In essence, the parts of the network would then engage in a complex tug-of-war, with each part of the network pulling toward the solution that satisfied its own demands. The resulting overall solution (the item retrieved from memory, or the decision reached) would then necessarily represent a balance point, or compromise, among these competing requirements. Connectionists refer to this process as **simultaneous multiple constraint satisfaction**.

In fact, we've already seen a process that works in roughly this fashion: In the feature net described in Chapter 3, there's no mechanism in place to coordinate the various detectors. Instead, each detector, on its own, does its thing—guided by the input (perhaps strong, perhaps weak) that it received, and by its level of activation prior to receiving any input. The *CH*-detector therefore tugs the network in one direction, the *CO*-detector tugs in a different direction, and the final outcome simply reflects the sum total of all these tugs. As we saw earlier, the resulting network, simple as it is, can accomplish a great deal: It acts as if it knows the rules of English spelling; it seems to have "expectations," and it acts as if it were making "inferences" to fill in missing information. But this is not because the network includes some centralized authority, or some sophisticated decision-maker. Instead, the network is a fully distributed system, and what it accomplishes is simply the result of the different elements within the system each doing their individual jobs.

Neural Nets

According to many advocates of the connection approach, another advantage of connectionist modeling is its *biological plausibility*. Thanks to the distributed processing, each part of the connectionist network has to deal with only a small part of the whole. As a result, each part of the network can be relatively simple—not a complex analyzer, but an uncomplicated receiver and accumulator of activation and, eventually, a source of further activation.

In the same way, the *brain's* functioning depends on the activities of many simple units, each accumulating activation and sending activation to its neighbors. We also know that many of the brain's parts are active at any particular point in time, strongly implying that the brain relies on parallel processing spread out over many neurons—just like a connectionist network.

For these (and other) reasons, advocates of the connectionist approach argue that their models make good biological sense and provide insights into how the brain itself functions. Indeed, because of this analogy between the models and the brain, connectionist nets are often referred to as **neural nets**. Let's be careful, though, in understanding this label: These are not networks made up of neurons, but instead networks hypothesized to function as we believe assemblies of neurons do.

Learning as the Setting of Connection Weights

In various ways, then, connectionist models do seem promising, and this has spurred investigators to develop models of this type for many different psychological tasks. Only time will tell, however, exactly what these models can accomplish, and with that, whether this line of research will be as fruitful as many now believe.

In the meantime, there is one large issue still be addressed: The success of distributed processing obviously depends on having the appropriate connections in place, so that activation will spread to the desired target rather than in some other direction. But how are the connections set up in the first place? How, in a connectionist account, does learning take place?

Let us first be clear about what it means, in network terms, to "know" something. In any associative network, connectionist or otherwise, knowledge is literally contained within the connections themselves. We already took a step in this direction when we discussed the unpacking of the nodes—that what it means to know "George Washington was a president" is to have a connection between a node for GEORGE WASHINGTON and a node for PRESIDENT. This is, of course, phrased in terms of local representations, with individual nodes having specific assigned referents. The basic idea, however, is the same in a distributed system. What it means to know this fact about Washington is to have a pattern of connections between the many nodes that together represent "Washington" and the many nodes that together represent "president." Once these connections are in place, activation of either of these patterns will lead to the activation of the other.

Notice, then, that knowledge refers to a potential rather than to a state. If you know that Washington was a president, then the connections are in place so that if the "Washington" pattern of activations occurs, this will lead to the "president" pattern of activations. And, of course, this state of readiness will remain even if you happen not to be thinking about Washington right now. In this way, "knowing" something, in network terms, corresponds to how the activation will flow, if there is activation on the scene. This is different from "thinking about" something, which corresponds to which nodes are active at a particular moment, with no comment about where that activation will spread next.

This conception of knowing has obvious implications for the nature of learning. The idea, in brief, is that learning must involve an adjustment in the connections among nodes, so that, after learning, activation flows in different ways than it did before. In a connectionist network, however, this adjustment of the connections cannot be done via some central authority's intervention. That's because, in a connectionist network, there is no central authority. Instead, the adjustment must be governed entirely at the local level. In other words, the adjustment of **connection weights**—the strength of the individual connections—must be controlled entirely by mechanisms in the immediate neighborhood of each connection and influenced only by information about what's happening in that neighborhood.

Moreover, let's be clear that any bit of learning requires the adjustment of a great many connection weights: We need to adjust the connections, for example, so that the thousands of nodes representing "Washington" manage, together, to activate the thousands of nodes representing "president." Thus, learning, just like everything else in the connectionist scheme, must be a distributed process, involving thousands of microscopic changes, taking place all over the network, with no attempt at (and, indeed, no mechanism for) any coordination of these adjustments.

This is, to be sure, an amazing proposal. In order to achieve learning in the network, the various adjustments in connection weights must, in some way, end up coordinated with each other. Otherwise, adjustments at one connection might cancel out adjustments made at another! Thus, if learning is to happen at all, we need to ensure that there is some coherence in the changes made across the network. And yet, as we have repeatedly said, there is no explicit mechanism in place to achieve this coordination. How, therefore, is learning possible? Here we arrive at one of the most important intellectual innovations driving connectionism forward. Connectionists have offered a number of powerful computing schemes, "learning algorithms," that seek to accomplish learning within this setup. The learning typically requires a large number of learning trials and some sort of feedback about the correctness or appropriateness of the response. But given this, connectionists have offered schemes, with names like the "delta rule" and "back propagation," that accomplish learning on the local level, without an executive, and that seem to make the entire system grow gradually and impressively smarter.

We leave the details of these learning algorithms to the side, both because they are mathematically complex and also because, when we talk about the state of the art, anything we say will be quickly out of date. We emphasize, though, that in all of these algorithms, the adjustment of connection weights depends entirely on local conditions. Moreover, let's bear in mind that individual nodes are extremely simple in their processing capacities. The interesting question, therefore, lies in whether the accumulation of such simple mechanisms can be used as the basis for much more complex, much more sophisticated cognition. This question is at the heart of current controversy.

Possible Limits on Connectionist Networks

Psychologists are divided in their assessments of connectionist models: Some view these models as an important step forward; others argue that the models are inadequate and that we should be pursuing other approaches. (For advocates of the connectionist approach, see Christiansen, Chater, & Seidenberg, 1999; Churchland & Sejnowski, 1992; McClelland & Seidenberg, 2000; Rumelhart, 1997; and Rumelhart & McClelland, 1986; for more critical views, see Fodor, 1997; Fodor & Pylyshyn, 1988; Holyoak, 1987; Lachter & Bever, 1988; Pinker, 1999; and Pinker & Prince, 1988.)

What arguments might sway us for or against the connectionist approach? First, as we have already noted, many argue that connectionist models make biological sense; these models fit well, they claim, with what we know about the nervous system. Second, there seems little doubt that connectionist models do offer a powerful means of information storage. Third, we need to take these models seriously simply because of what they can accomplish. Connectionist models have so far learned to recognize patterns and can generalize what they have learned in appropriate ways. Connectionist models can, it is claimed, learn the rules of English grammar, learn how to read, and even learn how to play strategic games such as backgammon. (Many of these accomplishments are summarized in McClelland, 1999; and Rumelhart & McClelland, 1986.) All of this has led to considerable enthusiasm for connectionist approaches.

Others, however, have expressed skepticism about these claims. There is, first of all, room for debate about the biological realism of connectionist models. Some aspects of these models (distributed processing, parallel activities) surely do make biological sense, but other aspects may not. (For example, it is not clear how some of the learning algorithms are to be translated into neural terms.) Second, some have argued that connectionist models can learn only when the programmers stack the deck in the right way. Because the models often learn by inspecting examples, it is possible to "help" the models enormously by providing just the right examples in just the right sequence. Perhaps, then, connectionist models can't learn as we learn; or more precisely, perhaps can learn what we learn only if we give them a great deal of help. (For concerns about the "psychological realism" of connectionist learning, see French, 1999; Lavric, Pizzagalli, Forstmeier, & Rippon, 2001; McCloskey & Cohen, 1989; and Pinker & Prince, 1988; for an example of how this debate unfolds, see G. F. Marcus, 1995, 1996; G. F. Marcus et al., 1999; McClelland & Seidenberg, 2000; Pinker, 1999; and Plunkett & Marchman, 1996.) Third, the existing connectionist models are fairly specific in their focus, modeling one or another well-defined task. But humans are capable of a huge variety of tasks, raising questions about how (or whether) connectionist models might rise from the miniature to the grand scale.

The state of the art, therefore, resembles what we saw with networks in general. There have been, to be sure, some remarkable successes for connectionist theory, with seemingly complex mental activities successfully modeled. However, the range of these successes is still limited, and questions have been raised about whether this learning matches the learning that humans do.

As a result of all this, many in the field have adopted a wait-and-see attitude about what connectionist modeling will eventually accomplish. (For discussion, see Gluck & Rumelhart, 1990; and Ramsey, Stich, & Rumelhart, 1991.) We leave this chapter, therefore, with some very obvious loose ends. There is no doubt that network theorizing can encompass an enormous range of memory data. Hand in hand with this, it is virtually certain that the "warehouse" of our long-term storage does rely on some sort of network representation, with activation spreading from node to node, just as we have described in this chapter. What remains unsettled, though, is whether we will need other mechanisms, and more theory, beyond that provided by the network. Does the associative network serve merely as the "library" of long-term storage? Or does it also serve as the librarian, the indexer, the guy who retrieves books from the stacks, and the patron using the library? Said differently, does the network provide a theory of how knowledge is represented (with other mechanisms then needed to explain how the knowledge is used), or does the network provide a theory that explains everything?

We don't yet have answers to these questions, either for propositional networks (like Anderson's ACT model) or connectionist nets. Perhaps this is unsurprising, given the scale of the questions that are at stake here. In the meantime, though, we should surely take comfort from the fact that, unsolved mysteries or no, we have at least part of the puzzle under control. Our theorizing is allowing us to handle a lot of data and is leading us to new discoveries. This is, on anybody's account, a positive and promising sign.

Chapter Summary

1. Many theorists have proposed that memory consists of a huge network of nodes, with each joined to others via connections or associations. An individual node becomes activated when it receives enough of an input signal to raise its activation level to its response threshold. Once activated, the node sends activation out through its connections to all the nodes connected to it.

2. The network approach easily accommodates many results. For example, hints are effective because the target node can receive activation from nodes identifying the previous encounter with the desired information while also receiving activation from nodes representing the hint. The benefits of context reinstatement we explained in roughly the same fashion.

3. Many specific predictions of network theorizing have been directly confirmed. For example, activating one node does seem to prime nearby nodes through the process of spreading activation. Similarly, search through the network does seem to resemble travel in the sense that greater travel distances (more connections to be traversed) require more time.

4. If a node has a high degree of fan, it will be less effective in activating neighboring nodes, because each neighbor will receive only a small fraction of the activation energy radiating out from the initial node. This can, in some circumstances, impede memory search, creating a cost of knowing too much. However, this cost is usually offset by the fact that, as knowledge grows, the target node is likely to receive input from many nodes, and not just one.

5. The quantity of knowledge in long-term storage can make it difficult to locate any particular bit of information when needed. However, search through memory can be guided by the structure of the network itself. Once in the vicinity of the target information, connections will guide activation toward the target. Such guidance requires having the right connections in place, and neither too many nor too few connections. However, many investigators believe that the right number of connections can be found so that search through the network may become a relatively mechanical affair. To launch the search, some nodes must be tied to the mechanisms of perception, and presentation of the appropriate stimulus will trigger these nodes.

6. To store all of knowledge, the network may need more than simple associations among ideas. One proposal is that the network stores propositions, with different nodes each playing the appropriate role within the proposition. In addition, a distinction between type nodes and token nodes may be needed for the network to store both generic knowledge and knowledge about individual objects and events.

7. To test network theories, investigators have often translated their theories into computer models. It is too soon to tell how successful these models will be, but the development of computer models has already spurred theoretical development. For example, any model based on a relatively mechanical process of spreading activation has difficulty explaining retrieval blocks or the tip-of-the-tongue phenomenon. However, an additional winner-takes-all mechanism may solve this problem.

8. Much recent effort has gone into the development of connectionist nets. These are distinctive in relying entirely on distributed processes and representations. In these models, all learning consists of the setting (and adjusting) of connection weights. One attraction of this mode of theorizing is biological realism; another is the fact that processing by a connectionist net is sensitive to many constraints simultaneously, just as the mind seems to be.

9. There continues to be controversy over what network models can accomplish. There is no doubt that associations and spreading activation do play a crucial role in long-term memory, but questions remain about whether these mechanisms are sufficient to explain memory storage and memory search, or whether, alternatively, some sort of guide or executive is needed to direct the operations of the network.

Concepts and Generic Knowledge

No adult takes any pride in knowing what a dog is, or a house, or a tree. These concepts are so ordinary, so common, that there seems to be nothing special about knowing, and being able to think about, these simple ideas. However, ordinary concepts like these are, in an important way, the building blocks out of which all our knowledge is created, and, as we've seen in previous chapters, we depend on our knowledge in many aspects of our day-to-day functioning. Thus we know what to pay attention to in a restaurant (for example) because we understand the basic concept of "restaurant." We're able to understand a simple story about a child checking her piggy bank because we understand the concepts of "money," "shopping," and so on.

The idea, then, is that we need concepts in order to have knowledge, and we need knowledge in order to function. In this fashion, our understanding of ideas like "dog" or "house" might seem commonplace, but it is an ingredient without which cognition cannot proceed.

But what exactly does it mean to understand simple concepts like these? How is this knowledge represented in the mind? In this chapter, we'll tackle these questions, and as we will see, describing these concepts is appreciably more difficult than one might guess.

- Basic concepts—like our concept of "chair" or "dog"—are the building blocks of all our knowledge. However, attempts at *defining* these concepts usually fail because we easily find exceptions to virtually any definition that might be proposed.

- This leads to the suggestion that knowledge of these concepts is cast in terms of *probabilities*, so that a creature that has wings and feathers, and that flies and lays eggs, is probably a bird.

- Many results are consistent with this probabilistic idea, and show that the more a test case resembles the "prototype" for a category, the more likely people are to judge the case as being in that category.

- Other results, however, indicate that our conceptual knowledge includes other beliefs— beliefs that link a concept to other concepts and also specify why the concept is as it is.

- We are driven, therefore, to a multipart theory of concepts: Our conceptual knowledge must include a prototype for each category and also a set of remembered exemplars. But we also seem to have a broad set of beliefs about each concept—beliefs that provide a "theory" for why the concept takes the form it does, and we use this theory in a wide range of judgments about the concept.

Definitions: What Do We Know When We Know What a Dog Is?

We all know what a dog is. If someone sends us to the pet shop to buy a dog, we are sure to succeed. If someone tells us that a particular disease is common among dogs, we know that our pet terrier is at risk and so are the wolves in the zoo. Clearly, our store of knowledge about dogs will support these not-very-exciting achievements. But what is that knowledge?

One possibility is that we know something akin to a dictionary definition. That is, what we know is of this form: "A dog is a creature that is (a) mammalian, (b) has four legs, (c) barks, (d) wags its tail." This definition would presumably serve us well. When asked whether a candidate creature is a dog, we could use our definition as a checklist, scrutinizing the candidate for the various defining features. When told that "a dog is an animal," we would know that we had not learned anything new, because this information is already contained, presumably, within our mental definition. If we were asked what dogs, cats, and horses have in common, we could scan our definition of each one looking for common elements.

The difficulty with this proposal, however, was made clear by an important 20th-century philosopher, Ludwig Wittgenstein. Wittgenstein (1953) noted that philosophers had been trying for thousands of years to define terms like "virtue" or "knowledge." There had been some success, inasmuch as various features had been identified as important aspects of these terms. However, even after thousands of years of careful thought, these terms were still without accepted, full definitions.

289

Perhaps this is unsurprising, since these are subtle, philosophically rich terms and so are naturally resistant to definition. Wittgenstein wondered, though, whether this really was the problem. He wondered whether we could find definitions even for simple, ordinary terms—for example, the word "game."

What is a game? Consider, for example, the game of hide-and-seek. What makes hide-and-seek a game? Hide-and-seek (a) is an activity most often practiced by children, (b) is engaged in for fun, (c) has certain rules, (d) involves multiple people, (e) is in some ways competitive, and (f) is played during periods of leisure. All these are plausible attributes of games, and so we seem well on our way to defining "game." But are these attributes really part of the definition of "game"? Consider (a) and (b): What about the Olympic Games? The competitors in these games are not children, and runners in marathon races do not look like they are having a great deal of fun. Consider (d) and (e): What about card games played by one person? These are played alone, without competition. Consider (f): What about professional golfers?

For each clause of the definition, we can find an exception: an activity that we call a game but that does not have the relevant characteristic. And the same is true for most any concept: We might define "shoe" as an item of apparel made out of leather, designed to be worn on the foot. But what about wooden shoes? What about a shoe, designed by a master shoemaker, that is intended only for display and never for use? What about a shoe filled with cement, which therefore cannot be worn? Similarly, we might define "dog" in a way that includes four-leggedness, but what about a dog that has lost a limb in some accident? We might specify "communicates by barking" as part of the definition of dog, but what about the Egyptian basenji, which has no bark? Examples like these make it clear that even simple terms, terms denoting concepts that we use easily and often, resist being defined. In each case, we can come up with what seems to be a plausible definition, but then it is absurdly easy to find exceptions to it.

Family Resemblance

What we need, therefore, is a way of identifying concepts that highlights what the various members of a category have in common (what all dogs have in common, for example), while simultaneously allowing exceptions to whatever rule we propose. One way to achieve this is by keeping the *content* of our definitions, but being much more flexible in how we *use* the definitions. Thus, we would not say, "A creature that has fur, four legs, and barks is a dog." That's because, as we've seen, there are exceptions to each of these requirements (a hairless Chihuahua? a three-legged dog? the barkless basenji?). But surely we *can* say, "A creature that has fur, four legs, and barks is *probably* a dog, and a creature without these features is *unlikely to be* a dog." This probabilistic phrasing preserves what is good about definitions—the fact that they do name sensible, relevant features. But this phrasing also allows some degree of uncertainty, some number of exceptions to the rule.

Wittgenstein's proposal was roughly along these lines. His notion was that members of a category have a **family resemblance** to each other. To understand this term, think about the resemblance pattern in an actual family—your own, perhaps. There are probably no "defining features" for your family—features that every family member has. Nonetheless, there are features that are *common* in the family, and so, if we consider family members two or even three at a time, we can always find some shared attributes. Thus, you, your brother, and your mother might all have the family's beautiful blonde hair, the same square shoulders, and also the same wide lips, and so, as a result, you three look alike to some extent. Your sister, on the other hand, doesn't have these features; she's a narrow-lipped brunette. Nonetheless, she's still recognizable as a member of the family, because she (like you and your father) has the family's typical eye shape and the family's distinctive chin.

One way to think about this resemblance pattern is by imagining the "ideal" for each family—someone who has *all* of the family's features. (In our example, this would be someone who is blonde, has square shoulders and wide lips, and also has just the right eye and chin shapes.) In many families, this person may not exist; there may be no one who has all of the family's features, and so no one who looks like the "perfect Smith" (or the "perfect Martinez" or the "perfect Goldstein"). Nonetheless, each member of the family has at least some features in common with this ideal, and therefore some features in common with other family members. This is why the family members resemble each other, and it's also how we manage to recognize these individuals as being within the family.

Wittgenstein proposed that the thousands of categories we can think about—categories like "dog" or "game" or "furniture"—work in the same fashion. There may be no features that are shared by all dogs, or all games, just like there are no features shared by everyone in your family. That's why a rigid definition isn't possible. Even so, we can identify "characteristic features" for each category—features that most category members have. And the more of these features that an object has, the more likely we are to believe it is in the category. Family resemblance is a matter of degree, not all-or-none (Figure 9.1).

There are several ways we might translate all of this into a psychological theory, but the most influential translation was proposed by Eleanor Rosch, in the mid-1970s (Rosch, 1973, 1978; Rosch & Mervis, 1975; Rosch, Mervis, Gray, Johnson, & Boyes-Braem, 1976), and it's to her model that we now turn.

Prototypes and Typicality Effects

One way to think about definitions is that they set the "boundaries" for a category: If a test case has certain attributes, then it is inside the category. If the test case does not have the defining attributes, then it is outside the category. (For discussion of this "classical" view, see E. E. Smith, 1988; and G. L. Murphy, 2003.)

| FIGURE 9.1 | What Attributes Define a Chair? |

"Attention, everyone! I'd like to introduce the newest member of our family."

Some chairs have four legs, some three, some none. Most chairs can be sat upon, but some are too small for sitting. It seems that chairs have a family resemblance to each other but not a definition.

Prototype theory begins with a different tactic: Perhaps the best way to identify a category, to characterize a concept, is to specify the "center" of the category rather than the boundaries. Just as we spoke earlier about the "ideal" family member, perhaps the concept of "dog" (for example) is represented in the mind by some representation of the "ideal" dog, the prototype dog. In this view, all judgments about dogs are made with reference to this ideal. For example, categorization (i.e., deciding whether something is a dog or not) would involve a comparison between a test case (the furry creature currently before your eyes) and the prototype, represented in your memory. If there is no similarity between these, then the creature before you is probably not in the category; if there is considerable similarity, then you draw the opposite conclusion.

What is a prototype? In some cases, the prototype may literally represent the ideal for the category (and so, for example, the prototype diet soft drink might have zero calories but still taste great). More commonly, though, the prototype will be an average of the various category members you have encountered. Thus, the prototype dog will be the average color of the dogs you have seen, the average size of the dogs you've seen, and so forth.

Notice, then, that different people will have different prototypes. If a prototype reflects the ideal for a category, then people may disagree about what that ideal would involve. If a prototype reflects the average of the cases you have encountered, then an American's prototype for "house" might have one form, while for someone living in Japan, the prototype "house" might be rather different. We will therefore need some flexibility in how we characterize prototypes. Nonetheless, in all cases the prototype will serve as the anchor, the benchmark, for our conceptual knowledge. When we reason about a concept, or use our conceptual knowledge, our reasoning is done with reference to the prototype.

Fuzzy Boundaries and Graded Membership

Our hypothesis, then, is that what it means to "know" a concept is simply to have some mental representation of the concept's prototype. How does this work? We've already described how prototypes would help us in the simple task of categorization: You categorize objects by comparing them to prototypes stored in memory. If, for example, the creature now before your eyes has many attributes in common with the dog prototype, it will easily and quickly be recognized as a dog. Dogs that have fewer attributes in common with the prototype will probably cause you uncertainty about their identity. Similarly, in deciding that a particular ceramic vessel is a cup and not a bowl, you might compare the vessel to both your cup prototype and your bowl prototype. By discovering that the vessel is more similar to one than to the other, you reach a decision.

This sounds plausible enough, but there is an odd implication here: Since the category is characterized by its *center* (the prototype), and not by its *boundaries*, there's no way we can say whether something is, strictly speaking, inside of the category or outside. (To be inside or outside, you need a boundary to be inside or outside *of*!) At best, therefore, each category will have what's called a **fuzzy boundary**, with no clear specification of category membership and nonmembership.

Hand in hand with this, on this view, not all category members are equal. In the classical view, an object was either in the category or not, with no issue of being "more" in the category or "less." But on the prototype view, with its fuzzy boundaries, categorization is a matter of more or less. Objects closer to the prototype are, in effect, "better" members of the category than objects farther from the prototype. Thus, categories that depend on a prototype have **graded membership**, with some dogs "doggier" than others, some books "bookier" than others, and so on for all the other categories you can think of.

Testing the Prototype Notion

In the **sentence verification task**, research participants are presented with a succession of sentences; their job is to indicate (by pressing the appropriate button) whether each sentence is true or false. In most experiments, what we are interested in is *how quickly* participants can do this task, and, in fact, their speed depends on several factors. As we saw in Chapter 8, response speed depends on the number of "steps" the participants must traverse to confirm the sentence. Participants also respond more quickly for true sentences than for false, and also more quickly for familiar categories. Most important for our purposes, though, the speed of response varies from item to item within a category. For example, response times are longer for sentences like "A penguin is a bird" than for "A robin is a bird"; longer for "An Afghan hound is a dog" than for "A German shepherd is a dog" (E. E. Smith, Rips, & Shoben, 1974).

Why should this be? According to a prototype perspective, participants make these judgments by comparing the thing mentioned (penguin, for example) to their prototype for that category (their bird prototype). When there is much similarity between the test case and the prototype, participants can make their decisions quickly; judgments about items more distant from the prototype take more time. Given the results, it seems that penguins and Afghans are more distant from their respective prototypes than are robins and German shepherds.

Other results can also be understood in these terms. For example, in a **production task** we ask people to name as many birds or dogs as they can (Mervis, Catlin, & Rosch, 1976). According to a prototype view, they will do this production task by first locating their bird or dog prototype in memory and then asking themselves what resembles this prototype. In essence, they will start with the center of the category (the prototype) and work their way outward from there. Thus, birds close to the prototype should be mentioned first, birds farther from the prototype later on.

Notice, then, that the first birds to be mentioned in the production task should be the birds that yielded fast response times in the verification task; that's because what matters, in both tasks, is proximity to the prototype. Likewise, the birds mentioned later in production should have yielded slower response times in verification. This is exactly what happens.

In fact, this sets the pattern of evidence for prototype theory: Over and over, in category after category, members of a category that are "privileged" on one task (e.g., yield the fastest response times) turn out also to be privileged on other tasks (e.g., are most likely to be mentioned). That is, various tasks *converge* in the sense that each task yields the same answer—i.e., indicates the same category members as special. (For some examples of these privileged category members, see Table 9.1.)

The Converging Evidence for Prototypes

We have mentioned two lines of experiments with converging data patterns, but there are many more. We list five of them here, to give you a sense of the evidence:

1. *Sentence verification.* As indicated, items close to the prototype are more quickly identified as category members. This presumably reflects the fact that category membership is determined by assessing the similarity to the prototype (Rosch, Simpson, & Miller, 1976).

TABLE 9.1	Participants' Typicality Ratings for the Category "Fruit" and the Category "Bird"

Fruit	Rating	Bird	Rating
Apple	6.25	Robin	6.89
Peach	5.81	Bluebird	6.42
Pear	5.25	Seagull	6.26
Grape	5.13	Swallow	6.16
Strawberry	5.00	Falcon	5.74
Lemon	4.86	Mockingbird	5.47
Blueberry	4.56	Starling	5.16
Watermelon	4.06	Owl	5.00
Raisin	3.75	Vulture	4.84
Fig	3.38	Sandpiper	4.47
Coconut	3.06	Chicken	3.95
Pomegranate	2.50	Flamingo	3.37
Avocado	2.38	Albatross	3.32
Pumpkin	2.31	Penguin	2.63
Olive	2.25	Bat	1.53

After Malt & Smith, 1984.

Note: Ratings were made on a 7-point scale, 7 corresponding to the highest typicality.

2. *Production.* As indicated, items close to the prototype are the earliest and the most likely to be mentioned in a production task. This presumably reflects the fact that the memory search supporting this task begins with the prototype and "works outward" (Barsalou, 1983, 1985; Barsalou & Sewell, 1985; Mervis et al., 1976).

3. *Picture identification.* This task is similar to the sentence verification task. Participants are told that they are about to see a picture that may or may not be a dog; they are asked to hit a "yes" or "no" button as quickly as they can. Pictures of dogs similar to the prototype (e.g., German shepherd or collie) are more quickly identified; pictures of dogs less similar to the prototype (e.g., Chihuahua or dachshund) are more slowly identified (Rosch, Mervis, et al., 1976; E. E. Smith, Balzano, & Walker, 1978).

4. *Explicit judgments of category membership.* Rosch (1975; also Malt & Smith, 1984) explicitly asked participants to judge how typical various category members were for the category. In these typicality studies, the participants are given instructions like these: "We all know that some birds are 'birdier' than others, some dogs are 'doggier' than others, and so on. I'm going to present you with a list of birds or of dogs, and I want you to rate each one on the basis of how 'birdy' or 'doggy' it is." People are easily able to render these judgments,

and quite consistently, they rate items as being very "birdy" or "doggy" when these instances are close to the prototype (as determined in the other tasks). They rate items as being less "birdy" or "doggy" when these are farther from the prototype. This suggests that people perform this task by comparing the test item to the prototype.

5. *Tasks asking people to think about categories.* The procedure here has three steps (Rosch, 1977a). First, we ask participants to make up sentences about a category. If the category were "birds," they might make up such sentences as, "I saw two birds in a tree," or "I like to feed birds in the park." Next, the experimenters rewrite these sentences, substituting for the category name either the name of a prototypical member of the category (e.g., robin) or a not-so-prototypical member (e.g., penguin). In our example, we would get "I like to feed robins in the park," and "I like to feed penguins in the park." Finally, we take these new, edited sentences to a different group of participants and ask this group to rate how silly or implausible the sentences seem.

The hypothesis is that, when we ask people to think about a category, they are in fact thinking about the prototype for that category. Therefore, in making up their sentences, participants will come up with statements appropriate for the prototype. It follows from this that the sentence's sensibility will be pretty much unchanged if we substitute a prototypical category member for the category name, since that will be close to what the participant had in mind in the first place. Substituting a nonprototypical member, on the other hand, may yield a peculiar, even ridiculous, proposition. This is fully in line with the data. When the new group of participants rate these sentences, they rate as quite ordinary the sentences into which we have placed a prototypical case ("I saw two robins in a tree") and reject as silly the sentences into which we have placed a nonprototypical case ("I saw two penguins in a tree").

Basic-Level Categories

Much of the research just reviewed derives from Eleanor Rosch's theorizing about the nature and function of mental prototypes. We should mention, though, that Rosch's work also contains another theme. As a way of introducing this point, consider the following task: We show you a picture of a chair, and we ask, "What is this?" What you are likely to say is that the picture shows a chair. You are far less likely to offer a more specific response ("It's a Windsor chair") or a more general response ("It's an item of furniture"), although these responses would also be correct. Likewise, we might ask, "How do people get to work?" In responding, you are unlikely to say, "Some people drive Fords; some drive Toyotas." Instead, your answer is likely to use more general terms, such as "cars" and "trains" and "buses."

In keeping with these observations, Rosch argued that there is a "natural" level of categorization, neither too specific nor too general, that we tend to use in our conversations and our reasoning. She refers to this level as **basic-level categorization**, and the "special status" of basic-level categories can be demonstrated in many ways. Basic-level categories are usually represented in our language via a single word, while more specific categories are identified only via a phrase. Thus, "chair" is a basic-level category and so is "apple." The subcategories of "lawn chair" or "kitchen chair" are not basic-level; nor is "Granny Smith apple" or "Golden Delicious apple." In addition, if asked to describe an object, we are likely spontaneously to use the basic-level term. If asked to explain what members of a category have in common with each other, we have an easy time with basic-level categories (what do all chairs have in common?) but some difficulty with more-encompassing categories (what does all furniture have in common?). And so on.

The importance of basic-level categories also shows up in our *memory errors*. In one study, participants read a story, and then, after a delay, their memory for the story was tested. If the story contained specific terms, participants often (falsely) recalled that they had heard something more general. For example, the sentence, "She noticed that her jeans were stained," was often misremembered as, ". . . her pants were stained." Conversely, if the story contained *general* terms, these were misremembered as being more specific than they actually were (and so participants remembered hearing about "dogs" when they had actually head about "animals"). In all cases, though, the errors tended to "revise" the story in the direction of basic-level categorization (Pansky & Koriat, 2004).

It seems, then, that basic-level categorization is important for a variety of purposes. Indeed, in studies of children who are learning how to talk, there are some indications that basic-level terms are acquired earlier than either the more specific subcategories or the more general, more-encompassing categories. Thus, basic-level categories do seem to reflect a natural way to categorize the objects in our world (Rosch, Mervis, et al., 1976; for discussion and some complications, see Corter & Gluck, 1992; M. Morris & Murphy, 1990; Tanaka & Taylor, 1991; and B. Tversky & Hemenway, 1991).

Exemplars

Let's return, though, to our main agenda. As we have seen, a broad spectrum of tasks reflects the "graded membership" of mental categories. Some members of the categories are better than others, and the "better" members are recognized more readily, mentioned more often, judged more typical, and so on. Thus, people give fast verifications for sentences like "An apple is a fruit" and slower responses to "An olive is a fruit." If asked to name fruits, people are likely to name "apple" fairly quickly; if they name "olive" at all, it will be much later. If asked to rate how "fruity" apples and olives are, they will give a higher rating for the former.

Likewise, it seems plain that typicality does guide many of our category judgments: In diagnosing diseases, for example, physicians often seem to function as if asking themselves, "How much does this case resemble a typical case of disease X? How closely does it resemble a typical case of disease Y?" The greater the resemblance to this or that diagnostic prototype, the more likely the diagnosis will be of that disease. (See, for example, Klayman & Brown, 1993.)

All of this is obviously in accord with prototype theory: Our conceptual knowledge is represented via a prototype, and we categorize by making comparisons to that prototype. It turns out, though, that prototype theory isn't the only way one can think about these data. Another perspective is available, providing a different way to explain typicality effects and the graded membership of categories. In this section, we examine this alternate view.

Analogies From Remembered Exemplars

Imagine that we place a wooden object in front of you and ask, "Is this a chair?" According to the prototype view, you will answer this question by calling up your chair prototype from memory and then comparing the candidate to that prototype. If the resemblance is great, you will announce, "Yes, this is a chair."

But you might make this decision in a different way: You might notice that this object is very similar to an object in your Uncle Jerry's living room, and you know that the object in Uncle Jerry's living room is a chair. After all, you've seen Uncle Jerry sitting in the thing, reading his newspaper. If Jerry's possession is a chair, and if the new object resembles Jerry's, then it is a safe bet that the new object is a chair too.

The idea here is that, in some cases, categorization can draw on knowledge about specific category members rather than on more general information about the overall category. In our example, the categorization is supported by memories of a specific chair, rather than remembered knowledge about chairs in general. This is referred to as **exemplar-based reasoning**, with an exemplar defined as a specific remembered instance—in essence, an example.

In crucial ways, the exemplar-based approach is very similar to the prototype view. According to each of these proposals, you categorize objects by comparing them to a mentally represented "standard." The difference between the views lies only in what that standard is: For prototype theory, the standard is the prototype—an average representing the entire category. For exemplar theory, the standard is provided by whatever example of the category comes to mind (and, of course, different examples may come to mind on different occasions). In either case, though, the process is then the same: You assess the similarity between a candidate object and this standard. If the resemblance is great, you judge the candidate as being within the relevant category; if the resemblance is minimal, you seek some alternative categorization.

Explaining Typicality Data With an Exemplar Model

We earlier suggested that the graded-membership pattern, so often seen in concept tasks, is consistent with the idea that concepts are represented in the mind via prototypes. It turns out, though, that an exemplar-based approach can also explain the graded-membership pattern. For illustration, consider a task in which we show people a series of pictures and ask them to decide whether each picture shows a fruit or not. We already know that they will respond more quickly for typical fruits than for less typical fruits, and we have seen how this result is handled by a prototype account. How could an exemplar model explain this finding?

According to exemplar theory, people make their judgments in this task by comparing the pictures to specific memories of fruits—that is, to specific, mentally represented examples. But how exactly will this work? Let's imagine that you're looking at a picture of some object and trying to decide whether it's a fruit or not. To make your decision, you'll try to think of a fruit exemplar that resembles the one in the picture; if you find a good match, then you know the object in the picture is a fruit. No match? Then it's not a fruit.

If the picture shows, say, an apple, then your memory search will be extremely fast: Apples are common in your experience (often seen, often eaten, often mentioned), and so you've had many opportunities to establish apple memories. Moreover, these memories will be well primed, thanks to your frequent encounters with apples. As a result, you'll easily find a memory that matches the picture, and so you will swiftly respond that, yes, the picture does show a fruit. But if the picture shows, say, a fig or a carob, then your memory search will be more difficult: You probably don't have as many memories that will match these pictures, and these memories aren't well primed. Hence your response will be appreciably slower.

A similar argument will handle the other tasks showing the graded-membership pattern—for example, the production task. Let's say that you are asked to name as many fruits as you can. You'll quickly name apples and oranges because these fruits are represented many times in your memory, thanks to the many encounters you've had with them. These memories are also well primed, making them easy to retrieve. Therefore apple memories and orange memories will readily come to mind. Fig and date memories, however, will have none of these advantages, and so will come to mind less easily. In this way, your production will favor the typical fruits—not because of prototyping, but because of the pattern of what's available in memory.

Exemplars Preserve Information About Variability

It seems, therefore, that exemplar-based views can easily explain typicality effects, largely by appealing to a typicality bias in people's memories: Items that are frequent in the world will be frequently represented (and well primed) in memory, and so will readily come to mind. This is all we need to explain the graded-membership pattern—with no appeal whatsoever to mental prototypes.

In this fashion, the graded-membership pattern favors neither the prototype nor the exemplar theory; both theories are compatible with the evidence. Other results, however, do favor the exemplar view. For example, we have noted that a prototype can be thought of as the average for a category, and as such, it provides a summary of what is typical or frequent for that category. But much information is lost in an average. For example, an average, by itself, doesn't tell you how variable a set is, and sometimes information about variability is rather useful (Rips, 1989; Rips & Collins, 1993). The average size of a pizza is 12 inches. The average size of a ruler is, of course, also 12 inches. Now let's imagine that I hand you a new object that is 19 inches across. Is it more likely that this new object is a pizza or a ruler? If you make this decision by comparing the test case to the averages, then you have no basis for a judgment; the test case departs from both averages by 7 inches. But of course you know that pizzas vary in size, and so a pizza could easily be 19 inches across. Rulers do not vary, and so the test case is almost certainly not a ruler.

In this situation, your judgment is plainly influenced by knowledge about variability. This knowledge would not be reflected in a prototype (which is just like an average), but it could be reflected via exemplars. If you remember both a 7-inch pizza and one that was 30 inches across, this tells you in an instant that a pizza can vary in its size (at least) from 7 to 30 inches. For that matter, if you reflect on the full set of pizzas you have seen, you can make a reasonable assessment of how variable the set has been.

In short, a set of exemplars preserves information about variability; a prototype does not. Since people do seem sensitive to variability information, this seems a strike against prototype theory and in favor of exemplars. (For further discussion of people's sensitivity to variability, see Fried & Holyoak, 1984; and Nisbett, Krantz, Jepson, & Kunda, 1983.)

The Pliability of Mental Categories

Other evidence also favors the exemplar perspective. For example, one might think that our conceptual knowledge is relatively *stable*, so that the concept of "giraffe" that I have today is the same as the concept I had yesterday (assuming that I haven't learned any new facts about giraffes). Likewise, the concept I use in identifying giraffes is presumably the same concept I use when talking about giraffes or drawing inferences about them. There is every reason to believe, however, that our concepts are more pliable, more flexible, than this, and this flexibility turns out to be more easily accommodated by the exemplar view.

In one study, participants were asked to judge how typical various birds were. Not surprisingly, for the category "birds," American participants rated robin and eagle as highly typical members of the category; swan and peacock got lower ratings. These results are exactly in line with others we have already discussed. However, these same participants were then asked to take a different point of view, and to redo the task. Specifically, they were asked to take a "Chinese point of view," and now they rated robin and eagle as much *less* typical for the category, and swan and peacock as more typical.

Similar results were obtained with other categories. In one procedure, college students were asked to think about the category of "gifts," and to rate different options (a new CD? a cookbook? a new shirt?) for how typical they were as gifts. Then the same students were asked to imagine that they were college faculty and, from this perspective, to rerate the typicality of various gifts. From the new perspective, the ratings were entirely different (Barsalou, 1988; Barsalou & Sewell, 1985).

How should we think about this result? One option is that people simply have many different prototypes—a prototype for "American bird" and one for "Chinese bird," a prototype for "student gift" and one for "faculty gift." According to this view, the procedures just described are simply urging the participants to move from one prototype to another as they do the various tasks.

However, some further evidence speaks against this proposal. So far, almost all of the categories we have considered involve the meanings of single words (e.g., "bird" or "gift"). But Barsalou (1988) notes that there are also **goal-derived categories** and completely **ad hoc categories**. Among goal-derived categories, we might include "things to eat on a diet" or "things to carry out of your house in case of a fire"; in ad hoc categories, we might include "things that could fall on your head" or "things you might see while in Paris." Interestingly, these categories also turn out to have a graded membership: People identify some category members as being more typical than others; they more quickly recognize the "typical" ones in a sentence verification task. If we interpret graded membership as indicating reliance on a prototype, then it seems that participants must have a prototype for these categories—a prototypical thing to see in Paris, a prototypical thing that could fall on your head, and so on.

Of course, we can proliferate categories like these endlessly: There is, for example, the category of "gifts to give your former high school friend who has just had her second baby," or the category of "things you can do to entertain a 4-year-old if she has a broken wrist." We surely don't want to argue that people have a ready-made prototype for each of these; that would be tantamount to assuming an infinite stockpile of prototypes. If categories like these do have prototypes, then people must be making up the prototypes on the spot.

At the least, all of this suggests that conceptual knowledge must include more than prototypes. People must also have some knowledge that allows them to "adjust" their prototypes, and to create new prototypes whenever they are needed. We can therefore conclude that prototype theory is, at best, incomplete as an account of conceptual knowledge; knowing a concept must involve more than having a prototype.

Things look simpler, though, if we adopt an exemplar-based view. In this view, category judgments depend on the specific exemplars that come to mind, and we have already noted that different exemplars may come to mind on different occasions. This is because the search for remembered exemplars, like any memory search, can be influenced by various forms of cueing or priming. Thus, the set of exemplars evoked by the cue "Chinese bird" may well be different from the set evoked by the cue "bird." With different exemplars coming to mind, different judgments will be rendered. Therefore, it is no surprise that typicality judgments are influenced by changes in perspective or in context.

With this view there is also no problem with ad hoc categories. In making judgments about these categories, people are relying on specific remembered cases (or, perhaps, specific imagined cases). Because there is no reliance here on prototypes, there is no issue of creating ad hoc prototypes on the spot. Indeed, according to the exemplar-based view, there is no difference between how people judge familiar categories and how they judge ad hoc categories: In both cases, they draw on a remembered (or imagined) instance and base their judgment on that instance. It is sensible, in this account, that participants behave similarly with familiar and unfamiliar categories.

Exemplar Use and Concept Learning

It appears, then, that a number of arguments speak in favor of exemplar-based accounts. These accounts provide an easy explanation for why people are often sensitive to category variability; they also help us understand why mental categories seem so flexible, and why we seem able to think about made-up categories in much the same ways that we think about familiar categories.

At the same time, prototypes also have their advantages. They do, after all, represent in an efficient and economical manner what's typical, or common, for a category. Perhaps, therefore, we don't want to treat prototypes and exemplars as mutually exclusive proposals. Perhaps, instead, our mental representation of a category includes both prototype *and* exemplar information, with each providing its own gains.

This sort of hybrid model may be particularly useful when we think about how people acquire new concepts. For example, think about a child's first trip to the zoo, and the child's first sight of a camel. On the basis of this encounter, the child has knowledge about that specific camel, but no information about camels in general—and so no information about the *category* of "camels." As a result, the child has no way of knowing whether the camel just seen was typical or not, and no way of knowing which of the camel's features will be shared by others of the species. At least for the moment, then, this remembered exemplar represents the full breadth of the child's camel knowledge. After the child has seen several camels, though, she can take the next step—"averaging" these together, potentially creating a camel prototype.

Notice, then, that novice category users may have no choice about relying on exemplars. A small number of examples of the category may be all they have, all they know about. More experienced category users, however, can "pool" the various examples they have encountered in order to create a prototype. And here, too, there may be no issue of choice: If someone has seen many different camels, then they may have trouble in recalling which camel was which. In other words, the various camels they've encountered may blur together in memory, creating a single memory that essentially averages across the various exemplars they've seen, just as a prototype would. (See Chapter 7 for more on how this blurring might take place.)

All of this suggests an obvious proposal: If we examine people who are just learning about a category, we should expect to find a heavy reliance on exemplars, with little evidence for prototype use. As people gain experience with the category, though, the data pattern may change, with a greater likelihood of relying on prototypes.

To explore these claims, a number of studies have examined the course of category learning. These studies use novel (usually fictional) categories, to ensure that the participants are unfamiliar with the category at the experiment's start. The participants are then shown pictures of category members, so that they can begin learning about them: "This animal is called a lepton. Here's a different lepton. This third animal is not a lepton. This fourth one isn't either." As this process unfolds, the participants are periodically tested: They are given cases without labels and asked, "Do you think this is a lepton or not?"

By choosing our cases with care, we can use these tests to find out what sort of representation the participants have in mind for the category of leptons. To make this concrete, let's suppose that most leptons have long necks; a long neck, therefore, is typical for the category. But not all leptons have long necks, and one or two of the leptons you've seen during training had relatively short necks. Now suppose that one of the test pictures shows a short-necked creature; is it a lepton? If you compare this picture to the lepton prototype, you'll say no, since the test case does not resemble the average (long-necked) lepton. But if you compare this picture to particular leptons you've seen (i.e., compare it to exemplars), then you may say yes, because you've seen other leptons just like this one. In this way, your response (your yes or no) will tell us whether you were relying on a prototype or on exemplars.

The pattern will reverse with a different type of test picture. This picture might show you the "ideal" lepton—one that has all of the features that are common in the species. We can arrange things in the experiment, though, so that this picture resembles none of the specific leptons you've seen so far. To continue the example, we have already said that having a long neck is common for this species, as is having a bushy tail and floppy ears. And, as part of your training, you've seen many long-necked leptons, and many bushy-tailed leptons, and many floppy-eared leptons. But you've never seen a lepton before that had all three of these features together, and so the test case now before your eyes is the first time you've seen the category's ideal—the "perfect" lepton. If you compare this case to the lepton prototype, you'll surely say, "Yes, it's a lepton." But if you compare the case to particular leptons you've seen (exemplars), then you may decide it's not a lepton. Again, your response will tell us what sort of representation was guiding your judgment.

Investigators have used this logic to ask what sort of representations participants have in mind at different stages of category learning. The results are consistent with the suggestion we offered earlier: Early in category learning, participants say yes to test pictures that resemble specific leptons they've already seen, even if the test pictures show creatures that aren't typical for the category. They're likely to say no to test pictures that don't resemble the creatures they've already seen, even if the pictures do show the category ideal. These results strongly suggest a reliance on exemplars. As the training proceeds, however, this pattern reverses. Now it doesn't matter if the test picture resembles particular leptons you've already seen. Participants say yes to the picture if it resembles the category average, and no otherwise. The obvious suggestion, then, is that a reliance on a prototype is gradually emerging as the participants' experience with the category grows. (For discussion and relevant data, see Homa, Dunbar, & Nohre, 1991; and Homa, Sterling, & Trepel, 1981; for some evidence, though, that not all categories show this pattern, see Minda & Smith, 2001; and J. D. Smith, 2002.)

It seems, then, that we are on the verge of a great compromise: Which is the better theory, one based on prototypes or one based on exemplars? The answer may be that both theories capture an element of the truth, with people shifting from exemplar-based to prototype-based knowledge as they gather more and more familiarity with a concept or category.

We must, however, attach a word of caution to this claim: Even if, through experience, we do construct a prototype for a category, this does not mean we cease relying on exemplars. Instead, some evidence suggests that, with familiar categories, we use *both* sorts of information. For example, Brooks, Norman, and Allen (1991; Brooks, 1990) have studied how expert dermatologists achieve their diagnoses. These physicians have viewed an enormous number of patients, and so they certainly have a basis for deriving a prototype for each diagnostic category. Nonetheless, the dermatologists show clear evidence of relying on exemplars: A correct diagnosis is more likely if the physicians have recently seen a specific case that resembles the one currently under scrutiny. Apparently, this prior case is still fresh in the doctors' memories and so comes readily to mind. Therefore, this prior case serves as a likely basis for analogy (and so a likely basis for diagnosis) for the new case now in view. Even the experts, in other words, rely on exemplars.

The Difficulties With Categorizing via Resemblance

Where are we so far? There is no question that typicality plays a huge role in our thinking about concepts. In many cases, the effect of typicality is due to our reliance on a prototype abstracted from our experiences with the category's members. In other cases, typicality arises from our use of specific exemplars, drawn from memory. Exemplar use is particularly likely, we have suggested, early in our learning about a category. Once we grow knowledgeable about a category, though, we have both exemplars and a prototype available to us, and we use both in an opportunistic fashion. In other words, if an object before your eyes happens to remind you of a specific prior experience, you can reason via an exemplar. If, instead, the object before you calls up some prototype knowledge, you will use that knowledge in your reasoning. In short, you rely on whichever sort of information comes to mind more readily. (For a discussion of the principles governing how these different species of conceptual knowledge are triggered, see Whittlesea, Brooks, & Westcott, 1994.) In either case, though, the process will be substantially the same, with a judgment based simply on the resemblance between this conceptual information, supplied by memory, and the novel case currently before you.

All of this seems straightforward enough. However, there are some results that do not fit easily into this picture. The time has come to broaden our conception of concepts.

Odd Number, Even Number

In the view we have been developing, judgments of typicality and judgments of category membership both derive from the same source: resemblance to an exemplar or to a prototype. If the resemblance is great, then a test case will be judged to be typical, and it will also be judged to be a category member. If the resemblance is small, then the test case will be judged atypical and probably not a category member. Thus, typicality and category membership should go hand in hand.

As we have seen, much evidence fits with this claim. It turns out, however, that we can also find situations in which there is no relation between typicality and category membership, and this is surely inconsistent with our claims so far. As a striking example of this pattern, consider a study by Armstrong, Gleitman, and Gleitman (1983). These researchers asked their research participants to do several of the concept tasks we have been discussing—for example, sentence verification, or explicit judgments about whether individuals were typical or not for their category. The twist, though, is that Armstrong et al. used categories for which there clearly is a definition—for example, the category "odd number." As a participant, therefore, you might be told, "We all know that some numbers are odder than others. What I want you to do is to rate each of the numbers on this list for how good an example it is for the category 'odd.'" Participants felt that this was a rather silly task, but nevertheless, they were able to render these judgments and, interestingly, were just as consistent with each other using these stimuli as they were with categories like "dog" or "bird" or "fruit" (see Table 9.2).

The obvious response to this experiment is that participants knew the definition of odd number but were playing along in response to the experimenters' peculiar request. Even so, the fact remains that participants' judgments about typicality were, in this case, disconnected from their judgments about category membership: They knew that all the test numbers were in the category of "odd number," but they still judged some to be more "typical" than others. Apparently, then, there is not

| TABLE 9.2 | Participants' Typicality Ratings for Well-Defined Categories |

Even number		Odd number	
Stimulus	Typicality rating	Stimulus	Typicality rating
4	5.9	3	5.4
8	5.5	7	5.1
10	5.3	23	4.6
18	4.4	57	4.4
34	3.6	501	3.5
106	3.1	447	3.3

After Armstrong et al., 1983.

Notes: Participants rated each item on how "good an example" it was for its category. Ratings were on a 0 to 7 scale, with 7 meaning the item is a "very good example." Participants rated some even numbers as being "better examples" of even numbers than others, although, mathematically, this is absurd: Either a number is even (divisible by 2 without a remainder), or it is not.

always a link between typicality and membership. (For further data pointing to the separation between typicality judgments and judgments of category membership, see Rips and Collins, 1993.)

To put this point slightly differently, the Armstrong et al. result signals a need for caution in interpreting the other results we've considered so far in this chapter. Thus, for example, we know that people are able to judge what a typical "dog" is, or a typical "tree," or a typical "bird," and we know that they rely on these assessments of typicality in many settings. But we cannot conclude from this that knowledge about typicality is *all* people know about these categories. That's because the Armstrong et al. data remind us that it's possible to have both a basis for judging typicality *and* other knowledge about the category; the presence of one of these doesn't rule out the possibility of the other. But what might this "other knowledge" be? This is clearly a point we'll need to tackle before we are through.

Lemons and Counterfeits

The example in the previous section (the category "odd number") is an unusual one—a technically defined, mathematical category. Do other categories show the same pattern? In fact, they do; and so, many results echo the messages just described: On the one side, people find it easy and "natural" to judge typicality. At the same time, they often find some basis for judging category membership that is independent of typicality—so that a test case can be a category member without being typical or can be typical without being a category member. This pattern is obviously troublesome for any theory proposing that typicality and category-membership judgments both derive from the same source.

For example, it is true that robins strike us as closer to the typical bird than penguins do. Nonetheless, most of us are quite certain that both robins and penguins are birds. Likewise, Moby Dick was definitely not a typical whale, but he certainly was a whale; Abraham Lincoln was not a typical American, but he was an American. These informal observations are easily confirmed in the laboratory. For example, participants judge whales to be more typical of the concept of "fish" than sea lampreys are, but these same participants respond (correctly) that sea lampreys are fish and whales are not (McCloskey & Glucksberg, 1978).

It seems, therefore, that category judgments are often not based on typicality. What are they based on? As a way of approaching the problem, let's think through some examples. Consider a lemon. Paint the lemon with red and white stripes. Is it still a lemon? Most people believe that it is. Now inject the lemon with sugar water, so that it has a sweet taste. Then run over the lemon with a truck, so that it is flat as a pancake. What have we got at this point? Do we have a striped, artificially sweet, flattened lemon? Or do we have a nonlemon? Most people still accept this poor, abused fruit as a lemon, but consider what this judgment entails: We have taken steps to make this object more and more distant from the prototype and also very different from any specific lemon you have ever encountered (and thus very different from any remembered exemplars). But this seems not to shake our faith that the object remains a lemon. To be sure, we have a not-easily-recognized lemon, an exceptional lemon, but it is still a lemon. Apparently, something can be a lemon with virtually no resemblance to other lemons. (For discussion of a similar case, with category members transformed by exposure to toxic waste, see Rips, 1989.)

Here is the opposite case. Consider a perfect counterfeit $20 bill. This bill will be enormously similar to the prototype for a real $20 bill and also highly similar to any remembered exemplar of a $20 bill. Yet we still consider it to be counterfeit, not real. Apparently, resemblance to other cases is not enough to qualify this bill for membership in the category of "real money." In fact, think about the category "perfect counterfeit." One can certainly imagine a prototype for this category, and of course, the prototype would have to be very similar to the prototype for the category of "real money." But despite this resemblance, you have no trouble keeping the categories distinct from each other: You know many things that are true for one category but not for the other, and you clearly understand, despite the near-identical prototypes, that counterfeit money is not the same thing as real money. You might be perceptually confused between a real bill and a counterfeit (because they do look alike), but you are not confused about the concepts, and you certainly know when you are thinking about one and when you are thinking about the other.

These examples underscore the distinction between typicality and category membership. In the case of the lemon, we see category membership even though the test case bears no resemblance to the prototype and, indeed, no resemblance to any of the other members of the lemon category. Conversely, one can have close resemblance to category members and high typicality without category membership (the counterfeit bill). If we take these cases at face value, then category membership cannot rest on typicality.

But can we take these cases at face value? Perhaps these cases are too playful. Perhaps people think about mutilated lemons in some artificial way, differently from how they think about more conventional concepts. Similarly, perhaps the Armstrong et al. participants realized they were doing something bizarre in judging the odd numbers and treated the task as a game, somehow different from their customary way of thinking about concepts. So again one might ask whether the data pattern would be different with more-typical concepts, in more-typical settings.

Relevant evidence for this point comes from work by Keil (1986). Keil was particularly interested in how children come to have concepts, and what children's concepts do or do not include. For our purposes, this approach is ideal because it allows us to ask about concept holders who are relatively untutored and relatively naive. These preschool children have not yet learned technical definitions for their concepts, nor have they been trained to reflect on, or manipulate, their mental categories. Thus, we can use the data from children as a way of asking about concepts "uncontaminated" by education or training.

In one of Keil's studies, preschool children were asked what it is that makes something a "coffeepot" or a "raccoon," and so on. As a way of probing their beliefs, the children were asked whether it would be possible to turn a toaster into a coffeepot. Children often acknowledged that this would be possible. One would have to widen the holes in the top of the toaster and fix things so that the water would not leak out of the bottom. One would need to design a place to put the coffee grounds. But the children saw no obstacles to these various manipulations, and they were quite certain that, with these adjustments in place, one would have created a bona fide coffeepot.

Things were different, though, when the children were asked a parallel question—namely, whether one could, with suitable adjustments, turn a skunk into a raccoon. The children understood that we could dye the skunk's fur, teach it to climb trees, and, in general, teach it to behave in a raccoonlike fashion. Even with these provisions, the children steadfastly denied that we would have created a raccoon. A skunk that looks, sounds, and acts just like a raccoon might be a very peculiar skunk, but it is a skunk nonetheless. (For related data, see Gelman & Wellman, 1991; and Keil, Smith, Simons, & Levin, 1998. Walker, 1993, offers an interesting extension of Keil's findings, including data on how people from other cultures make these judgments. For other evidence suggesting that we reason differently about naturally occurring items like raccoons, and manufactured items like coffeepots, see Estes, 2003.)

What lies behind these judgments? If people are asked why the abused lemon still counts as a lemon, they are likely to mention the fact that it grew on a lemon tree, is genetically a lemon, and so on. It is these "deep" features that matter, and not the lemon's current properties. Likewise, counterfeit money is defined as such not because of its current attributes, but because of its history: Real money was printed by the government, in special circumstances; counterfeit money was not. And so, too, for raccoons: In the child's view, being a raccoon is not merely a function of having the relevant features; there is something deeper to raccoonhood than that. What is this "something deeper"? In the eyes of the child, the key to being a raccoon involves (among other things) having a raccoon mommy and a raccoon daddy. Thus, a raccoon, just like lemons and counterfeit money, is defined in ways that refer to deep properties and not to mere appearances.

It appears, then, that some properties are essential for being a lemon or a raccoon, and if an object has these essential properties, it doesn't matter what the object looks like. Likewise, without these essential properties, an item is not in the category, no matter what its appearance. (This is the case of the counterfeit bill.) In addition, notice that these claims about an object's "essential properties" depend on a web of other beliefs—beliefs about cause and effect and about how things come to be as they are. For example, concern about a raccoon's parentage comes into play in your thinking about raccoons only because you have certain beliefs about how biological species are created, and about the role of inheritance in biological species. You do not worry about parentage when you are contemplating other categories, because you do not have the belief that inheritance matters for those categories. (In thinking through whether someone is really a doctor, you are unlikely to worry about whether she has a doctor mommy and a doctor daddy. Perhaps she does, and perhaps she doesn't, but this is simply irrelevant to whether she is or is not a doctor.)

Likewise, in judging the category of counterfeit bills, you consider "circumstances of printing" only because of your other beliefs—beliefs, in this case, about ownership, authenticity, and monetary systems. You wouldn't consider circumstances of printing if asked whether a copy of the Lord's Prayer is "counterfeit" or not (or authentic, or legitimate). Your beliefs tell you that the Lord's Prayer is the Lord's Prayer no matter where (or by whom) it's printed. What's crucial for the prayer is whether the words are the correct words, and so again, what's essential for the category depends on the category and on other beliefs you have about that category.

All of this invites several questions: How should we think about a category's "essential properties"? What are these "other beliefs" that seem to guide your thinking about what's essential for a particular category and what's superfluous? And how does typicality (which, without question, does have a powerful influence in many settings) fit into this enlarged picture? We'll turn to these issues in a moment; first, though, we need to consider an objection that might be raised to the argument we've just presented.

The Complexity of Similarity

Both the prototype and the exemplar views depend, at their base, on judgments of resemblance—resemblance to the prototype or to some remembered instance. And there is no doubt that resemblance does have a strong influence on category judgments; this is, as we discussed earlier, reflected in a great many experimental results showing, over and over, that resemblance to a prototype or exemplar does guide our judgments. Yet, as we have now seen, an object can be in a category even if it has no resemblance to other category members (think about the mutilated lemon or the disguised skunk). Likewise, an object can be excluded from a category even with enormous resemblance to other category members (a counterfeit bill). Therefore, we cannot base category membership on resemblance alone.

Perhaps, though, we can rescue the resemblance notion: An abused lemon doesn't resemble the lemon prototype perceptually, but it does resemble the lemon prototype in the ways that matter. For example, the abused lemon has a DNA pattern that resembles the DNA pattern of the prototype. Likewise, the abused lemon has seeds inside it that, if planted, would grow into lemon trees; this, too, is a property of the prototype. Therefore, if we could focus on these essential properties and ignore the superficial attributes, then we could preserve the claim that category membership depends on properties shared with the prototype or shared with exemplars. In this way, we could preserve the claim that category membership depends on resemblance.

The problem, though, lies in explaining what we mean by "resembling the prototype *in the ways that matter.*" How do we decide which properties of the prototype are really important, and so should be given a lot of weight when judging resemblance, and which properties we can ignore as irrelevant? This seems once again to demand that our judgments be guided by some further knowledge—including beliefs about what it is that really matters for that category. And this brings us right back to where we were: In order to use our category knowledge, we've got to have other beliefs about what is essential for the category and what's not.

As a different way of making this point, let's be clear about what "resemblance" involves. One might think that two objects will be seen to resemble each other if the two objects share properties; both objects are big, for example, or both are green, or slow-moving, or whatever. And presumably, the more properties shared, the greater the resemblance. But it turns out that resemblance is far more complicated than this. Part of the complexity comes from the fact that *the properties we consider*, in evaluating resemblance, depend heavily on the context; and therefore resemblance depends on the context. For example, how much do snakes and raccoons resemble each other? Most people think the resemblance is low, but this judgment changes if both of these animals are put in the context of "pet." Then their perceived similarity increases appreciably, because both are perceived as atypical but possible pets, and in the process, their similarity to each other goes up (Barsalou, 1982). Likewise, how similar to each other are Italy and Switzerland? These countries are judged to be rather different, but their apparent similarity goes up if we make it a three-way comparison among, say, Italy, Switzerland, and Brazil. This third country calls attention to the attribute shared by the first two: "in Europe." This attribute initially contributed little to the perceived similarity between Italy and Switzerland, but given the appropriate context, it can play a large role (A. Tversky, 1977).

If, therefore, we want to explain resemblance in terms of shared properties, we're going to need some further theory to explain how we choose which properties to include when making the comparison. As a more extreme demonstration of this point, consider plums and lawn mowers (G. L. Murphy & Medin, 1985). How similar are these to each other? Actually, these two have many properties in common: Both weigh less than a ton, both are found on Earth, both cannot hear well, both have an odor, both are used by people, both can be dropped, both cost less than a thousand dollars, both are bigger than a grain of sand, and so on. (For discussion, see Goldstone, 1996; N. Goodman, 1972; Markman & Gentner, 2001; and Medin, Goldstone, & Gentner, 1993.) Of course, we ignore most of these shared features in judging these two entities, and so, as a result, we regard plums and lawn mowers as rather different from each other. But that brings us back to a familiar question: How do we decide which features to ignore when assessing similarity, and which features to consider? How do we decide, in comparing a plum and a lawn mower, which of their features are essential (and so do matter for similarity) and which are superficial (and can be ignored)?

We have already suggested an answer to these questions: A decision about which features are trivial and which are crucial depends, at least in part, on your beliefs about the concept in question. We know, for example, that what matters for being a lawn mower is suitability for getting a particular job done. Costing less than a thousand dollars is irrelevant to this function. (Imagine a lawn mower covered with diamonds; it would still be a lawn mower, wouldn't it?) Therefore, cost is an unimportant feature for lawn mowers. Cost is a critical attribute, however, for other categories (consider the category "luxury item"). Similarly, we were unimpressed by the fact that plums and lawn mowers both weigh less than a ton: Weight is not critical for either of these categories. But weight is crucial in other settings (imagine a paperweight made out of gaseous helium). Apparently, then, the importance of an attribute—cost, or weight, or whatever—varies from category to category, and varies, in particular, according to your beliefs about what matters for that category.

To tie this back to issues of categorization, imagine that a furry creature stands before you, and you reason, "This creature reminds me of the animal I saw in the zoo yesterday. The sign at the zoo indicated that the animal was a gnu, so this must be one, too." This sounds like a simple case of categorization via exemplars. But of course, the creature before your eyes is not a perfect match for the gnu in the zoo, and so you might reason this way, "The gnu in the zoo was a different color and slightly smaller. But I bet that does not matter. Despite the new hue, this is a gnu too."

In this case, you have decided that color isn't a critical feature, and you categorize despite the contrast on this dimension. Things will go differently, though, in this case: "This stone in my hand reminds me of the ruby I saw yesterday. Therefore, I bet this is a ruby too. Of course, the ruby I saw yesterday was red, and this stone is green, but . . . ." You surely would not draw this conclusion because, in this case, you know that it is wrong to ignore hue. Rubies are red. If a stone isn't red, it isn't a ruby. Color might not matter for gnus, but it does matter here, and our category judgments respect this fact.

Concepts as Theories

Let's pause to take stock. Early in the chapter, we saw many results indicating that our use of concepts is heavily influenced by typicality. Typicality plays a role when we are categorizing objects we have just met; it also guides us when we are reasoning about our concepts. Our theory, therefore, needs to explain how these typicality effects emerge, and the best way to do this, we suggested, is by including prototypes or exemplars in the theory. Indeed, we saw indications (e.g., in our discussion of category learning) that our theory must include both prototypes *and* exemplars.

At the same time, however, our theory of concepts also needs more than prototypes and exemplars. This is evident, for example, in the fact that some category judgments (counterfeit money, the mutilated lemon) are entirely independent of typicality. Therefore, our theory needs some other element to guide these judgments.

Even when typicality is crucial, its role depends on *resemblance*. That is, typicality plays its role thanks to a judgment of resemblance between the object being assessed and some standard in memory (an exemplar or the prototype). But judgments of resemblance, in turn, depend on other knowledge—for example, knowledge about which attributes to pay attention to in judging resemblance, and which to regard as trivial. So here, too, we need some other element in the theory, guiding the assessment of resemblance.

It seems plain, therefore, that we're moving toward a multipart theory of concepts: On the one side, there are prototypes and exemplars, often shaping how we reason in tasks requiring conceptual knowledge, and the source of the well-documented typicality effects. On the other side, there are other beliefs and other knowledge, guiding and supplementing our use of prototypes.

But how should we characterize these other beliefs? And within this broader context, exactly what role is played by prototypes and exemplars?

Categorization Heuristics

In your day-to-day thinking about the world, it seems plausible that you'd want to rely on strategies that are as accurate as possible, strategies that would rarely lead you to error. There is a danger, though, that such strategies might be relatively laborious and slow. If so, you might be better off with a **heuristic** strategy, one that gives up the guarantee of accuracy in order to gain some efficiency. After all, which would you prefer: to be right *all* of the time, but needing 18 hours for every judgment you make; or to be right *most* of the time, but able to make your judgments in a matter of moments?

We've met this trade-off between efficiency and accuracy in several other contexts (e.g., in Chapters 3 and 5), and in truth it is a widespread feature of our mental lives, one that will come up again in later chapters. But in any case, the proposal to be offered here should be obvious: Categorization via resemblance is a heuristic strategy, a relatively efficient (even if imperfect) way to think about categories. What makes this strategy efficient? In most cases, resemblance to a prototype or an exemplar can be judged on the basis of relatively superficial features rather than on the basis of more abstract knowledge about a category. This emphasis on superficial characteristics is precisely what we want for a categorization heuristic: These traits can generally be judged swiftly, allowing comparisons that are quick and easy.

Like any other heuristic, however, the use of typicality will occasionally lead to error: If you rely on the bird prototype to categorize flying creatures, you may misidentify a bat. That is the price one pays for heuristic use. But if the heuristic is well chosen, these errors will be relatively rare, and on this point, too, a reliance on typicality seems sensible. Prototypes, by their very nature, represent the most common features of a category, and so prototypes will be representative of most category members. Thus, categorization via prototypes will usually be accurate: Most members of the category do resemble the prototype, even if some members do not. And, of course, the same points apply to a reliance on exemplars: As we have seen, the exemplars coming to mind will usually be examples of typical category members and so, more often than not, will resemble the new category members you encounter.

This view of things, therefore, preserves a central insight of both the prototype and the exemplar views: As we have seen, we cannot equate typicality with membership in a category. But even so, membership and typicality are clearly related to each other: Creatures closely resembling the prototype bird are not guaranteed to be birds, but they are highly likely to be birds. This is what allows us to use typicality as a fast and efficient basis for judging category membership.

Explanatory Theories

The previous section gives us a picture of what role prototypes and exemplars serve, and therefore why they are so important. They are, in short, the sort of category knowledge we rely on when we want a judgment that is quick and efficient. Over and over, though, we have argued that there is more to category knowledge than this. What is the "more"?

Our discussion has already provided some hints about this issue: In cases we have already considered, a person's understanding of a concept seems to involve a network of interwoven beliefs, linking the target concept to a number of other concepts: To understand what counterfeit is, you need to know what money is, and probably what a government is, and what crime is. To understand what a raccoon is, you need to understand what parents are, and with that, you need to know some facts about life cycles, heredity, and the like.

Perhaps, therefore, we need a different overall approach. We have been trying, throughout this chapter, to characterize concepts one by one, as though each concept could be characterized independently of other concepts. We talked about the prototype for bird, for example, without any thought about how this prototype is related to the animal prototype or the egg prototype. Perhaps, though, we need a more holistic approach, one in which we place more emphasis on the interrelationships among concepts. This would allow us to include in our accounts the wide network of beliefs in which concepts seem to be embedded.

To see how this might play out, consider the concept "blood pressure." It would be surprising if this concept could be characterized in isolation from a set of other terms, such as "circulation" or "heart" or "arteries." To understand blood pressure, one must understand these other terms, and one needs a web of beliefs about how these various terms are interrelated (Banks, Thompson, Henry, & Weissmann, 1986; Carey, 1985). This set of beliefs is surely less sophisticated, and probably less accurate, than a medically correct, scientific model of blood pressure. Nonetheless, our beliefs serve the same function as a scientific model: These beliefs unify our understanding of these various terms and provide a global cause-and-effect account that corresponds to our understanding of the processes involved.

Other, less technical concepts can be understood in similar terms. The concept "raccoon," for example, might include a raccoon prototype and also some exemplars, but it would also include a set of beliefs about raccoons: our belief that raccoons are biological creatures (and therefore made of flesh and blood, and also the offspring of adult raccoons, etc.), and also our belief that raccoons are wild animals (and therefore usually not pets, usually living in the woods), and so on. As in the case of blood pressure, these beliefs may not be sophisticated, and they may sometimes be inaccurate, but nonetheless they provide us with a broad cause-and-effect understanding of why raccoons are as they are. (Various authors have suggested different proposals for how exactly we should conceptualize this web of beliefs. See, among others, Johnson-Laird, 1987; Keil, 1989, 2003; Komatsu, 1992; Lakoff, 1987; Markman & Gentner, 2001; Medin & Ortony, 1989; G. L. Murphy, 2003; Neisser, 1987; Rips & Collins, 1993; and Wisniewski & Medin, 1994.)

The proposal, in short, is that people have something like a "theory" about raccoons—what they are, how they act, and why they are as they are—and likewise a "theory" about most of the other concepts they hold. The theories are less precise, less elaborate, than a scientist's theory, but they serve the same function: They provide a crucial knowledge base that we rely on in most of our thinking about an object, event, or category; and they allow us to understand any new facts we might encounter about the relevant object or category.

Theories and Category Coherence

We have, in the preceding pages of this chapter, been building an argument that these "theories" play in important role in our conceptual knowledge. If this is right, then we should be able to find clear examples of the theories influencing our ordinary concept use, and it turns out that we can. Let's look at three cases: First, we'll consider evidence that these theories play a large part in determining how easily, or how quickly, we learn new concepts. Second, we'll look at how the theories influence us when we're trying to decide whether a novel case is included within a conceptual category or not. And third, we'll consider the role of theories in shaping how we reason about a concept.

Consider the concept "bird." Birds generally have wings and feathers, build nests in trees, and can fly. And, of course, there are clear links among these various features: If birds didn't have wings or feathers, then they wouldn't be able to fly; and if they didn't fly, they probably wouldn't build nests in trees. In this way, then, a bird's traits form a coherent package, with the traits linked together by cause-and-effect relationships.

It turns out that people are alert to this coherence among features and *use* this coherence in a variety of ways. One demonstration of this lies in the fact that people can learn a new category much more readily if the features are coherent in this fashion. As a concrete example, imagine that you were given a group of objects and had to decide whether each belonged in Category A or Category B. Category A, you were told, included all the objects that were metal, had a regular surface, were of medium size, and were easy to grasp. Category B, on the other hand, included objects made of metal, with irregular surfaces, small, and hard to grasp. This sorting task would be difficult and cumbersome—unless we gave you another piece of information: namely, that Category A includes objects that could serve as substitutes for a hammer. With this clue, you can immediately draw on your cause-and-effect understanding about hammers, and in this way you can see *why* the features are as they are. This allows much more rapid learning of the new category, and indeed, when research participants were given this "theme," they learned the category more rapidly and more accurately (Medin, 1989; Wattenmaker, Dewey, Murphy, and Medin, 1986; for more recent findings on this point, see Heit & Bott, 2000; Kaplan & Murphy, 2000; and Rehder & Ross, 2001).

Many other cases show the same pattern, with the suggestion that, across our lifetimes, we will more easily learn, and more easily work with, concepts for which the features hang together in a sensible way. That is, we will more easily learn concepts if we can see why the features are as they are and, in many cases, why the presence of one feature demands the presence of some other feature. All of this, in turn, rests on a broader set of cause-and-effect beliefs: We understand why "wings" and "can fly" go together for the category of "birds" because we understand (roughly) how wings contribute to flying. We understand why "metal" and "easy to grasp" go together for the category of "hammer substitutes" because we understand how each of these qualities contributes to the overall functioning of the hammer. Thus, our *beliefs* and our broader understanding are what give the category its coherence, and as we have said, the coherence makes the category easier to learn. Putting these pieces together, then, our beliefs are what make the category easy to learn.

The Use of Theories in Categorization

The influence of our beliefs and background knowledge is also evident in how people categorize things—that is, their decisions about whether a test case is or is not in a particular category. As an informal example, imagine that you saw someone at a party jump fully clothed into a pool. Odds are good that you would decide this person belongs in the category "drunk," but why is this? Jumping into a pool in this way is surely not part of the *definition* of being drunk, nor is it part of the *prototype* (Medin & Ortony, 1989). But each of us also has certain beliefs about how drunks behave; we have, in essence, a "theory" of drunkenness. This theory allows us to think through what being drunk will cause someone to do and not to do, and on this basis, we would surely decide that, yes, someone who jumped into the pool fully clothed probably was inebriated. (For a different example, see Figure 9.2.)

A reliance on theories can be demonstrated more formally in how people stretch their concepts to cover new cases. In one study, trained clinical psychologists were asked to diagnose several cases (Kim & Ahn, 2002). These (hypothetical) cases had been carefully designed so that they had some of the symptoms associ-

---

| FIGURE 9.2 | What Makes Someone a Bachelor? |

Various potential bachelors

Alfred is an unmarried adult male, but he has been living with his girlfriend for the last 23 years. Their relationship is happy and stable. Is Alfred a bachelor?

Bernard is an unmarried adult male and does not have a partner. But Bernard is a monk, living in a monastery. Is Bernard a bachelor?

Charles is a married adult male, but he has not seen his wife for many years. Charles is earnestly dating, hoping to find a new partner. Is Charles a bachelor?

Donald is a married adult male, but he lives in a culture that encourages males to take two wives. Donald is earnestly dating, hoping to find a new partner. Is Donald a bachelor?

The term "bachelor" is often considered to have a firm definition: A bachelor is an unmarried adult male. However, this noun can be understood only in the context of certain expectations about marriage and marriageable age. As you read the examples shown here, think about what it is that guides your judgments. (After Fillmore, 1982) ated with certain disorders (anorexia nervosa, for example, or depression) but not other symptoms of those disorders. The question, then, was whether the clinicians would still apply the diagnostic label, despite the missing symptoms.

The answer turned out to depend not just on which symptoms were missing, but also on the individual clinician's beliefs about those symptoms. Specifically, the clinicians gave a symptom more weight if they believed the symptom was closely related to the root causes of the illness being diagnosed; therefore, they offered the diagnosis if a "causally central" symptom was present, but did not offer the diagnosis if the symptom was absent. In concrete terms, imagine a clinician who believes that depression is an important cause of anorexia. For this person, a patient who has anorexia-like symptoms but no visible depression probably doesn't have anorexia; she is missing a key ingredient. In contrast, another clinician may believe that depression is a common by-product of anorexia, but not a root cause. For this clinician, someone with anorexia-like symptoms but no visible depression might well be diagnosed as anorexic.

In this fashion, the clinicians are not simply comparing these new cases to a prototype, nor are they applying a definition. Instead, the clinicians are, in effect, using their (sometimes idiosyncratic) theories about the diagnostic category in order to decide which symptoms really matter. And that, of course, is the point: Categorization, it seems, depends on theories. (For related data, and a slightly different view of the data, see Rehder & Hastie, 2001; also see Ahn, Marsh, Luhmann, & Lee, 2002.)

Inferences Based on Theories

Here is one more way in which theories guide our everyday concept use: If you meet my pet, Boaz, and decide that he's a dog, then you instantly know a great deal about Boaz—the sorts of things he's likely to do (bark, beg for treats, chase cats) and the sorts of things he's unlikely to do (climb trees, play chess, hibernate all winter). Likewise, if you have decided (correctly) that Boaz is a dog, and if you now learn something new about Boaz, you may be able to make broad use of that knowledge. If, for example, you learn that Boaz has sesamoid bones, you may draw the conclusion that all dogs have sesamoid bones, and perhaps other animals do too.

These examples serve to remind us of one of the reasons why categorization is so important: Categorization allows you to make broad use of your knowledge, by applying that knowledge (e.g., knowledge about dogs in general) to the new cases you encounter (e.g., Boaz). Conversely, categorization allows you to draw broad conclusions from your experience (so that things you learn about Boaz can be applied to other dogs you meet). All of this, we emphasize, is possible only because you realize that Boaz *is a dog*; without this simple realization, you wouldn't be able to use your knowledge in this way. But how exactly does this use of knowledge proceed?

Early research indicated that inferences about categories were often guided by typicality: In one study, participants who were told a new fact about robins were willing to infer that the new fact would also be true for ducks. If they were told a new fact about ducks, however, they would not extrapolate to robins (Rips, 1975). Apparently, people were willing to make inferences from the typical case to the whole category, but not inferences from an atypical case to the category. This provides one more argument that typicality does play a crucial role in our thinking about concepts.

However, factors beyond typicality also influence these inferences. People are, for example, also influenced by *similarity*: If told that my dog, Boaz, has sesamoid bones, people are more comfortable concluding that wolves also have sesamoid bones than they are in concluding that cows do. The *diversity* of cases being considered also matters: If people are told that crows and ducks are vulnerable to a particular disease, they are quite willing to believe that all birds are vulnerable to the disease. If, on the other hand, people are told that crows and blackbirds are vulnerable to a disease, then they're less willing to draw the general conclusion that all birds are vulnerable (Osherson, Smith, Wilkie, López, & Shafir, 1990). Presumably, this is because crows and ducks are quite different from each other, while crows and blackbirds are less so, and the more diverse the cases being considered, the stronger the conclusion.

It turns out, though, that people's beliefs about cause and effect also play a role here, and so, once again, we meet a case of concept use being guided by the background knowledge and beliefs that accompany each concept. For example, if told that gazelle's blood contains a certain enzyme, people are willing to conclude that lion's blood contains the same enzyme. However, if told that lion's blood contains the enzyme, people are less willing to conclude that gazelle's blood does too. Why is this? In the first case, but not in the second, people find it easy to imagine the property being transmitted from gazelles to lions via the food chain. Likewise, if told that grass contains a certain chemical, people are willing to believe that cows have the same chemical inside them. This makes no sense in terms of similarity (since cows and grass are surely rather different from each other!), but it makes perfect sense if people are thinking of the inference in terms of cause and effect, relying on their beliefs about these various concepts ("gazelles," "lions," and so on) and how these categories are related to each other (Medin, Coley, Storms, & Hayes, 2003; see Heit, 2000, for a broad review of research on this type of inference).

Related results come from experiments in which people are making judgments *within* a single category. In one study, participants were told certain facts about Lake Victoria Shrimp—facts about their body weight, for example, or about their sleep cycles. In addition, some of the participants were given other information—namely, that some of the shrimp have high levels of a certain chemical in their brains, and that this causes both a high body weight and an accelerated sleep cycle (Rehder & Hastie, 2004).

Participants were then told about a new observation: a particular shrimp that had been examined and had mucus in its body that was slightly acidic. They were asked, "What proportion of all the Lake Victoria Shrimp do you think will have mucus that is slightly acidic?" Their answers clearly depended on their causal beliefs. Participants who had been given causal information (namely, information that the chemical caused the high body weight and the odd sleep cycle) were more willing to extrapolate from this new fact. It is as if they reasoned, "Well, I know that high levels of this chemical cause many properties in the shrimp, so I suppose it causes the acidic mucus as well."

The idea, therefore, seems to be that causal beliefs serve to unite a category's features, to make the features seem more coherent. And the more coherent the features, the more likely participants are to expect *other* features to join the package. Hence, more coherence leads to more extrapolation.

Expertise Effects

Let's once again pause to take stock. There is no question that typicality plays a huge role in shaping how we use our conceptual knowledge. That fact led us to a proposal in which typicality was at the heart of conceptual knowledge; that was the proposal cast in terms of prototypes and exemplars. However, we quickly found limitations on this proposal, and that led us to the view that conceptual knowledge must also include other information: knowledge about how each concept is linked to other concepts, and also knowledge about how the features associated with a concept are linked to each other. And now, when we look directly for evidence of this "other knowledge," we easily find it—in how people learn new concepts, how they categorize new cases they encounter, and how they reason about their categories.

This proposal about theories and background knowledge also has another important implication: We may think about different concepts in different ways. For example, most people believe that *natural kinds* (groups of objects that exist naturally in the world, like bushes or alligators or stones or mountains) are as they are because of forces of nature, forces that are relatively consistent across the years. As a result, the properties of these objects are relatively predictable: There are, in effect, certain properties that a bush must have, to survive as a bush; certain properties that a stone must have, because of its chemical composition. Things are different, though, for *artifacts*, objects made by us. If we wished to make a table with 15 legs rather than 4, or one made out of gold rather than wood, or even a table with a top that wasn't flat, we could do this. The design of tables, after all, is up to us; and the same is true for most artifacts.

This leads to the proposal that people will reason differently about natural kinds and artifacts—because they have different beliefs about why categories of either sort are as they are. We have already seen one result consistent with this idea: the finding that children would agree that toasters could be turned into coffeepots, but not that skunks could be turned into raccoons. Plainly, the children had different ideas about artifacts (like toasters) than they had about animate objects (like skunks). Other results confirm this pattern: In general, people tend to assume more homogeneity when reasoning about biological kinds (like raccoons or skunks) than when reasoning about artifacts (Atran, 1990; Coley, Medin, & Atran, 1997; Rehder & Hastie, 2001)

As a related point, this emphasis on background knowledge and beliefs strongly suggests that people will change how they use their concepts if their background knowledge changes—and this, too, turns out to be correct. For example, a number of studies have compared "ordinary" concept users with "experts"—commercial fisherman in making judgments about fish, or expert botanists in making judgments about trees. The experts are clearly influenced by their (extensive) background knowledge. In one procedure, the tree experts were asked to imagine that gingko trees get disease X, and they were asked how likely it would be, on this basis, that all trees could get disease X. The response was clearly guided by the experts' knowledge: "Gingkos are so resistant to disease that if they get it, it must be a very powerful disease" (Medin et al., 2003, p. 519). The results are similar with commercial fisherman: They are much less influenced by a fish's appearance than a novice is. Instead, they pay attention to multiple relations—including the fish's habitat, its preferred food, and so on (Shafto & Coley, 2003).

Concepts: Putting the Pieces Together

Where, then, does all of this leave us? One might think that there's nothing glorious or complicated about knowing what a dog is, or an airplane, or a lemon. Our use of these concepts is effortless and ubiquitous, and so is our use of the thousands of other concepts in our repertoire. No one over the age of 4 takes special pride in knowing what an odd number is, nor do we find it challenging to make the elementary sorts of judgments we've considered throughout this chapter.

As we have seen, though, human conceptual knowledge is impressively complex. At the very least, this knowledge contains several parts. There is probably a prototype for each concept, and a set of remembered exemplars, and we can use these for a range of fast and easy judgments about the relevant category. In addition, we seem to have a set of beliefs about each concept we hold, and also, as we have now discussed, an understanding of how these beliefs fit together. Much of this knowledge reflects our understanding of cause-and-effect relationships in the world—and so, why it is that drunks act as they do, or how it could be that chemicals found in gazelles might be transmitted to lions. These cause-and-effect beliefs influence how we categorize items, and also how we reason about the objects in our world.

Apparently, then, even our simplest concepts require a multifaceted representation in our minds, and at least part of this representation (the "theory") seems reasonably sophisticated. It is all this richness, presumably, that makes human conceptual knowledge extremely powerful and flexible, and also so easy to use in a remarkable range of circumstances.

Chapter Summary

1. People cannot provide definitions for most of the concepts they use; this suggests that knowing a concept, and being able to use it competently, does not require knowing a definition. However, when trying to define a term, people mention properties that are indeed closely associated with the concept. One proposal, therefore, is that our knowledge specifies what is typical for each concept, rather than naming properties that are truly definitive for the concept. Concepts based on typicality will have a family resemblance structure, with different category members sharing features, but with no features shared by the entire group.

2. Concepts may be represented in the mind via prototypes, with each prototype representing what is most typical for that category. This implies that categories will have fuzzy boundaries and graded membership, and many results are consistent with this prediction. The results converge in identifying some category members as "better" members of the category. This is reflected in sentence verification tasks, production tasks, explicit judgments of typicality, and so on.

3. In addition, basic-level categories seem to be the categories we learn earliest and use most often. Basic-level categories (like "chair") are more homogeneous than their superordinate categories ("furniture") and much broader than their subordinate categories ("armchair"), and they are also usually represented by a single word.

4. Typicality results can be also be explained with a model that relies on specific category exemplars, and with category judgments made by the drawing of analogies to these remembered exemplars. The exemplar model also has other advantages. It can explain our sensitivity to category variability, and can also explain the pliability of categories, including our ability to view categories from a new perspective, and also our ability to create ad hoc categories.

5. One proposal is that conceptual knowledge includes both prototypes and exemplars. When first learning a category, one knows only a few exemplars, but then a prototype can be derived as experience with the category grows. This does not imply, however, that exemplar use falls away as category knowledge grows; instead, expert category users have both exemplar knowledge and a category prototype.

6. Sometimes categorization does not depend at all on whether the test case resembles a prototype or a category exemplar. This is evident with some abstract categories ("odd number"), and some weird cases (a mutilated lemon), but it is also evident with more mundane categories ("raccoon"). In these examples, categorization seems to depend on knowledge about a category's essential properties.

7. Knowledge about essential properties is not just a supplement to categorization via resemblance. Instead, knowledge about essential properties may be a prerequisite for judgments of resemblance. With this knowledge, we are able to assess resemblance with regard to just those properties that truly matter for the category, and not be misled by irrelevant or accidental properties.

8. The properties that are essential for a category vary from one category to the next. The identification of these properties seems to depend on beliefs we have about the category, including causal beliefs that specify why the category features are as they are. These beliefs are implicit theories, and they describe the category not in isolation but in relation to various other concepts.

9. Prototypes and exemplars may serve as categorization heuristics, allowing efficient and usually accurate judgments about category membership. These heuristics may not be adequate, though, for some of the ways we use our category knowledge; for these, our implicit theories about the concept play a pivotal role.

Language

In Chapters 8 and 9, we said a lot about generic and conceptual knowledge. One type of knowledge, though, seems worth singling out for special consideration: our knowledge of language.

Scholars have long been intrigued by language, and it's not hard to see why. Virtually every human being knows and uses a language; some of us know and use several languages. Indeed, to find a human without language, we need to seek out people in extraordinary circumstances—people who have suffered serious brain damage or people who have grown up completely isolated from other humans. In sharp contrast, no other species has and uses a language comparable to ours in complexity, sophistication, or communicative power. In a real sense, then, knowing a language is a key part of being a human—a near-universal achievement in our species, yet unknown in its full-blown form in any other species.

Language seems no less central if we consider how it is used and what it makes possible. We use language to convey our ideas to each other, and our wishes, and our needs. Without language, our social interactions would be grossly impoverished, and cooperative endeavors would be a thousand times more difficult. Without language, the transmission of information and the acquisition of knowledge would be enormously impaired. (How much have you learned by listening to others or by reading?) Without language, there would be no science and no culture. Language is thus at the heart of, and essential for, a huge range of human activities and achievements. What is this tool, therefore, that is universal for our species, unique to our species, and crucial for so much of what our species does?

323

- Language can be understood as having a hierarchical structure—with phonemes put together to form morphemes, these put together to form words, and these put together to form sentences.

- At each level, we can endlessly combine and recombine units, but the combinations seem to be governed by rules of various sorts, so that some combinations of elements are rare; others seem prohibited outright.

- A different set of principles describes how people interpret the sentences they hear or read; in this interpretation, people are guided by many factors, including syntax, semantics, and contextual information.

- In interpreting sentences, people seem to use a "compile as you go" strategy, trying to figure out the role of each word the moment it arrives. This approach is often efficient, but it can lead to error.

- Our extraordinary skill in using language is made possible in part by the fact that large portions of the brain are specialized for language use, making it clear that we are, in a literal sense, a "linguistic species."

- Finally, language surely influences our thoughts, but in an indirect fashion: Language is one of many ways to draw our attention to this or that aspect of the environment. This obviously shapes our experience, which in turn shapes our cognition.

Phonology

It is convenient to think of language as having a hierarchical structure (Figure 10.1). At the top of the hierarchy, there are **sentences**—coherent sequences of words that express the intended meaning of a speaker. Sentences are composed of phrases, which are in turn composed of words. Words are composed of **morphemes**, the smallest language units that carry meaning. Meaning is largely carried by **content morphemes**, such as "umpire" or "talk" in Figure 10.1. However, **function morphemes** also add information crucial for interpretation, signaling the relations among words and also providing information about a word's grammatical role within a sentence. Examples of function morphemes in Figure 10.1 are the past-tense morpheme "ed" or the plural morpheme "s."

In spoken language, morphemes are conveyed by sounds called **phonemes**, and the study of these sounds is called **phonology**. Some phonemes are easily represented by letters of the alphabet, but others are not, and that is why the symbols look strange in the bottom row of Figure 10.1; the symbols correspond to the actual sounds produced, independent of how those sounds are expressed in our (or any other) alphabet.

The Production of Speech

Let's start at the bottom of this hierarchy and work our way up. We'll start, in short, with speech sounds.

324

| FIGURE 10.1 | The Hierarchy of Linguistic Units |

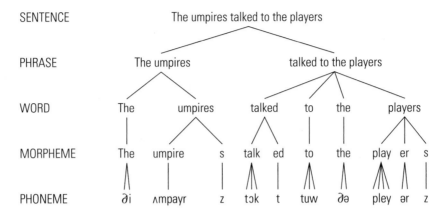

It is often useful to think of language as having a hierarchical structure. At the top of the hierarchy, there are sentences. These are composed of phrases, which are themselves composed of words. The words are composed of morphemes, the smallest language units that carry meaning. When the morphemes are pronounced, the units of sound are called phonemes. In describing phonemes, the symbols correspond to the actual sounds produced, independent of how these sounds are expressed in ordinary writing.

In ordinary breathing, air flows quietly out of the lungs, through the larynx, and up through the nose and mouth (Figure 10.2). However, noises are produced if this passageway is constricted in any fashion that impedes or interrupts the airflow. There are many forms that this constriction can take, allowing humans to produce a wide range of different sounds.

For example, within the larynx there are two flaps of muscular tissue called the "vocal folds." (These structures are also called the "vocal cords," although they are not cords at all.) The vocal folds can be rapidly opened and closed, producing a buzzing sort of vibration known as **voicing**. You can feel this vibration by putting your palm on your throat while you produce a [z] sound. You will feel no vibration, though, if you hiss like a snake, producing a sustained [s] sound. The [z] sound is voiced, the [s] is not.

You can also produce sound by narrowing the air passageway within the mouth itself. For example, hiss like a snake again and pay attention to your tongue's position. To produce this sound, you have placed your tongue's tip near the roof of your mouth, just behind your teeth. The [s] sound is the sound of the air rushing through the narrow gap you have created.

If the gap is elsewhere, a different sound results. For example, to produce the [sh] sound (as in "shoot" or "shine"), the tongue is positioned so that it creates a

FIGURE 10.2   The Production of Speech

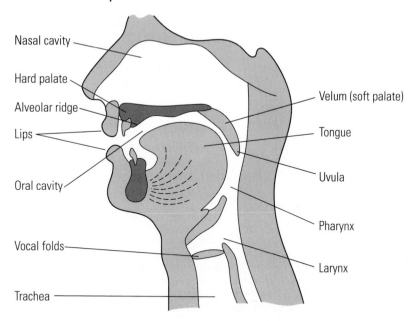

In ordinary breathing, air flows out of the lungs, through the larynx, and up through the nose and mouth. To produce speech, this passageway must be constricted in a fashion that impedes or interrupts the airflow. For example, the uvula can be closed to block air from moving into the nasal cavity. Likewise, the tongue and lips control the movement of air through the oral cavity.

narrow gap a bit further back in the mouth; air rushing through this gap causes the desired sound. Alternatively, the narrow gap can be more toward the front. Pronounce an [f] sound; in this case, the sound is produced by air rushing between your bottom lip and your top teeth.

Other sounds are produced by air moving through the nose rather than the mouth. Try humming an [m] sound while opening and closing your lips. This will cause some changes in the quality of the sound, but there is no interruption in the sound when your lips close. But now try humming an [m] sound and, while humming, pinch your nose shut. With air unable to move through your nose, the sound ceases.

All these aspects of speech production allow us to categorize the various speech sounds. Thus, linguists distinguish, first, between sounds that are voiced—produced with the vocal folds vibrating—and those that are not. The sounds of [v], [z], and [n] (to name a few) are voiced; [f], [s], [t], and [k] are unvoiced. (You can confirm this by running the hand-on-throat test while producing each of these sounds.) Second, sounds can be categorized according to where the airflow is restricted; this is referred to as **place of articulation**. Thus, you close your lips to produce "bilabial" sounds, like [p] or [b]; you place your top teeth close to your bottom lip to produce "labiodental" sounds, like [f] or [v]; and you place your tongue just behind your upper teeth to produce "alveolar" sounds, like [t] or [d].

Sounds can also be categorized according to how the airflow is restricted; this is referred to as **manner of production**. Thus, as we have seen, air is allowed to move through the nose for some speech sounds but not for others. Similarly, for some speech sounds, the flow of air is fully stopped for a moment (e.g., [p], [b], and [t]). For other sounds, the air passage is restricted, but some air continues to flow (e.g., [f], [z], and [r]).

This categorization scheme allows us to describe any speech sound in terms of a few simple features. For example, the [p] sound is produced (a) without voicing, (b) with a bilabial place of articulation, and (c) with air moving through the mouth (not the nose), and with a full interruption to the flow of air. If any of these features changes—voicing, place of articulation, or manner of production—so does the sound's identity.

Put differently, these few features, in varying combinations, allow us to make all the sounds our language needs. In English, these features are combined and recombined to produce 40 or so different phonemes. Other languages use as few as a dozen phonemes; still others, many more. (For example, there are 141 different phonemes in the language of Khoisan, spoken by the Bushmen of Africa; Halle, 1990.) In all cases, though, the phonemes are created by simple combinations of the features just described.

The Complexity of Speech Perception

These features of speech production also correspond to what listeners hear when they are listening to speech. Phonemes that differ only in one production feature sound similar to each other; phonemes that differ in multiple features sound more distinct. This is reflected in the pattern of errors people make when they try to understand speech in a noisy environment. Their misperceptions are usually off by just one feature, so that [p] is confused with [b] (a difference only in voicing), [p] with [t] (a difference only in place of articulation), and so on (G. A. Miller & Nicely, 1955; Wang & Bilger, 1973).

This makes it seem like the perception of speech may be a straightforward matter: A small number of features is sufficient to characterize any particular speech sound. All the perceiver needs to do, therefore, is detect these features, and with this done, the speech sounds are identified.

As it turns out, though, speech perception is far more complicated than this. For one problem, consider Figure 10.3, which shows the moment-by-moment sound amplitudes produced by a speaker uttering a brief greeting. It is these amplitudes, in the form of air-pressure changes, that reach the ear, and so, in an important sense, the figure shows the pattern of input with which "real" speech perception begins.

| FIGURE 10.3 | The Actual Pattern of Speech |

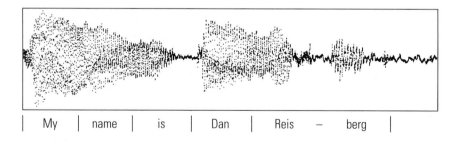

| My | name | is | Dan | Reis | – | berg |

Shown here are the moment-by-moment sound amplitudes produced by a speaker uttering a greeting. Notice that there is no gap between the sounds carrying the word "my" and the sounds carrying "name." Nor is there a gap between the sounds carrying "name" and the sounds carrying "is." Therefore, the listener needs to figure out where one sound stops and the next begins, a process known as "segmentation."

Notice that, within this stream of speech, there are no markers to indicate where one phoneme ends and the next begins. Likewise, there are generally no gaps, or signals of any sort, to indicate the boundaries between successive syllables or successive words. Therefore, as a first step prior to phoneme identification, you need to "slice" this stream into the appropriate segments—a step known as **speech segmentation**.

For many people, this pattern comes as a surprise. As perceivers of speech, we are usually convinced that there are pauses between words, marking the word boundaries. This turns out, however, to be an illusion, and we are "hearing" pauses that, in truth, aren't there. The illusion is revealed when we physically measure the speech stream (as we did in order to create Figure 10.3) or when we listen to speech we can't understand—for example, speech in a foreign language. In this latter circumstance, we lack the skill needed to segment the stream, and so we are unable to "supply" the word boundaries. As a consequence, we hear what is really there: a continuous, uninterrupted flow of sound. That is why speech in a foreign language often sounds so fast.

Speech perception is further complicated by a phenomenon known as **coarticulation** (A. Liberman, 1970; also Daniloff & Hammarberg, 1973). This term refers to the fact that, in producing speech, one does not utter one phoneme at a time. Instead, the phonemes "overlap." While you are producing the [s] sound in "soup," for example, your mouth is getting ready to say the vowel. While uttering the vowel, you are already starting to move your tongue and lips and teeth into position for producing the [p].

This overlap in production allows speech to be faster and considerably more fluent. But this overlap also has important consequences for the sounds produced, and so the [s] you produce while getting ready for one upcoming vowel is actually different from the [s] you produce while getting ready for a different vowel. As a result, we can't point to a specific acoustical pattern and say, "This is the pattern of an [s] sound." Instead, the acoustical pattern is different in different contexts. Speech perception therefore has to "read past" these context differences in order to identify the phonemes produced.

Aids to Speech Perception

These complications—the need for segmentation in a continuous speech stream, the variations caused by coarticulation, and also the variations from speaker to speaker or from occasion to occasion—render speech perception surprisingly complex. As one measure of this complexity, note that speech recognition by computer is still relatively primitive. Speech recognition programs do exist, but they are quite limited. Some of these programs "understand" a wide range of speech but only from a single speaker. (That is, the programs have great difficulty with speaker-to-speaker variation.) Other programs can "understand" many different speakers but can handle only a limited vocabulary.

Obviously, though, humans manage quite well to perceive speech. How do we do it? One perhaps surprising factor lies in the fact that the speech we encounter, from day to day, is rather limited in its range. Each of us knows tens of thousands of different words, but most of these words are rarely used. In fact, it has been estimated that the 50 most commonly used words in English make up more than half of the words we actually hear (G. A. Miller, 1951).

In addition (and perhaps more important), our speech perception benefits from the fact that we generally supplement what we hear with expectations and knowledge, and this guides our interpretation of speech that is difficult to perceive. In some cases, we are guided by knowledge of what sounds often go together and what sounds don't, and we can use that knowledge to draw reasonable inferences about what the input must have been. (For more on how this might work, see Chapter 3.) In other cases, we're guided by knowledge of a broader sort, so that (for example) if you hear someone say, "He put mustard on his [cough] dog," you easily infer what the word is, thanks to your knowledge about the foods of our culture.

How much are we helped by context? Pollack and Pickett (1964) tape-recorded a number of naturally occurring conversations. From these recordings, they spliced out individual words and presented these, now in isolation, to their research participants. Remarkably, the participants were able to identify only half of these words. If restored to their context, though, these same stimuli were easy to identify. Apparently, the benefits of context are considerable!

Categorical Perception

With or without the benefits of context, though, humans are, without question, exquisitely talented in deriving information from the speech signal. Indeed, there is every indication that we have evolved highly specialized mechanisms for this purpose and, more broadly, specialized mechanisms for the perception, acquisition, and use of language. (We will describe some of these specializations later in the chapter.)

The power of our speech recognition abilities is well revealed in the phenomenon of **categorical perception**. This term refers to the fact that we are much better at hearing the differences *between* categories of sounds than we are at hearing the variations *within* a category of sounds. Said differently, we are very sensitive to the differences between, say, a [t] sound and a [d], or the differences between a [g] or a [k]. But we're surprisingly *insensitive* to differences within each of these categories, and so we have a hard time distinguishing, say, one [p] sound from another, somewhat different, [p] sound. And, of course, this pattern is precisely what we want, because it allows each listener to categorize sounds with considerable accuracy, without hearing (and thus being distracted by) inconsequential variations within the category.

Let's examine categorical perception in terms of an example. Consider the consonants [p] and [b]. These consonants are identical in their place of articulation and manner of production (both involve a complete interruption of the flow of air, caused by closing the lips). These consonants differ, though, in the feature of voicing: [b] is voiced, [p] is not. But let's be more precise about what that means: Place your hand flat on your throat, and pronounce the word "pit." If you pay close attention, you will notice that the sound of the word begins slightly before you feel the vibration in your throat. In fact, there is (approximately) a 60-ms gap between the word's start (i.e., when you release your lips, which is when the air starts moving) and the onset of voicing. Technically, a [p] is pronounced with a 60-ms **voice-onset time**, or VOT.

Place your hand on your throat again, and now pronounce the word "bit." This time, you will detect no gap between the word's start and the onset of voicing. For the phoneme [b], the VOT is essentially zero.

The English language uses only these two VOTs: one of 60 ms or so, and one of zero. But what about other VOTs—a VOT of 30 ms, perhaps, or 45 msec? How are these perceived? Acoustically, such stimuli would be somewhere between an ordinary [b] and an ordinary [p]. Will people therefore perceive them as a sort-of-*p* and a sort-of-*b*? Or will they perhaps be uncertain about what the sound is?

To find out, we can use a computer to create *synthetic speech* that has the appropriate characteristics, and then play the synthetic speech for English speakers. More specifically, in many procedures the experimenters have used computers to create a *series* of compromise sounds: The first stimulus is a bilabial stop with a zero VOT (this is just an ordinary [b] sound). A second stimulus is a bilabial stop with a 10-ms VOT (this is a [b] with the voicing just slightly delayed). A third stimulus has a 20-ms VOT; a fourth has a 30-ms VOT (and so is midway between a [p] and a [b]); and so on, up to a bilabial stop with a 60-ms VOT (i.e., an ordinary [p]). We can now attach a vowel to each of these synthetic consonants and ask people to identify the resulting syllables. More precisely, we might add an "[a]" sound, and then ask them whether each stimulus is the syllable "ba" or the syllable "pa."

Figure 10.4A shows the pattern we might expect. After all, our stimuli are gradually shading from a clear "ba" to a clear "pa." Therefore, as we move through the series, one might expect people to be less and less likely to identify each stimulus as a "ba," and correspondingly more and more likely to identify each as a "pa." In the terms we used in Chapter 9, this would be a "graded-membership" pattern: Test cases close to the "ba" prototype should be reliably identified as "ba." As we move away from this prototype, though, cases should be harder and harder to categorize.

The graded-membership pattern emerged again and again in Chapter 9, but it doesn't show up here. The actual data are shown in Figure 10.4B. As you can see, all of the sounds with short VOTs are perceived as "ba." Moreover, in terms of their categorizations, research participants seem indifferent to whether the syllable resembles the "ba" prototype (with a 0-ms VOT) or not (e.g., a 20-ms VOT); both of these are equally likely to be identified as a "ba." Likewise, all of the long-VOT sounds are perceived as "pa." And, again participants seem indifferent to the contrast between a prototypical "pa" (e.g., 60-ms VOT) or a lousy exemplar (40-ms VOT); again, these are equally likely to be identified as "pa." (For the classic presentation of this pattern, see Liberman, Harris, Hoffman, & Griffith, 1957; for reviews, see Handel, 1989; and Yeni-Komshian, 1993. For studies of this pattern in children, see Werker & Desjardins, 1995. We should also mention that the steep cutoff, visible in Figure 10.4, occurs at slightly different points for different participants; nonetheless, every participant shows the pattern of a well-defined category boundary.)

In a variation of this procedure, we can present these stimuli two by two. This time, the participants are simply asked whether the two stimuli they hear are the same or different. In this **discrimination** task, participants often respond "same" if they are presented with the following pair of stimuli: one with a 10-ms VOT and one with a 30-ms VOT. It seems, then, that participants cannot reliably hear this difference, suggesting that all "ba" syllables really do sound alike. Likewise, people have difficulty in hearing the difference between a stimulus with a 40-ms VOT and one with a 60-ms VOT. Apparently, all "pa" syllables do sound alike. But the problem is not that the participants are insensitive to these 20-ms differences. They do quite well, in fact, in hearing the difference between a 20-ms VOT and a 40-ms VOT. Discriminations *across the category boundary* are relatively easy. (For more on these and other issues of speech perception, see Diehl, Lotto, & Holt, 2004.)

Combining Phonemes

Categorical perception tells us that people hear what category a phoneme is in—but little else. In other words, people seem oblivious to whether a "pa" has a shorter-than-normal VOT, or a slightly longer-than-normal one. All they hear is that it is a "pa"—which is, of course, precisely the information they need!

FIGURE 10.4 Categorical Perception

A

Hypothetical identification data

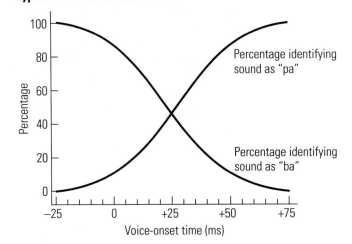

Percentage identifying sound as "pa"

Percentage identifying sound as "ba"

B

Actual identification data

Percentage identifying sound as "pa"

Percentage identifying sound as "ba"

In ordinary speech, the syllable "ba" is pronounced with a zero voice-onset time (VOT). That is, voicing begins at the same time as the air begins to flow. The syllable "pa" is pronounced with a 60- or 70-ms VOT; that is, voicing begins approximately 60 or 70 ms after the air begins to flow. With computer speech, we can produce a variety of compromises between these two sounds, and the top panel shows a plausible prediction about how these sounds will be perceived: As the sound becomes less and less like an ordinary "ba," people should be less and less likely to perceive it as a "ba." The bottom panel, however, shows the actual data: Research participants seem indifferent to small variations in the "ba" sound, and they categorize a sound with a 10- or 15-ms VOT in exactly the same way that they categorize a sound with a zero VOT. The categorizations also show an abrupt categorical boundary between "pa" and "ba," although there is no corresponding abrupt change in the stimuli themselves. (After Lisker & Abramson, 1970)

What about more complicated sounds? We have already noted that speech sounds have relatively few features, yet from these, English speakers fashion 40 different phonemes. Those 40 phonemes, in turn, can be combined and recombined to form tens of thousands of different morphemes, which can themselves be combined to create word after word after word.

These combinations don't happen, however, in a helter-skelter fashion. Instead, there is a pattern to the combinations: Some combinations seem common, others are rare; others seem prohibited outright. For example, English speakers easily recognize "fingst" as a made-up word, because it involves a cluster of consonant sounds that is essentially unknown in our language. Likewise, English dictionaries contain few words beginning "tl . . ."—apparently a combination forbidden in our language. In both cases, though, these are not limits on what human ears can hear or human tongues can produce; we see this in the fact that other languages do allow these combinations. (Consider, for example, the German word, *angst*, or the Northwest Indian language Tlingit.)

Apparently, then, each language has its own principles governing how phonemes are combined—principles, for example, that prohibit the "tl" or "ngst" combinations in English. In addition, other principles govern the pattern of change that must occur when two morphemes are joined together. For example, consider the "s" ending that marks the English plural—as in "books," "cats," "tapes," and so on. In the cases just listed, the plural is pronounced as an [s]. In other contexts, though, the plural ending is pronounced differently. Say these words out loud: "bags," "duds," "pills." If you listen carefully, you will realize that these words actually end with a [z] sound, not an [s]. The choice between these—a [z] pronunciation or an [s]—depends on how the base noun ends. If it ends with a voiced sound, then the [z] ending is used to make the plural. If the base noun ends with an unvoiced sound, then the plural is created with an [s]. (For more on these phonological rules, see Chomsky & Halle, 1968; and Halle, 1990.)

Could it be that we've simply memorized when to use the [s] sound and when the [z]? We can rule out this proposal in light of how people handle new, made-up cases. For example, I have one wug, and now I acquire another. Now, I have two . . . what? Memorization of cases you've met in the past won't help you here (since you've never heard of a wug before). Yet, without hesitation, people pronounce "wugs" using the [z] ending—in accord with the standard pattern. Clearly, then, the pattern does not depend on the memorization of specific instances. Instead, the pattern must be understood in terms of a general principle that people somehow understand and can apply to new cases as they come up.

Three important points can be drawn from these simple observations, and they are points we will meet again and again in this chapter. First, we must acknowledge the **generativity** of language—that is, the capacity to create an endless series of new morphemes, new words, and new sentences, all built up from a small set of fundamental units (e.g., the 40 phonemes of English). Second, this generativity is, in an important sense, bounded: The various combinations and recombinations seem to be governed by certain principles—for example, principles that prohibit certain combinations (such as "tl" for English speakers) and that shape other combinations (e.g., how the plural marker will be pronounced at the end of a word). Thus there is generativity, but generativity within a framework.

Third, think about what it means to "know English" (or, for that matter, to know any language). Obviously, speakers of English know the relevant vocabulary and grammar. But they also know more than that—including the principles that govern phonological combination. This surely isn't conscious knowledge; most English speakers could not articulate the principles that determine why they pronounce "wugs" with a [z] sound rather than an [s]. Nonetheless, the speakers honor the principles with remarkable consistency in their day-by-day use of the language.

Words and the Nature of Linguistic Rules

Phonemes are assembled to form morphemes, and morphemes are assembled to form words. But what *are* words, and what is it that we know when we "know a word"?

Some words (such as "if," "and," or "only") take their meaning only from their role within a larger proposition. Other words (like "house" or "bird" or "running") seem to refer to objects or events in the world. Even for these simpler cases, though, there is room for debate about what one knows when one "knows the word." A large part of this debate runs parallel to the points we encountered when we discussed *concepts* in Chapter 9. After all, many words do express single concepts, and more generally, one can understand a word's meaning only if one understands the relevant concepts.

For present purposes, therefore, let us just say that a large part of "knowing a word" is knowing the relevant concept (and then we can rely on the previous chapter for a discussion of what it means to know a concept). In addition, knowing a word must also include some other elements—such as the word's phonological representation (what it sounds like), and also its grammatical role. (For more on what it means to know a word, see G. A. Miller, 1999.)

Building New Words

A typical American high school graduate is said to know about 45,000 different words (G. A. Miller, 1991). For college graduates, the estimate is higher: 75,000–100,000 words (Oldfield, 1963). However, these estimates are very rough at best, because the size of someone's vocabulary is actually quite fluid.

Why is this? One important reason is that new words are created all the time. This happens, for instance, whenever a new style of music or clothing demands a correspondingly new descriptive vocabulary. The world of computers offers other examples: "E-commerce" is a relatively recent arrival in the language, as is "geek." Someone who wants to know something will often "google" for it, and "spam" has now become a verb (and not just a type of canned meat).

Moreover, when these new words arrive in the language, they don't arrive as isolated entries. That's because language users immediately know how to create many variations on the word, by adding the appropriate morphemes. Imagine, for example, that you have just heard the word "hack" for the first time. You know instantly that someone who likes to hack is a "hacker" and the activity is called "hacking," and you understand someone who says, "I've been hacked."

In this way, you can use morphemes to alter the words as they enter your vocabulary, allowing you to use these words in new ways. In addition, you can use morphemes to create entirely new words. For example, the word "wave" has long been in our language, but, with a few added morphemes, the term "unmicrowavable" is of recent vintage (Pinker, 1994).

Thus we again see the generativity of language: Just as we can recombine phonemes to create new morphemes, we can recombine morphemes to create new words; and this is an important part of what allows the language to *grow*.

This reliance on morpheme combinations also provides an enormous advantage for any language learner: As a novice English speaker, for example, you don't have to memorize, as separate vocabulary items, each word and its plural ("hat" and "hats," "cow" and "cows," "garden" and "gardens") Instead, you need to learn only the base nouns, plus the plural morpheme "s." This essentially cuts your memorization load in half: Rather than learning 1,000 singular nouns + 1,000 plural nouns, you just need to learn 1,000 nouns + 1 rule. In the same fashion, you don't need to memorize, as separate entries in your mental dictionary, "look" and "looked," "climb" and "climbed." Instead, you need to learn only the base words, plus the past tense morpheme "ed."

Once again, though, combinations of morphemes are not done in a helter-skelter fashion. Instead, a number of principles govern the combinations of morphemes. For example, if someone adds a feature to a display to make the display "cute," they have added "cuteness." If they do this multiple times, they've added "cutenesses." This term ("cute" + "ness" + the plural) may sound awkward, but it does sound acceptable to most people. Notice, though, that the combination cannot be done the other way around ("cute" + the plural + "ness"): The word "cutesness" sounds unacceptable to most people, and they may not even be certain what it means. Morphemes, like other units in the language, can be combined in some ways, but not in others.

Prescriptive Rules, Descriptive Rules

What is it that controls the combination of morphemes? If some combinations are "prohibited," then prohibited by whom? Likewise, we earlier suggested that there seems to be a "rule" governing the construction of plurals, so that "bugs" is pronounced with a [z] sound, while "bucks" is pronounced with an [s]. What sort of rule is this?

Let's first be clear about what these rules and prohibitions are *not*. We were all taught, at some stage of our education, how to talk and write "properly." We were all taught never to say "ain't." Many of us were scolded for writing in the passive voice; others were reprimanded for splitting infinitives. Many of us were counseled to say, "For whom are you looking?" rather than, "Who are you looking for?"; "It is I!" rather than, "It's me."

The rules at stake in these cases are called **prescriptive rules**, rules describing how language is "supposed" to be. Often these rules are used to mark the difference between social classes, so that "upper-class" people speak in one way, whereas "lower-class" people don't talk so good. Thus, if one wishes to avoid being stigmatized, or if one wishes for membership in the elite, one tries to use the rules and to speak "proper" English.

However, one should be skeptical about these prescriptive rules. All languages change with the passage of time, and so what was considered proper usage in one time period is likely to be different from what is proper a generation later. (Four hundred years ago, proper English required that people use the word "thou" when addressing close friends or children; otherwise, people said "you.") What, therefore, should we count as "proper English"—English as it was spoken in colonial times (so that "thou" is proper usage)? or English as it was spoken in the early 20th century (so that split infinitives are frowned upon, but "thou" is considered old-fashioned)? or English as it was spoken in the late 20th century (so that the prohibition on split infinitives is considered old-fashioned)? It is difficult to find clear answers to these questions, since it is hard to argue that the English of 1928 is better than the English of 1992 or 2005; as a result, prescriptive rules clearly need to be taken with a grain of salt.

The rules we are concerned with in this chapter are rules of a different sort—not *prescriptive* rules but **descriptive**—that is, characterizing the language as it is ordinarily used by fluent speakers and listeners. There are strong regularities in the way English is used, and the rules we are discussing describe these patterns. No value judgment is offered (nor should one be) about whether these patterns constitute "proper" or "good" English. These patterns simply describe how English is or, perhaps we should say, what English is.

Notice also how we go about discovering these regularities. In some cases, it is important to track what is said and what is not said in ordinary language use. However, this provides evidence only of a limited sort, because the *absence* of a word or construction from ordinary usage is difficult to interpret: If Leo never uses the word "boustrephedon," is this because he doesn't know the word or because he simply has no interest in talking about boustrephedon? If Miriam never uses the word "unmicrowavable," is this because she regards the word as illegitimate or merely because she is in the habit of using some other term to convey this idea?

In addition, the pattern of spontaneous speech is filled with performance errors. Sometimes you start a sentence with one idea in mind, but then change your idea as you are speaking. You might end up saying something like, "He went my father went yesterday," even though you realize, as you are uttering it, that the sentence contains an error. On other occasions, you slip in your production, and so end up saying something different from what you had intended. You might say, "They were I mean weren't fine," even though you notice (and regret) the slip the moment you produce it.

These speech errors are of considerable importance if we are studying the ways in which speech is actually produced. However, these slips are a nuisance if we are trying to study linguistic knowledge: In most cases, you would agree that you had, in fact, made an error. In many cases, you even know how to repair the error, in order to produce a "correct" sentence. Clearly, therefore, your original performance, with its errors, doesn't reflect the full extent of your linguistic knowledge.

Because of considerations like these, we sometimes need to examine language **competence** rather than language **performance**, with "competence" defined as the pattern of skills and knowledge that might be revealed under optimal circumstances (Chomsky, 1957, 1965). One way to reveal this competence is via linguistic judgments: People are asked to reflect on one structure or another and to tell us whether they find the structure acceptable or not. Note that we are not asking people whether they find the structure to be clumsy, or pleasing to the ear, or useful. Instead, we are asking them whether the structure is something that one could say, if one wished. Thus, "cutenesses" seems acceptable, but "cutesness" does not. Likewise, "There's the big blue house" seems fine, but "There's house blue big the" does not. Or, to return to an earlier example, you might slip and say, "He went my father went yesterday," but you certainly know there is something wrong with this sequence. It's these "acceptability judgments" that reveal linguistic competence, and it's these judgments that, ultimately, our theory needs to explain.

It should be said that these judgments do involve a peculiar use of language: Normally we use language to communicate about some object or event; language is the medium of expression and not by itself the topic of discussion. In the judgments we are considering, though, language is the topic of scrutiny, and so, in our data collection, we are asking people to make a judgment *about* language rather than simply to use language. Judgments like these are called **metalinguistic judgments**, and these in turn are members of a broader category: **metacognitive judgments**. Metacognitive judgments are, in general, defined as judgments in which one must stand back from a particular mental activity and comment on the activity, rather than participating in it.

The Psychological Reality of Linguistic Rules

Metalinguistic judgments reveal a number of strong patterns: Certain combinations of phonemes are reliably regarded as acceptable; others are not. Likewise, certain combinations of morphemes are regarded as acceptable; others are not. In most cases, it is convenient to describe these patterns in terms of a rule: We've already described some of these rules, but others are easy to find (see Figure 10.5).

What is the nature of these rules? One possibility is that the rules are consciously known and deliberately followed, just as most people know the spelling

| FIGURE 10.5 | The Rules of English: An Example |

One of the rules of English concerns how words combine: If a noun has an irregular plural, then it can be combined with other morphemes in the plural form. (Thus a beaver can leave "teethmarks," combining the irregular plural "teeth" with another morpheme to create the larger word. Likewise, a house can be "mice-infested," building on the irregular plural "mice.") If a noun has a regular plural, though, it is combined with other morphemes only in the singular form. (A house might be "rat-infested," but not "rats-infested." A porcupine leaves "clawmarks," not "clawsmarks." And so on.)

rule "*i* before *e* except after *c*." (Never mind that this rule has many exceptions—like "either" or "neither." What matters is that people know the rule, can report the rule, and try explicitly to apply the rule.)

However, we can swiftly rule out this claim: Linguistic rules are surely not conscious. Indeed, before looking at Figure 10.5, you probably didn't realize there was a relation between regularity of plurals and how a word combines with other words. Nonetheless, you have followed this rule for most of your life—at least since you were 3 or 4 years old (Gordon, 1986).

A different possibility is that you know the rules unconsciously and apply them without realizing you are doing so. Evidence for this claim comes from studies of children learning language. For example, English-speaking children seem initially to learn the past tense in a word-by-word fashion, and so they memorize the fact that the past tense of "play" is "played," that the past tense of "climb" is "climbed," and so on. By age 3 or so, however, children realize that there is a pattern here, so that one doesn't have to memorize each word's past tense as a separate vocabulary item. Instead, they realize, you can produce the past tense by manipulating morphemes—that is, by adding the "ed" ending onto a word. Once children make this discovery, they are able to apply this principle to many new verbs, including verbs they have never encountered before. Thus, Berko (1958) showed children a picture and told them, "Here is a man who likes to rick. Yesterday, he did the same thing. Yesterday, he . . . ." Prompted in this way, 3-year-olds unhesitatingly supply the past tense: "ricked."

However, children seem to get carried away with this pattern, and so, at this age, children's spontaneous speech contains many **over-regularization errors.** Children say things like, "Yesterday, we goed," or "Yesterday, I runned." The same thing happens with other morphemes, and so children of this age also overgeneralize in their use of the plural ending: They say things like, "I have two foots," or "I lost three tooths."

Remarkably, these same children were correctly using the irregular forms ("feet," "teeth," "went," "ran") just a few months earlier, and so, to the casual viewer, it seems that the child's linguistic development is going backward—first using the correct forms, and then later using incorrect ones. Adding to the puzzle, it is clear that the child still remembers the irregular past tense; this is revealed in the fact that a child of this age will flip-flop between using the correct form and the incorrect one, using "went" in one sentence and "goed" in the very next sentence. Worse, the child will sometimes combine the correct and incorrect forms, and so one can hear children of this age voicing such peculiarities as, "He wented." (For a review, see Marcus et al., 1992.)

This pattern makes it clear that language learning is not a matter of imitation, since these over-regularizations are almost never produced by adults. Nor is language acquisition a matter of explicit instruction, since no adult would encourage children to make these errors. Instead, in describing these data, it is tempting simply to say that children are inducing a rule about how the past tense is formed. Before they learn the rule, their use of the past tense is reliably correct, but it is limited to those cases they've memorized. Once they learn the rule, this limit vanishes, and now they can form the past tense even for unfamiliar verbs. At this point, however, the children are plainly confused about when to use the rule and when not, and this is the stage at which they produce over-regularization errors—in essence, they are overusing the rule. Later on, they straighten out which verbs are regular (and for these, they use the rule) and which are irregular; once this is done, children are able to use the past tense in a mature fashion.

According to this view, the rule governing the past tense is literally in place in the child's mind (although unconsciously) and is governing the child's linguistic productions. The same is true for the rules governing plurals and those governing contractions, and many other rules as well. Each of these rules is "known" to the child (although not consciously), and is used in forming the relevant linguistic combinations.

It should be said, though, that there is considerable controversy attached to these claims. There is no doubt that children do produce over-regularization errors, and many authors interpret this as evidence for language rules. Other authors, however, have argued that these errors could also emerge from other mechanisms—for example, a pattern of associations among the various words the child has learned. According to this view, our linguistic judgments might well be *described* by rules, but this does not mean that we *know* the rules in any sense. (For glimpses of this debate, see Hajiwara, Sugioka, Ito, Kawamura, & Shiota, 1999; Lavric, Pizzagalli, Forstmeier, & Rippon, 2001; McClelland & Patterson, 2002a, 2002b; Pinker, 1999; Pinker & Ullman, 2002a, 2002b; and Rohde & Plaut, 1999.)

It is too soon to know how this debate will be resolved. In the meantime, though, several points are certain: Our linguistic behavior is, on anyone's account, highly creative (in the sense that new forms can always be generated) but also highly constrained (in the sense that many of the possible combinations of units are deemed unacceptable by speakers and hearers of the language). These constraints fall into patterns that are well described by rules, but whether the rules are literally represented in the mind, and thus govern our linguistic practices, remains to be seen.

Syntax

We have already mentioned that a few production features are all you need to create dozens of phonemes, and these phonemes then allow you to create tens of thousands of words. But now let's consider what you can do with those words: If you have 40,000 words in your vocabulary, or 60,000, or 80,000, how many sentences can you build from those words? How many sentences are you able to understand or to produce?

Sentences can range in length from the very brief ("Go!" or "I do.") to the absurdly long. Most sentences, though, contain 20 words or fewer. With this length limit, it has been estimated that there are 100,000,000,000,000,000,000 possible sentences in English (that's 10^{20}; Pinker, 1994). If printed in microscopic font, so that 1,000 sentences could fit on a page, this set of sentences would fill up roughly 250 trillion books. (For comparison, the world's largest library, the United States Library of Congress, contains one ten-millionth of that number of volumes.)

Once again, though, we find limits on which combinations (i.e., which sequences of words) are acceptable, and which not. Thus, in English one could say, "The boy hit the ball," but not "The boy hit ball the." Likewise, one could say, "The bird squashed the car," but not "The bird the car," or "The bird squashed the," or just "Squashed the car." Virtually any speaker of the language would agree these sequences have something wrong in them, so here, too, it is tempting to appeal to rules—rules that permit endless numbers of word combinations, but prohibit other combinations. These rules, governing the sequences of words in the formation of phrases and sentences, are called rules of **syntax**. Syntactic rules determine whether a sequence of words is **grammatical**—that is, conforms to the patterns acceptable within the language.

One might think that these rules depend on *meaning,* so that meaningful sequences are accepted as "sentences," while meaning*less* sequences are rejected as nonsentences. This suggestion, though, is plainly wrong. As one concern, many nonsentences are interpretable ("Me Tarzan.") In addition, consider these two sentences (which are surely the two most widely quoted bits of gibberish ever composed):

> 'Twas brillig, and the slithey toves
> did gyre and gimble in the wabe.

> Colorless green ideas sleep furiously.

(The first of these is part of Lewis Carroll's famous poem "Jabberwocky"; the second was penned by the important linguist Noam Chomsky.) These sentences are, of course, without meaning: Colorless things aren't green; ideas don't sleep; toves aren't slithey. Nonetheless, these sequences are sentences: Speakers of English, perhaps after a moment's reflection, do regard these sequences as grammatically acceptable in a way that "Furiously sleep ideas green colorless" is not. It seems, therefore, that we need principles of syntax that are separate from considerations of semantics or sensibility.

Phrase Structure

What are the principles of syntax? The answer begins with the fact that syntax does more than merely determine whether a sequence of words is a sentence or not. In addition (and more important), syntax specifies the structure of the sentence and, with that, specifies the role of each word within the sentence.

Consider the simple sentence, "The boy loves his dog." The sentence seems to break naturally into two parts: a **noun phrase**, "the boy," which identifies what the sentence is about; and a **verb phrase,** "loves his dog," which supplies some information about the boy. The verb phrase, in turn, also breaks easily into two parts: the verb, "loves," and then another noun phrase ("his dog") identifying what is loved.

Linguists describe this organization of the sentence in terms of **phrase-structure rules,** rules that identify the patterns within each of the sentence's main components. One phrase-structure rule stipulates that a sentence (S) always consists of a noun phrase (NP) followed by a verb phrase (VP). This is often diagrammed as an (upside-down) "tree structure," as shown in Figure 10.6, and the rule itself is often written this way:

$$S \rightarrow NP\ VP$$

Another phrase-structure rule, also reflected in Figure 10.6, is the one defining how a noun phrase can be expanded:

$$NP \rightarrow (det)\ A* N$$

| FIGURE 10.6 | A Phase-Structure Tree |

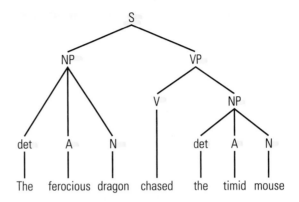

The syntax of a sentence is often depicted via a "tree" diagram. The diagram shows that the overall sentence itself (S) consists of a noun phrase (NP) followed by a verb phrase (VP). The noun phrase is composed of a determiner followed by an adjective and a noun. The verb phrase is composed of a verb followed by a noun phrase.

This means that a noun phrase consists of a *determiner* (like "a" or "one" or "the"), followed by an adjective (A), followed by a noun (N). Notice that you need not have a determiner; there is none in this sentence: "Trees like sunlight." This is why the symbol "det" is in parentheses, indicating that this term is optional. Likewise, there can be any number of adjectives, including none; this is indicated by the asterisk. Other phrase-structure rules are listed in Figure 10.7.

The phrase-structure rules have an important feature called **recursion.** A rule system is recursive if a symbol can appear both on the left side of a definition (the part being defined) and on the right side (the part providing the definition). Thus, a sentence always includes a noun phrase and a verb phrase (remember: S → NP VP; here it is the S that is being defined). The verb phrase, in turn, can be unpacked in several different ways, including

$$VP \rightarrow V\ NP$$

or

$$VP \rightarrow V\ S$$

Notice that in this last rule, S appears as part of the definition. This allows us to create sentences like this one:

I believe she is the thief.

Here, there is a sentence, "She is the thief," within a sentence. (The relevant phrase structure is shown in Figure 10.8; notice that we begin, as always, with an S node at

FIGURE 10.7   Syntactic Rewrite Rules

$$S \longrightarrow NP \quad VP$$
$$NP \longrightarrow (det) \quad A* \; N$$

$$VP \longrightarrow V \; (NP)$$
$$VP \longrightarrow V \; S$$
$$VP \longrightarrow V \; PP$$
$$VP \longrightarrow V \; AP$$
$$AP \longrightarrow A \; A$$

Most syntactic rules can be captured in terms of "rewrite rules." The top rule indicates that a sentence can consist of a noun phrase followed by a verb phrase. A verb phrase, however, can take several different forms: a verb by itself, or a verb followed by a noun phrase, or a verb followed by a prepositional phrase, and so on. Note that these rules are recursive: A sentence can contain a verb phrase, which can contain a sentence.

FIGURE 10.8   Recursion

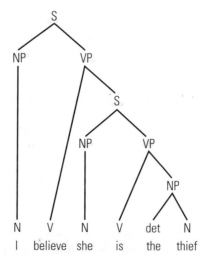

Shown here is the phrase-structure tree for a sentence that makes use of recursion. Recursion refers to the possibility for an element to appear as part of its own definition. Thus, sentences are defined as including verb phrases, but verb phrases can include sentences, leading to the possibility of sentences within sentences.

the top, but then unpack the S node in a fashion that leads to another S node, in the middle of the tree.)

We can then repeat this cycle of recursion, if we wish, with sentences including verb phrases that include sentences that include verb phrases that include sentences, as in

I fear that you believe Sam told her I am the thief.

Recursion provides an easy way to describe sentences like this one. In addition, recursion is one of the features of language supporting vast generativity, since one can, quite literally, use recursion to create an infinite number of sentences.

The Function of Phrase Structure

Phrase-structure rules help us to explain a range of facts. First, these rules provide part of our account for why some sequences of words are rejected as ungrammatical. As we have seen, these rules specify what must be included within a sentence, and they often specify an order for the sentence. Sequences of words that break these rules, therefore, can't be sentences.

Second, we mentioned earlier that phrase-structure rules capture the "natural" groupings of words within each sentence: Groups of words identified by the rules (e.g., the noun phrase, the verb phrase, and so on) really do seem to hang together. There are many ways to demonstrate this, including direct probes of people's intuitions about sentences. For example, where are the "natural" break points in this sentence: "The tall girl tackled the runner"? For most people, the sentence is sensibly split into "The tall girl" and "tackled the runner," and this is, of course, a split between the sentence's main noun phrase and its main verb phrase. If asked to split the sentence again, most people would divide it into "The tall girl," "tackled," and "the runner," fully in accord with the structure dictated by the rules.

Third, phrase-structure rules also seem to guide our interpretation of a sentence: The rule S → NP VP divides a sentence into the "doer" (the NP) and some information about that doer (the VP)—in other words, the rule divides the sentence into the subject and the predicate. If the verb phrase is rewritten VP → V NP, then the initial verb indicates the action described by the sentence, and the NP specifies the recipient of that action. In these ways, the phrase structure of a sentence provides an initial "road map" useful in understanding the sentence, as shown in Figure 10.9.

The role of phrase structure in guiding interpretation is particularly clear in cases of **phrase-structure ambiguity**. This term refers to the fact that sometimes two different phrase structures can lead to the same sequence of words, so that, if you encounter those words, you may not know which phrase structure is intended. If, as we just suggested, phrase structures guide interpretation, then in these cases there should be more than one way to interpret the sentence. This turns out to be correct; some examples are shown in Figure 10.10 and for the first of these we have

FIGURE 10.9 Phrase Structures Provide a Road Map for Understanding a Sentence

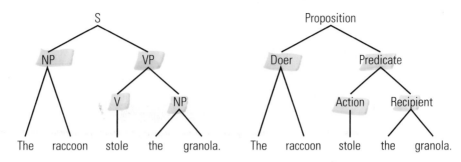

Phrase structures specify the syntactic relationships among a sentence's parts, but these syntactic relationships often provide a guide for how the sentence should be understood.

FIGURE 10.10 Phrase-Structure Ambiguity

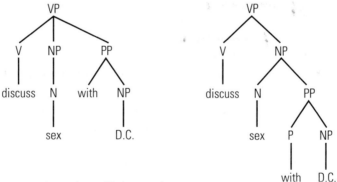

I saw the gorilla in my pajamas.
The shooting of the hunters was terrible.
They are roasting chickens.
Visiting relatives can be awful.
Two computers were reported stolen by the TV announcer.

Often the words of a sentence are compatible with more than one phrase structure; in this case, the sentence will be ambiguous. Thus, one can understand the first sentence as describing a discussion with Cavett, or as describing sex with Cavett; both analyses of the verb phrase are shown. Can you find both interpretations for the remaining sentences?

illustrated the two alternative phrase structures consistent with the sequence of words. Thus, ambiguity is predicted, on the basis of the phrase-structure rules, and the ambiguity is (often humorously) observed.

Movement Rules

It is clear, then, that phrase-structure rules are important. But there's more to syntax than this, and, in fact, we need to supplement the phrase-structure rules with rules of a second type, called **movement rules**. To put the idea in simple terms, phrase-structure rules allow us to "grow" a sentence tree, but then the movement rules allow us to "reshape" the tree by exchanging the positions of some of the tree's branches.

This reshaping serves various functions. For one, it allows us to shift the "focus" of a sentence, and so we might say, "The ball was hit by the boy" (focusing on the ball) rather than, "The boy hit the ball" (focusing on the boy). Movement rules also allow us to express the content of a sentence as a question rather than an assertion ("Who hit the ball?"). These rules also allow us to make a sentence more emphatic. (For example, to indicate our certainty about an event, we might say, "The boy *did* hit the ball.") In these ways, the movement rules create a "family" of sentences, differing in their focus and their attitude, but all based on the same basic content.

In light of all this, linguists find it useful to distinguish two views of a sentence. The phrase-structure rules allow us to generate the sentence's **underlying structure**, or d-structure.[1] Then the movement rules allow us to change the positions of various elements within the sentence, in order to create the sentence's **surface structure**, or s-structure. It is the d-structure that provides the starting point for semantic analysis, since it is this structure that makes clear who did what to whom. It is the s-structure, though, that is expressed in speech.

Linguistic Universals

Let's pause to take stock. We have slowly climbed up the linguistic hierarchy—from the basic features (like voicing or place of articulation) to phonemes, from there to morphemes, then to words, and finally to full sentences. At each step, we have seen how linguistic elements can be combined to create larger and more sophisticated units. In the process, we have seen how a relatively small number of elements can be used to create a vast (and, at some levels, infinite) number of combinations.

We have argued, though, that these combinations are rule-governed: The rules determine which units can be combined, and in what order. The rules also specify a

---

[1] Older texts refer to the underlying structure as the "deep structure" and to the movement rules as "transformations."

structure, within the larger units. And, remarkably, the rules are quite similar as we move from one language to the next.

Of course, languages differ. In English, adjectives are usually placed before the noun ("the blue house"); in Spanish, the adjective comes after the noun ("la casa azul"). Even so, there are a number of striking regularities across languages—even when we consider languages as diverse as, say, English, Japanese, and Turkish, or Mayan, Walbiri, and Kivunjo. Indeed, some have argued that these rules constitute **linguistic universals**—that is, principles applicable to every human language (Chomsky, 1965, 1975, 1986; see also Comrie, 1981; Cook, 1988; Greenberg, Ferguson, & Moravcsik, 1978; and Hawkins, 1988).

The proposed universals are of various sorts. Some are framed in terms of probabilities. Thus, in all the world's languages, some sequences of words are quite common, while other sequences are quite rare. As an example, it is possible in English to put a sentence's object before the sentence's subject ("A bear he shot"), but this isn't the normal pattern for English—the normal pattern, instead, is subject then verb then object. And it is not only English that shows this pattern: The subject of a sentence tends to precede the object in roughly 98% of the world's languages. The sequence of subject before verb is preferred in roughly 80% of the world's languages (Crystal, 1987).

Most universals, though, concern linguistic features that seem to come and go together. Thus, for example, if a language's preferred word order is subject-object-verb, the language is likely to form its questions by adding some words at the end of the question. If, in contrast, a language's preferred sequence is subject-verb-object (as in English), then the language will place its question words at the beginning of the question (as in, "Where did he . . . ?" or "When did they . . . ?").

The existence of these linguistic universals opens an intriguing possibility: Consider the fact that every human child learns how to speak. Indeed, children acquire language rather rapidly. A 2-year-old's linguistic skills are quite limited; a 4-year-old, in contrast, speaks perfectly well. Hence, the learning process is somehow compressed into a period lasting just a couple of years. Moreover, what is learned seems quite complex—with rules governing the combinations of phonemes and different rules governing the combinations of morphemes, and phrase-structure rules and movement rules. Finally, bear in mind that we have already considered evidence that language is not learned via simple imitation or via instruction by the parents. (Many considerations rule out these possibilities, including the over-regularization errors we considered earlier in the chapter.) How, then, is language learning possible?

A number of scholars have argued that language learning is possible only because the child enters this process with an enormous head start: a biological heritage that (somehow) stipulates the broad outline of human language. In this view, the child might begin the process already knowing the universal rules of language. The process of language learning would therefore be a process of figuring out exactly how the rules are realized within the language community in which the child is raised. The child needs to learn, for example, whether she lives in a community that prefers the subject-verb-object sequence or the subject-object-verb order. Having learned that, the child can then set the "switches" properly on the "language machinery" that she was born with and, in that way, be well on her way to speaking in the fashion that's appropriate for her language community—whether it's a community of Portuguese speakers or Urdu, Swedish, or Mandarin. Many have argued that this is the most plausible way to think about language learning, with the plausibility deriving from the fact that many of the rules we have discussed do seem, with the appropriate adjustments of parameters, universal. (For further discussion of these suggestions, see Bloom, 1994; Chomsky, 1957, 1965; and Lidz, Waxman, & Freedman, 2003.)

Sentence Parsing

We have talked about what it is that makes a sequence of words "acceptable" as a sentence, and we have also discussed the internal structure of a sentence. Just as important, though, how do we actually manage to comprehend the sentences we encounter? How do we manage to understand the speech that we hear, or the paragraphs that we read?

As we have discussed, a sentence's phrase structure conveys crucial information about who did what to whom. Thus, once you know the phrase structure, you are well on your way to understanding the sentence. But how do you figure out the phrase structure in the first place? This would be an easy question if sentences were uniform in their structure: "The boy hit the ball. The girl chased the cat. The elephant trampled the geraniums." But, of course, sentences are vastly more variable than this, and this makes the identification of a sentence's phrase structure appreciably more difficult.

How, therefore, do you **parse** a sentence—that is, figure out each word's syntactic role? One possibility is that you wait until the sentence's end, and only then go to work on figuring out the sentence's structure. With this strategy, your comprehension might be slowed a little (because of the wait for the sentence's termination), but you would avoid errors, because your interpretation could be guided by full information about the sentence's content.

A different possibility is that you parse the sentence as you are hearing it, trying to figure out the role of each word the moment you hear the word. This approach might be more efficient (since there's no waiting), but it will sometimes lead to error, in ways that we will describe in a moment.

Evidence favors the latter view; this turns out, therefore, to be one more case in which humans favor a strategy that is efficient but occasionally misleading, in comparison to a strategy that is less efficient but more accurate. (For other illustrations of this sort of trade-off, see Chapters 3, 7, 9, and 12.)

Garden Paths

We have already mentioned that sentences can sometimes be ambiguous, and indeed, even relatively simple sentences can be ambiguous if one is open-minded (or perverse) enough:

> Mary had a little lamb. (But I was quite hungry, so I had the lamb and also a bowl of soup.)

> Time flies like an arrow. (But fruit flies, in contrast, like a banana.)

Temporary ambiguity is also common inside a sentence. More precisely, the early part of a sentence is often open to multiple interpretations, but then the later part of the sentence clears things up. For instance, consider this example:

> The old man the ships.

In this sentence, there are two different ways to interpret the initial three words. Most people, though, read the initial bit as a three-word noun phrase: "the old man." However, this interpretation leaves the sentence with no verb. A different interpretation is demanded by the rest of the sentence, with the subject of the sentence being "the old" and with "man" as the verb. (Who mans the ships? It is the old, not the young. The old man the ships.) Likewise:

> The secretary applauded for his efforts was soon promoted.

Here one tends to read "applauded" as the sentence's main verb, but of course it isn't. Instead, this sentence is just a shorthand way of answering the question, "Which secretary was soon promoted?" (Answer: "The one who was applauded for his efforts.")

These last two examples are referred to as **garden-path sentences:** You are initially led to one interpretation (you are, as they say, "led down the garden path"), but this interpretation then turns out to be wrong. Hence, you need to reject your initial construal and seek an alternative. Here are two more examples:

> Fat people eat accumulates.

> Because he ran the second mile went quickly.

Garden-path sentences highlight the fact that there's some risk attached to the strategy of interpreting a sentence as it arrives. That's because the information you need in order to interpret these sentences arrives only late in the sequence, and so, to avoid an interpretive dead end, you would be well advised to remain neutral about the sentence's interpretation until you've gathered enough information. That way, you'd know that "the old man" couldn't be the sentence's subject, that "applauded" couldn't be the sentence's main verb, and so on. But this is plainly not what you do. Instead, you commit yourself fairly early to one interpretation and then try to "fit" subsequent words, as they arrive, into that interpretation. This strategy is probably efficient more often than not, but it does lead to the "double-take" reaction when late-arriving information forces you to abandon your interpretive efforts so far. (For more on this interpret-as-you-go tendency, see Just & Carpenter, 1987, 1992; Marslen-Wilson & Tyler, 1987; Morton, 1969, 1970; and Sedivy, Tanenhaus, Chambers, & Carlson, 1999.)

We can also use garden-path sentences as a research tool: What is it that leads us down the garden path? Why do we initially choose one interpretation, one parsing, rather than another? As we will see in a moment, garden-path sentences provide us with a useful means of addressing these questions.

Syntax as a Guide to Parsing

People use a bundle of different strategies in parsing the sentences they encounter. For one, they tend to assume that they will be hearing (or reading) *active* sentences rather than *passive*, and so they generally interpret a sentence's initial noun phrase as the "doer" of the action, and not the recipient. As it happens, most of the sentences we encounter are active, not passive, and so this assumption is correct more often than not (Svartik, 1966). However, this assumption works against us whenever we do encounter a passive sentence, and that is why active sentences are somewhat easier to understand than passive sentences (Hornby, 1974; Slobin, 1966).

Does this mean that speakers (and writers) should always avoid passive sentences? Surely not. The assumption of active voice is only one of the factors that guide parsing, and so, in some contexts, with other factors on the scene, passive sentences can be *easier* to understand, not harder (Pinker, 1994).

What are the other factors guiding parsing? It is not surprising that parsing is also influenced by the little function words that appear in a sentence and also by the various morphemes that signal syntactic role (Bever, 1970). For example, one quickly grasps the structure of, "He gliply rivitched the flidget." That's because the "–ly" ending indicates that "glip" is an adverb; the "-ed" ending identifies "rivitch" as a verb; and "the" signals that "flidget" is a noun—all excellent cues to the sentence's structure.

In addition, parsing seems to be guided by a number of other strategies, including an assumption of so-called **minimal attachment.** Roughly, this means that the listener or reader proceeds through a sentence seeking the simplest possible phrase structure that will accommodate the words heard so far. Consider the earlier sentence, "The secretary applauded for his efforts was soon promoted." As you read, "The secretary applauded," you had the option of interpreting this as a noun phrase plus the beginning of a separate clause modifying "secretary." This is, of course, the correct construal and is demanded by the way the sentence ends. However, the principle of minimal attachment led you to ignore this possibility, at least initially, and to proceed instead with a simpler interpretation—of a noun phrase + verb, with no idea of a separate embedded clause.

The tendency to misread the "secretary" sentence is also encouraged by some other factors. The embedded clause is in the passive voice (the secretary was applauded by someone else); your tendency to assume active voice, therefore, worked against the correct interpretation of this sentence. Likewise, this sentence deliberately omits the helpful function words. Notice that we didn't say, "The secretary who was applauded . . . ."

With all these factors stacked against you, it's no wonder you were led to the incorrect construal. Indeed, with all these factors in place, garden-path sentences can sometimes be enormously difficult to comprehend. For example, spend a moment puzzling over this (fully grammatical) sequence:

The horse raced past the barn fell.

(If you get stuck with this sentence, try adding commas after "horse" and after "barn.")

Semantics as a Guide to Parsing

The "secretary" sentence was also complicated by one additional factor: The sentence said, "The secretary applauded for his efforts . . . ." Many people assume, in reading this sentence, that the secretary is a woman, hence "his" must refer to someone else. The suggestion, therefore, is that parsing is also guided by semantic factors, and not just syntax, and this turns out to be correct.

For example, we have already noted that, in general, it is easier to understand an active sentence than it is to understand the corresponding passive sentence. However, this is true only if the sentence is "reversible," such as, "The dog chased the cat." This sentence is considered reversible because the opposite sentence ("The cat chased the dog") also makes sense. This is in contrast to sentences such as, "The elephant squashed the peanut." This sentence isn't reversible: Elephants can certainly squash peanuts, but peanuts can't squash elephants. In this case, therefore, you don't need the syntax to figure out who was the squasher and who was the squashed. And, indeed, for sentences like this, there is no processing advantage for the active form, relative to the passive (Slobin, 1966).

In addition, listeners and readers also seem sensitive to certain statistical properties in the language. If a word has several meanings, you tend to assume its most frequent meaning whenever you encounter the word. You therefore tend to assume that "train" means the thing on tracks rather than the activity one engages in to teach tricks to a dog. Likewise, you tend to assume that "tree" refers to a type of plant, rather than an activity (as in, "The hounds want to tree the raccoon"). Similarly, you tend to assume that adjectives, when they occur, will be followed by nouns. This isn't an obligatory pattern, but it is certainly a frequent pattern, and so the assumption seems safe.

Once again, we can see these factors in action in some of the garden-path sentences: The assumption that adjectives will be followed by nouns primes us to read the phrase "fat people" as an adjective–noun pair, and this gets us in trouble when we encounter, "Fat people eat accumulates." Likewise, our reliance on frequent meanings is part of our problem in understanding sentences like, "The old man ships," or "The new train quickly, but the old train more slowly."

The Extralinguistic Context

It's rare that we encounter a single, isolated sentence. Instead, sentences are uttered in some context, and the context can provide important aids for sentence parsing and sentence understanding. Thus, the garden-path problem is much less likely to occur in the following setting:

Aaron: Which horse fell?

Jon: The horse raced past the barn fell.

The **extralinguistic context** (factors outside of the language itself) is also important. To see how, consider the following sentence:

Put the apple on the towel into the box.

For many people, this sentence causes a temporary false interpretation. Early on, it seems to be an instruction to put an apple onto a towel; this understanding must be abandoned, though, when the words "into the box" arrive. Now listeners realize that the box is the apple's destination; "on the towel" is simply a specification of which apple is to be moved. (Which apple should be put into the box? The one that is on the towel.) In short, this is another example of a garden-path sentence—initially inviting one analysis, but eventually demanding another.

This confusion is avoided, however, if this sentence is uttered in the appropriate setting. Imagine that two apples are in view: one on a towel, and one not (Figure 10.11). In this context, a listener hearing the sentence's start ("Put the apple . . .") would immediately see the possibility for confusion (which apple is being referred to?) and so would expect the speaker to specify which apple is to be moved. When the phrase "on the towel" is uttered, then, the listener immediately and quite naturally understands it (correctly) as the needed specification. Hence, there is no confusion and no garden path (Eberhard, Spivey-Knowlton, Sedivy, & Tanenhaus, 1995; Tanenhaus & Spivey-Knowlton, 1996).

The Use of Language: What Is Left Unsaid

Earlier in this chapter, we argued that a rich set of rules is needed to explain why some sound combinations, some words, and some sentences are acceptable to speakers of a language, while others are not. These rules must be acquired by anyone who wishes to learn a language; indeed, these rules are a part of what it means to "know a language."

FIGURE 10.11 The Extralinguistic Context

"Put the apple on the towel into the box." Without the setting shown here, this sentence causes momentary confusion as the listener comes across "on the towel" before grasping the greater context of "into the box." But when the sentence is simultaneously presented with this picture, the listener finds "on the towel" useful in clearing up the ambiguity of "the apple."

As we have now seen, we need an additional set of principles to account for how the language is perceived and understood—either by the listener or by the reader. A number of syntactic principles seem relevant, as do several semantic principles. These factors then interact in an intricate fashion, so that our understanding of the sentences we hear (or see in print) seems guided by all of these principles at the same time.

All of this, however, still *understates* the complexity of language use and, with that, the complexity of the knowledge someone must have in order to "know a language." For illustration, note that we have said nothing about how one deals with pronouns, as in

Fred went swimming; Sam played tennis; later he napped.

Who napped? Here, a principle of "recency" seems crucial, and most people believe that it is Sam who napped. In other cases, though, other principles come into play:

Susan waved at Maria, but then she insulted her.

Who insulted whom? Here it is grammatical role that seems to matter, so that "she," the subject of the second phrase, seems to refer to "Susan," the subject of the first phrase. In short, then, we will need still other principles to deal with pronouns. (For a fuller treatment of pronouns, see Gordon & Scearce, 1995; and Just & Carpenter, 1987.)

We have also not mentioned another source of information useful in parsing: the rise and fall of speech intonation and the pattern of pauses. These rhythm and pitch cues are together called **prosody** and play an important role in speech perception. Prosody can reveal the mood of a speaker; it can also direct the listener's attention by, in effect, specifying the focus or theme of a sentence (Jackendoff, 1972). Prosody can also render unambiguous a sentence that would otherwise be entirely confusing (Beach, 1991). (Thus, garden-path sentences and ambiguous sentences are much more effective in print, where prosody provides no information.)

Finally, we have not even touched on several related puzzles. For one, how is language produced? How does one turn ideas, intentions, and queries into actual sentences? How does one turn the sentences into sequences of sounds? These are important issues, but for brevity's sake, we have held them to the side here. (For a review of these issues, see Dell, Burger, & Svec, 1997; and Fromkin, 1993.)

Likewise, what happens after one has parsed and understood an individual sentence? How is the sentence integrated with earlier sentences or subsequent sentences? Here, too, more theory is needed to explain the inferences we routinely make in ordinary conversation. If you are asked, for example, "Do you know the time?" you understand this as a request that you report the time—despite the fact that the question, understood literally, is a yes/no question about the extent of your temporal knowledge. In the same vein, consider this bit of conversation (Pinker, 1994):

Woman: I'm leaving you.

Man: Who is he?

We easily provide the soap-opera script that lies behind this exchange, but we do so by drawing on a rich fabric of additional knowledge, including knowledge of **pragmatics** (i.e., knowledge of how language is ordinarily used) and, in this case, also knowledge about the vicissitudes of romance. (For discussion, see Austin, 1962; Ervin-Tripp, 1993; Graesser, Millis, & Zwaan, 1997; Grice, 1975; Hilton, 1995; Kumon-Nakamura, Glucksberg, & Brown, 1995; and Sperber & Wilson, 1986.)

If you are intrigued by the topic of language, then these topics—pronouns, prosody, production, and pragmatics—certainly warrant further exploration. For our purposes, though, this fast mention of these topics merely serves to emphasize a central message of this chapter: Each of us uses language all the time—to learn, to gossip, to instruct, to persuade, to express affection. We use this tool as easily as we breathe; we spend more effort in choosing our clothes in the morning than we do in choosing the words we will utter. But these observations must not hide the fact that language is a remarkably complicated tool, and we are all exquisitely skilled in its use.

The Biology of Language

How is all of this possible? How is it that ordinary human beings—indeed, ordinary two-and-a-half-year-olds—manage the extraordinary task of mastering and fluently using language? We have already suggested part of the answer: Humans are equipped with extremely sophisticated neural machinery, specialized for learning, and then using, language. Let's take a quick look at this machinery.

Aphasias

Much of what we know about the neural basis for language comes from the study of brain damage. As we have seen in other chapters, brain damage can cause a variety of effects, depending on where and how widespread the damage is. For a number of brain sites, though, damage causes disruption of language—a disruption known as **aphasia**.

Aphasias take many different forms and are often quite specialized, with the particular symptoms largely dependent on the locus of the brain damage. As a rough summary of the data, however, investigators find it useful to distinguish two broad classes of aphasia. Damage to the left frontal lobe of the brain, and especially a region known as **Broca's area** (see Figure 10.12), usually produces a pattern of symptoms known as **nonfluent aphasia**. In extreme cases, a patient with this disorder becomes virtually unable to utter or write a word. In less-severe cases, only a part of the normal vocabulary is lost, but the patient's speech becomes labored and fragmented because finding and articulating each word requires special effort.

A different pattern is associated with damage to a brain site known as **Wernicke's area** (see Figure 10.12), and usually involves a pattern known as **fluent aphasia**. In these cases, patients seem able to produce speech but do not understand what is said to them, though they answer anyway. Unlike patients with nonfluent aphasias, those with fluent aphasias talk freely and rapidly, but although they utter many words, they say very little. The sentences they produce are reasonably grammatical, but they are "word salad," composed largely of the little filler words that provide scant information.

Let us be clear, though, that this broad distinction—between fluent and nonfluent aphasia—captures the data only in the broadest sense. That is because, as we have seen, language use (whether for production or comprehension) involves the coordination of many different steps, many different processes. These include processes needed to "look up" word meanings in one's "mental dictionary," processes needed to figure out the structural relationships within a sentence, processes needed to integrate information gleaned about a sentence's structure with the meanings of the words within the sentence, and so on. Each of these processes relies on its own set of brain pathways, and so damage to those pathways disrupts the process. As a result, the language loss observed in aphasia is often quite specific—with impairment just to a particular processing step (and then, as a consequence, disruption in subsequent processes that depend on that step; see Cabeza & Nyberg, 2000; Demonet, Wise, & Frackowiak, 1993; and Martin, 2003).

Thus, for example, some aphasic patients show a pattern quite different from what we have described so far. Some suffer from **anomia** and lose the ability to name various objects, as if their brain damage caused disruption to their mental

| FIGURE 10.12 | Brain Areas Crucial for the Perception and Production of Language |

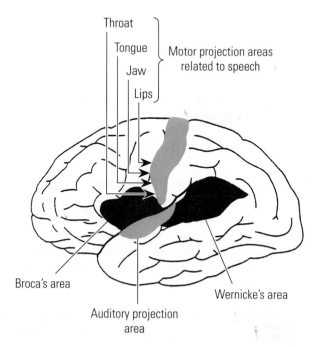

Many different brain regions are involved in the ordinary understanding or production of language. Many of these regions, however, are positioned close together; for most individuals, these regions are in the left cerebral hemisphere (as shown here). Broca's area is heavily involved in language production; Wernicke's area plays a crucial role in language comprehension.

dictionary. Anomias can be extraordinarily specific: Some patients can use concrete nouns but not abstract nouns; some can name animate objects but not inanimate ones; some patients lose the ability to name colors. Still other patients show a pattern called pure word deafness. These patients can speak, write, and read normally, and they can hear perfectly well, but they can't make any sense out of the language they hear. And so on. (For descriptions of the various aphasias, see Caplan, 1987, 1992; Dingwall, 1993; Gabrieli, 1998; and Hillis & Caramazza, 1991.)

These and other data make it clear that certain areas of the human brain are specialized for language processing, and indeed, each of these brain areas seems specialized for just one aspect of language processing. Apparently, then, our skill in using language rests in part on the fact that we have a considerable amount of neural apparatus devoted to precisely this task.

Language Learning

If we have skill in language use, where does this skill come from? If we have biological apparatus devoted to language processing, how does this apparatus come to be? For both of these questions, what is at issue is how language is learned—and, indeed, *whether* it is learned.

As we have mentioned, virtually all humans learn language, and they learn it very quickly: By the age of 3 or 4, almost every child is reasonably competent in communicating her wishes and desires and, for that matter, in communicating fairly sophisticated beliefs. Moreover, this rapid gain in skill proceeds in a roughly normal way in an astonishingly wide range of environments. Children who talk a lot with adults learn language, and so do children who talk very little with adults. Indeed, children learn language even if they have *no* linguistic contact with adults! Evidence on this last point comes from children born deaf, but with no opportunity to learn sign language. (In some cases this is because their caretakers don't know how to sign; in other cases, it is because their caretakers choose not to teach signing.) Even in these extreme cases, language emerges: Children in this situation invent their own gestural language (usually called "home sign"), and the language they invent shows many parallels to ordinary (spoken) language. For example, their invented language has many of the formal structures routinely seen in the world's existing languages; their invented language honors the linguistic universals we have already mentioned; and the pattern of emergence for these invented languages follows the same sequence as that observed in ordinary language learning (Feldman, Goldin-Meadow, & Gleitman, 1978; Goldin-Meadow, 2003; Senghas, Coppola, Newport, & Supalla, 1997).

We know also that language learning is not a matter of imitation. This is evident in the fact that deaf children learn language, but it is also reflected in the fact, mentioned earlier in the chapter, that children produce many forms (including the over-regularized past tense, as in "I goed to the store," or an over-regularized plural, as in "He has two feets") that adults never produce.

Likewise, language learning is not a matter of explicit instruction. Studies of child–adult interaction make it plain that adults rarely correct their children's grammar, nor do they reward children in any sense when the children speak "correctly." Instead, adults react to the *messages* that children convey in their language—and so (for example), respond positively to the message, "Love 'oo, Mommy," more concerned with the content than with the syntax. And in those rare occasions in which adults *do* correct children's grammar ("You shouldn't say 'holded', Susie. Say, 'she held'"), children seem largely oblivious to the correction (Bellugi, 1971).

These (and other) facts leave us with two possibilities. One option is that the acquisition of language is supported by extremely powerful learning mechanisms—mechanisms that can detect patterns, and induce rules, from truly minimal input. (For advocates of this view, see, for example, McClelland & Patterson, 2002a, 2002b; Pullum & Scholz, 2002; Saffran, 2003; and Seidenberg, 1997.) A second option, favored by many scholars, is that mechanisms of learning, no matter how powerful, will not be enough. We need, in addition, to help the process along with innate mechanisms—to guide the learning in exactly the right way, and perhaps also to provide skills that aren't learned at all, but that are hardwired into the structure of the human brain. Support for this view comes from many sources, including some facts we have already mentioned: the existence of linguistic universals, and the fact that language emerges even in children who have *no* linguistic input (and so nothing to learn *from*).

Moreover, some have argued that language *cannot* be learned, and the key argument here is often referred to as the "poverty of the stimulus" (Chomsky, 1957, 1965). The idea behind this argument is that the language children actually hear is compatible with more than one analysis: perhaps *this* is the appropriate phrase structure, and perhaps *that* is the appropriate structure. Nonetheless, adults seem reliably to settle on one of these interpretations—and all adults seem to settle on the same interpretation. If the language the child hears doesn't guide this choice of interpretation (because, again, the language is compatible with either analysis), then the choice must come from *within* the child—and that is the point. Independent of learning, the child seems biased toward certain interpretations of the language that he or she hears. And if these biases are independent of learning, they must be innate. (For a recent discussion of this argument, see Lidz et al., 2003; for a counterargument, see, for example, Pullum & Scholz, 2002.)

Finally, there is no question that genetic factors do contribute to the acquisition of language. This is reflected in the fact that some individuals seem to inherit a specific difficulty—traceable to just a single gene (a mutation of gene *FOXP2*)—that impairs their ability to learn language. Individuals with this syndrome, known as **specific language impairment,** have normal intelligence and no problems with the muscle movements needed to produce language. Nonetheless, they are generally slow to learn language and, throughout their lives, have difficulty in understanding and producing many sentences. They are also impaired on various tasks designed specifically to test their linguistic knowledge. They have difficulty, for example, completing passages like this one: "I like to blife. Today I blife. Tomorrow I will blife. Yesterday I did the same thing. Yesterday I ___." Most 4-year-olds know that the answer is, "Yesterday I blifed." But adults with a mutation of *FOXP2* cannot do this task—apparently having failed to learn this simple rule of language (Lai, Fisher, Hurst, Vargha-Khadem, & Monaco, 2001; Pinker, 1991, 1994; Tallal, Ross, & Curtiss, 1989).

All of this seems to suggest that language really is rooted in the biology of the human brain, and so we can close this section by circling back to a theme that was prominent at the chapter's start. We argued early on that language is something central to our species, and crucial for many of the activities our species engages in. As we have now seen, it is likewise clear that specializations for language are very much evident in the biology of our species, making it certain that, in an important sense, we are indeed linguistic creatures.

Language and Thought

One last topic will bring our consideration of language to a close. We have suggested, throughout this chapter, that humans are linguistic creatures, with language serving an essential role in many human activities, and with each of us having enormous skill in using language. We've also suggested that large portions of our brain are devoted to language processing, with each of the relevant brain regions providing its own specialized part of the whole.

Given this centrality of language, it should be no surprise that language has a powerful effect in shaping many aspects of our thought. Some of these effects are self-evident. For example, if a speaker says, "I saw a dog," the listener will, of course, be led to a different idea than if the speaker had said, "I saw a cat." In this perfectly obvious way, the language that we use (and, in this case, the language that we hear) can shape what we think.

Other influences of language are, however, perhaps more interesting. For instance, linguistic descriptions often provide a convenient label for a complex experience, and the labels, in turn, provide an economical way of coding, or chunking, that experience—with important consequences for memory (see Chapter 5). Thus, it is vastly easier to remember the label "tree" than it is to remember the corresponding image, easier to remember the label "trips to the zoo" than it is to remember all the details associated with those trips. In this fashion, labeling—made possible by language—has a powerful effect on memory.

Likewise, language can also influence our thinking—how we reason about things, for example, or how we make decisions. One illustration of this is in so-called framing effects (see Chapter 13). Thus, for just one case, a patient is more likely to choose a medical treatment if told that the treatment has a 50% chance of success than if told it has a 50% chance of failure—again, demonstrating a powerful effect of language.

But all of this, in turn, invites a further question: If language shapes thought, then do people who speak different languages end up *thinking differently*? Some of the early evidence on this question was offered by the anthropologist Benjamin Whorf, who was a strong proponent of the view that the specific language we speak forces us into certain modes of thought—a claim usually known as **linguistic relativity** (Whorf, 1956). The "results" Whorf offered, however, were quite weak. He tried to show, for example, that Hopi speakers think about time differently than English speakers do, but his only evidence came from the ways that the Hopi expressed themselves when talking about different kinds of events. This evidence is without value: Perhaps the Hopi think in just the same ways that English speakers do but express these thoughts differently because their language differs from English. In this case, the evidence indicates only that the way one expresses oneself is influenced by one's language—a conclusion that seems both unsurprising and not very interesting.

More recent researchers have tried to find more rigorous tests of Whorf's proposal. One line of work has examined how we perceive the colors in our world, building on the fact that some languages have many, many terms for colors (red, orange, yellow, mauve, puce, salmon, fawn, ocher, etc.), and others have few. Early data suggested that having a rich color vocabulary helps people to *remember* colors but does not change how the colors are *perceived* (Berlin & Key, 1969; R. Brown & Lenneberg, 1954; Heider, 1972; Rosch, 1977b). More recent findings, though, suggest that people who speak languages with a richer color vocabulary may, in fact, perceive colors differently—making finer and more sharply defined distinctions (Özgen, 2004; Roberson, Davies, & Davidoff, 2000).

In the same fashion, some recent studies start with the fact that different languages describe spatial arrangement in different ways—with some languages, for example, emphasizing absolute directions (akin to north or east, which are defined in a fashion independent of which way you're currently facing), while other languages emphasize relative directions (akin to left or right, which *do* depend on which way you are facing). Several studies have suggested that these language differences lead to corresponding differences in how people remember, and perhaps how they perceive, spatial position (Majid, Bowerman, Kita, Haun, & Levinson, 2004; Pederson et al., 1998).

These data are controversial—with some dispute, for example, about whether the experiments were executed and interpreted properly (Gallistel, 2002; Levinson, Kita, Haun, & Rasch, 2002; Li & Gleitman, 2002; Majid, 2002). If we take the data at face value, though, what do they tell us? One possibility—in line with Whorf's original hypothesis—is that language truly "restructures" cognition, so that the language you speak determines the concepts and categories you use and, as a result, shapes what you *can* think about. On this view, there are literally some ideas that a native Hopi speaker (for example) can contemplate, but that a native French speaker cannot, and vice versa.

A different possibility is more modest and, in truth, more plausible: The labels provided by language draw our attention to certain distinctions—so that, for example, by labeling some objects as "red," we draw attention to the distinction between red and not red. This drawing of attention makes it likely that we'll think about this distinction periodically, and, in essence, this provides *practice* in thinking about the distinction. Of course, this practice will probably lead to improvement in how easily or how skillfully we think about this distinction. As a result of all this, language will end up influencing our cognition, but not because there is a direct link between the two. Instead, language influences what we pay attention to, and this shapes experience, which influences how and how well we think. (For discussion of how this might work with *color*, see, for example, Özgen, 2004; and Özgen & Davies, 2002.)

If this latter view is correct, then the language we speak does influence our thoughts—but not because there is something special about language. Instead, language is just one of the ways we can guide someone's attention to this or that aspect of their experience. In addition, and quite unlike Whorf's claim, this view suggests that language-based influences on our thinking are *reversible*. The language you speak might well lead you to pay attention to some categories and not others, but the resulting biases can be altered if we draw your attention to different categories and thus create new experiences for you.

Consistent with this argument, Tzeltal speakers and English speakers do seem initially to think about space in different ways, but these differences can be erased if we use other (nonlinguistic) cues to lead speakers of either language to pay attention to other aspects of the spatial arrangement (Li & Gleitman, 2002). Likewise, English speakers and speakers of Mandarin Chinese seem initially to think about spatial relations differently—because their languages do bias them toward different interpretive habits. But the difference between English and Chinese speakers can be eradicated by a brief conversation with the research participants about other ways one might think about space. Thus, the language creates biases (again, by drawing attention to certain distinctions), but the biases can be reversed if attention is drawn in some way to other aspects of the situation (Boroditsky, 2001).

Finally, we can also find many instances in which there is no linkage between the language that one speaks and the way one perceives (or thinks about) the world (Landau & Munnich, 1998; Malt, Sloman, Gennari, Shi, & Wang, 1999; Munnich, Landau, & Dosher, 2001). This equivalence across language groups is a puzzle if language literally shapes how (and what) we can think, but it is sensible if language is only one of many factors biasing our attention and interpretation.

Where, then, does this leave us? Having a language certainly influences cognition, and so our human (and language-guided) thoughts are in many ways different from the thoughts of our nonlinguistic primate relatives (gorillas, chimps, bonobos, and so on). In addition, speaking a *specific* language (English or Tzeltal, Mandarin or French) does influence one's thoughts—but in ways that are not at all mysterious. Of course, someone can say, "Look at the bird," and thus guide your attention to the bird. In the same fashion, your language, by virtue of having a verbal label for a category, can call your attention to this category and thus shape your experience, and so your cognition. But this is a far cry from the claims offered by Whorf a half-century ago. Whorf's argument, as we've noted, was that language plays a unique role in shaping thought and has a lifelong impact in determining quite literally what we can or cannot think, what ideas we can or cannot entertain. There is no persuasive evidence in favor of this stronger claim.

Chapter Summary

1. All speech is built up from a few dozen phonemes; which phonemes are used varies from language to language. Phonemes in turn are built up from a small number of production features, including voicing, place of articulation, and manner of production. Phonemes can be combined to form more complex sounds, but combinations are constrained by a number of rules.

2. Speech perception is more than a matter of detecting the relevant features in the input sound stream. The perceiver needs to deal with speaker-to-speaker variation in how sounds are produced; he also needs to segment the stream of speech and cope with coarticulation. The process of speech perception is helped enormously by context, but we also have the impressive skill of categorical perception, which makes us keenly sensitive to differences between categories of speech sounds but insensitive to distinctions within each category.

3. People know many thousands of words, and for each, they know the sound of the word, its syntactic role, and its semantic representation. Our understanding of words is also generative, allowing us to create limitless numbers of new words. Some new words are wholly made up ("geek"), but more often, new words are created by combining morphemes. The combinations of morphemes, like the combinations of phonemes, are governed by rules. The rules are descriptive, not prescriptive, and are often best revealed by studies of metalinguistic judgments that display someone's linguistic competence, rather than by studies of their linguistic performance.

4. The psychological reality of language rules is suggested by many facts, including over-regularization errors. There is controversy over whether some representation of the rules is literally encoded in the mind, but there is no doubt that language use is highly creative but also highly constrained in a fashion that seems well described by rules.

5. The rules of syntax govern whether a sequence of words is grammatical. One set of rules consists of the phrase-structure rules, which can be understood as specifying how a sentence structure is created, or as specifying how an already existing sentence should be parsed. The word groups identified by phrase-structure rules do correspond to natural groupings of words, and the phrase-structure rules also guide interpretation.

6. Phrase-structure rules generate a sentence's underlying structure, but then movement rules (or transformations) shift the elements around to create the sentence's surface structure.

7. To understand a sentence, a listener or reader needs to parse the sentence, determining each word's syntactic role. Evidence suggests that people parse the sentence as they see or hear each word, and this sometimes leads them into parsing errors that must be repaired later; this is revealed by garden-path sentences. Parsing is guided by syntax, semantics, and the extralinguistic context.

8. The biological roots of language are revealed in many ways. The study of aphasias and neuroimaging data make it clear that some areas of the brain are specialized for learning and using language. The rapid learning of language, in a fashion dependent on neither imitation nor explicit instruction, also speaks to the biological basis for language; this rapid learning is certainly helped by the existence of linguistic universals—structural properties shared by all languages.

9. There has been considerable discussion about the ways in which thought might be shaped by the language one speaks. Language certainly guides and influences our thoughts, and the way a thought is formulated into words can have an effect on how we think about the thought's content. In addition, language can call our attention to a category, or to a distinction, and this makes it likely that we will have experience in thinking about the category or distinction. This experience, in turn, can promote fluency in these thoughts. However, these effects are not unique to language (because other factors can also draw our attention to the category), nor are they irreversible. Hence there is no evidence that language can shape what we *can* think.

Visual Knowledge

In Chapters 8, 9, and 10, we focused on knowledge about language and also on knowledge that can be expressed through language. But what about knowledge of other sorts? For example, you know what ammonia smells like, as well as apple pie and strawberries. How is this "smell knowledge" represented in the mind? Likewise, you remember the sound of a guitar or a fire engine's siren; you know what Judy's voice sounds like, and you can recall how it contrasts with Barbara's. What can we say about this auditory knowledge? You also have visual memories, and memories for pains and for tastes. In each case, how is this nonverbal knowledge encoded in memory?

Psychologists have examined many of these types of knowledge—memory for odors (Algom & Cain, 1991; Bensafi et al., 2003; Djordjevic, Zatorre, Petrides, & Jones-Gotman, 2004; A. N. Gilbert, Crouch, & Kemp, 1998; Lyman & McDaniel, 1990; P. Reed, 2000; Schab, 1990, 1991), for familiar voices (Nairn & Pusen, 1984; Van Lancker, Kreiman, & Emmorey, 1985; Van Lancker, Kreiman, & Wickens, 1985), for particular pitches (Levitin, 1994; Schellenberg & Trehub, 2003), for movements (Engelkamp, Zimmer, Mohr, & Sellen, 1994), and for pain (Algom & Lubel, 1994; Eich, Reeves, Jaeger, & Graff-Radford, 1985; Kahneman, Fredrickson, Schreiber, & Redelmeier, 1993; Kent, 1985; S. J. Linton & Melin, 1982; Rachman & Eyrl, 1989), to name just a few.

In this chapter, we will explore this nonverbal knowledge, with an emphasis on visual knowledge. We will ask how this knowledge is recorded in memory, and also how this

- Mental images are, in important ways, picturelike, representing in a direct fashion the spatial layout of the represented scene. It's not surprising, therefore, that there is considerable overlap between imagery and perception—in how each functions, and also in their neural bases.

- However, people can also use *spatial* imagery, which is not visual, and which may instead be represented in the mind in terms of movements, or perhaps in some more abstract format.

- Although they are picturelike, images (visual or spatial) are plainly not pictures; instead, images (like percepts) seem to be organized and already interpreted in a fashion that pictures are not.

- Even though images in working memory provide a distinctive form of representation, information about appearances in long-term memory may not be distinctive. In fact, long-term memory for sensory information seems to obey all the principles we described, in earlier chapters, for verbal or symbolic memories.

knowledge is used. Our focus on visual knowledge is motivated largely by the fact that far more is known about visual knowledge than about knowledge in any other modality. As we proceed, though, you should try to read this chapter on two different levels. At a concrete level, we will be surveying what is known about visual knowledge and visual imagery. At the same time, we will also be pursuing a broader agenda, as we seek to illustrate more generally how one can do research on nonverbal knowledge and what questions need to be asked about such knowledge.

Visual Imagery

How many windows are there in your house or your apartment? Who has bushier eyebrows—Eminem or George W. Bush? For most people, questions like these seem to elicit "mental pictures." You know what Eminem and Bush look like, and you call a "picture" of each before your "mind's eye" in order to make the comparison. Likewise, you call to mind a "map" of your apartment, and count the windows by inspecting this map. Many people even trace the map in the air, by moving their finger around, following the imagined map's contours.

Various practical problems also seem to evoke images. There you are in the store, trying on a new sweater. Will the sweater look good with your blue pants? To decide, you will probably try to visualize the blue of the pants, using your "mind's eye" to ask how they will look with the sweater. Similarly, a friend asks you, "Was Boaz in class yesterday?" You might try to recall by visualizing what the room looked like during the class; is Boaz "visible" in your image?

These examples illustrate the common, everyday use of visual images—as a basis for making decisions, as an aid to remembering. But what are these images? Surely there is no tiny eye somewhere deep in your brain; thus the phrase "mind's eye" cannot be taken literally. Likewise, mental "pictures" cannot be actual pictures; with no eye deep inside the brain, who or what would inspect such pictures?

365

Introspections About Images

Mental images have been described and discussed for thousands of years. However, it is only within the last century or so that psychologists have begun to gather systematic data about imagery. Among the earliest researchers was Francis Galton, who asked various people to describe their images and to rate them for vividness (Galton, 1883). In essence, Galton asked his research participants to introspect (or "look within"), and to report on their own mental contents. The self-report data he obtained fit well with common sense: The participants reported that they could "inspect" their images much as they would inspect a picture. In their images, scenes were represented as if viewed from a certain position and a certain distance. They also reported that they could "read off" from the image details of color and of texture. All of this implies a mode of representation that is, in many ways, picturelike, and that is of course quite consistent with our informal manner of describing mental images as "pictures in the head," to be inspected with the "mind's eye."

There was also another side of Galton's data: Galton's participants differed widely from each other. Many described images of photographic clarity, rich in detail, almost as if they were *seeing* the imaged scene, rather than visualizing it. Other participants, however, reported very sketchy images or no images at all. They were certainly able to think about the scenes or objects Galton named for them, but in no sense were they "seeing" these scenes. Their self-reports rarely included mention of color or size or viewing perspective; indeed, their reports were largely devoid of any visual qualities.

These observations are in themselves interesting: Do individuals really differ in the nature of their mental imagery? What consequences does such variety have? Are there tasks that the "visualizers" can do better than the "nonvisualizers" (or vice versa)? If so, this could provide crucial information about how visual imagery is used, and what it is good for.

Before we can answer these questions, though, we must address a methodological concern raised by Galton's data—a concern that we have met before: Perhaps we shouldn't take these self-reports at face value. Perhaps all of Galton's participants had the same imagery skill, but some were cautious in how they chose to describe their imagery, while others were more extravagant. In this way, Galton's data might reveal differences in how people *talk about* their imagery, rather than differences in the imagery per se. (For further discussion of this issue, see Chapters 1 and 15.)

This broad worry grows out of the fact that self-report data, by their nature, are always filtered through a person's verbal habits. What these data reveal, in other words, is not imagery itself, but *imagery as the person elects to describe it*. And there is always a danger that these descriptions will be misleading in some way, or incomplete, or perhaps just imprecise.

What seems required, therefore, is a more objective means of assessing imagery—one that does not rely on the subjectivity inherent in self-reports. With this more objective approach, we could assess the differences, from one individual to the next, evident in Galton's data. Indeed, with this more objective approach, we could hope to find out exactly what images are.

Chronometric Studies of Imagery

Imagery researchers have, in the last 50 years, been keenly sensitive to these concerns about self-report, and this is why imagery experiments usually don't ask participants to *describe* their images. Instead, to gain more objective data, these experiments ask people to *do something* with their images—to read information off of them, or to manipulate them in some way. We can then examine how accurate and how fast people are in their responses, and with appropriate comparisons, we can use these measurements as a basis for testing hypotheses about the nature of imagery. These **chronometric** ("time-measuring") **studies** give us a much more accurate portrait of mental imagery than could ever be obtained with self-report data.

For example, chronometric studies allow us to ask what sorts of information are prominent in a mental image and what sorts are not, and we can then use these evaluations as a basis for asking how "picturelike" mental images really are. To see the logic, think about how actual, out-in-the-world pictures are different from verbal descriptions. Concretely, consider what would happen if you were asked to *write a paragraph* describing a cat. It seems likely that you would mention the distinctive features of cats—their whiskers, their claws, and so on. Your paragraph probably would not include the fact that cats have heads, since this is too obvious to be worth mentioning. But now consider, in contrast, what would happen if we asked you to *draw a sketch* of a cat. In this format, the cat's head would be prominent, for the simple reason that the head is relatively large and up front. The claws and whiskers might be less salient, because these features are small and so would not take up much space in the drawing.

The point here is that the pattern of what information is included, and what information is prominent, depends on the mode of presentation. For a *description* of a cat, the features that are prominent will be those that are distinctive and strongly associated with the object being described. For a *depiction*, distinctiveness and association won't matter; instead, size and position will determine what is prominent and what is not.

Against this backdrop, let's now ask what information is available in a visual image. Is it the pictorially prominent features, which would imply a depictive mode of representation, or the verbally prominent ones, implying a descriptive mode? Self-reports about imagery surely indicate a picturelike representation; is this confirmed by the data?

In a study by Kosslyn (1976), participants were asked to form a series of mental images, and to answer yes/no questions about each. For example, they were asked to form a mental image of a cat and then were asked, Does the cat have a head? Does the cat have claws? Participants responded to these questions quickly, but strikingly, responses to the head question were quicker than those to the claws question. This difference suggests that information quickly available in the image follows the rules for pictures, not paragraphs. In contrast, a different group of participants was asked merely to think about cats (with no mention of imagery). These participants, asked the same questions, gave quicker responses to claws than to head—the reverse pattern of the first group. Thus, it seems that people have the option of thinking about cats via imagery, and also the option of thinking about cats without imagery; as the mode of representation changes, so does the pattern of information availability. (For more on when people rely on imagery for this task and when they don't, see Barsalou, Solomon, & Wu, 1998.)

Here is a different experiment, making a related point (Kosslyn, Ball, & Reiser, 1978). Participants were asked to memorize the fictional map shown in Figure 11.1 and, in particular, to memorize the locations of the various landmarks: the well, the straw hut, and so on. The experimenters made sure participants had the map memorized by asking them to draw a replica of the map from memory; once they could do this, the main experiment began. Participants were asked to form an image of the island, and to point their "mind's eye" at a specific landmark—let us say the

---

FIGURE 11.1   Map of a Fictional Island Used in Image-Scanning Experiments

Participants in the study first memorized this map, including the various landmarks (the hut, the well, the patch of grass, and so on). They then formed a mental image of this map for the scanning procedure. (After Kosslyn, 1983)

well. Another landmark was then mentioned, perhaps the straw hut, and participants were asked to imagine a black speck moving in a straight line from the first landmark to the second. When the speck "reached" the target, participants pressed a button, stopping a clock. This provides a measure of how long it takes to scan from the well to the hut. The same was done for the well and the palm tree, the hut and the rock, and so on, so that we end up with "scanning times" for each of the various pairs of landmarks.

Figure 11.2 shows the results. The data from this **image-scanning procedure** clearly suggest that participants scan across their images at a constant rate, so that doubling the scanning "distance" doubles the time required for the scan, and tripling the distance triples the time required.

Similar results are obtained if participants are given a task that requires them to "zoom in" on their images (e.g., a task that requires them to inspect the image for some small detail), or a task that requires them to "zoom out" (e.g., a task that requires a more global judgment). In these studies, response times are directly proportional to the amount of zoom required, suggesting once again that travel in the imaged world resembles travel in the actual world, at least with regard to timing. As

FIGURE 11.2   **Relationship Between Reaction Time and "Distance" on the Imaged Map**

Participants had to "scan" from one point on their mental image to another point; they pressed a button to indicate when their "mind's eye" had arrived at its destination. Response times in this task were closely related to the "distance" participants had to scan across on the image, implying that mental images are similar to actual pictures in how they represent positions and distance. (After Kosslyn, 1983)

a concrete example, participants in one study were asked to imagine a mouse standing next to an elephant, and they were then asked to confirm, by inspecting their image, that the mouse had whiskers. Participants were relatively slow in responding, presumably because they first needed time to zoom in on the image, in order to "see" the whiskers. Response times were faster if the participants were initially asked to imagine the mouse standing next to a paper clip. For this image, participants start with a "close-up" view, and so, in this setup, no zooming is needed to "see" the whiskers.

Whether you are scanning across a mental image, therefore, or zooming in on one, there is a clear relationship between "travel time" and "travel distance"—and, specifically, "traveling" a greater "distance" requires more time. This is, of course, the same relationship we would observe if we asked our participants to move their eyes across an actual map (rather than an image of one), or literally to zoom in on a real picture: In these cases, too, traveling a greater distance would require more time. All of this obviously points toward the similarity between mental images and actual out-in-the-world pictures.

More precisely, though, these mental imagery data are telling us a great deal about the *nature* of mental images: According to these results, images represent a scene in a fashion that preserves all of the distance relationships within that scene: Points close to each other in the scene are somehow "close" to each other in the image; points that are farther apart in the scene are somehow "farther apart" in the image. Thus, in a very real sense, the image preserves the spatial layout of the represented scene. With this, the image will necessarily represent information about all the shapes and sizes within the scene, and will also preserve a diverse set of spatial relationships (relationships such as one point being *between* two other points, or *aligned* with other points, and so on). It is in this fashion that images directly represent the *geometry* of the scene, and it is in this way that images *depict* the scene, rather than describing it, and so are much more similar to *pictures* or *maps* than they are to propositional descriptions.

Mental Rotation

Other results make a similar point with regard to the *transformation* of mental images. Consider the display shown in Figure 11.3A. In a series of experiments by Shepard, Cooper, and Metzler, participants were asked to decide whether displays like this one showed two different shapes or just one shape viewed from two different perspectives. In other words, is it possible to "rotate" the form shown on the left in Figure 11.3A so that it will end up looking just like the form on the right? What about the two shapes shown in Figure 11.3B, or the two in 11.3C?

To perform this mental rotation task, participants seem first to imagine one of the forms rotating into alignment with the other. Then, once the forms are oriented in the same way, participants can make their judgment. This step of imagined rotation takes some time, and in fact, the amount of time it takes depends on how

FIGURE 11.3	Stimuli for a Mental Rotation Experiment

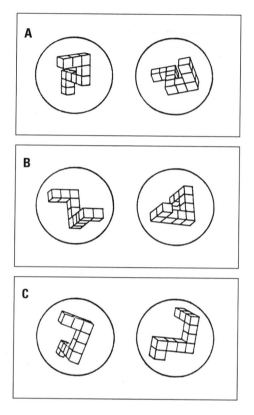

Participants had to judge whether the two stimuli shown in Panel A are the same as each other but viewed from different perspectives, and likewise for the pairs shown in B and C. Participants seem to make these judgments by imagining one of the forms rotating until its position matches that of the other form. (After Shepard & Metzler, 1971)

much rotation is needed. Figure 11.4 shows the data pattern, with response times clearly influenced by how far apart the two forms were in their initial orientations. Thus, once again, imagined "movement" resembles actual movement: The farther one has to imagine a form rotating, the longer the evaluation takes (Cooper & Shepard, 1973; Shepard & Metzler, 1971).

The mental rotation task can be used to answer a number of additional questions about imagery. For example, notice that the two forms in Figure 11.3A are identical except for a *picture-plane rotation*. In other words, if you were to cut out the left-hand drawing and spin it around (while leaving it flat on the table), you could align it with the drawing on the right. The relevant rotation, therefore, is a

FIGURE 11.4 **Data From a Mental Rotation Experiment**

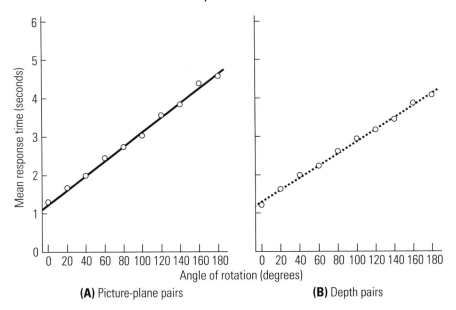

(A) Picture-plane pairs　　　　**(B)** Depth pairs

Panel A shows data from stimulus pairs requiring mental rotation in two dimensions, such that the imaged forms stay "within" the imagined picture plane. Panel B shows data from pairs requiring an imagined rotation in depth. The data are obviously similar, indicating that participants can imagine three-dimensional rotations as easily, and as swiftly, as they can imagine two-dimensional rotations. In both cases, the greater the degree of rotation required, the longer the response times. (After Shepard & Metzler, 1971)

rotation that leaves the pictures within the two-dimensional plane in which they are drawn. In contrast, the two forms shown in Figure 11.3B are identical except for a rotation in depth. No matter how you spin the picture on the left, it will not line up with the picture on the right. You can align these forms, but to do so you need to spin them around a vertical axis, in essence lifting them off the page.

People have no trouble with mental rotation in depth. They make very few errors (with accuracy levels around 95%), and the data resemble those obtained with picture-plane rotation. Figure 11.4A shows data from picture-plane rotation; Figure 11.4B shows data from pairs requiring depth rotation. In both cases, there is a clear relation between angle of rotation and response times, and the speed of rotation seems similar for both. Apparently, then, participants can represent three-dimensional forms in their images, and they can imagine these forms moving in depth. In some circumstances, therefore, visual images are not mental pictures; they are more like mental sculptures. (For a review, see Shepard & Cooper, 1982. For data on image scanning in three dimensions, see Pinker, 1980; and Pinker & Finke, 1980.)

Avoiding Concerns About Demand Character

Thus, in mental rotation, just as in mental scanning, distance relations seem to be preserved, and so the farther the imagined "travel," the longer it takes. We have interpreted these results as revealing the ways in which images represent spatial layout—with points that are more distant in the scene to be represented somehow farther apart in the image. But there is another way one might try to interpret the data: Participants in these studies obviously know that movement through the world takes time, and that moving a longer distance takes more time. Perhaps, therefore, the participants simply control the timing of their responses in order to re-create this "normal" pattern. On this view, the data shown in Figure 11.2 or 11.4 don't reveal any essential properties of mental imagery, and they don't, in particular, show that images "respect" spatial layout. Instead, these data show only that research participants can, if they wish, "simulate" in their responses the "proper" relationship between distance and time.

This proposal can be fleshed out in a variety of ways, but, to phrase things strongly, perhaps participants in these studies are not imagining rotations or scanning across an image at all. Instead, they might be thinking, "The experimenter just asked me to scan a long way, and I'd like to make it look like I'm obeying. I know that a long scan takes a long time, and so let me wait a moment before hitting the response button."

Why should participants act in this way? One reason is that participants in experiments usually want to be helpful, and that means that they do all they can to give the experimenter "good" data. As a result, they are very sensitive to the **demand character** of the experiment—that is, any cues that might signal how they are "supposed to" behave in that situation (Intons-Peterson, 1983, 1999; Intons-Peterson & White, 1981). A different possibility is that this sort of simulation is, in fact, what imagery is really all about. Perhaps, whenever someone tries to "imagine" something, they draw on their knowledge about how events in the world actually unfold, and then do their best to simulate the event. In this case, a longer scan or a greater rotation requires more time, not because there really is some "travel" involved, but because people know that these manipulations should take more time, and they do their best to simulate the process (Pylyshyn, 1981). Of course, this intention to simulate may well be unconscious, and likewise the knowledge. (The knowledge, in other words, may be "tacit knowledge"—knowledge the person doesn't even realize he has.) Nonetheless, the results would tell us about this knowledge-based simulation, and not any essential properties of imagery.

As it turns out, though, we can set aside these concerns, allowing us to maintain the claims that we've already sketched—namely, that the scanning and rotation data are as they are *because of how images represent spatial layout*. Several lines of evidence support this claim, including (crucially) the data we will turn to, later in the chapter, examining the neural bases for imagery. But, in addition, we can tackle directly the concern about demand character. In several studies, the experimenters have asked participants to make judgments about spatial layout but have taken care never to mention to participants that imagery was relevant to the task (e.g., Finke & Pinker, 1982). This should diminish the demand character of the procedure and should avoid any suggestion to participants that they should simulate some sort of "mental travel." Even without imagery instructions, though, the participants in these procedures spontaneously chose to form images and to scan across them, and their responses showed the standard pattern: longer response times observed with longer scans. Apparently, then, this result really does emerge whenever participants are using visual imagery—whether the result is encouraged by the experimenters' instructions or not.

Interactions Between Imagery and Perception

It seems, therefore, that there really are important correspondences between visual images and actual visual stimuli, and this leads to a question: If images are so much like pictures, then are the processes used to inspect images similar to those used to inspect stimuli? To put it more broadly, what is the relation between imaging and perceiving?

In a study by Segal and Fusella (1970, 1971), participants were asked to detect very faint signals—either dim visual stimuli or soft tones. On each trial, the participants' task was merely to indicate whether a signal had been presented or not. Participants did this in either of two conditions: either while forming a visual image before their "mind's eye," or while forming an auditory image before their "mind's ear." Thus we have a 2 × 2 design: two types of signals to be detected, and two types of imagery.

Let's hypothesize that there is some overlap between imaging and perceiving—that is, there are some mental structures, or mental processes, used by both activities. Therefore, if these processes or structures are occupied with imaging, they are not available for perceiving, and vice versa; and so we should expect competition if participants try to do both activities at once. That is exactly what Segal and Fusella observed: Their results, shown in Figure 11.5, indicate that forming a visual image interferes with seeing, and that forming an auditory image interferes with hearing (see also Farah & Smith, 1983).

Notice, though, that the Segal and Fusella participants were trying to visualize one thing while perceiving something altogether different. What happens if participants are trying to image a stimulus related to the one they are trying to perceive? Can visualizing a stimulus "pave the way" for perception? Farah (1985) had participants visualize a form (either an *H* or a *T*). A moment later, either an *H* or a *T* was actually presented, although at a very low contrast, making the letter difficult to perceive. Perception was facilitated if participants had just been visualizing the target form, and again, the effect was quite specific: Visualizing an *H* made it easier to perceive an *H*; visualizing a *T* made it easier to perceive a *T*. This result provides further confirmation of the claim that visualizing and perceiving draw on similar mechanisms, so that one of these activities can serve to prime the other. (For fur-

---

FIGURE 11.5 Can One Visualize and See at the Same Time?

	Percentage of detections			*Percentage of false alarms*	
	Visual signal	**Auditory signal**		**Visual signal**	**Auditory signal**
While visualizing	61%	67%	**While visualizing**	7.8%	3.7%
While maintaining an auditory image	63%	61%	**While maintaining an auditory image**	3.6%	6.7%

Participants were less successful in detecting a weak visual signal if they were simultaneously maintaining a visual image than if they were maintaining an auditory image. (The effect is small, but highly reliable.) The reverse is true with weak auditory signals: Participants were less successful in this detection if maintaining an auditory image than if visualizing. In addition, visual images often led to "false alarms" for participants trying to detect visual signals; auditory images led to false alarms for auditory signals. (After Segal & Fusella, 1970)

---

ther discussions, see Farah, 1989; and Heil, Rösler, & Hennighausen, 1993; also see McDermott & Roediger, 1994.)

Similar conclusions can be drawn from biological evidence. As we discussed in Chapter 2, we know a great deal about the specific brain structures required for vision; it turns out that many of the same structures are crucial for imagery. This can be documented in several ways, including the neuroimaging techniques that map the moment-by-moment pattern of activity in the brain. These techniques have revealed that visual perception relies heavily on tissue located in the occipital cortex (and so these brain areas are highly activated whenever someone is examining a visual stimulus). It turns out that activity levels are also high in these areas when participants are visualizing, confirming the claim that visual perception and visual imagery draw on similar structures in the brain (Behrmann, 2000; Farah, 1988; Isha & Sagi, 1995; Kosslyn, 1994; Miyashita, 1995; W. L. Thompson & Kosslyn, 2000).

More specifically, we mentioned in Chapter 2 that different areas of the occipital cortex are involved in different aspects of visual perception, and here, too, there are important parallels between the brain activity during perception and the activity during imagery. For example, Areas V1 and V2 in the visual cortex are involved in the earliest stages of visual perception, responding to the specific low-level features of the input. It is striking, therefore, that these same areas are particularly active whenever participants are maintaining high-resolution, detailed images, and, in fact, the amount of brain tissue showing activation increases as participants imagine larger and larger objects (Behrmann, 2000; Kosslyn & Thompson, 2003). In a similar fashion, Area MT/MST in the brain is highly sensitive to motion in ordinary visual perception, and it turns out that this same brain area is particularly activated when participants are asked to *imagine* movement patterns (Goebel, Khorram-Sefat, Muckli, Hacker, & Singer, 1998). Likewise, brain areas that are especially active during the perception of faces are also highly activated when people are *imagining* faces (O'Craven & Kanwisher, 2000).

As further evidence, consider studies of brain damage, usually damage resulting from stroke. We mentioned in Chapters 1, 2, and 3 that this damage can, in some cases, disrupt someone's ability to perceive; in Chapter 4, we saw that other forms of brain damage can disrupt the ability to pay attention to visual inputs. It turns out that these same forms of brain damage disrupt the ability to image, so that patients often have parallel gaps in their perception and their imagery: Patients who, because of a stroke, lose the ability to perceive color often seem to lose the ability to imagine scenes in color; patients who lose the ability to perceive fine detail seem also to lose the ability to visualize fine detail; and so on (Farah, 1988; Farah, Soso, & Dasheiff, 1992; Kosslyn, 1994; for some contrasting data, however, see Behrmann, 2000; Behrmann, Moscovitch, & Winocur, 1994; G. Goldenberg, Müllbacher, & Nowak, 1995; and Jankowiak, Kiinsbourne, Shalev, & Bachman, 1992).

In one remarkable case, a patient had suffered a stroke and, as a result, had developed the "neglect syndrome" we described in Chapter 4: If this patient was shown a picture, he seemed to see only the right side of it; if asked to read a word, he read only the right half. The same pattern of neglect was evident in the patient's imagery: In one test, the patient was urged to visualize a familiar plaza in his city and to list the buildings "in view" in the image. If the patient imagined himself standing at the southern edge of the plaza, he listed all the buildings on the plaza's west side, but none on the east. If the patient imagined himself standing on the northern edge of the plaza, he listed all the sights on the plaza's east side, but none on the west. In both cases, therefore, he neglected the right half of the imaged scene, just as he did with perceived scenes (Bisiach & Luzzatti, 1978; Bisiach, Luzzatti, & Perani, 1979).

Still more evidence comes from a technique called **transcranial magnetic stimulation** (TMS), which we encountered in Chapter 2. This technique creates a series of strong magnetic pulses at a specific location on the scalp; this causes a (temporary!) disruption in the brain region directly underneath this scalp area (Helmuth, 2001). In this fashion, it is possible to disrupt Area V1 temporarily in an otherwise normal brain; Area V1, recall, is the brain area where axons from the visual system first reach the cortex (see Chapter 2). Not surprisingly, using TMS in this way causes problems in vision, but it also causes parallel problems in visual imagery, providing a powerful argument that Area V1 is crucial both for the processing of visual information and for the creation and maintenance of visual images (Kosslyn et al., 1999).

Sensory Effects in Imagery

Clearly, the neural "machinery" needed for imagery overlaps with that needed for perception. If the machinery is occupied with one of these functions, it is not available for the other. If the machinery is disrupted (permanently, as by a stroke; or temporarily, as by TMS), then both activities are compromised. If we scrutinize activation patterns, we find that, to a large extent, the same brain structures are involved in visualizing and in vision. All of this indicates an intimate relationship between imagery and perception.

Against this backdrop, we would expect imagery and perception to share many traits, and research indicates that this is the case. This research, in other words, seems to indicate a **functional equivalence** between many aspects of visual imagery and aspects of visual perception—that is, a series of close parallels between how these two systems function.

For example, consider **visual acuity**—that is, the ability to see fine detail. In vision, acuity is much greater at the center of the visual field than it is in the visual periphery. Can we find a comparable pattern in imagery? Is it easier to discern detail at the image's center than at its periphery?

There are many ways to measure acuity, one of which is an assessment of "two-point acuity." In this test, observers are shown two dots. If the dots are 5 mm apart, can the observer see that there are two separate dots, or do the dots seem to fuse into one? How about a 4-mm separation? By determining the point at which the dots seem to fuse together, we can assess someone's ability to discern the small gap that actually separates the dots.

In vision, two-point acuity is greatest when people are looking directly at the dots; under these circumstances, even minuscule gaps can be detected. However, if we position the dots 10° away from someone's line of vision, acuity is far worse. What about imagery? In one study, participants were first shown two dots of the appropriate size. The dots were then removed, but participants were asked to imagine that the dots were still present. The participants then moved their eyes away from the imaged dots' position, and as they looked farther and farther away, they had to judge whether they could still "see" that the dots were separate. In this way, "two-point acuity" was measured with imaginary stimuli (Finke & Kosslyn, 1980).

The data show a remarkable correspondence between participants' performance with actually perceived dots and their performance with imagined dots. In both cases, acuity fell off abruptly if the dots were not in the center of vision, and indeed, the pattern of falloff was virtually the same in perception and in imagery. Moreover, in vision, acuity falls off more rapidly if participants look above or below the two dots, rather than to the left or right. This pattern was also observed in the imagery condition. Thus, qualitatively and quantitatively, the imagery data match the perceptual data.

Spatial Images and Visual Images

We are building an impressive case, therefore, for a close relationship between imagery and perception. Indeed, the evidence implies that we can truly speak of imagery as being *visual* imagery, drawing on the same mechanisms and having the same traits as actual vision. Other results, however, add some complications.

A number of studies have examined imagery in people blind since birth (Carpenter & Eisenberg, 1978; Kerr, 1983; Marmor & Zabeck, 1976; also see Jonides, Kahn, & Rozin, 1975; Paivio & Okovita, 1971; and Zimler & Keenan, 1983). Obviously the procedures need to be adapted in important ways—so that (for example) the stimuli to be imaged are presented initially as sculptures to be explored with the hands, rather than pictures to be examined visually. Once this is done, however, experimental procedures quite similar to those we have described can be carried out with the blind—procedures examining how the blind scan across an image, for example, or rotate one. And the data show what is by now a familiar pattern: In tests involving mental rotation or image scanning, blind individuals yield data quite similar to those obtained with sighted research participants—with response times proportionate to the "distance" traveled, and so on.

It seems unlikely that blind people are using visual imagery to perform these tasks. Therefore, they must have some other means of thinking about spatial layout and spatial relations. This "spatial imagery" might be represented in the mind in terms of a series of imagined movements, so that it is body imagery or motion imagery rather than visual imagery. (Reisberg & Logie, 1993, provide a discussion of motion-based imagery; also see Engelkamp, 1986, 1991; Logie, Engelkamp, Dehn, & Rudkin, 1999; and Saltz & Donnenwerth-Nolan, 1981.) Alternatively, perhaps spatial imagery is not tied to any sensory modality, but is part of our broader cognition about spatial arrangements and layout.

One way or another, though, it looks like we need to distinguish between *visual* and *spatial* imagery. Visual imagery represents spatial layout in terms of how things *look*. Spatial imagery, we have just suggested, can represent spatial layout in terms of *movements*, or *body feelings*, or perhaps in some more abstract format. Blind individuals presumably use spatial imagery to carry out the tasks we have been discussing in this chapter; it seems plausible that sighted people can use either visual or spatial imagery to carry out these tasks. (For a related, but somewhat different, distinction between *types* of imagery, see Kosslyn & Thompson, 1999, 2003; for other data, emphasizing the importance of the visual/spatial distinction, see Hegarty, 2004; and Klauer & Zhao, 2004.)

As further evidence for this distinction, consider the interference observed between imagery and vision. We have already noted that many studies have documented this interference: It is difficult to image one stimulus while looking at another. Other studies, though, have not shown this pattern (e.g., Baddeley & Lieberman, 1980; Logie & Marchetti, 1991; N. Morris, 1987; Quinn, 1988; Quinn & Ralston, 1986; Smyth & Pendleton, 1989). In these studies, there is *no* interference between imagery and simultaneous *visual* tasks (e.g., judging whether a light is bright or dim), but there *is* interference between imagery and *spatial/movement* tasks (moving your hand in a certain precisely defined way).

In short, then, the pattern of the interference data is mixed: Sometimes imagery is incompatible with simultaneous visual tasks, and this suggests that the imagery draws on the same resources as actual vision. But sometimes imagery is fully compatible with visual tasks, and is instead incompatible with simultaneous *spatial* tasks. The inevitable conclusion is that these experiments are revealing different types of imagery, and that one type is truly visual, while the other type is not.

A similar mix of results can be found in another domain: We have already noted the cases in which brain damage seems to produce similar patterns of disruption in seeing and imaging. Thus, patients who (because of brain damage) have lost their color vision also seem to lose the ability to imagine scenes in color; patients who have lost their ability to perceive motion also lose the ability to imagine movement. Results like these provide a powerful argument that the neural basis for vision overlaps heavily with that needed for imagining, and so damage to the relevant brain areas disrupts both activities. This obviously adds to the argument that the imagery is, in important ways, *visual*.

However, there are also exceptions to this pattern—cases in which brain damage causes problems in imagery but not perception, or vice versa. For example, Goldenberg et al., (1995) describe a patient whose bilateral occipital lobe lesions have produced blindness, but despite this profound visual deficit, the patient does well on many (but not all) mental imagery tasks. Similarly, a number of investigators have documented cases of patients who do well on imagery tasks despite severe visual agnosia (e.g., Bartolomeo et al., 1998; Behrmann, Moscovitch, & Winocur, 1994; Servos & Goodale, 1995).

Once again, these results seem to demand the conclusion that there are different types of imagery: Some types of imagery are truly visual, relying on parts of the brain devoted to vision, and so are disrupted when those brain areas are damaged. Other types of imagery, however, are not disrupted by this sort of brain damage and so, apparently, are not in any direct way visual.

The same points can also be made one more way: by looking at the sorts of imagery tasks that brain-damaged individuals can and cannot do. L.H. is a brain-damaged individual studied by Farah, Hammond, Levine, and Calvanio (1988). L.H.'s brain damage was the result of an automobile accident, but he recovered remarkably well. Even after his recovery, however, he continued to have trouble with a variety of visual tasks: In one test, the experimenter named a number of common objects (e.g., "football"), and L.H. had to report the color of each (for the football, "brown"). Control participants got 19 of 20 items correct; L.H. got only 10 correct. In another test, the experimenter named an animal (e.g., "kangaroo"), and L.H. had to indicate whether the animal had a long tail or a short one, relative to its body size. Again, control participants got 19 of 20 items correct on this test; L.H. got only 13 correct.

In contrast, L.H. does well in spatial tasks, including several of the tasks we have already described—image scanning, mental rotation, and the like. Thus, L.H. does poorly on tasks requiring judgments about visual appearance, or memory for visual appearance. He does quite well, however, on tasks requiring spatial manipulations, or memory for spatial positions. To make sense of L.H.'s profile, therefore, it seems once again crucial to distinguish between visual tasks and spatial ones and, correspondingly, between visual imagery and spatial imagery.

Individual Differences

Several lines of evidence, therefore, suggest that there are at least two types of imagery—one visual and one spatial. Visual imagery is disrupted by damage to brain areas needed for vision; spatial imagery is not. Visual imagery suffers interference from simultaneous visual (but not spatial) tasks; spatial imagery shows the opposite pattern. And spatial imagery is available to people who have been blind since birth, even though visual imagery is not.

It seems likely that both forms of imagery are available to sighted people, so that (for example) someone might do the image-scanning task by imagining what a speck would look like as it sped from the well to the grass hut, or they might do this task by imagining what it would feel like to move a pointer from the first of these landmarks to the second. The first of these approaches would presumably involve visual imagery; the second, spatial imagery.

All of this leads to a new question: When do people use one type of imagery, and when do they use the other? The answer has several parts. Some tasks surely require visual imagery rather than spatial. (Imagining colors, for example, is surely a visual task.) Other tasks may require spatial imagery rather than visual. Still other tasks (like image scanning) can go either way—that is, can be supported by imagery of either type. In this last sort of task, which form of imagery you use will depend on your preferences, aspects of the instructions, and (probably) a variety of other factors. The choice between these forms of imagery may also be influenced by each individual's ability levels. In essence, some people may be poor visualizers but good "spatializers"; these people would surely rely on spatial imagery, not visual, in most tasks. And, of course, for other people, this pattern would be reversed.

We need to be careful, though, in describing these individual differences. That's because people seem not to be "good visualizers" or "bad" *in general*, and likewise for "good spatializers" or "bad." Instead, each person has his or her own profile of strengths and weaknesses within these domains. Thus (for example) someone might be quite adept at scanning images, but less talented in, say, elaborating images. A person like this would therefore be quite skilled in imagery tasks that require a lot of scanning, but this person would look less able if the task demanded a lot of image elaboration. Likewise, someone might be good at image elaboration but poor at finding things in an image, and so this person would again look skilled in some imagery tasks but not others. And so on. (For discussion, see Kosslyn, Brunn, Cave, & Wallach, 1985.)

It would seem, therefore, that our analysis of imagery skill must be fairly fine-grained: Imagery tasks turn out to depend on a number of subskills, and someone can be good at some of these subskills but not others. Thus, rather than speaking of "good" and "bad" imagers in general, we need to be quite specific in describing which aspects of imagery a person can or cannot do well.

In addition, there is one more way in which individuals seem to differ in their imagery—namely, image vividness. Recall Galton's data, mentioned early on in this chapter. Some of Galton's participants described their imagery as rich and vivid—in short, very much like seeing. Others described their imagery as being relatively sparse, and not at all like vision. What should we make of these reports?

On the face of things, Galton's data suggest that people differ markedly in their conscious experience of imaging. People with vivid imagery report that their images truly are picturelike—usually in color, quite detailed, and with all of the depicted objects viewed from a particular distance and a particular viewing angle. People without vivid imagery, on the other hand, will say none of these things. Their images, they report, are not at all picturelike. It's meaningless to ask them, therefore, whether an image is in color or in black and white; their image simply isn't the sort of thing that could be in color or in black and white. Likewise, it's meaningless to ask whether their image is viewed from a particular perspective; their image is abstract in a way that makes this question inapplicable. In no sense, then, do these "nonimagers" feel like they are "seeing" with the "mind's eye." From their perspective, these figures of speech are (at best) loosely metaphorical. This stands in clear contrast to the reports offered by vivid imagers; for them, mental seeing really does seem like actual seeing.

Roughly 10% of the population will, in this fashion, "declare themselves entirely deficient in the power of seeing mental pictures" (Galton, 1883, p. 110). As William James (1890) put it, they "have no visual images at all worthy of the name" (p. 57). But what should we make of this? Is it truly the case that the various members of our species differ in whether or not they are capable of experiencing visual images?

To explore this issue, a number of studies have compared "vivid imagers" and "nonimagers" on tasks that depend on mental imagery, with the obvious prediction that people with vivid imagery will do better in these tasks, while those with sparse imagery will do worse. The results, however, have often been otherwise, with many studies finding no difference between vivid imagers and sparse imagers in how they do mental rotation, how quickly or accurately they scan across their images, or how effective their images are in supporting memory (e.g., Ernest, 1977; A. Katz, 1983; Marks, 1983; Richardson, 1980.)

There are several ways to read this data pattern. One possibility (as we suggested early in the chapter) is that these vividness reports do not reveal anything about the nature of imagery; instead, the reports reveal only how people *talk about* their imagery. On that basis, it is no surprise that there's little relationship between vividness reports and actual performance on imagery tasks.

A different (and more promising) interpretation of the data, though, builds on the distinction we have been discussing: When people describe their images as "vivid," they are, in essence, reporting how much their image experience is like seeing. The self-report, in other words, provides an assessment of *visual imagery*. Let's also propose (as seems likely) that there is little relationship between how good someone's visual imagery is, and how good that person's spatial imagery is. Thus people with vivid (visual) imagery might have excellent spatial imagery or poor; and the same is true for people with sparse (visual) imagery.

From this basis, we can make two predictions: First, there should be no relationship between image vividness and how well people perform on *spatial tasks*, such as tasks that require judgments about relative distance or position, or tasks that require manipulations like scanning or rotation or folding. That is because image vividness reflects *visual* imagery, and visual imagery, we've proposed, is unrelated to *spatial* performance.

Second, there *should* be a relationship between image vividness and how well people perform on *visual tasks*, tasks that hinge on close judgments about what something *looks like*.

Both of these predictions are correct. We've already mentioned the findings of no relationship between image vividness and tasks like image scanning or image rotation. In contrast, image vividness is related to tasks that require *visual* imagery. For example, consider the two-point acuity experiment already described. This experiment, at its heart, requires someone to imagine exactly *what something would look like*. Therefore, this task should be one performed more accurately by people with vivid mental imagery—and it is. People who describe their imagery as "vivid" yield data in this experiment in close correspondence to the perceptual data; people with less-vivid imagery do not show this correspondence (Finke & Kosslyn, 1980). Many other findings can be understood in similar terms (McKelvie, 1995).

All of this suggests that imagery self-reports are meaningful and do reveal genuine differences, from one person to the next, in the quality of their imagery experience. This in turn carries the fascinating implication that people may differ in the nature of their conscious experience, with at least some experiences (namely, vivid visual images) available to most, but not all, members of our species. This invites many questions: How do these differences in experience influence us? What can people "with imagery" do that people "without imagery" cannot? These points are not yet clear, although they are obviously a target for further research.

Images Are Not Pictures

At many points in this chapter, we have referred to mental images (especially *visual* images) as "mental pictures." That comparison is hardly new; the phrase was coined by Shakespeare four centuries ago and is embedded in the way most of us talk about our imagery. And, as we have seen, the comparison is in many ways appropriate: Images do seem to depict a scene in a fashion that seems quite pictorial. In other ways, though, this comparison may be misleading.

FIGURE 11.6 The Necker Cube

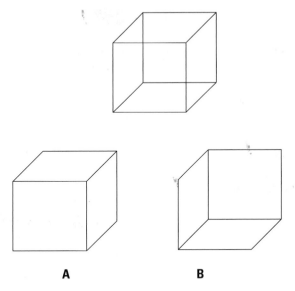

A   B

The cube shown at the top of this figure can be perceived as if viewed from above (in which case it is a transparent version of cube A) or as if viewed from below (i.e., a transparent version of Cube B).

To introduce this issue, let's review some points we first raised in Chapter 3, and with that, an example we first met in that chapter. The top of Figure 11.6 shows a figure known as the "Necker cube." The drawing of this cube—the stimulus itself—is ambiguous: It can be understood as a depiction of the (solid) cube shown as Cube A in the drawing, or it can be understood as a depiction of the cube shown as Cube B. The picture itself doesn't specify in any way whether it's Cube A or Cube B that's being shown, and so, in this sense, the picture is neutral with regard to interpretation, and fully compatible with either interpretation.

Unlike the picture, though, our *perception* of the cube is not neutral, is not indeterminate with regard to depth. Instead, at any moment in time, we perceive the cube either as similar to Cube A in the picture or as similar to Cube B. Our perception, in other words, "goes beyond the information given" by specifying a configuration in depth, a specification that, in this case, supplements an ambiguous drawing in order to create an unambiguous perception.

As we discussed in Chapter 3, the configuration in depth is just one of the ways that perception goes beyond the information given in a stimulus. Our perception of a stimulus also specifies a figure/ground organization, the form's orientation (e.g., identifying the form's "top"), and so on. These specifications serve to organize the form and have an enormous impact on the subjective appearance of the form, and with that, what the form is seen to resemble, and what the form will evoke in memory. (For more on these points, see Chapter 3.)

Let's be clear, then, that our **percepts** (our mental representations of the stimuli we are perceiving) are in some ways similar to pictures, but in other ways different. Like pictures, percepts are *depictions*, representing key aspects of the three-dimensional layout of the world. Percepts, in other words, are not descriptions of a stimulus; instead, percepts, just like pictures, show directly what a stimulus looks like. At the same time, though, percepts are also different from pictures: They are organized and unambiguous in a fashion that pictures are not.

It will be useful to have some terminology here. Let's refer to pictures as **neutral depictions**—showing what something looks like, but in a fashion that is neutral with regard to the various specifications we have mentioned. Let's refer to percepts as **organized depictions**—again showing what something looks like, but in a fashion that specifies how the form is organized. Finally, let's refer to the various specifications, organizing the form, as a **perceptual reference frame**, and so the difference between a neutral depiction and an organized one is that the latter is understood within a perceptual reference frame, but the former is not. (The "reference frame" terminology is adapted from Peterson, Kihlstrom, Rose, & Glisky, 1992.)

We're now ready (at last) to ask about mental images. Are they neutral depictions, the way pictures are, and so open to many different interpretations? Or are they organized depictions, the way percepts seem to be, and so, in a sense, already interpreted, already organized? One line of evidence comes from studies of ambiguous figures: In a study by D. Chambers and Reisberg (1985), participants were first shown a series of practice stimuli, to make sure that they understood what was meant by an ambiguous figure and could reinterpret these figures. They were then briefly shown a drawing of one more ambiguous figure (such as the Necker cube in Figure 11.6 or the duck/rabbit in Figure 11.7); and then, after this figure had been removed from view, they were asked to form a mental image of it. Once the image was formed, they were asked if they could reinterpret this image, just as they had reinterpreted the practice figures.

The results are easily summarized: Across several experiments, not one of the participants succeeded in reinterpreting his or her images: They reliably failed to find the duck in a "rabbit image" or the rabbit in a "duck image." Is it possible that they did not understand their task, or perhaps did not remember the figure? To rule out these possibilities, participants were given a blank piece of paper immediately after their failure at reinterpreting their images, and they were asked to draw the figure based on their image. Now, looking at their own drawings, all of the participants were able to reinterpret the configuration in the appropriate way. Thus, we have 100% failure in reinterpreting these forms with images, and 100% success, a moment later, with drawings.

Apparently, therefore, what participants "see" in their image is not a "picture"—neutral with regard to interpretation, and so open to new interpretations. Instead, images are inherently organized, just as percepts are; they are organized depictions,

FIGURE 11.7 The Duck/Rabbit

This figure can be perceived either as a duck or as a rabbit. With the picture in view, people readily find both interpretations of the figure. If people are imaging the figure, however, they have great difficulty finding a different interpretation. That is, people imaging the "duck" have great difficulty in discovering the "rabbit"; people imaging the "rabbit" have great difficulty in discovering the "duck."

not neutral ones. As such, images are entirely unambiguous, and strongly resistant to reinterpretation.

Learning From Images

In some ways, the results just cited are puzzling. The Chambers and Reisberg participants universally failed to make a simple discovery from an image, but we know from other evidence that discoveries from imagery are possible. After all, common experience tells us that mental images often surprise us or remind us of something. We routinely consult our images in solving problems or in making decisions. Indeed, the history of science is filled with examples of discoveries apparently inspired by an image (see, for example, A. Miller, 1986). Many laboratory studies have also shown that people can invent new forms, or new devices, by inspecting and manipulating their images (Anderson & Helstrup, 1993; Finke, 1990; Finke & Slayton, 1988; Pinker & Finke, 1980; also see Chapter 14). How should we think about this overall pattern? Why are discoveries from imagery sometimes possible and sometimes not?

We have just suggested that images (like percepts) are *organized* depictions, and so exist only within the context of a perceptual reference frame. Thus, we can think of the image as a *package* that includes both the depiction itself *and* the reference frame. If, therefore, someone is inspecting an image, seeking a discovery, it's this package that they are inspecting, and so the discoveries must be discoveries about this package. On this basis, the nature of the discoveries will be guided by both the depiction *and* the reference frame.

This implies, then, that discoveries about an image will be easy if those discoveries are compatible with both the depiction and the reference frame. Such discoveries will be relatively frequent, with no need for special hints or instructions. In contrast, discoveries about an image will be difficult if the discovery is compatible with the depiction but not with the reference frame. In that case, the discovery is compatible with only part of the "package" that is the image and, specifically, will require a *change* in the reference frame. These discoveries will be rare and will benefit enormously from hints. (An early version of this hypothesis was offered by Reisberg & Chambers, 1991; related ideas have been offered by M. Peterson et al., 1992; Verstijnen, Hennessey, van Leeuwen, Hamel, & Goldschmidt, 1998; and Verstijnen, van Leeuwen, Goldschmidt, Hamel, & Hennessey, 1998.)

To make this concrete, let's say that someone initially perceives Figure 11.7 as a rabbit, but then discovers that the form can also be seen as a child with her hair tied in pigtails. This discovery requires no change in the person's understanding of the form's basic shape (where its top is, where its front is, and so on), and therefore is compatible with both the depiction and its reference frame. According to our hypothesis, then, this discovery will be one that happens easily and often. And, in fact, it is (M. Peterson et al., 1992).

In contrast, let's say that someone initially perceives Figure 11.7 as a rabbit, but then manages to discover that the form can also be seen as a duck. This does involve a change in the person's organization of the form, including where the form's front is, and also the relationships among the form's parts. This discovery, therefore, is compatible with the depiction but does require a reference-frame change; that is, it does require the person to jettison one organization of the form and replace it with another. According to our hypothesis, this sort of discovery should be rare and dependent on hints, and, as we have seen, it is (D. Chambers & Reisberg, 1985; Peterson et al., 1992).

Further evidence comes from a study by Reisberg and Chambers (1991) in which participants were asked to memorize a series of "nonsense shapes." The tenth shape in the series, presented with no special notice, was the one depicted in Figure 11.8. Participants had 5 seconds in which to memorize this shape, and then the picture was removed. Participants were next asked to form an image of the shape, and then to imagine the shape rotated 90° clockwise. At this point the participants were told that the shape "resembles a familiar geographic form" and were asked to identify that form.

It seems likely that participants in this procedure understood the side topmost in the original drawing as being the shape's top. This understanding probably did not change when the participants imagined the rotation. In other words, when participants imagined the rotation, they rotated both the form and its reference frame. As a consequence, the participants were, in this experiment, imaging the correct geometry for Texas (in other words, they had the right depiction), but with the wrong understanding, specifying the wrong top. Therefore, discovering Texas in this image requires a reference-frame change—a shift in how the form is understood. As a result, we should predict that participants will not make this discovery. This is correct: Exactly zero participants were able to discover Texas in their image.

| FIGURE 11.8 | Limitations on Learning From Imagery |

Participants imaged this form, thinking of it merely as an abstract shape. When asked to imagine the form rotated by 90° clockwise, they failed to discover the familiar shape of Texas. Their understanding of the imaged form (and, in particular, their understanding of the form's "top") prevented them from recognizing the Lone Star State. When participants were explicitly instructed to change this understanding, however, many were able to discover Texas.

In a subsequent experiment, participants were led through the same procedure, but this time they were explicitly instructed in how to change their understanding of the imaged form. That is, they were told directly to think of the form's left edge as being the top. With this instruction, many participants were able to discover Texas in the image. Apparently, then, the obstacle to discovery is indeed how participants understand the image. When this understanding changes, there is a corresponding change in performance.

All of these results obviously fit with the claim that images are inherently understood in a certain way—a way that specifies, for example, which side of the form is the top, which side is the front, and so forth. This understanding then sets boundaries on what can be discovered about the image, so that (as we've seen) discoveries compatible with the imager's understanding of the form flow easily from the image, while discoveries incompatible with the understanding are rare.

Of course, imagers do have the option of changing how they understand the form. For example, we have just discussed a case in which participants, with explicit instruction, changed their assignment of the image's top. And once these changes occur, they have powerful effects: When the imager's understanding of the form changes, a range of new discoveries, compatible with the new understanding, become available. Evidence suggests, however, that these changes in reference frame are surprisingly difficult and often dependent on specific instructions, or specific training examples. Therefore, one's initial understanding of the form has a strong effect on what can be discovered from an image. (For further discussion, see Chapter 14; also Reisberg, 1996.)

Images and Pictures: An Interim Summary

Images, both visual and spatial, provide a distinctive means of representing the world, so that imagining a robot (for example) is quite different from thinking about the word "robot" or describing a robot to yourself, or merely contemplating the idea "robot." As one distinctive attribute, images truly seem to show what a form looks like, allowing judgments of what the form (perceptually) resembles. Other forms of representation do not have this trait. In this and other regards, therefore, images (both visual and spatial) are indeed picturelike.

At the same time, we have also highlighted ways in which images are *not* picturelike and, correspondingly, ways in which the processes of imagery are distinct from those of perception. As we have seen, images are inherently organized in a fashion that pictures are not. This is evident in the difficulty in reinterpreting images; it is also reflected in the pattern of discoveries that do or do not flow easily from an image. Results like these make it clear that images are understood within a perceptual reference frame and so, in this regard, contain more information than the corresponding picture.

As further illustration of this point, consider two pictures: One picture shows three rows of dots, with four dots in each row. The second picture shows four columns of dots, with three dots in each column. Needless to say, these two pictures would be identical. The corresponding images, though, turn out not to be identical. Research participants take longer, for example, to generate the second image, presumably because it contains a larger number of "units"—four columns, rather than three rows (Kosslyn, 1983). So here, too, we have an example of an image more specific than a picture: A picture such as Figure 11.9 contains no indication of whether

| FIGURE 11.9 | Columns or Rows

This picture shows "three rows of dots." The same picture also shows "four columns of dots." There is, in short, no difference between a picture of rows and a picture of columns. There is a difference, however, between a mental image of "three rows of dots" and a mental image of "four columns." The latter image, for example, takes longer to generate and is more difficult to maintain, presumably because it contains a larger number of units—four columns, rather than three rows.

we are looking at three rows of dots or four columns. A mental image of Figure 11.9, though, does specify this information.

Where does all this leave us? Images are plainly different from pictures in important ways. However, this cannot distract us from how much images have in common with pictures and, likewise, the enormous overlap between imagery and perception. In short, images share crucial properties with pictures, and so they are, in many ways, picturelike. Nonetheless, images are not pictures.

Long-Term Visual Memory

So far, our discussion has focused on "active" images—images currently being contemplated, images presumably held in working memory. What about visual information in long-term memory? For example, if you wish to form an image of an elephant, you need to draw on your knowledge of what an elephant looks like. What is this knowledge, and how is it represented in long-term storage? Likewise, if you recognize a picture as familiar, this is probably because you've detected a "match" between it and some memory of an earlier-viewed picture. What is the nature of this memory?

Image Information in Long-Term Memory

In Chapter 8, we suggested that your concept of "birthday" (for example) is represented by some number of nodes in long-term memory. When you think about birthdays, those nodes are activated; and conversely, when those nodes are activated, you are thinking about birthdays. Perhaps we can adapt this proposal to account for long-term storage of visual information (and likewise information for the other sensory modalities).

One possibility is that nodes in long-term memory can represent entire, relatively complete pictures. Thus, to think about a mental image of an elephant, you would activate the ELEPHANT PICTURE nodes; to scrutinize an image of your father's face, you would activate the FATHER'S FACE nodes; and so on.

However, evidence speaks against this idea. Research by Kosslyn (1980, 1983) suggests instead that mental images are stored in memory in a piecemeal fashion. To form an image, therefore, one first activates the nodes specifying the "image frame," which depicts the form's global shape. Then elaborations can be added to this frame, as the imager wishes, to create a full and detailed image.

Many results support this claim. For one, we know that images containing more parts take longer to create, just as we would expect if images are formed on a piece-by-piece basis (as with Figure 11.9). Second, we know that images containing more detail take longer to create, in accord with our hypothesis. Third, we also know that imagers have some degree of control over how complete and detailed their images will be, so that (depending on the task, the imagers' preferences, and so on) images can be quite sketchy or quite elaborate (Reisberg, 1996). This variation is easily explained if imagers first create an image frame and only then add as much detail as they want. (For further discussion of this issue, and also for an evaluation of some alternative views of image completeness, see D. Chambers & Reisberg, 1992.)

But how does the imager know *how to* construct the image—what its form should be and what it should include? The relevant information is drawn from **image files** in long-term memory. Each file contains the information you need in order to create a mental image—information about how to create the image frame, and then information about how to elaborate the frame in this way or that, if desired. How is this information represented within the image file? One proposal is that the image files contain something like a set of instructions, or even a "recipe," for creating an image. By analogy, someone could instruct you in how to create a picture by uttering the appropriate sentences: "In the top left, place a circle. Underneath it, draw a line, angling down . . . ." Such instructions would allow you to create a picture, but notice that there is nothing pictorial about the instructions themselves; the instructions are sentences, not pictures. In the same way, the instructions within an image file allow you to create a representation that, as we have already seen, is picturelike in important ways. In long-term memory, however, this information may not be at all picturelike.

Verbal Coding of Visual Materials

The proposal before us, therefore, is that visual information is represented in long-term memory in a fashion that isn't itself "visual." Instead, visual information can be represented via propositions, with these providing a "recipe" to be used, when needed, for creating an image.

In some cases, though, visual information can be represented in long-term storage by means of an even simpler format—namely, a verbal label. For example, consider memory for color. It is appreciably easier to remember a color if one has a label for it, so that individuals with large color vocabularies have better color memories. This leads to striking contrasts if we gather data in different cultures, capitalizing on the fact that some languages have many words for describing and categorizing colors, while other languages have only a few. It turns out that color memory is superior in those cultures with a greater number of color terms (R. Brown & Lenneberg, 1954; Rosch, 1977b). This is because, in many cases, people are remembering a verbal description for the stimuli, rather than the colors themselves. (For more on the influence of color labels on color memory and color perception, see Chapter 10.)

A related point was made by Carmichael, Hogan, and Walters (1932). Their research participants were shown pictures like those in the center column of Figure 11.10. Half of the participants were shown the top form and told, "This is a picture of eyeglasses." The other half were told, "This is a picture of a barbell." The participants were later required to reproduce, as carefully as they could, the pictures they had seen. Those who had understood the picture as spectacles produced drawings

FIGURE 11.10   The Influence of Verbal Labels on Visual Memory

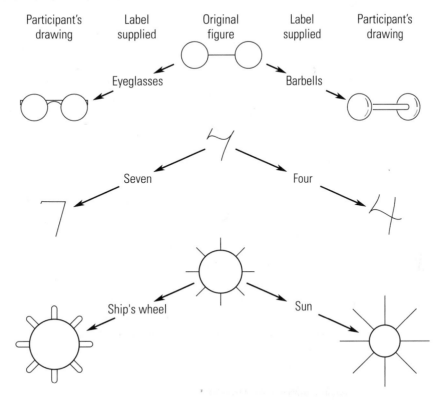

Participants were shown the figures in the middle column. If the top figure was presented with the label "eyeglasses," participants were later likely to reproduce the figure as shown on the left. If the figure was presented with the label "barbells," they were likely to reproduce it as shown on the right. (And so on for the other figures.) One interpretation of these data is that participants were remembering the verbal label and not the drawing itself and then, at the time of test, reconstructed what the drawing must have been based on the remembered label.

that resembled spectacles; those who understood the picture as weights distorted their drawings appropriately. This is again what one would expect if the participants had memorized the description, rather than the picture itself, and were re-creating the picture on the basis of this description.

It seems, then, that in some cases visual information may be stored in memory not via imagery, but as a description of the previously viewed object. Moreover, this is a helpful strategy: Memory is improved when an appropriate label, or appropriate description, is available. (This is certainly true in the color-memory studies.) However, this strategy can backfire: People may end up recalling a picture in a fashion that is distorted by their understanding of it, or perhaps selective in ways that their description was selective. This phenomenon obviously resembles the schema effects described in Chapter 7.

A similar message emerges from tasks that require participants to reason about spatial position. In one study, participants were asked, "Which is farther north: Seattle or Montreal? Which is farther west: Reno, Nevada; or San Diego, California?" Many participants responded that Montreal is farther north, and that San Diego is farther west, but both of these responses are wrong. Montreal, for example, is at roughly the same latitude as Portland, Oregon, a city almost 200 miles south of Seattle (Stevens & Coupe, 1978).

This error arises because participants seem to be reasoning this way: Montreal is in Canada; Seattle is in the United States. Canada is north of the United States. Therefore, Montreal must be farther north than Seattle. This kind of reasoning is sensible, since it will often bring you to the correct answer. (That's because most parts of Canada are, in fact, farther north than most parts of the United States.) Even so, this reasoning will sometimes lead to error, and it does so in this case. (The logic is obviously the same for the Reno/San Diego question.)

Of course, what is of interest here is not the participants' knowledge about the longitude and latitude of these particular cities. What is important is that the sort of reasoning revealed in these studies hinges on propositional knowledge, and not on any sort of mental images or maps. Apparently, then, at least some of our spatial knowledge relies on a symbolic/propositional code. (For more on reasoning about geography, see Friedman & Brown, 2000a, 2000b.)

Imagery Helps Memory

We have so far been concerned with how visual information is represented in long-term memory. No matter how images are stored, however, it is also clear that images influence long-term memory in important ways and, in general, imagery *improves* memory.

For example, materials that evoke imagery are considerably easier to remember than materials that do not evoke imagery. This can be demonstrated in many ways, including the following two-step procedure: First, participants are presented with a list of nouns and asked to rate each noun, on a scale from 1 to 7, for how readily it evokes an image (Paivio, 1969; Paivio, Yuille, & Madigan, 1968). Examples of words receiving high ratings are "church," with an average rating of 6.63; or "elephant," rated at 6.83. Words receiving lower ratings include "context" (2.13) and "virtue" (3.33).

As a second step, we ask whether these imagery ratings, generated by one group of participants, can be used to predict memory performance with a new group of participants. The new participants are asked to memorize lists of words, using the words for which we have imagery ratings. The data reliably indicate that participants learn high-imagery words more readily than low-imagery words (Paivio, 1969; Paivio, Smythe, & Yuille, 1968).

In the same fashion, memory can be enormously aided by the use of imagery mnemonics. In one study, some participants were asked to learn pairs of words by rehearsing each pair silently. Other participants were instructed to make up a sentence for each pair of words, linking the words in some sensible way. Finally, other participants were told to form a mental image for each pair of words, with the image combining the words in some interaction. The results showed poorest recall performance by the rehearsal group, and intermediate performance by the group that generated the sentences. Both of these groups, though, did appreciably worse than the imagery group (G. H. Bower & Winzenz, 1970; for discussion of other mnemonic techniques, see Chapter 5).

If forming images helps memory, does it matter *what sort of image* one creates? Quite reliably, memory is best if the images one forms show the objects to be remembered interacting in some way, and not just side by side (Wollen, Weber, & Lowry, 1972). This is unsurprising: As we saw in Chapter 5, memory is improved in general if one can find ways to organize the material; interacting images provide one means of achieving this organization.

In addition, it's sometimes suggested that imagery mnemonics are most effective if the mental "picture" is in some fashion *bizarre*, rather than just showing some ordinary interaction. Evidence for this point, however, is mixed, with some studies showing an effect of bizarreness, and some studies showing the opposite. The explanation for this mixed pattern probably lies in the *sequence* of stimuli employed in these studies. If participants see only a succession of bizarre images, one after another, they cease thinking of the images as bizarre, and so bizarreness has no impact on the data. If, instead, the bizarre images are mixed together with more-common images, the bizarreness is noticed and contemplated, leading to a memory improvement. (For reviews, see Einstein, McDaniel, & Lackey, 1989; and McDaniel & Einstein, 1986, 1990.)

Dual Coding

There's no question, then, that imagery improves memory. But why is this? What memory aid does imagery provide?

One proposal is that imageable materials, such as high-imagery words, will be doubly represented in memory: The word itself will be remembered, and so will the corresponding picture. This pattern is referred to as **dual coding**, and the advantage of this should be obvious: When the time comes to retrieve these memories, either record, the verbal or the image, will provide the information you seek. This gives you a double chance of locating the information you need, thereby easing the process of memory search. Imagery mnemonics work in the same way, by encouraging people to lay down two different memory records—a propositional record of the material, plus an image—rather than one.

Of course, framing things in this way implies that we have at least two different types of memory in long-term storage: memories that are symbolic (and perhaps verbal), and memories that are imagery-based. Paivio (1971), the source of the dual-coding proposal, argued that these two types of memory differ from each other in important ways—including the information that they contain, and also the ways they are accessed. Access to symbolic memories, he suggested, would be easiest if the cue provided were a word, as in, "Do you know the word 'squirrel'?" Access to an image-based memory, in contrast, would be easiest if one began with a picture: "Do you recognize this pictured creature?" Moreover, Paivio argued, some types of information—for example, semantic associations—are more easily stored via symbolic memories. Other types of information, such as information about size or shape, are more readily accessed from the remembered images. (Also see Paivio & Csapo, 1969; and Yuille, 1983.)

Memory for Pictures

Paivio (1971) also proposed that there are two separate memory systems: one containing the symbolic memories, the other containing images. However, many psychologists would reject this claim, arguing instead that there is just a single, vast, long-term memory, capable of holding diverse contents. Within this single memory, each type of content would have its own traits, its own pattern of functioning. Nonetheless, there would still be one unified memory system, with images and verbal memories fully and intimately interwoven. (For discussion of this point, see Heil, Rösler, & Hennighausen, 1994.)

To put this differently, images and verbal memories may well be distinct from each other in how they are accessed, and also the types of information they contain. Even so, these two types of memory also have a great deal in common, reflecting the fact that both types of memory reside within a single memory system. Thus, many of the claims we made in Chapters 5, 6, and 7 apply with equal force to visual memories and verbal memories: Recall of both memory types, for example, is dependent on memory connections; priming effects can be observed with both types of memory; encoding specificity is observed in both domains; and so on.

As an illustration of this broad point, consider memory for pictures. In many ways, the principles governing picture memory are the same as the principles governing memory for other materials. For example, recall our discussion of schema effects in Chapter 7. There we argued that participants' memories are clearly influenced by generic knowledge—knowledge about how events unfold in general. In support of this claim, Chapter 7 relied largely on evidence for verbal memories, such as memory for sentences and stories. Similar effects, though, can easily be demonstrated with pictures.

In one study, Friedman (1979) showed participants pictures of scenes such as a typical kitchen or a typical barnyard. In addition, the pictures also contained some unexpected objects. The kitchen picture, for example, included a stove and a toaster, but also included items less often found in a kitchen, such as a fireplace. Participants were later given a recognition test, in which they had to discriminate between pictures they had actually seen and altered versions of these pictures, in which something had been changed.

In some of the test pictures, one of the familiar objects in the scene had been changed. For example, participants might be shown a test picture in which a different kind of stove appeared in place of the original stove, or one in which the toaster on the counter was replaced by a radio. Participants rarely noticed these changes, and so they tended (incorrectly) to respond "old" in these cases. This is sensible on schema grounds: Both the original and altered pictures were fully consistent with the kitchen schema, and so both would be compatible with a schema-based memory.

On the other hand, participants almost always noticed changes to the unexpected objects in the scene. If the originally viewed kitchen had a fireplace and the test picture did not, participants consistently detected this alteration. Again, this is predictable on schema grounds: The fireplace did not fit with the kitchen schema and so was likely to be specifically noted in memory. In fact, Friedman recorded participants' eye movements during the original presentations of the pictures. Her data showed that participants tended to look twice as long at the unexpected objects as they did at the expected ones; clearly these objects did catch the participants' attention. (For more on schema guidance of eye movements, see Henderson & Hollingworth, 2003; and Henderson, Weeks, & Hollingworth, 1999.)

In essence, then, what Friedman's participants seemed to remember was that they had seen something we might label "kitchen plus a fireplace"—a description that both identifies the relevant schema and also notes what was special about this particular instance of the schema. If recognition memory is tested with a kitchen without a fireplace, participants spot this discrepancy easily, because this picture does not fit with the remembered description. If tested with a kitchen plus or minus a toaster, this picture still fits with the "kitchen plus a fireplace" description, and so the alteration is likely not to be noticed. (See also Pezdek, Whetstone, Reynolds, Askari, & Dougherty, 1989.)

A different line of evidence also shows schema effects in picture memory: Recall our claim that, in understanding a story, people place the story within a schematic frame. As we have seen, this can often lead to intrusion errors, as people import their own expectations and understanding into the story, and so end up remembering the story as including more than it actually did.

A similar phenomenon can be demonstrated with picture memory: Intraub and her collaborators have documented a consistent pattern of **boundary extension** in picture memory (Intraub, Bender, & Mangels, 1992; Intraub & Bodamer, 1993; Intraub, Gottesman, & Bills 1998; Intraub & Richardson, 1989). That is, people remember a picture as including more than it actually did, in effect extending the boundaries of the remembered depiction. For example, participants shown the top panel in Figure 11.11 were later asked to sketch what they had seen. Two of the participants' drawings are shown at the bottom of Figure 11.11, and the boundary extension is clear: Participants remember the scene as less of a close-up view than it actually was, and correspondingly, they remember the scene as containing more of

FIGURE 11.11   Boundary Extension in Picture Memory

Participants were initially shown the photograph at the top of this figure. The two panels below show the scene as drawn from memory by two different participants. The participants clearly recalled the scene as a wide-angle shot, revealing more of the background than it actually did. (After Intraub & Richardson, 1989)

the backdrop than it actually did. This effect is observed whether participants initially see a few pictures or many, whether they are tested immediately or after a delay, and even when participants are explicitly warned about boundary extension and urged to avoid this effect.

Intraub has argued that this boundary extension arises from the way in which people perceive these pictures in the first place. In essence, people understand a picture by means of a perceptual schema (Hochberg, 1978, 1986). This schema places the picture in a larger context, informing the perceiver about the real-world scene only partially revealed by the picture. This leads to a series of expectations about what people would see if they could somehow look beyond the photograph's edges. All of this influences memory, as the memory interweaves what people saw with what they expected, or what they knew they might see if they explored further. In important ways, this effect resembles the intrusion errors, produced by knowledge schemata, observed with verbal memory.

Overall, then, it does look like picture memory follows the same rules, and is influenced by the same factors, as memory for verbal materials. Schema effects, for example, can be found in both domains, with people showing better memory for the schema itself than for details of the particular stimulus. Intrusion errors can be documented in both domains. Similarly, participants show primacy and recency effects when they learn a series of pictures (Tabachnick & Brotsky, 1976), just as they do when they learn a series of words (Chapter 5). Phenomena such as spread of activation and priming can be demonstrated with nonverbal materials (Kroll & Potter, 1984), just as they can be demonstrated with verbal materials (Chapter 8). In short, picture memory is distinct from other sorts of memory, but there is also enough commonality to sustain our suggestion of a single memory system, with diverse contents but with a uniform set of operating principles.

The Diversity of Knowledge

Notice, then, where the data are leading us: There can be no question that *active images*, held in working memory, are different from other mental contents. Active images contain different information than other representations do; they make different information prominent; they require a set of operations (like scanning, or rotation, or zooming) that are just irrelevant to other sorts of memory contents. For materials in working memory, therefore, we really do need different types of theory to describe images and other forms of mental representation.

The situation is completely different, however, when we turn to long-term memory and consider our long-term retention for what an elephant looks like, or our recollection of what an earlier-viewed picture contained. The *content* of these memories is different from, say, our memory for stories. But even so, the image-based memories seem to be stored in the same memory system as every other memory—and so are influenced by exactly the same principles.

In support of this claim, we can find many commonalities in the ways people remember diverse types of knowledge. Thus, memory for pictures, as we have just seen, shows primacy and recency effects, just as memory for word lists does. Likewise, memory for faces benefits from rehearsal (Sporer, 1988), just as memory for stories does. Similarly, a separation between *familiarity* and *source memory* (see Chapter 6) can be demonstrated as easily for remembered music or remembered faces (Brigham & Cairns, 1988; Brown, Deffenbacher, & Sturgill, 1977) as it can be for remembered words. And across all of these domains, schema effects are observed, in which memories for specific cases become entangled with more-generic knowledge. Across domains, priming effects are observed. And so on.

It would appear, therefore, that there really is just one long-term memory, with a set of rules consistently applicable to all its diverse contents. However, we must attach some reservations to this claim. In this chapter, we have focused entirely on visual memories, and one might well ask whether similar conclusions would emerge with other categories of knowledge. For example, do memories for tastes or smells benefit from rehearsal, show schema effects, and the like? Do memories for emotions, or for pain, benefit from deep processing? Do they show the effects we called (in Chapter 6) "implicit memory" effects? Little research speaks to these issues.

It is on this basis, then, that the claims about the singularity of long-term memory must remain tentative, and that is one of the reasons why, as we said at the very start, our agenda in this chapter has been both methodological and substantive. We have tried to show by example what it means to explore the idea that a certain content is distinctive in working memory, and also what it would mean to propose a separate system within long-term memory. We have also seen how things stand on these issues with regard to visual materials. However, the field awaits additional data before these issues can be resolved for other modalities.

Chapter Summary

1. People differ enormously in how they describe their imagery experience, particularly the vividness of that experience. However, these self-reports are difficult to interpret, and this ambiguity has led investigators to seek more objective means of studying mental imagery.

2. Chronometric studies indicate that the pattern of what information is more available and what is less available in an image closely matches the pattern of what is available in an actual picture. Likewise, the times needed to scan across an image, or to zoom in on an image to examine detail, or to imagine the image rotating, all correspond closely to the times needed for these operations with actual pictures. These results emerge even when the experimenter makes no mention of imagery, ruling out an account of these data in terms of the demand character of the experiments.

3. In many settings, visual imagery seems to involve mechanisms that overlap with those used for visual perception. This is reflected in the fact that imaging one thing can make it difficult to perceive something else, or that imaging the appropriate target can prime a subsequent perception. Visual images also show sensory effects similar to those observed in vision. Further evidence comes from neuroimaging and studies of brain damage; this evidence confirms the considerable overlap between the biological basis for imagery and that for perception.

4. Not all imagery, however, is visual. In some cases, imagery is disrupted by simultaneous spatial activities, and not by visual activity. This suggests that we may need to distinguish between visual and spatial imagery. This proposal is confirmed by studies of individuals with brain damage, some of whom seem to lose the capacity for visual imagery but retain their capacity for spatial imagery. This proposal may also help us understand the pattern of individual differences in imagery ability, with some individuals particularly skilled in visual imagery, and some in spatial.

5. Even when imagery is visual, mental images are picture*like*, and not actually pictures. Unlike pictures, mental images seem to be accompanied by a perceptual reference frame, which guides the interpretation of the image and also influences what can be discovered about the image. Discoveries flow easily from an image if the discoveries are compatible with the imaged geometry and its reference frame; discoveries are much more difficult if the sought-after form is compatible with the imaged geometry but not the reference frame.

6. To create a mental image, one draws on information stored in an image file in long-term memory. These image files can be thought of as recipes for the construction of a mental image, usually by first constructing a frame and then by elaborating the frame as needed. In addition, at least some information about visual appearance or spatial arrangement is stored in long-term memory in terms of verbal labels or conceptual frameworks. For example, information about the locations of cities may be stored in terms of propositions ("Montreal is in Canada; Canada is north of the United States") rather than being stored in some sort of mental map.

7. Imagery helps people to remember, and so word lists are more readily recalled if the words are easily imaged; similarly, instructions to form images help people to memorize. These benefits may be the result of dual coding: storing information in both a verbal format and a format that encodes appearances; this approach doubles the chances of recalling the material later on. When you're trying to remember combinations of ideas, it is best to imagine the objects to be remembered interacting in some way. There has been some dispute over whether bizarre images are more easily remembered than ordinary images, and evidence suggests that bizarre images will have an advantage only if the other images to be remembered are not bizarre.

8. Memory for pictures can be accurate, but it follows most of the same rules as any other form of memory; for example, it is influenced by schematic knowledge.

9. It is unclear what other categories of memory there may be. In each case, other kinds of memory are likely to have some properties that are distinctive and also many properties that are shared with memories of other sorts.

PART FIVE

THINKING

THROUGHOUT OUR LIVES, we draw conclusions based on things we have observed. We solve problems, figuring out ways to reach our goals. And we make decisions, choosing paths of action that (we hope) will lead us toward those goals.

In this section, we can consider all of these achievements. We'll compare the ways people *do* think with the ways that scholars suggest they *should* think. In this comparison, we'll find that human reasoning and judgment are often excellent, but we will encounter numerous examples of bad judgment, improper reasoning, and highly inefficient problem-solving.

How should we understand these intellectual shortcomings? One suggestion will be a recurrent theme in this section, and indeed it has been a recurrent theme throughout the book: In case after case, we have seen that humans rely on cognitive shortcuts—strategies that are reasonably efficient, but that risk error. These shortcuts played an important role in Chapter 3, when we discussed object recognition; in Chapter 7, when we discussed memory errors; and in Chapter 9, when we discussed categorization heuristics. Similar shortcuts will emerge again in this section, and as we'll see, they play an important part in governing and guiding human thought.

Another theme will also be evident several times in this section: Humans do make many errors in their judgment and reasoning, but this is not because we don't know how to think well. In fact, we think quite well if the circumstances or the problem manages to trigger the appropriate knowledge. Our discussion of this point will drive us toward a multilayered conception of thinking because we will need to describe how people think when their better strategies are triggered, and also how they think when the strategies are not triggered. Hand and hand with this, we will need to say more about what these triggers are, given that they are apparently capable of turning poor reasoning into excellent reasoning.

These considerations also point the way toward another important issue in this section: If sound reasoning and judgment can be triggered by suitable cues, are there things we can do to make this triggering more likely, so that people will judge and reason more effectively in their day-to-day lives?

Finally, how much of our thought is conscious? Are there benefits associated with conscious thought, as opposed to unconscious thought? We will tackle these questions in Chapter 15, but we'll do this largely by pulling together points we have made in earlier chapters; in this way, Chapter 15 will provide something of a review for the text at the same time that it tackles a series of enormously important theoretical questions.

Judgment: Drawing Conclusions From Evidence

So far, we have said a great deal about the acquisition and retention of knowledge, but little about what people do with their knowledge once they've acquired it. It is to this broad concern that we now turn. We begin with a discussion of judgment—processes through which we think about evidence, draw conclusions, and make inferences. The study of judgment takes part of its importance from the fact that the knowledge we need in our day-to-day lives is typically not supplied by the world in neat, ready-to-use packages. When we act on the basis of what we know, therefore, it is generally not because we have memorized a single relevant fact, nor is it because we have received some specific instruction about what to do in that situation. Instead, our actions are typically based on knowledge that we have, in effect, created ourselves—by drawing inferences from things we have seen, or by extrapolating from what we have experienced. Imagine that you wish to cheer up your friend Allen. Chances are that Allen has never said to you, "Flowers are a good way to cheer me up." Therefore, you will need to figure out what will do the trick, on the basis of things you have seen Allen do or heard him say. Likewise, should you vote for candidate X or candidate Y in the upcoming election? In this case, you have received instructions—you have seen X on television saying, "Vote for me!" and likewise for Y. You will probably ignore these

403

■ In a wide range of circumstances, people use cognitive shortcuts, or "heuristics," to make judgments. These heuristics tend to be relatively efficient, and they often lead to sensible conclusions. However, heuristic use can lead to error.

■ People use these heuristics even when they are trying to be careful in their judgment, and even when they are highly motivated to be accurate. The heuristics are used as often by experts as by ordinary people, and so expert judgments, too, are vulnerable to error.

■ However, heuristic use is far from inevitable, and we can easily identify circumstances in

which people rely on more sophisticated forms of reasoning—and so they judge covariation accurately, are sensitive to base rates, are alert to the problems of drawing a conclusion from a small sample of evidence, and so on.

■ We will consider when people use their more sophisticated ("System 2") reasoning and when they rely on the heuristics ("System 1"). Evidence suggests that System 2 comes into play only if the circumstances are right, and only if the case being judged contains the appropriate triggers for this form of reasoning.

instructions, though, in making your decision. Instead, you will try to recall what you have read about X and Y, and you will make inferences from this information about how each is likely to behave in the future.

In still other situations, we use our judgment simply because we want to figure things out, because we want to understand the pattern of our experiences. "Why was I in such a bad mood today?" "Does she really like me?" "What will the consequences of the election be?" In these cases, too, we build on what we already know, as we seek to draw some conclusion from the information available to us.

In this chapter, we will examine how these judgments are made. What strategies do we rely on in evaluating evidence? What factors influence us? Our focus will be on cases involving **induction**, which is typically a process in which one begins with specific facts or observations and then draws some general conclusion from them. In Chapter 13, we will consider the related topic of *deduction*, which usually involves the drawing of specific claims, on the basis of more general principles.[1] For example, you might know in general that people with allergies often suffer during the spring. What conclusions can you (deductively) draw from this concerning Aaron, who has allergies?

---

[1]Note that we're describing the patterns that induction or deduction *typically* or *usually* follow. That's because not all cases of induction fit the profile of "from specifics to general," and not all cases of deduction fit the pattern of "from general to specifics." What, therefore, is the real distinction between induction and deduction? As Johnson-Laird (2004) notes, the key difference lies in the fact that deductions, if they are valid, never go beyond the given information; and so, if the premises of a deductive argument are true, the conclusion is guaranteed to be true. Induction, in contrast, does go beyond the given information. Even if the initial facts are true, and even if the conclusion is carefully warranted, an inductive conclusion is only "probably true," and not guaranteed true.

Induction and deduction are key elements of our intellectual lives, and they are ubiquitous in human reasoning. But induction and deduction also play a role in more formal settings, and in those settings, induction and deduction proceed according to clear rules. The rules of deduction have been specified in detail by logicians; these rules tell us rather precisely which deductive conclusions are valid—that is, warranted by the available information—and which are not. Likewise, scientists and statisticians have formalized many rules of induction, and so, in scientific discourse one cannot offer any conclusion one chooses. Instead, certain statistical and methodological principles govern how evidence is to be summarized and interpreted. Thus, one's inductive inferences are justified only if they are made in accordance with these principles.

According to many scholars, logic specifies the *correct* way to reason deductively, and so logic provides a normative account of deduction, as opposed to a descriptive account. **Normative** accounts tell us how things *ought* to go; **descriptive** accounts tell us merely how things are. In the same way, statistics and scientific methodology provide normative rules for inductive reasoning, telling us how this form of reasoning *ought* to proceed.

Of course, most people have never studied logic or statistics, but even so we can ask how their reasoning compares with the normative procedures: In our informal, day-to-day judgments, do we think sensibly and draw the "correct" conclusions? Or is our thinking foolish, and are our conclusions unjustified? These questions will be very much in view as we consider research in this domain.

Availability

As we move through our daily lives, we make a huge variety of judgments. Sometimes these judgments concern familiar matters; other times we need to figure things out in an unfamiliar setting. Sometimes we make judgments about trivial topics; sometimes the judgments are quite important. We make judgments about social questions and practical problems, judgments about sports, judgments about political issues, and much more. Yet, across all of these domains, we seem to rely over and over on the same few strategies.

Much of what we know about these strategies grows out of seminal work by two enormously important researchers, Daniel Kahneman and Amos Tversky; Kahneman received the Nobel Prize (in Economics) in 2002 for this (and related) research.[2] Their proposal has evolved over the years, but from the start they emphasized the importance of two strategies: one called the "availability heuristic," and one called the "representativeness heuristic."

---

[2]Amos Tversky died in 1996; his death was unmistakably a tremendous loss to the field of psychology. Because the Nobel Prize is never awarded posthumously, the 2002 prize went to Kahneman alone.

Let's start with a concrete case. Imagine that you are trying to judge how likely it is that you'll do well in Organic Chemistry next semester. To figure this out, you might ask yourself: How well have my friends done in this course? How many have gotten good grades, and how many have done poorly? These questions depend on **frequency estimates**—assessments of how often (how frequently) various events have happened in the past.

Frequency estimates are crucial in many circumstances, including cases like the one just mentioned, and also cases in which you're trying to figure out cause-and-effect relationships. For example, you find yourself in a particularly good mood, and you wonder why. Could it be the sunny weather? One way to check on this is by asking how often in the past you've been in a good mood on sunny days. If good moods occur on 80% of the sunny days, and on only 40% of the rainy days, then this is an indication that the weather does matter for you. In this fashion, your conclusion will depend on frequency estimates, on how often good moods have been observed in this setting or in that one.

The problem, though, is that often we don't have frequency information at our fingertips. To continue the example, you've never had reason to count the occasions of good mood + sunny weather, or the occasions of good mood + rainy weather, and so you don't have easy access to the information you need for your judgment. How, therefore, should you proceed? One option is that you might do a quick scan through memory, seeking relevant cases. If you easily can think of happy days filled with bright sunshine, you'll probably conclude that there are a lot of cases in that category. If happy days filled with sun come to mind only slowly, or only with effort, you'll draw the opposite conclusion: This must be a rare category. The idea, in other words, is that you can use *availability*—the ease with which things come to mind, as an index for *frequency*. Kahneman and Tversky referred to this strategy—again, relying on availability in order to judge frequency—as the **availability heuristic**.

The Availability Heuristic

We have met the idea of *heuristics* in several other chapters. Heuristics are generally defined as reasonably efficient strategies that usually lead us to the right answers. The key word here, however, is "usually." Heuristics do allow errors, but that is simply the price one pays in order to gain efficiency. To avoid the errors, one would need a strategy that would be much slower and much more effortful.

The availability heuristic certainly fits this profile. Assessing availability is quick and easy: You try to think of relevant cases, and in a moment or two, you know whether the cases come quickly to mind or not. And this usually does provide accurate assessments of frequency. Which are more common pets among college students—dogs or cats? You'll probably answer this question by thinking about the specific dog owners and cat owners in your acquaintance. If you easily think of eight dog owners but recall only two or three cat owners, you'll conclude that dogs are the more common pet. And the odds are good that your estimate will be correct.

But it is easy to find cases in which this strategy will lead to error. For example, Tversky and Kahneman asked participants this question: "Are there more words in the dictionary beginning with the letter *R* ("rose," "rock," "rabbit") or more words with an *R* in the third position ("tarp," "bare," "throw")? Most participants asserted that there are more words beginning with *R* (A. Tversky & Kahneman, 1973, 1974), but the reverse is true, by a margin of at least two to one.

Why do people get this wrong, and by so much? The answer lies in availability. If you search your memory for words starting with *R*, many will come to mind. (Try it: How many *R*-words can you name in 10 seconds?) But if you search your memory for words with an *R* in the third position, fewer will emerge. (Again, try this for 10 seconds.) This difference, favoring the words beginning with *R*, arises simply because your memory is organized roughly like a dictionary is, with the words sharing a starting sound all grouped together. As a consequence, it's easy to search memory using "starting letter" as your cue; a search based on *R* in third position" is much more difficult. In this way, the organization of memory creates a bias in what's easily available, and this bias in availability leads to an error in frequency judgment.

The Wide Range of Availability Effects

Use of the availability heuristic seems sensible in the "*R*-word" task. After all, the task isn't very interesting, and participants probably don't want to spend much effort or time in choosing their response. But evidence suggests that people use this shortcut strategy in a wide range of other cases, including cases in which they're making judgments of some importance.

For example, consider the fact that people regularly overestimate the frequency of events that are, in actuality, quite rare (Attneave, 1953; Lichtenstein, Slovic, Fischhoff, Layman, & Combs, 1978). This probably plays a part in people's willingness to buy lottery tickets; they overestimate the likelihood of winning! Sadly, it also can play a role in more important domains. For example, there is evidence that physicians may, in many circumstances, overestimate the likelihood of a rare disease and, in the process, fail to pursue other, perhaps more appropriate, diagnoses. (For an example, see Elstein et al., 1986.)

What causes this pattern? Events that are unusual or peculiar are, by their nature, likely to catch your attention. You will therefore notice these events and think about them, ensuring that these events are well recorded in memory. This will, in turn, make these events easily available to you. As a consequence, if you rely on the availability heuristic, you will overestimate the frequency of these unusual events and, correspondingly, will overestimate the likelihood of similar events happening in the future.

Here's a different example of how the availability heuristic can lead us astray: Schwarz et al. (1991) asked their participants first to recall a number of examples in their lives in which they had acted in an assertive fashion. Half of the participants were asked to recall 6 examples; half were asked to recall 12 examples. Then, all the participants were asked some more general questions, including how assertive, overall, they thought they were.

What should we expect here? Participants will probably have an easy time coming up with 6 examples, and so, using the availability heuristic, they are likely to conclude, "Those examples came easily to mind; therefore, there must be a large number of these examples; therefore, I must be an assertive person." On the other side, participants asked for 12 examples are likely to have more difficulty generating this longer list, and so will conclude, "If these examples are so difficult to recall, I guess the examples can't be typical for how I act."

Consistent with these suggestions, participants who recalled fewer examples judged themselves to be more assertive. Notice, ironically, that the participants who recalled *more* examples actually had more evidence in their view for their own assertiveness. But it's not the quantity of evidence that matters. Instead, what matters is the ease of coming up with the examples. Participants who were asked for a dozen examples had a hard time with the task *because they had been asked to do something difficult.* But participants seemed not to realize this. They reacted only to the fact that the examples were difficult to generate and, using the availability heuristic, concluded that being assertive was relatively infrequent in their past.

In this example, availability is obviously being influenced by the experimenter's request (for 6 examples or 12). But availability can also be influenced by many other factors. Imagine that you have been asked to vote on how much money the government should spend on various research projects, all aimed at saving lives. It seems sensible that you would choose to spend your resources on the more frequent causes of death, rather than investigating rare problems, and that leads to our questions: Should we spend more on preventing death from motor vehicle accidents or death from stomach cancer? Which is more common? Should we spend more on preventing homicides, or diabetes? People reliably assert that motor vehicle accidents and homicide are the more frequent in each pair, although the opposite is true both times, as shown in Table 12.1 (Combs & Slovic, 1979; Slovic, Fischhoff, & Lichtenstein, 1982).

What produces this error? In estimating the likelihood of these events, people are heavily influenced by the pattern of media coverage. Homicide makes the front page, while diabetes does not; and this is reflected in participants' estimates of frequency. Indeed, their estimates for each of the causes of death correspond rather closely to frequency of report in the media, rather than to actual frequency of occurrence. Thus, once again, we find an influence of availability. Just as some information is less available to us via the selectivity of memory, some information is less available via the selectivity of the media. And it is the available data that people use, making the media bias as important as the memory bias.

TABLE 12.1	Availability Bias in Estimates of Frequency of Death From Various Causes

Most overestimated	**Most underestimated**
All accidents	Smallpox vaccination
Motor vehicle accidents	Diabetes
Pregnancy, childbirth, and abortion	Stomach cancer
Tornadoes	Lightning
Flood	Stroke
Botulism	Tuberculosis
All cancer	Asthma
Fire and flames	Emphysema
Venomous bite or sting	
Homicide	

From Slovic, Fischhoff, & Lichtenstein, 1982.

Note: People estimated how many deaths are caused by each of these factors. Their judgments were clearly influenced by how often each factor is reported in the media: Stomach cancer is usually not reported; homicide and death from fires are often reported.

Representativeness

Availability, it seems, influences us in a wide range of judgments, and overall, this is probably a good thing. That's because, in many cases, events or objects that are more frequent in the world are more available to us, and so it is useful to rely on information about availability as a substitute for information about frequency. As we have seen, however, this strategy can go astray, and in some circumstances, availability-based judgments can be highly misleading.

The same points can be made about the **representativeness heuristic**, a strategy that people use when they want to extrapolate from the information they've gathered, making inferences or predictions based on their experience. This heuristic can be described in several ways, but at its essence the heuristic amounts to an assumption that the categories we think about are relatively homogeneous. This assumption then has several consequences. For one, the assumption leaves us willing to believe that each member of a category is "representative" of the category—that is, has all of the traits that we associate with that category. Thus, if someone is a lawyer, we give in to the stereotype and expect her to have the traits we associate with lawyers. Conversely, if someone looks like (our idea of) a typical lawyer, we conclude she is a lawyer.

This assumption of homogeneity also leaves us quite willing to draw conclusions from a relatively small sample: If each member of a group is representative of the group, then it's fair to draw conclusions about the whole after one or two observations, and thus we agree to statements such as, "If you've seen one lawyer, you've seen 'em all."

Of course, these reasoning patterns will often lead us to the correct conclusions, because many categories we encounter are homogeneous. If, after one or two nights at a Marriot, you conclude that all hotel rooms have Bibles in them, your conclusion is warranted. If you conclude that Sue probably is comfortable with math because she is, after all, an engineer, this conclusion, too, is probably correct; engineers are likely to be reasonably homogeneous in this particular dimension. But as with all heuristics, it is easy to find cases in which this sort of reasoning can lead to error.

Reasoning From the Population to an Instance

Imagine tossing a coin over and over, and let's say that the coin has landed heads up six times in a row. Many people (and many gamblers) believe that, in this situation, the coin is more likely to come up tails than heads on the next toss. But this conclusion is wrong, and this belief is commonly referred to as the "gambler's fallacy." The "logic" leading to this fallacy seems to be that, if the coin is fair, then a series of tosses should contain equal numbers of heads and tails. If no tails have appeared for a while, then some are "overdue" to bring about this balance.

But how could this be? The coin has no "memory," so it has no way of knowing how long it has been since the last tails. More generally, there simply is no mechanism through which the history of the previous tosses could influence the current one. Therefore, the likelihood of a tail on toss number 7 is 50-50 (i.e., .50), just as it was on the first toss, and as it is on every toss.

Where, then, does our (mistaken) belief come from? The explanation lies in our assumption of category homogeneity. We know that, over the long haul, a fair coin will produce equal numbers of heads and tails. Thus, the category of "all tosses" has this property. Our assumption of homogeneity, though, leads us to expect that any "representative" of the category will also have this property—that is, any sequence of tosses will also show the 50-50 split. But this isn't true: Some sequences of tosses are 75% heads, some are 5% heads, some are 100% heads. It is only when we combine all these sequences that the 50-50 split emerges.

A different way to say this appeals to the notion of sample size. If we examine a large number of cases (i.e., a large sample), we will find patterns close to those in the overall population. This is what statisticians refer to as the "law of large numbers," a law that states (roughly) that the larger the sample you consider is, the greater the resemblance will be between the properties of the sample and the properties of the population at large. There is, however, no "law of small numbers": There is no tendency for small samples to approximate the pattern of the population. Indeed, small samples can often stray rather far from the population values. But people seem not to appreciate this, and they act as though they expect small samples to show the pattern of the whole.

These mistaken beliefs about sample size are revealed directly in an early study by Kahneman and Tversky (1972). Participants were given the following problem:

> In a small town nearby, there are two hospitals. Hospital A has an average of 45 births per day; Hospital B is smaller, and has an average of 15 births per day. As we all know, overall the number of males born is 50%. Each hospital recorded the number of days in which, on that day, at least 60% of the babies born were male. Which hospital recorded more such days: (a) Hospital A, (b) Hospital B, (c) both equal?

The majority of the participants chose the response "(c) both equal," but this answer is statistically unwarranted. All of the births in the country add up to a 50-50 split between male and female babies. The larger the sample one examines is, the more likely one is to approximate this ideal. Conversely, the smaller the sample one examines is, the more likely one is to stray from this ideal. Days with 60% male births, straying from the ideal, are therefore more likely in the smaller hospital, Hospital B.

If you don't see this, consider a more extreme case. Hospital C has 1,000 births per day; Hospital D has exactly 1 birth per day. Which hospital records more days with at least 90% male births? This value will be observed in Hospital D rather often since, on many days, all the babies born (one out of one) will be male! This value is surely less likely, though, in Hospital C: 900 male births, with just 100 female, would be a remarkable event indeed. In this case, it seems clear that the smaller hospital can more easily stray far from the 50-50 split.

In the hospital problem, just like in the gambler's fallacy, participants seem not to take sample size into account. They seem to think a particular pattern is just as likely with a small sample as with a large sample, although this is plainly not true. This belief, however, is just what one would expect if people were making the assumption that each instance of a category—or, in this case, each subset of a larger set—should show the properties associated with the entire set.

Reasoning From a Single Case to the Entire Population

If people believe categories are homogeneous, then they will expect each subset of the category, and each individual within the category, to have the properties of the category overall; this is the error we were just discussing. But if people believe categories to be homogeneous, they'll also make the opposite error: They will expect the overall category to have the properties of the individuals, and so they will be quite willing to extrapolate from a few instances to the entire set. This is the error alluded to earlier—the error of "seen one lawyer, seen 'em all." This error is easy to document, even when people are explicitly told that the instance they are considering is *not* representative of the larger group.

Hamill, Wilson, and Nisbett (1980) showed their participants a videotaped interview in which a person identified as a prison guard discussed his job. In one condition, the guard was compassionate and kind, and he expressed great concern for rehabilitation. In the other condition, the guard expressed contempt for the prison inmates, and he scoffed at the idea of rehabilitation. Before seeing either of these videotapes, some participants were told that this guard was quite typical of those at the prison; other participants were told that he was quite *atypical*, chosen for the interview precisely because of his extreme views. Still other participants were given no information about whether the interviewed guard was typical or not.

Participants were later questioned about their views of the criminal justice system, and the data show that they were clearly influenced by the interview they had seen: Those who had seen the humane guard indicated that they now believed prison guards to be decent people in general; those who had seen the inhumane guard reported more negative views of guards. What is remarkable, though, is that participants seemed largely to ignore the information about whether the interviewed guard was typical or not. Those who were explicitly told the guard was atypical were influenced by the interview just as much, and in the same way, as those who were told that the guard was typical.

Similar data are easily observed outside of the laboratory. Consider what Nisbett and Ross (1980) have referred to as "man who" arguments. You are shopping for a new car. You have read various consumer magazines and decided, on the basis of their reports of test data and repair records, that you will buy a Smacko-brand car. You report this to your father, who is aghast. "Smacko?! You must be crazy. Why, I know a man who bought a Smacko, and the transmission fell out 2 weeks after he got it. Then the alternator went. Then the brakes. How could you possibly buy a Smacko?"

What should you make of this argument? The consumer magazines tested many cars and reported that 2% of all Smackos break down. In your father's "data," 100% of the Smackos (one out of one) break down. Should this "sample of one" outweigh the much larger sample tested by the magazine? Your father presumably believes he is offering a persuasive argument, but what is the basis for this? The only basis we can see is the presumption that the category will resemble the instance; only if that were true would reasoning from a single instance be appropriate.

If you listen to conversations around you, you will regularly hear "man who" (or "woman who") arguments. "What do you mean cigarette smoking causes cancer?! I have an aunt who smoked for 50 years, and she runs in marathons!" Often these arguments seem persuasive. But these arguments have force only by virtue of the representativeness heuristic—our assumption that categories are homogeneous, and therefore our peculiar willingness to take a small sample of data as seriously as a larger sample.

Anchoring

Availability and representativeness are two of the intellectual shortcuts we often use—but they are not the only ones. Another widely used heuristic is **anchoring and adjustment** (A. Tversky & Kahneman, 1974; for more recent work, see Epley &

Gilovich, 2001). The proposal here is that, even when we don't know the answer to a question, we often do have an idea about what "ballpark" the answer is in. What we can therefore do is use that initial idea as an "anchor," and then reach our answer by making some suitable adjustment to that anchor.

For example, in what year was George Washington elected president? Most Americans don't know, but they did memorize in school that the United States declared its independence in 1776; Washington's election, therefore, must have been sometime after this, and so, by suitable adjustment of the 1776 date, one can offer a proposal for Washington's election year.

This is—like the other heuristics—often a useful strategy. The problem, though, is that people tend to adjust too little, and so they are more influenced by the initial anchor than they should be. Thus, participants in one study estimated that Washington had been elected in 1779 (an adjustment of 3 years away from the anchor of 1776); he was in fact elected 7 years later than this (Epley & Gilovich, 2001).

The same pattern is evident if people are given anchors that are deliberately too low or too high. In each case, people adjust, but because they don't adjust enough, low anchors lead to low estimates, and high anchors to high estimates. In one study, some participants were first asked whether Gandhi lived to the age of 140; after they'd made this easy judgment, they were asked to estimate how long he actually did live. Their average, on estimate, was that he lived to be 67 years old. Other participants were first asked whether Gandhi lived past the age of 9; then they, too, had to estimate how long he lived. Given this much lower anchor, they gave appreciably lower estimates, judging on average that he lived to age 50 (Strack & Mussweiler, 1997).

The anchoring heuristic seems to be widely used, and that is one reason why it is important. But, in addition, anchoring has another consequence: When judgment errors arise for *other* reasons, anchoring serves to cement them in place. Imagine, for example, that you're trying to judge which is more frequent in the United States—death by homicide, or death by diabetes. You know perfectly well that homicides tend to be front-page news; diabetes, on the other hand, is rarely reported, unless the victim happens to be someone famous. Because you are aware of this bias, and aware of how it might have shaped your initial estimate, you might seek to adjust that estimate, and it is here that anchoring plays its role. The initial response, even though misguided, will influence subsequent judgments, making it difficult to undo the error. (For related claims, see Wilson & Brekke, 1994.)

Detecting Covariation

We seem to be moving toward an unsettling indictment of human judgment. Over and over, people draw on a small set of strategies (summarized in Table 12.2), and these strategies usually serve them well. But these strategies also leave people wide open to error, and so, for example, they are influenced by availability even when

TABLE 12.2 Strategies for Judgment

Heuristic	Purpose	How to use it	Drawback
Availability	For judging frequency	Try to think of relevant cases. If the cases come to mind quickly and easily, conclude the category is a frequent one.	Ease of thinking of cases is often influenced by factors other than actual frequency in the world.
Representativeness	For making inferences about the traits of a specific case or of a category	Assume the relevant category is homogeneous. On this basis, assume that each individual in the category, and each subset of the category, will have the properties evident in the category overall. Likewise, assume that the entire category will have the properties evident in each instance you observe.	Many of the categories we think about are not homogeneous, and so small samples of evidence will sometimes not reflect the properties of the whole.
Anchoring and adjustment	For making a variety of quantitative estimates	Start with a known anchor— an estimate that's in the same ballpark as the right answer. Then adjust that anchor to make it a better approximation of the right answer.	We often *under*adjust, and so we are too much influenced by the initial anchor.

there's an obvious bias in what's available. Likewise, they take small samples of evidence too seriously and treat evidence as though it were representative, even if told explicitly that it is not. People "anchor" their judgments, even when they know the anchor to be arbitrary.

Is this grim picture correct? Is human judgment as poor as the evidence so far suggests? We will have more to say about this before we are through. First, though, we need to add some additional "charges" to the indictment.

Many of the judgments people make hinge on questions about covariation. This term has a technical meaning, but for our purposes, we can define it this way: X and Y "covary" if X tends to be on the scene whenever Y is, and if X tends to be absent whenever Y is absent. For example, exercise and stamina covary: People who do the first tend to have a lot of the second. Owning audio CDs and going to concerts also covary, although less strongly than exercise and stamina. (Some people own many CDs but rarely go to concerts.) Note, then, that covariation is a matter of degree: Covariation can be strong or weak. Covariation can also be either negative or positive. Exercise and stamina, for example, covary positively (as exercise increases, so does stamina). Exercise and body fat, in contrast, covary negatively (as exercise increases, body fat decreases).

Why is covariation important? Covariation is what we look at in assessing the quality of a diagnostic technique. Can we diagnose schizophrenia on the basis of some blood test? We can find out by asking whether schizophrenic symptoms covary with some blood value. Covariation is also what we look at to test a hypothesis about cause and effect. Does education lead to a higher-paying job? If so, then degree of education and salary should covary. Likewise, does taking aspirin prevent heart attacks? If so, then aspirin use and heart attacks should covary negatively, with the presence of one being associated with the absence of the other.

In these ways, assessing covariation is of crucial importance for scientific data analysis, and it is no less important in day-to-day reasoning. Do your colleagues at work act in a friendlier fashion when you are formal or when you're casual? Can you study more effectively if you have a period of physical exercise early in the day? These are, once again, questions about covariation, and they are the sorts of questions we frequently ask. So how well do we do when we think about covariation?

Illusions of Covariation

Psychologists have developed a wide variety of tests to measure personality characteristics or behavioral inclinations. One well-known example is the Rorschach test, in which participants are shown inkblots and asked to describe them. Psychologists then examine the descriptions, looking for certain patterns. A mention of humans in motion is said to indicate imagination and a rich inner life; responses that describe the white spaces around the inkblot are taken as indications of rebelliousness.

Is this valid? Do specific responses really covary with certain personality traits? And how astutely do people detect this covariation? To attack these questions, Chapman and Chapman (1971) created a number of Rorschach protocols—that is, written transcripts of a person's responses. The protocols were actually fictional, made up for this study, but they were designed to resemble real Rorschach responses. The Chapmans also made up fictional descriptions of the people who had supposedly offered these responses: One protocol was attributed to someone who "believes other people are plotting against him." Another protocol was attributed to someone who "has sexual feelings toward other men."

The Chapmans randomly paired the protocols and the personality descriptions—one protocol and one description, the next protocol and a different description. These randomly assembled protocol–profile pairs were then shown to a group of undergraduates, students who had no prior experience with the Rorschach test and who did not know the theory behind the test. These students were asked to examine the pairs, and to determine what responses covaried with what traits. In particular, the students were asked which responses covaried with homosexuality.

Before pressing on, we should emphasize that the Chapmans' research was done more than three decades ago, at a time when many psychologists viewed homosexuality as a "disorder" to be diagnosed. Psychologists have long since abandoned this utterly indefensible view, and so we discuss the Chapmans' research because it is a classic study of covariation, and not because it tells us anything about homosexuality.

Returning to the study itself, we know that, thanks to the random pairing, there was no covariation in this set of "data" between protocols and descriptions. Nonetheless, the students reported seeing a pattern of covariation. Certain responses, they reported, seemed consistently good indicators that the respondent was a homosexual. For example, they reported that homosexual respondents were particularly likely to perceive buttocks in the inkblots. Therefore, mention of buttocks was a reasonable indicator, they claimed, of homosexuality.

Of course, there was no pattern in these randomly assembled data, and therefore the covariation the students were perceiving was illusory—"observed" in the data even though it was plainly not there. And oddly enough, the covariation "perceived" by these students was identical to that alleged at the time by professional clinicians. On the basis of extensive experience with patients, clinicians were convinced that certain Rorschach responses were valid indicators of homosexuality, and the responses they mentioned were exactly the ones nominated by the participants in the laboratory study. The clinicians, like the Chapmans' participants, reported that use of the "buttocks" response did covary with sexual orientation, with homosexuals much more likely to use this response.

Is it just a coincidence that the **illusory covariation** "detected" by the laboratory participants matches the actual covariation observed by the clinicians? It turns out to be no coincidence at all, because the pattern observed by the clinicians *is also illusory*. We know this because researchers have examined the Rorschach responses from homosexuals and heterosexuals and asked statistically whether the "buttocks" responses are more likely from one group than the other. It turns out that the two groups do not differ at all in the likelihood of this response, and so there is no covariation between sexual orientation and the use of the response. Thus, the clinicians are seeing a "pattern" that really isn't there. With all of their training, with their years of experience, and when they are making consequential professional judgments, the clinicians are caught by the same illusion that the lab participants are. (For related evidence, see Arkes & Harkness, 1983; Schustack & Sternberg, 1981; Shaklee & Mims, 1982; and Smedslund, 1963.)

Theory-Driven and Data-Driven Detection of Covariation

In day-to-day work, a professional can accumulate great quantities of experience. A physician sees many cases of the flu; a salesperson sees many customers; a teacher, many students. Therefore, each of these individuals has a great opportunity to accumulate "professional wisdom" within his or her area of special expertise. The clear message of the Chapmans' data, though, is that we might be wary of this "professional wisdom." Their data remind us that professional training does not make someone immune to illusions. Professionals, just like everyone else, are fully capable of projecting their beliefs onto the evidence and perceiving patterns that aren't there.

Given all this, perhaps we should be cautious when a police officer assures us that crimes are more frequent under a full moon, or when a hairstylist tells us that a certain shampoo cures split ends. In each of these cases, a professional is making a claim about covariation, and we all tend to trust such claims, because they are based on so much firsthand experience. Nonetheless, we might want to ask how these conclusions were drawn. Was the evidence systematically recorded and rigorously reviewed? Or are these claims simply derived in an informal way, from the professional's "global impression" of the facts? If the latter, one might argue that these claims—even though they come from "experts"—should be regarded with skepticism, since they could turn out merely to be further examples of illusory covariation. (For other evidence echoing this concern about "professional wisdom," see the studies reviewed by Shanteau, 1992.)

For that matter, if experts show these effects, what about the rest of us? Do we all project our own biases onto the data, seeing only the pattern of covariation we expect to see? It's certainly true that people have many false beliefs about covariation. For example, many people are convinced that there is a relationship between a person's handwriting and personality, yet no serious study has documented this covariation. Apparently, therefore, this is another example of illusory covariation (King & Koehler, 2000). Likewise, many people believe they can predict the weather by paying attention to their arthritis pain ("My knee always acts up when a storm is coming"). This, too, turns out to be groundless, and so it is another example that people are prone to perceive covariation when in truth there is none (Redelmeier & Tversky, 1996).

Can we be more precise about what it is that causes these illusions? In a study by Jennings, Amabile, and Ross (1982), college students were asked to make covariation judgments in two types of situations: situations in which they had no prior expectations or biases, and situations in which they did. For example, in the "prior belief" (or "theory-based") case, the participants were asked to estimate how strong the covariation is between (a) children's dishonesty as measured by false report of athletic performance, and (b) children's dishonesty as measured by the amount of cheating in solving a puzzle. If a child is dishonest according to one of these indices, is he or she also dishonest according to the other? Or, as a different example, participants estimated the covariation between (a) how highly a student rated U.S. presidents' performance in the last decade, and (b) how highly the student rated business leaders' performance in the last decade. If you think highly of our presidents, do you also think highly of the business community?

The participants presumably made these judgments by reflecting on their prior experience and their intuitions; no new data were presented in the experimental procedure. Participants expressed these judgments by selecting a number between 0 and 100, where 0 indicated that the two traits were unrelated (i.e., did not covary), and 100 indicated that the traits covaried perfectly. Participants could also use negative values (to–100) to indicate the belief that the two traits covary, but with the presence of one indicating the absence of the other.

The participants were also asked to make a comparable judgment in a "no prior belief" (or "data-based") case—that is, with variables they had never met or considered before. For example, they were presented with ten pictures, each showing a man holding a walking stick. The heights of the men varied in the pictures, as did the length of the walking stick, and participants had to judge whether these two variables covaried, again choosing a value between –100 and +100.

Figure 12.1 shows the results from the data-based cases—that is, the cases in which participants had no prior beliefs. Here, the estimates of covariation were reasonably regular: The stronger the covariation, the stronger the estimate. The judg-

| FIGURE 12.1 | Assessments of Covariation in the Absence of Expectations |

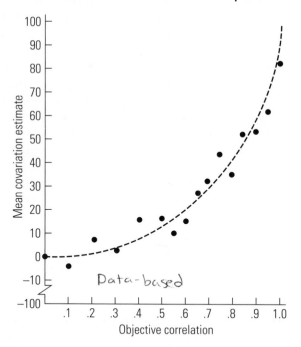

When participants enter a situation with no expectations about the data, their estimates of covariation are quite orderly: The estimates grow stronger and stronger as the actual (objective) correlation grows stronger and stronger. In addition, participants give low estimates unless the actual correlation is very strong. (After Jennings, Amabile, & Ross, 1982)

ments also tended to be rather conservative: Estimates exceeded +30 only when the objective correlation was very strong.

Figure 12.2 shows a very different picture for the theory-based cases. The participants tended to be far more extravagant in these estimates, with estimates of +60 and +80. They were also far less regular in the theory-based cases, with only a weak relation between the magnitude of the estimated covariation and the magnitude of the actual covariation. For example, the "children's dishonesty" pair, mentioned earlier, is shown as the black square in the figure. In this case, the objective correlation, statistically measured, is fairly small; that is, children who are dishonest in one context are often honest in other contexts. Participants estimated this covariation to be quite large, though, with an average

| FIGURE 12.2 | Assessments of Covariation in the Presence of Expectations |

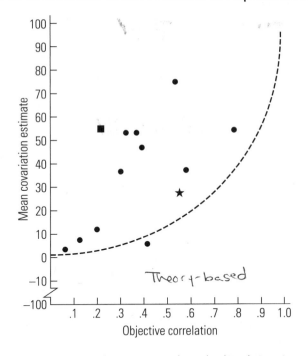

When participants enter a situation with expectations about the data, their estimates of covariation are often inaccurate. In this instance, participants were asked to assess the covariation in 16 cases. The square and the star indicate the two cases discussed in the text. Participants often estimated the covariation as strong even when it was quite weak, or as weak even when it was strong. The systematic pattern observed in Figure 12.1 is clearly absent here. (For purposes of comparison, this figure includes the curve describing the data from Figure 12.1.) (After Jennings, Amabile, & Ross, 1982)

estimate of almost +60. For the "presidents and business leaders" case (the black star in the figure), the objective correlation is much stronger than in the "dishonesty" pair, but participants estimated it to be much weaker.

At the very least, then, participants are performing differently in the theory-based and data-based judgments. The former judgments are often extravagant; the latter tend to be conservative. The data-based judgments track the objective facts fairly well; the theory-based judgments do not. Given these results, it is difficult to avoid the conclusion that theory biased what the participants "saw" in the data, and led them to see much stronger (or weaker) covariation than was there. (Other relevant data are reviewed by Allan, 1993; Alloy & Tabachnik, 1984; and Baron, 1988.)

What Causes Illusory Covariation?

What causes these errors? Plainly, people *can* judge covariation in the absence of prior beliefs; we see that in Figure 12.1. Therefore we need to ask why beliefs and expectations mislead participants in judgments of covariation? One promising proposal focuses on the *evidence* people consider, rather than the process itself (Baron, 1988; Evans, 1989; Gilovich, 1991; Jennings, Amabile, & Ross, 1982). Specifically, the claim is that, in making these judgments, people consider only a subset of the evidence, and it's a subset that's shaped by a tendency known as "confirmation bias." This virtually guarantees mistaken judgments, since of course, even if the judgment process were 100% fair, a biased input would lead to a biased output.

The term **confirmation bias** actually encompasses several different mechanisms (Nisbett & Ross, 1980; Tweney, Doherty, & Mynatt, 1981), but what these mechanisms have in common is that, collectively, they make people more alert and more responsive to evidence that confirms their beliefs in comparison to evidence that might challenge their beliefs.

We will have more to say about confirmation bias in Chapter 13, and there we will consider some of the data documenting the breadth and the power of this bias. For now, though, let's think through how confirmation bias applies to the assessment of covariation. Let us say, for the sake of discussion, that you have the belief that big dogs tend to be vicious. As a result of this belief, whenever you are thinking about dogs, or looking at dogs, confirmation bias will lead you to notice the big dogs that are, in fact, vicious, and the little dogs that are friendly. Your memory schemata will also help you to remember episodes that fit with this belief and will work against your remembering counterexamples. (Recall that one effect of memory schemata is to "regularize" our past experiences, bringing our recollections into line with our schema-based expectations; see Chapter 7.)

Thanks to these mechanisms, a biased sample of dogs is available to you—both in the dogs you perceive (because of a bias in attention) and also in the dogs you remember (because of the bias in attention and the effects of memory schemata). Therefore, if you are asked to estimate covariation between dog size and temperament, you will probably overestimate the covariation. This isn't because you are ignoring the facts, nor is it because you're incompetent in thinking about covariation. The problem instead lies in your "data"; and if the data are biased, so will be your judgment.

How alarmed should we be by these facts? It's worth bearing in mind that many social stereotypes are based on illusory covariation (e.g., the anti-Semitic illusion that being overconcerned with money "covaries" with being Jewish, or the racist illusion that being lazy "covaries" with being Black). In cases like these, the perception of illusory covariation obviously has ugly consequences. Likewise, if you're convinced that money makes people happy, and so you design your life in hopes of maximizing your wealth, then here, too, an illusion of covariation is having powerful effects. (For a glimpse of the data on the actual relationship between having money and being happy, see Myers, 2000.) Thus, the stakes are often high in judgments involving covariation, making our errors in this domain rather troubling.

Base Rates

Another line of evidence is also relevant here and highlights a type of information we often overlook in our assessment of covariation. As a way of entering this issue, consider the following problem (Kahneman & Tversky, 1973; Nisbett & Ross, 1980):

> I have a friend who is a professor. He likes to write poetry, is rather shy, and is small in stature. Which of the following is his field: (a) Chinese studies or (b) psychology?

In response to this question, most people conclude that the friend is in Chinese studies, and presumably this judgment is based on something like the representativeness heuristic: The example describes someone close to many people's stereotype of a Chinese scholar, and so they draw the appropriate conclusion.

However, this judgment overlooks an important bit of information. As you can probably guess, the number of psychologists in the world is much greater than the number of scholars in Chinese studies. To see how this matters, let us assume, just for the sake of argument, that virtually all Chinese scholars—let's say 90%—fit the stereotype. Let us assume further that only 5% of the psychologists fit the stereotype. In this case, "fitting the stereotype" would be high-quality diagnostic information—information that does indeed indicate that you are in one category rather than another.

But now let's factor in how many psychologists there are in total, and how many Chinese scholars. We've already suggested that there are relatively few Chinese scholars in the world; even if 90% of these fit the description, this is still 90% of a small number. In contrast, merely 5% of the psychologists fit the description, but this will be 5% of a much larger number. To make this concrete, let's say there are 10,000 Chinese scholars in the U.S., and 200,000 psychologists. In this case, 9,000 Chinese scholars fit the description (90% of 10,000), but 10,000 psychologists do as well (5% of 200,000). Therefore, even though the *proportion* of Chinese scholars fitting the description is larger than the proportion of psychologists (90% vs. 5%), the *number* of psychologists who fit the description is greater than the number of Chinese scholars fitting the description (10,000 vs. 9,000). As a result, chances are that the friend is a psychologist, because the description is compatible with more psychologists than Chinese scholars.

To put this more generally, you need two types of information in order to make judgments like this one: both the diagnostic information and also the **base rate**— the overall likelihood that a particular case will be in this category or that one, independent of the diagnostic information. Often the base rate is expressed as a probability or as a percentage, and so, in our example, the base rate for "being a Chinese scholar," from the total group being considered, is 4.8%.[3]

Base rates are always important to consider, and in some cases, they can overturn a conclusion suggested by the diagnostic information. This is evident in our "Chinese studies" example and is true in many other cases as well. Imagine that we are testing a new drug and discover that 70% of the patients who take this drug recover from the malady being treated. Does that mean the drug is effective? The answer depends on the base rate: In general, how many patients recover? If the answer is 70%, then the drug is having no effect whatsoever. Likewise, do good-luck charms help? Let's say that you wear your lucky socks whenever your favorite team plays, and the team has won 85% of its games. We again need to ask about base rates: How many games has your team won over the last few years? Perhaps the team has won 90% overall, but only 85% when you are wearing your lucky socks; in that case, your socks are actually a jinx.

Base-Rate Neglect

In a classic study, Kahneman and Tversky (1973) asked participants this question: If someone is chosen at random from a group of 70 lawyers and 30 engineers, what is his profession likely to be? Participants understood perfectly well that the person is likely to be a lawyer. When asked to estimate the probability of this outcome, they sensibly responded .70. Thus, in this setting, participants made full and accurate use of the base-rate information.

Other participants were given no base-rate information, but were given diagnostic information. Specifically, they were told that a "panel of psychologists" had administered personality tests to a group of engineers and lawyers. The participants were then given "thumbnail descriptions" of these individuals, allegedly based on the tests, and they were asked to use this information to judge whether a particular individual was more likely to be an engineer or a lawyer.

---

[3]In our example, we said that there were 10,000 Chinese scholars in the country, and 200,000 psychologists. That means the *proportion* of Chinese scholars, out of all the people we're considering, is 10,000/210,000. Expressed as a decimal, that fraction equals 0.0476, or roughly 4.8%.

The thumbnail descriptions provided to the participants were carefully designed so that some evoked the participants' engineer stereotype, while others evoked a lawyer stereotype. For example, a description favoring the engineer stereotype described a man whose hobbies include home carpentry, sailing, and mathematical puzzles and who has no interest in political or social issues. Not surprisingly, participants were easily able to use this information, and their judgments sensibly reflected the content of the thumbnail sketches.

Overall, then, it appears that participants are responsive to base rates if this is the only information they have, indicating that they know the base rates are relevant to this judgment. Likewise, they make appropriate use of the diagnostic information, if this is all they have. But now let's ask, What happens if we provide participants with both sorts of information: the base rates and the diagnostic information?

Participants in a third group were again provided with the thumbnail descriptions, but they were told, in addition, that the individuals being described had been selected at random from a group of 30 engineers and 70 lawyers. We have just seen evidence that participants understand the value of both pieces of information: the thumbnail sketch and the overall composition of the group. Therefore, we should expect the participants, when given both, to consider both, and to combine these two sources of information as well as they can. Thus, if the base rate and the diagnostic information both favor the lawyer response, participants should offer this response with some confidence. If the base rate indicates one response and the diagnostic information the other response, then participants should temper their estimates accordingly.

However, this is not what the participants do. When they are provided with both types of information, participants ignore the base rate and rely only on the diagnostic information. Thus, in the lawyer/engineer problem, participants' responses were completely determined by the degree of resemblance between the individual described and their stereotype of a lawyer or an engineer. Indeed, they responded the same way if the base rates were as already described (70 lawyers, 30 engineers) or if the base rates were reversed (30 lawyers, 70 engineers). This reversal had no impact whatsoever on participants' judgments, confirming that they were indeed ignoring the base rates.

Before pressing on, we should emphasize that this neglect of base rates is not observed in all circumstances, and we will have more to say about this later in the chapter. Nonetheless, people often do underutilize base-rate information, even in cases in which the judgment being made is enormously consequential, and even when the person making the judgment is an "expert" in the relevant field. For example, medical doctors are carefully trained in how to reach a diagnosis, and they obviously make important decisions. Even so, physicians, just like the rest of us, often fail to take base rates into account when evaluating a patient's symptoms (Dawes, 1988; Eddy, 1982; Klayman & Brown, 1993). In other words, doctors (and other professionals as well) show the same patterns of reasoning that we have already observed in the lab—with errors, in this case, that can lead to serious misassessments of a patient's status.

Assessing the Damage

We seem to be painting a grim portrait of human judgment. We have discussed several sources of error, and we have suggested that these errors are rather widespread. Most of the studies we have cited have been run at prestigious universities, and so the participants (students at those universities) are, presumably, intelligent and motivated. The errors occur nonetheless. (For reviews, see Arkes, 1991; Einhorn & Hogarth, 1981; and Gilovich, 1991.)

Even experts make these errors. We have discussed poor diagnostic reasoning in physicians and illusory correlations in experienced therapists. Likewise, if we add just a little subtlety to our problems, analogous errors can be observed even among those with considerable training in statistics and methodology (Kahneman & Tversky, 1982a; A. Tversky & Kahneman, 1971, 1983; also see Mahoney & DeMonbreun, 1978; and Shanteau, 1992). And, as we've seen, people make these errors even when the stakes are high. In a number of studies, participants have been offered cash bonuses if they perform accurately. These incentives do have an impact on performance (Arkes, 1991; Gilovich, 1991; Hertwig & Ortmann, 2003), but even so, many errors remain. In addition, we have discussed errors in the context of medical diagnosis; other studies have documented similar errors in the professional work of highly motivated financial managers (e.g., Hilton, 2003). In these cases, the stakes are high indeed, yet the errors can still be documented.

More-Sophisticated Judgment Strategies

Could it be that human judgment is so fundamentally flawed? If so, this might help explain why warfare, racism, neglect of poverty, and environmental destruction are widespread; perhaps these consequences are the inevitable outcome of our inability to understand the facts and to draw decent conclusions. Likewise, it's no wonder that people are so ready to believe in telepathy, astrology, and a variety of bogus cures (Gilovich, 1991; King & Koehler, 2000).

Before we draw these dismaying conclusions, however, we need to acknowledge that there is another side to our story, and with that, evidence showing that sometimes people rise above the simple strategies we have described and avoid the errors we have catalogued. This will in turn demand a new line of questioning—asking why people sometimes rely on judgment shortcuts (with the attendant risk of error), and why people sometimes use more-sophisticated strategies.

Let's start, though, by documenting the simple but crucial fact that sometimes human judgment does rise above the heuristics we have described so far. For example, we argued earlier that people often rely on availability when they are trying to judge frequency, asking themselves, "How easily can I think of cases of type X?" in order to decide, "How common is type X?" But people don't always do this. Sometimes, people are alert to the fact that they don't know very much about a category, and this dissuades them from relying on the availability heuristic. For example, how many sumo wrestlers are there in your state? If you relied on availability in answering this question, you might answer "zero" (assuming that none of your friends are sumo wrestlers). But in this situation you are probably alert to your own lack of expertise, and so you will seek some other basis for making this judgment. (For experimental demonstrations of this, see Oppenheimer, 2004; N. Schwarz, 1998; and Winkielman & Schwarz, 2001.)

Similarly, consider the common reliance on the representativeness heuristic. This reliance is evident in many ways, including the fact that people are far too willing to draw conclusions from a small sample of evidence (we saw this in the power of "man who" arguments). Closely related is the fact that people seem not to understand that large samples of evidence are less influenced by chance factors than small samples are. (We saw this in the "Hospital A or B problem," discussed earlier.) These findings seem to indicate that people just do not understand the importance of *sample size* when evaluating a pattern of evidence.

Other evidence, however, makes it clear that people *do* understand sample size. As an illustration, imagine the following dialogue:

> Bart: I've got a great system for choosing lottery numbers! I chose a number yesterday, and I won!
>
> Lisa: Come on—that doesn't mean your system's great; maybe you just got lucky.

In this setting, Lisa's response sounds perfectly fine; we all know that lucky accidents do happen, and so Bart's boast does sound unjustified. But now consider this bit of dialogue:

> Marge: I've got a great system for choosing lottery numbers! I've tried it 11 times, and I won every time!
>
> Homer: Come on—that doesn't mean your system's great; maybe you just got lucky each time.

This time, Homer's response sounds odd, and Marge's boast does seem sensible. Yes, lucky accidents do happen, but they don't keep happening over and over. If something does happen over and over, therefore, it's probably not an accident.

These are very easy points to grasp, and it's precisely this ease of understanding that's important here, because it reveals a comprehension of some crucial facts about sample size. Specifically, you understand these bits of dialogue only because you already know that it's dangerous to draw conclusions from a small sample of evidence. This is why you side with Lisa, not Bart. Likewise, you side with Marge because you understand that it's legitimate to draw conclusions from a larger sample; you know that a pattern in a larger set is less likely to be the result of accident.

Experimental data also make it clear that, in some circumstances, people are alert to the size of the data set they are considering. For example, Nisbett, Krantz, Jepson, and Kunda (1983) asked participants in one study to imagine that they had encountered a new bird, the "shreeble." The one shreeble observed so far was blue, and on this basis, participants were asked how likely they thought it was that all shreebles were blue. These participants were also asked to imagine that they had encountered a new element, "floridium." Only one sample of floridium had been examined, and when heated, it burned with a blue flame. Given this evidence, the participants were asked how likely they thought it was that all floridium, when heated, burns with a blue flame. Finally, in still other trials, the same participants were told about a previously unknown tribe living on a Pacific island. One member of the tribe had been observed and was obese. With this information, the participants were asked how likely they thought it was that all members of this tribe were obese.

For floridium, participants were quite willing to believe that a single instance allows generalization to the whole set, and so they asserted that all floridium would burn blue when heated. Participants were less willing to extrapolate from a single case when thinking about shreebles, and even less willing when thinking about obese islanders. For these categories, the participants were willing to draw conclusions only after they were told about several observations (several shreebles or several tribespeople) in addition to the initial case.

Clearly, therefore, people sometimes *are* sensitive to sample size, and so, apparently, they do not always use the representativeness heuristic. People could, in principle, have made their judgment about shreebles by relying on a "man who" argument (or, more precisely, "bird who"): "I know a shreeble that is blue; therefore all shreebles . . . ." But instead, people sensibly realize that shreebles may vary, and so draw no conclusion until they have more evidence. Obviously, use of the heuristic is not inevitable.

Finally, it is striking that people make all the errors we have described in this chapter but readily acknowledge their errors when someone points them out. Once someone points out the bias built into availability errors, people quickly agree that they have made a mistake in relying on availability. On their own, people usually ignore base rates, but with a few sentences of reminder, they agree that base rates should be considered (Stanovich, 1999). It's clear, then, that people do understand the proper way to make judgments and, with just a brief reminder, easily see their errors. Plainly, then, people do have the capacity to make judgments that are not rigidly tied to heuristic use—at the same time that, undeniably, heuristic use is extremely common.

Dual-Process Models

How should we think about all of this? It's certain that people do often rely on heuristics and, as a result, fall into certain errors—ignoring base rates, misjudging covariation, being overly influenced by what's easily available, or drawing conclusions from a tiny sample of evidence. Therefore, our theories about thinking must include some discussion of the heuristics. But, on the other side, people easily grasp what's wrong with heuristic use and, in some circumstances, do not make the errors associated with the heuristics. Plainly, therefore, people have some means of going beyond the heuristics, and this, too, must be represented in our theories.

These considerations have led many theorists to propose **dual-process models** of thinking—models that acknowledge the fact that people have two distinct ways of thinking about the evidence they encounter (e.g., Evans, 2003; Kahneman, 2003; Shafir & LeBoeuf, 2002). The various dual-process models differ in many specifics, but all propose that people have one way of thinking that is fast, effortless, and automatic; the heuristics we have described all fall into this category. The models then propose that people have another way of thinking that is slower, effortful, and applied only with deliberate intention. This is the sort of thinking that allows people to rise above the heuristics, and to reach decisions that are more laborious, but also more likely to be correct.

Different names have been proposed for the two systems. In their early writings, Kahneman and Tversky distinguished between *intuition* and *reasoning* (Kahneman, 2003); others have distinguished *association-driven thought* from *rule-driven thought* (e.g., Sloman, 1996). We will rely, though, on the more neutral terms suggested by Stanovich and West (2000), and therefore use **System 1** as the label for the fast and automatic sort of thinking, and **System 2** as the label for the slower, more effortful thinking.

In these terms, then, the proposal is that, in a wide range of situations, people rely on System 1 thinking. This is a good thing, because System 1 is fast, easy, and often leads to the correct answer. However, System 1's strategies are not perfect and so will, in many settings, lead to error; this is, in essence, the price one pays for being quick and efficient. Fortunately, though, System 2 thinking, although more cumbersome, is more accurate, and so System 2 can often catch (and overrule) System 1's errors.

All of this demands that we now tackle a question that we raised earlier: In any particular judgment, what governs whether we use System 1 or System 2? Why is it that we sometimes rely on the shortcuts and sometimes shift into more-cautious strategies?

The Importance of Circumstances

One obvious proposal is that people can *choose* when to rely on System 1 and when to rely on System 2. Presumably, people would elect to use the more efficient System 1 when making judgments that weren't particularly important, but would shift to the less efficient, more accurate, System 2 whenever a judgment really mattered.

However, we have already seen many indications that this proposal is not correct. As we have discussed, people rely on the fast-and-loose heuristics even when incentives are offered for accuracy; even when making important professional judgments; even when making medical diagnoses that may, in some cases, literally be matters of life and death. Surely people would choose to use System 2 in all these cases if they could, and yet they still rely on the heuristics, and still fall into error. On these grounds, it is difficult to argue that using System 2 is a matter of conscious choice.

Instead, the evidence suggests that System 2 comes into play only if appropriately triggered by certain cues in the problem, and only if the circumstances are right. In addition, evidence suggests that System 2 can become more responsive as a result of training. After the appropriate training, System 2 appears to be "primed," so that it is more easily triggered by situational cues.

What are the circumstances that matter for System 2's operation? We've already suggested that System 2 judgments are slower than System 1's, and on this basis, it's not surprising that heuristic-based judgments (and so heuristic-based *errors*) are more likely when judgments are made under time pressure (Finucane, Alhakami, Slovic, & Johnson, 2000). We've also said that System 2 judgments require *effort*, and this leads to the expectation that this form of thinking will be more likely if the person can focus attention on the judgment being made. This turns out to be correct: A reliance on heuristics and automatic interpretive habits is more likely if people are distracted, or not fully alert (D. T. Gilbert, 1989).

In addition, we've described System 2 as serving to *correct* or *overrule* the biased, shortcut conclusions reached by System 1. Phrased differently, one might say that System 1 is governed largely by *habit*, and System 2's job is often to override or inhibit the habit. As we discussed in Chapter 4, though, some people have more capacity than others to inhibit their own mental habits when they want to or need to. We argued, in the earlier chapter, that this ability to inhibit one's own habits is linked to working-memory capacity, which in turn is linked to many standardized tests of mental ability—including the IQ test and SAT scores.

Putting these pieces together, we might expect that people with high IQs, or high SATs, would be more successful in using System 2 to overrule the automatic (habit-based) conclusions of System 1. Many studies confirm this prediction. Thus, for example, people with higher SATs are more likely to consider base rates, less likely to be influenced by "man who" stories, and better able to judge covariation (Stanovich & West, 1998; also Feldman Barrett, Tugade, & Engle, 2004). We emphasize that high-SAT individuals still commit these judgment errors, but even so, they are less likely to commit the errors than those with low SATs.

The Importance of Data Format

There are surely no surprises in the factors just mentioned. It is not astonishing, for example, that people make more errors when they are pressed for time or distracted. Nor is it amazing that smart people make fewer errors than less-smart people. What is impressive, though, is that these factors are far from the whole story. We know this because even smart, undistracted, unpressured people make these errors. So we need to ask, What *else* is needed to elicit System 2 reasoning, and thus to avoid the mistakes?

The answer lies in the characteristics of the specific judgment that is being made. In effect, certain characteristics in a judgment seem to trigger System 2's operation. If these triggers are present, System 2 reasoning will be observed even with time pressure and distraction, and even with people who are not intellectual giants. But if the triggers are not present, then System 1 is likely to prevail.

For example, we earlier discussed the widespread neglect of base-rate information. Presumably, this is a result of System 1 thinking, with people relying on various heuristics in judging covariation and, in the process, not taking base rates into account. However, the error is avoided, and sensitivity to base rates is markedly increased, if the base rates are presented in the right way.

In many experiments, people have been presented with base rates cast in terms of probabilities or proportions: "There is a .01 chance that people like Mary will have this disease." "Only 5% of the people in this group are Chinese scholars." But this same information can be conveyed in terms of counts, or *frequencies*: "Of 100 people like Mary, only one will have this disease." "For every 1,000 people we consider, only 50 will be Chinese scholars."

It turns out that judgments are improved if people are given the information in "frequency format." Specifically, people are more likely to use base rates if they are phrased in terms of frequencies ("10 out of every 1,000 cases") rather than as a probability or percentage ("1%"). Likewise, people are more accurate in using diagnostic information cast as a frequency ("8 correct out of 10") than they are in using the same information cast as a probability or percentage ("80%"; Gigerenzer & Hoffrage, 1995; also Brase, Cosmides, & Tooby, 1998; and Cosmides & Tooby, 1996).

There is some debate, though, about *why* frequency information is advantageous. Some scholars have explained this in terms of the biology of the brain: Our ancient ancestors, they claim, often had occasion to think in terms of frequencies, and so natural selection favored those ancestors who were more skilled in thinking in these terms (e.g., Gigerenzer & Hoffrage, 1995). We are, of course, the descendants of these individuals, and so, as a result, we are now well adapted to thinking about frequencies, but not to thinking about proportions or probabilities.

Other researchers have offered different perspectives. As one alternative, a phrasing in terms of frequencies (X number *out of a larger group of* Y number) calls attention to the fact that we need to think about *groups* of observations, and subsets within those groups; it may be this cue that improves judgment, rather than the actual frequencies themselves (Evans, Handley, Perham, Over, & Thompson, 2000; Fiedler, Brinkmann, Betsch, & Wild, 2000; Girotto & Gonzalez, 2001; Lewis & Keren, 1999; Mellers & McGraw, 1999; Mellers, Hertwig, & Kahneman, 2001).

Even with this controversy, there is no question that participants' performance in dealing with judgment problems is influenced by the data format and, in particular, is improved if the data are cast in terms of frequencies (although, we note, errors still occur, even with frequencies). This may be for evolutionary reasons; it may be for some other reason. In either case, this result helps us to understand why human judgment about evidence is sometimes so poor, and sometimes reasonably accurate: It depends on how the problem is presented, with some presentations being more "user-friendly" than others.

Codable Data

As we have seen, people have a reasonable understanding of some fundamental statistical concepts. That was the point of our fictional dialogues, earlier, between Bart and Lisa, and between Marge and Homer. The dialogue captured the fact that people readily understand that accidents do happen (and hence one must be wary of a single observation, which could, after all, be the result of a fluke). They also understand that accidents don't keep happening over and over (and so one should take seriously a larger sample of evidence in which an observation has been repeated many times).

Why, therefore, don't people use this understanding more often? One reason is that we often just don't realize that our statistical concepts are *applicable* to a judgment we're trying to make. Often we don't realize that the evidence we're contemplating can be understood as a *sample of data* drawn from a larger set of potential observations. Likewise, we often don't see that *chance* played a role in shaping the evidence we're considering. As a result, we do not bring our (System 2) understanding to bear on the evidence, and instead we rely on (System 1) heuristics.

This leads to the expectation that we're likely to rise above our simple heuristics if the role of chance is conspicuous in the evidence we're considering, and if it's obvious how to interpret, or "code," the evidence in terms of a set of independent observations (Nisbett et al., 1983). The data confirm these claims: Manipulations that highlight the role of chance do increase the likelihood of a person's reasoning in a statistically appropriate manner. For example, Gigerenzer, Hell, and Blank (1988) presented participants with an urn containing 100 pieces of paper. Thirty of the pieces of paper, the participants were told, contained descriptions of engineers; 70 contained descriptions of lawyers. The participants themselves were then required to draw the "thumbnail descriptions" out of the urn, and to render a judgment about the likelihood that the individual selected was a lawyer. This manipulation emphasized for participants the role of chance in the selection of these descriptions and, accordingly, much improved the quality of their judgment; that is, it diminished their neglect of base rates. (For related data, see Baratgin & Noveck, 2000; Gigerenzer, 1991; Nisbett et al., 1983; and A. Tversky & Kahneman, 1982.)

We find the same pattern with the "codability" of the data. In some domains, like sports, it is obvious that the information we receive can be understood in statistical terms. It's clear that a team's performance in the game's first quarter is just a sample of evidence and may or may not reflect its performance in other samples (other quarters, or other games). It's also clear how to measure performance (points, or other sports statistics). For these reasons, the evidence is already "packaged" in a way that leads us to think in statistically sophisticated terms, and so it's no surprise that sports evidence, and other easily coded evidence, often evokes System 2 thinking (Jepson, Nisbett, & Krantz, 1983).

In contrast, other evidence is less easily coded in these terms. If an employer interviews a job candidate, the employer may or may not realize that the 10 minutes of interview can be thought of as just a "sample" of evidence, and that other impressions might come from other samples (e.g., reinterviewing the person on a different day, or seeing the person in another setting). It's also not clear how to quantify the employer's impressions during the interview—how to measure how responsible the candidate seemed, or how motivated, or how clever. In the eyes of most people, evidence like this doesn't lend itself easily to statistical treatment, leading to the expectation that this sort of evidence won't evoke System 2 thinking. Instead, the employer is likely to rely on simple heuristics in thinking about the job candidate—and to make less justifiable decisions in the process.

A number of studies confirm these broad claims. In general, people are more accurate, less prone to heuristic use, and less prone to errors, when confronting evidence that is easily understood in statistical terms. When judging events that are readily interpreted in terms of single, repeatable observations, people are better at judging covariation, more likely to be sensitive to the size of the sample of evidence, and so on (Holland, Holyoak, Nisbett, & Thagard 1986; Kunda & Nisbett, 1986).

Background Knowledge

Sometimes a specific problem will evoke better reasoning, not because of cues explicit in the problem, but because of knowledge that the person brings to the problem and, with that, beliefs that the person has about how the parts of the problem are related. We have already seen an example of this—in the study involving floridium, shreebles, and obese islanders (Nisbett et al., 1983). Participants came into this study with the knowledge that one sample of a chemical element is likely to resemble all other samples of that element, and so they were willing to extrapolate from just a single observation about the (fictional) element floridium. But the same participants also knew that birds of a single species can vary in color (think of how the pattern of coloration varies from one parrot to the next), and that humans within a group can surely vary in their height and weight. It was because of this background knowledge that participants hesitated to draw conclusions based on a single bird or a single tribesperson.

A different example involves base rates. Imagine that participants are asked to predict whether a particular student will pass an exam or not, and are given some diagnostic information, plus the base-rate information that, in the past, only 30% of the students who have taken this exam passed (Ajzen, 1977; also A. Tversky & Kahneman, 1982). In this case, the participants will draw on their broad understanding of exams and passing rates, and probably conclude that the exam must be relatively difficult. In other words, they are likely to perceive a cause-and-effect relationship between the base rate and the case they're trying to judge ("30% pass rate" implies "hard exam," which will cause difficulties for anyone taking the exam). As a result, they're likely to use the base rate in making their judgment.

On the other side, though, base rates are usually ignored when participants don't see any cause-and-effect relationship between the base rate and the case they are interested in. As an illustration, imagine, once again, that participants are asked to predict whether a particular student will pass an exam, and they are given diagnostic information about the student. As before, they are also given a base rate, but this time the base rate is presented differently: They are told that the student they are judging was drawn from a sample of students selected by a researcher; in this sample, it turns out, only 30% of the students are likely to pass. Here, the base rate is the same as it was before (a 30% pass rate), but the rate seems arbitrary; it might have been different if the researcher had chosen a different group of students. Statistically this makes no difference, and the base rate is as useful in this situation as it was in the first setting we considered. But with no causal link perceived, the base rate is neglected. (Also see Kunda, 1999, especially pp. 137–143; Oppenheimer, 2004; and Winkielman & Schwarz, 2001.)

In this and other experiments, then, people are likely to consider factors (like base rates, or sample size, or sample bias) that they think played a cause-and-effect role in shaping the particular case they are considering. In this way, System 2's influence depends on what people happen to believe about the "causal history" of the evidence being considered—that is, how that evidence came to be as it is. This, in turn, obviously depends on the background knowledge people bring into the situation, background knowledge about what causes what in the world.

Training Participants to Use Statistics

Let's pause to take stock. It is remarkably easy to find evidence for heuristic use, even when people are making highly consequential judgments. But people are also capable of more-sophisticated judgment strategies, strategies that in many cases can correct the errors sometimes produced by heuristic use. This demands that we ask *when* people use these System 2 strategies to correct the heuristics, and so far our answer to this question has two parts: One group of factors depends on the broad context (the presence or absence of time pressure or distraction, how capable the person is of inhibiting his or her own mental habits). A second group of factors depends on the specific task (the format of the data, whether the evidence is easily coded, whether the person has beliefs that would call up statistical concepts in interpreting the evidence, and so on).

But there is one more factor that also influences System 2's use: *training.* This is because, with appropriate education, it becomes easier to trigger the use of System 2, and thus to diminish the problems associated with System 1.

Fong, Krantz, and Nisbett (1986) provided participants with just a half-hour of training, focusing on the importance of sample size. The participants were reminded that accidents do happen, but that accidents don't keep happening over and over. Therefore, a small sample of data might be the result of some accident, but a large sample probably isn't. Consequently, large samples are more reliable, more trustworthy, than small samples.

Some of the participants in this study were taught about these issues in a fairly abstract way. Other participants were given examples during the training, showing them how considerations of sample size applied to real-world cases (e.g., a public opinion poll). Both forms of training were remarkably effective: After training, the participants (adults and high school students) were appreciably more likely to apply considerations of sample size to test cases, and their application of this principle tended to be reasonable and appropriate. (See also Fong & Nisbett, 1991.)

If a half-hour's training in statistics improves participants' judgment, what about an entire course in statistics? Fong et al. conducted a telephone survey of "opinions about sports," calling students who were taking an undergraduate course in statistics. Half of the students were contacted during the first week of the semester; half were contacted during the last week. Note, though, that there was no indication to the students that the telephone interview was connected to their course; as far as the students knew, they had been selected entirely at random.

The students in this study were asked several questions to increase the likelihood that they would indeed think they were simply being interviewed about sports, and to ensure that they didn't perceive the relation between the interview and their statistics course. Then they were asked a question that depended on a somewhat subtle consideration of sample size. (The question involved a comparison between how well a baseball player did in his first year and how well he did in the remainder of his career.) The participants' reasoning about this question was influenced by their training: For those contacted early in the term, only 16% gave answers that showed a consideration of sample size. For those contacted later, the number of answers influenced by sample size more than doubled (to 37%). The quality of the answers also increased, with students more likely to articulate the relevant principles correctly at the end of the semester than at the beginning.

It seems, then, that students' reasoning about evidence can be improved, and the improvement applies to problems in new domains and in new contexts. Training in statistics, it appears, can have widespread benefits. (For more on education effects, see Agnoli & Krantz, 1989; Lehman & Nisbett, 1990; and Schunn & Anderson, 1999.)

Thinking About Evidence: Some Conclusions

How, then, should we think about the results described throughout this chapter? As we have seen, it is easy to document judgment errors in bright, motivated undergraduates or in highly trained professionals. But we have also seen evidence of more-sophisticated judgment—and thus cases in which people are sensitive to sample size and sample bias, cases in which people judge covariation accurately and do consider base rates.

It's this pattern that demands a dual-process model, distinguishing between System 1 thinking and System 2 thinking. People surely don't want to use System 2 all the time; that would be too slow, too effortful, too inefficient. But they probably do want to use System 2 when the stakes are high and a judgment really matters. It's therefore troubling that System 2's use is not a matter of choice and so, even when we're motivated to use System 2 (e.g., because the judgment is an important one), we often use System 1 nonetheless. System 2 seems to enter the scene only when circumstances allow it, and only when this system is appropriately triggered.

It's therefore very encouraging that *training* seems to improve judgment and seems to make judgment errors less likely. The training presumably helps by making our understanding of statistical principles more prominent in memory and, therefore, easier to trigger. The training probably also helps us to see how our statistical intuitions apply to a range of new cases. Thus, with training, one realizes that an interview can be thought of as a small sample of data and perhaps should be trusted less than some other source of information based on a larger sample of evidence. Likewise, one can think of an athlete's rookie year in these terms, or a dancer's audition. Once the situation is coded in this fashion, the application of statistical rules is more straightforward and more likely.

We close this chapter, therefore, on an optimistic note. Errors in judgment are ubiquitous and often consequential. But these errors are not the result of some deep flaw in our capacity for making judgments. Instead, the errors arise largely because the situation does not trigger our (System 2) abilities for making sensible, defensible, judgments. And, crucially, education can improve this state of affairs, allowing us to use better judgment in a wide range of settings. Indeed, with suitable training, it may be possible to use judgment strategies that are both accurate *and* efficient.

Put differently, it seems that judgment—as one might have expected—is a *skill*, a skill that we all have to some extent, and a skill that can be improved by the appropriate type of education. Errors in drawing conclusions, and in making inferences, are remarkably widespread, but the path is open to reducing these errors and to improving the quality of human judgment.

Chapter Summary

1. In induction, one typically begins with specific observations and draws some general conclusion from them; in deduction, one usually starts with a general claim and asks what follows from this claim. Induction often begins with a frequency estimate, serving as an initial description of the data. In many cases, people make frequency estimates by using the availability heuristic, in which they judge an observation to be frequent if they can easily think of many examples of that observation. The more available an observation is, the greater the frequency is judged to be.

2. Judgments via availability are often accurate, but they do risk error. This is because many factors can influence availability, including the pattern of what is or is not easily retrievable from memory, bias in what we notice in our experiences, and also bias in what the media report. Even if people detect these biases, they often fail to adjust for them, because of anchoring.

3. People also rely on the representativeness heuristic when they extrapolate from observations they have made. This heuristic rests on the assumption that categories are relatively homogeneous, so that any case drawn from the category will be representative of the entire group. Because of this assumption, people expect a relatively small sample of evidence to have all the properties that are associated with the entire category; one example of this is the gambler's fallacy. Similarly, people seem insensitive to the importance of sample size, and so they believe that a small sample of observations is just as informative as a large sample. In the extreme, people are willing to draw conclusions from just a single observation, as in "man who" arguments.

4. People are also likely to make errors in judging covariation. In particular, their beliefs and expectations sometimes lead them to perceive illusory covariations. These errors have been demonstrated not just in novices working with unfamiliar materials but also in experts dealing with the sorts of highly familiar materials they encounter in their professional work.

5. People are accurate in assessing covariation if they have no prior beliefs or expectations about the data. This suggests that people do understand the concept of covariation and understand (roughly) how to assess covariation. When people have prior beliefs, though, their judgments of covariation are sometimes extreme and often erratic. This may be attributable to the fact that confirmation bias causes people to notice and remember a biased sample of the evidence, which leads to bad covariation judgments.

6. People also seem insensitive to base rates and, again, this can be demonstrated both in novices evaluating unfamiliar materials and in experts making judgments in their professional domains.

7. Use of heuristics is widespread, and so are the corresponding errors. However, we can also find cases in which people rely on more-sophisticated judgment strategies, and so are alert to sample size and sample bias, and do consider base rates. This has led many theorists to propose dual-process models of thinking. One process (often called System 1) relies on fast, effortless short-cuts; another process (System 2) is slower and more effortful, but less likely to lead to error.

8. System 1 thinking is more likely when people are pressed for time or distracted. System 1 thinking also seems more likely in people with lower working-memory capacity. However, System 1 thinking can be observed even in high-intelligence individuals, and even in the absence of time pressure or distraction. System 1 thinking can be observed even when the matter being judged is both familiar and highly consequential.

9. System 2 thinking seems more likely when the data are described in terms of frequencies rather than probabilities, and also when the data are easily coded in statistical terms (as a *sample* of data, with *chance* playing a role in shaping the sample). System 2 thinking is also more likely if people bring to a situation background knowledge that helps them to code the data, and to understand the cause-and-effect role of sample bias or base rates. Training in statistics also makes System 2 thinking more likely, leading us to the optimistic view that judging is a *skill* that can be improved through suitable education.

Reasoning: Thinking through the Implications of What You Know

In Chapter 12, we discussed how humans make judgments about evidence, and in most cases the judgments involved some element of uncertainty: You have no way to know if the "shreeble" you've examined is typical or not. In judging covariation, you're not sure if the evidence, provided by your memory, reflects reality or doesn't. At issue, then, was how we draw conclusions from a somewhat shaky base.

Often, though, we try to draw conclusions from claims that seem solidly established. Perhaps you're already convinced, for example, that Thai food tends to be spicy, or that relationships based only on physical attraction rarely last. You might then want to ask, What follows from this? What implications do these claims have for your other beliefs or actions? These questions rely on deduction—a process through which we start with claims or assertions that we count as "given," and ask what follows from these premises.

Among its other roles, deduction allows us to make predictions about upcoming events: If you are meeting a particular 6-year-old for the first time, you can anticipate many of her characteristics, on the basis of your knowledge of 6-year-olds in general. These anticipations rely on

- People often show a pattern of "confirmation bias," so that (for example) they usually take confirming evidence at face value but scrutinize disconfirming evidence with care, seeking flaws or ambiguity.

- Errors in logical reasoning are easy to document, and they follow patterns suggesting that people are guided by principles other than those of logic.

- People's reasoning is also heavily influenced by the *content* of what they're reasoning about, although the exact reasons for this remain uncertain.

- Overall, it appears that our theory of reasoning (like our theory of judgment) must contain multiple elements: People sometimes use logic; they sometimes rely on content-specific reasoning strategies, and sometimes on shortcuts. They sometimes also rely on mental models.

- People seem not to base most decisions on utility calculations. Instead, they try to make decisions that they feel they can explain and justify. This is why people are so sensitive to the framing of a decision, and also why decision-making is influenced by the same factors that, as we have seen, influence judgment and reasoning in general.

- We can easily document patterns in decision-making that seem to be errors—including self-contradictions and cases in which people fail to predict their own values. The chapter closes, therefore, with a consideration of whether or not people make decisions in the "right way."

deductions from your general knowledge. Likewise, if you are going for a job interview, you can predict many of the questions you'll be asked, and again these predictions are deduced from your general knowledge.

Predictions like these are obviously useful in our day-to-day lives, and this is one of the reasons why deduction is so important. But in addition, the ability to deduce predictions from our beliefs provides a way of keeping our beliefs in touch with reality: If our predictions turn out to be wrong, this tells us that something is off track in our beliefs—and that things we thought to be solidly established aren't so solid after all. Conversely, if a set of beliefs leads to correct predictions, this obviously lends support to those beliefs.

Does our reasoning respect these principles? If we encounter evidence confirming our beliefs, does this strengthen our convictions? If evidence challenging our beliefs should come our way, do we adjust? And what if we realize, from the start, that we are uncertain about a belief? Perhaps we have drawn a tentative conclusion and want to check on the conclusion before taking action. What evidence do we seek to verify or disprove our view? Our discussion of reasoning will begin with these crucial questions.

Confirmation and Disconfirmation

How should one go about testing a belief? What evidence might strengthen the belief? What would undermine it? These *normative* questions—about how one *ought* to reason—have been discussed at length by philosophers, and one important point emerging from their discussion concerns the ambiguity of confirming evidence and, with that, the great value of disconfirming evidence. To see this, consider the rooster, who is said to believe that his crowing each morning brings the sun into the sky. Plenty of evidence confirms his belief: Day after day he has crowed, and each time the sun has risen. Despite these confirmations, though, we believe the rooster's hypothesis to be false. Apparently, confirmations—no matter how numerous—cannot show a belief to be true.

Disconfirmations, on the other hand, can be enormously informative. Thus it might be useful for the rooster to ask, "What if I'm wrong? How else might I think about the evidence?" This might lead the rooster to the obvious experiment: to let one morning pass without crowing. The sun's arrival on that morning would surely tell the rooster a great deal.

Confirmation Bias

It seems, then, that in order to test a belief, it's often useful to *challenge* the belief, seeking out evidence that might be incompatible with the belief. Likewise, consideration of alternative hypotheses is usually helpful: In asking, "Is there another way to explain the facts?" one will often discover that the evidence is indeed ambiguous.

However, despite the usefulness of disconfirmation, and the utility of considering alternatives, people generally do neither. Instead, people display a strong tendency to seek out confirming evidence and to rely on that evidence in drawing their conclusions. This bias emerges in numerous forms: First, when people are assessing a belief or a hypothesis, they are far more likely to seek evidence that confirms the belief than evidence that might disconfirm it. Second, when disconfirming evidence is made available to them, people often fail to use it in adjusting their beliefs. Third, when people encounter confirming evidence, they take it at face value; when they encounter disconfirming evidence, in contrast, they reinterpret the evidence to diminish its impact. Finally, people regularly fail to consider alternative hypotheses that might explain the available data just as well as their current hypothesis does. (For reviews of the available evidence, see Evans, 1982; Gilovich, 1991; Higgins & Bargh, 1987; Rothbart, Evans, & Fulero, 1979; Schulz-Hardt, Frey, Lüthgens, & Moscovici, 2000; Stangor & McMillan, 1992; and Tweney, Doherty, & Mynatt, 1981.)

In a classic demonstration of confirmation bias, Wason (1966, 1968) presented research participants with a series of numbers, such as "2, 4, 6." The participants were told that this trio of numbers conformed to a specific rule, and their task was to figure out what the rule was. Participants were allowed to propose their own trios of numbers ("Does '8, 10, 12' follow the rule?"), and in each case the experimenter responded appropriately ("Yes, it does follow the rule" or "No, it doesn't"). Then, once participants were satisfied they had discovered the rule, they announced their "discovery."

The rule was, in fact, quite simple: The three numbers had to be in ascending order. Thus "1, 3, 5" follows the rule; so does "18, 19, 236." The trio "6, 4, 2" does not follow the rule, nor does "10, 10, 10." Despite this simplicity, participants had considerable difficulty in discovering the rule, often requiring many minutes. This was in part due to the kinds of information they requested, as they sought to evaluate candidate rules: To an overwhelming extent, they sought to confirm the rules they had proposed; requests for disconfirmation were relatively rare. And, importantly, those few participants who *did* seek out disconfirmation for their hypotheses were more likely to discover the rule! It seems, then, that confirmation bias was strongly on the scene in this experiment, and interfered with performance. (For related data, see Mahoney & DeMonbreun, 1978; Mitroff, 1981; and Mynatt, Doherty, & Tweney, 1977, 1978.)

Memory for Disconfirming Evidence

Confirmation bias also emerges in how people *remember* the evidence they have encountered. In some cases, people seem to remember the evidence consistent with their beliefs but conveniently forget facts that challenge their views. (For a classic finding, see J. M. Levine & Murphy, 1943.) Many studies, though, have failed to find this bias, suggesting that, in general, memory is not selective in this way (for reviews, see Eagly, Kulesa, Chen, & Chaiken, 2001; Gilovich, 1991; and Kunda, 1999).

However, there is a substantial difference in how people think about (and therefore remember) facts that are consistent with their beliefs and facts that are inconsistent. When people encounter confirming evidence, they tend to accept it at face value. When people encounter disconfirming evidence, in contrast, they're likely to scrutinize the evidence with special care, seeking flaws or ambiguities. If possible, they find ways to reinterpret the evidence so that it doesn't challenge their beliefs. Ironically, all this mental activity sometimes makes people *more likely* to remember disconfirming evidence than they are to remember confirming evidence (which receives much less scrutiny). However, the disconfirming evidence is remembered in a fashion that robs this evidence of its force, and so leaves the person's beliefs intact.

As an illustration, one study examined people who had placed bets on professional football games (Gilovich, 1983; also Gilovich & Douglas, 1986). The gamblers all believed that they had good strategies for picking winning teams, and their faith in these strategies was undiminished by a series of losses. Why is this? It is because the gamblers didn't remember their losses as "losses." Instead, they remembered them as mere flukes, or oddball coincidences. "I was right. New York was going to win, if it hadn't been for that crazy injury to their running back . . . ." "I was correct in picking St. Louis. They would have won except for that goofy bounce the ball took after the kickoff . . . ." In this way, winning bets were remembered as wins, but losing bets were remembered as "near wins" (Gilovich, 1991). No wonder, then, that the gamblers maintained their views, despite the (seemingly) contrary evidence provided by their own empty wallets.

Belief Perseverance

Even when disconfirming evidence is undeniable and out in plain view, people sometimes do not use it, creating a phenomenon called **belief perseverance**.

Participants in one study were asked to read a series of suicide notes; their task was to figure out which notes were authentic, collected by the police, and which were fake, written by other students as an exercise. As participants offered their judgments, they were provided with feedback about how well they were doing—that is, how accurate they were in detecting the authentic notes. The trick, though, was that the feedback was predetermined and had nothing to do with the participants' actual judgments. Some participants were told that they were well above average in this task (again, independent of their judgments); other participants were told the opposite—that they were much below average (L. Ross, Lepper, & Hubbard, 1975; also L. Ross & Anderson, 1982).

Later on, participants were debriefed. They were told that the feedback they had received was utterly bogus and had nothing to do with their performance. Indeed, they were shown the experimenter's instruction sheet, which had assigned them in advance to the *success* or *failure* group. They were then asked a variety of additional questions, including questions for which they had to assess their own "social sensitivity." Specifically, they were asked to rate their actual ability, as they perceived it, in tasks like the suicide-note task.

Let's emphasize that participants were making these judgments about themselves after they had been told the truth about the feedback. That is, they had been told clearly and explicitly that the feedback was randomly determined and had no credibility whatsoever. Nonetheless, participants were plainly influenced by the feedback: Those who had received the "above average" feedback continued to think of their social sensitivity as being above average, and likewise their ability to judge suicide notes. Those who had received the "below average" feedback showed the opposite pattern. The participants, in other words, persevered in their beliefs even when the basis for the belief had been completely discredited.

How does all of this connect to confirmation bias? Imagine yourself in the place of one of the participants, and let's say that we have told you that you are particularly bad at the suicide-note task. As you digest this new "information" about yourself, you'll probably ask yourself, "Could this be true? Am I perhaps less sensitive than I think I am?" To check on this possibility, you might search through your memory, looking for evidence that will help you evaluate this suggestion.

What sort of evidence will you seek? This is where confirmation bias comes into play. Because of this bias, chances are good that you will check on the researcher's information by seeking other facts or other prior episodes in your memory that might confirm your lack of social perception. As a result, you will soon have two sources of evidence for your social insensitivity: the (bogus) feedback provided by the researcher, and the supporting information you came up with yourself, thanks to your (selective) memory search. Thus, even if the researcher discredits the information he provided, you will still have the information you provided, and on this basis, you might maintain your belief. (For discussion, see Nisbett & Ross, 1980; also H. Johnson & Seifert, 1994.)

Of course, in this experiment, participants could be led either to an enhanced estimate of their own social sensitivity, or to a diminished estimate, depending on which false information they were given in the first place. Presumably, this is because the range of episodes in participants' memories is rather wide: In some previous episodes they have been sensitive, and in some they haven't been. Therefore, if they search through their memories seeking to confirm the hypothesis that they have been sensitive in the past, they will find confirming evidence. If, on the other hand, they search through memory seeking to confirm the opposite hypothesis, this too will be possible. In short, they can confirm either hypothesis, via a suitably selective memory search. This obviously highlights the dangers built into a selective search of the evidence and, more broadly, the danger associated with confirmation bias.

Logic

Why are people so vulnerable to confirmation bias? There are several possible explanations, but one, simply, is that people just aren't very logical in their thinking. Is this correct? One way to find out is to examine how well people do if we explicitly invite them to think things through in a logical manner. That will allow us to ask, in a straightforward way, whether thought tends to be logical or not.

Reasoning About Syllogisms

A number of theorists have proposed that thought does follow the rules of logic (Boole, 1854; Henle, 1962, 1978; Mill, 1874; Piaget, 1952). If we make reasoning errors, therefore, it is not because of some flaw in our thinking. Instead, the errors must come from other sources—carelessness, perhaps, or a misreading of the problem.

It turns out, however, that errors in logical reasoning are ubiquitous. If we are careless, or misread problems, we do so with great frequency. Much of the research relevant to this claim comes from studies employing categorical syllogisms. These are a type of logical argument that begin with two assertions—the problem's premises—each containing a statement about a category. These statements usually involve quantifiers, such as "some," "all," or "none." A premise might state, "All men are mortal," or "Some houses are not wooden."

The syllogism can then be completed with the conclusion that follows from these premises. Examples of categorical syllogisms are shown in Figure 13.1. These

FIGURE 13.1	Examples of Categorical Syllogisms

All M are B.
All D are M.
　　Therefore all D are B.

All X are Y.
Some A are X.
　　Therefore some A are Y.

Some A are not B.
All A are G.
　　Therefore some G are not B.

All of the syllogisms shown here are valid; that is, if the two premises are true, then the conclusion must be true.

are all **valid** syllogisms; that is, the conclusion does follow from the premises in each case. Here is an example of an invalid syllogism:

All P are M.
All S are M.
Therefore, all S are P.

To see that this is invalid, try translating it into concrete terms, such as, "All plumbers are mortal," and "All sadists are mortal." Both of these are surely true, but it doesn't follow from this that "All sadists are plumbers."

As you can see, syllogisms can involve concrete statements (such as, "All men are mortal") or abstract statements ("All A are B"). The logic of a syllogism, however, depends only on its form: No matter how we fill in "All A are B," the logical status of this statement remains the same. (Indeed, this dependence on only the *form* of a statement is the basis for the term "formal logic.")

Research participants who are asked to reason about syllogisms do remarkably poorly. Chapman and Chapman (1959) gave their participants a number of syllogisms, including the one just discussed, with premises of "All P are M," and "All S are M." The vast majority of participants, 81%, endorsed the invalid conclusion, "All S are P." Another 10% endorsed other invalid conclusions; only 9% got this problem right. Other studies, with other problems, yield similar data—with error rates regularly as high as 70% to 90%. (Gilhooly, 1988, provides a review.) Participants' performance is somewhat better when the syllogisms are spelled out in concrete terms, but here, too, performance remains relatively low (Wilkins, 1928).

Participants also show a pattern dubbed **belief bias:** If a syllogism's conclusion happens to be something people believe to be true anyhow, they are more likely to judge the conclusion as following logically from the premises. Conversely, if the conclusion happens to be something they believe to be false, they are likely to reject the conclusion as invalid (Evans, Over, & Manktelow, 1993; Klauer, Musch, & Naumer, 2000; Newstead, Pollard, Evans, & Allen, 1992; Oakhill & Garnham, 1993).

In displaying belief bias, participants are endorsing claims they believe to be true, based on the totality of their knowledge, and rejecting claims they believe to be false. In many ways, this seems a reasonable thing to do (Evans & Feeney, 2004), but it is not what these logic problems require: Logic is instead concerned with more "local" issues of reasoning—specifically, whether a particular conclusion is warranted by a particular set of premises. Thus, when people show the belief-bias pattern, they are failing to distinguish between good arguments (those that are logical and persuasive) and bad ones: They are willing to endorse a bad argument if it happens to lead to conclusions they already believe to be true, and they are willing to reject a good argument if it leads to conclusions already believed to be false.

Matching and Conversion

Why do people make so many errors on logic problems? One problem seems to be a reliance on a **matching strategy**, a strategy of endorsing conclusions if the words in the conclusion "match" those in the premises. Thus, if a participant sees a premise such as "All A are B," and then another premise such as "All D are B," then the participant is likely to accept a conclusion like "All A are D," because this conclusion "matches" the wording and structure of the premises. Likewise, a participant who sees premises like "Some A are not X" and "Some B are not X" is likely to accept a conclusion like "Some A are not B"—again, because of the "match" in wording and structure (Gilhooly, 1988; Gilhooly, Logie, Wetherick, & Wynn, 1993; Johnson-Laird, 1983; Wetherick, 1989; an earlier version of this idea, dubbed the "atmosphere hypothesis," was proposed by Woodworth & Sells, 1935).

Another pattern is also prominent in people's errors: People often interpret "All A are B" as though it were identical to "All B are A." (Of course this isn't warranted: "All trees are plants" isn't the same as "All plants are trees.") Likewise, people treat the following as equivalent: "Some F are not G" and "Some G are not F." These errors are referred to as **conversion errors**, because people are "converting" these statements from one form into another.

Where, then, does this leave us? Errors in logical reasoning are extremely common, and the errors don't look at all like the product of carelessness. Instead, there is a systematic pattern to the errors—a pattern captured in the phenomena of belief bias, the matching strategy, and conversion errors. This pattern indicates that our reasoning is guided by certain principles, but the principles are not the rules of logic! Put differently, it appears that scholars have simply been mistaken when they have argued that systems of formal logic describe the actual rules of thought.

Reasoning About Conditional Statements

Similar conclusions derive from research on a different aspect of logic—namely, reasoning about conditional statements. These are statements of the familiar "If X, then Y" format, with the first statement providing a condition under which the second statement is guaranteed to be true.

The rules of logic specify clearly how one should reason about conditional statements. For example, one logical rule, called *modus ponens*, justifies conclusions in this case:

> If P is true, then Q is true.
> P is true.
> Therefore, Q must be true.

People generally reason well with problems resting on *modus ponens*, such as "If Luke waves at me, I'll be happy. Luke did wave at me. What follows from this?" People have some difficulty, though, with the logical rule called *modus tollens*, which justifies the conclusion in this case:

> If P is true, then Q is true.
> Q is false.
> Therefore, P must be false.

In very simple cases, people do understand this rule: "If Luke waves at me, I'll be happy. I'm not happy. Therefore, it must be the case that Luke didn't wave at me; if he had, I'd be happy." If we add any complexity at all, though, people are easily confused by problems resting on *modus tollens*, often rejecting conclusions if they are based on this rule (Braine & O'Brien, 1991; Rips, 1983, 1990; Taplin & Staudenmayer, 1973).

People also make other logical errors—including the error called **affirming the consequent** and the error called **denying the antecedent** (Figure 13.2). As a result of all this, performance tends to be rather poor when people are asked to reason about conditional statements. Indeed, some studies have documented error rates, when people try to draw conclusions about conditionals, as high as 80% or 90%.

Just as with syllogisms, errors are more common if people are asked to reason about abstract problems ("If P, then Q"), in comparison to performance with concrete problems ("If John plays baseball, then he is tense"). Errors are also more common if the logic problems involve negatives ("If John does not play baseball, then he won't be late"). Moreover, and again just like syllogisms, belief bias can be demonstrated: People will endorse a conclusion if they happen to believe it to be true, even if the conclusion doesn't follow from the stated premises. Conversely, people will reject a conclusion if they happen to believe it to be false, even if the conclusion is logically demanded by the premises. Across the board, though, reasoning about conditionals is quite poor (Evans, 1982; Evans, Newstead, & Byrne, 1993; Rips, 1990; Wason & Johnson-Laird, 1972).

| **FIGURE 13.2** | Errors in Logic |

Affirming the consequent
(1) If A is true, then B is true.
 B is true.
 Therefore A is true.

Denying the antecedent
(2) If A is true, then B is true.
 A is not true.
 Therefore B is not true.

Many people accept these arguments as valid, but they are not. To see this, consider some concrete cases:

(3) If the object in my hand is a frog, then the object is green.
 The object in my hand is green.
 Therefore it is a frog.

(4) If the object in my hand is a frog, then the object is green.
 The object in my hand is not a frog.
 Therefore it is not green.

Both of these arguments are invalid. The object could, for example, be a lime—green, but not a frog, contradicting argument 3, and not a frog, but nonetheless green, contradicting argument 4.

People commonly make the errors called "affirming the consequent" and "denying the antecedent." However, a moment's reflection, guided by a concrete case, makes it clear that reasoning in these patterns is, in fact, incorrect.

The Four-Card Task

Psychologists have used many paradigms to study how people reason about "if-then" statements, but much of the research involves Wason's **four-card task** (sometimes called the **selection task**). In this task, research participants are shown four playing cards, as in Figure 13.3 (after Wason, 1966, 1968). The participants are told that each card has a number on one side and a letter on the other. Their task is to evaluate this rule: "If a card has a vowel on one side, it must have an even number on the other side." Which cards must be turned over to put this rule to the test?

Many people assert that the "A" card must be turned over, to check for an even number. Others assert that the "6" card must be turned over, to check for a vowel. Still others assert that both of these must be turned over. In Wason's research, 46% of the participants turned over the "A" and the "6"; 33% turned over just the "A." The correct answer, however, was obtained by only 4% of the participants—turning over

| FIGURE 13.3 | The Four-Card Task |

Each card has a letter on one side and a number on the other side. Which cards must be turned over to check this rule: "If a card has a vowel on one side, it must have an even number on the other side"?

the "A" and the "7." In brief, then, performance is atrocious in this problem, with 96% of the participants giving wrong answers.

Why is "A and 7" the right answer? If we turn over the "A" card, and find an even number, that's consistent with the rule. But if we turn it over and find an odd number, that's inconsistent. Therefore, by turning over the "A," we'll discover if this card is consistent with the rule or not. In other words, there's something to be learned by turning over this card. What about the "J"? The rule makes no claims about what is on the flip side of a consonant card, so no matter what we find on the other side, it satisfies the rule. Therefore, there's nothing to be learned by turning over this card; we already know (without flipping the card over) that it's consistent with the rule. How about the "6"? If we find a vowel on the reverse side of this card, this fits with the rule. If we find a consonant on the reverse, this also fits, since, again, the rule makes no claims about what is on the reverse of a consonant card. Therefore, we'll learn nothing by turning over the "6"; no matter what we find, it satisfies the rule. Finally, if we turn over the "7" and a consonant is on the other side, this fits with the rule. If there's a vowel on the other side, this doesn't fit. Therefore, we do want to turn over this card, because there is a chance that we might find something informative.

The Effects of Problem Content

As we have mentioned, performance in the four-card task is usually atrocious—with more than 90% of the participants giving the wrong answer. However, some studies, using variations on this problem, have found much better performance. For example, Griggs and Cox (1982) asked their participants to test this rule: "If a person is drinking beer, then the person must be over 19 years of age." As in the other studies, the participants were shown four cards and asked which cards they would need to turn over to test the rule (Figure 13.4). In this version, participants

FIGURE 13.4 An Easier Version of the Four-Card Task

| DRINKING A BEER | 22 YEARS OF AGE | DRINKING A COKE | 16 YEARS OF AGE |

Participants do reasonably well with this version of the four-card task. Here, each card has a person's age on one side, and what the person is drinking on the other side. The participants' task is to select the cards that one would have to turn over in order to test the following rule: "If a person is drinking beer, then the person must be over 19 years of age."

did quite well: 73% (correctly) selected the card labeled "Drinking a beer," and also the card labeled "16 years of age." They did not select "Drinking a Coke" or "22 years of age." Griggs and Cox also tested their participants with the "standard" version of the test (if vowel, then even number), and none of their participants got this problem right. (For discussion, see Cheng & Holyoak, 1985; Evans, 1982; Evans, Newstead, et al., 1993; Griggs, 1983; Johnson-Laird, Legrenzi, & Legrenzi, 1972; Legrenzi, Girotto & Johnson-Laird, 1993; and Wason, 1983.)

Notice that this effect of *content* is another argument against the proposal that logic describes the rules of thought. Logic, after all, depends only on the form or syntax of the assertions being considered, and not at all on their content. Thus, in terms of logic, there's no difference at all among the following three cases:

If you sleep, you dream.
You sleep.
Therefore, you dream.

If Fred eats, then Carla is happy.
Fred eats.
Therefore, Carla is happy.

If Boaz chases the squirrel, then Snowflake runs and hides.
Boaz chases the squirrel.
Therefore, Snowflake runs and hides.

These three cases obviously use different words, but they all have the same form, and it's only the form that matters for logic.

If our thought followed the rules of logic, then the same should be true for thought: It should be the form of the argument that matters, quite independent of the content. But that is not the pattern of the data. When people show the pattern of belief bias, for example, they are clearly being influenced by the content of what they're reasoning about, and not just the logical form. And certainly in the four-card problem, the content matters a lot. The logical form of the original problem (cast in terms of vowels and even numbers) is identical to the form of the "over 19 and drinking beer" version. Even so, the data are very different for these two versions, and so, quite plainly, the content of these problems does matter for performance. This seems highly problematic for the claim that logic (or any other formal system) reflects the way people typically think. Instead, the evidence is driving us toward the view that thought is influenced by the content, the meaning, and the pragmatics of the material we are contemplating.

Detecting Cheaters

But how does the content influence us? More specifically, why are some versions of the four-card problem difficult and others easy? Different investigators have offered different views of this issue, and the data do not yet allow a clear choice among these views; indeed, in the end, we may need to seek some combination of these different views in order to encompass the full data pattern.

What are our options? One proposal comes from an evolutionary perspective on psychology, a perspective we first met in Chapter 12. According to this perspective, many questions in psychology are better understood if we think about how the relevant skills, or relevant processes, have been shaped by evolutionary pressures over the last million years or so. To apply this perspective to the broad topic of reasoning, several investigators have argued this way: Our ancient ancestors didn't have to reason about whether or not all *A* are *B*, nor did they have to reason about vowels and even numbers. Instead, our ancestors had to worry about issues like social interactions, including issues of betrayal and cheating: "I asked you to do something. Have you done it, or have you betrayed me?" "None of our clan is supposed to eat more than one share of meat; is Joe perhaps cheating and eating too much?"

If our ancestors needed to reason about these issues, then any individuals who were particularly skilled in this reasoning might have had a survival advantage, and so, little by little, those who were skillful would become more numerous, and those without the skill would die off. In the end, only those skillful at social reasoning would be left. And, of course, we are the biological heirs of these survivors, and so we inherited their skills.

According to this proposal, therefore, people in the modern world will reason well about a logical rule whenever they understand that rule as involving cheating, betrayal, or the like (Cosmides, 1989; Cummins, 2004; Cummins & Allen, 1998; Gigerenzer & Hug, 1992). In this case, the skills that people have (thanks to their biology) will be well matched to the reasoning problem, and this will lead to good performance.

This claim is certainly consistent with the data we have seen so far: The "over 19 and drinking beer" problem, for example, involves the detection of "cheaters" and yields good performance. Other results also confirm that good performance is observed with problems that can be understood as "detecting cheaters"—even if the problems involve unfamiliar situations or principles (Cosmides, 1989; Gigerenzer & Hug, 1992; but also see N. Liberman & Klar, 1996).

Pragmatic Reasoning Schemata

Other investigators have offered different hypotheses about the four-card problem. Cheng and Holyoak (1985), for example, have proposed that thinking generally depends on pragmatically defined rules that people have learned from their day-to-day experience. Thus, for example, people learn from experience that certain rules apply to any situation that involves *permission*. These rules include, "If one wishes to take a certain action, then one must have permission," and "If one has permission to take a certain action, then one may take the action." These rules are obviously similar to the rules of logic, and so they can be used to guide reasoning. Let's emphasize, though, that these rules only support thinking about situations of the right sort—situations involving permission. In this way, these pragmatic reasoning rules are more concrete than the rules of logic.

People also have **pragmatic reasoning schemata** for other sorts of situations—situations involving *obligations*, or situations involving *cause-and-effect* relationships. In these cases, too, the pragmatic reasoning rules, gained from experience, guide people in the sorts of reasoning they need to do in their everyday existence (Cheng & Holyoak, 1985; Cheng, Holyoak, Nisbett, & Oliver, 1986; Nisbett, 1993).

How does all of this apply to the four-card problem? The original version of this problem contained no practical or meaningful relations; the rule of "if a vowel, then an even number" is completely arbitrary. The problem is therefore unlikely to evoke a reasoning schema, and this leaves participants at a loss: With their primary reasoning strategy not called into play, it is no wonder that they do poorly on this task.

According to this view, we should be able to improve performance on the four-card task by altering the problem so that it will trigger a pragmatic reasoning schema. Then people will be able to employ their usual means of reasoning and should perform quite well. To this end, participants in one experiment were shown the cards illustrated in Figure 13.5. Their task was to decide which cards to turn over to test the rule, "If the form says 'ENTERING' on one side, then the other side includes cholera among the list of diseases."

For half of the participants, this problem was given with no further rationale. The prediction here is that no schema will be evoked and performance should be poor. The other participants, however, were given a rationale designed to trigger the permission schema. These participants were told that the cards listed diseases

| FIGURE 13.5 | The Role of a Rationale in the Four-Card Problem |

| ENTERING | TRANSIT | CHOLERA | OTHER |

Participants were asked which cards they would need to turn over to find out if the following rule is true: "If the form says 'ENTERING' on one side, then the other side includes cholera among the list of diseases." Participants perform well on this problem if they are provided with a rationale; otherwise they perform poorly.

against which airline passengers had been inoculated. In addition, they were told that cholera inoculation was required of all passengers seeking to enter the country. These participants were then given the same rule as stated above, but now the rule can be understood in permission terms—something like, "If a passenger wishes to enter the country, he or she must first receive a cholera inoculation." With this rationale in view, the problem should trigger a schema, and participants should perform well.

The data were consistent with these predictions: Participants did rather well with the rationale versions of this problem, averaging about 90% correct. Without the rationale, they did poorly (about 60%). Thus, in this and in other experiments, people do seem to reason well if a reasoning schema is called into play, but otherwise they reason poorly.

Necessity and Sufficiency

Here's another approach to the four-card data—one that begins with the fact that "if-then" sentences are actually ambiguous (Ahn & Graham, 1999). Sometimes the condition (the "if" part) identifies a **necessary condition** for the rest of the sentence (something that *must be true* for the rest of the sentence to be true). Other times, the condition isn't necessary, but instead simply identifies one of many ways to make the conclusion true.

For example, consider these two sentences:

If Jacob passed his driver's test, then he can drive Bo to the park.

If Solomon is eligible for jury duty, then he is over 21.

The first sentence describes a necessary condition, because passing the test is a prerequisite for driving to the park. (If Jacob hasn't passed, then he cannot drive.) The second sentence, though, doesn't describe a necessary condition, because even if

Solomon isn't eligible for jury service, he might still be over 21. (Perhaps Sol isn't a citizen, or perhaps he's a convicted felon. In those cases, he wouldn't be eligible, but that tells us nothing about his age.)

Likewise, sometimes an "if-then" sentence describes a **sufficient condition**—something that, if true, guarantees that the claim being made is true. In other cases, however, the condition isn't sufficient. Again, consider our two examples. We've already said that Jacob's passing the driver's test is *necessary* for driving Bo, but it's not sufficient. That's because, even if Jacob has passed the test, other things might still prevent the drive. (What if Jacob doesn't have a car? What if Bo is on vacation in Fiji?) In contrast, the sentence about Solomon does describe a sufficient condition: If Sol is eligible, then we can be certain he's over 21, no matter what else we do or don't know about Solomon.

As these examples suggest, you need to reason in different ways about necessary or sufficient conditions. For illustration, when a sentence describes a necessary condition, then if the "if" clause is *false*, the conclusion must be false. (For Jacob, "has not passed" means "cannot drive.") But when the sentence describes a sufficient condition, then if the "if" clause is false, the conclusion might still be true. (For Sol, "is not eligible" is not, by itself, enough to tell us "not over 21.")

How does this connect to the four-card problem? Some versions of the problem (like the "drinking beer" version, or problems involving permission) invite an interpretation that involves *sufficiency*, and this triggers a pattern of reasoning that's very similar to the way logicians define the "if-then" relationship. It's no wonder, then, that these problems lead to a high proportion of "correct" answers (answers in line with those endorsed by logicians). Other problems invite different interpretations, and so trigger different patterns of reasoning. And still other problems (like the original "vowel and even number" version) are ambiguous with regard to interpretation, and so different participants interpret the problem in different ways, yielding a somewhat chaotic pattern of results. (For related proposals, see Almor & Sloman, 2000; Girotto, 2004; Oaksford & Chater, 1995; Polk & Newell, 1995; and Sperber, Cara, & Girotto, 1995.)

Where, then, does all of this leave us? There is no question that some versions of the four-card problem produce miserable levels of performance, while other versions yield excellent performance. Is this because of a biologically rooted skill of thinking about "cheating," or a skill, gained from experience, of reasoning about pragmatically defined goals? Or is it a reflection of the way that the problem's content leads us to interpret the "if-then" relationship? It is difficult to say, largely because these conceptions overlap heavily in their predictions about which versions of the task will be easy and which will be hard. It is no surprise, therefore, that researchers have not been able to devise tests that will allow us to choose one of these theoretical accounts over the others. In the meantime, though, one thing is clear: A purely formal account of our reasoning—one that emphasizes only the logical form of the problems we face, and not the content of those problems—does not mesh with the way humans reason.

Deductive Logic: An Interim Summary

Before pressing on, let's summarize where we are. We've been asking, in essence, how people reason: What rules do people rely on? What principles do people follow? The answer to these questions seems to have several parts. First, it's obvious that some people, in some circumstances, can use the rules of logic. Logic teachers, for example, can obviously use these rules. Even those untutored in logic can handle simple logic problems. Imagine, for example, that we tell people, "If G is true, then H is true. G happens to be true." With no difficulty, and even with this abstract, unfamiliar problem, people draw the conclusion (based on *modus ponens*) that H, too, must be true—fully in accordance with the rules laid out by logicians.

More commonly, people rely on less-formal reasoning strategies, although, as we have seen, there is debate over what the other strategies are. Perhaps these other strategies are reasoning skills specifically shaped by evolution, skills that we use whenever we are thinking about cheaters, betrayal, or the like. Perhaps, instead, the other strategies are pragmatic reasoning schemata, used whenever a problem can be understood in terms of pragmatic goals. Or perhaps the reasoning skills are more general, but still dependent on the problem's content as an aid toward figuring out whether the situation involves necessary conditions, sufficient conditions, or both. In all cases, though, these other reasoning strategies are sophisticated enough so that they generally yield conclusions identical to those endorsed by logical rules.

But this isn't all. Our account of reasoning also needs a third layer, describing the way people reason when these relatively sophisticated reasoning strategies are not triggered. For example, people seem to rely on the matching strategy if they don't know how else to proceed. Likewise, if people can't figure out a problem, they try to help themselves by "smuggling in" other knowledge, external to the problem. In this case, they show the pattern that we earlier called "belief bias." This inclusion of other knowledge isn't warranted according to logic, but it may be someone's best bet, if no other plan is available.

Putting all of this together, the suggestion is that the rules of logic, some sort of content-specific reasoning strategies, and various shortcuts may all coexist in our mental repertoire, and each will surface in appropriate circumstances. Some of these approaches to reasoning (like the matching strategy) are relatively primitive, but it seems that the more "sophisticated" strategies come into play only when appropriately triggered—by cues signaling that a problem involves permission, or content specifying that the condition is a *sufficient* one, and so forth.

Note the parallels between all of this and the pattern we saw in Chapter 12: In both judgment and reasoning, it seems, our theory requires multiple parts. In both cases, sophisticated thinking is possible even for people who have not been formally trained. However, this sophisticated thinking isn't always used, and it seems to play a role only in the "right" circumstances (e.g., if the problem contains the right triggers). And in both cases, people often rely on relatively primitive strategies when they don't see how else to tackle the problem. These may produce error, but they probably work more often than not, and at least they are efficient.

Mental Models

It seems, then, that different reasoning strategies exist side by side in the mind and are called into play in different situations. If we sometimes reason poorly, this is largely because we are using inappropriate strategies. If we can change the situation (so that different strategies are triggered), reasoning can be much improved.

It is against this backdrop that we consider one further reasoning strategy that people use—a strategy of creating, and then reasoning about, **mental models**. To see how these models work, let's return for the moment to categorical syllogisms, like this one:

> All of the artists are beekeepers.
> Some of the beekeepers are chemists.

What follows from these premises? One way to think about this problem is to imagine a room full of people. Some of the people in the room are artists (perhaps you imagine them as wearing sweatshirts with a big *A* on the front). Others in the room are not artists (they have no sweatshirts). Perhaps you then imagine all of the artists as having a bee perched on their heads, and perhaps you also imagine some nonartists as having bees on their heads as well. (After all, the premise said that all artists are beekeepers, but it didn't say that all beekeepers are artists.) Continuing in this fashion, you will end up imagining a little world, or a mental model, in which all of the premises are fulfilled. You can then inspect this model in order to ask what else is true about it: Once the premises are fulfilled, what other claims are entailed? Does it follow, for example, that some artists are chemists? (As it turns out, this conclusion doesn't follow from these premises, and so it would be invalid. You might confirm this by constructing a suitable mental model—"staffing" the imagined room as needed.) Other premises can also be represented in this fashion. For example, if the premise were, "No artists are beekeepers," you could imagine a room divided by a barrier, with the artists on one side and the beekeepers on the other.

Johnson-Laird and his colleagues have argued that mental models are widely used in reasoning. Broadly put, the idea is that one first constructs a mental model of a problem (or perhaps multiple models). Next, one scrutinizes the model, seeking to discover what conclusions follow from the modeled premises. Finally, one can check on these conclusions by trying to construct counterexamples—models that are compatible with the premises, but not with the proposed conclusion. If no counterexamples are found, then one concludes that the conclusion is valid (Johnson-Laird, 1990, 2001, 2004; Johnson-Laird & Byrne, 1989, 1991; also Klauer et al., 2000).

Participants in reasoning studies sometimes, on their own, mention the use of such models. One participant commented, "I thought of all the little artists in the room and imagined that they all had beekeeper's hats on." As more formal evidence, though, the mental-model approach leads to a number of predictions about reasoning performance, and many of these predictions have been confirmed. For example, some premises can be modeled in more than one way (see Figure 13.6). People trying to reason about these premises will have to examine multiple models, or else keep track of mental models with "optional" parts. One would expect this to make a problem more difficult, and this is indeed the case: The greater the number of models needed in reasoning through the problem, the more likely errors are to occur (Johnson-Laird, Byrne, & Tabossi, 1989; Johnson-Laird & Steedman, 1978).

Researchers have also suggested a role for mental models in other forms of reasoning, including reasoning about conditional problems (Evans, 1993; Johnson-

---

FIGURE 13.6   Mental Models of a Premise

Many premises can be modeled in more than one way. For example, shown here are several possible models for the premise, "Some of the artists are beekeepers." In other words, each row within the figure depicts a situation in which this premise is true. Artists are shown with As on their shirts; nonartists don't have As. Beekeepers are shown with bees on their heads; nonbeekeepers are bare-headed.

Laird, Byrne, & Schaeken, 1992; Legrenzi et al., 1993). For example, imagine that we tell you, "If it is sunny, the boys play baseball." You might then construct a mental model of this conditional—perhaps by contemplating a sunny day, with the boys out on the field. Imagine that we now add, "Today it is sunny." This is obviously consistent with the model you've constructed, implying that is okay to draw conclusions from this model. Therefore, you correctly conclude, "Today the boys play baseball."

Evidence suggests that people do sometimes reason about conditionals in this fashion. Hence, mental models take their place as part of the repertoire of human reasoning strategies. This obviously invites future researchers to explore more fully the pattern of triggers that lead us on one occasion to use one strategy, and on another occasion some other strategy. (For further discussion of mental models, see Evans, 1993; Ford, 1995; Goldvarg & Johnson-Laird, 2000; Johnson-Laird et al., 1992; Johnson-Laird, Legrenzi, Girotto, Legrenzi, & Caverni, 1999; Johnson-Laird & Savary, 1999; and Rips, 1986, 1989.)

Decision-Making

We turn now to one last category of reasoning: reasoning about choices. How do we choose what courses to take next semester or what movie to see on Saturday? How do we choose which candidate to support in an election? How do we choose an apartment or a job? Choices like these fill our lives, leading us to ask, How do people make decisions?

Utility Theory

Each of us has his or her own values—things we like, things we prize, or conversely, things we hope to avoid. Likewise, each of us has a series of goals—things we hope to accomplish or things we hope to see—including both near-term goals (what we hope to accomplish soon) and longer-term goals. The obvious suggestion, then, is that we use these values and goals in making decisions: In choosing courses for next semester, for example, you will choose courses that are interesting (something you value) and also courses that help fill the requirements for your major (one of your goals). In choosing a medical treatment, you will hope to avoid pain, and you will also hope to retain all of your physical capacities as long as possible.

To put this a bit more formally, each decision will have certain costs attached to it (i.e., consequences that will carry us farther from our goals) and also certain benefits (consequences moving us toward our goals and providing us with things we value). In deciding, we weigh the costs against the benefits and seek a path that will minimize the former and maximize the latter. When we have several options open to us, we will presumably choose the one that provides the most favorable balance of benefits and costs.

This weighing of benefits against costs allows us to accommodate the fact that many decisions involve trade-offs of one sort or another. Should you go to Miami for your vacation this year, or to Tucson? The weather is better in Tucson, but the flight to Miami is less expensive. Hence, you must trade off the more desirable weather against the more attractive plane fare. Likewise, should you drive a less comfortable car, if it happens to pollute less? Here, the trade-off is between your comfort and protection of the environment.

Notice that these trade-offs involve factors that are, to say the least, highly disparate—comfort versus pollution, the pleasure made possible by good weather versus the $50 you might save in airfare. Can you really translate your pleasure into dollar amounts? Is your pleasure worth more than, or less than, $50? Likewise, how do you compare a 10% reduction in comfort with a 0.0001% reduction in pollution levels? In these examples (and, indeed, in most decisions), comparing these factors seems like the proverbial comparison of apples and oranges: The values at stake seem incommensurable.

Somehow, though, we do make these comparisons. We have to, if we are going to make these choices. Presumably, we compare them in a rather subjective way, by asking how important each factor is to us. This is often expressed as the subjective utility of each factor, meaning, quite simply, the value of that factor for us. These utilities can then be summed (e.g., the utility of a pleasant vacation minus the "disutility" of spending more on airfare) to evaluate the overall utility for each outcome. These summed utilities for the various options can then be compared to each other, with the goal of selecting the option with the greatest overall utility.

In most decisions, though, there is also a degree of uncertainty or risk. Is Professor X an interesting instructor? Four of your friends have said she is, but two have said she is not. How should you factor these mixed reviews into your decision? Should you go to Miami for your vacation? At this time of year, let's say there is a 20% chance of rain. Do you want to take that chance?

One way to think about these risks follows a model formalized by von Neumann and Morgenstern (1947). Within their model, one calculates the expected value of each option using this simple equation:

Expected value = (probability of a particular outcome) × (utility of the outcome)

Thus, imagine that I offer to sell you a lottery ticket. The ticket costs $5 but gives you a one-in-a-hundred chance of winning $200. In this case, the expected value of the ticket is (.01 × $200), or $2. At a cost of $5, then, I'm selling the ticket for more than it is worth.

With more-complicated decisions, you will calculate the expected value of each factor and then add these up to compute the overall expected value associated with a particular choice. Let's say that you are choosing courses for next year. Course 1 looks interesting but also has a heavy workload. To evaluate this course, therefore, you will first need to estimate the subjective utility of taking an interesting course and also the disutility of being burdened by a heavy workload. Next, you will have to factor in the uncertainties. Perhaps there is a 70% chance that the course will be interesting, but a 90% chance that it will have a heavy workload. In this case, the overall utility for this course will be (.70 × the utility of an interesting course) minus (.90 × the disutility of a heavy workload). You could then make similar calculations for the other courses available to you and choose the one with the greatest expected value.

All of this points the way toward a theory of choice, and it is a theory endorsed by most modern economists: The claim is that, in making choices, we seek to maximize utility—that is, to gain as much as we can of those things we value, and to avoid those things we don't like. We do this by consistently selecting the option with the greatest expected utility, calculated as described. (For discussion, see von Neumann & Morgenstern, 1947; also Baron, 1988; and Savage, 1954.)

Before continuing, though, let's be clear that the term "utilities" is used here in a very broad sense, referring to whatever it is that is important to you. Hence, there is no connection between, say, seeking to maximize utilities and being greedy or materialistic. If you happen to value money, then the attempt to maximize utilities will turn out to be an attempt to gather wealth. But if you happen to value leisure, or happiness in those around you, or a reduction of world hunger, then these will be the utilities you seek to maximize. Thus, there is no stigma attached to the notion of utility maximization, and it surely seems sensible to make decisions that move you, as efficiently as possible, toward your goals.

Framing of Outcomes

There is no doubt that many of our choices and decisions do follow the principle of **utility maximization**. Which would you rather have—$90 or $100? Which gamble would you prefer—a 1% chance of winning a prize, or a 5% chance of winning the same prize? In each case, we are (rather obviously) sensitive to both the value of the "payoff" associated with a decision (i.e., its utility) and also the probability of a payoff.

However, an enormous number of studies show that, in many circumstances, we are not utility maximizers and, more broadly, that we are profoundly influenced by factors having little to do with utilities. In the process, we regularly make choices that are flatly inconsistent with other choices we have made. We will first review a number of these cases, and then we'll turn to how a theory of choice might accommodate them.

Consider the question posed in Figure 13.7. Research participants show a clear preference between these options, and 72% choose Program A (A. Tversky & Kahneman, 1987). Now consider the question posed in Figure 13.8. This problem is the same as the one in Figure 13.8: 200 people saved out of 600 is identical to 400 people dead out of 600. Therefore, the utilities involved in this problem have not changed one whit. Nonetheless, this change in how the problem is phrased—that is, the **frame** of the decision—has a strong impact on participants' choices. In the "lives

| FIGURE 13.7 | The Asian Disease Problem: Positive Frame |

Imagine that the United States is preparing for the outbreak of an unusual Asian disease, which is expected to kill 600 people. Two alternative programs to combat the disease have been proposed. Assume that the exact scientific estimates of the consequences of the programs are as follows:

If Program A is adopted, 200 people will be saved.

If Program B is adopted, there is a ⅓ probability that 600 people will be saved, and a ⅔ probability that no people will be saved.

There is clearly no right answer to this question; one could defend selecting the "risky" choice (Program B) or the less rewarding but less risky choice (Program A). The clear majority of people, however, lean toward Program A, with 72% choosing it over Program B. Note that this problem is "positively" framed in terms of lives "saved."

saved" frame (Figure 13.7), they favor Program A by almost a 3-to-1 margin. In the "will die" frame (Figure 13.8), this pattern of preferences reverses, and 78% opt for Program B.

It should be emphasized that there is nothing wrong with participants' individual choices. In either Figure 13.7 or Figure 13.8, there is no "right answer," and one can persuasively defend either the decision to avoid risk by selecting Program A, or the decision to take the chance by selecting Program B. The problem, though, lies in the contradiction created by choosing Program A in one context and Program B in the other context. Indeed, if a single participant is given both frames, on slightly different occasions, the participant is quite likely to contradict himself. For that matter, if a propagandist wanted to manipulate voters' evaluations of these programs, framing provides an effective way to do this.

Framing effects of this sort are easy to demonstrate. Figure 13.9 shows another example, in which people are asked to choose between two different medical treatments. When participants were given the "survival" frame, only 18% chose radiation over surgery. When participants were given the "mortality" frame, this number more than doubled—with 44% now favoring radiation (A. Tversky & Kahneman, 1987).

As one final example, consider the two problems shown in Figure 13.10 When participants are given the first problem, almost three quarters of them (72%) choose the first option—the sure gain of $100. Participants contemplating the second problem generally choose the second option, with only 36% selecting the sure loss of $100 (A. Tversky & Kahneman, 1987). Note, though, that the problems are once again identical. Both pose the question of whether you would rather end up with a certain $400, or with an even chance between $300 and $500. Despite this equivalence, participants treat these problems very differently, preferring the sure thing in one case, and the gamble in the other.

| FIGURE 13.8 | The Asian Disease Problem: Negative Frame |

Imagine that the United States is preparing for the outbreak of an unusual Asian disease, which is expected to kill 600 people. Two alternative programs to combat the disease have been proposed. Assume that the exact scientific estimates of the consequences of the programs are as follows:

If Program A is adopted, 400 people will die.

If Program B is adopted, there is a ⅓ probability that nobody will die, and a ⅔ probability that 600 people will die.

This problem is identical in content to the one shown in Figure 13.7: 400 dead out of 600 people is the same as 200 saved out of 600. Nonetheless, people react to the problem shown here rather differently than they do to the one in Figure 13.7: In the "lives saved" version, 72% choose Program A. In the "will die" version, 78% choose Program B. Thus, by changing the phrasing, we reverse the pattern of people's preferences.

Across these (and many other) examples, there is a consistent pattern to framing effects. If the frame casts a choice in terms of losses, decision-makers tend to be **risk-seeking**; that is, they are quite willing to gamble, presumably in hopes of avoiding or reducing the loss. To see this in action, look back at Figure 13.8. Here, the Asian disease problem is cast in terms of lives lost, and so this leads to risk-seeking choices: People choose the gamble that's inherent in Program B, apparently attracted by the (thin) possibility that, with this program, they may avoid the loss. Likewise, Problem 2 in Figure 13.10 casts your options in terms of financial losses, and this, too, triggers risk-seeking: Here people reliably choose the 50-50 gamble over the sure loss.

The pattern of preferences reverses, though, if the frame casts the exact same choice in terms of gains. When contemplating gains, decision-makers tend to be **risk-averse**, not risk-seeking. In other words, they are not willing to gamble, choosing instead to hold tight to what they already have. Thus, Figure 13.7 casts the Asian disease problem in terms of gains (the number of people saved), and this leads people to prefer the risk-free choice (Program A) over the gamble offered by Program B. (And likewise for Problem 1 in Figure 13.10.)

This pattern is powerful and easy to demonstrate: People are reliably risk-seeking when contemplating losses, and reliably risk-averse when contemplating gains. And we should emphasize that there is nothing wrong with either of these strategies by itself: If someone prefers to be risk-seeking, this is fine; if someone prefers to be risk-averse, this is okay too. The problem arises, though, when people flip-flop between these strategies, depending on how the problem is framed. The flip-flopping, as we have seen, leaves people wide open to manipulation, to inconsistency, and to self-contradiction.

| FIGURE 13.9 | Framing Effects in Medical Decision-Making |

Survival Frame

Surgery: Of 100 people having surgery, 90 live through the postoperative period, 68 are alive at the end of the first year, and 34 are alive at the end of 5 years.

Radiation: Of 100 people having radiation therapy, all live through the treatment, 77 are alive at the end of the first year, and 22 are alive at the end of 5 years.

Mortality Frame

Surgery: Of 100 people having surgery, 10 die during surgery, 32 die by the end of the first year, and 66 die by the end of 5 years.

Radiation: Of 100 people having radiation therapy, none die during the treatment, 23 die by the end of the first year, and 78 die by the end of 5 years.

The options shown in the "survival" frame are identical to the options shown in the "mortality" frame. The only difference between the frames is in how the options are described. With the survival frame, only 18% of the participants choose radiation over surgery. With the mortality frame, this number more than doubles, with 44% now choosing radiation.

Framing of Questions and Evidence

So far we have shown that people are influenced by how a problem's outcomes are framed. We can demonstrate related effects by changing how the question itself is framed. For example, imagine that you serve on a jury in a relatively messy divorce case; the parents are battling over who will get custody of their only child. The two parents have the attributes listed in Figure 13.11. To which parent will you award sole custody of the child?

Research participants asked this question tend to favor Parent B, by a 64% to 36% margin. After all, this parent does have a close relationship with the child, and has a good income. Note, though, that we have asked to which parent you would *award* custody. Things are different if we ask participants to which parent they would *deny* custody. This is, in obvious ways, the same question: If you are awarding custody to one parent, you are simultaneously denying it to the other parent. But in this case, 55% of the participants choose to deny custody to Parent B (and so, by default, end up awarding custody to A). Thus, the decision is simply reversed: With the "award" question, the majority of participants awards custody to B. With the "deny" question, the majority denies custody to B, and so gives custody to A.

This effect has been observed in a number of contexts, including problems involving monetary gambles, problems involving which courses a student will take,

FIGURE 13.10 Framing Effects in Monetary Choices

Problem 1

Assume yourself richer by $300 than you are today. You have to choose between

   a sure gain of $100

   50% chance to gain $200 and 50% chance to gain nothing.

Problem 2

Assume yourself richer by $500 than you are today. You have to choose between

   a sure loss of $100

   50% chance to lose nothing and 50% chance to lose $200.

These two problems are identical. In both cases, the first option leaves you with $400, while the second option leaves you with an even chance between $300 and $500. Despite this identity, people prefer the first option in Problem 1 (72% select this option) and the second option in Problem 2 (64% select this option). Once again, by changing the frames, we reverse the pattern of preferences.

and also problems involving decisions about political candidates (Shafir, 1993; also Downs & Shafir, 1999). As a related effect, people rate a basketball player more highly if the player has made 75% of his free throws, compared to their ratings of a player who has missed 25% of his free throws. They are more likely to endorse a medical treatment with a "50% success rate" than they are to endorse one with a "50% failure rate." And so on (I. Levin & Gaeth, 1988; I. Levin, Schnittjer, & Thee, 1988; also see Dunning & Parpal, 1989).

None of this makes any sense from the perspective of utility theory, since these differences in framing have no impact on the expected utilities of the options. Yet these differences in framing can dramatically change people's choices and, in many cases, can actually reverse their pattern of preferences. (For further, related evidence, see Mellers, Chang, Birnbaum & Ordóñez, 1992; Schneider, 1992; Schwarz, 1999; and Wedell & Bockenholt, 1990.)

Maximizing Utility Versus Seeing Reasons

How should we think about all of this? One broad possibility is that people are trying to use (something like) utility calculations when making their decisions, but just aren't very good at it. As a result, people can be pulled off track by various distractions or complications, including how the consequences of a decision are framed, or how the question they're pondering is framed.

| FIGURE 13.11 | The Influence of How a Question Is Formed |

Imagine that you serve on the jury of an only-child sole-custody case following a relatively messy divorce. The facts of the case are complicated by ambiguous economic, social, and emotional considerations, and you decide to base your decision entirely on the following few observations. To which parent would you award sole custody of the child?

Parent A   average income
average health
average working hours
reasonable rapport with the child
relatively stable social life

Parent B   above-average income
very close relationship with the child
extremely active social life
lots of work-related travel
minor health problems

When asked the question shown here, 64% of the participants decided to award custody to Parent B. Other participants, however, were asked a different question: "To which parent would you deny sole custody?" Asked this question, 55% of the participants chose to deny custody to B (and so, by default, to award custody to A). Thus, with the "award" question, a majority votes for granting custody to B; with the "deny" question, a majority votes for granting custody to A.

A different possibility, though, is more radical: Perhaps, in making decisions, the maximization of utility is not our goal. Instead, our goal is simply to make decisions that we feel good about, decisions that we think are reasonable and justified. This view of decision-making is called **reason-based choice**, and to see how the account plays out, consider a study by Shafir, Simonson, and Tversky (1993). Half their participants were asked to consider Scenario A in Figure 13.12. In this scenario, 66% of the participants said that they would buy the Sony; only 34% said that they would instead wait until they had learned about other models. Other participants, though, were presented with Scenario B.

How should someone choose in this second situation? We already know, from Scenario A, that most people think that purchasing the Sony is preferable to continued shopping. In Scenario B, therefore, there are, from a utility perspective, just two possibilities: Either the Aiwa (like the Sony) is also preferable to continued shopping, or it's not. If the Aiwa, like the Sony, *is* preferable to more shopping, then, plainly, a continuation of shopping is the worst choice of the three, and so the decision must be between the Aiwa and the Sony. If the Aiwa is *not* preferable to more shopping, then we know it's also less attractive than the Sony (because we've

| FIGURE 13.12 | The Influence of Other Alternatives on Decision Making |

Scenario A

Suppose you are considering buying a compact disk player and have not yet decided which model to buy. You pass a store that is having a one-day clearance sale. They offer a popular Sony player for just $99, well below the list price. Do you

    a. buy the Sony player
    b. wait until you learn more about the various models

Scenario B

Suppose you are considering buying a compact disk player and have not yet decided which model to buy. You pass a store that is having a one-day clearance sale. They offer a popular Sony player for just $99, and a top-of-the-line Aiwa player for just $169, both well below the list price. Do you

    a. buy the Sony player
    b. buy the Aiwa player
    c. wait until you learn more about the various models

When subjects were given the choice shown in Scenario A, 66% chose to buy the Sony player, and only 34% chose to continue shopping. In Scenario B, however, 46% of the subjects chose to continue shopping, and only 27% chose the Sony. Thus, in the first context, subjects think that the Sony is a better choice than shopping but, in the second choice, they think that shopping is a better choice than the Sony.

already said that the Sony *is*, according to the first scenario, more attractive than more shopping). Therefore, the Sony appears to be better than either of the alternatives, and people should choose it.

Clearly, then, people should either make a decision between the Aiwa and the Sony, or they should just choose the Sony. However, neither of those is what people do. Instead, when given the three choices, 27% choose the Aiwa, 27% choose the Sony, and a much larger number, 46%, choose to wait until they've learned about other models. From a utility perspective, this makes no sense. But it is understandable if people are looking for *reasons* for their decisions: When only the Sony is available, there are compelling arguments for buying it. (It's a popular model, it's available at a good price; it's available at that price for just 1 day.) But when both the Sony and the Aiwa are available, it's harder to find persuasive arguments for buying one rather than the other. (Both, after all, are available at a good price, for just 1 day. The Sony is cheaper, which is attractive, but the Aiwa is top-of-the-line.) With no good argument in view for buying one of these models, people buy neither.

These data come from laboratory studies, in which people are making hypothetical and unfamiliar decisions. Can we observe the same pattern outside of the lab? Redelmeier and Shafir (1995) gave medical doctors a problem identical in format to the Aiwa/Sony problem just discussed. Specifically, they described a patient's history, and then, in one condition, offered two options for treatment—(a) that the patient should be given a specific medication, or (b) that the patient should be referred to orthopedics for possible surgery. In a second condition, they offered *three* options for treatment—(a) that the patient should be given a specific medication, or (b) that the patient should be given a specific alternative medication, or (c), that the patient should be referred to orthopedics for possible surgery.

The results in this study were virtually identical to the Aiwa/Sony results: When the medical doctors were choosing between one drug and surgery, many thought the drug was worth a try, and only 53% referred to patient for surgery. When the doctors had three choices, though, they found it difficult to justify choosing either drug over the other, and so most—72%—opted for surgery instead. This is, of course, the same pattern we have already seen: When the doctors couldn't justify one drug option over the other, they chose neither. (Also see J. Schwartz, Chapman, & Brewer, 2004; for a related demonstration with medical doctors, see Tversky & Shafir, 1992a.)

The Reasoning in Reason-Based Choice

The claim of reason-based choice suggests that we make a decision only when we see compelling reasons for that decision. On that basis, our decision-making is obviously dependent on our capacity to find reasons, and to judge those reasons persuasive. Therefore, any factor that influences our thinking in general (our ability to make judgments, our ability to reason) should have a direct impact on decision-making.

For example, we suggested earlier that confirmation bias plays a large role whenever we're evaluating an argument. We would expect, therefore, that confirmation bias will also influence decision-making, and it does. To see this in action, let's reconsider a problem already discussed: the divorce/custody problem shown in Figure 13.11. Half the people presented with this problem are asked to which parent they would award custody. These people, influenced by confirmation bias, therefore ask themselves, "What would justify giving custody to one parent or another?" This draws their attention to one subset of the parental attributes—for example, Parent B's close relationship with the child, and this in turn leads them to favor awarding custody to B.

The other half of the participants are asked to which parent they would deny custody and, with confirmation bias in place, this leads them to ask, "What would justify denying custody to one parent or another?" This question draws attention to a different subset of attributes—for example, Parent B's travel schedule or health problems. Thus, these participants easily find a basis for denying custody to B. (For related discussion, see Legrenzi et al., 1993.)

Likewise, in Chapter 12 we argued for dual-process models of judgment. If decision-making depends on our capacity to make judgments, then we will also need dual-process models of decision-making. This turns out to be correct: Depending on how a decision is cast, people sometimes rely on fast, intuitive strategies in evaluating their options, and sometimes rely on more-careful, more-calculating strategies (Hsee & Rottenstreich, 2004). Thus we can find a distinction between System 1 and System 2 in decision-making, exactly as we would expect if decision-making relies on our more general abilities to find and evaluate arguments.

Similarly, we know that judgment often relies on shortcut strategies, like the representativeness heuristic. If decision-making depends on judgment, then decision-making, too, should show a reliance on representativeness. This also is easy to confirm. Several studies have asked people to choose between different *experiences*, and the results show a consistent pattern. People seem to evaluate experiences (and so make their decisions) on the basis of a small number of "representative moments" within the experience, much as one might try to summarize a week's vacation in Rome with just one or two snapshots (Kahneman, 2003; Kahneman, Fredrickson, Schreiber, & Redelmeier, 1993; Schreiber & Kahneman, 2000). As a result, people often seem remarkably insensitive to the *duration* of the event, because this dimension is not captured by the remembered "snapshots." In effect, then, one or two moments are being treated as if they were representative of a larger set of moments, and the size of the set (i.e., how many moments, total, were contained in the event) is neglected. This obviously resembles the pattern described in Chapter 12, in which one or two individuals are treated as if they are representative of a larger set, with no attention to the set's size. In this fashion, decision-making seems to involve a judgment strategy virtually identical to the representativeness heuristic.

Mental Accounting

It seems, therefore, that the choices people make are governed by familiar principles: confirmation bias and a reliance on System 1 thinking, including the representativeness heuristic. None of this makes sense on the basis of utility calculations, but it is just what we would expect from the perspective of reason-based choice.

This emphasis on the *justification* of a decision, however, demands a new line of questions: What principles guide people as they search for justifications for their choices? What determines whether a potential justification seems persuasive or not? (For a glimpse of some of the research on these issues, see Connolly & Koput, 1996; Hsee, 1999; Medin & Bazerman, 1999; and Messick, 1999.)

One important principle, relevant to these questions, appears to be **mental accounting**. This term refers to the fact that people seem to think about their gains and losses as if they were in separate "accounts," separate "budget categories." Decisions are then made with reference only to the appropriate account. To see this in action, imagine that you are at an electronics store, and about to purchase a pair of headphones for $125 and a calculator for $15. The calculator salesman tells you that the same calculator is on sale for $10 at a different store, located 20 minutes away. Would you make the trip to the other store? Most people decide they would (Thaler, 2000; A. Tversky & Kahneman, 1981).

But now imagine a different scene. Imagine that you are about to purchase a pair of headphones for $15 and a calculator for $125. The calculator salesman tells you that the same calculator is on sale for $120 at a different store, located 20 minutes away. Would you make the trip to the other store? Most people decide they would *not*.

In either of these cases, the total purchase will be $140 if you buy everything at the first shop, and $135 if you buy the calculator at the second shop. In both cases, therefore, the decision depends on whether a savings of $5 justifies a 20-minute trip. But people react to the two problems quite differently, as if they were dividing their purchases into different accounts. If the $5 savings comes from the smaller account, then it seems like a great deal (the calculator is 33% cheaper!). If the savings comes from the more expensive account, it seems much less persuasive (a mere 4% savings on a $125 calculator; for related data, see Figure 13.13).

Emotion

An emphasis on how people justify decisions also calls our attention to another group of factors, factors that concern *emotion*. As one example, should someone trade in his bicycle for a newer, shinier, version of the same bicycle? Most people say yes. Should someone trade in his wedding ring for a newer, shinier, version of the same ring? Most people say no, because the emotional meaning associated with a wedding ring makes this decision rather different from the bicycle decision (Medin, Schwartz, Blok, & Birnbaum, 1999; also see Kahneman, Diener, & Schwarz, 1999;

| FIGURE 13.13 | The Role of Separate Accounts in Decision-Making |

Imagine that two students are visiting a gambling casino. In front of the casino, Student A finds $25 cash and puts the money in his wallet. Student A and Student B each pay the $25 entrance fee and enter the casino. Inside the casino, Student B finds $25 cash and puts the money into his wallet. Both students have not yet decided whether to gamble.

The students are then given an opportunity to place a $25 bet that has a 50% chance of winning $25 and a 50% chance of losing $25. Which student is more likely to place the bet? Or are they both equally likely?

Roughly three quarters of the participants shown this problem said that Student B was more likely to place the bet, presumably because Student A has already "assigned" the $25 he found to the "entrance-fee account" and so no longer has any "windfall" money to spend. Student B is still holding his "windfall" and feels free to gamble with this money. (Brendl, Markman, & Higgins, 1998)

G. Loewenstein, Weber, Hsee, & Welch, 2001; and Slovic, Finucane, Peters, & Mac-Gregor, 2002).

In the same vein, in judging risks, people often seem to base their judgments not on some sort of calculation, but instead largely on their feelings. Thus, for example, someone's assessment of how risky nuclear power really is turns out to be closely related to the amount of dread they experience when thinking about a nuclear accident (Fischhoff, Slovic, & Lichtenstein, 1978). Indeed, some authors have suggested that many judgments, and much decision-making, rest on an "affect heuristic" (Finucane, Alhakami, Slovic, & Johnson, 2000; Slovic et al., 2002). The idea of this heuristic is that people often make judgments like, "How risky is this?" or "How promising is this?" or "How much should I pay for this?" largely by asking themselves, much more simply, "How good (or bad) does this make me feel?"

Related to this is the fact that decision-making is also influenced by the complex emotion of *regret.* Specifically, people seem powerfully motivated to avoid regret, and so one of the strong forces in guiding a decision is to choose a course of action that minimizes the chances for regret later on. Indeed, this may be one of the reasons why people care so much about making decisions they feel they can explain and justify: This may be the best defense against subsequent regret. (For more on the avoidance of regret, see Connolly & Zeelenberg, 2002; Gilovich & Medvec, 1995; Gilovich, Medvec, & Kahneman, 1998; Kahneman & Miller, 1986; Kahneman & Tversky, 1982b; Medvec, Madey, & Gilovich, 1995; and Mellers, Schwartz, & Ritov, 1999.)

In fact, Damasio (1994) has argued that it is emotional *experience*, and not just a calm, detached emotional appraisal, that plays a pivotal role in decision-making. Damasio starts by pointing out that certain memories can cause a clear bodily reaction: In remembering a scary movie, for example, we might once again become tense, and our palms might begin to sweat. In remembering a romantic encounter, we might once again become aroused. And so on. In the same fashion, *anticipated* events can also produce bodily arousal, and Damasio suggests that we use these bodily sensations—or **somatic markers**, as he calls them—as a guide to decision-making. In making a choice, he argues, we literally rely on our "gut feelings" to assess our various options, and this pulls us toward options associated with positive feelings and away from ones that trigger negative feelings.

Damasio argues, in addition, that a particular region of the brain—the orbitofrontal cortex (at the base of the frontal lobe, just above the eyes)—is crucial in our use of these somatic markers, because it is this brain region that allows us to interpret the emotions associated with various stimuli and various ideas. Evidence comes from patients who have suffered damage to the orbitofrontal cortex: In one study, participants were required to choose cards from one stack or another; each card, when turned over, showed the amount of money the participant had won or lost on that trial. The cards in one stack often showed large payoffs, but sometimes they showed huge penalties, and so, overall, it was better to choose cards from the other stack (which had smaller payoffs but much smaller penalties). Participants without orbitofrontal damage gradually figured this out as they worked their way through the task, and so they ended up making most of their choices from the less risky stack. Participants *with* orbitofrontal damage, on the other hand, continued (unwisely) to favor the risky deck (Damasio, 1994).

Apparently, then, the brain-damaged patients were less sensitive to risks and penalties, but why is this? Damasio's claim is that it is because they were not able to interpret the somatic markers associated with the risk—and so didn't detect or use the "gut feeling" that could have warned them against a dangerous choice. This proposal gains support from another aspect of the experiment: As the gambling task progressed, the experimenters measured the participants' moment-by-moment bodily arousal. After some experience with the risky cards, participants *without* brain damage showed increased levels of arousal *before* they turned over a card in the risky stack. Apparently they were anticipating the danger before it arrived, and reacting emotionally to the perceived risk. Patients *with* brain damage, however, showed no emotional response before they turned over each card (although they did react once the card was in view). This fits with the claim that they were not anticipating the emotional response to each card, and so anticipation (via the use of somatic markers) could not influence their assessment of risk (Damasio, 1994).

Predicting Our Own Values

This emphasis on emotion and regret also raises another set of questions: How good are people at making decisions that will maximize their contentment and minimize their regret? The answer—surprisingly—is that we're not that good at these important steps, in large part because we are not that good at predicting our own future reactions.

For example, we have noted that, in their decision-making, people are often influenced by the possibility of regret. Specifically, people consistently try to avoid making decisions that they might regret afterward. Notice, though, that this strategy rests on a prediction about the future: "If I do X and it turns out badly, how much will I regret the decision later?" It's relevant, therefore, that people are often inaccurate in forecasting their future regrets, and tend to *overestimate* how much they'll later regret their errors (D. Gilbert, Morewedge, Risen, & Wilson, 2004). As a result, people probably give more weight to regret avoidance than they should, since they're working to avoid something that, in the end, really won't be that bad.

In the same way, imagine that you are choosing between two apartments that you might rent for next year. One is cheaper and larger but faces a noisy street. Will you just grow used to the noise, so that it ceases to bother you? If so, then you should take the apartment. Or will the noise grow more and more obnoxious to you as the weeks pass? If so, you should pay the extra money for the other apartment. Notice, then, that this decision also involves a prediction about the future—in this case, a prediction about how your likes and dislikes will change as time goes by.

Several studies suggest that people are rather inept at making this sort of prediction, and in particular, people tend to underestimate the likelihood that they'll simply get used to new possessions or new features in their environment (Kahneman & Snell, 1992; G. Loewenstein & Schkade, 1999; Schkade & Kahneman, 1998; Wilson, Wheatley, Meyers, Gilbert, & Axsom, 2000). Thus, to name a few examples, researchers have shown that people generally mispredict how they will feel after "breaking up with a romantic partner, losing an election, receiving a gift, learning they have a serious illness, failure to secure a promotion, scoring well on an exam," and so on (D. Gilbert & Ebert, 2002, p. 503). For negative events, people are often convinced that things that bother them now will continue to bother them in the future, underestimating their ability to adapt. Similarly, for positive events, people seem to assume that things that please them now will continue to bring pleasure in the future (and so they're willing to pay for the better car, or the higher-quality speakers, assuming that these will give them continued pleasure in the long term). But here, too, people underestimate their ability to adapt and, as a result, probably end up spending money for things that, sadly, provide only short-term pleasure.

Related to this, people are often unsure that their decisions will be good ones (again, because they underestimate the likelihood that they'll adjust, and so grow content with *whatever* they choose). To protect themselves, therefore, people often take steps to preserve their flexibility in the future. ("If I don't like this model, can I return it?" "If the computer isn't fast enough, can I exchange it?") Ironically, this flexibility may interfere with the processes that lead people to grow satisfied with their acquisitions, and so, in the end, taking steps to preserve flexibility may actually leave people less content with their choices, rather than more (D. Gilbert & Ebert, 2002).

Normative Theories of Decision-Making

Where, then, does all of this leave us? In Chapter 12 and in the first half of this chapter, we saw that people often make errors in judgment and reasoning. It now appears that people also make errors in decision-making and so, in some cases, choose options that are far from optimal. In other cases, people rely on decision-making strategies that leave them open to manipulation and self-contradiction.

Could it be that people are really that incompetent in making the choices that fill their lives? To address this question, perhaps we need to consider how people *should* make decisions. We began our discussion of decision-making with utility theory, and as we have seen, this seems not to be the right way to describe how people make decisions. Instead, decision-making is more a matter of argument and justification: We make the decisions that we can best explain and defend to ourselves and to others. We choose the options that will leave us, in the end, content that we have made a rational choice.

On this basis, utility theory seems wrong as a *descriptive* theory of decision-making, but perhaps utility theory looks better as a *normative* theory—a theory of how people *should* make decisions. After all, decisions based on utility calculations will consistently maximize our chances of gaining the things we value and of reaching our goals (Baron, 1988, 1998; Larrick, Nisbett, & Morgan, 1993). Likewise, decisions based on utility calculations should, in principle, be immune to framing effects, and so avoid the self-contradictions that leave decision-makers vulnerable to external manipulation as they shift from one decision frame to another.

These considerations seem to imply that utility theory is the proper way to make decisions, and if so, one could argue that people, relying on reason-based choice, consistently make their decisions in the *wrong way*. Let's be clear, though, that other normative theories can also be defended. For example, it is obvious that we all wish to reach our goals and gain the things we value. But we also have other needs. For example, people generally don't want to feel foolish or capricious; instead, we all want to feel like our lives make some sense and have some integrity. Therefore, it is important to feel that the choices we have made have been reasonable choices and that, if these choices were ever challenged, we could explain and defend our selections.

From this perspective, if a decision brings us utility but leaves us feeling insecure or uncomfortable, then it is a bad decision, and one ought to avoid making such a decision. Notice the "ought": This is an assertion about how decisions *should* be made; it is, in other words, a normative assertion, and so we are moving toward a normative theory in which considerations of utility are not our only concern.

Moreover, some would argue that there are decisions that shouldn't be reduced to questions of utility. For example, consider choices involving morality—choices about theft or homicide, or choices about respecting other people's rights. Should one calculate the utility of "doing the moral thing"? If so, then perhaps there is some other utility (e.g., a large enough bribe) that would outweigh the demands of morality. For many people, this seems an inappropriate way to talk about moral values, but it is the right way to talk about moral decisions if utility theory is our normative theory. (For an intriguing exploration of this point, see Baron & Leshner, 2000.)

Moral values can be treated differently, however, within a theory of decision-making resting on justification. From this perspective, one shouldn't ask the "economic" question, "What gain would justify an immoral act?" Instead, one should ask the question, "What argument, or principle, would justify such an act?" Thus, in this view, there may be no payoff, no matter how large, to justify immorality. Instead, the only justification for an immoral action would be something like an even stronger, more compelling, moral claim.

This seems an attractive position, and it suggests that reason-based choice can be defended as a normative theory. Thus, in making decisions based on justification, we do expose ourselves to certain problems, but we're still making decisions the "right way."

Let's be clear, though, that we are not hoping to settle here the choice between these two normative views—one based on utilities, one based on justification. After all, on anyone's account, utility theory has much to recommend it. We hope, though, that these comments have at least made it clear that the choice between these views is not straightforward; good arguments can be presented on either side of the debate.

There is, in any case, ample evidence that we don't make decisions in accord with utility theory. Instead, it does seem that our decisions are guided by principles of justification: We make decisions that seem sensible and defensible to us. Over the last few paragraphs, we have tried to indicate that how these decisions should be evaluated, from the standpoint of a normative theory, is a matter open to discussion.

Chapter Summary

1. Reasoning often shows a pattern of confirmation bias: People tend to seek evidence that might confirm their beliefs rather than evidence that might challenge their beliefs. When evidence challenging a belief is in view, it tends to be underused or reinterpreted. One manifestation of confirmation bias is belief perseverance, a pattern in which people continue to believe a claim even after the basis for the claim has been discredited. This is probably because people engage in a biased memory search, seeking to confirm the claim. The evidence provided by this search then remains even when the original basis for the claim is removed.

2. People's performance with logic problems such as categorical syllogisms or problems involving conditional statements is often quite poor. The errors are not the product of carelessness; instead, many errors are due either to belief bias or to conversion of the problems. Performance is also poor in the four-card task.

3. People perform quite well, however, with some variations of the four-card problem. This makes it clear that reasoning is not guided by formal rules, but is instead influenced by problem content. One proposal is that this effect should be understood in evolutionary terms, with people skilled at reasoning about issues of cheating or betrayal; this is a type of reasoning, it is claimed, for which we are biologically well prepared. A different proposal is that our reasoning relies on pragmatic reasoning schemata; these summarize our experience in reasoning about situations involving permission, obligation, and so on. Reasoning performance will be good, therefore, if one of these schemata is triggered. Yet another proposal is that the content of a problem influences how we interpret the "if-then" relationship, with important consequences in how we reason about that relationship.

4. Apparently theories of reasoning need multiple layers. People can be trained to reason according to the rules of formal logic. In addition, people without training do have reasonably sophisticated reasoning skills, but these skills play a role only if they are triggered by the problem's content. People also have less-sophisticated strategies that they employ when their reasoning skills are not triggered. Finally, people can also reason using mental models, in which they construct an imagined model of a situation and then inspect this model to evaluate possible conclusions.

5. According to utility theory, people make decisions by calculating the expected utility or expected value of each of their options. Decisions made in this way will always maximize the decision-makers' chances of achieving the things they value, but even so, much evidence suggests that decisions are not made in this way. Instead, decisions are often influenced by factors that have nothing to do with utilities—for example, how the question is framed or how the possible outcomes are described. If the outcomes are described as potential gains, decision-makers tend to be risk-averse; if they are described as potential losses, decision-makers tend to be risk-seeking.

6. Some investigators have proposed that our goal in making decisions is not to maximize utility but, instead, to make decisions that we think are reasonable or justified. Therefore, we are influenced by any factor that makes an argument in favor of an option seem more compelling. Thus, confirmation bias influences decision-making, just as it influences reasoning in general. Representativeness shapes how we evaluate our options in decision-making, and so on.

7. Decision-makers also seem to think about their gains and losses as though they were in separate accounts, and decisions are made only with reference to the appropriate account. Decisions are also clearly influenced by emotion. This influence is evident in decision-makers' efforts toward avoiding regret; it is also evident in decision-maker's reliance on their own bodily sensations as a cue for evaluating their various options.

8. Decision-makers are surprisingly inept, however, at predicting their own future reactions. This is true both for predictions of regret (e.g., how much regret one will feel if a decision turns out badly) and for predictions of values (e.g., whether one will still like the new car, or still be annoyed by the street noise in an apartment, after some time has passed).

9. Decision-making guided by perceived justification may lead to self-contradiction, and may leave us open to external manipulation (because of frame effects). But this approach to decision-making may be appropriate nonetheless, and discussion about the normative theory of decision-making (how we should make decisions) is ongoing.

Solving Problems

In Chapter 12, we considered the processes through which people form new beliefs, based on information they have encountered. In Chapter 13, we examined how people reason about these beliefs—what inferences they draw, and how they adjust their beliefs (or fail to) as new evidence comes in. We then considered how people use their beliefs as a basis for choosing among options or for selecting a course of action. In other words, we considered how people make decisions.

Once we have taken all these steps, though—that is, we've formed a belief, drawn out its implications, and chosen a course of action—what happens next? In some cases, this is a straightforward matter. If you decide to buy one jacket rather than another, your next steps will be easy: You go to the store and get the jacket. In many other cases, though, what you select is a *goal*, and that still leaves the question of how you will reach that goal. This is the domain of **problem-solving**, the process through which you figure out how to reach your goals, starting from your current state.

We solve problems all the time. "I want to reach the store, but Tom borrowed my car. How should I get there?" "I really want Amy to notice me; how should I arrange it?" "I'm trying to prove this theorem. How can I do it, starting from these premises?" In this chapter, we will examine how people solve problems like these—including practical problems and academic ones, trivial problems and consequential ones, the well-defined and the diffuse. We will begin by considering strategies relevant to problems of all sorts. We will then turn to more-specialized strategies, applicable to only some sorts of problems.

473

- Often we solve problems by using general heuristics that help us to narrow our search for the problem's solution. One of these is means–end analysis, which often leads us to divide problems into a series of simpler subproblems.

- In other cases, we solve problems by drawing analogies based on problems we've solved in the past. As helpful as they are, however, analogies are often underused.

- Training can improve someone's skill in problem-solving. The training can draw someone's attention to a problem's deep structure, which promotes analogy use. Training can also help someone see how a problem can be divided into subproblems.

- Experts consistently attend to a problem's deep structure and are quite sensitive to a problem's parts. Experts also benefit from their highly cross-referenced knowledge in their domain of expertise.

- Problem-solving is often stymied by how people approach the problem in the first place, and that leads to a question of how people find new and creative approaches to problems.

- When closely examined, creative approaches seem to be the result of the same processes that are evident in "ordinary" problem-solving—processes hinging on analogies, heuristics, and the like. Hence, the creative *product* is often extraordinary, but the creative *process* may not be.

General Problem-Solving Methods

It is obvious that some problems require special expertise: If you are trying to achieve some bit of genetic engineering, you need the relevant training in biology and biochemistry. If you are trying to repair a computer, you need knowledge of electronics. Some problems, though, draw on more general skills and strategies that are available to all of us. What are these strategies?

Problem-Solving as Search

Many researchers find it useful to compare problem-solving to a process of search, as though you were navigating through a maze, seeking a path toward your goal. Some paths will (eventually) lead to the goal, but others will lead to dead ends or to the wrong goal. Some paths will be relatively direct; others will be long and circuitous. In all cases, though, your job is to select the best path, allowing you to get from your starting point to your target.

Building on this idea of "problem-solving as search," Newell and Simon (1972) described problem-solving as starting with an **initial state** (the knowledge and re-sources you have at the outset) and working toward a **goal state**. To move from the initial state to the goal, the problem-solver has a set of **operators**—that is, tools or actions that can change her current state. In addition, there is likely to be a set of **path constraints**, ruling out some options or some solutions. These constraints might take the form of resource limitations (limited time or money) or other limits (e.g., ethical limits on what you can do).

Given an initial state, the operators, and the path constraints, there is a limited number of intermediate states that one can reach, en route to the goal. For example, consider the "Hobbits and Orcs" problem, described in Figure 14.1. Figure 14.2 shows the states one can reach, early on, in solving this problem. Notice that these states can be depicted as a tree, with each step leading to more and more branches. All of these branches together form the **problem space**—that is, the set of all states that can be reached in solving this problem. In these terms, what one is seeking, in solving a problem, is quite literally a path through this space, leading, step-by-step, from the initial state to the goal.

One option in solving a problem would be to trace through the entire problem space, exploring each branch in turn. This approach would guarantee that you would eventually find the solution (if the problem were solvable at all). For most of the problems we face, however, this sort of "brute force" approach would be hopeless. Consider, for example, the game of chess: Your goal is to win the game, so how should you proceed? Let's say that you move first. In opening the game, you have exactly 20 moves available to you. For each of these, your opponent has 20 possible responses. Therefore, for the first cycle of play, there are 400 possibilities (20×20) for how things might go. If you are going to choose the best move, you need to inspect all 400 of these possibilities.

Your best move, however, probably depends on what you are planning to do next—it depends on what defense you are looking to establish or what attack you are planning to launch. Therefore, in evaluating your options, you will probably want to ask, "Will this lead me where I want to go?" and that requires some looking ahead. Before you select your move, then, you might want to think through three or four cycles of play, and not just one.

There are 400 possibilities for how the first cycle can unfold, but there are more options for subsequent cycles, as the pieces get spread out, leaving more room to

---

FIGURE 14.1 | The "Hobbits and Orcs" Problem

Five Orcs and five Hobbits are on the east bank of the Muddy River. They need to cross to the west bank and have located a boat. In each crossing, at least one creature must be in the boat, but no more than three creatures will fit in the boat.

And, of course, if the Orcs ever outnumber the Hobbits, on either side of the river, they will eat the Hobbits! Therefore, in designing the crossing, we must make certain that the Hobbits are never outnumbered, either on the east bank of the river or on the west.

How can the creatures get across without any Hobbits being eaten?

This problem has been used in many studies of problem-solving strategies. Can you solve it?

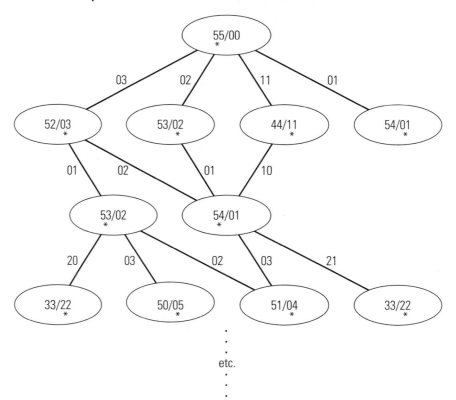

| FIGURE 14.2 | The Problem Space for the "Hobbits and Orcs" Problem |

Each circle shows a possible problem state. The state 54/01, for example, indicates that five Hobbits and 4 Orcs are on the east bank; there are no Hobbits, but one Orc, on the west bank. The star shows the position of the boat. The numbers alongside of each line indicate the number of creatures in the boat during each river crossing. The move 02, for example, transports no Hobbits, but two Orcs. The problem states shown here are all the legal states. (Other states, and other moves, would result in some of the Hobbits being eaten.) Thus, there are four "legal" moves one can make, starting from the initial state. From these, there are four possible moves one can make, but these lead to just two problem states (53/02, and 54/01). From these two states, there are four new states that can be reached, and so on. We have here illustrated the first three moves that can be made in solving this problem; the shortest path to the problem's solution involves 11 moves.

move. Let's estimate, therefore, that there are 30 different moves you might make next and, for each of these, 30 possible responses from your opponent. Thus, for two cycles of play, there are 360,000 (400 × 30 × 30) possible outcomes. If, at that point, there are now 40 options open to you, and 40 possible responses for each, three cycles of play leave us with 576,000,000 different options; four cycles of play,

921,600,000,000 options. If you are truly seeking the best possible move, maybe you should consider all 921 billion of these to find the best one. (For further discussion, see Gilhooly, 1988; and Newell & Simon, 1972.)

This proliferation of moves obviously rules out the strategy of "check every option." If you needed 1 second to evaluate each sequence, you would still need 256 million hours to evaluate the full set of possibilities for four cycles of play. And, of course, there is nothing special about chess. Let's say that you are having dinner with Percy and you want him to think you are witty. Your problem is to find things to say that will achieve this goal. How many possibilities are there for sentences you might utter? How many possible rejoinders are available to Percy? How many responses could you then make? Again, the number is vast. If you consider them all, searching for the best choice, you will impress Percy with your long pauses, but not with your wit.

In light of these calculations, it would obviously be helpful if you could somehow narrow your search, so that you consider only a subset of your options, rather than searching the entire problem space. Of course, this would involve an element of risk: If you consider only some options, you take the risk of overlooking the best option. However, you may have no choice about this, since the alternative—the strategy of considering every option—would be absurd for most problems.

In essence, then, what you need is a problem-solving heuristic. Heuristics, you will recall, are strategies that are reasonably efficient, but at the cost of occasional errors. In the domain of problem-solving, a heuristic is a strategy that guides you through the problem space—narrowing your search appreciably, but (one hopes) in a fashion that still leads you to the problem's solution. What problem-solving heuristics do we employ?

General Problem-Solving Heuristics

Several problem-solving heuristics are revealed if we simply ask people to think out loud while working on a problem such as the "Hobbits and Orcs" problem in Figure 14.1, or the "Tower of Hanoi" problem, in Figure 14.3. By inspecting the running commentaries—or **problem-solving protocols**—that people produce while they are working on these problems, we can identify some of the strategies that these problem-solvers rely on.

For example, one often-used heuristic is the so-called **hill-climbing strategy**. To understand the term, imagine that you are hiking through the woods and trying to figure out which trail leads to the mountaintop. You obviously need to climb uphill to reach the top, and so whenever you come to a fork in the trail, you select the path that is going uphill. The hill-climbing strategy works the same way: At each point, you simply choose the option that moves you in the direction of your goal.

This strategy is helpful for some problems: Imagine that there is a bad smell in your house, and you are trying to figure out where it's coming from. You might stand at the doorway between the kitchen and the dining room, and then decide in

FIGURE 14.3   The "Tower of Hanoi" Problem

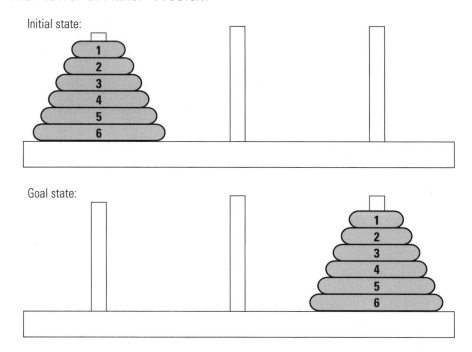

Initial state:

Goal state:

The rings on the left pole need to be moved so that they end up on the right pole, as shown. The rings must be moved one at a time, and with each move, a ring can be placed only on a *larger* ring. Thus, Ring 1 can be placed on top of Ring 2, but Ring 2 can never be placed on Ring 1. Can you solve this?

which direction the smell is stronger. If it is stronger in the kitchen, then that is the direction to explore. If the smell gets stronger as you approach the sink, then you explore that area. By always moving in the direction of the stronger smell, you will eventually discover the smell's source.

This strategy, however, is of limited use, largely because many problems require that you start by moving *away* from your goal; only then, from this new position, can the problem be solved. We have illustrated this in Figure 14.4, and other examples are easy to find. For instance, if you want Mingus to notice you more, it might help if you go away for a while; that way, he will be more likely to notice you when you come back. This ploy would never be discovered, though, if you relied on the hill-climbing strategy.

Despite these limitations, people do often rely on a hill-climbing strategy. As a result, they have difficulties whenever a problem requires them to move "backward in order to go forward"—that is, whenever the problem requires them to move

| FIGURE 14.4 | Limits on the Hill-Climbing Strategy |

According to the hill-climbing strategy, the dog should, at each step, choose a path that moves it closer and closer to the goal. However, this strategy will fail here because the dog needs first to move away from the bone (toward the open gate) in order to reach the bone.

(briefly) away from their goal in order (ultimately) to reach the goal. For example, solving the "Hobbits and Orcs" problem (Figure 14.1) requires, at various points, that one carry creatures from the east bank back to the west—i.e., from the goal state back to the initial state. These points of "backward movement" turn out to be very difficult for people. Often, at these points, people become convinced they are on the wrong track, and they seek some other solution to the problem: "This must be the wrong strategy; I'm going the wrong way." (See, for example, Jeffries, Polson, Razran, & Atwood, 1977; and J. Thomas, 1974.)

Fortunately, though, people also have other, more sophisticated, heuristics available to them. For example, people often rely on a strategy called **means–end analysis**. To use this strategy, one starts by comparing the current state and the goal state. One then asks, "What means do I have available to get from here to there?" To see how this plays out, consider this commonsense example, offered by Newell and Simon (1972):

> I want to take my son to nursery school. What's the difference between what I have and what I want? One of distance. What changes distance? My automobile. My automobile won't work. What is needed to make it work? A new battery. What has new batteries? An auto repair shop. I want the repair shop to put in a new battery; but the shop doesn't know I need one. What is the difficulty? One of communication. What allows communication? A telephone . . . (p. 416)

As this example illustrates, a means–end analysis can actually provide two different benefits. First, the analysis obviously highlights *differences* between where you are right now and where you want to be, and in this way it helps you see exactly what you need to do to solve the problem. Second, a means–end analysis will, as in this example, often lead you to break up a problem into smaller **subproblems**, each with its own goal. By solving the subproblems, one by one, the larger problem is addressed. In fact, some have suggested that this identification of subproblems is itself a powerful problem-solving heuristic: By breaking a problem into smaller pieces, we make the initial problem easier to solve. (We'll return to this idea later, when we consider some of the ways that people can be trained to become better problem-solvers.)

A related idea is that one can often solve a problem by using the *goal* as the starting point, rather than the problem's initial state, so that, in essence, one solves the problem by **working backward** from the goal. This strategy is quite useful, for example, for the water-lilies problem described in Figure 14.5. Here, too, one is using means–end analysis, but now in reverse—asking how the goal state can be made more similar to the current state.

A variety of evidence suggests that means–end analysis and working backward are commonly used strategies. For example, both strategies appear frequently in people's problem-solving protocols. And this turns out to be sensible, because these two strategies are often effective and are applicable to a large number of problems.

Mental Models and Mental Images

In many cases, it helps to translate a problem into concrete terms, perhaps relying on a mental image or a mental model (Cooper, 1990; Palmer, 1977; Shepard & Feng, 1972). Not surprisingly, images and mental models are particularly useful if the problem hinges on spatial arrangements: In this case, you can use your "mind's eye" to envision how the elements will look, once in their appropriate positions, and you can also visualize how the elements might look if rearranged. It's perhaps for this reason that the histories of science, art, and engineering are all filled with

---

FIGURE 14.5 The Water-Lilies Problem

Water lilies are growing on Blue Lake. The water lilies grow rapidly, so that the amount of water surface covered by lilies *doubles* every 24 hours.

On the first day of summer, there was just one water lily. On the 90th day of the summer, the lake was entirely covered. On what day was the lake *half covered*?

Working backward from the goal is useful in solving this problem. Can you solve it?

FIGURE 14.6	The Bookworm Problem

Solomon is proud of his 26-volume encyclopedia, placed neatly, with the volumes in alphabetical order, on his bookshelf. Solomon doesn't realize, though, that there's a bookworm sitting on the front cover of the *A* volume. The bookworm begins chewing his way through the pages, on the shortest possible path toward the back cover of the *Z* volume.

Each volume is 3 inches thick (including pages and covers), so that the entire set of volumes requires 78 inches of bookshelf. The bookworm chews through the pages + covers at a steady rate of ¾ of an inch per month. How long will it take before the bookworm reaches the back cover of the *Z* volume?

People who try an algebraic solution to this problem often end up with the wrong answer.

instances in which great discoveries or innovations appear to have emerged from the use of imagery (A. Miller, 1986; S. Reed, 1993; Shepard, 1988; also see Finke, 1990, 1993; and Finke & Slayton, 1988).

As a simple example of how models and images can help us, consider the bookworm problem described in Figure 14.6. Most people try an algebraic solution to this problem (width of each volume, multiplied by the number of volumes, divided by the worm's eating rate) and end up with the wrong answer. People generally get this problem right, though, if they start by visualizing the arrangement (as depicted in Figure 14.7). With this done, they can discern the actual positions of the worm's starting point and end point, and this usually takes them to the correct answer.

Pictures and Diagrams

It's likely that someone could figure out the bookworm problem either by inspecting a picture (like the one in Figure 14.7) or by inspecting a mental image of the problem's layout, and indeed, for many purposes, pictures and images may be interchangeable. Consistent with this idea, several studies have found no difference between problem-solving via picture and problem-solving via imagery (J. R. Anderson, 1993; R. Anderson & Helstrup, 1993; S. Reed, 1993).

For other purposes, though, there are important differences between mental images and pictures, with some problems more readily solved via imagery, and other problems showing the reverse. For example, mental images have the advantage of being more easily modified than diagrams: If one wishes to make a form larger or a different shape, this is easy in imagination; one can, after all, imagine anything one wishes. Likewise, one can easily imagine moving patterns; it is much harder to depict motion with a diagram. Therefore, if a problem solution depends on motion, then the problem may be more easily solved with imagery than with a picture.

FIGURE 14.7 Diagram for the Bookworm Problem

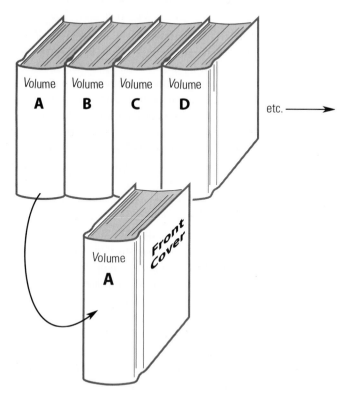

When the bookworm problem is illustrated, as shown here, people more easily solve it. Notice that a worm, starting on the front cover of the *A* volume, would not have to chew through volume *A*'s pages in moving toward the *Z* volume. Likewise, at the end of the worm's travel, he would reach the back cover of the *Z* volume before penetrating the *Z* volume!

At the same time, however, it takes some effort to create and maintain a mental image (see Chapter 11); this can divert attention away from the problem under scrutiny, and so this provides an advantage for problem-solving via pictures. Likewise, elaborate or detailed forms are difficult to image clearly. If a problem depends on such forms, then, problem-solving via image will be difficult.

In addition, we argued in Chapter 11 that mental images are always created with a particular understanding in mind for how the imaged form is organized; we referred to this understanding as a "perceptual reference frame." Moreover, we saw that this reference frame sets boundaries on what can be discovered within the image: Discoveries that are compatible with the reference frame happen easily; discoveries not compatible with the reference frame are rare. (See Chapter 11 for the specifics of these claims, and the supporting evidence.)

Let's be clear, though, that these limits apply to mental images, not to pictures. When a picture is perceived by someone, it is perceived within a particular reference frame, but crucially, the picture itself has no reference frame. In other words, the picture itself is neutral with regard to interpretation, and so open to multiple interpretations. This is obviously an advantage for problem-solving: Because the picture is open to reinterpretation, one can often make new discoveries about the pictured form.

For this reason, it's often useful for a problem-solver to draw a picture based on an image of the problem's setting or form. In many cases, this "external representation" will allow discoveries that weren't possible from the original image—even though the two representations, the drawing and the image, supposedly depict the same thing. This advantage of "externalizing" is easily demonstrated in the laboratory, both with visual images and with auditory ones (see Chapter 11; also Reisberg, 2000). This advantage can also be demonstrated in real-world settings—for example, with architects who gain by sketching out their designs, rather than trying to work out the design entirely "in their heads" (Verstijnen, Hennessey, van Leeuwen, Hamel, & Goldschmidt, 1998; for more on the role of pictures and other external aids in support of problem-solving, see Cary & Carlson, 1999; Chen, 1995; Novick, Hurley, & Francis, 1999; and Ormerod & Chronicle, 1999).

Relying on Past Knowledge

Our discussion so far has focused on strategies that apply to problem-solving in general, problem-solving of all sorts. But problem-solving also draws on more specialized strategies, as well as on knowledge about particular domains.

Problem-Solving via Analogy

Often, in solving a problem, we are reminded of some other problem we have already solved, and this will tell us, by analogy, how to solve the problem now before us. In this way, we can derive the unknown solution from one that is already known.

There is no question that analogies are useful. In the history of science, analogies have often played an important role—with scientists furthering their understanding of the heart by comparing it to a pump, extending their knowledge of gases by comparing the molecules to billiard balls, and so on (Gentner & Jeziorski, 1989). Likewise, many writers have recommended the use of analogies as a teaching tool. Thus, the atom is described to students as (very roughly) resembling the solar system, memory is compared to a library, and the like. Are these analogies helpful? Donnelly and McDaniel (1993) presented some of their participants with literal accounts of new scientific materials; other participants were given analogies of these same materials (Figure 14.8). When all the participants were later asked to make inferences about these new ideas, those instructed via analogy did better. (For important limitations on this finding, though, see Donnelly & McDaniel, 2000.)

FIGURE 14.8 Analogies Are a Useful Way to Convey New Information

Literal Version

Collapsing stars spin faster and faster as they fold in on themselves and their size decreases. This phenomenon of spinning faster as the star's size shrinks occurs because of a principle called "conservation of angular momentum."

Analogy Version

Collapsing stars spin faster as their size shrinks. Stars are thus like ice-skaters, who pirouette faster as they pull in their arms. Both stars and skaters operate by a principle called "conservation of angular momentum."

Question:

What would happen if a star "expanded" instead of collapsing?
  a. Its rate of rotation would increase.
  b. Its rate of rotation would decrease.
  c. Its orbital speed would increase.
  d. Its orbital speed would decrease.

Participants were presented with new materials either in a literal version or in an analogy version. Later, participants were asked questions about these materials. Those instructed via analogy reliably did better. (After Donnelly & McDaniel, 1993)

In addition, it is easy to demonstrate that analogies do help in solving problems. For example, the tumor problem (Figure 14.9) is quite difficult, but people generally solve it if they are able to use an analogy: Gick and Holyoak (1980) first had their participants read about a related situation (Figure 14.10), and then presented them with the tumor problem. When participants were encouraged to use

FIGURE 14.9 The Tumor Problem

Suppose you are a doctor faced with a patient who has a malignant tumor in his stomach. To operate on the patient is impossible, but unless the tumor is destroyed, the patient will die. A kind of ray, at a sufficiently high intensity, can destroy the tumor. Unfortunately, at this intensity the healthy tissue that the rays pass through on the way to the tumor will also be destroyed. At lower intensities the rays are harmless to healthy tissue, but will not affect the tumor. How can the rays be used to destroy the tumor without injuring the healthy tissue?

The tumor problem, designed by Duncker (1945), has been studied extensively. Can you solve it? One solution is to aim multiple low-intensity rays at the tumor, each from a different angle. The rays will meet at the site of the tumor and so, at just that location, will sum to full strength.

FIGURE 14.10 The "General and Fortress" Problem

A small country was ruled from a strong fortress by a dictator. The fortress was situated in the middle of the country, surrounded by farms and villages. Many roads led to the fortress through the countryside. A rebel general vowed to capture the fortress. The general knew that an attack by his entire army would capture the fortress. He gathered his army at the head of one of the roads, ready to launch a full-scale direct attack. However, the general then learned that the dictator had planted mines on each of the roads. The mines were set so that small bodies of men could pass over them safely, since the dictator needed to move his own troops and workers to and from the fortress. However, any large force would detonate the mines. Not only would this blow up the road, but it would also destroy many neighboring villages. It seemed impossible to capture the fortress. However, the general devised a simple plan. He divided his army into small groups and dispatched each group to the head of a different road. When all was ready, he gave the signal and each group marched down a different road. Each group continued down its road to the fortress, so that the entire army arrived together at the fortress at the same time. In this way, the general captured the fortress and overthrew the dictator.

This problem is analogous in its structure to the tumor problem (Figure 14.9). If people read this problem and then try the tumor problem, they are far more likely to solve the latter. (After Gick & Holyoak, 1980)

this hint, 75% were able to solve the tumor problem. For participants not given the hint, only 10% solved the tumor problem.

Difficulties in Finding an Appropriate Analogy

Despite the clear benefit of using analogies, people routinely fail to use them. For example, Gick and Holyoak had another group of participants read the "general and fortress" story, but no further hints were given. In particular, these participants were not told that this story was relevant to the tumor problem. Only 30% solved the tumor problem—far fewer than the 75% explicitly told that the fortress story was relevant to their task.

Similarly, S. Reed (1977; S. Reed, Ernst, & Banerji, 1974) first had participants solve the "jealous husbands" problem shown in Figure 14.11; the participants were then asked to solve the "Hobbits and Orcs" problem (Figure 14.1). When the close relationship between these two problems was pointed out to the participants, they were considerably faster in solving the "Hobbits and Orcs" problem. But if this relationship was not explicitly pointed out, they showed no benefit at all from this "training." (See also Hayes & Simon, 1977; B. Ross, 1984, 1987, 1989; and Weisberg, DiCamillo, & Phillips, 1978.)

FIGURE 14.11   The "Jealous Husbands" Problem

Three jealous husbands and their wives, who have to cross a river, find a boat. However, the boat is so small that it can hold no more than two persons. Find the simplest schedule of crossings that will permit all six persons to cross the river so that no woman is left in the company of any other woman's husband unless her own husband is present. It is assumed that all passengers on the boat debark before the next trip and that at least one person has to be in the boat for each crossing.

If the experimenter points out the relationship between the "jealous husbands" problem and the "Hobbits and Orcs" problem (Figure 14.1), then participants benefit from first solving the "jealous husbands" problem. If this relationship is not pointed out to participants, however, they show no benefit from this "training." (After S. Reed et al., 1974)

Apparently, then, people do use analogies if suitably instructed, but spontaneous, uninstructed use of analogies seems relatively rare. Why is this? Part of the answer lies in how people search through their memories when seeking an analogy. In solving a problem about tumors, people seem to ask themselves, "What else do I know about tumors?" This will help them remember other situations in which they thought about or learned about tumors, but of course this memory search won't lead them to the "general and fortress" problem. This (potential) analogue will therefore lie dormant in memory and provide no help. Likewise, Hobbit problems remind people of other Hobbit problems, even though problems on other topics might point the way to a solution.

Consistent with this perspective, people solving Hobbit problems will spontaneously use analogies if the previously studied problems also involved Hobbits. In this case, the (rather obvious) relation between the current problem and the prior problems guarantees that the former will call the latter to mind. People are less likely to draw analogies if they have previously solved problems involving actors of a different sort. (For relevant evidence, see Bassok, 1996; Bassok, Wu, & Olseth, 1995; Cummins, 1992; Holyoak & Koh, 1987; Novick, 1988; B. Ross, 1984, 1987; Spencer & Weisberg, 1986; and Wharton, Holyoak, Downing & Lange, 1994.)

Similarities between the current problem and a previously studied case also help people in another way: In order to create, or even to understand, an analogy, people need to get beyond the superficial features of the problem and think instead about the principles governing the problem. Put differently, people can use analogies only if they figure out how to **map** the prior case onto the problem now being solved—only if they realize, for example, that converging groups of soldiers correspond to converging beams, and that a fortress-to-be-captured corresponds to a tumor-to-be-destroyed. This mapping process is sometimes difficult, and failures to figure out the mapping are common, providing another reason why people regularly fail to find, and fail to use, analogies. (For discussion of how this process of mapping unfolds, see French, 2002; Gentner, 1983, 1989; Holyoak, 1984; Holyoak & Thagard, 1989; Markman, 1997; and VanLehn, 1998.)

Of course, mapping one problem onto another is easier if the two problems are similar in their particulars: If you have recently solved one "Hobbits and Orcs" problem, it is easy to apply this experience to a new "Hobbits and Orcs" problem: What you earlier learned about Hobbits can be mapped onto the new Hobbits, and what you earlier discovered about boats is immediately applicable to the boat in the current problem. If, instead, you have recently solved the "jealous husbands" problem (see Figure 14.11), then the principles learned in this experience might be applicable to the new problem, but only via a step of translation (Hobbits become husbands; "cannot outnumber" is replaced with "cannot be left alone with"). This is therefore further reason why analogy use is facilitated by similarity between the target problem and the analogous case drawn from memory. (For discussion of still other factors impeding or facilitating the use of analogies, see Bassok et al., 1995; Blanchette & Dunbar, 2000; Gick & Holyoak, 1980; Needham & Begg, 1991; and Novick & Holyoak, 1991.)

Strategies to Make Analogy Use More Likely

These claims point toward several suggestions for how we might promote analogy use, and thus improve problem-solving. Let's start with the memory search. When considering the tumor problem presented in Figure 14.9 (for example), people seem to ask themselves, "What else do I know about tumors?" But surely there is nothing inevitable about this, and presumably people could, with suitable instruction, learn to ask themselves a different question, along the lines of, "How can I bring forces to bear on a specific target without losing the forces while they're on their way to the target?" With this question, people might well be reminded of a suitable analogue, even if the analogue differs from the current problem in a dozen superficial ways.

Similarly, let's be clear that analogies usually depend on a problem's "deep structure"—the pattern of causal relationships within the problem, and how the problem's parts are interrelated. The problem's "surface structure"—how the causal relationships are manifested—is largely irrelevant. Perhaps we can promote analogy use, therefore, by urging people to pay attention to the deep structure from the very start, rather than attending to the problem's superficial content. In this way, a proper orientation, when working on a problem, might help both in the locating of analogues and also in the mapping of one problem onto another.

Several studies have confirmed these optimistic predictions. For example, we have seen that people are unlikely, on their own, to notice the analogy between the "general and fortress" problem (for which they know the solution) and the tumor problem (which they are currently trying to solve). In a related procedure, though, people were initially given two analogous stories, prior to the test problem, rather than just one (Gick & Holyoak, 1983). These participants were much more likely to draw analogies from these stories in solving the tumor problem, compared to participants who had read only one (potential) analogue.

Why are two analogues better than one? The two analogues both involved the same principles (one was the "general and fortress" problem; the other problem involved the use of many small hoses to put out a large fire). This may have been enough to call the participants' attention to these principles (e.g., the use of converging forces). This would, in turn, highlight the underlying structure of the stories, paving the way for the analogy.

A similar point emerges from an experiment by Cummins (1992). She presented participants with a series of algebra word problems. Participants in one group were asked to analyze these training problems, one by one; these participants tended to categorize the problems in terms of superficial features and were unlikely, later on, to apply these analogies to new problems. Participants in a second group were explicitly asked to *compare* the training problems to each other. These participants tended to describe and categorize the problems in terms of their structures; in other words, they paid attention to each problem's underlying dynamic. These participants were much more likely to use these problems as a basis for analogies when later solving new problems.

Likewise, Needham and Begg (1991) presented their participants with a series of training problems. Some participants were told that they would need to recall these problems later on and were encouraged to work hard at remembering them. Other participants were encouraged to work at *understanding* each solution, so that they would be able to explain it later to another person.

When the time came for the test problems, participants in the second group were much more likely to transfer what they had earlier learned. As a result, those who had taken the "understand" approach were able to solve 90% of the test problems; participants who had taken the "memorize" approach solved only 69%. (For related data, see Lane & Schooler, 2004; Lee & Hutchison, 1998; and J. Loewenstein, Thompson, & Gentner, 1999.)

For purposes of problem-solving, therefore, there is a preferred way to learn. In essence, you want to attend to the structure of a problem rather than to its surface; this increases the likelihood of finding analogies later on, and thus the likelihood of benefiting from analogies. One way to achieve this is by comparing problems to each other, seeking parallels and points of similarity. The same benefit is observed if you simply spend time thinking about why a problem's solution *is* a solution— that is, why the solution gets the job done. People are also helped by getting the right training problems—problems that call attention to underlying structures. Thus, there seem to be many ways to promote analogy use—ways that provide people both with the relevant analogues and with the "sagacity to apply the knowledge to a new problem" (Needham & Begg, 1991; after W. James, 1890).

Expert Problem-Solvers

In obvious ways, then, our discussion of problem-solving has important implications for education. To make this concrete, let's say that we want students to be better problem-solvers; how should we proceed? First, we could teach our students some of the heuristics that appear useful for problem-solving in general. Second, analogies are plainly helpful in problem-solving, and so we could provide students with experience in the relevant domains so that they would have a basis from which to draw analogies. Third, we now see that this training may have little effect unless we take steps to ensure that students will use this knowledge when it is needed. To this end, we need to encourage students to approach the training problems in an appropriate way, to make certain the training problems will be retrievable from memory later on, and also to provide a basis for seeing the mapping between the training and test problems.

Will these training steps truly improve problem-solving? One way to ask is by examining *expert* problem-solvers; if they use the techniques we have already discussed, this obviously supports the claim that these techniques are valuable and should be the focus of training. If, on the other hand, experts use some other techniques, then perhaps these, too, could be developed with novices, through the appropriate education.

In fact, expert problem-solvers do use many of the techniques we've discussed. For example, we have claimed that it is helpful to think about problems in terms of their deep structure, and this is, it turns out, the way experts think about problems. This is evident in many studies, including one in which novices and experts were asked to categorize simple physics problems (Chi, Feltovich, & Glaser, 1981). The novices tended to place together all the problems involving inclined planes, all the problems involving springs, and so on, in each case focusing on the surface form of the problem, independent of what physical principles were needed to solve the problem. In contrast, the experts (Ph.D. students in physics) ignored these details of the problems and, instead, sorted according to the physical principles relevant to the problem's solution. (Also see Chi, Glaser, & Farr, 1988; Cummins, 1992; Hardiman, Dufresne, & Mestre, 1989; Hinsley, Hayes, & Simon, 1977; and Reeves & Weisberg, 1994.)

We have also claimed that attention to a problem's structure promotes analogy use. Therefore, if experts are more attentive to this structure, then experts should be more likely to use analogies. Several studies indicate that this is correct. For example, Novick and Holyoak (1991) examined their participants' skill in using mathematical analogies (an example is shown in Figure 14.12). They first provided the participants with a training problem; the participants then tried to solve several analogous problems.

Novick and Holyoak assessed "math expertise" by looking at the participants' quantitative SAT scores, and found a positive relation between these scores and the

| FIGURE 14.12 | Using Analogies to Solve Mathematical Problems |

The Garden Problem

Mr. and Mrs. Renshaw were planning how to arrange vegetable plants in their new garden. They agreed on the total number of plants to buy, but not on how many of each kind to get. Mr. Renshaw wanted to have a few kinds of vegetables and 10 of each kind. Mrs. Renshaw wanted more different kinds of vegetables, so she suggested having only 4 of each kind. Mr. Renshaw didn't like that because if some of the plants died, there wouldn't be very many left of each kind. So they agreed to have 5 of each vegetable. But then their daughter pointed out that there was room in the garden for 2 more plants, although then there wouldn't be the same number of each kind of vegetable. To remedy this, she suggested buying 6 of each vegetable. Everyone was satisfied with this plan. Given this information, what is the fewest number of vegetable plants the Renshaws could have in their garden?

Solution for the Garden Problem   Since at the beginning Mr. and Mrs. Renshaw agree on the total number of plants to buy, 10, 4, and 5 must all go evenly into that number, whatever it is. Thus the first thing to do is find the smallest number that is evenly divisible by those 3 numbers, which is 20. So the original number of vegetable plants the Renshaws were thinking of buying could be any multiple of 20 (that is, 20 or 40 or 60 or 80, etc.). But then they decide to buy 2 additional plants that they hadn't been planning to buy originally, so the total number of plants they actually end up buying must be 2 more than the multiples of 20 listed above (that is, 22 or 42 or 62 or 82, etc.). This means that 10, 4, and 5 will now no longer go evenly into the total number of plants. Finally, the problem states that they agree to buy 6 of each vegetable, so the total number of plants must be evenly divisible by 6. The smallest total number of plants that is evenly divisible by 6 is 42, so that's the answer.

The "Marching Band" Problem

Members of the West High School Band were hard at work practicing for the annual homecoming parade. First they tried marching in rows of 12, but Andrew was left by himself to bring up the rear. The band director was annoyed because it didn't look good to have one row with only a single person in it, and of course Andrew wasn't very pleased either. To avoid this problem, the director told the band members to march in columns of 8. But Andrew was still left to march alone. Even when the band marched in rows of 3, Andrew was left out. Finally, in exasperation, Andrew told the band director that they should march in rows of 5 in order to have all the rows filled. He was right. This time all the rows were filled and Andrew wasn't alone any more. Given that there were at least 45 musicians on the field but fewer than 200 musicians, how many students were there in the West High School Band?

The Seashell Problem

Samantha's mother asked her how many seashells she had in her collection. Samantha said she wasn't sure, but it was a lot—somewhere between 80 and 550. And she could count them by sevens without having any left over. However, if she counted them by threes, there was one shell left over. Things were even worse if she counted the shells by fives, by sixes, by nines, or by tens—there were always four shells left over. Samantha's mother promptly told her how many seashells she had in her collection. What number did Samantha's mother come up with?

Participants first solved the garden problem, and then they were tested with the band and seashell problems. Participants with greater math expertise (measured via SAT scores) were more likely to rely on analogies in solving these problems, and so were more likely to apply what they had learned in the training problems to the subsequent test problems. (After Novick & Holyoak, 1991) ability to form mathematical analogies. There was no relation between analogy use and verbal SATs, or between analogy use and what they called "general analogy skill." What seems to matter in drawing analogies, therefore, is not some sort of generalized skill. Instead, analogy use depends specifically on expertise within the relevant domain. (For related results, see Clement, 1982; and Novick, 1988.)

Chunking and Subgoals

Experts also have another advantage, and it once again leads us to a suggestion about how to *train* people so that they can become better problem-solvers. We mentioned earlier in the chapter that it is often helpful to break a problem into subproblems, so that the problem can be solved part by part, rather than all at once. With that, it is often helpful to create subgoals while working on a problem, and to work on reaching these, rather than aiming only at the problem's ultimate goal. It turns out that these, too, are techniques often used by experts, and, crucially, these techniques are supported by the experts' understanding of the problem's deep structure.

Classic evidence on this point comes from studies of chess experts (De Groot, 1965, 1966; also Chase & Simon, 1973), and the data show that these experts are particularly skilled in *organizing* a chess game—in seeing the structure of the game, understanding its parts, and perceiving how these parts are related to each other. This is revealed, for example, in how chess masters remember board positions: In one procedure, chess masters were able to remember the positions of 20 pieces after viewing the board for just 5 seconds; not surprisingly, novices remembered many fewer. In addition, there was a strong pattern to the experts' recollection: In recalling the layout of the board, the experts would place four or five pieces in their proper positions, then pause, then recall another group, then pause, and so on. In each case, the group of pieces was one that made "tactical sense"—for example, the pieces involved in a "forked" attack, a chain of mutually defending pieces, and the like.

Plainly, the masters had memorized the board in terms of higher-order units, and not the individual pieces. These units, in turn, were defined according to their strategic function within the game. Consistent with this suggestion, the masters showed no memory advantage if asked to memorize random configurations of chess pieces. In this case, there were no sensible groupings, and so the masters were unable to organize (and thus memorize) the board. (Also see Gobet & Simon, 1996a, 1996b; but then see Gobet & Simon, 2000; and Lassiter, 2000. For evidence that chess experts actually *see more*, with each glance at the board, see Reingold, Charness, Pomplun, & Stampe, 2001.)

In Chapter 5, we saw that memory is generally improved if one can repackage the materials to be remembered into a small number of memory "chunks," and this is obviously relevant to the result being considered here. What the chess experts are doing, in essence, is organizing the board into meaningful chunks, and this produces their superior memory for the board's layout. Similar memory advantages have been reported in other domains—for example, masters in the game of Go memorizing board positions (J. Reitman, 1976) or experts in electronics memorizing circuit diagrams (Egan & Schwartz, 1979).

Crucially, though, this perception of higher-order units doesn't just help memory; it also helps organize the expert's thinking. By focusing on the units and how they're related to each other, the expert keeps track of broad strategies without getting bogged down in the details. Likewise, these units help set subgoals for the expert: Having perceived a group of pieces as a coordinated attack, the expert sets the subgoal of preparing for the attack. Having perceived another group of pieces as "the early development of a pin," the expert creates the subgoal of avoiding the pin. In these ways, the higher-order units lend structure to the expert's thinking and guide the expert in choosing the next move.

Can nonexperts be trained to use subgoals in this way? Participants in one study were shown a new mathematical procedure, useful for calculating probabilities. For some of the participants, key steps of the procedure were labeled in a fashion that highlighted the function of those steps; for other participants, no labels were provided (Catrambone, 1998). Importantly, these labels had been chosen so that they didn't merely add detail to the solution; instead, the labels were chosen so as to highlight the problem's structure, and so potentially helped the participants to divide the procedure into meaningful parts, and to see the role of each part within the larger solution. And, in fact, the labels were quite useful: Participants given the labels were better able to use this new procedure in solving novel problems, including novel problems that (superficially) differed from the training problems in a variety of ways.

The Nature of Expertise

We have now suggested that experts have several advantages in comparison to novices, including a greater use of analogies, and a greater reliance on subgoals. And, as we have seen, various training programs can convey these advantages to nonexperts, making them better problem-solvers.

Let's be clear, though, that a few training sessions, encouraging the use of analogies or subgoals, won't turn someone into a problem-solving expert. That's because experts also have some other advantages, including the simple fact that they know much more about their domains of expertise than novices do. Indeed, Hayes (1985) estimates that it takes at least 10 years to become an expert in a domain, presumably because it takes that long to accumulate the relevant experience. (Also see Holding, 1985.)

In addition, experts don't just have *more* knowledge; they also have different *types* of knowledge than novices do. We have already suggested, for example, that chess masters are particularly conversant with higher-order patterns on the chessboard—patterns often involving six or seven different pieces. Indeed, the expert may know a huge number of these patterns; it has been estimated that a chess master has roughly 50,000 different chess patterns in memory, compared to the 1,000 patterns known to someone who is merely a "good" player (Chase & Simon, 1973; also Bédard & Chi, 1992). Similar claims have been made for experts in a variety of other domains (Gilhooly, 1988).

There are also indications that experts *organize* their knowledge more effectively than novices. In particular, studies indicate that experts' knowledge is heavily cross-referenced, so that each bit of information has associations to many other bits (e.g., Bédard & Chi, 1992; Eylon & Reif, 1984; Heller & Reif, 1984). As a result, not only do experts know more, but they have faster, more effective access to what they know.

These differences in what experts know have immediate implications for what experts *do*—that is, how they proceed when they are tackling a problem. For example, we mentioned earlier that novices often find it useful, in solving a problem, to work backward from the goal—to seek operators that will gradually make the goal state more and more similar to their current state. In contrast, experts are less likely to use this working-backward strategy (Bédard & Chi, 1992; Gick, 1986; Larkin, McDermott, Simon, & Simon, 1980; Sweller, Mawer, & Ward, 1983); instead, they work forward, from the initial state toward the goal.

One might think that the experts are using a risky strategy: If you start at the initial state and work forward, it is possible that the path you have selected might not lead where you want to go. However, this risk is relatively small for experts: Because they quickly recognize what type of problem they are working on, they realize what type of solution will be appropriate. Therefore, they are essentially guaranteed, as they work forward from their initial state, that they are moving in the right direction.

Notice, then, that experts work forward on a problem only because they recognize the type of problem and know how to tackle it. On this basis, we might expect that even experts will resort to the working-backward strategy with unfamiliar problems, problems that they cannot categorize. This is correct: When experts don't recognize a problem, they work backward from the goal to their current state, exactly as a novice would (Bhaskar & Simon, 1977; Gick, 1986). Thus, the expert's strategy choice is, in the end, dependent on the expert's knowledge base. (For a different example, showing how experts' strategies are influenced by their knowledge, see Proffitt, Coley, & Medin, 2000.)

Finally, one other advantage for the experts should also be mentioned: In addition to their advantages in knowledge, experts are also, rather obviously, well practiced in working in their domain, well practiced in solving problems. As we discussed in Chapter 4, this allows the expert to "automatize" many tasks. Similarly, the expert has established certain routines for dealing with commonplace tasks or, as some would say, has "proceduralized" these tasks. In many cases, therefore, an expert will realize that a problem is functionally identical to problems met earlier and so will give the problem no further thought, relying instead on the well-rehearsed routine. (For discussion, see J. R. Anderson, 1982, 1983, 1987.)

Defining the Problem

As we have seen, one of the features of expertise lies in how experts conceptualize a problem. Novices often define problems in terms of their superficial features, and this approach guides how the novices think about the problem and how they try to solve it. Experts, in contrast, usually define a problem in their area of expertise in terms of the problem's deep structure or underlying dynamic. As a result, the experts are more likely to realize what other problems are analogous to the current problem, and they are more likely to benefit from analogies.

Notice, therefore, that there are plainly better and worse ways to define a problem—ways that will lead to a solution, and ways that will obstruct it. But what does it mean to "define" a problem? And what determines how we define the problems we encounter? We turn next to these crucial questions.

Ill-Defined and Well-Defined Problems

For many problems, the initial state, goal state, and operators are clearly defined from the start. In the "Hobbits and Orcs" problem (Figure 14.1), you know exactly where all the creatures stand at the beginning of the problem. You know exactly where you want the creatures to be at the problem's end. And you know exactly what operators you have available.

Many problems—including problems we encounter in our day-to-day lives—are rather different. We all hope for peace in the world, but what exactly will this goal look like? There will be no fighting, of course, but what other traits will the goal have? Will the nations currently on the map still be in place? How will disputes be settled? How will resources be allocated? It is also unclear what the operators should be for reaching this goal. Should we try making diplomatic adjustments? Or would economic measures be more effective—perhaps some pattern of commerce through which nations become more dependent on each other?

Problems like this one are said to be **ill-defined**, with no clear statement at the outset of how the goal should be characterized or what steps one might try in reaching that goal. Many problems are ill-defined—"having a good time while on vacation," "saving money for college," "choosing a good paper topic" (Halpern, 1984; Kahney, 1986; W. Reitman, 1964; Schraw, Dunkle, & Bendixen, 1995; Simon, 1973).

Problem-solvers have several options available when they confront ill-defined problems. An obvious option is one we have already met: Establish subgoals. For many ill-defined problems, there may be well-defined subproblems; and by solving each of these, one can move toward solving the overall problem. A different strategy is to add some structure to the problem—by adding extra constraints or extra assumptions. In this way, you might gradually render the problem **well-defined** instead of ill-defined—with a narrower set of options perhaps in how you might approach the problem, but with a clearly specified goal state and, eventually, with a manageable set of operators to try.

Functional Fixedness

Even for well-defined problems, there is often more than one way to understand the problem. We have already met an example of this, in the contrast between superficial and deeper-level descriptions of a problem. But other examples are easy to find.

For example, consider the candle problem presented in Figure 14.13. To solve this problem, you need to cease thinking of the box as a container. You need instead to think of it as a potential platform, and so solving the problem depends heavily on how the box is represented.

As a way of emphasizing this point, we can compare two groups of research participants: One group is given the equipment shown in Figure 14.13: some matches, a box of tacks, and a candle. This configuration (implicitly) underscores

---

| FIGURE 14.13 | The Candle Problem |

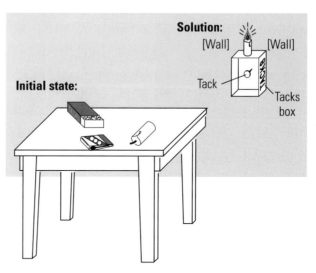

You are given the objects shown: a candle, a book of matches, and a box of tacks. Your task is to find a way to attach the candle to the wall of the room, at eye level, so that it will burn properly and illuminate the room.

What makes this problem difficult is the tendency to think of the box of tacks as a box—that is, as a container. The problem is readily solved, though, once you think of the box as a potential platform.

the box's conventional function—namely, as a container. As a result, this configuration increases **functional fixedness**—that is, the tendency to be rigid in how one thinks about an object's function. With this fixedness in place, the problem is rarely solved.

Other participants are given the same tools, but configured differently. They are given some matches, a pile of tacks, the box (now empty), and a candle. In this setting, the participants are less likely to think of the box as a container for the tacks, and so they are less likely to think of the box *as a container*. And, in this setting, they are more likely to solve the problem (Duncker, 1945; also Adamson, 1952; Glucksberg & Danks, 1968; and Weisberg & Suls, 1973).

Functional fixedness is also evident in studies of the two-string problem (Figure 14.14). Few participants solve this problem, presumably because they are thinking of the pliers as a tool for grabbing and holding. To solve the problem, the pliers need to play a much simpler role, serving only as a weight, and participants will realize this only if they ignore the pliers' customary function. And, once again, we can

---

FIGURE 14.14   The Two-String Problem

You enter a room in which two strings are hanging from the ceiling. Your task is to tie the two strings together. Unfortunately, though, the strings are positioned far enough apart so that you can't grab one string and hold on to it while reaching for the other. How can you tie them together?

To solve the problem, you should tie the pliers to one string, then push them gently away from the other string. Then grab the second string, and wait until the pliers, as a pendulum, swing back to you. (After Maier, 1931)

make this problem even more difficult if we take steps to emphasize the pliers' standard function—if, for example, we use the pliers to pull a tack out of the tabletop while instructing the participant in the overall task. Under these circumstances, fixedness is maximal, and virtually no participants solve the problem.

Einstellung

In the cases just described, people seem to represent a problem in a fashion that emphasizes a particular function for some crucial object—a representation that emphasizes the pulling function of pliers, or the containing function of a box. If we can change that representation, people immediately benefit; that is, they are able to solve the problem. Changing this representation, though, turns out not to be easy, and people instead display a counterproductive rigidity, a rigidity we have referred to as "functional fixedness."

People also display other forms of rigidity in problem-solving, and this rigidity in general is referred to as **Einstellung**, the German word for "attitude." The idea is that, in solving a problem, people develop a certain attitude or perspective and then approach all subsequent problems with the same rigid attitude. Functional fixedness provides one example of an Einstellung effect, but the classic demonstration of this effect employs the so-called water-jar problem. You are initially given three jars: A, which holds 18 ounces; B, which holds 43 ounces; and C, which holds 10 ounces. You have access to an unlimited supply of water. You also have a large, uncalibrated bucket. Your task is to pour exactly 5 ounces of water into the bucket. How would you do it?

The solution is to fill Jar B (43 ounces), then to pour water from Jar B into Jar A (which holds 18). Now Jar B contains 25 ounces of water. From this, fill Jar C (which holds 10 ounces); 15 ounces of water remains in B. Dump Jar C, then fill it again from B. Now, 5 ounces of waters remains in Jar B, so you are done.

Once participants have solved this problem, we give them a new problem. Jar A now holds 9 ounces, B holds 42, and C holds 6. The goal is to end up with 21 ounces. We then give participants a third problem: Jar A holds 21; B holds 127; C holds 3; the goal is 100 ounces.

The series of problems is carefully designed such that all can be solved in the same way: One starts by filling the largest jar (B), pouring from it once into the middle-sized jar (A), then pouring from it twice into the smallest jar (C), leaving the desired amount.

After solving four problems of this form, participants are given one more problem: Jar A holds 18 ounces; Jar B holds 48 ounces; Jar C holds 4 ounces. The goal is 22 ounces. Participants generally solve this problem the same way they have solved the previous problems. They apparently fail to see that a different, more direct route to the goal is possible—by filling A, filling C, and then combining these (18 + 4). Their prior success in using the same procedure over and over renders them blind to the more efficient alternative.

More troubling, consider what happens if participants are given the training problems just described, all solved via the same path, and then are given this problem: Jar A holds 28 ounces; B holds 76; C holds 3. The goal is 25 ounces. The participants attack this problem by using their tried-and-true method: B, minus A, minus C twice. But this time the method fails (yielding 42 ounces, instead of the desired 25). When participants realize this, they are often stymied; their well-practiced routine won't work here, and they fail to see the much simpler path that would work (28 minus 3 equals 25). Remarkably, 64% of the participants fail to solve this problem, thanks to their history of using a now inapplicable strategy (Luchins, 1942; Luchins & Luchins, 1950, 1959).

In a sense, the participants are doing something sensible here: Once you discover a strategy that "gets the job done," you might as well use that strategy. Correspondingly, once you discover a strategy that works, there is little reason to continue hunting for other, alternative strategies. It is a little unsettling, though, that this mechanization of problem-solving prevents people from discovering other, simpler strategies. Worse, this mechanization actually interferes with problem-solving: Once they have learned one strategy for solving water-jar problems, people seem less able to discover new strategies. When a new problem arrives that cannot be solved with the prior formula, performance suffers.

Problem-Solving Set

In the water-jar experiments, people develop a strategy within the experiment itself, and then continue applying that strategy in a rigid, mechanical fashion. In other cases, people seem to make certain assumptions about a problem from the very start—assumptions about how the problem should be handled and what sorts of strategies are likely to be productive. These starting assumptions are referred to as a **problem-solving set**, and if the set turns out to be inappropriate, problem-solving suffers.

An often-discussed example of a problem-solving set involves the nine-dot problem illustrated in Figure 14.15. In tackling this problem, people seem to be guided by several different ideas about how they should proceed: First, people seem to have the idea that the lines they draw should stay inside the "square" defined by the dots. Second, people seem to assume that the lines they draw must begin and end on dots. Third, people have the idea that they'll need to maximize the number of dots "canceled" with each move, and so, as a result, they seek solutions in which each line cancels a full row or column of dots. It turns out, though, that these starting assumptions are all wrong, and so, guided by these mistaken beliefs, people find this problem quite hard (Kershaw & Ohlsson, 2004; MacGregor, Ormerod, & Chronicle, 2001).

In cases like the nine-dot problem, problem-solving sets seem to be bad things, blocking the discovery of a solution. This point must be balanced, though, with an equal emphasis on the *benefits* of a problem-solving set. This is because most prob-

FIGURE 14.15 The Nine-Dot Problem

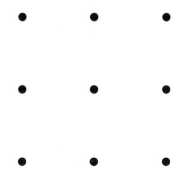

Draw four straight lines, passing through all nine of these dots, without lifting your pencil from the page.

Most people have difficulty with this problem, probably because of an inappropriate problem-solving set.

lems offer an immense number of options as you seek the solution—an enormous number of moves you might try, or approaches you might consider. A problem-solving set helps you, therefore, by narrowing your options, which, in turn, eases the search for a solution. In solving the candle problem (Figure 14.13), for example, you didn't waste any time wondering whether Martians might be summoned to hold the candle in place. You also didn't waste time trying to think of ways to melt the thumbtacks, in order to transform them into a candelabra. These are obviously silly options, so you brushed past them. But what identifies them as silly? It is your problem-solving set, which tells you, among other things, which options are plausible, which are physically possible, and the like.

In sum, there are benefits and costs to a problem-solving set. A set can blind you to important options and thus can, in some cases, be an enormous obstacle to problem solution. But a set also blinds you to a wide range of futile or impractical options, and this is a good thing: It allows you to focus, much more productively, on options likely to work out. Therefore, the key is not to approach a problem without a set. Instead, all depends on finding the right set.

Creativity

Approaching a problem with the right set (the right assumptions, the right representation) can help us in important ways. Approaching a problem with the wrong set, on the other hand, can make the problem enormously difficult. Worse, if one does start with the wrong representation, it is often hard to shift gears, thanks to phenomena like fixedness or Einstellung. This obviously demands that we ask; How does one find an appropriate problem-solving set? How does one figure out how to approach a problem?

Case Studies of Creativity

We have already noted that a problem's solution can, in many cases, be suggested by an analogy to a previously solved problem. In the same fashion, a *set* can also be suggested by analogy: If the current problem reminds you of a previously solved case, you are likely to adopt the same set that worked previously: You will make the same assumptions, and try the same operations, as you did on the prior occasion. What if no analogy comes to mind? In this case, you will be forced to use some less insightful, more laborious strategy—perhaps trial and error, or hill-climbing, or working backward from the problem's solution.

Surely, though, there is more to problem-solving than this. What about cases of insight, or cases in which one suddenly finds a new and creative way to approach a problem? These don't seem like cases of searching through memory for an analogy or cases based on heuristic use. What, then, can we say about these cases?

One way to approach these questions is by examining individuals who have undeniably been enormously creative—great artists like Picasso or Bach, or innovative scientists like Charles Darwin or Marie Curie. These are people who found innovative ways to approach their work, whether that work was in art or in science. Perhaps, therefore, by studying these people we can find out how new approaches to a problem can be found, how new sets can be established. We might then be able to draw hints from this about the nature of creativity when it arises—on a much smaller scale—in day-to-day life. With that, we'll be able to tackle the question with which we began this section—the question of how one finds a good approach to a problem, rather than a futile one; an appropriate problem-solving set, rather than one that will block progress.

Many researchers have examined the creativity of individuals like Picasso or Darwin, and this inquiry reveals that highly creative people tend to have certain things in common, so that, perhaps, we can think of these shared elements as "prerequisites" for great creativity. These individuals, first of all, need to have knowledge and skills in their domain: If one doesn't know a lot of chemistry, one cannot be a creative chemist. If one is not a skilled storyteller, one cannot be a creative novelist, and so on. Second, to be creative, one must be the "right sort of person." That is, one must have certain intellectual capacities (e.g., creative people tend to be highly intelligent) and also certain personality traits, including a willingness to take risks, a willingness to ignore criticism, an ability to tolerate ambiguous findings or situations, and an inclination not to "follow the crowd." Third, highly creative people tend to be motivated by the pleasure of their work, rather than by the promise of external rewards. With this, highly creative people tend to work extremely hard on their endeavors, and to produce a lot of their product, whether that product is poems, paintings, or scientific papers. Fourth, there is an important sense in which highly creative people have been "in the right place at the right time"—that is, in environments that allowed them freedom, that provided them with the appropriate supports, and that offered them problems that were "ripe" for solution with the resources available. (For discussion of these "prerequisites," and how they apply to a succession of enormously creative individuals, see Amabile, 2001; Gruber & Wallace, 2001; Nakamura & Csikszentmihalyi, 2001; Sternberg, 2001; Sternberg & Dess, 2001; Stokes, 2001; and Ward, 2001.)

All of this still leaves us asking, however, about what it is that goes on inside the creative mind. If one has all the prerequisites just listed, what happens next, to produce the creative step forward? One proposal was offered many years ago by Wallas (1926), who argued that creative thought proceeds through four stages. In the first stage, **preparation**, the problem-solver gathers information about the problem. This stage is typically characterized by periods of effortful, often frustrating, work on the problem, generally with little progress. In the second stage, **incubation**, the problem-solver sets the problem to the side and seems not to be working on it. Wallas argued, though, that the problem-solver was continuing to work on the problem during this stage, albeit unconsciously. Thus, the problem solution is continuing to develop, unseen, just as the baby bird develops, unseen, inside the egg. This period of incubation leads to the third stage, **illumination**, in which some key insight or new idea emerges, paving the way for the fourth stage, **verification**, in which one confirms that the new idea really does lead to a problem solution and works out the details.

The Moment of Illumination

Most modern psychologists are highly skeptical about Wallas's proposal. As one concern, historical evidence suggests that many creative discoveries don't include the four steps or, if they do, include them in a complex, back-and-forth sequence (Weisberg, 1986). In addition, the stages, when examined, turn out to be considerably less impressive, less "magical," than Wallas implied. For example, let's consider Wallas's third stage, illumination.

It is certainly true that, in solving problems, people sometimes do have "Aha!" experiences, in which they feel like they have made a great leap forward. But what exactly does this experience involve? Wallas proposed that this moment indicates the arrival of the solution—or, at least, the arrival of the insight that would lead to the solution. But is this right?

Metcalfe (1986; Metcalfe & Weibe, 1987) gave her participants a series of "insight problems," like those shown in Figure 14.16. As participants worked on each problem, they rated their progress, using a judgment of "warmth" ("I'm getting warmer . . . , I'm getting warmer. . . ."). These ratings did capture the "moment of insight": Initially, the participants didn't have a clue how to proceed and gave

| FIGURE 14.16 | Studies of Insight Problems |

Problem 1

A stranger approached a museum curator and offered him an ancient bronze coin. The coin had an authentic appearance and was marked with the date 544 B.C. The curator had happily made acquisitions from suspicious sources before, but this time he promptly called the police and had the stranger arrested. Why?

Problem 2

A landscape gardener is given instructions to plant four special trees so that each one is exactly the same distance from each of the others. How should the trees be arranged?

As participants worked on these problems, they were asked to judge their progress, using an assessment of "warmth" ("I'm getting warmer . . . , I'm getting warmer . . . , I'm getting hot!"). For the first problem, you must realize that no one in the year 544 B.C. knew that it was 544 B.C.; that is, no one could have known that Christ would be born exactly 544 years later. For the second problem, the gardener needs to plant one of the trees at the top of a hill, and then plant the other three at the base of the hill, with the three together forming an equilateral triangle, and with the four forming a triangle-based pyramid (i.e., a tetrahedron).

warmth ratings of 1 or 2. Then, rather abruptly, they saw how to solve the problem, and at that instant their warmth ratings shot up to the top of the scale.

To understand this pattern, though, we need to look separately at those participants who subsequently announced the correct solution to the problem, and those who announced an *incorrect* solution. As you can see in Figure 14.17, the pattern is the same for these two groups. Thus, some participants abruptly announced that they were getting "hot" and moments later, solved the problem. Other participants made the same announcement and, moments later, slammed into a dead end. Indeed, if there is any difference at all between these two groups, it appears that the participants who are on the wrong track are more confident in their progress than those who are on the right track.

In short, then, when we say, "Aha!" it means only that we've discovered a new approach, one that we've not yet considered. This is by itself important, because often a new approach is just what we need. But there is nothing remarkable about the "moment of illumination." This moment doesn't signal the fact that we have at last discovered the problem's solution, or even that we have discovered a path leading to the solution. Instead, it means only that we've discovered something new to try, with no guarantee whatsoever that this "something new" will be helpful. (For more on insight, illumination, and how one overcomes a problem-solving impasse, see Chronicle, MacGregor, & Ormerod, 2004; Jones, 2003; Knoblich, Ohlsson, & Raney, 2001; and Sternberg & Davidson, 1995.)

FIGURE 14.17   Participants' Self-assessments of Progress While Solving
Insight Problems

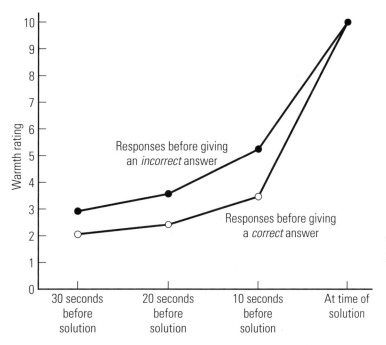

Initially, participants had little idea about how to proceed with these problems and gave very
low "warmth" ratings. Then, abruptly, they saw how to solve the problem, and at that moment
their warmth ratings shot up to the top of the scale. Importantly, though, the same pattern
was observed for participants who then announced a correct solution to the problem and for
those who then announced an *incorrect* solution. Thus, it seems that participants really can't
tell when they are on the verge of correctly solving a problem. Sometimes, they shout, "Aha!"
only to slam into a dead end a moment later.

Incubation

What about Wallas's second stage, the stage of incubation? In this stage, problem-
solvers seem to set the problem aside, but they (allegedly) continue to work on it
unconsciously and, as a result, make considerable progress.

Many people find this an appealing idea, since most of us have had an experience along these lines: You are working on a problem but getting nowhere. After a
while, you give up and turn your thoughts to other matters. Sometime later,
though, you try the problem again and are able to solve it. Or perhaps, later on, you
are thinking about something altogether different when the solution suddenly pops
into your thoughts.

Many examples of this pattern have been recorded, with a number of authors pointing out that great scientific discoveries have often been made in this manner (e.g., Kohler, 1969). As a more modest example, consider the tip-of-the-tongue (TOT) phenomenon, which we described in Chapter 8. In this phenomenon, you are struggling to think of a specific word but can't. Often your best strategy is to give up and try again later. When you do, there is a reasonable likelihood that the word will come to you.

Let's be careful, though, in how we interpret these observations. As one large concern, laboratory studies indicate that time away from a problem sometimes helps in finding the problem's solution, but usually doesn't. At best, therefore, the incubation effect is highly unreliable, and researchers have made little progress in determining when a benefit from interruption will be observed, and when it won't. (See, among others, Dominowski & Jenrick, 1972; Dorfman, Shames, & Kihlstrom, 1996; Gilhooly, 1999; Goldman, Wolters, & Winograd, 1992; Olton, 1979; Olton & Johnson, 1976; and C. Peterson, 1974.)

In addition, in those few cases in which interruption does promote problem-solving, why is this? Wallas's explanation, of course, is that the interruption allows unconscious problem-solving activity. Others, however, offer more prosaic hypotheses. In some studies, the interruption may simply provide an opportunity for problem-solvers to gather new information. Perhaps, during the time away from the problem, they stumble across some clue in the environment, or in their own memories, that will help them when they return to the problem. In this case, time away will aid problem solution, but not because of any unconscious work on the problem.

In other cases, the interruption may simply allow problem-solvers a fresh start on a problem. Their early efforts with a problem may have been tiring, or frustrating, and the interruption may provide an opportunity for this frustration or fatigue to dissipate. Likewise, their early efforts with a problem may have been dominated by a particular approach, a particular set. If they put the problem aside for a while, it is possible for them to forget these earlier tactics, and this will then free them to explore other, more productive, avenues.

In fact, there is some evidence for this "forgetting" account of incubation. S. M. Smith and Blankenship (1989, 1991) gave their participants puzzles to solve like those shown in Figure 14.18. To make these problems even more difficult, clues were given, but for many of the problems the clues were designed to be misleading. Control participants had a minute to work on each puzzle; other participants worked on each puzzle for 30 seconds, then were interrupted, and later returned to the puzzle for an additional 30 seconds.

This interruption did improve performance, so that problem solution was more likely for the "incubation" group. Crucially, though, Smith and Blankenship also tested participants' memory for the misleading clues, and found that the incubation participants were less likely to remember the clues. Smith and Blankenship argued that this forgetting is what created the "incubation" advantage: After the in-

FIGURE 14.18 Puzzles Used in a Study of Incubation

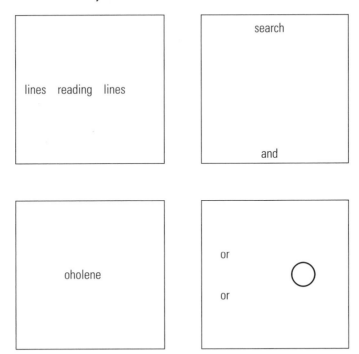

Participants had to figure out what familiar phrase was represented by each picture. For example, the first picture represents the phrase "reading between the lines"; the second represents the phrase "search high and low"; the third represents "a hole in one"; the fourth represents "double or nothing." For some stimuli, these pictures were accompanied by helpful clues (e.g., the last picture might be accompanied by the word "nothing"). For other stimuli, the clues were misleading (e.g., the third picture might be accompanied by the clue "chemical"). Time away from these puzzles, however, allowed participants to forget the misleading cues, and as a result, they were no longer misled by the clues and were more likely to solve the puzzles. (After S. M. Smith & Blankenship, 1989, 1991)

terruption, participants were no longer misled by the bad clues, and their performance improved accordingly. (Also see J. R. Anderson, 1981; and S. M. Smith & Vela, 1991. For more on why time off can aid memory search, see Chapter 8.)

The Nature of Creativity

Where does all of this leave us? We entered this section with the question of how one chooses the proper set, the proper approach, when solving a problem. We linked this to the question of creativity simply because one essential element of creativity is the ability to define problems in a new and valuable fashion—a fashion that opens up new possibilities, or points the way toward solutions for problems that had previously been regarded as insoluble. Hence, if we understand creativity, we understand (among other things) how one finds new and productive ways to define and approach a problem.

It would seem, though, that the cognitive processes involved in creativity are essentially the same processes involved in other, more mundane, forms of problem-solving—and this is, in some ways, an amazing claim. After all, one stands in awe of creative geniuses like da Vinci, Einstein, or Beethoven. So remarkable are their accomplishments, so different from what you and I produce, that it is natural to assume their thought processes are no less distinctive. You and I, equipped with heuristics, analogies, and subgoals, have troubles enough with Hobbits and Orcs. It seems unlikely, therefore, that these same intellectual tools could have led to the creativity obvious in great works of art, great innovations of science, or great inventions. The presumption, then, is that this creativity must arise from some other source—some different form of thinking, some other approach to problem-solving.

The evidence, however, is otherwise. When we examine Darwin's notebooks or Picasso's early sketches, we discover that they relied on analogies and hints and heuristics, and a lot of hard work, just as the rest of us do (Gruber, 1981; Weisberg, 1986). Likewise, when we examine processes like illumination, or incubation, we realize that these processes are less mysterious than they first seem. As we have seen, the "Aha!" feeling of illumination reflects only the fact that a person has discovered new things to try, new approaches to explore, in working on a problem. These new approaches may have been triggered by analogy, or by an association in memory, and crucially, these new approaches bring no guarantee of success. In many cases, people stumble onto a new approach and shout "Aha!" only to discover that the new approach leads them no closer to their goal.

Similarly, the topic of incubation has fascinated many authors, and much has been written about the role of incubation within the creative process. However, the evidence for incubation is uneven: It is unclear whether time off from a problem provides any consistent benefit, in contrast to continued effort on the same problem. Even when an "incubation" effect is observed, there is no persuasive evidence that this involves an unconscious process of problem-solving. Instead, incubation seems best explained in terms of dissipation of fatigue, opportunity for discovering new clues, forgetting of previous false starts, and the like.

In addition, further evidence suggests that highly creative people—just like the rest of us—find their solutions by scrounging through memory, relying on the same sort of spreading activation that serves all memory search (see Chapter 8). To be sure, highly creative people do have an advantage here: We mentioned earlier that experts tend to have memories that are highly cross-referenced, allowing them to find and use associations that other people might miss. Similarly, highly creative people do seem to have an advantage in finding novel associations for an idea; this is the base for what is commonly called "divergent thinking" (Guilford, 1967, 1979; see Figure 14.19); it is also related to the advantage that creative people sometimes

FIGURE 14.19 Creativity as Divergent Thinking

Tests of divergent thinking require you to think of new uses for simple objects, or new ways to think about familiar ideas. How many different uses can you think of for a brick?

As a paperweight.
As the shadow-caster in a sun dial (if positioned appropriately).
As a means of writing messages on a sidewalk.
As a stepladder (if you want to grab something just slightly out of reach).
As a nutcracker.
As a pendulum useful for solving the two-string problem.

Choose five names, at random, from the telephone directory. In how many different ways could these names be classified?

According to the number of syllables.
According to whether there is an even or odd number of vowels.
According to whether their third letter is in the last third of the alphabet.
According to whether they rhyme with things that are edible.

Guilford argued that creativity lies in the ability to take an idea in a new, unprecedented direction. Among its other items, his test of creativity asks people to think of new uses for a familiar object. Some possible responses are listed here.

have in locating "remote associates" in memory (Mednick, 1962; Mednick & Mednick, 1967; see Figure 14.20).

Even with these advantages in memory search, however, highly creative individuals do seem to be using the same search processes as everyone else: spreading activation, triggering associated ideas in memory. Yes, they are better at the process than the rest of us are, and so they're less likely to trigger the same memories again and again, and more likely to trigger new ideas. But even so, the fact remains that there's no "special" creativity mechanism here; there's just a greater level of skill in using the "standard machinery" of memory search.

In light of all of this, is it possible that there really is nothing special about the mental processes underlying creativity? To be sure, the creative *product* is extraordinary, but could it be that this product is the result of the same processes, the same forms of thinking, as more "ordinary" thought? Many authors have endorsed this idea, arguing that we need no special mental mechanisms to explain creativity. (See, for example, J. Goldenberg, Mazursky, & Solomon, 1999; Klahr & Simon, 2001; Langley & Jones, 1988; Simonton, 2003; Sternberg, 1988; and Weisberg, 1986, 1988.) The "ingredients" of creativity, in other words, are available to all of us—or perhaps would be available, if we simply acquired expertise in the relevant domain.

| FIGURE 14.20 | Creativity as the Ability to Find New Connections |

For each trio of words, think of a fourth word that is related to each of the first three. For example, for the trio "snow, down, out," the answer would be "fall" (snowfall; downfall; fallout).

1.	off	top	tail
2.	ache	sweet	burn
3.	dark	shot	sun
4.	arm	coal	peach
5.	tug	gravy	show

Mednick argued that creativity lies in the ability to find new connections among ideas. This ability is measured in the Remote Associates Test, for which some sample items are shown here. The solutions are (1) "spin" (spin-off, topspin, tailspin); (2) "heart"; (3) "glasses"; (4) "pit"; (5) "boat."

What, then, is so special about Newton or Michelangelo or Bach? The possibility before us is that these individuals did not rely on some special intellectual tools or some extraordinary thought processes in attaining their towering greatness. What distinguished these extraordinary individuals, therefore, was simply that they had *all* of the right tools, and *all* of the right ingredients, and it was this combination of ordinary elements that allowed their extraordinary achievements.

In other words, great scientists, artists, and inventors may rely on the same strategies as anyone else. What makes these people great is that they have the heuristics, and the expertise, and the appropriately cross-referenced memory, and the right training and opportunities, and the appropriate personality, and plenty of motivation. Very few people have all these ingredients, and it is the convergence of these elements that may, perhaps, be the recipe for achieving monumental creativity.

Chapter Summary

1. Problem-solving is often likened to a process of search in which one seeks a path leading from a starting point to the goal. In many problems, though, there are far too many paths to allow a search of each, and this is why problem-solving heuristics are crucial. Heuristics applicable to a wide range of problems include hill-climbing, means–end analysis, and working backward from the goal.

2. Problem-solving is also often aided by mental models, visual images, or diagrams. For some purposes, these work equally well, but each has its own advantages. Visual images are easily adjusted if one wishes to change the size or position of some element. Diagrams, in contrast, have the advantage of standing independent of our interpretation of them, and thus they can facilitate reinterpretation.

3. Analogies to earlier-solved problems are often helpful, but nonetheless, analogies seem to be underused by many problem-solvers. Analogy use is most likely if the current problem is similar in superficial ways to the (potential) analogue; these similarities help remind the problem-solver of the analogue, and also help him map the analogue onto the current problem. Analogy use can be promoted, however, by suitable instruction. For example, people are more likely to find analogues (and so more likely to solve problems) if they focus on a problem's deep structure, rather than its surface characteristics.

4. Experts in a domain generally pay more attention to a problem's underlying structure, rather than its surface form, and this helps the experts find and use analogies. Focusing on the problem's underlying structure also helps the experts to break the problem into subproblems.

5. The likelihood of solving a problem is enormously influenced by how someone perceives or defines the problem. The problem definition can include unnoticed assumptions about the form the solution must take, assumptions about the use or function of elements contained within the problem, and also assumptions about what types of procedures one should try in solving the problem. These various forms of problem-solving sets are usually helpful, because they guide the problem-solver away from pointless lines of attack on the problem. But the problem-solving set can also be an obstacle to problem-solving—if, for example, the solution requires a change in the set. Thus, problem-solving sets in the form of functional fixedness or Einstellung can often be significant obstacles to problem solution.

6. Investigators interested in creativity have often relied on detailed case studies of famous creative individuals. These case studies are said to reflect four stages of problem-solving: preparation, incubation, illumination, and verification.

7. However, researchers are skeptical about these four stages, and careful studies of creativity have provided little evidence to suggest that creativity involves special or exotic processes. For example, incubation is often mentioned as a form of unconscious problem-solving, but studies indicate that the benefits of incubation, when they occur, can be understood in simpler terms: recovery from fatigue, or the forgetting of unfruitful earlier approaches. In the same way, the moment of illumination seems to indicate only that the problem-solver has located a new approach to a problem; in many cases, this new approach ends up leading to a dead end.

8. In light of these data, many authors have suggested that creativity may simply be the extraordinary product that results from an assembly of ordinary elements—elements that include cognitive processes (memory search through spreading activation, heuristics, etc.), and also emotional and personality characteristics that foster the processes and circumstances needed for creativity.

Conscious Thought, Unconscious Thought

It was a bit more than a century ago that the field of psychology emerged as a separate discipline, distinct from philosophy or biology. And in those early years of our field, the topic of consciousness was a central concern: In Wilhelm Wundt's laboratory in Germany, researchers sought to understand the "elements" of consciousness. William James, in America, sought to understand the "stream" of consciousness.

However, the young field of psychology soon rejected this focus on consciousness, arguing that this research was subjective and unscientific. By the early 20th century, therefore, the topic of consciousness was largely gone from mainstream psychological research, and little was written on the topic for the next 50 years.

Over the last few decades, though, it has become clear that a scientific investigation of consciousness is possible, and armed with new tools and new conceptualizations, researchers have made enormous advances in their understanding of what consciousness is, how it functions, and how the brain makes consciousness possible. Ironically, much of this progress has come not from examining consciousness directly, but from studying what happens in the absence of conscious awareness. This strategy has allowed us to detail the sorts of circumstances in which consciousness seems not to be needed, and this, in turn, has allowed valuable insights into when consciousness *is* needed and,

- Throughout this text, we have discussed processes that provide an unnoticed support structure for cognition. We begin, therefore, by reviewing themes from earlier chapters, in order to ask what sorts of things are accomplished within the "cognitive unconscious."

- Overall, it appears that we can perform a task unconsciously if we arrive at the task with an already-established routine, directly applicable to that task, and if the routine can be guided by strong habits or by powerful cues within the situation.

- This reliance on unconscious operations is fast and efficient, but also inflexible and difficult to control. It frees us to pay attention to higher-order aspects of a task, but also leaves us ignorant about the sources of our ideas, beliefs, and memories.

- From a biological perspective, we know that most operations of the brain are made possible by highly specialized modules. These modules can be interrelated by means of workspace neurons, literally connecting one area of the brain to another, and allowing the integration of different processing streams.

- The workspace neurons create a "global workspace," and this is literally what makes consciousness possible; the operations of this workspace fit well with many things we know to be true about consciousness.

- However, profound questions remain about how (or whether) the global workspace makes possible the subjective experience that for many theorists is the defining element of consciousness.

with that, just what it is that consciousness contributes to our mental lives. This understanding of what consciousness is *for* has then illuminated questions about what consciousness *is*.

Let's acknowledge at the start, though, that there is still much about consciousness that we do not understand and, indeed, still disagreement about how consciousness should be defined and how it should be studied. With that, there is still disagreement about whether we should distinguish different types of consciousness or, at least, different sorts of things that might be included under the broad label of "consciousness."

We will return to these conceptual issues later in the chapter. For now, we'll proceed with this rough definition: Consciousness is a state of awareness of sensations or ideas, such that we can reflect on those sensations and ideas, know what it "feels like" to experience these sensations and ideas, and can, in many cases, report to others that we are aware of the sensations and ideas. As we'll see later, this broad definition has certain problems, but it will provide an adequate initial guide for our discussion.

The Cognitive Unconscious

As it turns out, much of the information that we need for our discussion of consciousness is already out in view—presented and discussed in previous chapters. Therefore, in this final chapter, we will draw repeatedly on topics covered earlier. By weaving these strands together, we will see that we already have a great deal to say about the topic of consciousness.

More specifically, we have seen throughout this book that our intellectual lives require an elaborate "support structure." Thinking, remembering, and categorizing (to name just a few of our intellectual achievements) all feel like they're quick and effortless, but as we have discussed, these activities depend on a great deal of work taking place "behind the scenes," and in a sense, describing this behind-the-scenes action has been one of the main concerns of this text.

Psychologists refer to this behind-the-scenes activity as the **cognitive unconscious**—activity of which we are completely unaware but that makes possible our ordinary interactions with the world. Let's begin by cataloguing some of the things that go on in the cognitive unconscious.

Unconscious Processes, Conscious Products

Several investigators have proposed that the cognitive unconscious includes all the *processes* involved in our mental lives, and so we are typically unaware of these processes. We are, however, aware of the *products* that result from these processes— the beliefs or conclusions or perceptions—even though we're not aware of the steps that brought us to those beliefs or those perceptions. (For discussion of the process/product distinction, see G. A. Miller, 1962; Neisser, 1967; Nisbett & Wilson, 1977; E. Smith & Miller, 1978; and White, 1988.)

For example, consider these mundane bits of memory retrieval: What is your mother's first name? What is your father's first name? Odds are that the answers just popped into your mind. You presumably had no awareness of searching through memory, of "traveling" from node to node within a network. You surely had no awareness of activation spreading out from the node for MOTHER'S NAME— activation that then facilitated the retrieval of your father's name. Yet, as we saw in Chapter 8, there is reason to believe that all of these processes were relevant to this bit of memory retrieval. The processes, however, were hidden from your view; all that you were aware of was the product—in this case, the two sought-after names.

Unconscious processes are also crucial in other domains. Imagine, for example, that we show one group of people the stimulus "CORN," and we show a second group of people the stimulus "CQRN." As we discussed in Chapter 3, both groups are likely to perceive the stimulus as "CORN" and, in all likelihood, won't know whether they were in the first group (and so correctly perceived the stimulus) or in the second (and so, guided by an inference, *mis*perceived the stimulus). Notice, therefore, that the experience of the two groups is the same; both groups have the experience of "seeing" the word "CORN." This seems a clear case, then, in which people are aware of the product of a mental process (they know that their perceptual apparatus reported that the stimulus was "CORN"), but not aware of the process (and so cannot tell whether the stimulus was actually perceived or merely inferred).

Similar themes emerged in Chapter 7, when we discussed memory errors. As we saw in that chapter, there is virtually no relationship between how confident people are in their memory, and the accuracy of that memory. In other words, people cannot tell when they are genuinely remembering something, and when they have instead inferred (or assumed or imagined) that something happened. This is, therefore, another case in which people are aware of a product (a belief about the past) but not the process (and so they cannot tell apart events that come into their mind because of a bona fide memory, and events that come into their mind because of an inference or assumption).

The Influence of Unconscious Attributions

The role of the cognitive unconscious is also evident in studies of implicit memory (Chapter 6). In these studies, participants are plainly being influenced by events they cannot consciously recall. Moreover, this influence often seems to require several steps of reasoning: "That name rings a bell, and I'm not sure why. But the experimenter is asking me about famous names, and there are other famous names on this list in front of me. I guess, therefore, that this one must also be the name of some famous person." This inference surely sounds like something that we want to count as "thinking," but it is thinking, the evidence suggests, of which we are entirely unaware.

A similar pattern is evident in cases involving source confusion (Chapter 6). In these cases, someone seems to reason this way: "That face looks familiar to me, and the police think it's likely that this is the person who robbed me. I guess, therefore, that the face is familiar because I saw this person at the robbery." But, of course, it's not this reasoning that the person is aware of. Instead, the person simply (and sometimes falsely) "remembers" seeing the person at the robbery, and so can end up, in some circumstances, an unwitting victim of his own mistaken inference.

These examples suggest that our unconscious thinking can be rather sophisticated, with layers of inference and reasoning. This sophistication is particularly evident when the unconscious thinking involves a **causal attribution**—that is, reasoning about the cause to which we should attribute some fact. ("The name rings a bell because it belongs to someone famous." "The face looks familiar because I saw that person at the robbery.")

As another example of unconscious causal reasoning, consider an early experiment by Nisbett and Schachter (1966). Their participants were asked to endure a series of electric shocks, with each shock slightly more severe than the one before. The question of interest was how far into the series the participants would go. What was the maximum shock they would voluntarily accept?

Before beginning the series of shocks, some of the participants were given a pill that, they were told, would diminish the pain but would also have several side effects: The pill would cause their hands to shake, butterflies in the stomach, irregular breathing, and the like. Of course, none of this was true. The pill was a placebo and had no analgesic properties, nor did it produce any of these side effects. Even so, this inert pill was remarkably effective: Participants given the pill and told about its side effects were willing to accept four times as much amperage as control participants.

Why was the placebo so effective? Nisbett and Schachter proposed that their control participants noticed that their hands were shaking, that their stomachs were upset, and so on. (These are standard reactions to electric shock.) The participants then used these self-observations as evidence in judging that they were quite uncomfortable in the experiment. It is as if participants said to themselves, "Oh look, I'm trembling! I guess I must be scared. Therefore, these shocks must really be bothering me." This led them to terminate the shock series relatively early. Placebo participants, in contrast, attributed these same physical symptoms to the pill. "Oh look, I'm trembling! That's just what the experimenter said the pill would do. I guess I can stop worrying, therefore, about the trembling. Let me look for some other indication of whether the shock is bothering me." As a consequence, these participants were less influenced by their own physical symptoms, and less influenced by what, in Chapter 13, we called "somatic markers." They detected these markers but discounted them, attributing them to the pill, not to the shock. In essence, they overruled the evidence of their own anxiety and so misread their own internal state. (For related studies, see Nisbett & Wilson, 1977; Wilson, 2002; and Wilson & Dunn, 2004.)

Of course, participants' reasoning about the pill was entirely unconscious. We know that they were thinking about the pill, because participants who received the pill (plus the instructions about the side effects) behaved in a fashion dramatically different from other participants. But the participants seemed to be entirely unaware of this thinking: When they were specifically asked why they had accepted so much shock, they rarely mentioned the pill. When asked directly, "While you were taking the shock, did you think about the pill at all?" they responded with answers like, "No, I was too worried about the shock to think of anything else."

Note also the *complexity* of the unconscious thinking in this experiment. The participants are reasoning about themselves in an intellectually sophisticated manner: observing "symptoms," generating hypotheses about those symptoms, drawing conclusions, and so on. As it turns out, in this case the participants reached erroneous conclusions, because they had been misled about the pill by the experimenter. But that takes nothing away from what they are doing intellectually—and unconsciously.

Mistaken Introspections

It does seem useful, then, to distinguish between the (unconscious) processes involved in thought and the (conscious) products that result from these processes. It turns out that this distinction isn't always clear-cut, but even so, the distinction does support a useful rule of thumb about what we're aware of in our mental lives and what we're not. Thus, we arrive at a conclusion, but the steps leading to the conclusion are hidden from view. We reach a decision, but again, we are unable to introspect about the processes leading to that decision.

Sometimes, however, the processes of thought do seem to be conscious. Sometimes you reason carefully and deliberately, weighing each step, scrutinizing each bit of logic. This surely sounds like a case in which your thoughts are conscious. Remarkably, though, this sense of knowing one's own thoughts may, in some cases, be an illusion. You feel like the processes were conscious, so that you know why you reached a conclusion, or why you made a particular decision, but you may be mistaken!

We have just discussed one example of this pattern: In the Nisbett and Schachter (1966) study, participants steadfastly denied that their willingness to undergo shock was influenced by the pill they had taken. Apparently, then, the participants had some beliefs about why they had acted as they did, and their beliefs were *wrong*—systematically ruling out a factor (the pill) that, in truth, was having an enormous impact.

Related examples are easy to find. Participants in one study read a brief excerpt from the novel *Rabbit Run*. They were then asked to describe what emotional impact the excerpt had on them, and they were also asked why the excerpt had the impact it did: Which sentences or which images, within the excerpt, led to the emotional "kick"? The participants were impressively unanimous in their judgments, with 86% pointing to a particular passage (describing the messiness of a baby's crib) as playing an important role in creating the emotional tone of the overall passage. However, it appears that the participants' judgments were simply wrong. Another group of participants read the same excerpt, but minus the passage about the crib. These participants reacted to the overall excerpt in exactly the same way as had the earlier group. Apparently the passage about the crib was not crucial at all (Nisbett & Wilson, 1977; for other, more recent data, see Bargh & Chartrand, 1999; Greenwald & Banaji, 1995; and Uleman & Bargh, 1989).

In studies like these, participants think they know why they acted as they did, but they are mistaken. Their self-reports are offered with full confidence, and in many cases the participants report that they carefully and deliberately thought about their actions, and so the various causes and influences were, it seems, out in plain view. Nonetheless, from our perspective as researchers, we can see that these introspective reports are wrong—omitting factors we know to be crucial, highlighting factors we know to be irrelevant.

But what is it that produces these mistaken (but highly confident) introspections? The answer starts with the fact that we've already showcased—namely, that the processes of thought are often unconscious. People seeking to introspect, therefore, have no special "window" through which they can peer to discover why they acted as they did. What happens, therefore, when they try to introspect? It seems likely that they end up reasoning in roughly this fashion: "Why did I act that way? Well, let me think about why, in general, people would act in a certain way in this situation. Then let me build, from that general knowledge, a plausible after-the-fact inference about why I acted as I did." In terms we used in Chapter 7, the participants are engaging in reconstruction—building on generic knowledge to reconstruct what must have occurred in a particular episode. (For more on this process of "self-interpretation," see Cooney & Gazzaniga, 2003.)

Let's emphasize, though, that the research participants don't realize that this is what they are doing. Instead, they are convinced they are simply remembering their own mental processes. These reconstructions, in other words, *feel like* introspections. Ironically, therefore, this is one more case in which people are conscious of the product and not the process. They are aware of the conclusion ("I acted as I did because . . .") but not aware of the process that led them to the conclusion. Hence they continue to believe (falsely) that the conclusion rests on an introspection, when, in truth, it rests on an after-the-fact reconstruction. Hand in hand with this, they continue to believe confidently that they know themselves, even though, in reality, their self-perception is (in these cases at least) focusing on entirely the wrong factors.

Unconscious Guides to Conscious Thinking

It is undeniable, however, that sometimes we are aware of our own thoughts. Sometimes we make decisions based on a clear, well-articulated "inner dialogue" with ourselves. Sometimes we make discoveries based on a visual image that we carefully (and consciously!) scrutinized. Even here, though, there is a role for the cognitive unconscious, because even here an elaborate unconscious support structure is needed—a support structure that exists at the "fringe" or the "horizon" of our conscious thoughts (Husserl, 1931; W. James, 1890).

Evidence for this unnoticed fringe comes from many sources, including a wide variety of cases in which our thoughts seem guided, or influenced, by an "unseen hand." For example, in our description of problem-solving (Chapter 14), we emphasized the role of *set*—unnoticed assumptions and definitions that guide our search for the problem's solution. Even when the problem-solving is conscious and deliberate, even when we "think out loud" about the steps of the problem solution, we are guided by a set. For the most part this is a good thing, because the set keeps us focused, protecting us from distracting and unproductive lines of thought. But, as we have seen, the set can sometimes be an obstacle to problem-solving, and the fact that the set is unconscious makes it all the more difficult to overcome the obstacle: The problem-solver cannot easily pause and reflect on the set, and so cannot alter the problematic beliefs or abandon the misleading assumptions.

Similarly, in our discussion of decision-making (Chapter 13), we emphasized the importance of the decision's *frame*. You might be completely focused on the decision, and fully aware of your options and your efforts toward choosing among them. Nonetheless, the evidence suggests that you will be heavily influenced by the unnoticed framing of the decision—the way the options are described, and the way the question itself is posed. You don't think about the framing itself, but the framing unmistakably colors your thoughts about the decision and plays a large role in determining the outcome of those thoughts.

Related points emerged in our discussion of mental imagery. Here, too, an unnoticed support structure is on the scene, guiding how the image is to be understood. In Chapter 11, we referred to this support structure as a "perceptual reference frame," and there we argued that this frame guides your thinking about the image (e.g., what you can discover about the image) and also renders the image unambiguous. The reference frame itself is unnoticed, but it powerfully determines the understanding of the conscious image, how the image subjectively appears, and what the image will call to mind.

The argument is the same with *verbal* representations. As we discussed in Chapter 10, words and sentences can often be interpreted in more than one way. But when we form our thoughts into words, the thoughts are unambiguous. Thus, when you think, "I was looking for the sage," you are not puzzled about whether you are hunting for some herbs to flavor the turkey or for a wise fellow. Likewise, if you were to think, "I saw the man with the binoculars," you might not even detect the ambiguity. In both cases, you are protected from confusion by a context of other ideas, beliefs, and expectations. These other ideas might not be noticed directly, and so the context they provide is an unconscious one. Even so, these other ideas set the context for the idea you are consciously focusing on, and they guide your understanding of the conscious idea.

One way to demonstrate these unconscious influences is by *priming*. In essence, the idea is that a previous stimulus or event can create a context in which we are likely to interpret a stimulus in one way or another, or a context in which we're more receptive to some ideas than to others. This provides a clear illustration of how an unconscious framework can guide our conscious thought.

In Chapter 8, for example, we discussed the influence that priming can have on lexical decisions: Having just seen the word "nurse," for example, you will be quicker in identifying "doctor." In essence, the presentation of "nurse" primes the nodes representing "doctor," and these nodes, now warmed up, are more easily (and more quickly) activated. Remarkably, though, the same effect can be observed even if "nurse" is presented so briefly that it's not consciously seen (Marcel, 1983a, 1983b). In this case, "nurse" serves as a **subliminal prime**, an unnoticed, undetected stimulus that still creates a context guiding subsequent perception.

In all of these ways, then, our deliberate, conscious thinking—about problems, decisions, images, or words—is guided by an unnoticed framework. Thus, we are aware that we are thinking about the sage, but not aware of how this thinking is shaped by assumptions or associations lying in the background. We are conscious that we are working on a problem, but not conscious of how our set guides our approach to the problem. We consciously recognize a stimulus, not realizing that our recognition was primed by a stimulus we didn't consciously see. In case after case, the unconscious mental framework protects us from uncertainty and ambiguity, and shapes both the content and the sequence of our thoughts.

Automatic Actions

We're obviously assembling a large catalogue of mental achievements that can go forward without consciousness. This catalogue grows still larger when we consider another category of unconscious thought—a category that grows out of our discussion of automaticity (in Chapter 4) and also our discussion of routinizing problem solutions (Chapter 14).

We noted in Chapter 4 that practice in a task has many consequences. Among them, practice allows us to perform the task without any need for close control of the performance and, correspondingly, without any need for close monitoring of the performance. In the end, we may be able to do the task "on autopilot," without being aware of the task at all.

An extreme example is provided by a study by Spelke, Hirst, and Neisser (1976). They asked their participants to do the seemingly impossible task of reading an encyclopedia while simultaneously listening to a series of words and writing down each word they heard. After many weeks of practice, participants were able to do this, and their reading speed and comprehension were just as good while taking dictation as they were when reading was the sole task. Likewise, their accuracy in taking dictation was just as good while reading as it was without. But this remarkable achievement did not depend on conscious awareness; instead, the participants were doing the dictation task on autopilot. Specifically, participants claimed that they had no idea what the dictated words were; they had written them down, they said, in an entirely mechanical fashion. When given a memory test for these words, the participants insisted they couldn't remember anything, and could only respond on this test by guessing. But their "guesses" turned out to be impressively accurate, indicating that the participants did, in fact, remember the words. Other tests showed that the participants had even understood the sequences within the dictated material, sequences that turned the word lists into miniature stories. In short, it seems that the participants had comprehended the dictated material without being aware of it, without consciousness.

Blind Sight and Amnesia

One last line evidence for unconscious achievements comes from patients who have suffered one or another form of brain damage. Consider, for example, the cases of memory pathology that we described in Chapter 6. Patients suffering from Korsakoff's syndrome often have no conscious awareness of events they have witnessed or things they have done. If asked directly about these events, the patients will insist that they have no recollection. If asked to perform tasks that require recollection, the patients will fail. Yet the patients do remember these events in some sense: On tests of *implicit* memory, the amnesic patients seem quite normal, making it clear that they are influenced, in their present beliefs and behaviors, by the specific content of the prior episodes. Thus, it seems that people with amnesia can remember and can be influenced by their memories, with no conscious awareness that they are recalling the past. This is a pattern that Jacoby and Witherspoon (1982) dubbed "memory without awareness."

A similar pattern is evident in the phenomenon of **blind sight**. This is a pattern observed in patients who have experienced damage to the striate cortex. As a result of this brain damage, these patients are, for all practical purposes, blind: If asked to move around a room, they will bump into objects; they do not react to flashes of bright light; and so on. In one experiment, however, visual stimuli were presented to these patients, and they were forced to guess whether the stimuli were (for example) *X*s or *O*s, circles or squares. Quite reliably, these patients "guessed" correctly (Rees, Kreiman, & Koch, 2002; Weiskrantz, 1986, 1997). Similarly, if the patients were forced to guess where various objects were placed and to reach toward those objects, they tended to reach in the right direction with the appropriate hand position (given the shape and size of the target object). The patients did this, all the while asserting that they could not see the targets, and insisting that they were reaching out at random. Thus it seems that these patients can, in a sense, "see," but they are not aware of seeing. (For related data, also showing a sharp distinction between a patient's conscious perception of the world and her ability to use visual information in guiding her actions, see Goodale & Milner, 2004.)

The Disadvantages of Unconscious Processing

Where, then, does all of this leave us? Clearly, a huge range of activities, including rather complex activities, can be accomplished unconsciously. So why do we need consciousness at all? What function is served by consciousness? And related to this, what things can't we do unconsciously?

The Nature of Unconscious Performance

One way to tackle these questions is by scrutinizing the various activities we can perform without consciousness, and asking what they have in common. In rough terms, three broad factors can be identified. First, the various cases of unconscious processing all seem to rely on well-established routines, or well-defined "processing modules" that have the specific job of carrying out a particular identifiable function. In some cases, the processing module has been created through practice; this was reflected in our discussion of automaticity, and in our comments (Chapter 14) about experts' reliance on the routinization of complex tasks. In other cases, the module is well rooted in our biology, but then shaped by experience. A good example would be the pattern-recognition network, which automatically makes a range of inferences, guided by the spelling patterns of language, without our realizing it is doing so. In all cases, though, the unconscious performance is made possible by a specific set of well-honed skills that we bring to the situation. Perhaps, then, to do things unconsciously, we need to bring just the right "tools" to the job, and must already be well practiced in using those tools.

Second, it seems that each of these modules, relevant to unconscious performance, is relatively specialized, doing a well-defined job in an identifiable domain. We are, for example, unaware of the machinery needed for memory search—but notice that this is machinery needed *for memory search*; it has that specific job to do. We are likewise unaware of the processes needed to detect processing fluency—again, processes that have a clearly defined function.

Third, and perhaps most important, in all the cases of conscious processing that we've considered, people seem to be doing just what the situation requires—guided either by the situation itself, or by prior habit. When people have (unconsciously) drawn conclusions, the conclusions tend to be the ones favored by familiarity or by the situation itself. Likewise, when people have made responses—like reaching for an object that they cannot consciously see, or noting the meaning of a word they did not consciously perceive—they are making the familiar response, the ordinary response for that situation.

All of this leads to an obvious proposal about unconscious processing, and also an obvious proposal about *conscious* processing. Let's turn at last to that proposal.

The Limits of Unconscious Performance

Perhaps we can perform tasks unconsciously—even sophisticated, complex tasks—if we arrive at the task with an already-established routine, directly applicable to that task, and if the routine can be guided entirely by strong habits, or powerful cues within the situation. These routines can be highly efficient, but they are also inflexible, relying on customary, habitual, or stimulus-governed actions, and not subject to control.

All of this implies that there will be clear limits on our unconscious processes. Specifically, the inflexibility in our unconscious routines will make it difficult—and perhaps impossible—to tune or adjust the routine. Indeed, the inflexibility makes it difficult for us to turn off the routine, even when we want to. As an illustration, consider the workings of memory: The inferences used to fill gaps in memory (both during encoding and during retrieval) are often helpful, but they can, on occasion, lead to memory error (Chapter 7). Knowing this, however, is no protection at all. Just as one cannot choose to avoid a perceptual illusion, one cannot choose to avoid memory error. The process of making inferences is automatic and effortless, and it is also irresistible.

Similarly, the inflexibility in routine makes it all too easy for us to become victims of habit, relying on our customary actions or customary thought patterns, even when we hope to avoid them. This is one of the reasons why problem-solving sets (Chapter 14) are so powerful and so difficult to break out of. It is also the reason why **action slips**—doing something different from what you intend—take the form that they do: In most cases, these slips involve your doing what's *normal* or *habitual* in a situation, rather than what you want to do on that occasion. For example, you are in the car, driving to the store. You intend to turn left at the corner, but, distracted for a moment, you turn right, taking the route that you frequently take on your way to school. Action slips like this one almost invariably involve the intrusion of a strong and familiar habit, slipping into what's "normal," even if it's not, at that moment, what you intend (Norman, 1981; Reason, 1990; also see Langer, 1989). All of this is just what we would expect if routine is forceful, automatic, and uncontrolled.

The Advantages of Unconscious Performance

At the same time, unconscious performance—inflexible as it often is—also has its advantages. For one, it allows mental tasks to run much more quickly, and we have seen many indications that speed is a desirable feature in our intellectual functioning. (This is, of course, one of the reasons we so often draw on mental shortcuts of one sort or another; see Chapters 9, 12, 13, and 14.) In addition, the routine allows a withdrawal of attention from the task, and this allows you to devote your attention instead to other, more pressing, matters.

What makes this withdrawal of attention possible? When you're first learning a task, you need to monitor each step, so that you'll know when it's time to start the next step. Then you need to *choose* the next step and get it started. Obviously, this gives you close control over how things proceed, but this need for supervision of the task makes the performance quite demanding.

After some practice, however, things are different. The steps needed for the task are still there, but you don't think about them one by one. That's because you have stored in memory a complete routine that specifies what all the steps should be, and when each step should be initiated. All you need to do, therefore, is launch the routine, and from that point forward, you simply repeat the familiar sequence. Thus, with no need for monitoring or decisions, you can do the task without paying close attention to it.

In this way, practice allows you to perform a task while allocating your resources elsewhere, and this has important benefits. When you're in the midst of a conversation, for example, you need, again and again, to search through memory to find suitable words for expressing your intended meaning. In this setting, you'd be distracted and slowed if you had to think through the mechanics of this memory search. Better, then, to keep those mechanics hidden from view. What you want to have in your awareness are the words resulting from the search, and not the search itself.

It seems, then, that the invisibility of our mental processes is often a good thing: It allows us to keep our attention focused on the things that matter (like choosing what ideas to convey in the conversation) without having to worry about the details (like how to find the exact words in memory). In Chapter 14, we discussed how this focus on "higher-order" aspects of a task is useful for experts; we now see that it is just as useful for nonexperts performing ordinary tasks.

The Function of Consciousness

Thus, unconscious processing carries both advantages and disadvantages: Routine is efficient and requires few mental resources, but it is also inflexible and difficult to control. Similarly, our lack of awareness for our own mental processes probably buys us speed and certainly spares us distraction, but it also leaves us ignorant about our mental processes in a fashion that can sometimes be disruptive—making it impossible for us to distinguish genuine memories from reconstructions, or actual perceptions from mere inferences, even when we want to.

It is a small step from these points to a proposal for the purpose of consciousness. Before we take that step, though, we need to add one last perspective on these issues.

The Cognitive Neuroscience of Consciousness

In the last decade or so, there has been an avalanche of intriguing books and papers concerned with the relationship between consciousness and brain function. Some of the relevant research has focused on cases of brain damage, including the cases of amnesia or blind sight mentioned earlier in this chapter. Other research has asked, roughly, what changes in the brain when someone becomes conscious of a stimulus; in other words, what are the **neural correlates** of consciousness? Research in this category often relies on the neuroimaging techniques we described in Chapter 2, and also on various techniques for measuring the electrical activity of the brain. (For broad reviews of this research, see, for example, A. P. Atkinson, Thomas, & Cleeremans, 2000; Baars & Franklin, 2003; Bogen, 1995; Chalmers, 1998; Crick & Koch, 1995; Dehaene & Naccache, 2001; and Rees et al., 2002.)

In light of this research, a number of different theories have been offered about how consciousness emerges from the brain's activity, but many researchers have endorsed one version or another of the **neuronal workspace hypothesis**. In broad outline, here is the proposal: As we first discussed in Chapter 2, different areas within the brain seem highly specialized in their function. The various aspects of visual perception, for example, depend on multiple brain areas, with one area specialized for the perception of color, another for the perception of movement, another for the perception of faces, and so on. Each of these areas does its own job, and the activity in each area is highly transient: The neurons respond to the current inputs and then move on, ready to respond to the next set of inputs.

For many purposes, though, we need to sustain the activity in these various systems (e.g., for prolonged scrutiny), and we also need to integrate the activity of the different systems into a coherent whole. What makes this possible is *attention*. Biologically, attention seems to amplify the activity within neural systems, and also to sustain that activity. In addition, as we described in Chapter 2, attention seems to link the activity of different neural systems, binding these into a single representation: Specifically, we have just said that various neural systems each respond to different aspects of a stimulus. If we are paying attention to that stimulus, however, the neurons in the various systems all fire in synchrony with each other, and they all fire at a rate known as the gamma rate (see Chapter 2). When neurons fire in this synchronized fashion, the brain seems to register this as a linkage among the different processing areas, thus binding together the aspect detected by one neural system (e.g., *movement*) with the aspected detected by another system (e.g., *red*). In this fashion, the brain registers that it was a red object that was moving.

This large-scale integration of different neural processes is supported by "workspace neurons," neurons that literally connect one area of the brain to another. And, with that said, we're now ready for our hypothesis: The integrated activity, made possible by the workspace neurons, is what makes consciousness possible; indeed, according to some authors, this integrated activity is literally the biological basis for consciousness (e.g., Dennett, 2001). Notice, though, that the workspace neurons don't carry the *content* of consciousness. The content—the sense of seeing something red, the sense of seeing something moving—is presumably represented in the same neurons, the same processing modules, that analyzed the perceptual information in the first place. But what the workspace neurons do is glue these bits together, thus creating a unified experience and allowing the exchange of information from one module to the next. (For a number of specific versions of this hypothesis, see Baars, 1988; Baars & Franklin, 2003; Cooney & Gazzaniga, 2003; Crick & Koch, 1995; Dehaene & Naccache, 2001; Engel & Singer, 2001; and Roser & Gazzaniga, 2004.)

The Function of the Neuronal Workspace

The proposal, then, is that the neuronal workspace, supported by attention, provides the biological basis for conscious experience. Stimuli become conscious when they are linked to each other in the dynamic, coherent representation that the workspace provides.

What does this linkage do for us? What does it make possible? For one, it provides a basis for explaining some basic facts about conscious experience itself. For instance, it is important that our conscious experience feels unitary and coherent: We are not aware of redness and also aware of movement, and of roundness, and of closeness. Instead, we are aware of a single experience, in which the red apple rolls slowly by us. Of course, this integrated coherence is just what the workspace allows: one representation, constructed from the coordinated activity of many processing components (Roser & Gazzaniga, 2004).

The workspace also makes possible a range of important behaviors (Dehaene & Naccache, 2001). First, the workspace, supported by attention, allows us to maintain a mental representation in an active state for an extended period of time. In other words, the workspace makes it possible for us to continue thinking about a stimulus, or an idea, even after the specific trigger for that idea is removed. In this way, we can link the workspace to working memory (Chapter 5), and to the brain areas associated with working memory's function—specifically, the prefrontal cortex (or PFC; Goldman-Rakic, 1987; for other evidence specifically linking activation in the PFC to conscious awareness, see McIntosh, Rajah, & Lobaugh, 1999).

In addition, the workspace allows us to compare what's going on in one neural system with what's going on in others. This allows us to reflect on *relationships* and *combinations* among various inputs, or ideas, and this in turn allows us to produce new combinations of ideas, or new combinations of operations. Thus, the neural mechanisms underlying consciousness are just the right sort to allow us, consciously, to produce novel thoughts and novel behaviors.

This sensitivity to relationships also allows us to detect conflict—if, for example, two simultaneous stimuli are triggering incompatible responses, or if a stimulus is triggering a response incompatible with our goals. This is clearly linked to what we said earlier about the limits of unconscious processes, and the advantages of conscious thinking: Unconscious processes, we said, rely on separate, self-contained processing modules. These processes are relatively inflexible and guided by prior habits, or specific cues within the situation, rather than by current goals. Indeed, if there were some conflict between prior habit and current goals, this would have no influence on the unconscious process. Conscious thought, in contrast, can rise above habit and can resist the responses triggered by the situation. Indeed, conscious thought, guided by a sense of one's goals, can launch exactly the behavior that will lead to those goals.

Again, the neuronal workspace has just the right properties to support these conscious achievements: Linking the processing modules makes it possible to detect conflict and, crucially, to adjust processing in one system in light of what is going on in another system. Biologically, this ability to adjust is probably made possible by brain circuits involving the **anterior cingulate cortex** (ACC), a structure that we know (from other data) plays a crucial role in detecting and resolving conflicts among different brain systems (Botvinick, Braver, Barch, Carter, & Cohen, 2001; for more connecting the functioning of the ACC to conscious awareness, see Dehaene et al., 2003; but for some complications, see Mayr, 2004).

The idea, then, is that conscious processing is instantiated through the neuronal workspace, and it is the coordination of separate processing modules, provided by the workspace, that allows flexibility, novel behaviors, and also the possibility of rising above habit, or resisting the behaviors cued by the immediate situation. To put all of this differently, the workspace underlies the functioning that we ascribed (in Chapter 5) to the "central executive," the system that seems to control many aspects of our actions and thoughts. In this way, we can link our claims about consciousness to our claims about how the mind controls its own activity.

Consciousness as Justification for Action

Dehaene and Naccache (2001) also argue that conscious experience has another function, and this function, too, is made possible by the characteristics of the neuronal workspace. Specifically, they argue that conscious experience is what allows us to produce *spontaneous* and *intentional* behavior.

To understand this point, consider the blind-sight patients. We have so far emphasized the fact that these patients are sensitive to some visual information, and this tells us something important: Apparently, some aspects of vision can go forward with no conscious awareness, and with no conscious supervision. But it's also striking that these patients insist that they are blind, and their behaviors are consistent with this self-assessment: They are fearful of walking across a room (lest they bump into something), they fail to react to many stimuli, and so on.

Note the puzzle here: If, as it seems, these patients can see, why don't they *use* the information that they gain by vision—for example, to guide their reaching or to navigate across the room? The evidence suggests that these patients see enough so that they reach correctly, when they do reach. Why, then, don't they reach out on their own, when they want to grab something? Why do they reach (in the right direction, with the right hand shape) only when the experimenter insists that they try? Or, to put this more generally, why don't they use their (unconscious) perception of the visual world to guide their actions? Is it possible that perceptual information has to be *conscious* before someone puts that information to use? (For further discussion of this puzzle, see Dennett, 1992; Goodale & Milner, 2004; and Weiskrantz, 1997.)

Roughly the same questions can be asked about people who suffer from amnesia. We have emphasized how much amnesic patients do remember, when properly tested (i.e., with tests of implicit memory). But it's also important that people with amnesia do not use this (implicitly) remembered information. Thus, for example, amnesic patients will insist that they do not know the route to the hospital cafeteria, and so they won't go to the cafeteria on their own. However, if we demand that they *guess* which way one turns to get to the cafeteria, they typically guess correctly. Once again, therefore, we might ask, Why don't the amnesic patients spontaneously use their (implicit) memories? Why do they reveal their knowledge only when we insist that they guess? Is it possible that remembered information has to be conscious before it is put to use?

Closely related questions arise when we consider data from people with no brain damage—such as ordinary college students. Participants in one study were shown a list of words and then, later on, were tested in either of two ways (Graf, Mandler, & Haden, 1982): Some were explicitly asked to recall the earlier list and were given word stems as cues: "What word on the prior list began 'CLE'?" Other participants were tested indirectly: "Tell me the first word that comes to mind beginning 'CLE.'"

The results show rather poor memory in the explicit test, but much better performance in the implicit test. This observation echoes many findings we have reviewed: We often have implicit memories for episodes we have explicitly forgotten. But note that there is something peculiar in this result: Participants could, in principle, proceed this way: "I don't recall any words from the list beginning 'CLE.' Perhaps I'll just guess. Let's see: What words come to mind that begin 'CLE'?" In this way, participants could use their implicit memory to supplement what they remember explicitly. If they did this, then the performance difference between the two conditions would be erased; performance on the explicit test would be just as good as performance on the implicit test. Given the results, however, participants are obviously not using this strategy. For some reason, participants in this situation seem unable or unwilling to use their implicit memories to guide explicit responding.

What is going on in all of these cases? Here is one plausible answer: In many situations, we need to take action based on remembered or perceived information. In some cases, the action is overt (walking across the room or making a verbal response); other times, the action is mental (reaching a decision or drawing a conclusion). In either setting, though, it seems not enough merely to have access to the relevant information. In addition, we also seem to need some justification, some reason, to take the relevant information seriously.

By analogy, imagine that you are trying to remember some prior event, and some misty thoughts about that event come to mind. You vaguely recall that friends were present on the target occasion; you have a dim idea that food was served. You might refuse to voice these thoughts, though, because you are not convinced that these thoughts are *memories*. (Perhaps they are chance associations or dreams you once had.) Thus, you will report your memory only if you're satisfied that you are, in fact, remembering. In other words, in order to report on your recollection, you need more than the remembered information. You also need some reason to believe that the remembered information is credible.

What convinces us that the remembered information is credible? The answer, perhaps, is our conscious experience. The idea, in other words, is that we will generally take action, based on some information, only if we are conscious of the information, and only if the conscious experience has the right qualities. More specifically, when the experience that accompanies a memory, or a perception, is rich and detailed, this convinces us that the presented information is more than a passing fantasy, more than a chance association, more than a mere hunch. In that situation, we're likely to take the information seriously, and take action based on the information. However, when the conscious presentation is impoverished, as it seems to be in blind sight or in amnesia, we fail to take seriously the information provided to us by our own eyes, or our own memory, and so we are paralyzed into inactivity. (For related discussion, see M. K. Johnson, 1988; and Johnson, Hashtroudi, & Lindsay, 1993.)

How can these points be linked to the biological claims about the neuronal workspace? One possibility is that the integration of information, within the workspace, provides exactly the corroboration we need in deciding to take a memory or perception seriously. The integration allows us to see that the information provided by vision is confirmed by touch, that the information gained from our senses is consistent with our other beliefs, and so on. It's then this convergence of cues that persuades us that the perception or memory is real, and not just a passing thought.

In Shakespeare's play, Macbeth asks himself whether the dagger he sees is real or "a dagger of the mind, a false creation proceeding from a heat-oppressed brain" (Act 2, Scene 1). He tries to decide by checking the visual information against other cues, asking whether the dagger is "sensible to feeling as to sight." The idea we're discussing here is the same: It is the confluence of inputs, provided by the neuronal workspace, that we use to decide whether ideas and perceptions and memories are "false creations," or true to reality. And it is only after we decide that they are real that we use them as a basis for action.

Consciousness: What Is Left Unsaid

Let's put all of these pieces together. From a biological perspective, we know that the various operations in the brain are made possible by the simultaneous action of numerous, specialized brain regions, each performing its own part of the whole. We also know that attention serves to unite these various modules, via the neuronal workspace. This workspace integrates the diverse elements, allowing comparisons and combinations of the processing components. The integration also allows the detection of conflict—when one module is pulling toward one response, and a different module is pulling toward another. And when conflict is detected (thanks to the anterior cingulate cortex), steps can then be taken to overcome the problem—by, for example, inhibiting a habitual act so that the preferred (but nonhabitual) act can dominate.

All of this fits well with the points we would make from a psychological perspective: We have seen that an enormous amount of mental work can be done—and perhaps has to be done—by unconscious processes. These processes rely on separate, self-contained modules and are enormously efficient, but they are also inflexible. We also know that these separate processes are influenced by attention. Specifically, paying attention to an input or to an idea brings the input or idea into consciousness, where we can hold it or compare it with other ideas, potentially allowing the executive control that lets us be flexible, and lets us rise above habit, in ways not possible in unconscious processing.

The proposal, therefore, is that consciousness is intertwined with the processes through which we pay attention; indeed, there may be little difference in many circumstances between "paying attention" to something and "becoming conscious" of it. Then, when we do pay attention to an idea or an input or a memory, this provides an integration and organization of separate processing streams, which, as we have discussed, creates the potential for flexibility, new ideas, and sustained attention. It also creates the sort of rich representation needed to justify the launching of action.

These ideas provide powerful suggestions about what conscious is *for*. But can we build from this to ask what conscious *is*? This turns out to be a hard question—in part because (as we indicated at the chapter's start) scholars still disagree about some of the fundamental conceptual issues in this domain. For example, many investigators insist that consciousness can be understood only from a first-person perspective—what it actually *feels like* to have certain experiences. In our discussion, in contrast, we have focused instead on what consciousness *allows*—that is, the behaviors (and thoughts and decisions) that are made possible by consciousness. Is this focus appropriate? Or does it leave out the essential element of consciousness—the subjectivity that seems to distinguish a conscious being from a "zombie" who acts just like a conscious being, but with no "inner experience"? In other words, in focusing on what consciousness makes possible, and not on how consciousness feels, have we perhaps dodged what Chalmers (1996, 1998) has called the "hard problem" of consciousness? (For a glimpse of how philosophers wrestle with these issues, see, for example, Block, 2001; Chalmers, 1996, 1998; and Dennett, 2001. For an example of psychologists exploring the distinction between "executive control" and "conscious experience," see Feldman Barrett, Tugade, & Engle, 2004.)

Along with these ideas, some theorists have suggested that we need to distinguish *types* of conscious experience, and it is plausible that our discussion in this chapter has addressed some types and not others. For example, Block (1997) has argued for a distinction between "phenomenal" and "access" consciousness—the first concerned with the subjective experience of being conscious, and the second concerned with the functional consequences of consciousness. Clearly, this chapter has been more concerned with the second of these than the first. Likewise, Pinker (1997; also see Jackendoff, 1987) offers a three-way distinction: First, there is "sentience" (or, on Damasio's, 1999, account, "core consciousness"); this term covers the subjective feelings of what it is like, in the here and now, to experience something—what chocolate really tastes like, how red actually looks, what it is to feel pain, and so on. Second, there is "access to information," which is the ability to use and report on one's own mental experience. Third is "self-knowledge" (or, in Damasio's terms, "extended consciousness"), which is, as the term implies, awareness of oneself as an individual, and which includes people's memories and also their sense of the future. Again, this chapter has focused on only one of these (the second) and neglected the other two.

In light of these various concerns, it seems likely that, in this chapter, we have discussed *part of* the problem of consciousness, and left other parts untouched. Indeed, it is possible that some aspects of consciousness can be studied by means of data collection and scientific research, while other aspects require other forms of inquiry (e.g., philosophical analysis). Even so, there can be no question that the data we have reviewed in this chapter, and the conclusions that flow from these data, provide powerful insights into the nature of consciousness, and these data will certainly inform any future discussions of this profound and complex issue. This by itself—the mere fact that research can address these issues—has to be a source of enormous satisfaction for investigators working on these difficult and intriguing problems.

Chapter Summary

1. An enormous amount of cognitive processing happens "behind the scenes," in the cognitive unconscious. In many cases, we are conscious only of the products that result from our mental processes; the processes themselves are unconscious.

This is reflected in the fact that we are not conscious of searching through memory; we are aware only of the results produced by that search. Similarly, we cannot tell when we have truly perceived a word and when we have merely inferred the word's presence.

2. Unconscious processing can be rather sophisticated. For example, implicit memory influences us without our being aware that we are remembering at all; however, this influence is often mediated by a complex process through which we attribute a feeling of familiarity to a particular cause. Unconscious attributions can also shape how we interpret and react to our own bodily states.

3. Even when our thinking is conscious, we are still influenced by unconscious guides that shape and direct our thought. This is evident in the effects of framing in decision-making and the effects of perceptual reference frames in perception and imagery.

4. The automaticity produced by practice can lead to yet another category of unconscious thought. With sufficient practice, we become largely unaware of the steps involved in an action, and we may not even be aware of the outcomes of that action. Still further evidence for unconscious achievements comes from the study of blind sight and amnesia; in both cases, patients seem to have knowledge (gained from perception or from memory) but no conscious awareness of that knowledge.

5. The cognitive unconscious allows enormous efficiency, but at the cost of flexibility or control. Likewise, the cognitive unconscious keeps us from being distracted by the details of our mental processes, but in some cases there is a cost to our ignorance about how our mental processes unfolded, and how we arrived at a particular memory or particular perception. These trade-offs point the way toward the function of consciousness: Conscious thinking is less efficient but more controllable, and also better informed by information about process.

6. The neuronal workplace hypothesis begins with the fact that most of the processing in the brain is carried out by separate, specialized modules. When we pay attention to a stimulus, however, the neurons in the various modules are linked by means of workspace neurons. This linkage amplifies and sustains the processing within individual modules, and allows integration and comparison of the various modules. This integration, it is proposed, is what makes consciousness possible. The integration provides the basis for the unity in our experience; it also allows flexibility and the detection of conflict.

7. Consciousness may also serve to give us a sense that we have adequate justification for taking an action. This may be why amnesic patients seem unable to take action based on what they (unconsciously) recall and why blind-sight patients seem unable to respond to what they (unconsciously) see.

8. Several theorists have argued that we must distinguish types of conscious experience. The considerations in this chapter bear more directly on "access" consciousness, which is the matter of how information is accessed and used within the mind. The chapter has had less to say about "phenomenal" consciousness, which is concerned with the subjective experience of being conscious.

7 plus-or-minus 2   A number often offered as an estimate of the holding capacity of *working memory*.

ACC   See *anterior cingulate cortex*.

acquisition   The process of placing new information into *long-term memory*.

action slip   An error in which someone performs some behavior, or makes some response, that is different from the behavior or response intended.

activation level   A measure of the current activation state for a *node* or *detector*. Activation level is increased if the node or detector receives the appropriate input from its associated nodes or detectors; activation level will be high if input has been received frequently or recently.

acuity   The ability to discern fine detail. See also *visual acuity*.

ad hoc category   A mental category made up on the spot, in response to a specific question.

affirming the consequent   An error often made in logical reasoning. The error begins with these two premises: (a) "If A then B," and (b) "B is true." The error consists of drawing the false conclusion that (c) "A must therefore be true." Compare with *denying the antecedent*.

agnosia   A disturbance in a person's ability to identify familiar objects.

all-or-none law   The principle stating that a *neuron* or *detector* either *fires* completely or does not fire at all; no intermediate responses are possible.

ambiguous figure   A drawing that can be readily perceived in more than one way.

amnesia   A broad inability to remember events within a certain category, due in many cases to brain damage.

amygdala   An almond-shaped structure in the *limbic system* that plays a central role in emotion and in the evaluation of stimuli.

anarthria   A disorder characterized by an inability to control the muscles needed for ordinary speech. Anarthric individuals cannot speak, although other aspects of language functioning are unimpaired.

anchoring and adjustment   A commonly used strategy for making judgments, in which one begins with an "anchor" (an estimate roughly in the ballpark of the desired answer) and "adjusts" the anchor to make it more realistic.

anomia   A disruption of language abilities, usually resulting from specific brain damage, in which the individual loses the ability to name objects, including highly familiar objects.

anterior cingulate cortex (ACC)   A brain structure known to play a crucial role in detecting and resolving conflicts among different brain systems.

anterograde amnesia   An inability to remember experiences that occurred *after* the event that triggered the memory disruption. Often contrasted with *retrograde amnesia*.

aphasia   A disruption to language capacities, often caused by brain damage.

apraxia   A disturbance in the initiation or organization of voluntary action.

area V1   The site on the *occipital lobe* where axons from the *lateral geniculate nucleus* first reach the cerebral *cortex*.

articulatory rehearsal loop   One of the low-level assistants, hypothesized as part of the *working-memory system*. This loop draws on *subvocalized* (covert) speech, which serves to create a record in the *phonological buffer*. Materials in this buffer then fade, but they can be refreshed by another cycle of covert speech, with this cycle initiated by working memory's *central executive*.

association cortex   The traditional name for the portion of the human *cortex* outside of the *primary motor* and *primary sensory projection areas*.

associations   Functional connections that are hypothesized to link *nodes* within a mental network or *detectors* within a detector network; these associations are often hypothesized as the "carriers" of activation, from one node or detector to the next.

attended channel   In *selective attention* experiments, research participants are exposed to simultaneous inputs and instructed to ignore all of these except one. The attended channel is the input to which participants are instructed to pay attention. Often contrasted with *unattended channel*.

autobiographical memory   The aspect of memory that records the episodes and events in a person's life.

A1

automaticity   A state achieved by some tasks and some forms of processing, in which the task can be performed with little or no attention. Automatized actions can, in many cases, be combined with other activities without interference. Automatized actions are also often difficult to control, leading many to refer to them as "mental reflexes."

availability heuristic   A strategy used to judge the frequency of a certain type of object, or the likelihood of a certain type of event. The first step is to assess the ease with which examples of the object or event come to mind; this "availability" of examples is then used as an index of frequency or likelihood.

axon   The part of a *neuron* that transmits a signal to another location.

base-rate information   Information about the broad likelihood of a particular type of event (also referred to as "prior probability"). Often contrasted with *diagnostic information.*

basic-level categorization   A level of categorization hypothesized as the "natural" and most informative level, neither too specific nor too general. It is proposed that we tend to use basic-level terms (such as "chair," rather than the more general "furniture" or the more specific "armchair") in our ordinary conversation and in our reasoning.

behaviorist theory   Broad principles concerned with how behavior changes in response to different configurations of stimuli (including stimuli often called "rewards" and "punishments"). In its early days, behaviorist theory sought to avoid mentalistic terms.

belief bias   A tendency, within logical reasoning, to endorse a conclusion if the conclusion happens to be something one believes is true anyhow. In displaying this tendency, people seem to ignore both the premises of the logical argument and logic itself, and rely instead on their broader pattern of beliefs about what is true and what is not.

bigram   A pair of letters. For example, the word "FLAT" contains the bigrams *FL, LA,* and *AT.*

binding problem   The problem of reuniting the various elements of a scene, given the fact that these elements are initially dealt with by different systems in the brain.

binocular rivalry   A pattern that arises when the input to one eye cannot be integrated with the input to the other eye. In this circumstance, the person tends to be aware of only one eye's input at a time.

bipolar cell   A *neuron* in the eye. Bipolar cells receive their input from the *photoreceptors* and transmit their output to the retinal *ganglion cells.*

blind sight   A pattern resulting from brain damage, in which the person seems unable to see in all or part of his/her field of vision, but can correctly respond to visual inputs when required to by an experimenter.

BOLD (blood oxygenation level dependent)   A measure of how much oxygen the brain's hemoglobin is carrying in specific parts of the brain; this provides a quantitative basis for comparing activity levels in different brain areas.

bottom-up processing   See *data-driven processing.*

boundary extension   A tendency for people to remember pictures as being less "zoomed in" (and thus having wider boundaries) than they actually are.

Broca's area   An area usually in the left *frontal lobe* of the brain; damage here typically causes *nonfluent aphasia.*

Capgras syndrome   A rare disorder, resulting from specific forms of brain damage, in which the afflicted person recognizes the people in his or her world, but denies that they are who they appear to be. Instead, the person insists, these familiar individuals are well-disguised impostors.

categorical perception   The tendency to hear speech sounds "merely" as members of a category—the category of "z" sounds, or the category of "p" sounds, and so on. As a consequence, one tends to hear sounds *within* the category as being rather similar to each other; sounds from different categories, however, are perceived as quite different.

categorical syllogism   A logical argument containing two *premises* and a conclusion, and concerned with the properties of, and relations between, categories. An example is, "All trees are plants. All plants require nourishment. Therefore all trees require nourishment." This is a valid syllogism, since the truth of the premises guarantees the truth of the conclusion.

causal attribution   An interpretation of a thought or behavior in which one decides what caused the behavior.

ceiling level   A level of performance in a task that is near the maximum level possible. (In many tasks, this is performance near 100%.)

cell body   The area of the cell containing the nucleus and the metabolic machinery that sustains the cell.

center–surround cell A *neuron* in the visual system that has a "donut-shaped" *receptive field*; stimulation in the center of the receptive field has one effect on the cell, whereas stimulation in the surrounding ring has the opposite effect.

central executive The hypothesized director of the *working-memory system*. This is the component of the system needed for any interpretation or analysis; in contrast, mere storage of materials can be provided by *working memory*'s assistants, which work under the control of the central executive.

central fissure The separation dividing the *frontal lobes* on each side of the brain from the *parietal lobes*.

cerebellum The largest area of the *hindbrain*, crucial for the coordination of bodily movements and balance.

cerebral hemisphere One of the two hemispherical brain structures—one on the left side, one on the right—that comprise the major part of the *forebrain* in mammals.

change blindness A pattern in which perceivers either do not see, or take a long time to see, large-scale changes in a visual stimulus. This pattern reveals how little we perceive, even from stimuli in plain view, if we are not specifically attending to the target information.

chronometric study Literally "time measurement" study; generally, a study that measures the amount of time a task takes, often used as a means of examining the task's components, or used as a means of examining which brain events are simultaneous with specific mental events.

chunk The hypothetical storage unit in *working memory*; it is estimated that working memory can hold 7 ± 2 chunks. An unspecified quantity of information can be contained within each chunk, since the content of each chunk depends on how the memorizer has organized the materials to be remembered.

coarticulation A trait of speech production in which the way a sound is produced is altered slightly by the immediately previous and immediately following sounds. Because of this "overlap" in speech production, the acoustic properties of each speech sound vary according to the context in which that sound appears.

cognitive neuroscience The study of the biological basis for cognitive functioning.

cognitive unconscious The broad set of mental activities of which we are completely unaware that makes possible our ordinary thinking, remembering, reasoning, and so on.

commissure One of the thick bundles of fibers via which information is sent back and forth between the two *cerebral hemispheres*.

competence The pattern of skills and knowledge that might be revealed under optimal circumstances. Often contrasted with *performance*.

computerized axial tomography (CT scanning) A *neuroimaging technique* that uses X-rays to construct a precise three-dimensional image of the brain's anatomy.

concept-driven processing A type of processing in which the sequence of mental events is influenced by a broad pattern of knowledge and expectations (sometimes referred to as *top-down processing*). Often contrasted with *data-driven processing*.

conditional statement A statement of the format "If X then Y," with the first statement (the "if" clause) providing a condition under which the second statement (the "then" clause) is guaranteed to be true.

cone A photoreceptor that is able to discriminate hues, and that has high *acuity*. Cones are concentrated in the *retina*'s *fovea* and become less frequent in the visual periphery. Often contrasted with *rod*.

confirmation bias A family of effects in which people seem more sensitive to evidence that confirms their beliefs than they are to evidence that challenges their beliefs. Thus, if people are given a choice about what sort of information they would like in order to evaluate their beliefs, they request information that is likely to confirm their beliefs. Likewise, if they are presented with both confirming and disconfirming evidence, they are more likely to pay attention to, to be influenced by, and to remember the confirming evidence, rather than the disconfirming.

conjunction error An error in perception in which someone correctly perceives what features are present, but misperceives how the features are joined, so that (for example) a red circle and a green square might be misperceived as a red square and a green circle.

connection weight The strength of a connection between two *nodes* in a network. The greater the connection weight, the more efficiently activation will flow from one node to the other.

connectionism An approach to theorizing about the mind that relies on *parallel distributed processing* among elements that provide a *distributed representation* of the information being considered.

content morpheme A *morpheme* that carries meaning. Often contrasted with *function morpheme*.

context reinstatement A procedure in which someone is led to the same mental and emotional state they were in during some previous event; context reinstatement can often promote accurate recollection.

contralateral control A pattern in which the left half of the brain controls the right half of the body, and the right half of the brain controls the left half of the body.

conversion error An error in which people convert statements from one form into another—for example, treating "All A are B" as though it were identical to "All B are A," or treating "If A then B" as though it were identical to "If B then A."

convolutions The wrinkles visible in the *cortex* that allow the enormous surface area of the human brain to be stuffed into the relatively small volume of the skull.

cornea The transparent tissue at the front of each eye that plays an important role in focusing the incoming light.

corpus callosum The largest of the *commissures* linking the left and right *cerebral hemispheres*.

cortex The outermost surface of the brain.

CT scanning See *computerized axial tomography*.

covariation A relationship between two variables such that the presence (or magnitude) of one variable can be predicted from the presence (or magnitude) of the other. Covariation can be positive or negative: If positive, then increases in one variable occur when increases in the other occur. If negative, then decreases in one variable occur when decreases in the other occur.

data-driven processing A type of processing in which the sequence of mental events is determined largely by the pattern of incoming information (sometimes referred to as *bottom-up processing*). Often contrasted with *concept-driven processing*.

decay theory of forgetting The hypothesis that, with the passage of time, memories may fade or erode.

deduction A process through which we start with claims, or general assertions, and ask what follows from these *premises*. Often contrasted with *induction*.

deep processing A mode of thinking about material in which one pays attention to the meaning and implications of the material; deep processing typically leads to excellent memory retention. Often contrasted with *shallow processing*.

Deese–Roediger–McDermott (DRM) procedure A commonly used experimental procedure for eliciting and studying memory errors. In this procedure, a person sees or hears a list of words that are all related to a single theme; however, the word that names the theme is not itself included. Nonetheless, people are very likely to remember later that the theme word was presented.

degree of fan The number of *associative links* radiating out from a *node*. If there are more links (high degree of fan), then each of the associated nodes will receive only a small fraction of the activation flowing outward from the node.

demand character Cues within an experiment that signal to the participant how he or she is "supposed to" respond.

dendrites The part of a *neuron* that usually detects the incoming signal.

denying the antecedent An error often made in logical reasoning. The error begins with these two premises: (a) "If A then B," and (b) "A is false." The error consists of drawing the false conclusion that (c) "B must therefore also be false." Often contrasted with *affirming the consequent*.

descriptive account An account that tells us how things are, as opposed to how they should be. Often contrasted with *normative account*.

detector A *node* within a processing network that *fires* primarily in response to a specific target contained within the incoming perceptual information.

diagnostic information Information about an individual case indicating whether the case belongs in one category or another. Often contrasted with *base-rate information*.

dichotic listening A task in which participants hear two simultaneous verbal messages—one presented via headphones to the left ear, a second presented to the right ear. In typical experiments, participants are asked to pay attention to one of these inputs (the *attended channel*) and urged to ignore the other.

digit-span task A task often used for measuring *working memory*'s storage capacity. Participants are read a series of digits (e.g., "8 3 4") and must immediately repeat them back. If they do this successfully, they are given a slightly longer list (e.g., "9 2 4 0"), and so forth. The length of the longest list a person can remember in this fashion is that person's digit span.

direct memory testing A form of memory testing in which people are asked explicitly to remember some previous event. *Recall* and standard *recognition* testing are both forms of direct memory testing. Often contrasted with *indirect memory testing.*

distributed representation   A mode of representing ideas or contents in which there is no one *node* representing the content, and no one place where the content is stored. Instead, the content is represented via a pattern of simultaneous activity across many nodes. Those same nodes will also participate in other patterns, and so those same nodes will also be part of other distributed representations. Often contrasted with *local representation.*

divided attention   The skill of performing multiple tasks simultaneously.

double dissociation   An argument used by researchers to prove that two processes, or two structures, are truly distinct. To make this argument, one must show that each of the processes or structures can be disrupted without in any way interfering with the other.

dual-coding theory   A theory that imaginable materials, such as high-imagery words, will be doubly represented in memory: The word itself will be remembered, and so will the corresponding mental image.

dual-process model   Any model of thinking that claims we have two distinct means of making judgments—one of which is fast, efficient, but prone to error, and one that is slower, more effortful, but also more accurate.

early selection   A proposal that *selective attention* operates at an early stage of processing, so that the unattended inputs receive little analysis.

edge enhancement   A process created by *lateral inhibition* in which the *neurons* in the visual system give exaggerated responses to edges of surfaces.

Einstellung   The phenomenon in *problem-solving* in which people develop a certain attitude or perspective on a problem, and then approach all subsequent problems with the same rigid attitude.

elaborative rehearsal   A way of engaging materials to be remembered, such that one pays attention to what the materials mean and how they are related to each other, or to other things in the surroundings, or to other things one already knows. Often contrasted with *maintenance rehearsal.*

encoding specificity   The tendency, when memorizing, to place in memory both the materials to be learned and also some amount of the context of those

materials. As a result, these materials will be recognized as familiar, later on, only if the materials appear again in a similar context.

excitatory connection   A link from one *node*, or one *detector*, to another, such that activation of one node activates the other. Often contrasted with *inhibitory connection.*

executive control   The mental resources and processes used to set goals, choose task priorities, and avoid conflict among competing habits or responses.

exemplar-based reasoning   Reasoning that draws on knowledge about specific category members, rather than drawing on more-general information about the overall category.

expected value   An estimate of the value of choosing a particular option, calculated as the likely value of that option, if it is obtained, multiplied by the probability of gaining that value. (Also referred to as "expected utility.")

explicit memory   A memory revealed by *direct memory testing*, and typically accompanied by the conviction that one is remembering a specific prior episode. Often contrasted with *implicit memory.*

extralinguistic context   The social and physical setting in which a *sentence* is encountered; usually, cues within this setting guide the interpretation of the sentence.

false alarm   A detection even though the specified target is actually absent.

false memory   A memory, sincerely reported, that misrepresents how an event actually unfolded. In some cases, a false memory can be wholly false, and report an event that never happened at all.

family resemblance   The notion that members of a category (all dogs, or all games) resemble each other. In general, family resemblance relies on some number of *features* shared by any group of category members, even though these features may not be shared by all members of the category. Therefore, the basis for family resemblance may shift from one subset of the category to another.

feature   One of the small set of elements out of which more-complicated patterns are composed.

feature net   A system for recognizing patterns that involves a network of *detectors*, with detectors for features as the initial layer in the system.

figure/ground organization   The processing step in which the perceiver determines which aspects of the stimulus belong to the central object (or "figure") and which aspects belong to the background (or "ground").

filter A hypothetical mechanism that would block potential distractors from further processing.

fixation target A visual mark (such as a dot or a plus sign) at which one points one's eyes (or "fixates"). Fixation targets are used to help people control their eye position.

flashbulb memory A memory of extraordinary clarity, typically for some highly emotional event, retained despite the passage of many years.

fluent aphasia A disruption of language, caused by brain damage, in which afflicted individuals are able to produce speech, but the speech is not meaningful, and the individuals are not able to understand what is said to them. Often contrasted with *nonfluent aphasia*.

fMRI scanning See *functional magnetic resonance imaging*.

forebrain One of the three main structures (along with the *hindbrain* and the *midbrain*) of the brain; the forebrain plays a crucial role in supporting intellectual functioning.

form perception The process through which one sees what the basic shape, size, and position of an object are.

four-card task See *selection task*.

fovea The center of the *retina*; when one looks at an object, one is lining up that object with the fovea.

frame Aspects of how a decision is phrased that are, in fact, irrelevant to the decision, but that influence people's choices nonetheless.

free recall A method of assessing memory. The person being tested is asked to come up with as many items as possible from a particular source (such as "the list you heard earlier," or "things you saw yesterday"), in any sequence.

frequency estimate People's assessment of how often they have encountered examples of a particular category and how likely they are to encounter new examples of that category.

frontal lobe The lobe in each *cerebral hemisphere* that includes the *prefrontal area* and the *primary motor projection area*.

function morpheme A *morpheme* that signals a relation between words within a sentence, such as the morpheme "s" indicating a plural, or the morpheme "ed" indicating past tense. Often contrasted with *content morpheme*.

functional fixedness A tendency to be rigid in how one thinks about an object's function. This generally involves a strong tendency to think of an object only in terms of its *typical* function.

functional magnetic resonance imaging (fMRI) A neuroimaging technique that uses magnetic fields to construct a detailed three-dimensional representation of the activity levels in different areas of the brain at a particular moment in time.

fusiform face area (FFA) A brain area apparently specialized for the perception of faces.

fuzzy boundary A distinction between categories that identifies each instance only as more or less likely to be in a category, rather than specifying whether each instance is or is not included in the category.

gamma-band oscillation A particular rhythm of *firing* that seems to signal in the nervous system when different parts of the visual system are all responding to the same stimulus.

ganglion cell A *neuron* in the eye. The ganglion cells receive their input from the *bipolar cells*, and then the *axons* of the ganglion cells gather together to form the *optic nerve*, carrying information back to the *lateral geniculate nucleus*.

garden-path sentence A sentence that initially leads the reader to one understanding of how the sentence's words are related, but that then requires a change in this understanding in order to comprehend the sentence. Examples are "The old man ships," or "The horse raced past the barn fell."

generativity The idea that one can combine and recombine basic units to create (or "generate") new and more-complex entities. Linguistic rules, for example, are generative, and so govern how a limited number of words can be combined and recombined to produce a vast number of sentences.

generic knowledge Knowledge of a general sort, as opposed to knowledge about specific episodes. Often contrasted with *episodic knowledge*.

geon One of the basic shapes proposed as the building blocks of all complex three-dimensional forms. Geons take the form of cylinders, cones, blocks, and the like, and are combined to form "geon assemblies." These are then combined to produce entire objects.

goal state The state one is working toward in trying to solve a problem. Often contrasted with *initial state*.

graded membership The idea that some members of a category are "better" members, and therefore are more firmly in the category than other members.

grammatical Conforming to the rules that govern the sequence of words acceptable within the language.

heuristic A strategy that is reasonably efficient and works most of the time. In using a heuristic, one is in effect choosing to accept some risk of error in order to gain efficiency.

hill-climbing strategy A commonly used strategy in *problem-solving*. If people use this strategy, then whenever their efforts toward solving a problem give them a choice, they will choose the option that carries them closer to the goal.

hindbrain One of the three main structures (along with the *forebrain* and the *midbrain*) of the brain; the hindbrain sits atop the spinal cord and includes several structures crucial for controlling key life functions.

hippocampus A structure in the *temporal lobe* that is involved in *long-term memory* and spatial memory.

hypothalamus A small structure at the base of the *forebrain* that plays a vital role in the control of motivated behaviors such as eating, drinking, and sexual activity.

ill-defined problem A problem for which the goal state is specified only in general terms, and the operators available for reaching the goal state are not obvious at the start. Often contrasted with *well-defined problem*.

illumination The third in a series of stages often hypothesized as crucial for creativity. The first stage is *preparation*; the second, *incubation*. Illumination is the stage in which some new key insight or new idea suddenly comes to mind.

illusion of truth An effect of *implicit memory* in which claims that are familiar end up seeming more plausible.

illusory covariation A pattern that people "perceive" in data, leading them to believe that the presence of one factor allows them to predict the presence of another factor. However, this perception occurs even in the absence of any genuine relationship between these two factors. As an example, people perceive that a child's willingness to cheat in an academic setting is an indicator that the child will also be willing to cheat in athletic contests. However, this perception is incorrect, and so the covariation that people perceive is "illusory."

image file Visual information stored in *long-term memory*, specifying what a particular object or shape looks like. Information within the image file can

then be used as a "recipe" or set of instructions for how to construct an active image of this object or shape.

image-scanning procedure An experimental procedure in which participants are asked to form a specific mental image, and then asked to scan, with their "mind's eye," from one point in the image to another. By timing these scans, the experimenter can determine how long "travel" takes across a mental image.

implicit memory A memory revealed by *indirect memory testing* usually manifest as *priming* effects in which current performance is guided or facilitated by previous experiences. Implicit memories are often accompanied by no conscious realization that one is, in fact, being influenced by specific past experiences. Often contrasted with *explicit memory*.

inattentional blindness A pattern in which perceivers seem literally not to see visual stimuli right in front of their eyes; this pattern is caused by the participants' attending to some other stimulus and not expecting the target to appear.

incidental learning Learning that takes place in the absence of any intention to learn and, correspondingly, in the absence of any expectation of a subsequent memory test.

incubation The second in a series of stages often hypothesized as crucial for creativity. The first stage is *preparation*; the third, *illumination*. Incubation consists of (hypothesized) events that occur when one puts a problem being worked on out of one's conscious thoughts, but continues nonetheless to work on the problem unconsciously. Many current psychologists are skeptical about this process, and propose alternative accounts for data ostensibly documenting incubation.

indirect memory testing A form of memory testing in which research participants are not told that their memories are being tested. Instead, they are tested in a fashion in which previous experiences can influence current behavior. Examples of indirect tests include *word-stem completion*, the *lexical-decision task*, and *tachistoscopic* recognition. Often contrasted with *direct memory testing*.

induction A pattern of reasoning in which one seeks to draw general claims from specific bits of evidence. Often contrasted with *deduction*.

information processing A particular approach to theorizing in which complex mental events, such as learning, remembering, and deciding, are understood as being built up out of a large number of discrete steps. These steps occur one by one, with each providing as its "output" the input to the next step in the sequence.

inhibitory connection   A link from one *node*, or one *detector*, to another, such that activation of one node decreases the *activation level* of the other. Often contrasted with *excitatory connection*.

initial state   The state one begins in, in working toward the solution of a problem. *Problem-solving* can be understood as the attempt to move, with various operations, from the initial state to the *goal state*.

input node   A *node*, within a network, that receives at least part of its activation from *detectors* sensitive to events in the external world.

insensitivity   A property of an experiment that makes the experiment unable to detect differences. An experiment can be insensitive, for example, if the procedure is too easy, so that *performance* is at *ceiling levels*.

intentional learning   The acquisition of memories in a setting in which people know that their memory for the information will be tested later.

interactive model   A model of cognitive processing that relies on an ongoing interplay between *data-driven* and *concept-driven processing*.

interference theory of forgetting   The hypothesis that materials are lost from memory because of interference from other materials also in memory. Interference that is caused by materials learned prior to the learning episode is called "proactive interference"; interference that is caused by materials learned after the learning episode is called "retroactive interference."

introspection   The process through which one "looks within," to observe and record the contents of one's own mental life.

intrusion error   A memory error in which one recalls elements not part of the original episode that one is trying to remember.

Korsakoff's syndrome   A clinical syndrome characterized primarily by dense *anterograde amnesia*. Korsakoff's syndrome is caused by damage to specific brain regions, and it is often precipitated by a form of malnutrition common among long-term alcoholics.

late selection   A proposal that *selective attention* operates at a late stage of processing, so that the unattended inputs receive considerable analysis.

lateral fissure   The separation dividing the *frontal lobes* on each side of the brain from the *temporal lobes*.

lateral geniculate nucleus (LGN)   An important way station in the thalamus that is the first destination for visual information sent from the eyeball to the brain.

lateral inhibition   A pattern in which cells, when stimulated, inhibit the activity of neighboring cells. In the visual system, lateral inhibition in the *optic nerve* creates *edge enhancement*.

lens   The transparent tissue located near the front of each eye that plays an important role in focusing the incoming light. Muscles control the degree of curvature of the lens, allowing the eye to form a sharp image on the *retina*.

lesion   A specific area of tissue damage.

lexical-decision task   A test in which participants are shown strings of letters and must indicate, as quickly as possible, whether each string of letters is a word in English or not. It is supposed that people perform this task by "looking up" these strings in their "mental dictionary."

limbic system   A set of brain structures including the *amygdala*, *hippocampus*, mammillary bodies, and parts of the *thalamus*. The limbic system is believed to be involved in the control of emotional behavior and motivation, and it also plays a key role in learning and memory.

limited-capacity system   A group of processes in which resources are limited, so that extra resources supplied to one process must be balanced by a withdrawal of resources somewhere else, so that the total resources expended do not exceed some limit.

linguistic relativity   The proposal that the language that we speak shapes our thought, because the structure and vocabulary of our language create certain ways of thinking about the world.

linguistic universal   A rule that appears to apply to every human language.

local representation   A representation of information that is encoded in some small number of identifiable *nodes*. Local representations are sometimes spoken of as "one idea per node" or "one content per location." Often contrasted with *distributed representation*.

localization of function   The research endeavor of determining what specific job is performed by a particular region of the brain.

long-term memory   The storage system in which we hold all of our knowledge and all of our memories. Long-term memory contains memories that are not currently activated; those that are activated are represented in *working memory*.

longitudinal fissure   The separation dividing the brain's left *cerebral hemisphere* from the right.

M cells   Specialized cells within the *optic nerve* that provide the input for the *magnocellular cells* in the *lateral geniculate nucleus*. Often contrasted with *P cells*.

magnetic resonance imaging (MRI)   A *neuroimaging technique* that uses magnetic fields (created by radio waves) to construct a detailed three-dimensional representation of brain tissue. Like *CT scans*, MRI scans reveal the brain's anatomy, but they are much more precise than CT scans.

magnocellular cells   Cells in the *lateral geniculate nucleus* specialized for the perception of motion and depth. Often contrasted with *parvocellular cells*.

maintenance rehearsal   A rote, mechanical process, in which items are continually cycled through *working memory*, merely by being repeated over and over. Also called "item-specific rehearsal," and often contrasted with *elaborative rehearsal*.

manner of production   The way in which a speaker momentarily obstructs the flow of air out of the lungs to produce a speech sound. This obstruction can take several forms. For example, the airflow can be fully stopped for a moment, as it is in the [t] or [b] sound; or the air can continue to flow, as it does in the pronunciation of [f] or [v].

mask   A visual presentation used to interrupt the processing of another visual stimulus.

matching strategy   A shortcut apparently used in reasoning tasks; to use this strategy, the person selects a conclusion that contains the same words (e.g., "not", "some," "all") as the *premises*.

means–end analysis   A strategy used in *problem-solving* in which the person is guided, step-by-step, by a comparison of the difference, at that moment, between the current state and the *goal state*, and a consideration of the *operators* available.

memory reconstruction   See *reconstruction*.

memory rehearsal   Any mental activity that has the effect of maintaining information in *working memory*. Two types of rehearsal are often distinguished: *maintenance rehearsal* and *elaborative rehearsal*.

mental accounting   A process that seems to guide our decision-making, in which different choices and different resources are kept separate, so that gains in one "account" (for example) do not influence choices about a different account.

mental model   An internal representation in which an abstract description is translated into a relatively concrete representation, with that representation serving to illustrate how that abstract state of affairs might be realized.

mental rotation   A process that participants seem to use in comparing one imaged form to another. To make the comparison, participants seem to imagine one form rotating into alignment with the other, so that the forms can be compared.

metacognitive judgment   A judgment in which one must stand back from a particular mental activity, and comment on the activity, rather than participating in it.

metalinguistic judgment   A particular type of *metacognitive judgment*, in which one must stand back from one's ordinary language use, and comment on language or linguistic processes.

midbrain   One of the three main structures (along with the *forebrain* and the *hindbrain*) of the brain; the midbrain plays an important role in coordinating movements, and it also contains structures that serve as "relay" stations for information arriving from the sensory organs.

minimal attachment   A *heuristic* used in *sentence perception*. The listener or reader proceeds through the sentence seeking the simplest possible phrase structure that will accommodate the words heard so far.

misinformation effect   An effect in which research participants' reports about an earlier event are influenced by misinformation they received after experiencing the event. In the extreme, misinformation can be used to create *false memories* concerning an entire event that, in truth, never occurred.

mnemonic strategy   A technique designed to improve memory accuracy, and to make learning easier; in general, mnemonic strategies seek in one fashion or another to help memory by imposing an organization on the materials to be learned.

modal model   A nickname for a specific conception of the "architecture" of memory. In this model, *working memory* serves both as the storage site for material now being contemplated, and also the "loading platform" for *long-term memory*. Information can reach working memory through the processes of perception, or it can be drawn from long-term memory. Once in working memory, material can be further processed, or it can simply be recycled for subsequent use.

modus ponens   A logical rule stipulating that, from the two premises "If P then Q" and "P is true," one can draw the conclusion "Therefore, Q is true." Often contrasted with *modus tollens*.

modus tollens   A logical rule stipulating that, from the two premises "If P then Q" and "Q is false," one can draw the conclusion "Therefore, P is false." Often contrasted with *modus ponens*.

morpheme   The smallest language unit that carries meaning. Psycholinguists distinguish *content morphemes* (the primary carriers of meaning) from *function morphemes* (which specify the relations among words).

MRI   See *magnetic resonance imaging*.

movement rule   A rule that describes one aspect of our knowledge about *sentence* structure. Movement rules govern, for example, how the sentence "Can he do it?" is formed from the base of "He can do it."

necessary condition   A condition that *must* be fulfilled in order for a certain consequence to occur. However, necessary conditions may not guarantee that the consequence will occur, since it may be true that other conditions must also be met. Often contrasted with *sufficient condition*.

Necker cube   One of the classic *ambiguous figures*; the figure is a two-dimensional drawing that can be perceived either as a cube viewed from above or as a cube viewed from below.

neglect syndrome   *See* unilateral neglect syndrome.

neural correlate   An event in the nervous system that occurs at the same time as, and may be the biological basis of, a specific mental event or state.

neural net model   An alternative term for connectionist models, reflecting the hypothesized parallels between this sort of computer model and the functioning of the nervous system.

neural synchrony   A pattern of *firing* by *neurons* in which neurons in one brain area fire at the same time as neurons in another area; the brain seems to use this pattern as an indication that the neurons in different areas are firing in response to the same stimulus.

neuroimaging technique   A method for examining either the structure or the activation pattern within a living brain.

neuron   An individual cell within the nervous system.

neuronal workspace hypothesis   A specific claim about how the brain makes conscious experience possible; the proposal is that "workspace neurons" link together the activity of various specialized brain areas, and this linkage makes possible integration and comparison of different types of information.

neuropsychology   The branch of psychology concerned with the relation between various forms of brain dysfunction and various aspects of mental functioning. Neuropsychologists study, for example, *amnesia*, *agnosia*, and *aphasia*.

neurotransmitter   One of the chemicals released by *neurons* in order to stimulate adjacent neurons. See also *synapse*.

neutral depiction   A representation that directly reflects the layout and appearance of an object or scene (and so is, on this basis, a "depiction"), but without adding any specifications about how that depiction is to be understood (and so is, on this basis, "neutral"). Often contrasted with *organized depiction*.

node   An individual unit within an associative network. In a scheme employing *local representations*, nodes represent single ideas or concepts. In a scheme employing *distributed representations*, ideas or contents are represented by a pattern of activation across a wide number of nodes; the same nodes may also participate in other patterns and therefore in other representations.

nonfluent aphasia   A disruption of language, caused by brain damage, in which someone loses the ability to speak or write with any fluency. Often contrasted with *fluent aphasia*.

normative account   An account that tells how things ought to be, as opposed to how they are. Also referred to as "prescriptive account"; often contrasted with *descriptive account*.

noun phrase   One of the constituents of a phrase structure that defines a *sentence*.

object recognition   The steps or processes through which we identify the objects we encounter in the world around us.

occipital lobe   The rearmost lobe in each *cerebral hemisphere*, which includes the primary visual projection area.

operation span   A measure of *working memory*'s capacity. This measure turns out to be predictive of performance in many other tasks, presumably because these tasks all rely on working memory.

operator   A tool or action that one can use, in *problem-solving*, to move from the problem's *initial state* to the *goal state*.

optic nerve The bundle of nerve fibers, formed from the *retina*'s *ganglion cells*, that carries information from the eyeball to the brain.

organized depiction A representation that directly reflects the layout and appearance of an object or scene (and so is, on this basis, a "depiction"), but that also adds some specifications about how the depiction is to be understood (e.g., where the form's top is, what the form's *figure/ground organization* is). Often contrasted with *neutral depiction.*

over-regularization error An error in which one perceives or remembers a word or event as being closer to the "norm" than it really is. For example, misspelled words are read as though they were spelled correctly; atypical events are misremembered in a fashion that brings them closer to more-typical events; words with an irregular past tense (such as "ran") are replaced with a regular past tense ("runned").

P cells Specialized cells within the *optic nerve* that provide the input for the *parvocellular cells* in the *lateral geniculate nucleus.* Often contrasted with *M cells.*

parahippocampal place area (PPA) A brain area apparently specialized for the perception of places.

parallel distributed processing A system of handling information in which many steps happen at once (i.e., in parallel) and in which various aspects of the problem or task are represented only in a distributed fashion.

parallel processing A system in which many steps are going on at the same time. Usually contrasted with *serial processing.*

parietal lobe The lobe in each *cerebral hemisphere* that lies between the *occipital* and *frontal* lobes and includes some of the *primary sensory projection area,* as well as circuits that are crucial for the control of attention.

parsing The process through which one divides an input into its appropriate elements—for example, divides the stream of incoming speech into its constituent words.

parvocellular cells Cells in the *lateral geniculate nucleus* specialized for the perception of patterns. Often contrasted with *magnocellular cells.*

path constraint A limit that rules out some operation in *problem-solving.* Path constraints might take the form of resource limitations (limited time to spend on the problem, or limited money), or limits of other sorts (perhaps ethical limits on what one can do).

peg-word systems A type of *mnemonic strategy* using words or locations as "pegs" on which one "hangs" the materials to be remembered.

percept An internal representation of the world that results from perceiving; percepts are *organized depictions.*

perceptual reference frame The set of specifications about how a form is to be understood that provides the organization in an *organized depiction.*

performance The actual behavior someone produces (including the errors they make) under ordinary circumstances. Often contrasted with *competence.*

permastore A hypothesized state in which individual memories are held in storage forever (hence the state can be considered "permanent storage").

perseveration A pattern of responding in which one produces the same response over and over, even though one knows that the task requires a change in response. This pattern is often observed in patients with brain damage in the *frontal lobe.*

PET scanning See *positron emission tomography.*

phonemes The basic categories of sound used to convey language. For example, the words "peg" and "beg" differ in their initial phoneme—[p] in one case, [b] in the other.

phonological buffer A passive storage device that serves as part of the *articulatory rehearsal loop.* The phonological buffer serves as part of the mechanisms ordinarily needed for hearing. In rehearsal, however, the buffer is loaded by means of *subvocalization.* Materials within the buffer then fade, but they can be refreshed by new covert speech, under the control of the *central executive.*

phonology The study of the sounds that are used to convey language.

photoreceptor A cell on the *retina* that responds directly to the incoming light; photoreceptors are of two kinds: *rods* and *cones.*

phrase-structure ambiguity Ambiguity in how a *sentence* should be interpreted, resulting from the fact that more than one phrase structure is compatible with the sentence. An example of such ambiguity is, "I saw the bird with my binoculars."

phrase-structure rule A constraint that governs the pattern of branching in a phrase-structure tree. Equivalently, phrase-structure rules govern what the constituents must be for any syntactic element of a *sentence.*

place of articulation The position at which a speaker momentarily obstructs the flow of air out of the lungs to produce a speech sound. For example, the place of articulation for the [b] sound is the lips; the place of articulation for the [d] sound is created by the tongue briefly touching the roof of the mouth.

positron emission tomography (PET scanning)   A *neuroimaging technique* that determines how much glucose (the brain's fuel) is being used by specific areas of the brain at a particular moment in time.

postsynaptic membrane   The cell membrane of the *neuron* "receiving" information across the *synapse*. Often contrasted with *presynaptic membrane*.

pragmatic reasoning schema   A collection of rules, derived from ordinary practical experience, that defines what inferences are appropriate in a specific situation. These reasoning schemata are usually defined in terms of a goal or theme, and so one schema defines the rules appropriate for reasoning about situations involving "permission," whereas a different schema defines the rules appropriate for thinking about situations involving cause-and-effect relations.

pragmatic rule   A rule that governs how language is ordinarily used, as well as how this language will be interpreted. As an example, "Do you know the time?" is literally a question about one's knowledge, but this question is interpreted as a request that one report what time it is.

prefrontal area   The frontmost part of the *frontal lobe*, crucial for planning and the organization of behavior.

premise   A *proposition* that is assumed to be true in a logic problem; the problem asks what conclusion follows from its premises.

preparation   The first in a series of stages often hypothesized as crucial for creativity. The second stage is *incubation*; the third, *illumination*. Preparation is the stage in which one commences effortful work on the problem, often with little progress.

prescriptive rules   Rules describing how things are supposed to be instead of how they are. Often called *normative* rules, and contrasted with *descriptive rules*.

presynaptic membrane   The cell membrane of the *neuron* "sending" information across the *synapse*. Often contrasted with *postsynaptic membrane*.

primacy effect   An often-observed advantage in remembering the early-presented materials within a sequence of materials. This advantage is generally attributed to the fact that one can focus attention on these items, because, at the beginning of a sequence, one is obviously not trying to divide attention between these items and other items in the series. Often contrasted with *recency effect*.

primary motor projection areas   The strip of tissue, located at the rear of the *frontal lobe*, that is the departure point for nerve cells that send their signals to lower portions of the brain and spinal cord, which ultimately result in muscle movement.

primary sensory projection areas   The main points of arrival in the *cortex* for information arriving from the eyes, ears, and other sense organs.

priming   A process through which one input or cue prepares a person for an upcoming input or cue.

problem-solving   A process in which one begins with a goal and seeks some steps that will lead toward that goal.

problem-solving protocol   A record of how someone seeks to solve a problem; the record is created by simply asking the person to think aloud while working on the problem. The written record of this thinking-aloud is the protocol.

problem-solving set   The starting assumptions that a person uses when trying to solve a new problem. These assumptions are often helpful, because they guide the person away from pointless strategies. But these assumptions can sometimes steer the person away from worthwhile strategies, and so they can be an obstacle to problem-solving.

problem space   The set of all states that can be reached in solving a problem, as one moves, by means of the problem's *operators*, from the problem's *initial state* toward the problem's *goal state*.

process-pure task   A task that relies on only a single mental process. If tasks are "process-pure," then we can interpret the properties of task performance as revealing the properties of the underlying process. If tasks are not process-pure, however, we cannot interpret performance as revealing the properties of a specific process.

processing fluency   An improvement in the speed or ease of processing that results from prior practice in using those same processing steps.

production task   An experimental procedure used in studying concepts, in which the person is asked to name as many examples (e.g., as many fruits) as possible.

proposition   The smallest unit of knowledge that can be either true or false. Propositions are often expressed via simple sentences, but this is merely a convenience.

prosody The pattern of pauses and pitch changes that characterize speech production. Prosody can be used to emphasize elements of a spoken *sentence*, to highlight the sentence's intended structure, or to signal the difference between a question and an assertion.

prosopagnosia A syndrome in which patients lose their ability to recognize faces and to make other fine-grained discriminations within a highly familiar category, even though their other visual abilities seem relatively intact.

prototype theory The claim that mental categories are represented by means of a single "best example," or prototype, identifying the "center" of the category. In this view, decisions about category membership, and inferences about the category, are made with reference to this best example, often an average of the examples of that category that one has actually encountered.

pseudoword A letter string designed to resemble an actual word, even though it is not. Examples include "blar," "plome," and "tuke."

reason-based choice A proposal for how people make decisions. The central idea is that people make a choice when—and only when—they detect what they believe to be a persuasive reason for making that choice.

recall The task of memory *retrieval* in which the rememberer must come up with the desired materials, sometimes in response to a cue that names the context in which these materials were earlier encountered ("Name the pictures you saw earlier"), sometimes in response to a question that requires the sought-after information ("Name a fruit," or "What is the state capital of California?"). Often contrasted with *recognition.*

recency effect The tendency to remember materials that occur late in a series.

receptive field The portion of the visual field to which a cell within the visual system responds. If the appropriately shaped stimulus appears in the appropriate position, the cell's *firing* rate will change. The cell's firing rate will not change if the stimulus is of the wrong form or is in the wrong position.

recognition The task of memory *retrieval* in which the items to be remembered are presented and the person must decide whether or not the item was encountered in some earlier circumstance. Thus, for example, one might be asked, "Have you ever seen this person before?" or "Is this the poster you saw in the office yesterday?" Often contrasted with *recall.*

recognition by components model A model (often referred to by its initials, RBC) of *object recognition.* In this model, a crucial role is played by *geons,* the (hypothesized) basic building blocks out of which all the objects we recognize are constructed.

recognition threshold The briefest exposure to a stimulus that still allows accurate recognition of that stimulus. For words, the recognition threshold typically lies between 10 and 40 ms. Words shown for longer durations are usually easily perceived; words shown for briefer durations are typically difficult to perceive.

reconstruction A process in which one draws on broad patterns of knowledge in order to figure out how a prior event actually unfolded. In some circumstances, we rely on reconstruction to fill gaps in what we recall; in other circumstances, we rely on reconstruction because it requires less effort than actual *recall.*

recursion A property of rule systems that allows a symbol to appear both on the left side of a definition (the part being defined) and on the right side (the part providing the definition). Recursive rules within *syntax,* for example, allow a *sentence* to include another sentence as one of its constituents, as in the following example: "Solomon says that Jacob is talented."

rehearsal loop See *articulatory rehearsal loop.*

relational rehearsal A form of mental processing in which one thinks about the relations, or connections, between ideas. This rehearsal will later guide memory search.

repetition priming A pattern of *priming* that occurs simply because a stimulus is presented a second time; processing is more efficient on the second presentation.

representativeness heuristic A strategy often used in making judgments about categories. This strategy is broadly equivalent to making the assumption that, in general, the instances of a category will resemble the prototype for that category and, likewise, that the prototype resembles each instance.

response selector A (hypothesized) mental resource needed for the selection and initiation of a wide range of responses, including overt responses (e.g., moving in a particular way) and covert responses (e.g., initiating a memory search).

response threshold   The quantity of information, or quantity of activation, needed in order to trigger a response.

response time   The amount of time (usually measured in milliseconds) needed for a person to respond to a particular event (such as a question, or a cue to press a specific button).

restoration effect   A perceptual illusion in hearing, in which one "hears" sounds that are actually missing from the stimulus presented.

retention interval   The amount of time that passes between the initial learning of some material and the subsequent memory *retrieval* of that material.

retina   The light-sensitive tissue that lines the back of the eyeball.

retrieval   The process of locating information in memory and activating that information for use.

retrieval block   A circumstance in which a person seems unable to retrieve a bit of information that he or she knows reasonably well.

retrieval failure   A mechanism that probably contributes to a great deal of forgetting. Retrieval failure occurs when a memory is, in fact, in long-term storage, but one is unable to locate that memory when trying to retrieve it.

retrieval path   A connection (or series of connections) that can lead to a sought-after memory in long-term storage.

retrograde amnesia   An inability to remember experiences that occurred *before* the event that triggered the memory disruption. Often contrasted with *anterograde amnesia*.

risk aversion   A tendency toward avoiding risk. People tend to be risk-averse when contemplating gains, choosing instead to hold tight to what they already have. Often contrasted with *risk seeking*.

risk seeking   A tendency toward seeking out risk. People tend to be risk-seeking when contemplating losses, because they are willing to gamble in hopes of avoiding (or diminishing) their losses. Often contrasted with *risk aversion*.

rod   A *photoreceptor* that is sensitive to very low light levels, but that is unable to discriminate hues, and that has relatively poor *acuity*. Often contrasted with *cone*.

schema (pl. schemata)   A pattern of knowledge describing what is typical or frequent in a particular situation. For example, a "kitchen schema" would stipulate that a stove and refrigerator are likely to be present, whereas a coffeemaker may be or may not be present, and a piano is likely not to be present.

selection task   An experimental procedure, commonly used to study reasoning, in which a person is presented with four cards, with certain information on either side of the card. The person is also given a rule that may describe the cards, and the person's task is to decide which cards must be turned over to find out if the rule describes the cards or not. Also called the "four-card task."

selective attention   The skill through which one pays attention to one input or one task, while ignoring other stimuli that are also on the scene.

self-reference effect   The tendency to have better memory for information relevant to one's self than for other sorts of material.

self-report data   A form of evidence in which the person is asked directly about his or her own thoughts or experiences.

sentence   A sequence of words that conforms to the rules of syntax (and so has the right constituents in the right sequence).

sentence verification task   An experimental procedure, used for studying memory, in which participants are given simple sentences (e.g., "Cats are animals") and must respond as quickly as possible whether the sentence is true or false.

serial position   A data pattern summarizing the relationship between some performance measure (often, likelihood of *recall*) and the order in which the test materials were presented. In memory studies, the serial position curve tends to be U-shaped, with people best able to recall the first-presented items (the *primacy effect*) and also the last-presented items (the *recency effect*).

serial processing   A system in which only one step happens at a time (and so the steps go on in a series). Usually contrasted with *parallel processing*.

shadowing   A task in which research participants are required to repeat back a verbal input, word for word, as they hear it.

shallow processing   A mode of thinking about material in which one pays attention only to appearances and other superficial aspects of the material; shallow processing typically leads to poor memory retention. Often contrasted with *deep processing*.

short-term memory   An older term for what is now called *working memory*.

simultaneous multiple constraint satisfaction   An attribute of much of our thinking, in which we seem able to find solutions to problems, or answers to questions, that satisfy several requirements ("multiple constraints"), using a search process that seems to be guided by all of these requirements at the same time.

single-cell recording   A technique for recording the moment-by-moment *activation level* of an individual *neuron*, within a healthy, normally functioning brain.

somatic markers   States of the body used in decision-making. For example, a tight stomach and an accelerated heart rate when someone is thinking about an option can signal that person that the option has risk associated with it.

source confusion   A memory error in which one misremembers where a bit of information was learned, or where a particular stimulus was last encountered.

source memory   A form of memory that allows one to recollect the episode in which learning took place, or the time and place in which a particular stimulus was encountered.

span test   A procedure used for measuring *working memory*'s holding capacity. In newer studies, the *operation span* test is used.

spatial attention   The mechanism through which we allocate processing resources to particular positions in space, so that we more efficiently process any inputs from that region in space.

specific language impairment   A genetically rooted syndrome in which individuals seem to have normal intelligence but problems in learning the rules of language.

speech segmentation   The process through which a stream of speech is "sliced" into its constituent words and, within words, into the constituent *phonemes*.

spreading activation   A process through which activation travels from one *node* to another, via *associative links*. As each node becomes activated, it serves as a source for further activation, spreading onward through the network.

state-dependent learning   A phenomenon in which learning seems linked to the person's mental, emotional, or biological state during the learning. As a result of this linkage, the learning is most likely to show its effects when the person is again in that mental, emotional, or biological state.

storage   The state in which a memory, once acquired, remains dormant until it is retrieved.

Stroop interference   A classic demonstration of *automaticity* in which people are asked to name the color of ink used to print a word, and the word itself is a different color name. For example, research participants might see the word "yellow" printed in blue ink and be required to say "blue." Considerable interference is observed in this task, with participants apparently unable to ignore the word's content, even though it is irrelevant to their task.

subcortical   Beneath the surface of the brain (i.e., underneath the *cortex*).

subliminal prime   A *prime* that is presented so quickly that it is not consciously detected; such primes nonetheless can have an impact on subsequent perceptions or thoughts.

subproblem   A subdivision of a problem being solved. Subproblems are produced when a person tries to solve a problem by breaking it into components or steps, each with its own goal, but so that solving all the subproblems results in solution of the overall problem.

subthreshold activation   Activation levels below *response threshold*. Subthreshold activation, by definition, will not trigger a response; nonetheless, this activation is important because it can accumulate, leading eventually to an *activation level* that exceeds the response threshold.

subvocalization   Covert speech, in which one goes through the motions of speaking, or perhaps forms a detailed motor plan for speech movements, but without making any sound.

sufficient condition   A condition that, if satisfied, guarantees that a certain consequence will occur. However, sufficient conditions may not be necessary for that consequence (since the same consequence might occur for some other reasons). Often contrasted with *necessary condition*.

summation   The addition of two or more separate inputs so that the effect of these combined inputs is greater than the effect of any one of the inputs by itself.

surface structure   The representation of a *sentence* that is actually expressed in speech. In some treatments, this structure is referred to as "s-structure." Often contrasted with *underlying structure*.

synapse   The area that includes the *presynaptic membrane* of one *neuron*, the *postsynaptic membrane* of another neuron, and the tiny gap between them. The presynaptic membrane releases a small amount of *neurotransmitter* that drifts across the gap and stimulates the postsynaptic membrane.

syntax Rules governing the sequences and combinations of words in the formation of phrases and *sentences*.

System 1 A commonly used name for judgment and reasoning strategies that are fast and effortless, but prone to error.

System 2 A commonly used name for judgment and reasoning strategies that are slower and require more effort than System 1 strategies do, but are less prone to error.

tachistoscope A device that allows the presentation of stimuli for precisely controlled amounts of time, including very brief presentations.

temporal lobe The lobe of the *cortex* lying inward and down from the temples. The temporal lobe in each *cerebral hemisphere* includes the primary auditory projection area, *Wernicke's area*, and, subcortically, the *amygdala* and *hippocampus*.

thalamus A part of the lower portion of the *forebrain* that serves as a major relay and integration center for sensory information.

threshold The activity level at which a cell or *detector* responds, or "*fires.*"

time-sharing A process through which one rapidly switches attention from one task to another, creating the appearance of doing two things at the same time.

TMS See *transcranial magnetic stimulation*.

token node A *node* that represents a specific example or instance of a category, and therefore is used in propositions concerned with specific events and individuals. Often contrasted with *type node*.

top-down processing See *concept-driven processing*.

TOT phenomenon An often-observed effect in which people are unable to remember a particular word, even though they are certain that the word (typically identified via its definition) is in their vocabulary. People in this state often can remember the starting letter for the word and its number of syllables, and insist that the word is on the "tip of their tongue" (hence the "TOT" label).

transcendental method A logic for theorizing first proposed by the philosopher Immanuel Kant. To use this method, one first observes the effects or consequences of a process, and then asks, What must the concept have been in order to bring about these effects?

transcranial magnetic stimulation (TMS) A technique in which a series of strong magnetic pulses at a specific location on the scalp cause temporary disrup-

tion in the brain region directly underneath this scalp area.

type node A *node* that represents a general category, and therefore is embedded in propositions that are true for the entire category. Often contrasted with *token node*.

typicality The degree to which a particular case (an object, or a situation, or an event) is typical for its kind.

unattended channel A stimulus (or group of stimuli) that a person is not trying to perceive. Ordinarily, little information is understood or remembered from the unattended channel. Often contrasted with *attended channel*.

underlying structure An abstract representation of the *sentence* to be expressed; sometimes called "deep structure" (or "d-structure"). Often contrasted with *surface structure*.

unilateral neglect syndrome A pattern of symptoms in which patients ignore all inputs coming from one side of space. Patients with this syndrome put only one of their arms into their jackets, eat food from only one half of their plates, read only one half of words (e.g., they might read "output" as "put"), and so on.

utility A measure of the value that an individual puts on a particular outcome; this measure can then be used to compare various outcomes, allowing choices to be based on these comparisons.

utility maximization The proposal that people make decisions by selecting the option that has the greatest *utility*.

V1 See *area V1*.

valid argument An argument for which the conclusion follows from the *premise*, in accord with the rules of logic or the principles of statistics and research methods.

verb phrase One of the constituents of a phrase structure that defines a *sentence*.

verification One of the four steps commonly hypothesized as part of creative *problem-solving*; in this step, one confirms that a new idea really does lead to a problem solution, and works out the details.

viewpoint-dependent recognition A process in which the ease or success of *recognition* depends on the perceiver's particular viewing angle or distance, with regard to the target object.

viewpoint-independent recognition A process in which the ease or success of *recognition* does *not* depend on the perceiver's particular viewing angle or distance, with regard to the target object.

visual acuity   A measure of one's ability to see fine detail.

visuospatial buffer   One of the low-level assistants used as part of the *working-memory system*. This buffer plays an important role in storing visual or spatial representations, including visual images.

voice-onset time (VOT)   The time period that elapses between the start of a speech sound and the onset of *voicing*. VOT is the main feature distinguishing "voiced" consonants (such as [b], with a near-zero VOT) and "unvoiced" consonants (such as [p], with a VOT of approximately 60 ms).

voicing   One of the properties that distinguishes different categories of speech sounds. A sound is considered "voiced" if the vocal folds are vibrating while the sound is produced. If the vocal folds start vibrating sometime after the sound begins (i.e., with a long *voice-onset time*), the sound is considered "unvoiced."

weapon-focus effect   A pattern, often alleged for witnesses to violent crimes, in which one pays close attention to some crucial detail (such as the weapon, within a crime scene) to the exclusion of much else.

well-defined problem   A problem for which the *goal state* is clearly specified at the start, and the operators available for reaching that goal are clearly identified. Often contrasted with *ill-defined problem*.

Wernicke's area   An area usually in the left *frontal lobe* of the brain; damage here typically causes *fluent aphasia*.

what system   The system of visual circuits and pathways leading from the visual *cortex* to the *temporal lobe* and especially involved in object recognition. Often contrasted with the *where system*.

where system   The system of visual circuits and pathways leading from the visual *cortex* to the *parietal lobe*, and especially involved in the spatial localization of objects and in the coordination of movements. Often contrasted with the *what system*.

winner-takes-all system   A process in which a stronger node inhibits weaker ones, so that the stronger node comes more and more to dominate the weaker nodes.

word-stem completion   A task in which people are given the beginning of a word (e.g., "TOM") and must provide a word that starts with the letters provided. In some versions of the task, only one solution is possible, and so performance is measured by counting the number of words completed. In other versions of the task, several solutions are possible for each stem, and performance is assessed by determining which of the responses fulfill some other criterion.

word-superiority effect   The data pattern in which research participants are more accurate and more efficient in recognizing words (and wordlike letter strings) than they are in recognizing individual letters.

working backward   A commonly used *problem-solving* strategy in which the person begins with the *goal state* and tries to figure out what transformations or operations would make this state more similar to the problem's starting point (the *initial state*).

working memory   The storage system in which information is held while that information is being worked on. All indications are that working memory is a system, and not a single entity, and that information is held here via active processes, not via some sort of passive storage. Formerly called "short-term memory."

working-memory system   A system of mental resources used for holding information in an easily accessible form. The *central executive* is at the heart of this system, and the executive then relies on a number of low-level assistants, including the *visuospatial buffer* and the *articulatory rehearsal loop*.

Ackerman, P. L., Beier, M. E., & Boyle, M. O. (2002). Individual differences in working memory within a nomological network of cognitive and perceptual speed abilities. *Journal of Experimental Psychology: General, 131,* 567–589.

Adamson, R. (1952). Functional fixedness as related to problem solving: A repetition of three experiments. *Journal of Experimental Psychology, 44,* 288–291.

Aggleton, J. P., & Shaw, C. (1996). Amnesia and recognition memory: A re-analysis of psychometric data. *Neuropsychologia, 34,* 51–62.

Agnoli, F., & Krantz, D. H. (1989). Suppressing natural heuristics by formal instruction: The case of the conjunction fallacy. *Cognitive Psychology, 21,* 515–550.

Ahn, W.-K., & Graham, L. M. (1999). The impact of necessity and sufficiency in the Wason four-card task. *Psychological Science, 10,* 237–242.

Ahn, W.-K., Marsh, J., Luhmann, C. C., & Lee, K. (2002). Effect of theory-based feature correlations on typicality judgments. *Memory & Cognition, 30,* 107–118.

Ajzen, I. (1977). Intuitive theories of events and the effects of base-rate information on prediction. *Journal of Personality & Social Psychology, 35,* 303–314.

Algom, D., & Cain, W. (1991). Remembered odors and mental mixtures: Tapping reservoirs of olfactory knowledge. *Journal of Experimental Psychology: Human Perception and Performance, 17,* 1104–1119.

Algom, D., & Lubel, S. (1994). Psychophysics in the field: Perception and memory for labor pain. *Memory & Cognition, 55,* 133–141.

Allan, L. (1993). Human contingency judgments: Rule based or associative. *Psychological Bulletin, 114,* 435–448.

Alloy, L. B., & Tabachnik, N. (1984). Assessment of covariation by humans and animals: The joint influence of prior expectations and current situational information. *Psychological Review, 91,* 112–149.

Allport, A. (1989). Visual attention. In M. Posner (Ed.), *Foundations of cognitive science* (pp. 631–682). Cambridge, MA: MIT Press.

Allport, D., Antonis, B., & Reynolds, P. (1972). On the division of attention: A disproof of the single channel hypothesis. *Quarterly Journal of Experimental Psychology, 24,* 225–235.

Almor, A., & Sloman, S. A. (2000). Reasoning versus text processing in the Wason selection task: A nondeontic perspective on perspective effects. *Memory & Cognition, 28,* 1060–1070.

Altmann, E. M., & Gray, W. D. (2002). Forgetting to remember: The functional relationship of decay and interference. *Psychological Science, 13,* 27–33.

Amabile, T. M. (2001). Beyond talent: John Irving and the passionate craft of creativity. *American Psychologist, 56,* 333–336.

Anand, P., & Sternthal, B. (1991). Perceptual fluency and affect without recognition. *Memory & Cognition, 19,* 293–300.

Anderson, J. R. (1974). Verbatim and propositional representation of sentences in immediate and long-term memory. *Journal of Verbal Learning and Verbal Behavior, 13,* 149–162.

Anderson, J. R. (1976). *Language, memory, and thought.* Hillsdale, NJ: Erlbaum.

Anderson, J. R. (1980). *Cognitive psychology and its implications.* San Francisco: Freeman.

Anderson, J. R. (Ed.). (1981). Cognitive skills and their acquisition. Hillsdale, NJ: Erlbaum.

Anderson, J. R. (1982). Acquisition of cognitive skill. *Psychological Review, 89,* 369–406.

Anderson, J. R. (1983). *The architecture of cognition.* Cambridge, MA: Harvard University Press.

Anderson, J. R. (1987). Skill acquisition: Compilation of weak-method problem solutions. *Psychological Review, 94,* 192–210.

Anderson, J. R. (1993). Problem solving and learning. *American Psychologist, 48*, 35–44.

Anderson, J. R. (1996). ACT: A simple theory of complex cognition. *American Psychologist, 51*, 355–365.

Anderson, J. R., & Bower, G. H. (1972). Recognition and retrieval processes in free recall. *Psychological Review, 79*, 97–123.

Anderson, J. R., & Bower, G. H. (1973). *Human associative memory.* Washington, DC: Winston.

Anderson, J. R., & Reder, L. M. (1999a). The fan effect: New results and new theories. *Journal of Experimental Psychology: General, 128*, 186–197.

Anderson, J. R., & Reder, L. M. (1999b). Process, not representation: Reply to Radvansky (1999). *Journal of Experimental Psychology: General, 128*, 207–210.

Anderson, M. C., & Bell, T. (2001). Forgetting our facts: The role of inhibitory processes in the loss of propositional knowledge. *Journal of Experimental Psychology: General, 130*, 544–570.

Anderson, M. C., Bjork, R., & Bjork, E. (1994). Remembering can cause forgetting: Retrieval dynamics in long-term memory. *Journal of Experimental Psychology: Learning, Memory and Cognition, 20*, 1063–1087.

Anderson, M. C., Bjork, R. A., & Bjork, E. L. (2000). Retrieval-induced forgetting. Evidence for a recall-specific mechanism. *Psychonomic Bulletin & Review, 7*, 522–530.

Anderson, M. C., & McCulloch, K. C. (1999). Integration as a general boundary condition on retrieval-induced forgetting. *Journal of Experimental Psychology: Learning, Memory and Cognition, 25*, 608–629.

Anderson, M. C., & Spellman, B. (1995). On the status of inhibitory mechanisms in cognition: Memory retrieval as a model case. *Psychological Review, 102*, 68–100.

Anderson, R., & Helstrup, T. (1993). Visual discovery in mind and on paper. *Memory & Cognition, 21*, 283–293.

Arkes, H. (1991). Costs and benefits of judgment errors: Implications for debiasing. *Psychological Bulletin, 110*, 486–498.

Arkes, H., & Harkness, A. (1983). Estimates of contingency between two dichotomous variables. *Journal of Experimental Psychology: General, 112*, 117–135.

Armstrong, S. L., Gleitman, L. R., & Gleitman, H. (1983). What some concepts might not be. *Cognition, 13*, 263–308.

Arrigo, J. M., & Pezdek, K. (1997). Lessons from the study of psychogenic amnesia. *Current Directions in Psychological Science, 6*, 148–152.

Ashbridge, E., Walsh, V., & Cowey, A. (1997). Temporal aspects of visual search studied by transcranial magnetic stimulation. *Neuropsychologia, 35*, 1121–1131.

Atkinson, A. P., Thomas, M. S. C., & Cleeremans, A. (2000). Consciousness: Mapping the theoretical landscape. *Trends in Cognitive Sciences, 4*, 372–382.

Atkinson, R. C., & Shiffrin, R. M. (1968). Human memory: A proposed system and its control processes. In K. W. S. Spence & J. T. Spence (Eds.), *The psychology of learning and motivation* (pp. 89–105). New York: Academic Press.

Atran, S. (1990). *Cognitive foundations of natural history.* New York: Cambridge University Press.

Attneave, F. (1953). Psychological probability as a function of experienced frequency. *Journal of Experimental Psychology, 46*, 81–86.

Austin, J. (1962). *How to do things with words.* Cambridge, MA: Harvard University Press.

Awh, E., Dhaliwal, H., Christensen, S., & Matsukura, M. (2001). Evidence for two components of object-based selection. *Psychological Science, 12*, 329–334.

Ayers, M. S., & Reder, L. M. (1998). A theoretical review of the misinformation effect: Predictions from an activation-based model. *Psychonomic Bulletin & Review, 5*, 1–21.

Baars, B. J. (1988). Momentary forgetting as a "resetting" of a conscious global workspace due to competition between incompatible contexts. In M. J. Horowitz (Ed.), *Psychodynamics and cognition* (pp. 269–293). Chicago: University of Chicago Press.

Baars, B. J., & Franklin, S. (2003). How conscious experience and working memory interact. *Trends in Cognitive Sciences, 7*, 166–172.

Baddeley, A. D. (1976). *The psychology of memory.* New York: Basic Books.

Baddeley, A. D. (1986). *Working memory.* Oxford, England: Clarendon.

Baddeley, A. D. (1992). Is working memory working? The fifteenth Bartlett lecture. *Quarterly Journal of Experimental Psychology, 44A*, 1–31.

Baddeley, A. (1996). Exploring the central executive. *Quarterly Journal of Experimental Psychology: Human Experimental Psychology, 49A*, 5–28.

Baddeley, A. D. (1999). *Essentials of human memory.* Hove, England: Psychology Press.

Baddeley, A. (2000). The episodic buffer: A new component of working memory? *Trends in Cognitive Sciences, 4,* 417–423.

Baddeley, A. D., Aggleton, J. P., & Conway, M. A. (Eds.). (2002). *Episodic memory: New directions in research.* New York: Oxford University Press.

Baddeley, A. D., Gathercole, S., & Papagno, C. (1998). The phonological loop as a language learning device. *Psychological Review, 105,* 158–173.

Baddeley, A. D., & Hitch, G. (1974). Working memory. In G. Bower (Ed.), *Recent advances in learning and motivation* (pp. 47–90). New York: Academic Press.

Baddeley, A. D., & Hitch, G. (1977). Recency re-examined. In S. Dornic (Ed.), *Attention and performance VI* (pp. 646–667). Hillsdale, NJ: Erlbaum.

Baddeley, A. D., & Lieberman, K. (1980). Spatial working memory. In R. Nickerson (Ed.), *Attention and performance VIII* (pp. 521–539). Hillsdale, NJ: Erlbaum.

Baddeley, A. D., Logie, R. H., Nimmo-Smith, I., & Brereton, J. (1985). Components of fluent reading. *Journal of Memory and Language, 24,* 119–131.

Bahrick, H. (1984). Semantic memory content in permastore: 50 years of memory for Spanish learned in school. *Journal of Experimental Psychology: General, 113,* 1–29.

Bahrick, H., Bahrick, L., Bahrick, A., & Bahrick, P. (1993). Maintenance of foreign language vocabulary and the spacing effect. *Psychological Science, 4,* 316–321.

Bahrick, H., Bahrick, P. O., & Wittlinger, R. P. (1975). Fifty years of memory for names and faces: A cross-sectional approach. *Journal of Experimental Psychology: General, 104,* 54–75.

Bahrick, H., & Hall, L. (1991). Lifetime maintenance of high school mathematics content. *Journal of Experimental Psychology: General, 120,* 20–33.

Bahrick, H., Hall, L. K., & Berger, S. A. (1996). Accuracy and distortion in memory for high school grades. *Psychological Science, 7,* 265–271.

Balch, W., Bowman, K., & Mohler, L. (1992). Music-dependent memory in immediate and delayed word recall. *Memory & Cognition, 20,* 21–28.

Banks, W. P., Thompson, S., Henry, G., & Weissmann, T. (1986). *Mental models of physiological function in health and illness.* Presentation at the 27th annual meeting of the Psychonomic Society, November 1986, New Orleans.

Baratgin, J., & Noveck, I. A. (2000). Not only base rates are neglected in the engineer-lawyer problem: An investigation of reasoners' underutilization of complementarity. *Memory & Cognition, 28,* 79–91.

Bargh, J. A. (1989). Conditional automaticity: Varieties of automatic influence in social perception and cognition. In J. Uleman & J. Bargh (Eds.), *Unintended thought* (pp. 3–51). New York: Guilford.

Bargh, J. A., & Chartrand, T. L. (1999). The unbearable automaticity of being. *American Psychologist, 54,* 462–479.

Baron, J. (1988). *Thinking and reasoning.* Cambridge, England: Cambridge University Press.

Baron, J. (1998). *Judgment misguided: Intuition and error in public decision making.* New York: Oxford University Press.

Baron, J., & Leshner, S. (2000). How serious are expressions of protected values? *Journal of Experimental Psychology: Applied, 6,* 183–194.

Barsalou, L. (1982). Context-independent and context-dependent information in concepts. *Memory & Cognition, 10,* 82–93.

Barsalou, L. (1983). Ad hoc categories. *Memory & Cognition, 11,* 211–227.

Barsalou, L. (1985). Ideals, central tendency, and frequency of instantiation. *Journal of Experimental Psychology: Learning, Memory and Cognition, 11,* 629–654.

Barsalou, L. (1988). The content and organization of autobiographical memories. In U. Neisser & E. Winograd (Eds.), *Remembering reconsidered* (pp. 193–243). Cambridge, England: Cambridge University Press.

Barsalou, L., & Sewell, D. R. (1985). Contrasting the representation of scripts and categories. *Journal of Memory and Language, 24,* 646–665.

Barsalou, L. W., Solomon, K. O., & Wu, L.-L. (1998). Perceptual simulation in conceptual tasks. In M. K. Hiraga, C. Sinha, & S. Wilcox (Eds.), *Cultural, typological, and psychological perspectives in cognitive linguistics* (pp. 209–228). Amsterdam: John Benjamins.

Bartlett, F. C. (1932). *Remembering: A study in experimental and social psychology.* Cambridge, England: Cambridge University Press.

Bartolomeo, P., Bachoud-Levi, A.-C., De Gelder, B., Denes, G., Barba, G. D., Brugieres, P., et al. (1998). Multiple-domain dissociation between impaired visual perception and preserved mental imagery in a patient with bilateral extrastriate lesions. *Neuropsychologia, 36*(3), 239–249.

Bartz, W. H. (1976). Rehearsal and retrieval processes in recall and recognition. *Bulletin of the Psychonomic Society, 8*, 258.

Bassok, M. (1996). Using content to interpret structure: Effects on analogical transfer. *Current Directions in Psychological Science, 5*, 54–57.

Bassok, M., Wu, L.-L., & Olseth, K. (1995). Judging a book by its cover: Interpretive effects of content on problem-solving transfer. *Memory & Cognition, 23*, 354–367.

Beach, C. M. (1991). The interpretation of prosodic patterns at points of syntactic structural ambiguity: Evidence for cue trading relations. *Journal of Memory and Language, 30*, 644–663.

Bechara, A., Damasio, H., & Damasio, A. R. (2003). Role of the amygdala in decision-making. *Annals of the New York Academy of Sciences, 985*, 356–369.

Bechara, A., Tranel, D., Damasio, H., Adolphs, R., Rockland, C., & Damasio, A. (1995). Double dissociation of conditioning and declarative knowledge relative to the amygdala and hippocampus in humans. *Science, 269*, 1115–1118.

Bédard, J., & Chi, M. (1992). Expertise. *Current Directions in Psychological Science, 1*, 135–139.

Begg, I., Anas, A., & Farinacci, S. (1992). Dissociation of processes in belief: Source recollection, statement familiarity, and the illusion of truth. *Journal of Experimental Psychology: General, 121*, 446–458.

Begg, I., Armour, V., & Kerr, T. (1985). On believing what we remember. *Canadian Journal of Behavioral Science, 17*, 199–214.

Begg, I., & Wickelgren, W. A. (1974). Retention functions for syntactic and lexical vs. semantic information in sentence recognition memory. *Memory & Cognition, 2*, 353–359.

Behrmann, M. (2000). The mind's eye mapped onto the brain's matter. *Current Directions in Psychological Science, 9*, 50–54.

Behrmann, M., Moscovitch, M., & Winocur, G. (1994). Intact visual imagery and impaired visual perception in a patient with visual agnosia. *Journal of Experimental Psychology: Human Perception and Performance, 20*, 1068–1087.

Behrmann, M., & Tipper, S. (1999). Attention accesses multiple reference frames: Evidence from visual neglect. *Journal of Experimental Psychology: Human Perception and Performance, 25*, 83–101.

Bekerian, D. A., & Baddeley, A. D. (1980). Saturation advertising and the repetition effect. *Journal of Verbal Learning & Verbal Behavior, 19*, 17–25.

Bellugi, U. (1971). Simplification in children's language. In R. Huxley & E. Ingram (Eds.), *Language acquisition: Models and methods.* New York: Academic Press.

Bensafi, M., Porter, J., Pouliot, S., Mainland, J., Johnson, B., Zelano, C., et al. (2003). Olfactomotor activity during imagery mimics that during perception. *Nature Neuroscience, 6*, 1142–1144.

Berko, J. (1958). The child's learning of English morphology. *Word, 14*, 150–177.

Berlin, B., & Key, P. (1969). *Basic color terms: Their universality and evolution.* Berkeley: University of California Press.

Besner, D., & Stolz, J. A. (1999a). Unconsciously controlled processing: The Stroop effect reconsidered. *Psychonomic Bulletin & Review, 6*, 449–455.

Besner, D., & Stolz, J. A. (1999b). What kind of attention modulates the Stroop effect? *Psychonomic Bulletin & Review, 6*, 99–104.

Besner, D., Stolz, J. A., & Boutilier, C. (1997). The Stroop effect and the myth of automaticity. *Psychonomic Bulletin and Review, 4*, 221–225.

Bever, T. (1970). The cognitive basis for linguistic structures. In J. R. Hayes (Ed.), *Cognition and the development of language* (pp. 279–362). New York: Wiley.

Bhaskar, R., & Simon, H. (1977). Problem solving in semantically rich domains: An example from engineering thermodynamics. *Cognitive Science, 1*, 193–215.

Biederman, I. (1985). Human vision understanding: Recent research and a theory. *Computer Vision, Graphics, and Image Processing, 32*, 29–73.

Bisiach, E. (1996). Unilateral neglect and the structure of space representation. *Current Directions in Psychological Science, 5*, 62–65.

Bisiach, E., & Luzzatti, C. (1978). Unilateral neglect of representational space. *Cortex, 14*, 129–133.

Blanchette, I., & Dunbar, K. (2000). How analogies are generated: The roles of structural and superficial similarity. *Memory & Cognition, 28*, 108–124.

Block, N. (1997). Biology vs. computation in the study of consciousness. *Behavioral and Brain Sciences, 20*, 1.

Block, N. (2001). Paradox and cross purposes in recent work on consciousness. *Cognition, 79*, 197–219.

Bloom, P. (Ed.). (1994). *Language acquisition.* Cambridge, MA: MIT Press.

Blount, G. (1986). Dangerousness of patients with Capgras Syndrome. *Nebraska Medical Journal, 71,* 207.

Blum, D., & Yonelinas, A. P. (2001). Transfer across modality in perceptual implicit memory. *Psychonomic Bulletin & Review, 8,* 147–154.

Bobrow, S., & Bower, G. H. (1969). Comprehension and recall of sentences. *Journal of Experimental Psychology, 80,* 455–461.

Bogen, J. E. (1995). On the neurophysiology of consciousness: I. An overview. *Consciousness & Cognition: An International Journal, 4,* 52–62.

Boole, G. (1854). *An investigation of the laws of thought, on which are founded the mathematical theories of logic and probabilities.* London: Maberly.

Bornstein, B. (1963). Prosopagnosia. In L. Halpern (Ed.), *Problems of dynamic neurology* (pp. 283–318). Jerusalem: Hadassah Medical Organization.

Bornstein, B., & LeCompte, D. (1995). A comparison of item and source forgetting. *Psychonomic Bulletin & Review, 2,* 254–259.

Bornstein, B., Sroka, H., & Munitz, H. (1969). Prosopagnosia with animal face agnosia. *Cortex, 5,* 164–169.

Boroditsky, L. (2001). Does language shape thought? Mandarin and English speakers' conceptions of time. *Cognitive Psychology, 43,* 1–22.

Botvinick, M. M., Braver, T. S., Barch, D. M., Carter, C. S., & Cohen, J. D. (2001). Conflict monitoring and cognitive control. *Psychological Review, 108,* 624–652.

Bower, G. H. (1970). Analysis of a mnemonic device. *American Scientist, 58,* 496–510.

Bower, G. H. (1972). Mental imagery and associative learning. In L. W. Gregg (Ed.), *Cognition in learning and memory* (pp. 51–88). New York: Wiley.

Bower, G. H., Black, J. B., & Turner, T. J. (1979). Scripts in memory for text. *Cognitive Psychology, 11,* 177–220.

Bower, G. H., Karlin, M. B., & Dueck, A. (1975). Comprehension and memory for pictures. *Memory & Cognition, 3,* 216–220.

Bower, G. H., & Reitman, J. S. (1972). Mnemonic elaboration in multilist learning. *Journal of Verbal Learning and Verbal Behavior, 11,* 478–485.

Bower, G. H., & Winzenz, D. (1970). Comparison of associative learning strategies. *Psychonomic Science, 20,* 119–120.

Bower, J. M., & Parsons, L. M. (2003). Rethinking the "lesser brain." *Scientific American, 289*(August), 50–57.

Braine, M., & O'Brien, D. (1991). A theory of if: A lexical entry, reasoning program, and pragmatic principles. *Psychological Review, 98,* 182–203.

Brainerd, C. J., & Reyna, V. F. (1998). When things that were never experienced are easier to "remember" than things that were. *Psychological Science, 9,* 484–490.

Brainerd, C. J., Reyna, V. F., & Mojardin, A. H. (1999). Conjoint recognition. *Psychological Review, 106,* 160–179.

Bransford, J. (1979). *Human cognition: Learning, understanding and remembering.* Belmont, CA: Wadsworth.

Bransford, J., Barclay, J. R., & Franks, J. J. (1972). Sentence memory: A constructive versus interpretive approach. *Cognitive Psychology, 3,* 193–209.

Bransford, J., & Franks, J. J. (1971). The abstraction of linguistic ideas. *Cognitive Psychology, 2,* 331–350.

Bransford, J., & Johnson, M. K. (1972). Contextual prerequisites for understanding: Some investigations of comprehension and recall. *Journal of Verbal Learning and Verbal Behavior, 11,* 717–726.

Bransford, J., & Johnson, M. K. (1973). Considerations of some problems of comprehension. In W. G. Chase (Ed.), *Visual information processing* (pp. 383–438). New York: Academic Press.

Brase, G. L., Cosmides, L., & Tooby, J. (1998). Individuation, counting and statistical inference: The role of frequency and whole-object representations in judgment under uncertainty. *Journal of Experimental Psychology: General, 127,* 3–21.

Braver, T. S., & Cohen, J. D. (2001). Working memory, cognitive control, and the prefrontal cortex: Computational and empirical studies. *Cognitive Processing, 2,* 25–55.

Bremner, J. D., Shobe, K., & Kihlstrom, J. F. (2000). False memories in women with self-reported childhood sexual abuse: An empirical study. *Psychological Science, 11,* 333–337.

Brendl, C. M., Markman, A. B., & Higgins, E. T. (1998). Mental accounting as self-regulation: Representativeness to goal-derived categories. *Zeitschrift fuer Sozialpsychologie, 29(2),* 89–104.

Brennen, T., Baguley, T., Bright, J., & Bruce, V. (1990). Resolving semantically induced tip-of-the-tongue states for proper nouns. *Memory & Cognition, 18,* 339–347.

Brewer, W. (1988). Memory for randomly sampled autobiographical events. In U. Neisser & E. W. Winograd (Eds.), *Remembering reconsidered* (pp. 21–90). Cambridge, England: Cambridge University Press.

Brewer, W., & Treyens, J. C. (1981). Role of schemata in memory for places. *Cognitive Psychology, 13,* 207–230.

Brewin, C. R. (1998). Intrusive autobiographical memories in depression and post-traumatic stress disorder. *Applied Cognitive Psychology, 12,* 359–370.

Brewin, C. R., Andrews, B., & Gotlib, I. (1993). Psychopathology and early experience: A reappraisal of retrospective reports. *Psychological Bulletin, 113,* 82–98.

Brigham, J., & Cairns, D. L. (1988). The effect of mugshot inspections on eyewitness identification accuracy. *Journal of Applied Social Psychology, 18,* 1394–1410.

Brigham, J., & Wolfskiel, M. P. (1983). Opinions of attorneys and law enforcement personnel on the accuracy of eyewitness identification. *Law and Human Behavior, 7,* 337–349.

Broadbent, D. E. (1958). *Perception and communication.* London: Pergamon.

Brooks, L. (1968). Spatial and verbal components of the act of recall. *Canadian Journal of Psychology, 22,* 349–368.

Brooks, L. (1990). Concept formation and particularizing learning. In P. Hanson (Ed.), *Information, language and cognition* (pp. 141–167). Vancouver, BC: University of British Columbia Press.

Brooks, L., Norman, G., & Allen, S. (1991). Role of specific similarity in a medical diagnostic task. *Journal of Experimental Psychology: General, 120,* 278–287.

Brown, A. (1991). A review of the tip-of-the-tongue experience. *Psychological Bulletin, 109,* 204–223.

Brown, A., & Mitchell, D. (1994). A reevaluation of semantic versus nonsemantic processing in implicit memory. *Memory & Cognition, 22,* 533–541.

Brown, A., Neblett, D., Jones, T., & Mitchell, D. (1991). Transfer of processing in repetition priming: Some inappropriate findings. *Journal of Experimental Psychology: Learning, Memory and Cognition, 17,* 514–525.

Brown, A. L. (1979). Theories of memory and the problems of development: Activity, growth, and knowledge. In L. S. Cermak & F. I. M. Craik (Eds.), *Levels of processing in human memory* (pp. 225–258). Hillsdale, NJ: Erlbaum.

Brown, A. S. (2002). Consolidation theory and retrograde amnesia in humans. *Psychonomic Bulletin & Review, 9,* 403–425.

Brown, A. S., & Halliday, H. E. (1990). *Multiple-choice tests: Pondering incorrect alternatives can be hazardous to your knowledge.* Paper presented at the meeting of the Psychonomic Society, November 1990, New Orleans.

Brown, E., Deffenbacher, K., & Sturgill, W. (1977). Memory for faces and the circumstances of encounter. *Journal of Applied Psychology, 62,* 311–318.

Brown, R., & Kulik, J. (1977). Flashbulb memories. *Cognition, 5,* 73–99.

Brown, R., & Lenneberg, E. H. (1954). A study in language and cognition. *Journal of Abnormal and Social Psychology, 49,* 454–462.

Brown, R., & McNeill, D. (1966). The "tip of the tongue" phenomenon. *Journal of Verbal Learning and Verbal Behavior, 5,* 325–337.

Bruce, D., & Winograd, E. (1998). Remembering Deese's 1959 articles: The Zeitgeist, the sociology of sciences, and false memories. *Psychonomic Bulletin & Review, 5,* 615–624.

Bruck, M., & Ceci, S. J. (1999). The suggestibility of children's memory. *Annual Review of Psychology, 50,* 419–440.

Bruner, J. S. (1973). *Beyond the information given.* New York: Norton.

Buchanan, T. W., & Adolphs, R. (2004). The neuroanatomy of emotional memory in humans. In D. Reisberg & P. Hertel (Eds.), *Memory and emotion* (pp. 42–75). New York: Oxford University Press.

Bundesen, C., Kyllingsbaek, S., & Larsen, A. (2003). Independent encoding of colors and shapes from two stimuli. *Psychonomic Bulletin & Review, 10,* 474–479.

Burke, A., Heuer, F., & Reisberg, D. (1992). Remembering emotional events. *Memory & Cognition, 20,* 277–290.

Burton, A. M., Young, A., Bruce, V., Johnston, R., & Ellis, A. (1991). Understanding covert recognition. *Cognition, 39,* 129–166.

Busey, T. A., Tunnicliff, J., Loftus, G. R., & Loftus, E. F. (2000). Accounts of the confidence-accuracy relation in recognition memory. *Memory & Cognition, 7*, 26–48.

Buzsáki, G., & Draguhn, A. (2004). Neuronal oscillations in cortical networks. *Science, 304*, 1926–1929.

Cabeza, R., & Nyberg, L. (2000). Imaging cognition II: An empirical review of 275 PET and fMRI studies. *Journal of Cognitive Neuroscience, 12*, 1–47.

Cann, A., & Ross, D. (1989). Olfactory stimuli as context cues in human memory. *American Journal of Psychology, 2*, 91–102.

Cantor, J., & Engle, R. (1993). Working-memory capacity as long-term memory activation: An individual-differences approach. *Journal of Experimental Psychology: Learning, Memory and Cognition, 19*, 1101–1114.

Capgras, J., & Reboul-Lachaux, J. (1923). L'illusion des "sosies" dans un delire systematise chronique. *Bulletine de Societe Clinique de Medicine Mentale, 11*, 6–16.

Caplan, D. (1987). *Neurolinguistics and linguistic aphasiology.* New York: Cambridge University Press.

Caplan, D. (1992). *Language: Structure, processing and disorders.* Cambridge, MA: MIT Press.

Carey, S. (1985). *Conceptual change in childhood.* Cambridge, MA: Bradford/MIT Press.

Carmichael, L. C., Hogan, H. P., & Walters, A. A. (1932). An experimental study of the effect of language on the reproduction of visually perceived form. *Journal of Experimental Psychology, 15*, 73–86.

Carpenter, P., & Eisenberg, P. (1978). Mental rotation and the frame of reference in blind and sighted individuals. *Perception & Psychophysics, 23*, 117–124.

Carpenter, P., Just, M., & Shell, P. (1990). What one intelligence test measures: A theoretical account of the processing in the Raven Progressive Matrices Test. *Psychological Review, 97*, 404–431.

Carrasco, M., Ling, S., & Read, S. (2004). Attention alters appearance. *Nature Neuroscience, 7*, 308–313.

Carrasco, M., Penpeci-Talgar, C., & Eckstein, M. (2000). Spatial covert attention increases contrast sensitivity across the CSF: Support for signal enhancement. *Vision Research, 40*, 1203–1215.

Cary, M., & Carlson, R. A. (1999). External support and the development of problem-solving routines. *Journal of Experimental Psychology: Learning, Memory and Cognition, 25*, 1053–1070.

Catrambone, R. (1998). The subgoal learning model: Creating better examples so that students can solve novel problems. *Journal of Experimental Psychology: General, 127*, 355–376.

Cattell, J. M. (1885). Über die Zeit der Erkennung and Benennung von Schriftzeichen, Bildern and Farben. *Philosophische Studien, 2*, 635–650.

Cave, K. R., & Bichot, N. P. (1999). Visuospatial attention: Beyond a spotlight model. *Psychonomic Bulletin and Review, 6*, 204–223.

Ceci, S., & Bruck, M. (1995). *Jeopardy in the courtroom: A scientific analysis of children's testimony.* Washington, DC: American Psychological Association.

Challis, B., & Brodbeck, D. (1992). Level of processing affects priming in word fragment completion. *Journal of Experimental Psychology: Learning, Memory and Cognition, 18*, 595–607.

Chalmers, D. (1996). *The conscious mind.* New York: Oxford University Press.

Chalmers, D. (1998). What is a neural correlate of consciousness? In T. Metzinger (Ed.), *Neural correlates of consciousness: Empirical and conceptual issues* (pp. 17–39). Cambridge, MA: MIT Press.

Chambers, D., & Reisberg, D. (1985). Can mental images be ambiguous? *Journal of Experimental Psychology: Human Perception and Performance, 11*, 317–328.

Chambers, D., & Reisberg, D. (1992). What an image depicts depends on what an image means. *Cognitive Psychology, 24*, 145–174.

Chambers, K. L., & Zaragoza, M. S. (2001). Intended and unintended effects of explicit warnings on eyewitness suggestibility: Evidence from source identification tests. *Memory & Cognition, 29*, 1120–1129.

Chandler, C. (1994). Studying related pictures can reduce accuracy, but increase confidence, in a modified recognition test. *Memory & Cognition, 22*, 273–280.

Chapman, J., & Chapman, L. J. (1959). Atmosphere effect re-examined. *Journal of Experimental Psychology, 58*, 220–226.

Chapman, L. J., & Chapman, J. (1971). Test results are what you think they are. *Psychology Today, 5*, 106–110.

Charniak, E. (1972). *Toward a model of children's story comprehension.* Unpublished doctoral dissertation, Massachusetts Institute of Technology, Cambridge, MA.

Chase, W., & Ericsson, K. A. (1978). *Acquisition of a mnemonic system for digit span.* Paper presented at the annual meeting of the Psychonomic Society, San Antonio, Texas.

Chase, W., & Ericsson, K. A. (1979). *A mnemonic system for digit span: One year later.* Paper presented at the annual meeting of the Psychonomic Society, Phoenix, Arizona.

Chase, W., & Ericsson, K. A. (1982). Skill and working memory. In G. H. Bower (Ed.), *The psychology of learning and motivation* (pp. 1–58). New York: Academic Press.

Chase, W., & Simon, H. (1973). Perception in chess. *Cognitive Psychology, 4,* 55–81.

Chen, Z. (1995). Analogical transfer: From schematic pictures to problem solving. *Memory & Cognition, 23,* 255–269.

Cheng, P., & Holyoak, K. J. (1985). Pragmatic reasoning schemas. *Cognitive Psychology, 17,* 391–416.

Cheng, P., Holyoak, K. J., Nisbett, R. E., & Oliver, L. M. (1986). Pragmatic versus syntactic approaches to training deductive reasoning. *Cognitive Psychology, 18,* 293–328.

Cherry, E. C. (1953). Some experiments on the recognition of speech with one and with two ears. *Journal of the Acoustical Society of America, 25,* 975–979.

Chi, M. (1976). Short-term memory limitations in children: Capacity or processing deficits? *Memory & Cognition, 4,* 559–572.

Chi, M., Feltovich, P., & Glaser, R. (1981). Categorization and representation of physics problems by experts and novices. *Cognitive Science, 5,* 121–152.

Chi, M., Glaser, R., & Farr, M. (Eds.). (1988). *The nature of expertise.* Hillsdale, NJ: Erlbaum.

Chomsky, N. (1957). *Syntactic structures.* The Hague, Netherlands: Mouton.

Chomsky, N. (1965). *Aspects of a theory of syntax.* Cambridge, MA: MIT Press.

Chomsky, N. (1975). *Reflections on language.* London: Temple-Smith.

Chomsky, N. (1986). *Knowledge of language: Its nature, origin and use.* New York: Praeger.

Chomsky, N., & Halle, M. (1968). *The sound pattern of English.* New York: Harper & Row.

Christen, F., & Bjork, R. A. (1976). *On updating the loci in the method of loci.* Paper presented at the meeting of the Psychonomic Society, November 1976, St. Louis.

Christiansen, M. H., Chater, N., & Seidenberg, M. S. (Eds.). (1999). Connectionist models of human language processing: Progress and prospects [Special issue]. *Cognitive Science, 23*(4).

Christianson, S.-Å. (1989). Flashbulb memories: Special, but not so special. *Memory & Cognition, 17,* 435–443.

Christianson, S.-Å. (1992). Emotional stress and eyewitness memory: A critical review. *Psychological Bulletin, 112,* 284–309.

Chronicle, E. P., MacGregor, J. N., & Ormerod, T. C. (2004). What makes an insight problem? The roles of heuristics, goal conception, and solution recoding in knowledge-lean problems. *Journal of Experimental Psychology: Learning, Memory, & Cognition, 30,* 14–27.

Churchland, P. (1989). *A neurocomputational perspective: The nature of mind and the structure of science.* Cambridge, MA: MIT Press.

Churchland, P., & Sejnowski, T. J. (1992). *The computational brain.* Cambridge, MA: MIT Press.

Clancy, S. A., Schacter, D. L., McNally, R. J., & Pitmann, R. K. (2000). False recognition in women reporting recovered memories of sexual abuse. *Psychological Science, 11,* 26–31.

Claparède, E. (1951). Reconnaissance et moiité. In D. Rapaport (Ed.), *Organization and pathology of thought* (pp. 58–75). New York: Columbia University Press. (Original work published in 1911)

Clement, J. (1982). *Analogical reasoning patterns in expert problem solving.* Paper presented at the 4th Annual Conference of the Cognitive Science Society, August 1982, Ann Arbor.

Cobb, S. (1941). *Foundations of neuropsychiatry.* Baltimore: Williams & Wilkins.

Cohen, A., & Rafal, R. D. (1991). Attention and feature integration: Illusory conjunctions in a patient with a parietal lobe lesion. *Psychological Science, 2,* 106–110.

Cohen, N. J., & Squire, L. R. (1980). Preserved learning and retention of pattern analyzing skill in amnesics: Dissociation of knowing how and knowing that. *Science, 210,* 207–210.

Coley, J. D., Medin, D. L., & Atran, S. (1997). Does rank have its privilege? Inductive inferences within folkbiological taxonomies. *Cognition, 64,* 73–112.

Collins, A. M., & Loftus, E. F. (1975). A spreading activation theory of semantic processing. *Psychological Review, 82,* 407–428.

Collins, A. M., & Quillian, M. R. (1969). Retrieval time from semantic memory. *Journal of Verbal Learning and Verbal Behavior, 8,* 240–247.

Combs, B., & Slovic, P. (1979). Causes of death: Biased newspaper coverage and biased judgments. *Journalism Quarterly, 56*, 837–843, 849.

Comrie, B. (1981). *Language universals and linguistic typology.* Chicago: University of Chicago Press.

Connolly, T., & Koput, K. (1996). Naturalistic decision making and the new organizational context. In Z. Shapira (Ed.), *Organizational decision making* (pp. 282–303). Cambridge, England: Cambridge University Press.

Connolly, T., & Zeelenberg, M. (2002). Regret in decision making. *Current Directions in Psychological Science, 11*, 212–216.

Connors, E., Lundregan, T., Miller, N., & McEwan, T. (1996). *Convicted by juries, exonerated by science: Case studies in the use of DNA evidence to establish innocence after trial.* Alexandria, VA: National Institute of Justice.

Conrad, C. (1972). Cognitive economy in semantic memory. *Journal of Experimental Psychology, 92*, 149–154.

Conway, A. R. A., Cowan, N., & Bunting, M. (2001). The cocktail party phenomenon revisited: The importance of working memory capacity. *Psychonomic Bulletin & Review, 8*, 331–335.

Conway, A. R. A., Kane, M. J., & Engle, R. W. (2003). Working memory capacity and its relation to general intelligence. *Trends in Cognitive Sciences, 7*, 547–552.

Conway, M., Anderson, S., Larsen, S., Donnelly, C., McDaniel, M., McClelland, A. G. R., et al. (1994). The formation of flashbulb memories. *Memory & Cognition, 22*, 326–343.

Conway, M., Cohen, G., & Stanhope, N. (1991). On the very long-term retention of knowledge acquired through formal education: Twelve years of cognitive psychology. *Journal of Experimental Psychology: General, 120*, 395–409.

Conway, M., Cohen, G., & Stanhope, N. (1992). Why is it that university grades do not predict very long term retention? *Journal of Experimental Psychology: General, 121*, 382–384.

Conway, M., Collins, A. F., Gathercole, S., & Anderson, S. J. (1996). Recollections of true and false autobiographical memories. *Journal of Experimental Psychology: General, 125*, 69–98.

Conway, M., & Fthenaki, K. (1999). Disruption and loss of autobiographical memory. In L. S. Cermak (Ed.), *Handbook of neuropsychology: Memory.* Amsterdam: Elsevier.

Conway, M., & Holmes, A. (2004). Psychosocial stages and the accessibility of autobiographical memories across the life cycle. *Journal of Personality, 72*, 461–480.

Conway, M., & Pleydell-Pearce, C. W. (2000). The construction of autobiographical memories in the self-memory system. *Psychological Review, 107*, 261–288.

Conway, M., & Ross, M. (1984). Getting what you want by revising what you had. *Journal of Personality and Social Psychology, 39*, 406–415.

Cook, V. J. (1988). *Chomsky's universal grammar: An introduction.* Cambridge, MA: Basil Blackwell.

Cooney, J. W., & Gazzaniga, M. S. (2003). Neurological disorders and the structure of human consciousness. *Trends in Cognitive Sciences, 7*, 161–165.

Cooper, L. (1990). Mental representation of three-dimensional objects in visual problem solving and recognition. *Journal of Experimental Psychology: Learning, Memory and Cognition, 16*, 1097–1106.

Cooper, L., & Shepard, R. N. (1973). Chronometric studies of the rotation of mental images. In W. G. Chase (Ed.), *Visual information processing* (pp. 75–176). New York: Academic Press.

Corbetta, M., Kincade, J., Ollinger, J. M., McAvoy, M. P., & Shulman, G. L. (2000). Voluntary orienting is dissociated from target detection in human posterior parietal cortex. *Nature Neuroscience, 3*, 292–297.

Corter, J., & Gluck, M. (1992). Explaining basic categories: Feature predictability and information. *Psychological Bulletin, 111*, 291–303.

Cosmides, L. (1989). The logic of social exchange: Has natural selection shaped how humans reason? Studies with the Wason selection task. *Cognition, 31*, 187–276.

Cosmides, L., & Tooby, J. (1996). Are humans good intuitive statisticians after all? Rethinking some conclusions from the literature on judgment. *Cognition, 58*, 1–73.

Courtney, S. M., Petit, L., Maisog, J. M., Ungerleider, L. G., & Haxby, J. V. (1998). An area specialized for spatial working memory in human frontal cortex. *Science, 279*, 1347–1351.

Craik, F. I. M., & Lockhart, R. S. (1972). Levels of processing: A framework for memory research. *Journal of Verbal Learning and Verbal Behavior, 11*, 671–684.

Craik, F. I. M., Moscovitch, M., & McDown, J. (1994). Contributions of surface and conceptual information to performance on implicit and explicit memory tasks. *Journal of Experimental Psychology: Learning, Memory and Cognition, 20*, 864–875.

Craik, F. I. M., & Tulving, E. (1975). Depth of processing and the retention of words in episodic memory. *Journal of Experimental Psychology: General, 104*, 269–294.

Craik, F. I. M., & Watkins, M. J. (1973). The role of rehearsal in short-term memory. *Journal of Verbal Learning and Verbal Behavior, 12*, 599–607.

Crick, F., & Koch, C. (1995). Are we aware of neural activity in primary visual cortex? *Nature, 375*, 121–123.

Crombag, H. F. M., Wagenaar, W. A., & van Koppen, P. J. (1996). Crashing memories and the problem of "source monitoring." *Applied Cognitive Psychology, 10*, 95–104.

Crystal, D. (1987). *The Cambridge encyclopedia of language.* Cambridge, MA: Cambridge University Press.

Csibra, G., Davis, G., Spratling, M. W., & Johnson, M. H. (2000). Gamma oscillations and object processing in the infant brain. *Science, 290*, 1582–1585.

Cummins, D. (1992). Role of analogical reasoning in induction of problem categories. *Journal of Experimental Psychology: Learning, Memory and Cognition, 18*, 1103–1124.

Cummins, D. D. (2004). The evolution of reasoning. In J. P. Leighton & R. J. Sternberg (Eds.), *The nature of reasoning* (pp. 339–374). New York: Cambridge University Press.

Cummins, D., & Allen, C. (Eds.). (1998). *The evolution of mind.* New York: Oxford University Press.

Curran, T., & Hintzman, D. L. (1995). Violations of the independence assumption in process dissociation. *Journal of Experimental Psychology: Learning, Memory, & Cognition, 21*, 531–547.

Cutler, B. L., Penrod, S. D., & Dexter, H. R. (1990). Juror sensitivity to eyewitness identification evidence. *Law and Human Behavior, 14*, 185–191.

Damasio, A. R. (1994). *Descartes' error: Emotion, reason, and the human brain.* New York: Putnam.

Damasio, A. R. (1999). *The feeling of what happens: Body and emotion in the making of consciousness* (1st ed.). New York: Harcourt Brace.

Damasio, A., Damasio, H., & Van Hoesen, G. W. (1982). Prosopagnosia: Anatomic basis and behavioral mechanisms. *Neurology, 32*, 331–341.

Damasio, A. R., Tranel, D., & Damasio, H. (1989). Disorders of visual recognition. In H. Goodglass & A. R. Damasio (Eds.), *Handbook of neuropsychology,* Vol. 2 (pp. 317–332). New York: Elsevier.

Damasio, A. R., Tranel, D., & Damasio, H. (1990). Face agnosia and the neural substrates of memory. *Annual Review of Neuroscience, 13*, 89–109.

Daneman, M., & Carpenter, P. (1980). Individual differences in working memory and reading. *Journal of Verbal Learning and Verbal Behavior, 19*, 450–466.

Daneman, M., & Hannon, B. (2001). Using working memory theory to investigate the construct validity of multiple-choice reading comprehension tests such as the SAT. *Journal of Experimental Psychology: General, 130*, 208–223.

Daniloff, R., & Hammarberg, R. (1973). On defining coarticulation. *Journal of Phonetics, 1*, 185–194.

Dawes, R. M. (1988). *Rational choice in an uncertain world.* San Diego, CA: Harcourt Brace Jovanovich.

Deese, J. (1957). Serial organization in the recall of disconnected items. *Psychological Reports, 3*, 577–582.

Deese, J. (1959). On the prediction of occurrence of particular verbal intrusions in immediate recall. *Journal of Experimental Psychology, 58*, 17–22.

Deese, J., & Kaufman, R. A. (1957). Serial effects in recall of unorganized and sequentially organized verbal material. *Journal of Experimental Psychology, 54*, 180–187.

De Groot, A. (1965). *Thought and choice in chess.* The Hague, Netherlands: Mouton.

De Groot, A. (1966). Perception and memory versus thought: Some old ideas and recent findings. In B. Kleinmuntz (Ed.), *Problem solving* (pp. 19–50). New York: Wiley.

Dehaene, S., Artiges, E., Naccache, L., Martelli, C., Viard, A., Schurhoff, F., et al. (2003). Conscious and subliminal conflicts in normal subjects and patients with schizophrenia: The role of the anterior cingulate. *Proceedings of the National Academy of Sciences, USA, 100*, 13722–13727.

Dehaene, S., & Naccache, L. (2001). Toward a cognitive neuroscience of consciousness: Basic evidence and a workspace framework. *Cognition, 79*, 1–37.

Dell, G. S., Burger, L. K., & Svec, W. R. (1997). Language production and serial order: A function analysis and a model. *Psychological Review, 104*, 123–147.

Demonet, J. F., Wise, R. A., & Frackowiak, R. S. J. (1993). Language functions explored in normal subjects by positron emission tomography: A critical review. *Human Brain Mapping, 1*, 39–47.

Dempster, F. N. (1981). Memory span: Sources of individual and developmental differences. *Psychological Bulletin, 89*, 63–100.

Dennett, D. (1992). *Consciousness explained.* Boston: Little, Brown.

Dennett, D. (2001). Are we explaining consciousness yet? *Cognition, 79*, 221–237.

De Renzi, E., Faglioni, P., Grossi, D., & Nichelli, P. (1991). Apperceptive and associative forms of prosopagnosia. *Cortex, 27*, 213–221.

DeWitt, L., & Samuel, A. (1990). The role of knowledge-based expectations in music perception: Evidence from musical restoration. *Journal of Experimental Psychology: General, 119*, 123–144.

Diamond, R., & Carey, S. (1986). Why faces are and are not special: An effect of expertise. *Journal of Experimental Psychology: General, 115*, 107–117.

Diehl, R. L., Lotto, A. J., & Holt, L. L. (2004). Speech perception. *Annual Review of Psychology, 55*, 149–179.

Dinges, D., Whitehouse, W., Orne, E., Powell, J., Orne, M., & Erdelyi, M. (1992). Evaluation of hypnotic memory enhancement (hypermnesia and reminiscence) using multitrial forced recall. *Journal of Experimental Psychology: Learning, Memory and Cognition, 18*, 1139–1147.

Dingwall, W. O. (1993). The biological bases of human communicative behavior. In J. Berko Gleason & N. Bernstein Ratner (Eds.), *Psycholinguistics* (pp. 42–88). New York: Harcourt Brace Jovanovich.

Djordjevic, J., Zatorre, R. J., Petrides, M., & Jones-Gotman, M. (2004). The mind's nose: Effects of odor and visual imagery on odor detection. *Psychological Science, 15*, 143–148.

Dodson, C. S., Holland, P. W., & Shimamura, A. P. (1998). On the recollection of specific- and partial-source information. *Journal of Experimental Psychology: Learning, Memory and Cognition, 24*, 1121–1136.

Dominowski, R., & Jenrick, R. (1972). Effects of hints and interpolated activity on solution of an insight problem. *Psychonomic Science, 26*, 335–338.

Donnelly, C., & McDaniel, M. A. (1993). Use of analogy in learning scientific concepts. *Journal of Experimental Psychology: Learning, Memory and Cognition, 19*, 975–986.

Donnelly, C. M., & McDaniel, M. A. (2000). Analogy with knowledgeable learners: When analogy confers benefits and exacts costs. *Psychonomic Bulletin & Review, 7*, 537–543.

Dorfman, J., Shames, V. A., & Kihlstrom, J. F. (1996). Intuition, incubation, and insight: Implicit cognition in problem solving. In G. D. M. Underwood (Ed.), *Implicit cognition* (pp. 257–296). Oxford, England: Oxford University Press.

Downs, J., & Shafir, E. (1999). Why some are perceived as more confident and more insecure, more reckless and more cautious, more trusting and more suspicious, than others: Enriched and impoverished options in social judgment. *Psychonomic Bulletin & Review, 6*, 598–610.

Dudai, Y. (2004). The neurobiology of consolidations, or, how stable is the engram. *Annual Review of Psychology, 55*, 51–86.

Duncan, J. (1995). Attention, intelligence, and the frontal lobes. In M. S. Gazzaniga (Ed.), *The cognitive neurosciences* (pp. 721–733). Cambridge, MA: MIT Press.

Duncan, J., Bundesen, C., Olson, A., Humphreys, G., Chavda, S., & Shibuya, H. (1999). Systematic analysis of deficits in visual attention. *Journal of Experimental Psychology: General, 128*, 450–478.

Duncan, J., Burgess, P., & Emslie, H. (1995). Fluid intelligence after frontal lobe lesions. *Neuropsychologia, 33*, 261–268.

Duncan, J., Emslie, H., Williams, P., Johnson, R., & Freer, C. (1996). Intelligence and the frontal lobe: The organization of goal-directed behavior. *Cognitive Psychology, 30*, 257–303.

Duncker, K. (1945). *On problem-solving* (Psychological Monographs: General and Applied, Vol. 58, No. 5 [whole no. 270]). Washington, DC: American Psychological Association.

Dunning, D., & Parpal, M. (1989). Mental addition versus subtraction in counterfactual reasoning. *Journal of Personality and Social Psychology, 57*, 5–15.

Durgin, F. H. (2000). The reverse Stroop effect. *Psychonomic Bulletin & Review, 7*, 121–125.

Eagly, A. H., Kulesa, P., Chen, S., & Chaiken, S. (2001). Do attitudes affect memory? Tests of the congeniality hypothesis. *Current Directions in Psychological Science, 10*, 5–9.

Easterbrook, J. A. (1959). The effect of emotion on cue utilization and the organization of behavior. *Psychological Review, 66,* 183–201.

Eberhard, K. M., Spivey-Knowlton, M. J., Sedivy, J. C., & Tanenhaus, M. K. (1995). Eye movements as a window into real-time spoken language comprehension in natural contexts. *Journal of Psycholinguistic Research, 24,* 409–436.

Eddy, D. M. (1982). Probabilistic reasoning in clinical medicine: Problems and opportunities. In D. Kahneman, P. Slovic, & A. Tversky (Eds.), *Judgment under uncertainty: Heuristics and biases* (pp. 249–267). Cambridge, England: Cambridge University Press.

Edelstyn, N. M. J., & Oyebode, F. (1999). A review of the phenomenology and cognitive neuropsychological origins of the Capgras Syndrome. *International Journal of Geriatric Psychiatry, 14,* 48–59.

Egan, D., & Schwartz, B. (1979). Chunking in the recall of symbolic drawings. *Memory & Cognition, 7,* 149–158.

Egly, R., Driver, J., & Rafal, R. D. (1994). Shifting visual attention between objects and locations: Evidence from normal and parietal lesion subjects. *Journal of Experimental Psychology: General, 123,* 161–177.

Eich, E., Reeves, J., Jaeger, B., & Graff-Radford, S. (1985). Memory for pain: Relation between past and present pain intensity. *Pain, 23,* 375–380.

Eich, J. E. (1980). The cue-dependent nature of state dependent retrieval. *Memory & Cognition, 8,* 157–173.

Einhorn, H., & Hogarth, R. (1981). Behavioral decision theory: Processes of judgment and choice. *Annual Review of Psychology, 32,* 53–88.

Einstein, G. O., McDaniel, M. A., & Lackey, S. (1989). Bizarre imagery, interference, and distinctiveness. *Journal of Experimental Psychology: Learning, Memory, and Cognition, 15,* 137–146.

Elliott, M. A., & Müller, H. J. (2000). Evidence for 40-Hz oscillatory short-term visual memory revealed by human reaction-time measurements. *Journal of Experimental Psychology: Learning, Memory and Cognition, 26,* 7093–7718.

Ellis, H. D., & De Pauw, K. W. (1994). The cognitive neuropsychiatric origins of the Capgras delusion. In A. S. David & J. C. Cutting (Eds.), *The neuropsychology of schizophrenia* (pp. 317–335). Hillsdale, NJ: Erlbaum.

Ellis, H. D., & Lewis, M. B. (2001). Capgras delusion: A window on face recognition. *Trends in Cognitive Sciences, 5,* 149–156.

Ellis, H. D., & Young, A. (1990). Accounting for delusional misidentifications. *British Journal of Psychiatry, 157,* 239–248.

Elstein, A., Holzman, G., Ravitch, M., Metheny, W., Holmes, M., Hoppe, R., et al. (1986). Comparison of physicians' decisions regarding estrogen replacement therapy for menopausal women and decisions derived from a decision analytic model. *American Journal of Medicine, 80,* 246–258.

Engel, A. K., & Singer, W. (2001). Temporal binding and the neural correlates of sensory awareness. *Trends in Cognitive Sciences, 5,* 16–25.

Engelkamp, J. (1986). Motor programs as part of the meaning of verbal items. In I. Kurcz, E. Shugar, & J. H. Danks (Eds.), *Knowledge and language* (pp. 115–137). Amsterdam: North-Holland.

Engelkamp, J. (1991). Imagery and enactment in paired-associate learning. In R. H. Logie & M. Denis (Eds.), *Mental images in human cognition* (pp. 119–128). Amsterdam: Elsevier.

Engelkamp, J., Zimmer, H., Mohr, G., & Sellen, O. (1994). Memory of self-performed tasks: Self-performing during recognition. *Memory & Cognition, 22,* 34–39.

Engle, R. W., & Kane, M. J. (In press). Executive attention, working memory capacity, and a two-factor theory of cognitive control.

Epley, N., & Gilovich, T. (2001). Putting adjustment back in the anchoring and adjustment heuristic: Differential processing of self-generated and experimenter-provided anchors. *Psychological Science, 12,* 391–396.

Ericsson, K. A. (2003). Exceptional memorizers: Made, not born. *Trends in Cognitive Sciences, 7,* 233–235.

Ericsson, K., Chase, W. G., & Faloon, S. (1980). Acquisition of a memory skill. *Science, 208,* 1181–1182.

Ernest, C. (1977). Imagery ability and cognition: A critical review. *Journal of Mental Imagery, 2,* 181–216.

Ervin-Tripp, S. (1993). Conversational discourse. In J. B. Gleason & N. B. Ratner (Eds.), *Psycholinguistics* (pp. 237–270). New York: Harcourt Brace Jovanovich.

Estes, Z. (2003). Domain differences in the structure of artifactual and natural categories. *Memory & Cognition, 31,* 199–214.

Evans, J. S. B. T. (1982). *The psychology of deductive reasoning.* London: Routledge & Kegan Paul.

Evans, J. S. B. T. (1989). *Bias in human reasoning.* Hillsdale, NJ: Erlbaum.

Evans, J. S. B. T. (1993). The mental model theory of conditional reasoning: Critical appraisal and revision. *Cognition, 48,* 1–20.

Evans, J. S. B. T. (2003). In two minds: Dual-process accounts of reasoning. *Trends in Cognitive Sciences, 7,* 454–459.

Evans, J. S. B. T., & Feeney, A. (2004). The role of prior belief in reasoning. In J. P. Leighton & R. J. Sternberg (Eds.), *The nature of reasoning* (pp. 78–102). New York: Cambridge University Press.

Evans, J. S. B. T., Handley, S. J., Perham, N., Over, D. E., & Thompson, V. A. (2000). Frequency versus probability formats in statistical word problems. *Cognition, 77,* 197–213.

Evans, J. S. B. T., Newstead, S. E., & Byrne, R. M. J. (1993). *Human reasoning: The psychology of deduction.* London: Erlbaum.

Evans, J. S. B. T., Over, D., & Manktelow, K. (1993). Reasoning, decision making and rationality. *Cognition, 49,* 165–187.

Eylon, B., & Reif, F. (1984). Effects of knowledge organization on task performance. *Cognition and Instruction, 1,* 5–44.

Eysenck, M. W. (1982). *Attention and arousal: Cognition and performance.* Berlin: Springer.

Farah, M. J. (1985). Psychophysical evidence for a shared representational medium for mental images and percepts. *Journal of Experimental Psychology: General, 114,* 91–103.

Farah, M. J. (1988). Is visual imagery really visual? Overlooked evidence from neuropsychology. *Psychological Review, 95,* 307–317.

Farah, M. J. (1989). Mechanisms of imagery-perception interaction. *Journal of Experimental Psychology: Human Perception and Performance, 15,* 203–211.

Farah, M. J. (1990). *Visual agnosia: Disorders of object recognition and what they tell us about normal vision.* Cambridge, MA: MIT Press.

Farah, M. J., Hammond, K. M., Levine, D. N., & Calvanio, R. (1988). Visual and spatial mental imagery: Dissociable systems of representation. *Cognitive Psychology, 20,* 439–462.

Farah, M. J., & Smith, A. (1983). Perceptual interference and facilitation with auditory imagery. *Perception & Psychophysics, 33,* 475–478.

Farah, M. J., Soso, M., & Dasheiff, R. (1992). Visual angle of the mind's eye before and after unilateral occipital lobectomy. *Journal of Experimental Psychology: Human Perception and Performance, 18,* 241–246.

Farah, M. J., Wilson, K. D., Drain, M., & Tanaka, J. (1998). What is "special" about face perception? *Psychological Review, 105,* 482–498.

Feldman, H., Goldin-Meadow, S., & Gleitman, L. R. (1978). Beyond Herodotus: The creation of language by linguistically deprived deaf children. In A. Lock (Ed.), *Action, gesture, and symbol: The emergence of language* (pp. 351–414). London: Academic Press.

Feldman Barrett, L., Tugade, M. M., & Engle, R. W. (2004). Individual differences in working memory capacity and dual-process theories of the mind. *Psychological Bulletin, 130,* 553–573.

Fiedler, K., Brinkmann, B., Betsch, T., & Wild, B. (2000). A sampling approach to biases in conditional probability judgments: Beyond base rate neglect and statistical format. *Journal of Experimental Psychology: General, 129,* 399–418.

Fillmore, C. (1982). Towards a descriptive framework for spatial deixis. In R. J. Jarvella & W. Klein (Eds.), *Speech, place and action: Studies in deixis and related topics* (pp. 31–60). Chichester, England: Wiley.

Finke, R. (1990). Creative imagery: Discoveries and inventions in visualization. Hillsdale, NJ: Erlbaum.

Finke, R. (1993). Mental imagery and creative discovery. In B. Roskos-Ewoldsen, M. J. Intons-Peterson, & R. Anderson (Eds.), *Imagery, creativity, and discovery* (pp. 255–285). New York: North-Holland.

Finke, R., & Kosslyn, S. M. (1980). Mental imagery acuity in the peripheral visual field. *Journal of Experimental Psychology: Human Perception and Performance, 6,* 126–139.

Finke, R. A., & Pinker, S. (1982). Spontaneous imagery scanning in mental extrapolation. *Journal of Experimental Psychology: Learning, Memory, & Cognition, 8,* 142–147.

Finke, R., & Slayton, K. (1988). Explorations of creative visual synthesis in mental imagery. *Memory & Cognition, 16,* 252–257.

Finucane, M. L., Alhakami, A., Slovic, P., & Johnson, S. M. (2000). The affect heuristic in judgments of risks and benefits. *Journal of Behavioral Decision Making, 13,* 1–17.

Fischhoff, B., Slovic, P., & Lichtenstein, S. (1978). Fault trees: Sensitivity of estimated failure probabilities to problem representation. *Journal of Experimental Psychology: Human Perception & Performance, 4,* 330–344.

Fisher, R., & Craik, F. I. M. (1977). The interaction between encoding and retrieval operations in cued recall. *Journal of Experimental Psychology: Human Learning and Memory, 3,* 701–711.

Fisher, R., Geiselman, R., & Amador, M. (1989). Field tests of the cognitive interview: Enhancing the recollection of actual victims and witnesses of crime. *Journal of Applied Psychology, 74,* 722–727.

Flanagan, O. (1991). *The science of the mind* (2nd ed.). Cambridge, MA: MIT Press.

Fodor, J. (1997). Connectionism and the problem of systematicity (continued): Why Smolensky's solution still doesn't work. *Cognition, 62,* 109–119.

Fodor, J., & Pylyshyn, Z. W. (1988). Connectionism and cognitive architecture: A critical analysis. *Cognition, 28,* 3–71.

Fong, G., Krantz, D., & Nisbett, R. (1986). The effects of statistical training on thinking about everyday problems. *Cognitive Psychology, 18,* 253–292.

Fong, G., & Nisbett, R. (1991). Immediate and delayed transfer of training effects in statistical reasoning. *Journal of Experimental Psychology: General, 120,* 34–45.

Ford, M. (1995). Two modes of mental representation and problem solution in syllogistic reasoning. *Cognition, 54,* 1–71.

Fox, E. (1994). Interference and negative priming from ignored distractors: The role of selection difficulty. *Perception & Psychophysics, 56,* 565–574.

Fox, E. (1995). Negative priming from ignored distractors in visual selection: A review. *Psychonomic Bulletin & Review, 2,* 145–173.

French, R. M. (1999). Catastrophic forgetting in connectionist networks. *Trends in Cognitive Science, 3,* 128–135.

French, R. M. (2002). The computational modeling of analogy-making. *Trends in Cognitive Sciences, 6,* 200–205.

Freyd, J. J. (1996). *Betrayal trauma: The logic of forgetting childhood abuse.* Cambridge, MA: Harvard University Press.

Freyd, J. J. (1998). Science in the memory debate. *Ethics & Behavior, 8,* 101–113.

Fried, L. S., & Holyoak, K. J. (1984). Induction of category distributions: A framework for classification learning. *Journal of Experimental Psychology: Learning, Memory and Cognition, 10,* 234–257.

Friedman, A. (1979). Framing pictures: The role of knowledge in automatized encoding and memory for gist. *Journal of Experimental Psychology: General, 108,* 316–355.

Friedman, A., & Brown, N. R. (2000a). Reasoning about geography. *Journal of Experimental Psychology: General, 129,* 193–219.

Friedman, A., & Brown, N. R. (2000b). Updating geographical knowledge: Principles of coherence and inertia. *Journal of Experimental Psychology: Learning, Memory and Cognition, 26,* 900–914.

Friedman-Hill, S. R., Robertson, L. C., & Treisman, A. (1995). Parietal contributions to visual feature binding: Evidence from a patient with bilateral lesions. *Science, 269,* 853–855.

Fries, P., Reynolds, J. H., Rorie, A. E., & Desimone, R. (2001). Modulation of oscillatory neural synchronization by selective visual attention. *Science, 291,* 1560–1563.

Fromkin, V. (1993). Speech production. In J. B. Gleason & N. B. Ratner (Eds.), *Psycholinguistics* (pp. 271–300). New York: Harcourt Brace Jovanovich.

Frost, P. (2000). The quality of false memory over time: Is memory for misinformation "remembered" or "known"? *Psychonomic Bulletin & Review, 7,* 531–536.

Gabrieli, J. D. E. (1998). Cognitive neuroscience of human memory. *Annual Review of Psychology, 49,* 87–115.

Gabrieli, J., Fleischman, D., Keane, M., Reminger, S., & Morrell, F. (1995). Double dissociation between memory systems underlying explicit and implicit memory in the human brain. *Psychological Science, 6,* 76–82.

Gallistel, C. R. (2002). Language and spatial frames of reference in mind and brain. *Trends in Cognitive Sciences, 6,* 321–322.

Gallo, D. A., Roberts, M. J., & Seamon, J. G. (1997). Remembering words not presented in lists: Can we avoid creating false memories? *Psychonomic Bulletin & Review, 4,* 271–276.

Galton, F. (1883). *Inquiries into human faculty.* London: Dent.

Gardiner, J. M. (1988). Functional aspects of recollective experience. *Memory & Cognition, 16,* 309–313.

Garry, M., & Polaschek, D. L. L. (2000). Imagination and memory. *Current Directions in Psychological Science, 9,* 6–10.

Gathercole, S. E., & Pickering, S. J. (2000). Assessment of working memory in six- and seven-year-old children. *Journal of Educational Psychology, 92,* 377–390.

Gathercole, S. E., Service, E., Hitch, G., Adams, A.-M., & Martin, A. J. (1999). Phonological short-term memory and vocabulary development: Further evidence on the nature of the relationship. *Applied Cognitive Psychology, 13,* 65–77.

Gauthier, I. (2000). Expertise for cars and birds recruits brain areas involved in face recognition. *Nature Neuroscience, 3,* 191–197.

Gauthier, I. L., Skudlarski, P., Gore, J. C., & Anderson, A. W. (2000). Expertise for cars and birds recruits brain areas involved in face recognition. *Nature Neuroscience, 3,* 191–197.

Gazzaniga, M. S., Ivry, R. B., & Mangun, G. R. (1998). *Cognitive neuroscience: The biology of the mind.* New York: Norton.

Geiselman, R. E., Schroppel, T., Tubridy, A., Konishi, T., & Rodriguez, V. (2000). Objectivity bias in eyewitness performance. *Applied Cognitive Psychology, 14,* 323–332.

Gelman, S., & Wellman, H. (1991). Insides and essences: Early understandings of the non-obvious. *Cognition, 38,* 213–244.

Gentner, D. (1983). Structure mapping: A theoretical framework for analogy. *Cognitive Science, 7,* 155–170.

Gentner, D. (1989). The mechanisms of analogical learning. In S. Vosniadou & A. Ortony (Eds.), *Similarity, analogy, and thought* (pp. 199–241). Cambridge, England: Cambridge University Press.

Gentner, D., & Jeziorski, M. (1989). Historical shifts in the use of analogy in science. In B. Gholson, W. Shadish, R. Neimeyer, & A. Houts (Eds.), *Psychology of science: Contributions to metascience* (pp. 296–325). Cambridge, England: Cambridge University Press.

Gibson, E., Bishop, C., Schiff, W., & Smith, J. (1964). Comparison of meaningfulness and pronounceability as grouping principles in the perception and retention of verbal material. *Journal of Experimental Psychology, 67,* 173–182.

Gick, M. (1986). Problem-solving strategies. *Educational Psychologist, 21,* 99–120.

Gick, M., & Holyoak, K. J. (1980). Analogical problem solving. *Cognitive Psychology, 12,* 306–355.

Gick, M., & Holyoak, K. J. (1983). Schema induction and analogical transfer. *Cognitive Psychology, 15,* 1–38.

Gigerenzer, G. (1991). From tools to theories: A heuristic of discovery in cognitive psychology. *Psychological Review, 98,* 254–267.

Gigerenzer, G., Hell, W., & Blank, H. (1988). Presentation and content: The use of base rates as a continuous variable. *Journal of Experimental Psychology: Human Perception and Performance, 14,* 513–525.

Gigerenzer, G., & Hoffrage, U. (1995). How to improve Bayesian reasoning without instruction: Frequency formats. *Psychological Review, 102,* 684–704.

Gigerenzer, G., & Hug, K. (1992). Domain-specific reasoning: Social contracts, cheating and perspective change. *Cognition, 43,* 127–172.

Gilbert, A. N., Crouch, M., & Kemp, S. (1998). Olfactory and visual mental imagery. *Journal of Mental Imagery, 22,* 137–146.

Gilbert, D., & Ebert, J. E. J. (2002). Decisions and revisions: The affective forecasting of changeable outcomes. *Journal of Personality and Social Psychology, 82,* 503–514.

Gilbert, D., Morewedge, C. K., Risen, J. L., & Wilson, T. D. (2004). Looking forward to looking backward. *Psychological Science, 15,* 346–350.

Gilbert, D. T. (1989). Thinking lightly about others: Automatic components of the social inference process. In J. S. Uleman & J. A. Bargh (Eds.), *Unintended thought* (pp. 189–211). New York: Guilford.

Gilbert, S. J., & Shallice, T. (2002). Task switching: A PDP model. *Cognitive Psychology, 44,* 297–337.

Gilhooly, K. J. (1988). *Thinking: Direct, undirected and creative* (2nd ed.). New York: Academic Press.

Gilhooly, K. J. (1999). Creative thinking: Myths and misconceptions. In S. Della Sala (Ed.), *Mind myths: Exploring popular assumptions about the mind and brain* (pp. 138–156). New York: Wiley.

Gilhooly, K. J., Logie, R. H., Wetherick, N., & Wynn, V. (1993). Working memory and strategies in syllogistic-reasoning tasks. *Memory & Cognition, 21,* 115–124.

Gilovich, T. (1983). Biased evaluation and persistence in gambling. *Journal of Personality & Social Psychology, 44,* 1110–1126.

Gilovich, T. (1991). *How we know what isn't so.* New York: Free Press.

Gilovich, T., & Douglas, C. (1986). Biased evaluations of randomly determined gambling outcomes. *Journal of Experimental Social Psychology, 22,* 228–241.

Gilovich, T., & Medvec, V. H. (1995). The experience of regret: What, when and why. *Psychological Review, 102,* 379–395.

Gilovich, T., Medvec, V. H., & Kahneman, D. (1998). Varieties of regret: A debate and partial resolution. *Psychological Review, 105,* 602–605.

Girotto, V. (2004). Task understanding. In J. P. Leighton & R. J. Sternberg (Eds.), *The nature of reasoning* (pp. 103–128). New York: Cambridge University Press.

Girotto, V., & Gonzalez, M. (2001). Solving probabilistic and statistical problems: A matter of information structure and question form. *Cognition, 78,* 247–276.

Glanzer, M., & Cunitz, A. R. (1966). Two storage mechanisms in free recall. *Journal of Verbal Learning and Verbal Behavior, 5,* 351–360.

Glenberg, A., & Adams, F. (1978). Type I rehearsal and recognition. *Journal of Verbal Learning and Verbal Behavior, 17,* 455–463.

Glenberg, A., Smith, S. M., & Green, C. (1977). Type I rehearsal: Maintenance and more. *Journal of Verbal Learning and Verbal Behavior, 16,* 339–352.

Glisky, E. L., Polster, M. R., & Routhieaux, B. C. (1995). Double dissociation between item and source memory. *Neuropsychology, 9,* 229–235.

Gluck, M., & Rumelhart, D. (1990). *Neuroscience and connectionist theory.* Hillsdale, NJ: Erlbaum.

Glucksberg, S., & Danks, J. (1968). Effects of discriminative labels and of nonsense labels upon availability of novel function. *Journal of Verbal Learning and Verbal Behavior, 7,* 72–76.

Gobet, F., & Simon, H. A. (1996a). Recall of random and distorted chess positions: Implications for the theory of expertise. *Memory & Cognition, 24,* 493–503.

Gobet, F., & Simon, H. A. (1996b). The roles of recognition processes and look-ahead search in time-constrained expert problem solving: Evidence from Grand-master-level chess. *Psychological Science, 7,* 52–55.

Gobet, F., & Simon, H. A. (2000). Reply to Lassiter. *Psychological Science, 11,* 174–175.

Godden, D. R., & Baddeley, A. D. (1975). Context-dependent memory in two natural environments: On land and underwater. *British Journal of Psychology, 66,* 325–332.

Goebel, R., Khorram-Sefat, D., Muckli, L., Hacker, H., & Singer, W. (1998). The constructive nature of vision: Direct evidence from functional magnetic resonance imaging studies of apparent motion and motion imagery. *European Journal of Neuroscience, 10,* 1563–1573.

Goff, L. M., & Roediger III, H. L. (1998). Imagination inflation for action events: Repeated imaginings lead to illusory recollections. *Memory & Cognition, 26,* 20–33.

Goldenberg, G., Müllbacher, W., & Nowak, A. (1995). Imagery without perception—A case study of anosognosia for cortical blindness. *Neuropsychologia, 33,* 1373–1382.

Goldenberg, J., Mazursky, D., & Solomon, S. (1999). Creative sparks. *Science, 285,* 1495–1496.

Goldin-Meadow, S. (2003). *The resilience of language: What gesture creation in deaf children can tell us about how all children learn language.* New York: Psychology Press.

Goldman, P., Wolters, N., & Winograd, E. (1992). A demonstration of incubation in anagram problem solving. *Bulletin of the Psychonomic Society, 30,* 36–38.

Goldman-Rakic, P. S. (1987). Development of cortical circuitry and cognitive function. *Child Development, 58,* 601–622.

Goldman-Rakic, P. S. (1995). Architecture of the prefrontal cortex and the central executive. In J. Grafman & K. J. Holyoak (Eds.), *Structure and functions of the human prefrontal cortex* (Annals of the New York Academy of Sciences, Vol. 769, pp. 71–83). New York: New York Academy of Sciences.

Goldman-Rakic, P. S. (1998). The prefrontal landscape: Implications of functional architecture for understanding human mentation and the central executive. In A. C. Roberts & T. W. Robbins (Eds.), *The prefrontal cortex: Executive and cognitive functions* (pp. 87–102). New York: Oxford University Press.

Goldstone, R. (1996). Alignment-based nonmonotonicities in similarity. *Journal of Experimental Psychology: Learning, Memory and Cognition, 22,* 988–1001.

Goldvarg, Y., & Johnson-Laird, P. N. (2000). Illusions in modal reasoning. *Memory & Cognition, 28,* 282–294.

Golier, J. A., Yehuda, R., & Southwick, S. (1997). Memory and posttraumatic stress disorder. In P. S. Appelbaum, L. A. Uyehara, & M. R. Elin (Eds.), *Trauma and memory: Clinical and legal controversies* (pp. 225–242). New York: Oxford University Press.

Goodale, M. A. (1995). The cortical organization of visual perception and visuomotor control. In S. M. Kosslyn & D. Osherson (Eds.), *Visual cognition: An invitation to cognitive science* (2nd ed., pp. 167–213). Cambridge, MA: MIT Press.

Goodale, M. A., & Milner, A. D. (2004). *Sight unseen.* New York: Oxford University Press.

Goodman, G. S., Ghetti, S., Quas, J. A., Edelstein, R. S., Alexander, K. W., Redlich, A., D., et al. (2003). A prospective study of memory for child sexual abuse: New findings relevant to the repressed-memory controversy. *Psychological Science, 14,* 113–118.

Goodman, N. (1972). Seven strictures on similarity. In N. Goodman (Ed.), *Problems and projects* (pp. 437–446). New York: Bobbs-Merrill.

Gordon, P. (1986). Level-ordering in lexical development. *Cognition, 21,* 73–93.

Gordon, P., & Scearce, K. (1995). Pronominalization and discourse coherence: Discourse structure and pronoun interpretation. *Memory & Cognition, 23,* 313–323.

Gorenstein, G., & Ellsworth, P. (1980). Effect of choosing an incorrect photograph on later identification by an eyewitness. *Journal of Applied Psychology, 65,* 616–622.

Graesser, A. C., Millis, K. K., & Zwaan, R. A. (1997). Discourse comprehension. *Annual Review of Psychology, 48,* 163–189.

Graesser, A. C., Woll, S. B., Kowalski, D. J., & Smith, D. A. (1980). Memory for typical and atypical actions in scripted activities. *Journal of Experimental Psychology: Human Learning and Memory, 6,* 503–515.

Graf, P., Mandler, G., & Haden, P. E. (1982). Simulating amnesic symptoms in normals. *Science, 218,* 1243–1244.

Graf, P., & Masson, M. (Eds.). (1993). *Implicit memory: New directions in cognition, development and neuropsychology.* Hillsdale, NJ: Erlbaum.

Graf, P., & Schacter, D. L. (1985). Implicit and explicit memory for new associations in normal and amnesic subjects. *Journal of Experimental Psychology: Learning, Memory and Cognition, 11,* 501–518.

Grainger, J., & Whitney, C. (2004). Does the huamn mnid raed wrods as a wlohe? *Trends in Cognitive Sciences, 8,* 58–59.

Grant, H. M., Bredahl, L. C., Clay, J., Ferrie, J., Groves, J. E., McDorman, T. A., et al. (1998). Context-dependent memory for meaningful material: Information for students. *Applied Cognitive Psychology, 12,* 617–623.

Gray, J. R., Chabris, C. F., & Braver, T. S. (2003). Neural mechanisms of general fluid intelligence. *Nature Neuroscience, 6,* 316–322.

Graziano, M. S. A., Taylor, C. S. R., & Moore, T. (2002). Complex movements evoked by microstimulation of precentral cortex. *Neuron, 34,* 841–851.

Greenberg, J., Ferguson, C., & Moravcsik, E. (Eds.). (1978). *Universals of human language.* Stanford, CA: Stanford University Press.

Greene, E., Flynn, M., & Loftus, E. F. (1982). Inducing resistance of misleading information. *Journal of Verbal Learning and Verbal Behavior, 21,* 207–219.

Greenwald, A., & Banaji, M. (1995). Implicit social cognition: Attitudes, self-esteem and stereotypes. *Psychological Review, 102,* 4–27.

Grice, H. P. (1975). Logic and conversation. In P. Cole & J. L. Morgan (Eds.), *Syntax and semantics 3: Speech acts* (pp. 41–58). New York: Academic Press.

Griggs, R. (1983). The role of problem content in the selection task and in the THOG problem. In J. S. B. Evans (Ed.), *Thinking and reasoning: Psychological approaches* (pp. 17–43). London: Routledge & Kegan Paul.

Griggs, R., & Cox, J. R. (1982). The elusive thematic-materials effect in Wason's selection task. *British Journal of Psychology, 73,* 407–420.

Gruber, H. E. (1981). *Darwin on man: A psychological study of scientific creativity* (2nd ed.). Chicago: University of Chicago Press.

Gruber, H. E., & Wallace, D. B. (2001). Creative work: The case of Charles Darwin. *American Psychologist, 56,* 346–349.

Guilford, J. (1967). *The nature of human intelligence.* New York: Scribner.

Guilford, J. (1979). Some incubated thoughts on incubation. *Journal of Creative Behavior, 13,* 1–8.

Hagiwara, H., Sugioka, Y., Ito, T., Kawamura, M., & Shiota, J. (1999). Neurolinguistic evidence for rule-based nominal suffixation. *Language, 75,* 739–763.

Halle, M. (1990). Phonology. In D. Osherson & H. Lasnik (Eds.), *Language: An invitation to cognitive science* (pp. 43–68). Cambridge, MA: MIT Press.

Halligan, P., & Marshall, J. (1994). Toward a principled explanation of unilateral neglect. *Cognitive Neuropsychology, 2,* 167–206.

Halpern, D. (1984). *Thought and knowledge: An introduction to critical thinking.* Hillsdale, NJ: Erlbaum.

Hamann, S. (2001). Cognitive and neural mechanisms of emotional memory. *Trends in Cognitive Sciences, 5,* 394–400.

Hamill, R., Wilson, T. D., & Nisbett, R. E. (1980). Insensitivity to sample bias: Generalizing from atypical cases. *Journal of Personality and Social Psychology, 39,* 578–589.

Hancock, P. J. B., Bruce, V., & Burton, A. M. (2000). Recognition of unfamiliar faces. *Trends in Cognitive Sciences, 4,* 330–344.

Handel, S. (1989). *Listening: An introduction to the perception of auditory events.* Cambridge, MA: MIT Press.

Harber, K. D., & Pennebaker, J. W. (1992). Overcoming traumatic memories. In S.-A. Christianson (Ed.), *The handbook of emotion and memory: Research and theory* (pp. 359–387). Hillsdale, NJ: Erlbaum.

Hardiman, P., Dufresne, R., & Mestre, J. (1989). The relation between problem categorization and problem solving among experts and novices. *Memory & Cognition, 17,* 627–638.

Harley, T. A., & Bown, H. E. (1998). What causes a tip-of-the-tongue state? Evidence for lexical neighbourhood effects in speech production. *British Journal of Psychology, 89,* 151–174.

Harwood, D. G., Barker, W. W., Ownby, R. L., & Duara, R. (1999). Prevalence and correlates of Capgras syndrome in Alzheimer's disease. *International Journal of Geriatric Psychiatry, 14,* 415–420.

Hasher, L., Goldstein, D., & Toppino, T. (1977). Frequency and the conference of referential validity. *Journal of Verbal Learning and Verbal Behavior, 16,* 107–112.

Hasselmo, M. E. (1999). Neuromodulation: Acetylcholine and memory consolidation. *Trends in Cognitive Science, 6,* 351–359.

Haugeland, J. (Ed.). (1997). *Mind design 2: Philosophy, psychology, artificial intelligence* (2nd ed.). Cambridge, MA: MIT Press.

Hawkins, J. (Ed.). (1988). *Explaining language universals.* London: Basil Blackwell.

Hay, D., Young, A., & Ellis, A. (1991). Routes through the face recognition system. *Quarterly Journal of Experimental Psychology: Human Experimental Psychology, 43A,* 761–791.

Hayes, J. (1985). Three problems in teaching general skills. In S. Chipman, J. Segal, & R. Glaser (Eds.), *Thinking and learning skills* (pp. 391–406). Hillsdale, NJ: Erlbaum.

Hayes, J., & Simon, H. (1977). Psychological differences among problem solving isomorphs. In N. Castellan, D. Pisoni, & G. Potts (Eds.), *Cognitive theory* (pp. 21–42). Hillsdale, NJ: Erlbaum.

Hayward, W., & Williams, P. (2000). Viewpoint dependence and object discriminability. *Psychological Science, 11,* 7–12.

Heaps, C., & Nash, M. (1999). Individual differences in imagination influation. *Psychonomic Bulletin & Review, 6,* 313–318.

Heaps, C. M., & Nash, M. (2001). Comparing recollective experience in true and false autobiographical memories. *Journal of Experimental Psychology: Learning, Memory and Cognition, 27,* 920–930.

Hegarty, M. (2004). Mechanical reasoning by mental simulation. *Trends in Cognitive Sciences, 8,* 280–285.

Heider, E. R. (1972). Universals in color naming and memory. *Journal of Experimental Psychology, 93,* 10–20.

Heil, M., Rösler, F., & Hennighausen, E. (1993). Imagery-perception interaction depends on the shape of the image: A reply to Farah. *Journal of Experimental Psychology: Human Perception and Performance, 19,* 1313–1319.

Heil, M., Rösler, F., & Hennighausen, E. (1994). Dynamics of activation in long-term memory: The retrieval of verbal, pictorial, spatial and color information. *Journal of Experimental Psychology: Learning, Memory and Cognition, 20,* 169–184.

Heilman, K., Watson, R., & Valenstein, E. (1985). Neglect and related disorders. In K. Heilman & E. Valenstein (Eds.), *Clinical neuropsychology* (pp. 243–293). New York: Oxford University Press.

Heit, E. (2000). Properties of inductive reasoning. *Psychonomic Bulletin & Review, 7,* 569–592.

Heit, E., & Bott, L. (2000). Knowledge selection in category learning. In D. L. Medin (Ed.), *The psychology of learning and motivation: Advances in research and theory,* Vol. 39 (pp. 163–199). San Diego, CA: Academic Press.

Heller, J., & Reif, F. (1984). Prescribing effective human problem-solving processes: Problem description in physics. *Cognition and Instruction, 1*, 177–216.

Helmuth, L. (2001). Boosting brain activity from the outside in. *Science, 292*, 1284–1286.

Henderson, J. M. & Hollingworth, A. (2003). Global transsaccadic change blindness during scene perception. *Psychological Science, 14*, 493–497.

Henderson, J. M., Weeks, P. A., Jr., & Hollingworth. A. (1999). The effects of semantic consistency on eye movements during complex scene viewing. *Journal of Experimental Psychology: Human Perception and Performance, 25*, 210–228.

Henle, M. (1962). On the relation between logic and thinking. *Psychological Review, 69*, 366–378.

Henle, M. (1978). Foreword. In R. Revlin & R. Mayer (Eds.), *Human reasoning* (pp. xiii–xviii). New York: Wiley.

Hertwig, R., & Ortmann, A. (2003). Economists' and psychologists' experimental practices: How they differ, why they differ, and how they could converge. In I. Brocas & J. D. Carrillo (Eds.), *The psychology of economic decisions: Rationality and well-being*, Vol. 1 (pp. 253–272). New York: Oxford University Press.

Hicks, J. L., & Marsh, R. L. (1999). Remember-Know judgments can depend on how memory is tested. *Psychonomic Bulletin & Review, 6*, 117–122.

Higbee, K. L. (1977). *Your memory: How it works and how to improve it.* Englewood Cliffs, NJ: Prentice-Hall.

Higgins, E. T., & Bargh, J. A. (1987). Social cognition and social perception. *Annual Review of Psychology, 38*, 1–95.

Hilgard, E. R. (1968). *The experience of hypnosis.* New York: Harcourt Brace Jovanovich.

Hillis, A., & Caramazza, A. (1991). Category-specific naming and comprehension impairment: A double dissociation. *Brain, 114*, 2081–2094.

Hillyard, S. A., Vogel, E. K., & Luck, S. J. (1998). Sensory gain control (amplification) as a mechanism of selective attention: Electrophysiological and neuroimaging evidence. *Philosophical Transactions of the Royal Society: Biological Sciences, 353*, 1257–1270.

Hilton, D. (1995). The social context of reasoning: Conversational inference and rational judgment. *Psychological Bulletin, 118*, 248–271.

Hilton, D. J. (2003). Pychology and the financial markets: Applications to understanding and remedying irrational decision-making. In I. Brocas & J. D. Carrillo (Eds.), *The psychology of economic decisions: Rationality and well-being*, Vol. 1 (pp. 273–297). New York: Oxford University Press.

Hilts, P. J. (1995). *Memory's ghost: The strange tale of Mr. M and the nature of memory.* New York: Simon & Schuster.

Hinsley, D., Hayes, J., & Simon, H. (1977). From words to equations: Meaning and representation in algebra word problems. In P. Carpenter & M. Just (Eds.), *Cognitive processes in comprehension* (pp. 89–106). Hillsdale, NJ: Erlbaum.

Hirshman, E. (1998). On the logic of testing the independence assumption in the process-dissociation procedure. *Memory & Cognition, 26*, 857–859.

Hirst, W. (1986). The psychology of attention. In J. E. LeDoux & W. Hirst (Eds.), *Mind and brain* (pp. 105–141). Cambridge, England: Cambridge University Press.

Hirst, W., & Kalmar, D. (1987). Characterizing attentional resources. *Journal of Experimental Psychology: General, 116*, 68–81.

Hirst, W., Spelke, E., Reaves, C., Caharack, G., & Neisser, U. (1980). Dividing attention without alternation or automaticity. *Journal of Experimental Psychology: General, 109*, 98–117.

Hitch, G. J., Towse, J. N., & Hutton, U. (2001). What limits children's working memory span? Theoretical accounts and applications for scholastic development. *Journal of Experimental Psychology: General, 130*, 184–198.

Hochberg, J. (1978). *Perception* (2nd ed.). Englewood Cliffs, NJ: Prentice-Hall.

Hochberg, J. (1986). Representation of motion and space in video and cinematic displays. In K. J. Boff, L. Kaufman, & J. P. Thomas (Eds.), *Handbook of perception and human performance*, Vol. 1 (pp. 22:1–22:64). New York: Wiley.

Hodges, J. R., & Graham, K. S. (2001). Episodic memory: Insights from semantic dementia. In A. D. Baddeley, J. P. Aggleton, & M. A. Conway (Eds.), *Episodic memory: New directions in research* (pp. 132–152). New York: Oxford University Press.

Hoffman, D. D. (2000). *Visual intelligence: How we create what we see.* New York: Norton.

Holding, D. (1985). *The psychology of chess.* Hillsdale, NJ: Erlbaum.

Holland, J. H., Holyoak, K. F., Nisbett, R. E., & Thagard, P. R. (1986). *Induction.* Cambridge, MA: MIT Press.

Holmberg, D., & Homes, J. G. (1994). Reconstruction of relationship memories: A mental models approach. In N. Schwarz & S. Sudman (Eds.), *Autobiographical memory and the validity of retrospective reports* (pp. 267–288). New York: Springer.

Holmes, J. B., Waters, H. S., & Rajaram, S. (1998). The phenomenology of false memories: Episodic content and confidence. *Journal of Experimental Psychology: Learning, Memory and Cognition, 24,* 1026–1040.

Holyoak, K. J. (1984). Analogical thinking and human intelligence. In R. J. Sternberg (Ed.), *Advances in the psychology of human intelligence* (pp. 199–230). Hillsdale, NJ: Erlbaum.

Holyoak, K. J. (1987). Review of parallel distributed processing. *Science, 236,* 992.

Holyoak, K. J., & Koh, H. (1987). Surface and structural similarity in analogical transfer. *Memory & Cognition, 15,* 332–340.

Holyoak, K. J., & Thagard, P. (1989). Analogical mapping by constraint satisfaction. *Cognitive Science, 13,* 295–355.

Homa, D., Dunbar, S., & Nohre, L. (1991). Instance frequency, categorization, and the modulating effect of experience. *Journal of Experimental Psychology: Learning, Memory and Cognition, 17,* 444–458.

Homa, D., Sterling, S., & Trepel, L. (1981). Limitation of exemplar-based generalization and the abstraction of categorical information. *Journal of Experimental Psychology: Human Learning and Memory, 7,* 418–439.

Hornby, P. (1974). Surface structure and presupposition. *Journal of Verbal Learning and Verbal Behavior, 13,* 530–538.

Horowitz, M. J., & Reidbord, S. P. (1992). Memory, emotion, and response to trauma. In S.-A. Christianson (Ed.), *The handbook of emotion and memory: Research and theory* (pp. 343–357). Hillsdale, NJ: Erlbaum.

Howe, M. L., Rabinowitz, F. M., & Powell, T. L. (1998). Individual differences in working memory and reasoning-remembering relationships in solving class-inclusion problems. *Memory & Cognition, 26,* 1089–1101.

Howes, D., & Solomon, R. (1951). Visual duration thresholds as a function of word probability. *Journal of Experimental Psychology, 41,* 401–410.

Howes, M., Siegel, M., & Brown, F. (1993). Early childhood memories: Accuracy and affect. *Cognition, 47,* 95–119.

Hsee, C. K. (1999). Value seeking and prediction-decision inconsistency: Why don't people take what they predict they'll like the most? *Psychonomic Bulletin & Review, 6,* 555–561.

Hsee, C. K. & Rottenstreich, Y. (2004). Music, pandas, and muggers: On the affective psychology of value. *Journal of Experimental Psychology: General, 133,* 23–30.

Hubel, D. (1963). The visual cortex of the brain. *Scientific American, 209*(November), 54–62.

Hubel, D., & Wiesel, T. (1959). Receptive fields of single neurones in the cat's visual cortex. *Journal of Physiology, 148,* 574–591.

Hubel, D., & Wiesel, T. (1968). Receptive fields and functional architecture of monkey striate cortex. *Journal of Physiology, 195,* 215–243.

Hummel, J., & Biederman, I. (1992). Dynamic binding in a neural network for shape recognition. *Psychological Review, 99,* 480–517.

Hummel, J. E., & Stankiewicz, B. J. (1998). Two roles for attention in shape perception: A structural description model of visual scrutiny. *Visual Cognition, 5,* 49–79.

Humphreys, M. S., Dennis, S., Maguire, A. M., Reynolds, K., Bolland, S. W., & Hughes, J. D. (2003). What you get out of memory depends on the question you ask. *Journal of Experimental Psychology: Learning, Memory and Cognition, 29,* 797–812.

Hunt, R., & Ellis, H. D. (1974). Recognition memory and degree of semantic contextual change. *Journal of Experimental Psychology, 103,* 1153–1159.

Husserl, E. (1931). *Ideas.* New York: Collier.

Hutchison, K. A. (2003). Is semantic priming due to association strength or feature overlap? A *micro* analytic review. *Psychonomic Bulletin & Review, 10,* 785–813.

Hyde, T. S., & Jenkins, J. J. (1969). Differential effects of incidental tasks on the organization of recall of a list of highly associated words. *Journal of Experimental Psychology, 82,* 472–481.

Hyde, T. S., & Jenkins, J. J. (1973). Recall for words as a function of semantic, graphic, and syntactic orienting tasks. *Journal of Verbal Learning and Verbal Behavior, 12,* 471–480.

Hyman, I. E., Jr. (2000). Creating false autobiographical memories: Why people believe their memory errors. In E. Winograd, R. Fivush, & W. Hirst (Eds.), *Ecological approaches to cognition: Essays in honor of Ulric Neisser.* Hillsdale, NJ: Erlbaum.

Hyman, I. E., Jr., & Billings, F. J. (1998). Individual differences and the creation of false childhood memories. *Memory, 6*, 1–20.

Hyman, I. E., Jr., Husband, T., & Billings, F. (1995). False memories of childhood experiences. *Applied Cognitive Psychology, 9*, 181–198.

Intons-Peterson, M. J. (1983). Imagery paradigms: How vulnerable are they to experimenters' expectations? *Journal of Experimental Psychology: Human Perception & Performance, 9*, 394–412.

Intons-Peterson, M. J. (1999). Comments and caveats about "scanning visual mental images." *Cahiers de Psychologie Cognitive, 18*, 534–540.

Intons-Peterson, M., & White, A. (1981). Experimenter naiveté and imaginal judgments. *Journal of Experimental Psychology: Human Perception and Performance, 7*, 833–843.

Intraub, H., Bender, R., & Mangels, J. (1992). Looking at pictures but remembering scenes. *Journal of Experimental Psychology: Learning, Memory and Cognition, 18*, 180–191.

Intraub, H., & Bodamer, J. (1993). Boundary extension: Fundamental aspect of pictorial representation or encoding artifact? *Journal of Experimental Psychology: Learning, Memory and Cognition, 19*, 1387–1397.

Intraub, H., Gottesman, C. V., & Bills, A. J. (1998). Effects of perceiving and imagining scenes on memory for pictures. *Journal of Experimental Psychology: Learning, Memory and Cognition, 24*, 1–16.

Intraub, H., & Richardson, M. (1989). Wide-angle memories of close-up scenes. *Journal of Experimental Psychology: Learning, Memory and Cognition, 15*, 179–187.

Isha, A., & Sagi, D. (1995). Common mechanisms of visual imagery and perception. *Science, 268*, 1772–1774.

Jackendoff, R. (1972). *Semantic interpretation in generative grammar.* Cambridge, MA: MIT Press.

Jackendoff, R. (1987). *Consciousness and the computational mind.* Cambridge, MA: MIT Press.

Jacoby, L. L. (1978). On interpreting the effects of repetition: Solving a problem versus remembering a solution. *Journal of Verbal Learning and Verbal Behavior, 17*, 649–667.

Jacoby, L. L. (1983). Remembering the data: Analyzing interactive processes in reading. *Journal of Verbal Learning and Verbal Behavior, 22*, 485–508.

Jacoby, L. L. (1991). A process dissociation framework: Separating automatic from intentional uses of memory. *Journal of Memory and Language, 30*, 513–541.

Jacoby, L. L. (1998). Invariance in automatic influences of memory: Toward a user's guide for the process-dissociation procedure. *Journal of Experimental Psychology: Learning, Memory and Cognition, 24*, 3–26.

Jacoby, L. L., Allan, L., Collins, J., & Larwill, L. (1988). Memory influences subjective experience: Noise judgments. *Journal of Experimental Psychology: Learning, Memory and Cognition, 14*, 240–247.

Jacoby, L. L., & Dallas, M. (1981). On the relationship between autobiographical memory and perceptual learning. *Journal of Experimental Psychology: General, 3*, 306–340.

Jacoby, L. L., Jones, T. C., & Dolan, P. O. (1998). Two effects of repetition: Support for a dual process model of know judgments and exclusion errors. *Psychonomic Bulletin & Review, 5*, 705–509.

Jacoby, L. L., & Kelley, C. (1992). A process-dissociation framework for investigating unconscious influences: Freudian slips, projective tests, subliminal perception, and signal detection theory. *Current Directions in Psychological Science, 1*, 174–179.

Jacoby, L. L., Kelley, C. M., Brown, J., & Jasechko, J. (1989). Becoming famous overnight: Limits on the ability to avoid unconscious influences of the past. *Journal of Personality and Social Psychology, 56*, 326–338.

Jacoby, L. L., Levy, B. A., & Steinbach, K. (1992). Episodic transfer and automaticity: Integration of data-driven and conceptually-driven processing in rereading. *Journal of Experimental Psychology: Learning, Memory and Cognition, 18*, 15–24.

Jacoby, L. L., Lindsay, D. S., & Hessels, S. (2003). Item-specific control of automatic processes: Stroop process dissociations. *Psychonomic Bulletin & Review, 10*, 638–644.

Jacoby, L. L., & Witherspoon, D. (1982). Remembering without awareness. *Canadian Journal of Psychology, 36*, 300–324.

James, L. E., & Burke, D. M. (2000). Phonological priming effects on word retrieval and Tip-of-the-Tongue experiences in young and older adults. *Journal of Experimental Psychology: Learning, Memory and Cognition, 26,* 1378–1391.

James, W. (1890). *The principles of psychology,* Vol. 2. New York: Dover.

Jankowiak, J., Kinsbourne, M., Shalev, R. S., & Bachman, D. L. (1992). Preserved visual imagery and categorization in a case of associative visual agnosia. *Journal of Cognitive Neuroscience, 4,* 119–131.

Jeffries, R., Polson, P., Razran, L., & Atwood, M. (1977). A process model for missionaries-cannibals and other river-crossing problems. *Cognitive Psychology, 9,* 412–440.

Jennings, D. L., Amabile, T. M., & Ross, L. (1982). Informal covariation assessment: Data-based versus theory-based judgments. In D. Kahneman, P. Slovic, & A. Tversky (Eds.), *Judgments under uncertainty: Heuristics and biases* (pp. 211–230). Cambridge, England: Cambridge University Press.

Jepson, D., Krantz, D., & Nisbett, R. (1983). Inductive reasoning: Competence or skill? *Behavioral and Brain Sciences, 6,* 494–501.

Jobe, J., Tourangeau, R., & Smith, A. (1993). Contributions of survey research to the understanding of memory. *Applied Cognitive Psychology, 7,* 567–584.

Johnson, H., & Seifert, C. (1994). Sources of the continued influence effect: When misinformation affects later inferences. *Journal of Experimental Psychology: Learning, Memory and Cognition, 20,* 1420–1436.

Johnson, M. K. (1988). Reality monitoring: An experimental phenomenological approach. *Journal of Experimental Psychology: General, 117,* 390–394.

Johnson, M. K., Hashtroudi, S., & Lindsay, S. (1993). Source monitoring. *Psychological Bulletin, 114,* 3–28.

Johnson, M. K., Kim, J. K., & Risse, G. (1985). Do alcoholic Korsakoff's syndrome patients acquire affective reactions? *Journal of Experimental Psychology: Learning, Memory and Cognition, 11,* 27–36.

Johnson, S. K., & Anderson, M. C. (2004). The role of inhibitory control in forgetting semantic knowledge. *Psychological Science, 15,* 448–453.

Johnson-Laird, P. N. (1983). *Mental models.* Cambridge, MA: Harvard University Press.

Johnson-Laird, P. N. (1987). The mental representation of the meaning of words. *Cognition, 25,* 189–211.

Johnson-Laird, P. N. (1988). A computational analysis of consciousness. In A. Marcel & E. Bisiach (Eds.), *Consciousness in contemporary science* (pp. 357–368). Oxford, England: Oxford University Press.

Johnson-Laird, P. N. (1990). Mental models. In M. Posner (Ed.), *Foundations of cognitive science* (pp. 469–500). Cambridge, MA: Bradford.

Johnson-Laird, P. N. (2001). Mental models and deduction. *Trends in Cognitive Sciences, 5,* 434–442.

Johnson-Laird, P. N. (2004). Mental models and reasoning. In J. P. Leighton & R. J. Sternberg (Eds.), *The nature of reasoning* (pp. 169–204). New York: Cambridge University Press.

Johnson-Laird, P. N., & Byrne, R. (1989). Only reasoning. *Journal of Memory and Language, 28,* 313–330.

Johnson-Laird, P. N., & Byrne, R. (1991). *Deduction.* Hillsdale, NJ: Erlbaum.

Johnson-Laird, P. N., Byrne, R. M. J., & Schaeken, W. (1992). Propositional reasoning by model. *Psychological Review, 99,* 418–439.

Johnson-Laird, P. N., Byrne, R., & Tabossi, P. (1989). Reasoning by model: The case of multiple quantification. *Psychological Review, 96,* 658–673.

Johnson-Laird, P. N., Legrenzi, P., Girotto, V., Legrenzi, M. S., & Caverni, J.-P. (1999). Naive probability: A mental model theory of extensional reasoning. *Psychological Review, 106,* 62–88.

Johnson-Laird, P. N., Legrenzi, P., & Legrenzi, M. S. (1972). Reasoning and a sense of reality. *British Journal of Psychology, 63,* 395–400.

Johnson-Laird, P. N., & Savary, F. (1999). Illusory inferences: A novel class of erroneous deductions. *Cognition, 71,* 191–229.

Johnson-Laird, P. N., & Steedman, M. (1978). The psychology of syllogisms. *Cognitive Psychology, 10,* 64–99.

Jones, G. (2003). Testing two cognitive theories of insight. *Journal of Experimental Psychology: Learning, Memory and Cognition, 29,* 1017–1027.

Jonides, J., Kahn, R., & Rozin, P. (1975). Imagery instructions improve memory in blind subjects. *Bulletin of the Psychonomic Society, 5,* 424–426.

Jurica, P. J., & Shimamura, A. P. (1999). Monitoring item and source information: Evidence for a negative generation effect in source memory. *Memory & Cognition, 27,* 648–657.

Just, M., & Carpenter, P. (1987). *The psychology of reading and language comprehension.* Boston: Allyn & Bacon.

Just, M., & Carpenter, P. (1992). A capacity theory of comprehension: Individual differences in working memory. *Psychological Review, 99,* 122–149.

Just, M., Carpenter, P. A., & Hemphill, D. D. (1996). Constraints on processing capacity: Architectural or implementational? In D. Steier & T. Mitchell (Eds.), *Mind matters: A tribute to Allen Newell* (pp. 141–178). Mahwah, NJ: Erlbaum.

Kahneman, D. (1973). *Attention and effort.* Englewood Cliffs, NJ: Prentice-Hall.

Kahneman, D. (2003). A perspective on judgment and choice: Mapping bounded rationality. *American Psychologist, 58,* 697–720.

Kahneman, D., Diener, E., & Schwarz, N. (Eds.). (1999). *Well-being: The foundations of hedonic psychology.* New York: Russell Sage Foundation.

Kahneman, D., Fredrickson, B., Schreiber, C., & Redelmeier, D. (1993). When more pain is preferred to less: Adding a better end. *Psychological Science, 4,* 401–405.

Kahneman, D., & Miller, D. (1986). Norm theory: Comparing reality to its alternatives. *Psychological Review, 93,* 136–153.

Kahneman, D., & Snell, J. (1992). Predicting a changing taste: Do people know what they will like? *Journal of Behavioral Decision Making, 5,* 187–200.

Kahneman, D., & Tversky, A. (1972). Subjective probability: A judgment of representativeness. *Cognitive Psychology, 3,* 430–454.

Kahneman, D., & Tversky, A. (1973). On the psychology of prediction. *Psychological Review, 80,* 237–251.

Kahneman, D., & Tversky, A. (1982a). On the study of statistical intuitions. *Cognition, 11,* 237–251.

Kahneman, D., & Tversky, A. (1982b). The simulation heuristic. In D. Kahneman, P. Slovic, & A. Tversky (Eds.), *Judgment under uncertainty: Heuristics and biases* (pp. 201–208). New York: Cambridge University Press.

Kahney, H. (1986). *Problem solving: A cognitive approach.* Milton Keynes, England: Open University Press.

Kane, M. J., Bleckley, M., Conway, A. R. A., & Engle, R. W. (2001). A controlled-attention view of work-ing-memory capacity. *Journal of Experimental Psychology: General, 130,* 169–183.

Kane, M. J., & Engle, R. W. (2003). Working-memory capacity and the control of attention: The contributions of goal neglect, response competition, and task set to Stroop interference. *Journal of Experimental Psychology: General, 132,* 47–70.

Kane, M. J., Hambrick, D. Z., Tuholski, S. W., Wilhelm, O., Payne, T. W., & Engle, R. W. (2004). The generality of working memory capacity: A latent-variable approach to verbal and visuospatial memory span and reasoning. *Journal of Experimental Psychology: General, 133,* 189–217.

Kanizsa, G. (1979). *Organization in vision.* New York: Praeger.

Kaplan, A. S., & Murphy, G. L. (2000). Category learning with minimal prior knowledge. *Journal of Experimental Psychology: Learning, Memory, & Cognition, 26,* 829–846.

Kapur, N. (1999). Syndromes of retrograde amnesia. *Psychological Bulletin, 125,* 800–825.

Kassin, S. M. (1997). The psychology of confession evidence. *American Psychologist, 52,* 221–233.

Kassin, S. M., & Kiechel, K. L. (1996). The social psychology of false confessions: Compliance, internalization and confabulation. *Psychological Science, 7,* 125–128.

Katona, G. (1940). *Organizing and memorizing.* New York: Columbia University Press.

Katz, A. (1983). What does it mean to be a high imager? In J. Yuille (Ed.), *Imagery, memory and cognition* (pp. 39–63). Hillsdale, NJ: Erlbaum.

Katz, B. (1952). The nerve impulse. *Scientific American, 187*(November), 55–64.

Keil, F. C. (1986). The acquisition of natural-kind and artifact terms. In W. Demopoulos & A. Marras (Eds.), *Language, learning, and concept acquisition* (pp. 133–153). Norwood, NJ: Ablex.

Keil, F. C. (1989). *Concepts, kinds, and cognitive development.* Cambridge, MA: MIT Press.

Keil, F. C. (2003). Folkscience: Coarse interpretations of a complex reality. *Trends in Cognitive Sciences, 7,* 368–373.

Keil, F. C., Smith, W. C., Simons, D. J., & Levin, D. T. (1998). Two dogmas of conceptual empiricism: Implications for hybrid models of the structure of knowledge. *Cognition, 65,* 103–135.

Kelly, S. W., Burton, A. M., Kato, T., & Akamatsu, S. (2001). Incidental learning of real-world regularities. *Psychological Science, 12,* 86–89.

Kent, G. (1985). Memory of dental pain. *Pain, 21,* 187–194.

Kerr, N. H. (1983). The role of vision in "visual imagery" experiments: Evidence from the congenitally blind. *Journal of Experimental Psychology: General, 112,* 265–277.

Kershaw, T. C., & Ohlsson, S. (2004). Multiple causes of difficulty in insight: The case of the nine-dot problem. *Journal of Experimental Psychology: Learning, Memory, & Cognition, 30,* 3–13.

Kihlstrom, J. F., & Schacter, D. L. (2000). Functional amnesia. In F. Boller & J. Grafman (Eds.), *Handbook of neuropsychology* (2nd ed., Vol. 2, pp. 409–427). Amsterdam: Elsevier.

Kim, N. S., & Ahn, W.-K. (2002). Clinical psychologists' theory-based representations of mental disorders predict their diagnostic reasoning and memory. *Journal of Experimental Psychology: General, 131,* 451–476.

Kimberg, D. Y., D'Esposito, M., & Farah, M. J. (1998). Cognitive functions in the prefrontal cortex in working memory and executive control. *Current Directions in Psychological Science, 6,* 185–192.

King, R. N., & Koehler, D. J. (2000). Illusory correlations in graphological inference. *Journal of Experimental Psychology: Applied, 6,* 336–348.

Kinoshita, S. (2001). The role of involuntary aware memory in the implicit stem and fragment completion tasks: A selective review. *Psychonomic Bulletin & Review, 8,* 58–69.

Kintsch, W. (1994). Text comprehension, memory, and learning. *American Psychologist, 49,* 294–303.

Kirsner, K., Milech, D., & Standen, P. (1983). Common and modality-specific processes in the mental lexicon. *Memory & Cognition, 11,* 621–630.

Klahr, D., & Simon, H. A. (2001). What have psychologists (and others) discovered about the process of scientific discovery? *Current Directions in Psychological Science, 10,* 75–79.

Klauer, K. C., Musch, J., & Naumer, B. (2000). On belief bias in syllogistic reasoning. *Psychological Review, 107,* 852–884.

Klauer, K. C., & Zhao, Z. (2004). Double dissociations in visual and spatial short-term memory. *Journal of Experimental Psychology: General, 133,* 355–381.

Klayman, J., & Brown, K. (1993). Debias the environment instead of the judge: An alternative approach to reducing error in diagnostic (and other) judgment. *Cognition, 49,* 97–122.

Knoblich, G., Ohlsson, S., & Raney, G. E. (2001). An eye movement study of insight problem solving. *Memory & Cognition, 29,* 1000–1009.

Kohler, W. (1969). *The task of Gestalt psychology.* Princeton, NJ: Princeton University Press.

Komatsu, L. (1992). Recent views of conceptual structure. *Psychological Bulletin, 112,* 500–526.

Kopelman, M. D., & Kapur, N. (2001). The loss of episodic memories in retrograde amnesia: Single-case and group studies. In A. D. Baddeley, J. P. Aggleton, & M. A. Conway (Eds.), *Episodic memory: New directions in research* (pp. 110–131). New York: Oxford University Press.

Kosslyn, S. M. (1976). Can imagery be distinguished from other forms of internal representation? Evidence from studies of information retrieval times. *Memory & Cognition, 4,* 291–297.

Kosslyn, S. M. (1980). *Image and mind.* Cambridge, MA: Harvard University Press.

Kosslyn, S. M. (1983). *Ghosts in the mind's machine.* New York: Norton.

Kosslyn, S. M. (1994). *Image and brain: The resolution of the imagery debate.* Cambridge, MA: MIT Press.

Kosslyn, S. M., Ball, T. M., & Reiser, B. J. (1978). Visual images preserve metric spatial information: Evidence from studies of image scanning. *Journal of Experimental Psychology: Human Perception and Performance, 4,* 1–20.

Kosslyn, S. M., Brunn, J., Cave, K., & Wallach, R. (1985). Individual differences in mental imagery ability: A computational analysis. *Cognition, 18,* 195–243.

Kosslyn, S. M., Pascual-Leone, A., Felician, O., Camposano, S., Keenan, J. P., Thompson, W. L., et al. (1999). The role of area 17 in visual imagery: Convergent evidence from PET and rTMS. *Science, 284,* 167–170.

Kosslyn, S. M., & Thompson, W. L. (1999). Shared mechanisms in visual imagery and visual perception: Insights from cognitive neuroscience. In M. S. Gazzaniga (Ed.), *The new cognitive neurosciences* (pp. 975–986). Cambridge, MA: MIT Press.

Kosslyn, S. M., & Thompson, W. L. (2003). When is early visual cortex activated during mental imagery? *Psychological Bulletin, 129,* 723–746.

Kroll, J. F., & Potter, M. C. (1984). Recognizing words, pictures, and concepts: A comparison of lexical, object, and reality decisions. *Journal of Verbal Learning and Verbal Behavior, 23,* 39–66.

Kucera, H., & Francis, W. N. (1967). *Computational analysis of present-day American English*. Providence, RI: Brown University Press.

Kumon-Nakamura, S., Glucksberg, S., & Brown, M. (1995). How about another piece of pie: The allusional pretense theory of discourse irony. *Journal of Experimental Psychology: General, 124*, 3–21.

Kunda, Z. (1999). Social cognition: Making sense of people. Cambridge, MA: MIT Press.

Kunda, Z. (1990). The case for motivated reasoning. *Psychological Bulletin, 108*, 480–498.

Kunda, Z., & Nisbett, R. E. (1986). The psychometrics of everyday life. *Cognitive Psychology, 18*, 195–224.

Kyllonen, P. C., & Cristal, R. E. (1990). Reasoning ability is (little more than) working-memory capacity? *Intelligence, 14*, 389–433.

Lachter, J., & Bever, T. G. (1988). The relation between linguistic structure and associative theories of language learning—A critique of some connectionist learning models. *Cognition, 28*, 195–247.

Lai, C. S., Fisher, S. E., Hurst, J. A., Vargha-Khadem, F., & Monaco, A. P. (2001). A forkhead-domain gene is mutated in a severe speech and language disorder. *Nature, 413*, 519–522.

Lakoff, G. (1987). Cognitive models and prototype theory. In U. Neisser (Ed.), *Concepts and conceptual development* (pp. 63–100). Cambridge, England: Cambridge University Press.

Lamb, M. E. (1998). Assessments of children's credibility in forensic contexts. *Current Directions in Psychological Science, 7*, 43–46.

Lamble, D., Kauranen, T., Laakso, M., & Summala, H. (1999). Cognitive load and detection thresholds in car following situations: Safety implications for using mobile (cellular) telephones while driving. *Accident Analysis & Prevention, 31*, 617–623.

Lampinen, J. M., Copeland, S., & Neuschatz, J. S. (2001). Recollections of things schematic: Room schemas revisited. *Journal of Experimental Psychology: Learning, Memory and Cognition, 27*, 1211–1222.

Landau, B., & Munnich, E. (1998). The representation of space and spatial language: Challenges for cognitive science. In P. Oliver & K.-P. Gapp (Eds.), *Representation and processing of spatial expressions* (pp. 263–272). Mahwah, NJ: Erlbaum.

Lane, S. M., & Schooler, J. W. (2004). Skimming the surface: Verbal overshadowing of analogical retrieval. *Psychological Science, 15*, 715–719.

Lane, S., & Zaragoza, M. (1995). The recollective experience of cross-modality confusion errors. *Memory & Cognition, 23*, 607–610.

Laney, C., Campbell, H., Heuer, F., & Reisberg, D. (In press). Memory for thematically arousing events. *Memory & Cognition*.

Langer, E. (1989). *Mindfulness*. Reading, MA: Addison-Wesley.

Langley, P., & Jones, R. (1988). A computational model of scientific insight. In R. J. Sternberg (Ed.), *The nature of creativity* (pp. 177–201). Cambridge, England: Cambridge University Press.

Larkin, J., McDermott, J., Simon, D., & Simon, H. (1980). Expert and novice performance in solving physics problems. *Science, 208*, 1335–1342.

Larrick, R., Nisbett, R., & Morgan, J. (1993). Who uses the normative rules of choice? In R. Nisbett (Ed.), *Rules for reasoning* (pp. 277–294). Hillsdale, NJ: Erlbaum.

Lassiter, G. D. (2000). The relative contributions of recognition and search-evaluation processes in high-level chess performance: Comment on Gobet and Simon. *Psychological Science, 11*, 172–174.

Lavie, N. (1995). Perceptual load as a necessary condition for selective attention. *Journal of Experimental Psychology: Human Perception and Performance, 21*, 451–468.

Lavie, N. (1997). Visual feature integration and focused attention: Response competition from multiple distractor features. *Perception & Psychophysics, 59*, 543–556.

Lavie, N. (2001). Capacity limits in selective attention: Behavioral evidence and implications for neural activity. In J. Braun, C. Koch, & J. L. Davis (Eds.), *Visual attention and cortical circuits* (pp. 49–68). Cambridge, MA: MIT Press.

Lavie, N., Hirst, A., De Fockert, J. W., & Viding, E. (2004). Load theory of selective attention and cognitive control. *Journal of Experimental Psychology: General, 133*, 339–354.

Lavric, A., Pizzagalli, D., Forstmeier, S., & Rippon, G. (2001). Mapping dissociations in verb morphology. *Trends in Cognitive Sciences, 5*, 301–308.

Lee, A. Y., & Hutchison, L. (1998). Improving learning from examples through reflection. *Journal of Experimental Psychology: Applied, 4*, 187–210.

Legrenzi, P., Girotto, V., & Johnson-Laird, P. (1993). Focussing in reasoning and decision making. *Cognition, 49*, 37–66.

Lehman, D. R., & Nisbett, R. (1990). A longitudinal study of the effects of undergraduate education on reasoning. *Developmental Psychology, 26,* 952–960.

Leippe, M. R., Manion, A. P., & Romanczyk, A. (1992). Eyewitness persuasion: How and how well do fact finders judge the accuracy of adults' and children's memory reports? *Journal of Personality and Social Psychology, 63,* 181–197.

Levin, D. T., & Simons, D. J. (1997). Failure to detect changes to attended objects in motion pictures. *Psychonomic Bulletin & Review, 4,* 501–506.

Levin, I., & Gaeth, G. (1988). How consumers are affected by the framing of attribute information before and after consuming the product. *Journal of Consumer Research, 15,* 374–378.

Levin, I., Schnittjer, S., & Thee, S. (1988). Information framing effects in social and personal decisions. *Journal of Experimental Social Psychology, 24,* 520–529.

Levine, J. M., & Murphy, G. (1943). The learning and forgetting of controversial material. *Journal of Abnormal & Social Psychology, 38,* 507–517.

Levine, L. J. (1997). Reconstructing memory for emotions. *Journal of Experimental Psychology: General, 126,* 165–177.

Levinson, S. C., Kita, S., Haun, D. B. M., & Rasch, B. H. (2002). Returning the tables: Language affects spatial reasoning. *Cognition, 84,* 155–188.

Levitin, D. (1994). Absolute representation in auditory memory: Evidence from the production of learned melodies. *Perception & Psychophysics, 56,* 414–423.

Lewis, C., & Keren, G. (1999). On the difficulties underlying Bayesian reasoning: A comment on Gigerenzer and Hoffrage. *Psychological Review, 106,* 411–416.

Li, P., & Gleitman, L. R. (2002). Turning the tables: Language and spatial reasoning. *Cognition, 83,* 265–294.

Liberman, A. (1970). The grammars of speech and language. *Cognitive Psychology, 1,* 301–323.

Liberman, A., Harris, K., Hoffman, H., & Griffith, B. (1957). The discrimination of speech sounds within and across phoneme boundaries. *Journal of Experimental Psychology, 54,* 358–368.

Liberman, N., & Klar, Y. (1996). Hypothesis testing in Wason's selection task: Social exchange cheating detection or task understanding. *Cognition, 58,* 127–156.

Lichtenstein, S., Slovic, P., Fischhoff, B., Layman, M., & Combs, B. (1978). Judged frequency of lethal events. *Journal of Experimental Psychology: Human Learning and Memory, 4,* 551–578.

Lidz, J., Waxman, S., & Freedman, J. (2003). What infants know about syntax but couldn't have learned: Experimental evidence for syntactic structure at 18 months. *Cognition, 89,* B65–B73.

Light, L. L., & Carter-Sobell, L. (1970). Effects of changed semantic context on recognition memory. *Journal of Verbal Learning and Verbal Behavior, 9,* 1–11.

Linton, M. (1975). Memory for real-world events. In D. A. Norman & D. E. Rumelhart (Eds.), *Explorations in cognition* (pp. 376–404). San Francisco: Freeman.

Linton, M. (1978). Real world memory after six years: An in vivo study of very long term memory. In M. M. Gruneberg, P. E. Morris, & R. N. Sykes (Eds.), *Practical aspects of memory* (pp. 69–76). London: Academic Press.

Linton, M. (1982). Transformations of memory in everyday life. In U. Neisser (Ed.), *Memory observed: Remembering in natural contexts* (pp. 77–92). San Francisco: Freeman.

Linton, M. (1986). Ways of searching and the contents of memory. In D. C. Rubin (Ed.), *Autobiographical memory* (pp. 50–67). Cambridge, England: Cambridge University Press.

Linton, S. J., & Melin, L. (1982). The accuracy of remembering chronic pain. *Pain, 13,* 281–285.

Lisker, L., & Abramson, A. (1970). *The voicing dimension: Some experiments in comparative phonetics.* Paper presented at the Proceedings of the Sixth International Congress of Phonetic Sciences, Prague.

Lockhart, R. S., Craik, F. I. M., & Jacoby, L. (1976). Depth of processing, recall, and recognition. In J. Brown (Ed.), *Recall and recognition* (pp. 75–102). New York: Wiley.

Loewenstein, G., & Schkade, D. (1999). Wouldn't it be nice? Predicting future feelings. In D. Kahneman, E. Diener, & N. Schwarz (Eds.), *Well-being: The foundations of hedonic psychology* (pp. 85–105). New York: Russell Sage Foundation.

Loewenstein, G., Weber, E. U., Hsee, C. K., & Welch, N. (2001). Risk as feelings. *Psychological Bulletin, 127,* 267–286.

Loewenstein, J., Thompson, L., & Gentner, D. (1999). Analogical encoding facilitates knowledge transfer in negotiation. *Psychonomic Bulletin & Review, 6,* 586–597.

Loftus, E. F. (1979). *Eyewitness testimony.* Cambridge, MA: Harvard University Press.

Loftus, E. F. (1997). Memory for a past that never was. *Current Directions in Psychological Science, 6,* 60–64.

Loftus, E. F. (2003). Make-believe memories. *American Psychologist, 58,* 867–873.

Loftus, E. F., & Guyer, M. J. (2002). Who abused Jane Doe? The hazards of the single case history. *Skeptical Inquirer, 26,* 24–32.

Loftus, E. F., & Ketcham, K. (1991). *Witness for the defense: The accused, the eyewitness, and the expert who puts memory on trial.* New York: St. Martin's.

Loftus, E. F., & Palmer, J. C. (1974). Reconstruction of automobile destruction: An example of the interaction between language and memory. *Journal of Verbal Learning and Verbal Behavior, 13,* 585–589.

Loftus, E. F., & Pickrell, J. E. (1995). The formation of false memories. *Psychiatric Annals, 25,* 720–725.

Logan, G. D. (2003). Executive control of thought and action: In search of the wild homunculus. *Current Directions in Psychological Science, 12,* 45–48.

Logan, G. D. (2004). Working memory, task switching, and executive control in the task span procedure. *Journal of Experimental Psychology: General, 133,* 218–236.

Logie, R. H. (1995). *Visuo-spatial working memory.* Hillsdale, NJ: Erlbaum.

Logie, R. H., Engelkamp, J., Dehn, D., & Rudkin, S. (1999). Actions, mental actions, and working memory. In M. Denis, C. Cornoldi, J. Engelkamp, M. De Vega, & R. H. Logie (Eds.), *Imagery, language, and the representation of space* (pp. 161–184). Hove, England: Psychology Press.

Logie, R. H., & Marchetti, C. (1991). Visuo-spatial working memory: Visual, spatial or central executive. In R. H. Logie & M. Denis (Eds.), *Mental images in human cognition* (pp. 105–115). Amsterdam: Elsevier.

Lucas, M. (2000). Semantic priming without association: A meta-analytic review. *Psychonomic Bulletin & Review, 7,* 618–630.

Luchins, A. (1942). *Mechanization in problem solving: The effect of Einstellung.* (Psychological Monographs, Vol. 54, No. 6 [whole no. 248]). Evanston, IL: American Psychological Association.

Luchins, A., & Luchins, E. (1950). New experimental attempts at preventing mechanization in problem solving. *Journal of General Psychology, 42,* 279–297.

Luchins, A., & Luchins, E. (1959). *Rigidity of behavior: A variational approach to the effects of Einstellung.* Eugene: University of Oregon Books.

Lyman, B., & McDaniel, M. (1990). Memory for odors and odor names: Modalities of elaboration and imagery. *Journal of Experimental Psychology: Learning, Memory and Cognition, 16,* 656–664.

MacDonald, A. W., Cohen, J. D., Stenger, V. A., & Carter, C. S. (2000). Dissociating the role of dorsolateral prefrontal cortex and anterior cingulate cortex in cognitive control. *Science, 288,* 1835–1837.

MacGregor, J. N., Ormerod, T. C., & Chronicle, E. P. (2001). Information processing and insight: A process model of performance on the 9-dot and related problems. *Journal of Experimental Psychology: Learning, Memory and Cognition, 27,* 176–201.

Mack, A. (2003). Inattentional blindness: Looking without seeing. *Current Directions in Psychological Science, 12,* 180–184.

Mack, A., & Rock, I. (1998). *Inattentional blindness.* Cambridge, MA: MIT Press.

MacLeod, M. D., & Macrae, C. N. (2001). Gone but not forgotten: The transient nature of retrieval-induced forgetting. *Psychological Science, 12,* 148–152.

Mahoney, M., & DeMonbreun, B. (1978). Problem-solving bias in scientists. *Cognitive Therapy and Research, 1,* 229–238.

Maier, N. R. F. (1931). Reasoning in humans: II. The solution of a problem and its appearance in consciousness. *Journal of Comparative Psychology, 12,* 181–194.

Majid, A. (2002). Frames of reference and language concepts. *Trends in Cognitive Sciences, 6,* 503–504.

Majid, A., Bowerman, M., Kita, S., Haun, D. B. M., & Levinson, S. (2004). Can language restructure cognition? The case for space. *Trends in Cognitive Sciences, 8,* 108–114.

Malt, B. C., Sloman, S. A., Gennari, S., Shi, M., & Wang, Y. (1999). Knowing versus naming: Similarity and the linguistic categorization of artifacts. *Journal of Memory & Language, 40,* 230–262.

Malt, B. C., & Smith, E. E. (1984). Correlated properties in natural categories. *Journal of Verbal Learning and Verbal Behavior, 23,* 250–269.

Mandler, J. M., & Ritchey, G. H. (1977). Long-term memory for pictures. *Journal of Experimental Psychology: Human Learning and Memory, 3,* 386–396.

Marcel, A. J. (1983a). Conscious and unconscious perception: An approach to the relations between phenomenal experience and perceptual processes. *Cognitive Psychology, 15,* 238–300.

Marcel, A. J. (1983b). Conscious and unconscious perception: Experiments on visual masking and word recognition. *Cognitive Psychology, 15,* 197–237.

Marcus, G. B. (1986). Stability and change in political attitudes: Observe, recall, and "explain." *Political Behavior, 8,* 21–44.

Marcus, G. F. (1995). The acquisition of the English past tense in children and multilayered connectionist networks. *Cognition, 56,* 271–279.

Marcus, G. F. (1996). Why do children say "breaked"? *Current Directions in Psychological Science, 5,* 81–85.

Marcus, G. F., Pinker, S., Ullman, M., Hollander, M., Rosen, T., & Xu, F. (1992). *Overregularization in language acquisition* (Monographs of the Society for Research in Child Development, Vol. 57, No. 4 [serial no. 228]). Chicago: University of Chicago Press.

Marcus, G. F., Vijayan, S., Rao, S. B., & Vishton, P. M. (1999). Rule learning by seven-month-old infants. *Science, 283,* 77–80.

Markman, A. B. (1997). Constraints on analogical inference. *Cognitive Science, 21,* 373–418.

Markman, A. B., & Gentner, D. (2001). Thinking. *Annual Review of Psychology, 52,* 223–247.

Marks, D. (1983). Mental imagery and consciousness: A theoretical review. In A. Sheikh (Ed.), *Imagery: Current theory, research and application* (pp. 96–130). New York: Wiley.

Marmor, G. S., & Zabeck, L. A. (1976). Mental rotation by the blind: Does mental rotation depend on visual imagery? *Journal of Experimental Psychology: Human Perception and Performance, 2,* 515–521.

Marsh, R., & Landau, J. (1995). Item availability in cryptomnesia: Assessing its role in two paradigms of unconscious plagiarism. *Journal of Experimental Psychology: Learning, Memory and Cognition, 21,* 1568–1582.

Marslen-Wilson, W. D., & Teuber, H. L. (1975). Memory for remote events in anterograde amnesia: Recognition of public figures from news photographs. *Neuropsychologia, 13,* 353–364.

Marslen-Wilson, W. D., & Tyler, L. (1987). Against modularity. In J. L. Garfield (Ed.), *Modularity in knowledge representation and natural-language understanding* (pp. 37–62). Cambridge, MA: MIT Press.

Martin, R. C. (2003). Language processing: Functional organization and neuroanatomical basis. *Annual Review of Psychology, 54,* 55–89.

Mather, M., Shafir, E., & Johnson, M. K. (2000). Misremembrance of options past: Source monitoring and choice. *Psychological Science, 11,* 132–138.

Mayr, U. (2004). Conflict, consciousness, and control. *Trends in Cognitive Sciences, 8,* 145–148.

Mazzoni, G., Loftus, E. F., & Kirsch, I. (2001). Changing beliefs about implausible autobiographical events. *Journal of Experimental Psychology: Applied, 7,* 51–59.

Mazzoni, G., & Memon, A. (2003). Imagination can create false autobiographical memories. *Psychological Science, 14,* 186–188.

McCann, R., & Johnston, J. (1992). Locus of the single-channel bottleneck in dual-task interference. *Journal of Experimental Psychology: Human Perception and Performance, 18,* 471–484.

McClelland, J. L. (1999). Connectionist cognitive modeling. In R. A. Wilson & F. C. Keil (Eds.), *The MIT encyclopedia of the cognitive sciences* (pp. 137–141). Cambridge, MA: MIT Press.

McClelland, J. L. & Patterson, K. (2002a). Rules or connections in past-tense inflections: What does the evidence rule out? *Trends in Cognitive Sciences, 6,* 465–472.

McClelland, J. L. & Patterson, K. (2002b). "Words or rules" cannot exploit the regularity in exceptions: Reply to Pinker and Ullman. *Trends in Cognitive Sciences, 6,* 464–465.

McClelland, J. L., & Rumelhart, D. E. (1981). An interactive model of context effects in letter perception. Part 1. An account of basic findings. *Psychological Review, 88,* 375–407.

McClelland, J. L., & Seidenberg, M. S. (2000). Why do kids say goed and brang? *Science, 287,* 47–48.

McCloskey, M., & Cohen, N. J. (1989). Catastrophic interference in connectionist networks: The sequential learning problem. In G. H. Bower (Ed.), *The psychology of learning and motivation*, Vol. 23 (pp. 109–165). New York: Academic Press.

McCloskey, M., & Glucksberg, S. (1978). Natural categories. Well-defined or fuzzy sets? *Memory & Cognition, 6,* 462–472.

McDaniel, M., & Einstein, G. (1986). Bizarre imagery as an effective mnemonic aid: The importance of distinctiveness. *Journal of Experimental Psychology: Learning, Memory and Cognition, 12,* 54–65.

McDaniel, M., & Einstein, G. (1990). Bizarre imagery: Mnemonic benefits and theoretical implications. In R. Logie & M. Denis (Eds.), *Mental images in human cognition* (pp. 183–192). New York: North Holland.

McDermott, K., & Roediger, H. (1994). Effects of imagery on perceptual implicit memory tests. *Journal of Experimental Psychology: Learning, Memory and Cognition, 20,* 1379–1390.

McDermott, K. B., & Roediger, H. L. (1998). False recognition of associates can be resistant to an explicit warning to subjects and an immediate recognition probe. *Journal of Memory & Language, 39,* 508–520.

McEvoy, C. L., Nelson, D., & Komatsu, T. (1999). What is the connection between true and false memories? The differential role of interitem associations in recall and recognition. *Journal of Experimental Psychology: Learning, Memory and Cognition, 25,* 1177–1194.

McGaugh, J. L. (2000). Memory—A century of consolidation. *Science, 287,* 248–251.

McGuire, M. J., & Maki, R. H. (2001). When knowing more means less: The effect of fan on metamemory judgment. *Journal of Experimental Psychology: Learning, Memory and Cognition, 27,* 1172–1179.

McIntosh, A. R., Rajah, M. N., & Lobaugh, N. J. (1999). Interactions of prefrontal cortex in relation to awareness in sensory learning. *Science, 284,* 1531–1533.

McKelvie, S. (1995). The VVIQ as a psychometric test of individual differences in visual imagery vividness: A critical quantitative review and plea for direction. *Journal of Mental Imagery, 19*(3&4), 1–106.

McNally, R. J. (2003). Recovering memories of trauma: A view from the laboratory. *Current Directions in Psychological Science, 12,* 32–35.

McNally, R. J., Lasko, N., Clancy, S. A., Macklin, M. L., Pitman, R. K., & Orr, S. P. (2004). Psychophysiological responding during script-driven imagery in people reporting abduction by space aliens. *Psychological Science, 15,* 493–497.

Meadows, J. C. (1974). Disturbed perception of colours associated with localized cerebral lesions. *Brain, 97,* 615–632.

Medin, D. L. (1989). Concepts and conceptual structure. *American Psychologist, 44,* 1469–1481.

Medin, D. L., & Bazerman, M. H. (1999). Broadening behavioral decision research: Multiple levels of cognitive processing. *Psychonomic Bulletin & Review, 6,* 533–546.

Medin, D. L., Coley, J. D., Storms, G., & Hayes, B. K. (2003). A relevance theory of induction. *Psychonomic Bulletin & Review, 10,* 517–532.

Medin, D. L., Goldstone, R., & Gentner, D. (1993). Respects for similarity. *Psychological Review, 100,* 254–278.

Medin, D. L., & Ortony, A. (1989). Psychological essentialism. In S. Vosniadou & A. Ortony (Eds.), *Similarity and analogical reasoning* (pp. 179–195). New York: Cambridge University Press.

Medin, D. L., Schwartz, H., Blok, S. V., & Birnbaum, L. A. (1999). The semantic side of decision making. *Psychonomic Bulletin & Review, 6,* 562–569.

Mednick, S. (1962). The associative basis of the creative process. *Psychological Review, 69,* 220–232.

Mednick, S., & Mednick, M. (1967). *Examiner's manual, Remote Associates Test.* Boston: Houghton Mifflin.

Medvec, V. H., Madey, S. F., & Gilovich, T. (1995). When less is more: Counterfactual thinking and satisfaction among Olympic medalists. *Journal of Personality & Social Psychology, 60,* 603–610.

Mellers, B., Chang, S.-J., Birnbaum, M., & Ordóñez, L. (1992). Preferences, prices, and ratings in risky decision making. *Journal of Experimental Psychology: Human Perception and Performance, 18,* 347–361.

Mellers, B., Hertwig, R., & Kahneman, D. (2001). Do frequency representations eliminate conjunction effects? An exercise in adversarial collaboration. *Psychological Science, 12,* 269–275.

Mellers, B. A., & McGraw, A. P. (1999). How to improve Bayesian reasoning: Comment on Gigerenzer and Hoffrage. *Psychological Review, 106,* 417–424.

Mellers, B., Schwartz, A., & Ritov, I. (1999). Emotion-based choice. *Journal of Experimental Psychology: General, 128,* 332–345.

Mervis, C. B., Catlin, J., & Rosch, E. (1976). Relationships among goodness-of-example, category norms and word frequency. *Bulletin of the Psychonomic Society, 7,* 268–284.

Messick, D. M. (1999). Alternative logics for decision making in social settings. *Journal of Economic Behavior & Organization, 39,* 11–28.

Metcalfe, J. (1986). Premonitions of insight predict impending error. *Journal of Experimental Psychology: Learning, Memory and Cognition, 12,* 623–634.

Metcalfe, J., & Weibe, D. (1987). Intuition in insight and noninsight problem solving. *Memory & Cognition, 15,* 238–246.

Meyer, D. E., & Schvaneveldt, R. W. (1971). Facilitation in recognizing pairs of words: Evidence of a dependence between retrieval operations. *Journal of Experimental Psychology, 90,* 227–234.

Meyer, D. E., Schvaneveldt, R. W., & Ruddy, M. G. (1974). Functions of graphemic and phonemic codes in visual word recognition. *Memory & Cognition, 2,* 309–321.

Mill, J. S. (1874). *A system of logic* (8th ed.). New York: Harper.

Miller, A. (1986). *Imagery in scientific thought.* Cambridge, MA: MIT Press.

Miller, G. A. (1951). *Language and communication.* New York: McGraw-Hill.

Miller, G. A. (1956). The magical number seven plus or minus two: Some limits on our capacity for processing information. *Psychological Review, 63,* 81–97.

Miller, G. A. (1962). *Psychology: The science of mental life.* New York: Harper & Row.

Miller, G. A. (1991). *The science of words.* New York: Freeman.

Miller, G. A. (1999). On knowing a word. *Annual Review of Psychology, 50,* 1–19.

Miller, G. A., Bruner, J. S., & Postman, L. (1954). Familiarity of letter sequences and tachistoscopic identification. *Journal of General Psychology, 50,* 129–139.

Miller, G. A., Galanter, E., & Pribram, K. (1960). *Plans and the structure of behavior.* New York: Holt, Rinehart and Winston.

Miller, G. A., & Nicely, P. (1955). An analysis of perceptual confusions among some English consonants. *Journal of the Acoustical Society of America, 27,* 338–352.

Milliken, B., Joordens, S., Merikle, P., & Seiffert, A. (1998). Selective attention: A reevaluation of the implications of negative priming. *Psychological Review, 105,* 203–229.

Milliken, B., & Tipper, S. (1998). Attention and inhibition. In H. Pashler (Ed.), *Attention* (pp. 191–221). Hove, England: Psychology Press.

Milner, B. (1966). Amnesia following operation on the temporal lobes. In C. W. M. Whitty & O. L. Zangwill (Eds.), *Amnesia* (pp. 109–133). London: Butterworths.

Milner, B. (1970). Memory and the medial temporal regions of the brain. In K. H. Pribram & D. E. Broadbent (Eds.), *Biology of memory* (pp. 29–48). New York: Academic Press.

Minda, J. P., & Smith, J. D. (2001). Prototypes in category learning: The effects of category size, category structure and stimulus complexity. *Journal of Experimental Psychology: Learning, Memory and Cognition, 27,* 775–799.

Mitroff, I. (1981). Scientists and confirmation bias. In R. Tweney, M. Doherty, & C. Mynatt (Eds.), *On scientific thinking* (pp. 170–175). New York: Columbia University Press.

Miyashita, Y. (1995). How the brain creates imagery: Projection to primary visual cortex. *Science, 268,* 1719–1720.

Moore, C. M., & Egeth, H. (1997). Perception without attention: Evidence of grouping under conditions of inattention. *Journal of Experimental Psychology: Human Perception and Performance, 23,* 339–352.

Moray, N. (1959). Attention in dichotic listening: Affective cues and the influence of instructions. *Quarterly Journal of Experimental Psychology, 11,* 56–60.

Morris, M., & Murphy, G. (1990). Converging operations on a basic level in event taxonomies. *Memory & Cognition, 18,* 407–418.

Morris, N. (1987). Exploring the visuo-spatial scratch pad. *Quarterly Journal of Experimental Psychology, 39A,* 409–430.

Morton, J. (1969). Interaction of information in word recognition. *Psychological Review, 76,* 165–178.

Morton, J. (1970). A functional model of human memory. In D. Norman (Ed.), *Models of human memory* (pp. 203–254). New York: Academic Press.

Moscovitch, M. (1982). Multiple dissociations of function in amnesia. In L. S. Cermak (Ed.), *Human memory and amnesia* (pp. 337–370). Hillsdale, NJ: Erlbaum.

Most, S. B., Simons, D. J., Scholl, B. J., Jimnez, R., Clifford, E., & Chabris, C. F. (2001). How not to be seen: The contribution of similarity and selective ignoring to sustained inattentional blindness. *Psychological Science, 12,* 9–17.

Munnich, E., Landau, B., & Dosher, B. A. (2001). Spatial language and spatial representation: A cross-linguistic comparison. *Cognition, 81,* 171–207.

Murdock, B. B., Jr. (1962). The serial position effect of free recall. *Journal of Experimental Psychology, 64,* 482–488.

Murphy, G. L. (2003). *The big book of concepts.* Cambridge, MA: MIT Press.

Murphy, G. L., & Medin, D. L. (1985). The role of theories in conceptual coherence. *Psychological Review, 92,* 289–316.

Murphy, S. T. (2001). Feeling without thinking: Affective primacy and the nonconscious processing of emotion. In J. A. Bargh & D. K. Apsley (Eds.), *Unraveling the complexities of social life: A festschrift in honor of Robert B. Zajonc* (pp. 39–53). Washington, DC: American Psychological Association.

Murray, J. E., Yong, E., & Rhodes, G. (2000). Revisiting the perception of upside-down faces. *Psychological Science, 11,* 492–496.

Myers, D. G. (2000). *The American paradox: Spiritual hunger in an age of plenty.* New Haven, CT: Yale University Press.

Mynatt, C., Doherty, M., & Tweney, R. (1977). Confirmation bias in a simulated research environment: An experimental study of scientific inference. *Quarterly Journal of Experimental Psychology, 29,* 85–95.

Mynatt, C., Doherty, M., & Tweney, R. (1978). Consequences of confirmation and disconfirmation in a simulated research environment. *Quarterly Journal of Experimental Psychology, 30,* 395–406.

Nadel, L., & Jacobs, W. J. (1998). Traumatic memory is special. *Current Directions in Psychological Science, 7,* 154–157.

Nadel, L., & Moscovitch, M. (2001). The hippocampal complex and long-term memory revisited. *Trends in Cognitive Sciences, 5,* 228–230.

Nairn, J., & Pusen, C. (1984). Serial recall of imagined voices. *Journal of Verbal Learning and Verbal Behavior, 23,* 331–342.

Nakamura, J., & Csikszentmihalyi, M. (2001). Catalytic creativity: The case of Linus Pauling. *American Psychologist, 56,* 337–341.

Needham, D., & Begg, I. (1991). Problem-oriented training promotes spontaneous analogical transfer: Memory-oriented training promotes memory for training. *Memory & Cognition, 19,* 543–557.

Neely, J. H. (1977). Semantic priming and retrieval from lexical memory: Role of inhibitionless spreading activation and limited capacity attention. *Journal of Experimental Psychology: General, 106,* 226–254.

Neil v. Biggers, 409 U.S. 188 (1972).

Neisser, U. (1967). *Cognitive psychology.* New York: Appleton-Century-Crofts.

Neisser, U. (1981). John Dean's memory: A case study. *Cognition, 9,* 1–22.

Neisser, U. (1987). From direct perception to conceptual structure. In U. Neisser (Ed.), *Concepts and conceptual development* (pp. 11–24). Cambridge, England: Cambridge University Press.

Neisser, U., & Becklen, R. (1975). Selective looking: Attending to visually significant events. *Cognitive Psychology, 7,* 480–494.

Neisser, U., & Harsch, N. (1992). Phantom flashbulbs: False recollections of hearing the news about Challenger. In E. Winograd & U. Neisser (Eds.), *Affect and accuracy in recall: Studies of "flashbulb" memories* (pp. 9–31). Cambridge, England: Cambridge University Press.

Neisser, U., Winograd, E., & Weldon, M. S. (1991). *Remembering the earthquake: "What I experienced" vs. "How I heard the news."* Paper presented at the meeting of the Psychonomic Society, San Francisco, November 24, 1991.

Nelson, D., Schreiber, T., & Holley, P. (1993). The retrieval of controlled and automatic aspects of meaning on direct and indirect tests. *Memory & Cognition, 20,* 671–684.

Nelson, T. O. (1976). Reinforcement and human memory. In W. K. Estes (Ed.), *Handbook of learning and cognitive processes,* Vol. 3. Hillsdale, NJ: Erlbaum.

Newcombe, F., Ratcliff, G., & Damasio, H. (1987). Dissociable visual and spatial impairments following right posterior cerebral lesions: Clinical, neuropsychological and anatomical evidence. *Neuropsychologia, 25,* 149–161.

Newcombe, N. S., Drummey, A. B., Fox, N. A., Lie, E., & Ottinger-Alberts, W. (2000). Remembering early childhood: How much, how, and why (or why not). *Current Directions in Psychological Science, 9,* 55–58.

Newell, A., & Simon, H. (1972). *Human problem solving.* Englewood Cliffs, NJ: Prentice-Hall.

Newstead, S., Pollard, P., Evans, J., & Allen, J. (1992). The source of belief bias effects in syllogistic reasoning. *Cognition, 45,* 257–284.

Nickerson, R. S., & Adams, M. J. (1979). Long-term memory for a common object. *Cognitive Psychology, 11*, 287–307.

Nisbett, R. (Ed.). (1993). *Rules for reasoning.* Hillsdale, NJ: Erlbaum.

Nisbett, R., Krantz, D. H., Jepson, C., & Kunda, Z. (1983). The use of statistical heuristics in everyday inductive reasoning. *Psychological Review, 90*, 339–363.

Nisbett, R., & Ross, L. (1980). *Human inference: Strategies and shortcomings of social judgment.* Englewood Cliffs, NJ: Prentice-Hall.

Nisbett, R., & Schachter, S. (1966). Cognitive manipulation of pain. *Journal of Experimental Social Psychology, 2*, 277–236.

Nisbett, R., & Wilson, T. (1977). Telling more than we can know: Verbal reports on mental processes. *Psychological Review, 84*, 231–259.

Norman, D. A. (1981). Categorization of action slips. *Psychological Review, 88*, 1–15.

Norman, D., Rumelhart, D. E., & Group, T. L. R. (1975). *Explorations in cognition.* San Francisco: Freeman.

Norman, D., & Shallice, T. (1986). Attention to action: Willed and automatic control of behavior. In R. Davidson, G. Schwartz, & D. Shapiro (Eds.), *Consciousness and self-regulation* (pp. 1–18). New York: Plenum.

Novick, L. (1988). Analogical transfer, problem similarity and expertise. *Journal of Experimental Psychology: Learning, Memory and Cognition, 14*, 510–520.

Novick, L., & Holyoak, K. (1991). Mathematical problem solving by analogy. *Journal of Experimental Psychology: Learning, Memory and Cognition, 17*, 398–415.

Novick, L. R., Hurley, S. M., & Francis, M. (1999). Evidence for abstract, schematic knowledge of three spatial diagram representations. *Memory & Cognition, 27*, 288–308.

Oakhill, J., & Garnham, A. (1993). On theories of belief bias in syllogistic reasoning. *Cognition, 46*, 87–92.

Oaksford, M., & Chater, N. (1995). Information gain explains relevance which explains the selection task. *Cognition, 57*, 97–108.

Ochsner, K. N., & Schacter, D. L. (2000). A social cognitive neuroscience approach to emotion and memory. In J. C. Borod (Ed.), *The neuropsychology of emotion* (pp. 163–193). New York: Oxford University Press.

O'Connor, M., Walbridge, M., Sandson, T., & Alexander, M. (1996). A neuropsychological analysis of Capgras syndrome. *Neuropsychiatry, Neuropsychology, and Behavioral Neurology, 9*, 265–271.

O'Craven, K. M., Downing, P. E., & Kanwisher, N. (1999). fMRI evidence for objects as the units of attentional selection. *Nature, 401*, 584–587.

O'Craven, K. M., & Kanwisher, N. (2000). Mental imagery of faces and places activates corresponding stimulus-specific brain regions. *Journal of Cognitive Neuroscience, 12*, 1013–1023.

Ofshe, R. (1992). Inadvertent hypnosis during interrogation: False confession due to dissociative state; mis-identified multiple personality and the Satanic Cult Hypothesis. *International Journal of Clinical and Experimental Hypnosis, 40*, 125–136.

Ohman, A. (2002). Automaticity and the amygdala: Nonconscious responses to emotional faces. *Current Directions in Psychological Science, 11*, 62–66.

Oldfield, R. (1963). Individual vocabulary and semantic currency: A preliminary study. *British Journal of Social and Clinical Psychology, 2*, 122–130.

Oliphant, G. W. (1983). Repetition and recency effects in word recognition. *Australian Journal of Psychology, 35*, 393–403.

Olton, R. (1979). Experimental studies of incubation: Searching for the elusive. *Journal of Creative Behavior, 13*, 9–22.

Olton, R., & Johnson, D. (1976). Mechanisms of incubation in creative problem solving. *American Journal of Psychology, 89*, 617–630.

Oppenheimer, D. M. (2004). Spontaneous discounting of availability in frequency judgment tasks. *Psychological Science, 15*, 100–105.

Ormerod, T. C., & Chronicle, E. P. (1999). Global perceptual processing in problem solving: The case of the traveling salesperson. *Perception & Psychophysics, 61*, 1227–1238.

Osherson, D. N., Smith, E. E., Wilkie, O., Lopez, A., & Shafir, E. (1990). Category-based induction. *Psychological Review, 97*, 185–200.

Ost, J., Vrij, A., Costall, A., & Bull, R. (2002). Crashing memories and reality monitoring: Distinguishing between perceptions, imaginations and "false memories." *Applied Cognitive Psychology, 16*, 125–134.

Overton, D. (1985). Contextual stimulus effects of drugs and internal states. In P. D. Balsam & A.

Tomie (Eds.), *Context and learning* (pp. 357–384). Hillsdale, NJ: Erlbaum.

Owens, J., Bower, G. H., & Black, J. B. (1979). The "soap opera" effect in story recall. *Memory & Cognition, 7*, 185–191.

Özgen, E. (2004). Language, learning, and color perception. *Current Directions in Psychological Science, 13*, 95–98.

Özgen, E., & Davies, I. R. L. (2002). Acquisition of categorical color perception: A perceptual learning approach to the linguistic relativity hypothesis. *Journal of Experimental Psychology: General, 131*, 477–493.

Paivio, A. (1969). Mental imagery in associative learning and memory. *Psychological Review, 76*, 241–263.

Paivio, A. (1971). *Imagery and verbal processes.* New York: Holt, Rinehart & Winston.

Paivio, A., & Csapo, K. (1969). Concrete image and verbal memory codes. *Journal of Experimental Psychology, 80*, 279–285.

Paivio, A., & Okovita, H. W. (1971). Word imagery modalities and associative learning in blind and sighted subjects. *Journal of Verbal Learning and Verbal Behavior, 10*, 506–510.

Paivio, A., Smythe, P. C., & Yuille, J. C. (1968). Imagery versus meaningfulness of nouns in paired-associate learning. *Canadian Journal of Psychology, 22*, 427–441.

Paivio, A., Yuille, J. C., & Madigan, S. (1968). *Concreteness, imagery, and meaningfulness values for 925 nouns* (Journal of Experimental Psychology Monograph Supplement, Vol. 76, No. 1, Pt. 2). [Washington, DC]: American Psychological Association.

Palmer, S. (1977). Hierarchical structure in perceptual representation. *Cognitive Psychology, 9*, 441–474.

Palmer, S. (1999). *Vision science: Photons to phenomenology.* Cambridge, MA: MIT Press.

Palmer, S., Schreiber, C., & Fox, C. (1991). *Remembering the earthquake: "Flashbulb" memory for experienced vs. reported events.* Paper presented at the meeting of the Psychonomic Society, November 1991, San Francisco.

Pansky, A., & Koriat, A. (2004). The basic-level convergence effect in memory distortions. *Psychological Science, 15*, 52–59.

Paris, S. C., & Lindauer, B. K. (1976). The role of inference in children's comprehension and memory for sentences. *Cognitive Psychology, 8*, 217–227.

Parkin, A. J. (1984). Levels of processing, context, and facilitation of pronunciation. *Acta Psychologia, 55*, 19–29.

Pashler, H. (1991). Dual-task interference and elementary mental mechanisms. In D. E. Meyer & S. Kornblum (Eds.), *Attention and performance XIV* (pp. 245–264). Hillsdale, NJ: Erlbaum.

Pashler, H. (1992). Attentional limitations in doing two tasks at the same time. *Current Directions in Psychological Science, 1*, 44–47.

Pashler, H. (1994). Graded capacity-sharing in dual-task interference. *Journal of Experimental Psychology: Human Perception and Performance, 20*, 330–342.

Pashler, H. (1996). Structures, processes and the flow of information. In E. Bjork & R. Bjork (Eds.), *Handbook of perception and cognition*, 2nd ed., Vol. 10: *Memory* (pp. 3–29). San Diego, CA: Academic Press.

Pashler, H., & Johnston, J. (1989). Interference between temporally overlapping tasks: Chronometric evidence for central postponement with or without response grouping. *Quarterly Journal of Experimental Psychology, 41A*, 19–45.

Passolunghi, M. C., Cornoldi, C., & De Liberto, S. (1999). Working memory and intrusions of irrelevant information in a group of specific poor problem solvers. *Memory & Cognition, 27*, 779–790.

Payne, J. D., Nadel, L., Britton, W. B., & Jacobs, W. J. (2004). The biopsychology of trauma and memory. In D. Reisberg & P. Hertel (Eds.), *Memory and emotion* (pp. 76–128). New York: Oxford University Press.

Pederson, E., Danziger, E., Wilkins, D., Levinson, S., Kita, S., & Senft, G. (1998). Semantic typology and spatial conceptualization. *Language, 74*, 557–589.

Peretz, I., Gaudreau, D., & Bonnel, A.-M. (1998). Exposure effects on music preference and recognition. *Memory & Cognition, 26*, 884–902.

Peterson, C. (1974). Incubation effects in anagram solution. *Bulletin of the Psychonomic Society, 3*, 29–30.

Peterson, M., Kihlstrom, J. F., Rose, P., & Glisky, M. (1992). Mental images can be ambiguous: Reconstruals and reference-frame reversals. *Memory & Cognition, 20*, 107–123.

Pezdek, K., Finger, K., & Hodge, D. (1997). Planting false childhood memories: The role of event plausibility. *Psychological Science, 8*, 437–441.

Pezdek, K., & Hodge, D. (1999). Planting false childhood memories in children: The role of event plausibility. *Child Development, 70,* 887–895.

Pezdek, K., Whetstone, T., Reynolds, K., Askari, N., & Dougherty, T. (1989). Memory for real-world scenes: The role of consistency with schema expectation. *Journal of Experimental Psychology: Learning, Memory, and Cognition, 15,* 587–595.

Piaget, J. (1952). *The origins of intelligence in children.* New York: International Universities Press.

Pickel, K. L. (1999). Distinguishing eyewitness descriptions of perceived objects from descriptions of imagined objects. *Applied Cognitive Psychology, 13,* 399–413.

Pillemer, D. B. (1984). Flashbulb memories of the assassination attempt on President Reagan. *Cognition, 16,* 63–80.

Pillsbury, W. B. (1897). A study in apperception. *American Journal of Psychology, 8,* 315–393.

Pinker, S. (1980). Mental imagery and the third dimension. *Journal of Experimental Psychology: General, 109,* 354–371.

Pinker, S. (1991). Rules of language. *Science, 253,* 530–535.

Pinker, S. (1994). *The language instinct.* New York: Penguin.

Pinker, S. (1997). *How the mind works.* New York: Norton.

Pinker, S. (1999). *Words and rules: The ingredients of language.* New York: Basic Books.

Pinker, S., & Finke, R. (1980). Emergent two-dimensional patterns in images in depth. *Journal of Experimental Psychology: Human Perception and Performance, 6,* 244–264.

Pinker, S., & Prince, A. (1988). On language and connectionism: Analysis of a parallel distributed processing model of language acquisition. *Cognition, 28,* 73–193.

Pinker, S., & Ullman, M. (2002a). Combination and structure, not gradedness, is the issue: Reply to McClelland and Patterson. *Trends in Cognitive Sciences, 6,* 472–474.

Pinker, S., & Ullman, M. T. (2002b). The past and future of the past tense. *Trends in Cognitive Sciences, 6,* 456–463.

Plunkett, K., & Marchman, V. A. (1996). Learning from a connectionist model of the acquisition of the English past tense. *Cognition, 61,* 299–308.

Polk, T., & Newell, A. (1995). Deduction as verbal reasoning. *Psychological Review, 102,* 533–566.

Pollack, I., & Pickett, J. (1964). Intelligibility of excerpts from fluent speech: Auditory versus structural context. *Journal of Verbal Learning and Verbal Behavior, 3,* 79–84.

Poole, D. A., & Lindsay, D. S. (2001). Children's eyewitness reports after exposure to misinformation from parents. *Journal of Experimental Psychology: Applied, 7,* 27–50.

Pope, H. G., Hudson, J. I., Bodkin, J. A., & Oliva, P. (1998). Questionable validity of "dissociative amnesia" in trauma victims. *British Journal of Psychiatry, 172,* 210–215.

Porter, S., Yuille, J. C., & Lehman, D. R. (1999). The nature of real, implanted, and fabricated memories for emotional childhood events: Implications for the false memory debate. *Law and Human Behavior, 23,* 517–538.

Posner, M., & Snyder, C. (1975). Facilitation and inhibition in the processing of signals. In P. Rabbitt & S. Dornic (Eds.), *Attention and performance V* (pp. 669–682). New York: Academic Press.

Posner, M., Snyder, C., & Davidson, B. (1980). Attention and the detection of signals. *Journal of Experimental Psychology: General, 109,* 160–174.

Posner, M. I., Walker, J. A., Friedrich, F. A., & Rafal, R. D. (1987). How do the parietal lobes direct covert attention? *Neuropsychologia, 25,* 135–145.

Postman, L. (1964). Short-term memory and incidental learning. In A. W. Melton (Ed.), *Categories of human learning* (pp. 146–201). New York: Academic Press.

Postman, L. (1975). Verbal learning and memory. *Annual Review of Psychology, 26,* 291–335.

Postman, L., & Phillips, L. W. (1965). Short-term temporal changes in free recall. *Quarterly Journal of Experimental Psychology, 17,* 132–138.

Proffitt, J. B., Coley, J. D., & Medin, D. L. (2000). Expertise and category-based induction. *Journal of Experimental Psychology: Learning, Memory and Cognition, 26,* 811–825.

Pullum, G. K., & Scholz, B. C. (2002). Empirical assessment of stimulus poverty arguments. *Linguistic Review, 19,* 9–50.

Pylyshyn, Z. (1981). The imagery debate: Analogue media versus tacit knowledge. In N. Block (Ed.), *Imagery* (pp. 151–206). Cambridge, MA: MIT Press.

Quinlan, P. T. (2003). Visual feature integration theory: Past, present and future. *Psychological Bulletin, 129,* 643–673.

Quinn, G. (1988). Interference effects in the visuo-spatial sketchpad. In M. Denis, J. Engelkamp, & J. T. E. Richardson (Eds.), *Cognitive and neuropsychological approaches to mental imagery* (pp. 181–189). Dordrecht, Netherlands: Nijhoff.

Quinn, G., & Ralston, G. E. (1986). Movement and attention in visual working memory. *Quarterly Journal of Experimental Psychology, 38A,* 689–703.

Rachman, S., & Eyrl, K. (1989). Predicting and remembering recurrent pain. *Behavior Research and Therapy, 27,* 621–635.

Radvansky, G. A. (1999). The fan effect: A tale of two theories. *Journal of Experimental Psychology: General, 128,* 198–206.

Radvansky, G. A., & Zacks, R. T. (1991). Mental models and the fan effect. *Journal of Experimental Psychology: Learning, Memory and Cognition, 17,* 940–953.

Rajaram, S. (1993). Remembering and knowing: Two means of access to the personal past. *Memory & Cognition, 21,* 89–102.

Ramachandran, V. S., & Blakeslee, S. (1998). *Phantoms in the brain.* New York: Morrow.

Ramsey, W., Stich, S., & Rumelhart, D. (1991). *Philosophy and connectionist theory.* Hillsdale, NJ: Erlbaum.

Rao, G. A., Larkin, E. C., & Derr, R. F. (1986). Biologic effects of chronic ethanol consumption related to a deficient intake of carbohydrates. *Alcohol and Alcoholism, 21,* 369–373.

Rasmussen, T., and Milner, B. (1977). The role of early left brain injury in determining lateralization of cerebral speech functions. *Annals of the New York Academy of Sciences, 299,* 355–369.

Read, J. D. (1999). The recovered/false memory debate: Three steps forward, two steps back? *Expert Evidence, 7,* 1–24.

Read, J. D., & Bruce, D. (1982). Longitudinal tracking of difficult memory retrievals. *Cognitive Psychology, 14,* 280–300.

Reason, J. T. (1990). *Human error.* Cambridge, England: Cambridge University Press.

Reason, J. T., & Lucas, D. (1984). Using cognitive diaries to investigate naturally occurring memory blocks. In J. E. Harris & P. E. Morris (Eds.), *Everyday memory actions and absent-mindedness* (pp. 53–70). London: Academic Press.

Redelmeier, D. A., & Shafir, E. (1995). Medical decision making in situations that offer multiple alternatives. *Journal of the American Medical Association, 273,* 302–305.

Redelmeier, D. A., & Tversky, A. (1996). On the belief that arthritis pain is related to the weather. *Proceedings of the National Academic of Sciences, USA, 93,* 2895–2896.

Reed, J. M., & Squire, L. R. (1997). Impaired recognition memory in patients with lesions limited to the hippocampal formation. *Behavioral Neuroscience, 111,* 667–675.

Reed, P. (2000). Serial position effects in recognition memory for odors. *Journal of Experimental Psychology: Learning, Memory and Cognition, 26,* 411–422.

Reed, S. (1977). Facilitation of problem solving. In J. N. Castellan, D. Pisoni, & G. R. Potts (Eds.), *Cognitive theory* (pp. 3–20). Hillsdale, NJ: Erlbaum.

Reed, S. (1993). Imagery and discovery. In B. Roskos-Ewoldsen, M. J. Intons-Peterson, & R. Anderson (Eds.), *Imagery, creativity, and discovery: A cognitive perspective* (pp. 287–312). New York: North-Holland.

Reed, S., Ernst, G., & Banerji, R. (1974). The role of analogy in transfer between similar problem states. *Cognitive Psychology, 6,* 436–450.

Rees, G., Kreiman, G., & Koch, C. (2002). Neural correlates of consciousness in humans. *Nature Reviews Neuroscience, 3,* 261–270.

Reeves, L., & Weisberg, R. (1994). The role of content and abstract information in analogical transfer. *Psychological Bulletin, 115,* 381–400.

Rehder, B., & Hastie, R. (2001). Causal knowledge and categories: The effects of causal beliefs on categorization, induction, and similarity. *Journal of Experimental Psychology: General, 130,* 323–360.

Rehder, B., & Hastie, R. (2004). Category coherence and category-based property induction. *Cognition, 91,* 113–153.

Rehder, B., & Ross, B. H. (2001). Abstract coherent categories. *Journal of Experimental Psychology: Learning, Memory, & Cognition, 27,* 1261–1275.

Reicher, G. M. (1969). Perceptual recognition as a function of meaningfulness of stimulus material. *Journal of Experimental Psychology, 81,* 275–280.

Reingold, E. M., Charness, N., Pomplun, M., & Stampe, D. M. (2001). Visual span in expert chess players: Evidence from eye movements. *Psychological Science, 12,* 48–55.

Reinitz, M. T., Lammers, W., & Cochran, B. (1992). Memory-conjunction errors: Miscombination of stored stimulus features can produce illusions of memory. *Memory & Cognition, 20*, 1–11.

Reisberg, D. (1996). The non-ambiguity of mental images. In C. Cornold, R. H. Logie, M. Brandimonte, G. Kaufmann & D. Reisberg (Eds.), *Stretching the imagination: Representation and transformation in mental imagery* (pp. 119–171). New York: Oxford University Press.

Reisberg, D. (1999). *The (non) effect of warnings on DRM errors.* Unpublished class project in Psychology 121, Reed College.

Reisberg, D. (2000). The detachment gain: The advantage of thinking out loud. In B. Landau, J. Sabini, E. Newport, & J. Jonides (Eds.), *Perception, cognition and language: Essays in honor of Henry and Lila Gleitman* (pp. 139–156). Cambridge, MA: MIT Press.

Reisberg, D., Baron, J., & Kemler, D. (1980). Overcoming Stroop interference: The effects of practice on distractor potency. Journal *of Experimental Psychology: Human Perception and Performance, 6*, 140–150.

Reisberg, D., & Chambers, D. (1991). Neither pictures nor propositions: What can we learn from a mental image? *Canadian Journal of Psychology, 45*, 288–302.

Reisberg, D., & Heuer, F. (2004). Memory for emotional events. In D. Reisberg & P. Hertel (Eds.), *Memory and emotion* (pp. 3–41). New York: Oxford University Press.

Reisberg, D., & Logie, R. H. (1993). The in's and out's of working memory: Escaping the boundaries on imagery function. In B. Roskos-Ewoldsen, M. Intons-Peterson, & R. Anderson (Eds.), *Imagery, creativity and discovery: A cognitive approach* (pp. 39–76). Amsterdam: Elsevier.

Reitman, J. (1976). Skilled perception in Go: Deducing memory structures from inter-response times. *Cognitive Psychology, 8*, 336–356.

Reitman, W. (1964). Heuristic decision procedures, open constraints, and the structure of ill-defined problems. In M. Shelley & G. Bryan (Eds.), *Human judgments and optimality* (pp. 282–315). New York: Wiley.

Rensink, R. A. (2002). Change detection. *Annual Review of Psychology, 53*, 245–277.

Rensink, R. A., O'Regan, J. K., & Clark, J. J. (1997). To see or not to see: The need for attention to perceive changes in scenes. *Psychological Science, 8*, 368–373.

Repp, B. (1992). Perceptual restoration of a "missing" speech sound: Auditory induction or illusion? *Perception & Psychophysics, 51*, 14–32.

Reynolds, J. H., Pasternak, T., & Desimone, R. (2000). Attention increases sensitivity of V4 neurons. *Neuron, 26*, 703–714.

Rhodes, G., Brake, S., & Atkinson, A. (1993). What's lost in inverted faces? *Cognition, 47*, 25–57.

Riccio, D. C., Millin, P. M., & Gisquet-Verrier, P. (2003). Retrograde amnesia: Forgetting back. *Current Directions in Psychological Science, 12*, 41–44.

Richardson, J. (1980). *Mental imagery and human memory.* New York: St. Martin's.

Richardson-Klavehn, A., & Bjork, R. A. (1988). Measures of memory. *Annual Review of Psychology, 39*, 475–543.

Richardson-Klavehn, A., & Gardiner, J. M. (1998). Depth-of-processing effects on priming in stem completion: Tests of the voluntary-contamination, conceptual-processing, and lexical-processing hypotheses. *Journal of Experimental Psychology: Learning, Memory and Cognition, 24*, 593–609.

Riesenhuber, M., & Poggio, T. (1999). Hierarchical models of object recognition in cortex. *Nature Neuroscience, 2*, 1019–1025.

Riesenhuber, M., & Poggio, T. (2002). Neural mechanisms of object recognition. *Current Opinion in Neurobiology, 12*, 162–168.

Rinck, M. (1999). Memory for everyday objects: Where are the digits on numerical keypads? *Applied Cognitive Psychology, 13*, 329–350.

Rips, L. (1975). Inductive judgements about natural categories. *Journal of Verbal Learning and Verbal Behavior, 14*, 665–681.

Rips, L. (1983). Cognitive processes in propositional reasoning. *Psychological Review, 90*, 38–71.

Rips, L. (1986). Mental muddles. In M. Brand & R. Harnish (Eds.), *The representation of knowledge and belief* (pp. 258–286). Tucson: University of Arizona Press.

Rips, L. (1989). Similarity, typicality, and categorization. In S. Vosniadou & A. Ortony (Eds.), *Similarity and analogical reasoning* (pp. 21–59). Cambridge, England: Cambridge University Press.

Rips, L. (1990). Reasoning. *Annual Review of Psychology, 41*, 321–353.

Rips, L., & Collins, A. (1993). Categories and resemblance. *Journal of Experimental Psychology: General, 122*, 468–489.

Ritchie, J. M. (1985). The aliphatic alcohols. In A. G. Gilman, L. S. Goodman, T. W. Rall, & F. Murad (Eds.), *The pharmacological basis of therapeutics* (pp. 372–386). New York: Macmillan.

Roberson, D., Davies, I., & Davidoff, J. (2000). Color categories are not universal: Replications and new evidence from a stone-age culture. *Journal of Experimental Psychology: General, 129*, 369–398.

Roberts, K. P., & Blades, M. (1998). The effects of interacting in repeated events on children's eyewitness memory and source monitoring. *Applied Cognitive Psychology, 12*, 489–504.

Robertson, L., Treisman, A., Friedman-Hill, S., & Grabowecky, M. (1997). The interaction of spatial and object pathways: Evidence from Balint's syndrome. *Journal of Cognitive Neuroscience, 9*, 295–317.

Rock, I. (1983). *The logic of perception.* Cambridge, MA: MIT Press.

Roediger, H. L. (1980). The effectiveness of four mnemonics in ordering recall. *Journal of Experimental Psychology: Human Learning and Memory, 6*, 558–567.

Roediger, H. L., & Blaxton, T. A. (1987). Effects of varying modality, surface features, and retention interval on word fragment completion. *Memory & Cognition, 15*, 379–388.

Roediger, H. L., & McDermott, K. (1995). Creating false memories: Remembering words not presented in lists. *Journal of Experimental Psychology: Learning, Memory and Cognition, 21*, 803–814.

Roediger, H. L., & McDermott, K. (2000). Tricks of memory. *Current Directions in Psychological Science, 9*, 123–127.

Rohde, D. L. T., & Plaut, D. C. (1999). Simple recurrent networks can distinguish nonoccurring from ungrammatical sentences given appropriate task structure. Reply to Marcus. *Cognition, 73*, 297–300.

Rosch, E. (1973). On the internal structure of perceptual and semantic categories. In T. E. Moore (Ed.), *Cognitive development and the acquisition of language* (pp. 111–144). New York: Academic Press.

Rosch, E. (1975). Cognitive representations of semantic categories. *Journal of Experimental Psychology: General, 104*, 192–233.

Rosch, E. (1977a). Human categorization. In N. Warren (Ed.), *Advances in cross-cultural psychology* (pp. 1–49). London: Academic Press.

Rosch, E. (1977b). Linguistic relativity. In P. Johnson-Laird & P. Wason (Eds.), *Thinking: Readings in cognitive science* (pp. 501–519). New York: Cambridge University Press.

Rosch, E. (1978). Principles of categorization. In E. Rosch & B. B. Lloyd (Eds.), *Cognition and categorization* (pp. 27–48). Hillsdale, NJ: Erlbaum.

Rosch, E., & Mervis, C. B. (1975). Family resemblances. Studies in the internal structure of categories. *Cognitive Psychology, 7*, 573–605.

Rosch, E., Mervis, C. B., Gray, W., Johnson, D., & Boyes-Braem, P. (1976). Basic objects in natural categories. *Cognitive Psychology, 3*, 382–439.

Rosch, E., Simpson, C., & Miller, R. S. (1976). Structural bases of typicality effects. *Journal of Experimental Psychology: Human Perception and Performance, 2*, 491–502.

Roser, M., & Gazzaniga, M. S. (2004). Automatic brains—Interpretive minds. *Current Directions in Psychological Science, 13*, 56–59.

Ross, B. (1984). Remindings and their effects in learning a cognitive skill. *Cognitive Psychology, 16*, 371–416.

Ross, B. (1987). This is like that: The use of earlier problems and the separation and similarity effects. *Journal of Experimental Psychology: Learning, Memory and Cognition, 13*, 629–639.

Ross, B. (1989). Distinguishing types of superficial similarities: Different effects on the access and use of earlier problems. *Journal of Experimental Psychology: Learning, Memory and Cognition, 15*, 456–468.

Ross, D. F., Ceci, S. J., Dunning, D., & Toglia, M. P. (1994). Unconscious transference and lineup identification: Toward a memory blending approach. In D. F. Ross & J. D. Read (Eds.), *Adult eyewitness testimony: Current trends and developments* (pp. 80–100). New York: Cambridge University Press.

Ross, J., & Lawrence, K. A. (1968). Some observations on memory artifice. *Psychonomic Science, 13*, 107–108.

Ross, L., & Anderson, C. (1982). Shortcomings in the attribution process: On the origins and maintenance of erroneous social assessments. In D. Kahneman, P. Slovic, & A. Tversky (Eds.), *Judgment under uncertainty: Heuristics and biases* (pp. 129–152). New York: Cambridge University Press.

Ross, L., Lepper, M., & Hubbard, M. (1975). Perseverance in self perception and social perception:

Biased attributional processes in the debriefing paradigm. *Journal of Personality and Social Psychology, 32,* 880–892.

Ross, M., & Wilson, A. E. (2003). Autobiographical memory and conceptions of self: Getting better all the time. *Current Directions in Psychological Science, 12,* 66–69.

Rothbart, M., Evans, M., & Fulero, S. (1979). Recall for confirming events: Memory processes and the maintenance of social stereotypes. *Journal of Experimental Social Psychology, 15,* 343–355.

Rubin, D. C., & Kontis, T. S. (1983). A schema for common cents. *Memory & Cognition, 11,* 335–341.

Rubin, D. C., & Kozin, M. (1984). Vivid memories. *Cognition, 16,* 81–95.

Rueckl, J. G., & Oden, G. C. (1986). The integration of contextual and featural information during word identification. *Journal of Memory and Language, 25,* 445–460.

Rugg, M. D., & Yonelinas, A. P. (2003). Human recognition memory: A cognitive neuroscience perspective. *Trends in Cognitive Sciences, 7,* 313–319.

Rumelhart, D. E. (1997). The architecture of mind: A connectionist approach. In J. Haugeland (Ed.), *Mind design 2: Philosophy, psychology, artificial intelligence* (2nd rev. & enlarged ed.). Cambridge, MA: MIT Press.

Rumelhart, D. E., & McClelland, J. L. (Eds.). (1986). *Parallel distributed processing,* Vol. 1. Cambridge, MA: MIT Press.

Rumelhart, D. E., & Siple, P. (1974). Process of recognizing tachistoscopically presented words. *Psychological Review, 81,* 99–118.

Rundus, D. (1971). Analysis of rehearsal processes in free recall. *Journal of Experimental Psychology, 89,* 63–77.

Saffran, J. R. (2003). Statistical language learning: Mechanisms and constraints. *Current Directions in Psychological Science, 12,* 110–114.

Salame, P., & Baddeley, A. D. (1982). Disruption of short-term memory by unattended speech: Implications for the structure of working memory. *Journal of Verbal Learning and Verbal Behavior, 21,* 150–164.

Saltz, E., & Donnenwerth-Nolan, S. (1981). Does motoric imagery facilitate memory for sentences? A selective interference test. *Journal of Verbal Learning and Verbal Behavior, 20,* 322–332.

Samuel, A. G. (1987). Lexical uniqueness effects on phonemic restoration. *Journal of Memory and Language, 26,* 36–56.

Samuel, A. G. (1991). A further examination of attentional effects in the phonemic restoration illusion. *Quarterly Journal of Experimental Psychology: Human Experimental Psychology, 43,* 679–699.

Savage, J. (1954). *The foundation of statistics.* New York: Wiley.

Schab, F. (1990). Odors and the remembrance of things past. *Journal of Experimental Psychology: Learning, Memory and Cognition, 16,* 648–655.

Schab, F. (1991). Odor memory: Taking stock. *Psychological Bulletin, 109,* 242–251.

Schacter, D. (1987). Implicit memory: History and current status. *Journal of Experimental Psychology: Learning, Memory and Cognition, 13,* 501–518.

Schacter, D. (1996). *Searching for memory: The brain, the mind and the past.* New York: Basic Books.

Schacter, D. (1999). The seven sins of memory. *American Psychologist, 54,* 182–203.

Schacter, D., & Tulving, E. (1982). Amnesia and memory research. In L. S. Cermak (Ed.), *Human memory and amnesia* (pp. 1–32). Hillsdale, NJ: Erlbaum.

Schacter, D., Tulving, E., & Wang, P. (1981). *Source amnesia: New methods and illustrative data.* Paper presented at the meeting of the International Neuropsychological Society, Atlanta.

Schellenberg, E. G., & Trehub, S. E. (2003). Good pitch memory is widespread. *Psychological Science, 14,* 262–266.

Schkade, D. A., & Kahneman, D. (1998). Does living in California make people happy? A focusing illusion in judgments of life satisfaction. *Psychological Science, 9,* 340–346.

Schneider, S. (1992). Framing and conflict: Aspiration level contingency, the status quo, and current theories of risky choice. *Journal of Experimental Psychology: Learning, Memory and Cognition, 18,* 1040–1057.

Scholl, B. J. (2001). Objects and attention: The state of the art. *Cognition, 80,* 1–46.

Schooler, J. W. (In press). Discovering memories in the light of meta-consciousness. *Journal of Aggression, Maltreatment & Trauma.*

Schraw, G., Dunkle, M., & Bendixen, L. (1995). Cognitive processes in well-defined and ill-defined problem solving. *Applied Cognitive Psychology, 9,* 523–538.

Schreiber, C. A., & Kahneman, D. (2000). Determinants of the remembered utility of aversive sounds. *Journal of Experimental Psychology: General, 129,* 27–42.

Schulz-Hardt, S., Frey, D., Lüthgens, C., & Moscovici, S. (2000). Biased information search in group decision making. *Journal of Personality and Social Psychology, 78,* 655–669.

Schunn, C. D., & Anderson, J. R. (1999). The generality/specificity of expertise in scientific reasoning. *Cognitive Science, 23,* 337–370.

Schustack, M., & Sternberg, R. (1981). Evaluation of evidence in causal inference. *Journal of Experimental Psychology: General, 110,* 101–120.

Schwartz, B., E. A. Wasserman, & S. J. Robbins (2001). *Psychology of learning and behavior,* 5th ed. New York: Norton.

Schwartz, B. L. (1999). Sparkling at the end of the tongue: The etiology of tip-of-the-tongue phenomenology. *Psychonomic Bulletin & Review, 5,* 379–393.

Schwartz, J., Chapman, G., & Brewer, N. (2004). The effects of accountability on bias in physician decision making: Going from bad to worse. *Psychonomic Bulletin & Review, 11,* 173–178.

Schwarz, N. (1998). Accessible content and accessibility experiences: The interplay of declarative and experiential information in judgments. *Personality and Social Psychology Review, 2,* 87–99.

Schwarz, N. (1999). Self-reports: How the questions shape the answers. *American Psychologist, 54,* 93–105.

Schwarz, N., Bless, H., Strack, F., Klumpp, G., Rittenauer-Schatka, H., & Simons, A. (1991). Ease of retrieval as information: Another look at the availability heuristic. *Journal of Personality & Social Psychology, 61,* 195–202.

Scullin, M. H., Kanaya, T., & Ceci, S. J. (2002). Measurement of individual differences in children's susceptibility across situations. *Journal of Experimental Psychology: Applied, 8,* 233–246.

Seamon, J., Williams, P., Crowley, M., Kim, I., Langer, S., Orne, P., et al. (1995). The mere exposure effect is based on implicit memory: Effects of stimulus type, encoding conditions, and number of exposures on recognition and affect judgments. *Journal of Experimental Psychology: Learning, Memory and Cognition, 21,* 711–721.

Sedivy, J. C., Tanenhaus, M. K., Chambers, C. G., & Carlson, G. N. (1999). Achieving incremental semantic interpretation through contextual representation. *Cognition, 71,* 109–147.

Segal, S., & Fusella, V. (1970). Influence of imaged pictures and sounds in detection of visual and auditory signals. *Journal of Experimental Psychology, 83,* 458–474.

Segal, S., & Fusella, V. (1971). Effect of images in six sense modalities on detection of visual signal from noise. *Psychonomic Science, 24,* 55–56.

Seidenberg, M. S. (1997). Language acquisition and use: Learning and applying probabilistic constraints. *Science, 275,* 1599–1603.

Selfridge, O. (1955). *Pattern recognition and modern computers.* Proceedings of the Western Joint Computer Conference, Los Angeles, CA.

Selfridge, O. (1959). Pandemonium: A paradigm for learning. In D. Blake & A. Uttley (Eds.), *The mechanisation of thought processes: Proceedings of a symposium held at the National Physics Laboratory* (pp. 511–529). London: H. M. Stationery Office.

Seltzer, B., & Benson, D. F. (1974). The temporal pattern of retrograde amnesia in Korsakoff's Disease. *Neurology, 24,* 527–530.

Senghas, A., Coppola, M., Newport, E. L., & Supalla, A. (1997). *Argument structure in Nicaraguan Sign Language: The emergence of grammatical devices.* (Proceedings of the Boston University Conference on Language Development, 21.) Boston: Cascadilla.

Sergent, J., & Poncet, M. (1990). From covert to overt recognition of faces in a prosopagnosic patient. *Brain, 113,* 989–1004.

Servos, P., & Goodale, M. A. (1995). Preserved visual imagery in visual form agnosia. *Neuropsychologia, 33,* 1383–1394.

Shafir, E. (1993). Choosing versus rejecting: Why some options are both better and worse than others. *Memory & Cognition, 21,* 546–556.

Shafir, E., & LeBoeuf, R. A. (2002). Rationality. *Annual Review of Psychology, 53,* 491–517.

Shafir, E., Simonson, I., & Tversky, A. (1993). Reason-based choice. *Cognition, 49,* 11–36.

Shafto, P., & Coley, J. D. (2003). Development of categorization and reasoning in the natural world: Novices to experts, naive similarity to ecological knowledge. *Journal of Experimental Psychology: Learning, Memory and Cognition, 29,* 641–649.

Shaklee, H., & Mims, M. (1982). Sources of error in judging event covariations. *Journal of Experimental*

Psychology: Learning, Memory and Cognition, 8, 208–224.

Shanteau, J. (1992). The psychology of experts: An alternative view. In G. Wright & F. Bolger (Eds.), *Expertise and decision support* (pp. 11–23). New York: Plenum.

Shepard, R. N. (1988). The imagination of the scientist. In K. Egan & D. Nadaner (Eds.), *Imagination and education* (pp. 153–185). New York: Teachers College Press.

Shepard, R. N., & Cooper, L. A. (1982). *Mental images and their transformations.* Cambridge, MA: MIT Press.

Shepard, R. N., & Feng, C. (1972). A chronometric study of mental paper folding. *Cognitive Psychology, 3,* 228–243.

Shepard, R. N., & Metzler, J. (1971). Mental rotation of three-dimensional objects. *Science, 171,* 701–703.

Shobe, K. K., & Kihlstrom, J. F. (1997). Is traumatic memory special? *Current Directions in Psychological Science, 6,* 70–74.

Shore, D. I., & Klein, R. M. (2000). The effects of scene inversion on change blindness. *Journal of General Psychology, 127,* 27–43.

Sieroff, E., Pollatsek, A., & Posner, M. (1988). Recognition of visual letter strings following damage to the posterior visual spatial attention system. *Cognitive Neuropsychology, 5,* 427–449.

Silbersweig, D. A., Stern, E., Frith, C., Cahill, C., Holmes, A., Grootoonk, S., et al. (1995). A functional neuroanatomy of hallucinations in schizophrenia. *Nature, 378,* 176–179.

Simmons v. United States, 390 U.S. 377 (1968).

Simon, H. (1973). The structure of ill-defined problems. *Artificial Intelligence, 4,* 181–201.

Simon, H. (1974). How big is a chunk? *Science, 183,* 482–488.

Simons, D. J. (2000). Attentional capture and inattentional blindness. *Trends in Cognitive Science, 4,* 147–155.

Simons, D. J., & Chabris, C. F. (1999). Gorillas in our midst: Sustained inattentional blindness for dynamic events. *Perception, 28,* 1059–1074.

Simons, D. J., & Levin, D. T. (1998). Failure to detect changes to people during a real-world interaction. *Psychonomic Bulletin & Review, 5,* 644–649.

Simonton, D. K. (2003). Scientific creativity as constrained stochastic behavior: The integration of product, person, and process perspectives. *Psychological Bulletin, 129,* 475–494.

Slamecka, N. J., & Graf, P. (1978). The generation effect: Delineation of a phenomenon. *Journal of Experimental Psychology: Human Learning and Memory, 4,* 592–604.

Slobin, D. (1966). Grammatical transformations and sentence comprehension in childhood and adulthood. *Journal of Verbal Learning and Verbal Behavior, 5,* 219–227.

Sloman, S. A. (1996). The empirical case for two systems of reasoning. *Psychological Bulletin, 119,* 3–22.

Slovic, P., Finucane, M., Peters, E., & MacGregor, D. G. (2002). The affect heuristic. In T. Gilovich, D. Griffin, & D. Kahneman (Eds.), *Heuristics and biases* (pp. 397–420). New York: Cambridge University Press.

Slovic, P., Fischhoff, B., & Lichtenstein, S. (1982). Facts versus fears: Understanding perceived risk. In D. Kahneman, P. Slovic, & A. Tversky (Eds.), *Judgment under uncertainty: Heuristics and biases* (pp. 463–489). Cambridge, England: Cambridge University Press.

Smedslund, J. (1963). The concept of correlation in adults. *Scandinavian Journal of Psychology, 4,* 165–173.

Smith, E., & Miller, F. (1978). Limits on perception of cognitive processes: A reply to Nisbett & Wilson. *Psychological Review, 85,* 355–362.

Smith, E. E. (1988). Concepts and thought. In R. J. Sternberg & E. E. Smith (Eds.), *The psychology of human thought* (pp. 19–49). Cambridge, England: Cambridge University Press.

Smith, E. E., Balzano, G. J., & Walker, J. H. (1978). Nominal, perceptual, and semantic codes in picture categorization. In J. W. Cotton & R. L. Klatzky (Eds.), *Semantic factors in cognition.* Hillsdale, NJ: Erlbaum.

Smith, E. E., Rips, L. J., & Shoben, E. J. (1974). Structure and process in semantic memory: A featural model for semantic decisions. *Psychological Review, 81,* 214–241.

Smith, J. D. (2002). Exemplar theory's predicted typicality gradient can be tested and disconfirmed. *Psychological Science, 13,* 437–442.

Smith, M. (1982). *Hypnotic memory enhancement of witnesses: Does it work?* Paper presented at the meeting of the Psychonomic Society, Minneapolis.

Smith, S. (1979). Remembering in and out of context. *Journal of Experimental Psychology: Human Learning and Memory, 5,* 460–471.

Smith, S. (1985). Background music and context-dependent memory. *American Journal of Psychology, 6,* 591–603.

Smith, S. M., & Blankenship, S. E. (1989). Incubation effects. *Bulletin of the Psychonomic Society, 27,* 311–314.

Smith, S. M., & Blankenship, S. (1991). Incubation and the persistence of fixation in problem solving. *American Journal of Psychology, 104,* 61–87.

Smith, S. M., Glenberg, A., & Bjork, R. A. (1978). Environmental context and human memory. *Memory & Cognition, 6,* 342–353.

Smith, S. M., & Vela, E. (1991). Incubated reminiscence effects. *Memory & Cognition, 19,* 168–176.

Smith, S. M., & Vela, E. (2001). Environmental context-dependent memory: A review and meta-analysis. *Psychonomic Bulletin & Review, 8,* 203–220.

Smyth, M. M., & Pendleton, L. R. (1989). Working memory for movements. *Quarterly Journal of Experimental Psychology, 41A,* 235–250.

Spelke, E., Hirst, W., & Neisser, U. (1976). Skills of divided attention. *Cognition, 4,* 215–230.

Spellman, B. A., Holyoak, K. J., & Morrison, R. G. (2001). Analogical priming via semantic relations. *Memory & Cognition, 29,* 383–393.

Spence, C., & Read, L. (2003). Speech shadowing while driving: On the difficulty of splitting attention between eye and ear. *Psychological Science, 14,* 251–256.

Spencer, R., & Weisberg, R. (1986). Is analogy sufficient to facilitate transfer during problem solving? *Memory & Cognition, 14,* 442–449.

Sperber, D., Cara, F., & Girotto, V. (1995). Relevance theory explains the selection task. *Cognition, 57,* 31–95.

Sperber, D., & Wilson, D. (1986). *Relevance: Communication and cognition.* Cambridge, MA: Harvard University Press.

Spiegel, D. (1995). Hypnosis and suggestion. In D. L. Schacter, J. T. Coyle, G. D. Fischbach, M.-M. Mesulam, & L. E. Sullivan (Eds.), *Memory distortion: How minds, brains and societies reconstruct the past* (pp. 129–149). Cambridge, MA: Harvard University Press.

Spiro, R. J. (1977). Remembering information from text: The "state of schema" approach. In R. C. Anderson, R. J. Spiro, & W. E. Montague (Eds.), *Schooling and the acquisition of knowledge* (pp. 137–166). Hillsdale, NJ: Erlbaum.

Sporer, S. (1988). Long-term improvement of facial recognition through visual rehearsal. In M. Gruneberg, P. Morris, & R. Sykes (Eds.), *Practical aspects of memory: Current research and issues* (pp. 182–188). New York: Wiley.

Sporer, S., Penrod, S., Read, D., & Cutler, B. (1995). Choosing, confidence, and accuracy: A meta-analysis of the confidence-accuracy relation in eyewitness identification studies. *Psychological Bulletin, 118,* 315–327.

Squire, L., & McKee, R. (1993). Declarative and non-declarative memory in opposition: When prior events influence amnesic patients more than normal subjects. *Memory & Cognition, 21,* 424–430.

Srinivas, K. (1993). Perceptual specificity in nonverbal priming. *Journal of Experimental Psychology: Learning, Memory and Cognition, 19,* 582–602.

Srinivas, K., & Roediger, H. L. (1990). Classifying implicit memory tests: Category association and anagram solution. *Journal of Memory and Language, 29,* 389–412.

Stadler, M. A., Roediger, H. L., & McDermott, K. B. (1999). Norms for word lists that create false memories. *Memory & Cognition, 27,* 494–500.

Stangor, C., & McMillan, D. (1992). Memory for expectancy-congruent and expectancy-incongruent information: A review of the social and social developmental literatures. *Psychological Bulletin, 111,* 42–61.

Stanovich, K. E. (1999). *Who is rational? Studies of individual differences in reasoning.* Mahwah, NJ: Erlbaum.

Stanovich, K. E., & West, R. F. (1998). Who uses base rates and P(Du,H)? An analysis of individual differences. *Memory & Cognition, 26,* 161–179.

Stanovich, K. E., & West, R. F. (2000). Individual differences in reasoning: Implications for the rationality debate. *Behavioral and Brain Sciences, 23,* 645–665.

State of Oregon v. Classen, 285 Or 221 (1979).

Steblay, N. J. (1992). A meta-analytic review of the weapon focus effect. *Law and Human Behavior, 16,* 413–424.

Sternberg, R. J. (1988). A three-facet model of creativity. In R. J. Sternberg (Ed.), *The nature of creativity* (pp. 125–147). Cambridge, England: Cambridge University Press.

Sternberg, R. J. (2001). What is the common thread of creativity? Its dialectical relation to intelligence and wisdom. *American Psychologist, 56,* 360–362.

Sternberg, R. J., & Davidson, J. E. (Eds.). (1995). *The nature of insight.* Cambridge, MA: MIT Press.

Sternberg, R. J., & Dess, N. K. (2001). Creativity for the new millenium. *American Psychologist, 56,* 332.

Stevens, A., & Coupe, P. (1978). Distortions in judged spatial relations. *Cognitive Psychology, 10,* 422–437.

Strack, F., & Mussweiler, T. (1997). Explaining the enigmatic anchoring effect: Mechanisms of selective accessibility. *Journal of Personality & Social Psychology, 73,* 437–446.

Strayer, D. L., Drews, F. A., & Johnston, W. A. (2003). Cell phone induced failures of visual attention during simulated driving. *Journal of Experimental Psychology: Applied, 9,* 23–32.

Strayer, D. L., & Johnston, W. A. (2001). Driven to distraction: Dual-task studies of simulated driving and conversing on a cellular phone. *Psychological Science, 12,* 462–466.

Stroop, J. R. (1935). Studies of interference in serial verbal reaction. *Journal of Experimental Psychology, 18,* 643–662.

Sulin, R. A., & Dooling, D. J. (1974). Intrusion of a thematic idea in retention of prose. *Journal of Experimental Psychology, 103,* 255–262.

Sumby, W. H. (1963). Word frequency and serial position effects. *Journal of Verbal Learning and Verbal Behavior, 1,* 443–450.

Stuss, D. T., & Levine, B. (2002). Adult clinical neuropsychology: Lessons from studies of the frontal lobes. *Annual Review of Psychology, 53,* 401–433.

Svartik, J. (1966). *On voice in the English verb.* The Hague, Netherlands: Mouton.

Sweller, J., Mawer, R., & Ward, M. (1983). Development of expertise in mathematical problem solving. *Journal of Experimental Psychology: General, 112,* 639–661.

Symons, C. S., & Johnson, B. T. (1997). The self-reference effect in memory: A meta-analysis. *Psychological Bulletin, 121,* 371–394.

Tabachnick, B., & Brotsky, S. (1976). Free recall and complexity of pictorial stimuli. *Memory & Cognition, 4,* 466–470.

Talarico, J. M., & Rubin, D. C. (2003). Confidence, not consistency, characterizes flashbulb memories. *Psychological Science, 14,* 455–461.

Tallal, P., Ross, R., & Curtiss, S. (1989). Familial aggregation in specific language impairment. *Journal of Speech & Hearing Disorders, 54,* 167–173.

Tanaka, J. W., & Taylor, M. (1991). Object categories and expertise: Is the basic level in the eye of the beholder? *Cognitive Psychology, 23,* 457–482.

Tanenhaus, M. K., & Spivey-Knowlton, M. J. (1996). Eye-tracking. *Language & Cognitive Processes, 11,* 583–588.

Taplin, J., & Staudenmayer, H. (1973). Interpretation of abstract conditional sentences in deductive reasoning. *Journal of Verbal Learning and Verbal Behavior, 12,* 530–542.

Tarr, M. (1995). Rotating objects to recognize them: A case study on the role of viewpoint dependency in the recognition of three-dimensional objects. *Psychonomic Bulletin & Review, 2,* 55–82.

Tarr, M. (1999). News on views: Pandemonium revisited. *Nature Neuroscience, 2,* 932–935.

Tarr, M., & Bülthoff, H. (1998). Image-based object recognition in man, monkey and machine. *Cognition, 67,* 1–208.

Terr, L. C. (1991). Acute responses to external events and posttraumatic stress disorders. In M. Lewis (Ed.), *Child and adolescent psychiatry: A comprehensive textbook* (pp. 755–763). Baltimore: Williams & Wilkins.

Terr, L. C. (1994). *Unchained memories: The stories of traumatic memories, lost and found.* New York: Basic Books.

Thaler, R. H. (1999). Mental accounting matters. *Journal of Behavioral Decision Making, 12,* 183–206.

Thaler, R. (2000). Mental accounting matters. In Kahneman, D. & Tversky, A. (Eds.), Choices, values and frames. N.Y.: Russell Sage Foundation.

Thapar, A., & Greene, R. (1994). Effects of level of processing on implicit and explicit tasks. *Journal of Experimental Psychology: Learning, Memory and Cognition, 20,* 671–679.

Thomas, A. K., Bulevich, J. B., & Loftus, E. F. (2003). Exploring the role of repetition and sensory elaboration in the imagination inflation effect. *Memory & Cognition, 31,* 630–640.

Thomas, A. K., & Loftus, E. F. (2002). Creating bizarre false memories through imagination. *Memory & Cognition, 30,* 423–431.

Thomas, J. (1974). An analysis of behavior in the Hobbits-Orcs problem. *Cognitive Psychology, 6,* 257–269.

Thompson, P. (1980). Margaret Thatcher: A new illusion. *Perception, 9*, 483–484.

Thompson, W. B., & Mason, S. E. (1996). Instability of individual differences in the association between confidence judgments and memory performance. *Memory & Cognition, 24*, 226–234.

Thompson, W. L., & Kosslyn, S. M. (2000). Neural systems activated during visual mental imagery: A review and meta-analyses. In J. Mazziotta & A. Toga (Eds.), *Brain mapping II: The applications* (pp. 535–560). New York: Academic Press.

Thorndike, E., & Lorge, I. (1963). *The Thorndike/Lorge teacher's word book of 30,000 words.* New York: Columbia University Press.

Tong, F., Kakayama, K., Vaughan, J. T., & Kanwisher, N. (1998). Binocular rivalry and visual awareness in human extrastriate cortex. *Neuron, 21*, 753–759.

Tousignant, J., Hall, D., & Loftus, E. (1986). Discrepancy detection and vulnerability to misleading postevent information. *Memory & Cognition, 14*, 329–338.

Treisman, A. (1964). Verbal cues, language, and meaning in selective attention. *American Journal of Psychology, 77*, 206–219.

Treisman, A., & Gelade, G. (1980). A feature-integration theory of attention. *Cognitive Psychology, 12*, 97–136.

Treisman, A., & Gormican, S. (1988). Feature analysis in early vision: Evidence from search asymmetries. *Psychological Review, 95*, 15–48.

Treisman, A., Sykes, M., & Gelade, G. (1977). Selective attention and stimulus integration. In S. Dornic (Ed.), *Attention and performance VI* (pp. 333–361). Hillsdale, NJ: Erlbaum.

Tulving, E. (1983). *Elements of episodic memory.* Oxford, England: Oxford University Press.

Tulving, E. (1985). Memory and consciousness. *Canadian Psychologist, 26*, 1–12.

Tulving, E. (1993). What is episodic memory? *Current Directions in Psychological Science, 2*, 67–70.

Tulving, E. (2002). Episodic memory: From mind to brain. *Annual Review of Psychology, 53*, 1–25.

Tulving, E., & Gold, C. (1963). Stimulus information and contextual information as determinants of tachistoscopic recognition of words. *Journal of Experimental Psychology, 92*, 319–327.

Tulving, E., Mandler, G., & Baumal, R. (1964). Interaction of two sources of information in tachistoscopic word recognition. *Canadian Journal of Psychology, 18*, 62–71.

Tversky, A. (1977). Features of similarity. *Psychological Review, 84*, 327–352.

Tversky, A., & Kahneman, D. (1971). Belief in the law of small numbers. *Psychological Bulletin, 76*, 105–110.

Tversky, A., & Kahneman, D. (1973). Availability: A heuristic for judging frequency and probability. *Cognitive Psychology, 5*, 207–232.

Tversky, A., & Kahneman, D. (1974). Judgments under uncertainty: Heuristics and biases. *Science, 185*, 1124–1131.

Tversky, A., & Kahneman, D. (1981). The framing of decisions and the psychology of choice. *Science, 211*, 453–458.

Tversky, A., & Kahneman, D. (1982). Evidential impact of base rates. In D. Kahneman, P. Slovic, & A. Tversky (Eds.), *Judgment under uncertainty: Heuristics and biases* (pp. 153–160). New York: Cambridge University Press.

Tversky, A., & Kahneman, D. (1983). Extensional versus intuitive reasoning: The conjunction fallacy in probability judgment. *Psychological Review, 90*, 293–315.

Tversky, A., & Kahneman, D. (1987). Rational choice and the framing of decisions. In R. Hogarth & M. Reder (Eds.), *Rational choice: The contrast between economics and psychology* (pp. 67–94). Chicago: University of Chicago Press.

Tversky, A., & Shafir, E. (1992a). Choice under conflict: The dynamics of deferred decision. *Psychological Science, 3*, 358–361.

Tversky, B., & Hemenway, K. (1991). Parts and the basic level in natural categories and artificial stimuli: Comments on Murphy (1991). *Memory & Cognition, 19*, 439–442.

Tweney, R. D., Doherty, M. E., & Mynatt, C. R. (1981). *On scientific thinking.* New York: Columbia University Press.

Uleman, J., & Bargh, J. (Eds). (1989). *Unintended thought.* New York: Guilford.

Ungerleider, L. G., & Haxby, J. V. (1994). "What" and "where" in the human brain. *Current Opinions in Neurobiology, 4*, 157–165.

Ungerleider, L. G., & Mishkin, M. (1982). Two cortical visual systems. In D. J. Ingle, M. A. Goodale, & R. J. W. Mansfield (Eds.), *Analysis of visual behavior* (pp. 549–586). Cambridge, MA: MIT Press.

Valentine, T. (1988). Upside-down faces: A review of the effects of inversion upon face recognition. *British Journal of Psychology, 79*, 471–491.

Van Essen, D. C., & DeYoe, E. A. (1995). Concurrent processing in the primate visual cortex. In M. S. Gazzaniga (Ed.), *The cognitive neurosciences* (pp. 383–400). Cambridge, MA: MIT Press.

Van Lancker, D., Kreiman, J., & Emmorey, K. (1985). Familiar voice recognition: Patterns and parameters: I. Recognition of backward voices. *Journal of Phonetics, 13*, 19–38.

Van Lancker, D., Kreiman, J., & Wickens, T. (1985). Familiar voice recognition: Patterns and parameters: II. Recognition of rate altered voices. *Journal of Phonetics, 13*, 39–52.

VanLehn, K. (1998). Analogy events: How examples are used during problem solving. *Cognitive Science, 22*, 347–388.

Van Overschelde, J. P., & Healy, A. F. (2001). Learning of nondomain facts in high- and low-knowledge domains. *Journal of Experimental Psychology: Learning, Memory and Cognition, 27*, 1160–1171.

Verstijnen, I. M., Hennessey, J. M., van Leeuwen, C., Hamel, R., & Goldschmidt, G. (1998). Sketching and creative discovery. *Design Studies, 19*, 519–546.

Verstijnen, I. M., van Leeuwen, C., Goldschmidt, G., Hamel, R., & Hennessey, J. M. (1998). Creative discovery in imagery and perception: Combining is relatively easy, restructuring takes a sketch. *Acta Psychologica, 99*, 177–200.

Vicente, K., & Brewer, W. (1993). Reconstructive remembering of the scientific literature. *Cognition, 46*, 101–128.

Vitevitch, M. S. (2003). Change deafness: The inability to detect changes between two voices. *Journal of Experimental Psychology: Human Perception and Performance, 29*, 333–342.

von Neumann, J., & Morgenstern, O. (1947). *Theory of games and economic behavior.* Princeton, NJ: Princeton University Press.

Vuong, Q. C., & Tarr, M. (2004). Rotation direction affects object recognition. *Vision Research, 44*, 1717–1730.

Wagenaar, W. A. (1986). My memory: A study of autobiographical memory over six years. *Cognitive Psychology, 18*, 225–252.

Wagenaar, W. A., & Groeneweg, J. (1990). The memory of concentration camp survivors. *Applied Cognitive Psychology, 4*, 77–88.

Walker, S. (1993). Supernatural beliefs, natural kinds, and conceptual structure. *Memory & Cognition, 20*, 655–662.

Wallas, G. (1926). *The art of thought.* New York: Harcourt, Brace.

Wallis, G., & Bülthoff, H. (1999). Learning to recognize objects. *Trends in Cognitive Sciences, 3*, 22–31.

Wang, M., & Bilger, R. (1973). Consonant confusion in noise: A study of perceptual features. *Journal of the Acoustical Society of America, 54*, 1248–1266.

Ward, T. B. (2001). Creative cognition, conceptual combination, and the creative writing of Stephen R. Donaldson. *American Psychologist, 56*, 350–354.

Wason, P. (1966). Reasoning. In B. Foss (Ed.), *New horizons in psychology* (pp. 135–151). Middlesex, England: Penguin.

Wason, P. (1968). Reasoning about a rule. *Quarterly Journal of Experimental Psychology, 20*, 273–281.

Wason, P. (1983). Realism and rationality in the selection task. In J. S. B. Evans (Ed.), *Thinking and reasoning: Psychological approaches* (pp. 44–75). London: Routledge & Kegan Paul.

Wason, P., & Johnson-Laird, P. (1972). *Psychology of reasoning: Structure and content.* Cambridge, MA: Harvard University Press.

Watkins, M. J. (1977). The intricacy of memory span. *Memory & Cognition, 5*, 529–534.

Wattenmaker, W. D., Dewey, G. I., Murphy, T. D., & Medin, D. L. (1986). Linear separability and concept learning: Context, relational properties, and concept naturalness. *Cognitive Psychology, 18*, 158–194.

Waugh, N. C., & Norman, D. A. (1965). Primary memory. *Psychological Review, 72*, 89–104.

Weaver, C. (1993). Do you need a "flash" to form a flashbulb memory? *Journal of Experimental Psychology: General, 122*, 39–46.

Wedell, D., & Bockenholt, U. (1990). Moderation of preference reversals in the long run. *Journal of Experimental Psychology: Human Perception and Performance, 16*, 429–438.

Wegner, D., Wenzlaff, R., Kerker, R., & Beattie, A. (1981). Incrimination through innuendo: Can media questions become public answers? *Journal of Personality and Social Psychology, 40*, 822–832.

Weisberg, R. (1986). *Creativity: Genius and other myths.* New York: Freeman.

Weisberg, R. (1988). Problem solving and creativity. In R. J. Sternberg (Ed.), *The nature of creativity* (pp. 148–176). Cambridge, England: Cambridge University Press.

Weisberg, R., DiCamillo, M., & Phillips, D. (1978). Transferring old associations to new problems: A nonautomatic process. *Journal of Verbal Learning and Verbal Behavior, 17*, 219–228.

Weisberg, R., & Suls, J. (1973). An information processing model of Duncker's candle problem. *Cognitive Psychology, 4*, 255–276.

Weiskrantz, L. (1986). *Blindsight: A case study and implications.* New York: Oxford University Press.

Weiskrantz, L. (1997). *Consciousness lost and found.* New York: Oxford University Press.

Weldon, M. (1993). The time course of perceptual and conceptual contributions to word fragment completion priming. *Journal of Experimental Psychology: Learning, Memory and Cognition, 19*, 1010–1023.

Wells, G. L., & Bradfield, A. L. (1999). Distortions in eyewitnesses' recollections: Can the postidentification-feedback effect be moderated? *Psychological Science, 10*, 138–144.

Wells, G. L., Lindsay, R. C. L., & Ferguson, T. J. (1979). Accuracy, confidence, and juror perceptions in eyewitness identification. *Journal of Applied Psychology, 64*, 440–448.

Wells, G. L., Luus, C. A. E., & Windschitl, P. (1994). Maximizing the utility of eyewitness identification evidence. *Current Directions in Psychological Science, 3*, 194–197.

Wells, G. L., Olson, E. A., & Charman, S. D. (2002). The confidence of eyewitnesses in their identifications from lineups. *Current Directions in Psychological Science, 11*, 151–154.

Wells, G. L., Olson, E. A., & Charman, S. D. (2003). Distorted retrospective eyewitness reports as functions of feedback and delay. *Journal of Experimental Psychology: Applied, 9*, 42–51.

Werker, J., & Desjardins, R. (1995). Listening to speech in the first year of life: Experiential effects on phoneme perception. *Current Directions in Psychological Science, 4*, 76–80.

Wetherick, N. (1989). Psychology and syllogistic reasoning. *Philosophical Psychology, 2*, 111–124.

Wharton, C., Holyoak, K., Downing, P., & Lange, T. (1994). Below the surface: Analogical similarity and retrieval competition in reminding. *Cognitive Psychology, 26*, 64–101.

Wheeler, D. (1970). Processes in word recognition. *Cognitive Psychology, 1*, 59–85.

White, P. (1988). Knowing more than we can tell: "Introspective access" and causal report accuracy 10 years later. *British Journal of Psychology, 79*, 13–45.

Whitney, C. (2001). How the brain encodes the order of letters in a printed word: The SERIOL model and selective literature review. *Psychonomic Bulletin & Review, 8*, 221–243.

Whittlesea, B. W. A. (2002). False memory and the discrepancy-attribution hypothesis: The prototype-familiarity illusion. *Journal of Experimental Psychology: General, 131*, 96–115.

Whittlesea, B., Brooks, L., & Westcott, C. (1994). After the learning is over: Factors controlling the selective application of general and particular knowledge. *Journal of Experimental Psychology: Learning, Memory and Cognition, 20*, 259–274.

Whorf, B. L. (1956). *Language, thought, and reality.* Cambridge, England: Technology Press.

Wilkins, M. (1928). The effect of changed material on ability to do formal syllogistic reasoning. *Archives of Psychology, 16*, 83.

Wilson, T., & Brekke, N. (1994). Mental contamination and mental correction: Unwanted influences on judgments and evaluations. *Psychological Bulletin, 116*, 117–142.

Wilson, T. D. (2002). *Strangers to ourselves: Discovering the adaptive unconscious.* Cambridge, MA: Harvard University Press.

Wilson, T. D., & Dunn, E. W. (2004). Self-knowledge: Its limits, value, and potential for improvement. *Annual Review of Psychology, 55*, 493–518.

Wilson, T. D., Wheatley, T., Meyers, J. M., Gilbert, D., & Axsom, D. (2000). Focalism: A source of durability bias in affective forecasting. *Journal of Personality and Social Psychology, 78*, 821–836.

Winkielman, P., & Schwarz, N. (2001). How pleasant was your childhood? Beliefs about memory shape inferences from experienced difficulty of recall. *Psychological Science, 12*, 176–179.

Winnick, W., & Daniel, S. (1970). Two kinds of response priming in tachistoscopic recognition. *Journal of Experimental Psychology, 84*, 74–81.

Winograd, E., & Neisser, U. (Eds.). (1993). *Affect and accuracy in recall: Studies of "flashbulb" memories.* New York: Cambridge University Press.

Winograd, E., Peluso, J. P., & Glover, T. A. (1998). Individual differences in susceptibility to memory illusions. *Applied Cognitive Psychology, 12*, S5–S28.

Wiseman, S., & Neisser, U. (1974). Perceptual organization as a determinant of visual recognition memory. *American Journal of Psychology, 87*, 675–681.

Wisniewski, E., & Medin, D. (1994). On the interaction of theory and data in concept learning. *Cognitive Science, 18,* 221–282.

Wittgenstein, L. (1953). *Philosophical investigations* (G. E. M. Anscombe, Trans.). Oxford, England: Blackwell.

Wixted, J. (1991). Conditions and consequences of maintenance rehearsal. *Journal of Experimental Psychology: Learning, Memory and Cognition, 17,* 963–973.

Wolfe, J. M. (1999). Inattentional amnesia. In V. Coltheart (Ed.), *Fleeting memories: Cognition of brief visual stimuli* (MIT Press/Bradford Books Series in Cognitive Psychology) (pp. 71–94). Cambridge, MA: MIT Press.

Wolfe, J. M. (2003). Moving towards solutions to some enduring controversies in visual search. *Trends in Cognitive Sciences, 7,* 70–76.

Wollen, K. A., Weber, A., & Lowry, D. (1972). Bizarreness versus interaction of mental images as determinants of learning. *Cognitive Psychology, 3,* 518–523.

Wood, N., & Cowan, N. (1995). The cocktail party phenomenon revisited: How frequent are attention shifts to one's name in an irrelevant auditory channel? *Journal of Experimental Psychology: Learning, Memory and Cognition, 21,* 255–260.

Woodward, A. E., Bjork, R. A., & Jongeward, R. H., Jr. (1973). Recall and recognition as a function of primary rehearsal. *Journal of Verbal Learning and Verbal Behavior, 12,* 608–617.

Woodworth, R., & Sells, S. (1935). An atmosphere effect in formal syllogistic reasoning. *Journal of Experimental Psychology, 18,* 451–460.

Wright, D. B., & Davies, G. M. (1999). Eyewitness testimony. In F. T. Davies, R. S. Nickerson, R. W. Schwaneveldt, S. T. Dumais, D. S. Lindsay, & M. T. H. Chi (Eds.), *Handbook of applied cognition* (pp. 789–818). New York: Wiley.

Wright, D. B., & McDaid, A. T. (1996). Comparing system and estimator variables using data from real line-ups. *Applied Cognitive Psychology, 10,* 75–84.

Yarmey, A. (1973). I recognize your face but I can't remember your name: Further evidence on the tip-of-the-tongue phenomenon. *Memory & Cognition, 1,* 287–290.

Yates, F. A. (1966). *The art of memory.* London: Routledge and Kegan Paul.

Yeni-Komshian, G. (1993). Speech perception. In J. B. Gleason & N. B. Ratner (Eds.), *Psycholinguistics* (pp. 90–133). New York: Harcourt Brace Jovanovich.

Yin, R. (1969). Looking at upside-down faces. *Journal of Experimental Psychology, 81,* 141–145.

Yonelinas, A. P. (2001). Components of episodic memory: The contribution of recollection and familiarity. In A. D. Baddeley, J. P. Aggleton, & M. A. Conway (Eds.), *Episodic memory: New directions in research* (pp. 31–52). New York: Oxford University Press.

Yuille, J. (Ed.). (1983). *Imagery, memory, and cognition.* Hillsdale, NJ: Erlbaum.

Yuille, J., & Cutshall, J. L. (1986). A case study of eyewitness memory of a crime. *Journal of Applied Psychology, 71,* 291–301.

Yuille, J., & Kim, C. (1987). A field study of the forensic use of hypnosis. *Canadian Journal of Behavioral Sciences Review, 19,* 418–429.

Zajonc, R. B. (1980). Feeling and thinking. *American Psychologist, 35,* 151–175.

Zaragoza, M. S., & Mitchell, K. J. (1996). Repeated exposure to suggestion and the creation of false memories. *Psychological Science, 7,* 294–300.

Zaragoza, M. S., Payment, K. E., Ackil, J. K., Drivdahl, S. B., & Beck, M. (2001). Interviewing witnesses: Forced confabulation and confirmatory feedback increases false memories. *Psychological Science, 12,* 473–477.

Zihl, J., Von Cramon, D., & Mai, N. (1983). Selective disturbance of movement vision after bilateral brain damage. *Brain, 106,* 313–340.

Zimler, J., & Keenan, J. M. (1983). Imagery in the congenitally blind: How visual are visual images? *Journal of Experimental Psychology: Learning, Memory and Cognition, 9,* 269–282.

Figure 2.3: Mazziotta, J. et al. "PET Scan and Visual Stimulation." Copyright © Photo Researchers. Reprinted by permission.
Figure 2.5: Tong, F. et al. "Binocular Rivalry and Visual Awareness in Human Extrastriate Cortex," *Neuron*, Vol. 21, 753–759, October, 1998. Copyright © 1998 by Cell Press. Reprinted with permission.
Figure 2.7: Cobb, S. "Primary sensory projection areas of the human cortex," *Foundations of Neuropsychiatry*, Second Edition. Copyright © 1941 by Lippincott, Williams & Wilkins.
Figure 2.8: "Sensory Homunculus." Reprinted with permission of the Natural History Museum, London.
Figure 2.11: Figure 5.18 from *Psychology*, Sixth Edition, by H. Gleitman, A. J. Fridlund and D. Reisberg. Copyright © 2004, 1999, 1995, 1991, 1986, 1981 by W.W. Norton & Co., Inc. Used by permission of W.W. Norton & Co., Inc.
Figure 2.12: Figure 27A from *Psychology*, Fifth Edition, by H. Gleitman, A. J. Fridlund and D. Reisberg. Copyright © 1999, 1995, 1991, 1986, 1981 by W.W. Norton & Co., Inc. Used by permission of W.W. Norton & Co., Inc.
Figure 2.14: Copyright © by John L. Howard.
Figure 3.3: Figure 6.46 from *Psychology*, Fifth Edition, by H. Gleitman, A. J. Fridlund and D. Reisberg. Copyright © 1999, 1995, 1991, 1986, 1981 by W.W. Norton & Co., Inc. Used by permission of W.W. Norton & Co., Inc.
Figure 3.6: Figure 6.27 from *Psychology*, Fifth Edition, by H. Gleitman, A. J. Fridlund and D. Reisberg. Copyright © 1999, 1995, 1991, 1986, 1981 by W.W. Norton & Co., Inc. Used by permission of W.W. Norton & Co., Inc.
Figure 3.13: McClelland, J. L. and Rumelhat, D. E. "An interactive model of context effect in letter perception." *Psychological Review, 88*, 375–407. Copyright © 1981 by the American Psychological Association. Reprinted with permission.
Figure 3.15: Biederman, I. "Human vision understanding: Recent research and a theory," *Computer Vision, Graphics and Image Processing, 32*, 29–73. Copyright © 1985 by Academic Press. Reprinted with permission.
Figure 4.1: Figure page 231 from *Psychology*, Sixth Edition, by H. Gleitman, A. J. Fridlund and D. Reisberg. Copyright © 2004, 1999, 1995, 1991, 1986, 1981 by W.W. Norton & Co., Inc. Used by permission of W.W. Norton & Co., Inc.

Figure 5.7: "Cognitive functions in the prefrontal cortex", *Psychological Science*, v. 10il, 1998 (6), 185–192.
Figure 7.1: Photograph from "Role of schemata in memory for places," by W. F. Brewer and J. C. Treyens. *Cognitive Psychology, 13*, 207–230.
Figure 9.1: Copyright © The New Yorker Collection, 1977, Jeff Kaufman from cartoonbank.com. All Rights Reserved.
Figure 9.2: Fillmore, C. "Towards a descriptive framework for spatial deixis," Speech, place and action: Studies in deixis and related topics, R. J. Jarvella and W. Klein (Eds.). Copyright © 1982 by John Wiley and Sons, Limited. Reprinted by permission.
Figure 11.1: Copyright © by Stephen M. Kosslyn.
Figure 11.3: Shepard, R. N. and Metzler, J. "Mental rotation of three dimensional objects," *Science, 171*, 701–3. Copyright © 1971 by the American Association for the Advancement of Science. Reprinted by permission.
Figure 11.11: Intraub, H. and Richardson, M. "Boundary extension in picture memory," *Journal of Experimental Psychology, 15*, 179–87. Reprinted by permission.
Figure 13.7: Tversky, A. and Kahneman, D. "Rational choice and the framing of decisions," *Journal of Business, 59:4*, pt. 2. Copyright © 1986 by the University of Chicago Press. Reprinted by permission.
Figure 13.8: Tversky, A. and Kahneman, D. "Rational choice and the framing of decisions," *Journal of Business, 59:4*, pt. 2. Copyright © 1986 by the University of Chicago Press. Reprinted by permission.
Figure 13.9: Tversky, A. and Kahneman, D. "Rational choice and the framing of decisions," *Journal of Business, 59:4*, pt. 2. Copyright © 1986 by the University of Chicago Press. Reprinted by permission.
Figure 13.10: Tversky, A. and Kahneman, D. "Rational choice and the framing of decisions," *Journal of Business, 59:4*, pt. 2. Copyright © 1986 by the University of Chicago Press. Reprinted by permission.
Figure 14.12: Novick, L. and Holyoak, K. J. Appendix A (adapted), page 414, *Journal of Experimental Psychology: Learning Memory and Cognition, 17*, 1991, 398–415. Copyright © by the American Psychological Association. Reprinted by permission.

Note: Italicized page locators indicate figures; notes and tables are denoted with *n* and *t*.